INSIDERS'GUIDE®

INSIDERS' GUIDE® SERIES

INSIDERS' GUIDE® TO THE BERKSHIRES

GAE ELFENBEIN

INSIDERS'GUIDE®

GUILFORD, CONNECTICUT
AN IMPRINT OF THE GLOBE PEQUOT PRESS

INSIDERS'GUIDE®

Text design by LeAnna Weller Smith
Maps created by XNR Productions Inc.
© The Globe Pequot Press

ISSN 1549-7291
ISBN 0-7627-2725-X

Manufactured in the United States of America
First Edition/First Printing

Mount Greylock from the Mohawk Trail. BERKSHIRE VISITORS BUREAU/A. BLAKE GARDNER

Tanglewood. WALTER H. SCOTT

The Round Stone Barn at Hancock Shaker Village. BERKSHIRE VISITORS BUREAU/A. BLAKE GARDNER

Spires in Pittsfield. BERKSHIRE VISITORS BUREAU/A. BLAKE GARDNER

Williams College on Main Street, Williamstown. BERKSHIRE VISITORS BUREAU/STEVE ZIGLAR

Biking on Ashuwillticook Rail Trail. BERKSHIRE VISITORS BUREAU/A. BLAKE GARDNER

Onota Lake. BERKSHIRE VISITORS BUREAU/A. BLAKE GARDNER

Canterbury Farms. BERKSHIRE VISITORS BUREAU/A. BLAKE GARDNER

Harbour House Inn B&B. BERKSHIRE VISITORS BUREAU/A. BLAKE GARDNER

Sleigh ride at the Pittsfield Winter Carnival, Onota Lake. BERKSHIRE VISITORS BUREAU/A. BLAKE GARDNER

Pumpkin picking at Ioka Valley Farm. BERKSHIRE VISITORS BUREAU/A. BLAKE GARDNER

Great Barrington. BERKSHIRE VISITORS BUREAU/A. BLAKE GARDNER

Wheatleigh, the award-winning hotel in Lenox. BERKSHIRE VISITORS BUREAU/WHEATLEIGH

Williamstown. BERKSHIRE VISITORS BUREAU/A. BLAKE GARDNER

CONTENTS

Acknowledgments xxiii
How to Use This Book 1
Area Overview 3
History 18
Getting Here, Getting Around 23
Accommodations 32
Restaurants 74
Farms and Gardens 107
Nightlife 116
Shopping 124
Attractions 152
Arts and Culture 169
Kidstuff 208
Annual Events 221
Parks 232
Recreation 246
Day Trips and Weekend Getaways 291
Real Estate 301
Education and Child Care 311
Health Care and Wellness 320
Retirement 329
Media 340
Worship 347
Index 351
About the Author 360

Directory of Maps

Overview xix
North County xx
South County xxi
Central Berkshire xxii

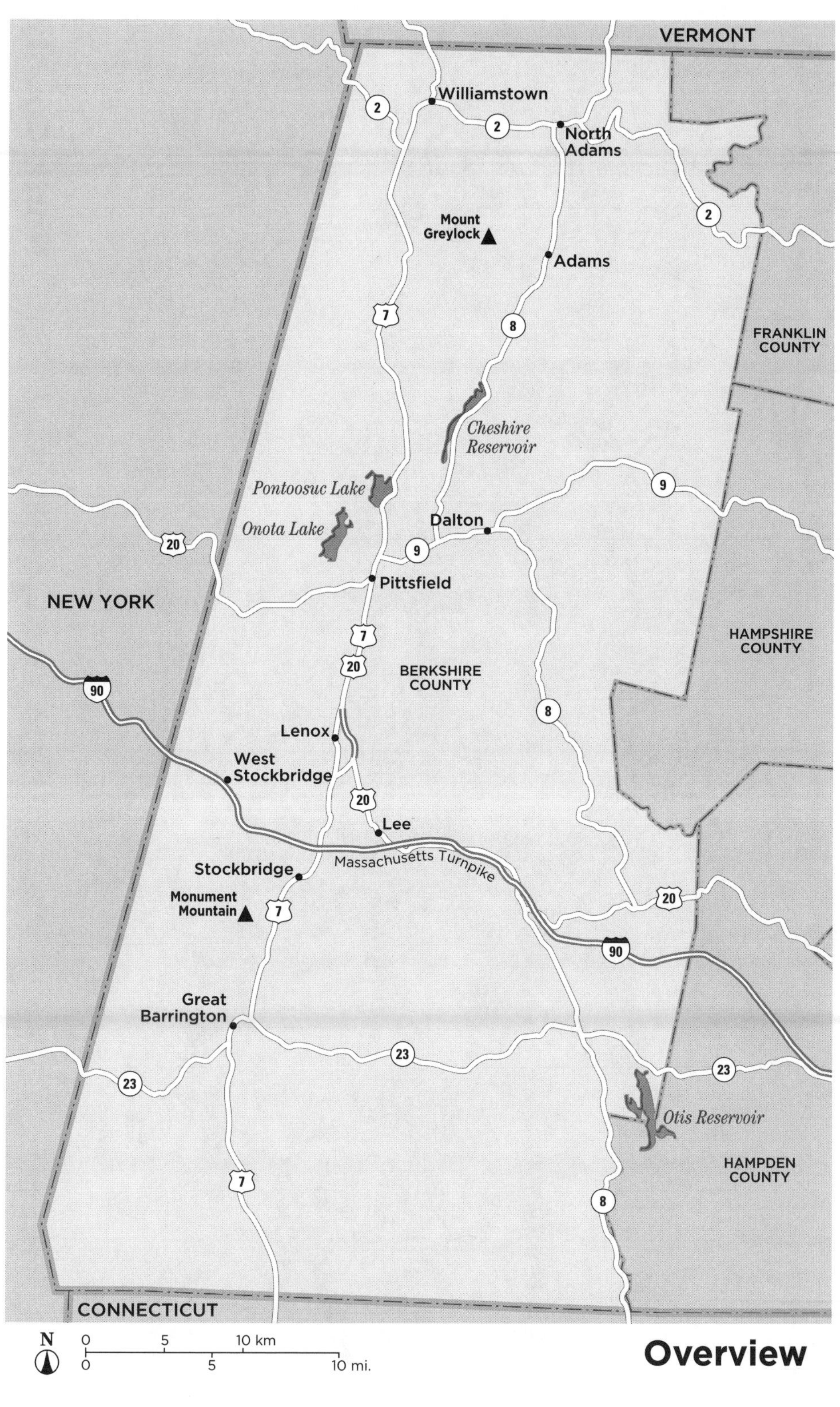
VERMONT
Williamstown
2
North Adams
Mount Greylock
Adams
7
8
FRANKLIN COUNTY
Cheshire Reservoir
Pontoosuc Lake
Onota Lake
9
Dalton
20
Pittsfield
NEW YORK
HAMPSHIRE COUNTY
7
20
BERKSHIRE COUNTY
90
8
Lenox
West Stockbridge
20
Lee
Massachusetts Turnpike
Stockbridge
Monument Mountain
7
20
90
Great Barrington
23
Otis Reservoir
HAMPDEN COUNTY
CONNECTICUT
N
0 5 10 km
0 5 10 mi.

Overview

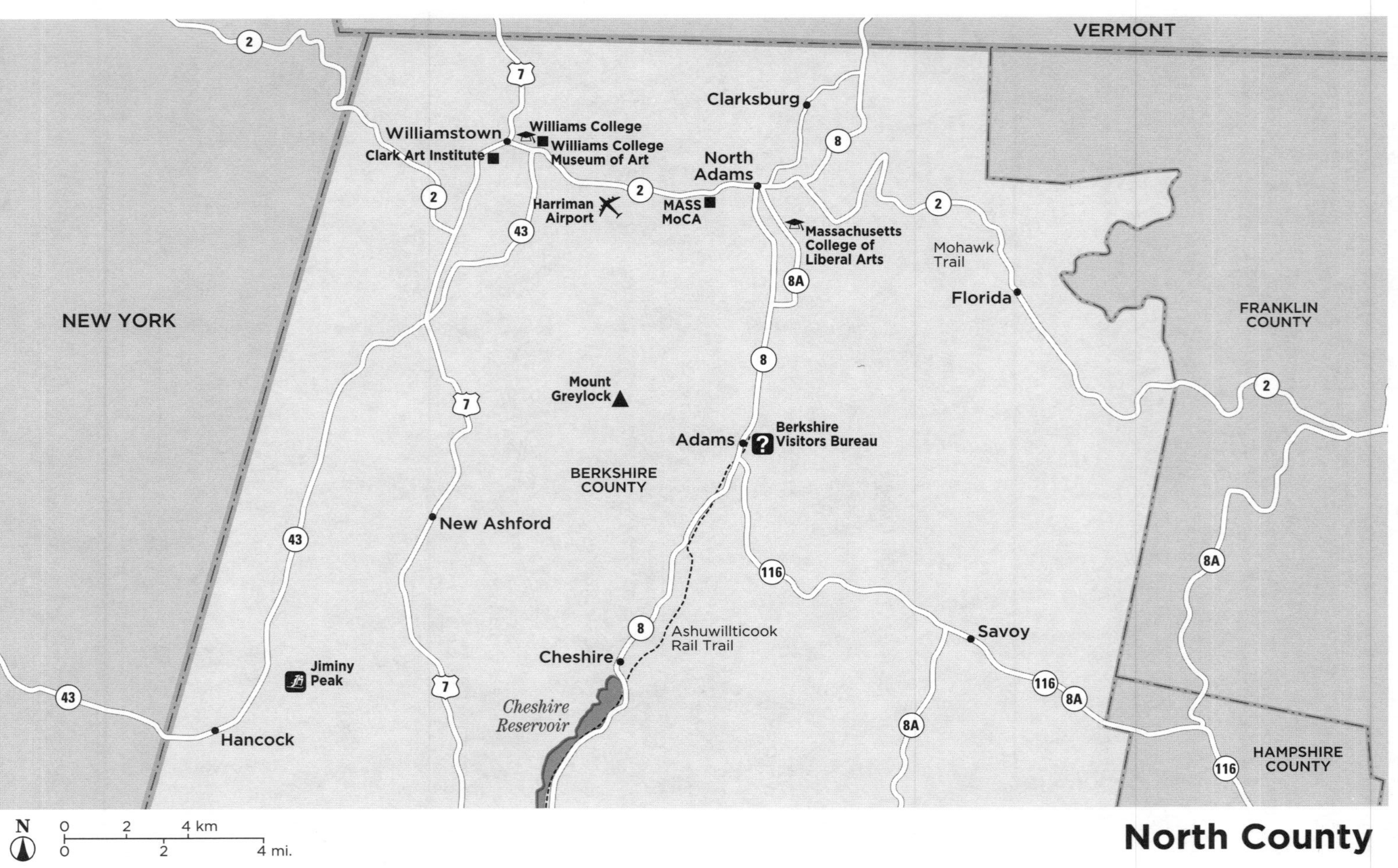

North County

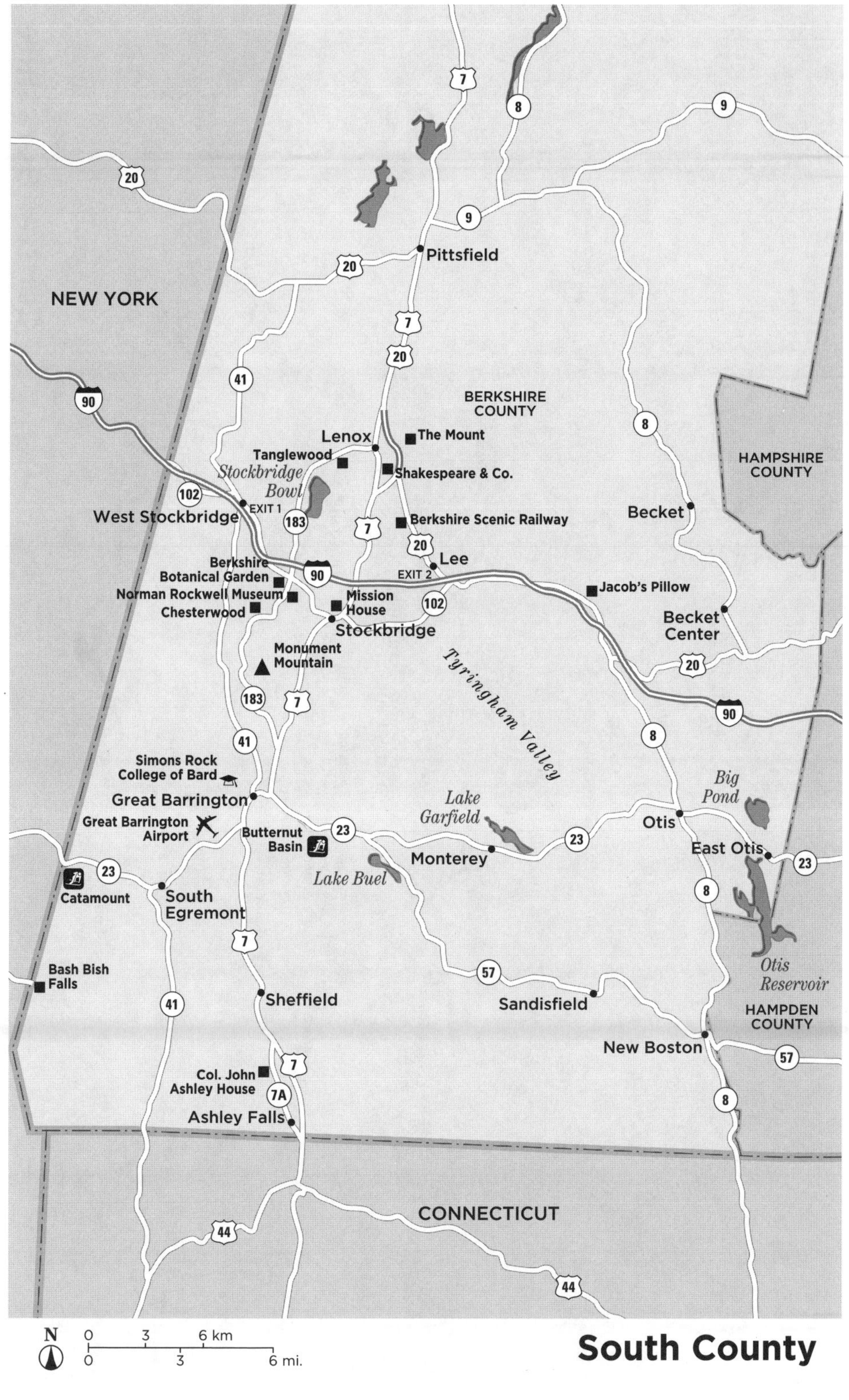

South County

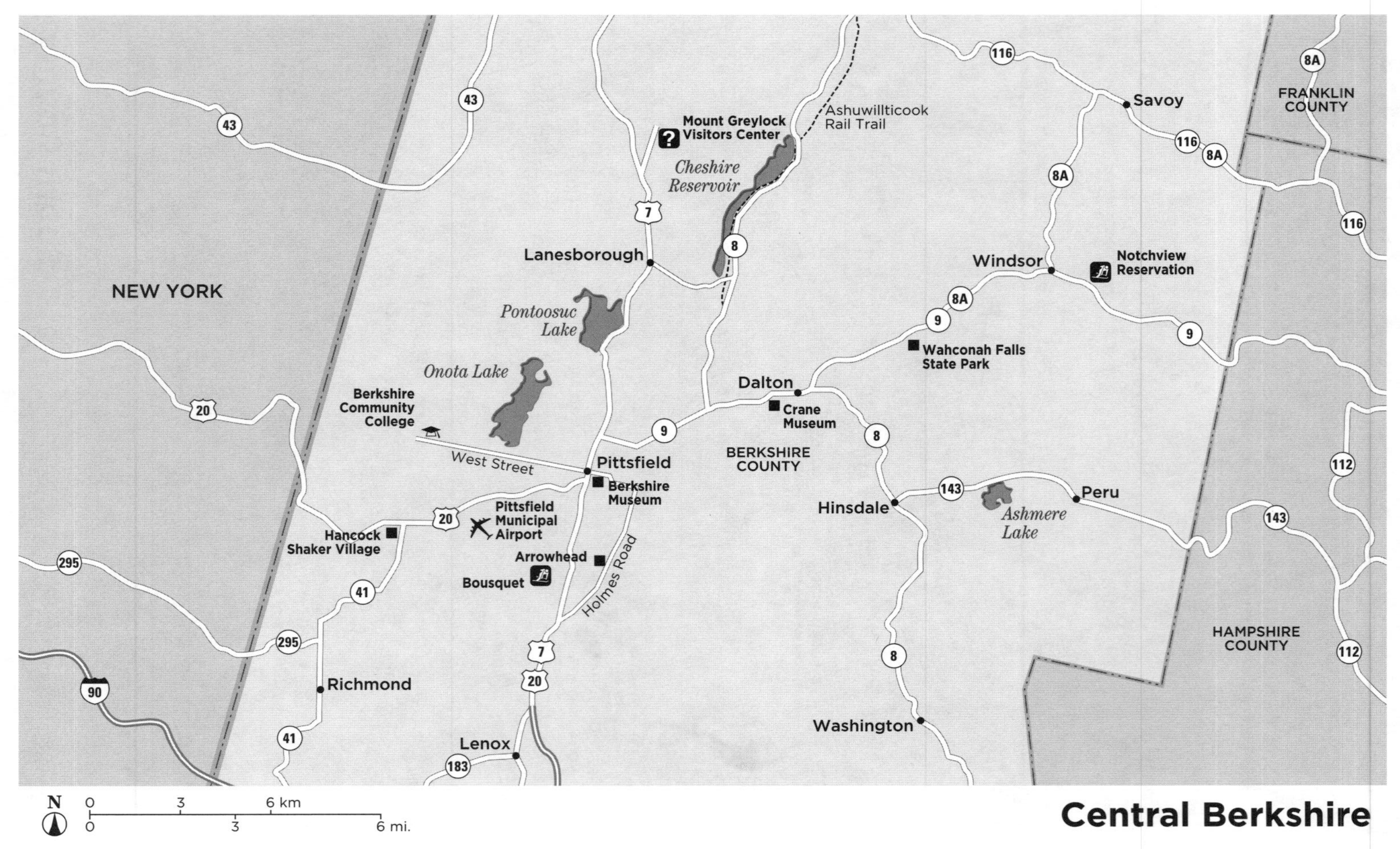

Central Berkshire

ACKNOWLEDGMENTS

Having covered the news in Berkshire County as a reporter for 15 years, I thought compiling the information for this Insiders' Guide would be a piece of cake. After all, my head is full of trivia, I have driven on practically every road between Vermont and Connecticut, I eat out a lot (a lot!), and I love to visit galleries, go to shows and concerts, and generally support the arts. What a great chance to put all that knowledge to use!

Then came the shock. I knew a lot, but I sure didn't know it all, even after living here for more than 30 years. And I soon realized there were some rather huge gaps in my knowledge, due largely to my aversion to physical activity and sports! As the process evolved, I leaned on lots of people for help—and now's the chance to thank them. For their help with golf, I am indebted to Glen Drohan and Bob McDonough. Ce Swanson and Tom Hurlbut bailed me out when I was confronted with the section on fishing. K. C. Westwood helped me with genealogy and other tidbits about the research available in the county. And without the help of Tad Ames at the Berkshire Natural Resources Council, I wouldn't have had a clue about which hikes and vistas to recommend. The writings of historians Bernard Drew and Gerard Chapman were of tremendous help to me in chronicling the development of this area.

Of course, I have to thank all the publicists who were so helpful, with Ann Claffie of the Berkshire Visitors Bureau at the top of the list. As I interviewed innkeepers, the owners of B&Bs, restauranteurs, shop keepers, gallery owners, and artists of all kinds, my admiration for these entrepreneurs grew and I am grateful for their help. I also must thank my friends, the "Couch Tomatoes," who suffered my complaining and lack of attendance at social gatherings as I dealt with "the book." To my son Curt, way out there in California, thanks for being a great sounding board and for shoring up my confidence when it sagged! And to my father who at 92 was gracious and understanding when his daughter was "too busy" to take him on pleasure drives or spend more time with him—thanks, Dad! In all, working on this guide has turned out to be a challenge—and a gift. The Berkshires—and the people who live here—are even more special than I thought and I feel lucky to have found that out.

HOW TO USE THIS BOOK

Welcome to the first *Insiders' Guide to the Berkshires.* We hope, through this guide, to introduce visitors to the many faces of "America's Premier Cultural Resort" and to remind those who live here of the opportunities at their doorstep. The Berkshires truly have just about everything in a unique blend of natural beauty, historic sites, and cosmopolitan living. Colonial inns and multicultural restaurants; museums of national renown; world-class theater, dance, and art; family farms; and parks and recreational facilities are all here, as you will learn perusing the 23 chapters in this guide.

As explained in Area Overview, the term "Berkshires" has been used by some to include parts of New York State, Connecticut, and Massachusetts counties to the east. While the attractions in those areas can be found in Day Trips and Weekend Getaways, the rest of the information in this guide refers specifically to what's available in Berkshire County. With some exceptions, most of that information is presented geographically from south to north, beginning with South County. Due in part to the nearness of Boston, New York, and Connecticut, that area has the largest number of restaurants, shops, accommodations, and other attractions. But as tourism has expanded northward, so have businesses in those and other categories.

In Getting Here, Getting Around, you will learn that travel here is determined by the mountains that dominate the landscape. As shown on our maps, there are two main north-south routes and only a few east-west highways. But we have included a number of back roads that locals use for shortcuts—or just because there are some pretty great views along the way. Before planning to go from here to there, you might want to read in the Area Overview about the 30 towns and two cities that make up the county and then develop your own scenic routes and detours. The History chapter will give some insight into what makes many of those towns special and where there are interesting collections of historic documents and artifacts. For those interested in their family roots, sources for genealogical research also are included here.

Accommodations includes an assortment of hotels, inns, bed-and-breakfasts, and resorts as well as places to park an RV or pitch a tent. Check out the Attractions and Arts and Culture chapters before deciding when to come or where to book a room. For instance, if gallery-hopping is high on your list of interests, you will see in Arts and Culture that the majority are in South County and that many are open only in the summer. On the other hand, if you plan on visiting all the museums, which are scattered around the entire county and open year-round, a room in central Berkshire might be handy. If the music at Tanglewood is a priority, the Lenox area is probably what you want. But many of the rooms there are booked before that short season even starts, so you might want to check out lodging in Central or North County and allow extra time for travel.

Restaurants are presented geographically; most locals plan their outings that way unless going to a favorite restaurant just for the treat of dining out. For example, if you're planning on visiting the three museums in North County, it makes sense to have lunch and/or dinner up there, too, so peruse the restaurant listings in the North County section. If, however, the evening includes a performance at Shakespeare & Company or the Berkshire Theatre Festival, dinner in that neck of the woods is preferable. Incidentally, restaurants that offer entertainment, along with other happening places, will be found in the Nightlife chapter.

If the kids start complaining, hop over to Kidstuff, where all kinds of kid-friendly things are suggested, including visiting farms where they can pet the animals, pick pumpkins, or undertake other seasonal activities. But don't ignore the museums, which also run many programs just for kids. People interested in agriculture will find Farms and Gardens interesting. And they will learn about the growing number of places raising organic products that are being used by the best restaurants in the county. Folks who enjoy the outdoors will find plenty of information in the Parks chapter, where the many state parks and protected lands that are open for public use are described. Recreation covers all that is offered here year-round, including golf, fishing, skiing, biking, and hiking.

There are assisted-living homes in the area, where an elderly relative can stay while the rest of the family vacations. These and other offerings for older folks will be found in the Retirement chapter. In the Health Care and Wellness and Education and Child Care chapters we describe the services and opportunities that are part of the way of life in the Berkshires. And just in case you decide you want to settle here, the Real Estate chapter provides property values and lists brokers who will be eager to help you find your dream house.

Our Insiders' tips (represented by an i) and Close-ups are designed to enhance your visit to the Berkshires and let you in on local secrets. While we have tried to present as much information as possible, some chapters, notably Restaurants and Accommodations, can not be all-inclusive, by the very nature of their subjects. But we do tell you how to find out more through various Web sites and other sources, including newspapers and radio stations listed in the Media chapter.

We hope this guide will become dog-eared from use and full of notes as you travel around the county, and we hope that you will recommend it to others. We'd also like to hear any suggestions or comments you might have to improve our effort to make the most of your time in the Berkshires. You can contact us online at www.GlobePequot.com or write to us at:

The Globe Pequot Press
P.O. Box 480
Guilford, CT 06437-0480

AREA OVERVIEW 

The sights and sounds that make up the Berkshires are as varied as those who see and hear them. To the sportsman, the hills, lakes, and streams offer bounty to be caught, while the artist tries to capture them with paint or film. The gourmand pursues dining pleasures at an amazing array of restaurants, while the local farmer sees a market for the specialty produce he grows. The paper manufacturer treasures and protects the pure water that ensures the quality of his product, while the canoeist paddles softly through the valley, pausing to observe nature at play.

Each season has its yin and yang: snow to play in, roads to clear; blossoming hillsides, mud up to here; summer theater and concerts galore; foliage resplendent, traffic and tours; Federal architecture, Victorian mills; mansions and caves, Renoir and Rauschenberg; Jessye Norman and Suzanne Vega, Amadeus Mozart and Phillip Glass. In short, the Berkshires offer a buffet to be savored. Bon appetit!

Technically speaking, the Berkshires don't exist. There is a chain of mountains called the Berkshire Plateau or Highlands, but those hills are to the east of the area generally considered to be "The Berkshires." To the purists the Berkshires means Berkshire County—period. To others the Berkshires include the hill towns to the east and New York's Columbia County to the west. Some even throw in northern Connecticut.

The Battle of the Berkshires began back in the 1920s when the area started growing as a tourist destination and our neighbors tried to cash in on the action. At one point, the county's tourism agency threatened to sue folks over in New York State who insisted on being part of the Berkshires. Saying the claim was false advertising, the group actually got the *New York Times* to reject the imposters' ads. Things are a little more relaxed nowadays, probably because the area has become an established tourist destination. Thousands are drawn annually to enjoy the scenic beauty and menu of offerings, including some 200 restaurants, 12 public golf courses, world-renowned museums, first-class summer stock theater, major concert venues, film festivals, agricultural fairs, health spas, resorts and conference centers, and sporting events. The hospitality business is booming and promises to grow even more.

But there's even more to life here than that. The Berkshires are a special place where the past is part of the present, where one is reminded daily of man's relationship with nature. It's the kind of place some wish could be kept secret. Others believe the future of the county lies in continuing to promote the area as a tourist destination and a rare setting in which to make a living. Whatever the future holds, right now the Berkshires seem to have the best of both worlds.

i

Berkshures, Berkshyres, Berksheers. Which is it? Well, it's definitely not the middle one. Most folks pronounce it* **Berkshures. Berksheers** *is an accepted second choice.

THE LAY OF THE LAND

One thing all can agree on about the Berkshires is that there are mountains. In fact, the state's highest peak is found here: Mount Greylock at 3,491 feet. The base of Mount Greylock lies in five towns: Adams, North Adams, Williamstown, New Ashford, and Lanesborough. The Appalachian Trail crosses it. Hang gliders leap from it, and cyclists race up it. Folks pick blueberries on it, and snowmobiles and skiers tour it. Greylock's snow-covered hump is said to have been the inspiration for Herman Melville's white whale, Moby Dick. Five states can be seen from the monument on Mount Greylock's peak.

To the east of Mount Greylock lies Hoosac Mountain, which in the 1800s presented a formidable barrier to trains traveling between Boston and Troy, New York, via North Adams. But in 1851 engineers began to dig a tunnel through the solid rock mountain. Financed with state funds, the project ended up taking 24 years and costing $21,241,842—sort of the forerunner of Boston's Big Dig. The project might have lasted even longer if the inventor of nitroglycerin, George Mowbray, had not set up shop at the site. But handling that highly dangerous material helped drive the death toll during construction to 196. Even more lives might have been lost if it had not been discovered—after a wagon tipped over in winter—that nitroglycerin did not explode when frozen. From then on, only frozen nitroglycerin was used. When the first train steamed through from the Deerfield Valley, the 4.75-mile tunnel was the longest in the country. Until its completion, the project had been a major industry for the city of North Adams, which was dubbed the Tunnel City. The tunnel is still in use but cannot be seen in North Adams because it is located at the end of a private road. The entrance on the other side of the mountain is visible.

Mount Greylock is part of a range of mountains that runs up through the county, ending near Vermont about where the Green Mountains begin. On the west, the Taconic Mountains run along the New York border; on the east, the Berkshire Highlands mark the entrance to the neighboring hill towns and the next county. Today folks tend to view these hills as recreational resources—or challenges to deal with in winter—but in the 1800s they were a major source of income. Talc, soapstone, mica, copper, asbestos, iron, nickel, and even gold were pulled from the mines that dotted the county. Quarries ran full tilt, providing marble and granite for projects around the country. Some, like the Specialty Minerals lime quarry in Adams, are still in operation. Others have filled with water, creating often dangerous swimming holes. The complex minerals found in these hills have drawn many a rock hound to the area. A favorite exhibit at the Berkshire Museum features a collection of local minerals and gemstones that glow eerily when the ultraviolet lights are turned on. Some say the abundance of quartz in the Berkshire schist is responsible for the many writers, artists, musicians, and other creative folks who have thrived here.

i ***Don't be fooled into thinking you're in for a fast trip just by looking at a map. Hills often don't show on a road map, and going up, down, or around them can add a lot of driving time to what seemed like a short distance.***

Then there is the water—mainly the Hoosic and Housatonic Rivers, which created the fertile valleys for farming and provided a source of power for the mills of industrialization. Many of those mills are still operating; others are being adapted to new uses. One of the most exciting adaptations is the transformation of the former Sprague Electric complex in North Adams into the Massachusetts Museum of Contemporary Art (MASS MoCA). There are also countless lakes, mostly man-made, now surrounded by vacation homes, summer camps, or exclusive properties. Places to launch a boat, take a dip, or drop a line will be found in other chapters in this guide.

The weather is often described as "changeable." Locals say that if you don't like what you're getting now, wait a minute. The layered look is de rigueur, and most residents own at least one fleece vest for those days that start out chilly and end up warm—or vice versa. Most of the weather comes from the west, and the forecasts originate with the National Weather Service Bureau in Albany. Average temperatures range around 45 degrees Fahrenheit

in spring, 69 in summer, 50 in fall, and 24 in winter. Average annual snowfall is 75 inches. At least that's what the record books say.

WHO LIVES HERE, AND WHAT DO THEY DO?

Although 95 percent of the residents of Berkshire County are white, the melting pot is alive and well. Generations have grown from the early Dutch, French, and English settlers. Descendants of the immigrants who came here to work in the mills and quarries trace their roots back to Italy, Poland, and the Slavic nations. There are Jews, Greeks, Russians, Vietnamese, Koreans, Chinese, East Indians, Pakistanis, Lebanese, West Indians, Hispanics, and African Americans.

The workforce is a diverse mix of professionals, blue-collar, service, and hospitality workers; educators, artists, writers, composers, weavers, and musicians. Hundreds work in the county's health-care industry, which supports four hospitals and a host of nursing homes and assisted-living facilities. GE Plastics has fueled the growth of the 42-member Berkshire Plastics Network. Nationally known K-B Toys, started by two local brothers, maintains its headquarters here. Other well-known companies include Interprint, Laurin Publishing, General Systems, General Dynamics, and Berkshire Life Insurance. The paper industry and related businesses continue to be major employers, as do quarries.

Too mundane? How about special effects firms and Internet companies, including chic shopping Web site Eziba. Some folks keep one foot in the city and the other in the country, commuting physically or electronically. Many employers come here for seasonal retreat and end up moving their companies here permanently.

SOUTH, NORTH, AND IN BETWEEN

Newcomers and visitors will soon notice that most residents think of the county as three distinct areas: South County, North County, and the dividing island, Central Berkshire, which consists of Pittsfield, Dalton, and some peripheral towns. Some folks act as though the three areas are different states—to be entered only if necessary. Of course for many years, the dying industrial towns in North County were depressing, and who in beautiful South County would want to go there? But that is no longer the case, although not everyone has caught up with the times. In any event, South, Central, and North County are handy ways to present information to the traveler. Where appropriate, this guide will do that, beginning with brief descriptions of the 30 towns and two cities that make up Berkshire County. Hopefully you will be able to explore them all to better understand what draws and holds so many here.

i

All phone numbers in Berkshire County are in the 413 area. If you are calling outside your local calling area—i.e., a town or exchange that isn't adjacent to you—you will have to dial "1" and then "413." Local calling areas are listed in the front of the telephone directory.

South County

ALFORD

The smallest town in Berkshire County in area, Alford covers less than 11.6 square miles. It was settled in 1750 as a farming community and remains much the same today, despite a brief period of marble quarrying in the 1800s. The classic village center has no stores, gas stations, or hotels—only a church, town hall, and one-room schoolhouse. Reportedly, poet William Cullen Bryant courted his wife, Frances, in the Alford woods. Many of the town's gracious homes are owned by current or former city dwellers.

Berkshire County Vital Statistics

Size: 947.14 square miles

Population: 134,953 (2000 census)

Highest Point: The peak of Mount Greylock, the state's highest mountain, is 3,491 feet above sea level.

Lowest Point: The Hoosic River in Williamstown is 594 feet above sea level.

Climate: Average temperatures range around 45° F in the spring, 69° F in summer, 50° F in the fall and 24° F in winter.

Average Yearly Rainfall: 43.13 inches

Average Yearly Snowfall: 70 inches

Cities: North Adams and Pittsfield

Major Towns: Williamstown, Lenox, Lee, Great Barrington

Major Rivers: Housatonic, Hoosic, Williams

Important Agricultural Crops: Organically grown fruits and vegetables and free-range livestock and poultry

Wild foods: Blueberries, raspberries, blackberries

National Park Service Land: Appalachian Trail

State Parks: Bash Bish Falls, Beartown, Clarksburg, Jug End, Mount Everett, Mount Greylock, Mount Washington, Natural Bridge, October Mountain, Otis, Pittsfield, Sandisfield (York Lake), Savoy Mountain, Taconic Trail, Wahconah Falls, Western Gateway, Windsor

Places of Special Interest: Arrowhead, Berkshire Botanical Garden, Berkshire Museum, Chesterwood, Clark Art Institute, Col. John Ashley House, Jacob's Pillow, MASS MoCA, Mission House Museum and Gardens, Naumkeag, Norman Rockwell Museum, Tanglewood, Ventfort Hall, Williams College Museum of Art

ASHLEY FALLS

The traveler coming into Berkshire County from Connecticut on new U.S. Highway 7 will fly right by Ashley Falls. Those not in a hurry would do better to take the old highway to see the 18th- and 19th-century homes that grace this charming village. This scenic route winds past farms, with great views of the mountains and river valley. The county's oldest house, the furnished 1735 home of Colonel John Ashley, is located on Cooper Road. The visitor center at Bartholomew's Cobble, a 278-acre preserve with hiking trails and scenic views throughout, is worth a visit even if hiking is not on your agenda.

BECKET

Fans of modern dance probably already know that Becket is the home of the Jacob's Pillow Dance Festival, founded by dance pioneer Ted Shawn in 1932. During summer, thousands visit the festival for world-class performances, and for that reason it is included with South County

Visitors: Approximately 2,250,000 visit the Berkshires annually.

Airports: Pittsfield Municipal Airport, Great Barrington Airport, Harriman Airport (North Adams)

Rail Service (Passenger): Amtrak

Rail Service (Freight): Conrail, Housatonic Railroad (Pittsfield-Canaan, Connecticut)

Sales Tax: 5% (clothing exempt)

Colleges: Berkshire Community College, Massachusetts College of Liberal Arts, Simon's Rock College of Bard, Williams College

Daily Newspapers: *Berkshire Eagle* (Pittsfield), *Transcript* (North Adams)

Major Interstate: Interstate 90 (Massachusetts Turnpike)

Major Highways: Massachusetts 7 and 8 (north-south); 2, 20, and 23 (east-west)

Room count: 5,000

Tourist specialties: Four-season recreation, world-class performing and visual arts, museums, historic homes, natural beauty, galleries, outlet shopping, upscale specialty stores, health spas

Major Employers: Berkshire Health Systems, Crane & Company, General Dynamics, GE Plastics, Williams College, North Adams Regional Hospital

Famous Residents: Susan B. Anthony, W. Murray Crane (Governor and U.S. Senator), W. E. B. DuBois (scholar and civil rights activist), Daniel Chester French, Nathaniel Hawthorne, Oliver Wendell Holmes, Serge Koussevitsky, Henry Wadsworth Longfellow, Herman Melville, Norman Rockwell, Edith Wharton, Secretary of the Navy William Whitney

Information: Berkshire Visitors Bureau: (800) 237-5747

Berkshire Chamber of Commerce: (413) 499-4000

Southern Berkshire Chamber of Commerce: (413) 528-4284

towns. But Becket, which encompasses about 50 square miles, is also considered part of Central Berkshire because one end of it is there. Settled in 1765, Becket was a lumbering center until the mills and related industries were wiped out by a disastrous flood in 1927. The town also benefited briefly from the discovery of blue granite. A bedroom community for Lee and Pittsfield, Becket is full of lakes and vacation homes. More than half the houses in town were built during a 1970s and 1980s construction boom. Becket can also lay claim as the highest point on I-90, which the Appalachian Trail crosses on its own bridge.

EGREMONT

With Catamount Ski & Ride nearby and a cluster of interesting shops along the highway, one might get the impression that Egremont thrives on the four-season tourist trade. In fact, agriculture is the livelihood for most of its residents, a tradition harking back to the 18th century. For a time around the turn of the 20th century, automobile axles were made in Egremont by the Dalzell factory. Eventually the company moved to Michigan to be nearer its customers, which included the Ford Motor Company. Egremont's nearness to New York has made it popular among second-home owners, who have bought up about a third of the properties in town.

GREAT BARRINGTON

Founded in 1766, Great Barrington has evolved into the cosmopolitan and commercial hub of "arty" South County. A base population of around 7,400 swells in summer when tourists and second-home owners from New York City, Connecticut, and the Boston area arrive. Parking is at a premium, and traffic crawls as shoppers explore upscale shops and take in a host of entertainment and cultural venues. Alternative lifestyles abound. Great Barrington might be considered the eating-out capital of Berkshire County—at last count there were around 85 restaurants, three of them specializing in sushi. The town is also known as a mecca for antiques collectors and dealers. Butternut Basin offers skiing in winter and outdoor events in summer. Although things quiet down somewhat after foliage season, a large student population at nearby private schools keeps the town hopping, so don't be surprised to see lots of brightly colored hair and multipierced personages. The Southern Berkshire Chamber of Commerce organizes various activities throughout the year, as do local churches, civic organizations, and schools. The Housatonic River winds through town, and volunteers have constructed and landscaped a walking path that follows much of it. Great Barrington is a leader in recycling and other environmental and social issues, due in large part to many groups of dedicated volunteers. Farms in the surrounding fertile valley offer seasonal produce at their own stands, cooperatives, or markets and supply many restaurants. Notable architecture includes Searles Castle right in the center of town, impressive 19th-century stone churches, and the town's original railroad station. Great Barrington was the first town in the country to have electric streetlights, thanks to local inventor William Stanley's transformer. It also is the birthplace of black scholar and civil rights activist W. E. B. DuBois.

HOUSATONIC

Bearing the name of the river that flows through it, Housatonic is home to several large mills, including one that is still producing paper. Empty mills loom large, but there are several businesses located in parts of them, including nationally known Country Curtains. Considered part of Great Barrington, Housatonic is kind of an offbeat town with a great bakery and several galleries and restaurants. It is one of the few places along the Housatonic River that has a public bathing area.

LEE

Settled in 1769, Lee was incorporated in 1777 and named for General Charles Lee, second in command to George Washington. Harnessing the power of the Housatonic River, the community supported some textile manufacturing in the 19th century, but paper built the town. The first paper mill was built in 1806, and by 1857 there were 25. The first practical demonstration in the United States of papermaking from wood pulp rather than rags took place in 1867 at the Smith Paper Company, which grew to be the largest producer in the world. Fine specialty papers are still produced in mills owned by world-renowned Mead and Schweitzer-Mauduit. An extremely hard and fine grade of marble was found here in 1852, creating another industry. The marble was used in the U.S. Capitol and was a major component in many of the 274 historic buildings in town. More than 9,000 headstones in Arlington National Cemetery are made of Lee marble. A lime quarry is still operating here. Although a 60-store outlet village opened on the outskirts a few years ago, the town businesses continue to thrive and in fact may be benefitting

from the additional tourist trade. A trolley carries shoppers to and fro. An infusion of state aid has transformed a dowdy downtown into an attractive street with wheelchair-accessible sidewalks and Victorian-type lighting fixtures. The picturesque center of town was featured in *Before & After*, a major film shot locally that featured Liam Neeson and Meryl Streep. Several business parks have been developed on the outskirts of town, capitalizing on the nearby Massachusetts Turnpike exit. Lee celebrates its history with Founders' Day, an annual event in September that features sidewalk sales, parades, and other activities.

i

If you've held a dollar bill, taken a Tums, written a letter on Mead stationery, opened the plastic pouring spout on a carton of orange juice, or bought a plastic "jewel case" for your compact discs, you've had a piece of the Berkshires in your hand! Crane & Co. makes the paper for currency, Specialty Minerals mines the limestone for Tums, Mead is located in Lee, the container spout is made from a mold created here, and the CD cases are made in Pittsfield!

LENOX

It's hard to believe that Lenox, with its chic shops, fascinating galleries, cutting-edge restaurants, and magnificent estates, was once a rough and tumble mining town. History says that veins of iron so honeycombed the main street that in 1862 a house sank into the earth up to its second story. The area also yielded a fine grade of sand used in glass manufacturing. (Learn more about this period by checking out the Lenox Historical Society Museum in the historic Lenox Academy on Main Street. It is open Saturday from 11:00 A.M. to 3:00 P.M.) The gorgeous views and open land available in the late 1800s attracted the mega-rich, who built elaborate summer "cottages" all over town, each one outdoing the next. Many of those estates have been adapted to other uses, which are listed in the Attractions chapter. Lenox is the summer home of the Boston Symphony and Shakespeare & Company is creating a campus that will include a historically correct replica of the Rose Theatre. Once a year, members of the horsey set carry on a Victorian tradition by decorating their carriages—called tubs—with flowers and ribbons and holding a parade. In springtime, Lilac Park bursts with the scent and color of hundreds of its namesake, planted by a local resident. The park provides a large area for kids to play and for various organizations to hold bazaars and fairs, including the annual fall Apple Squeeze sponsored by the chamber of commerce. Birders and other nature lovers enjoy walks and lectures at the Pleasant Valley Wildlife Sanctuary.

LENOXDALE

Actually part of Lenox, this small manufacturing community was originally named Furnace for an iron smelt built there. The Lenox railroad station is actually in Lenoxdale and is now a museum operated by the Berkshire Scenic Railway. This small private company operates a tourist train on a portion of the old track still owned by the Housatonic Railroad. The state is investing $3.6 million to upgrade all the track between Lenoxdale and Stockbridge, hoping to revive tourist excursions in a year or so. Sometimes thought of as the poor stepchild of Lenox, Lenoxdale has been refurbished and is coming into its own.

MONTEREY

Lake Garfield, one of the county's most beautiful, is located in Monterey, as are parts of Beartown State Forest and Lake Buel. Situated on the Mill River, this scenic town became a popular resort after the Civil War. More than half the town's 800 homes are seasonally occupied. Bidwell

House Museum, a fully furnished elegant 18th-century parsonage with accompanying gardens, is worth a visit. A tornado in the 1990s struck one part of town, killing several students at a private school and destroying acres of trees. The scars can still be seen on some of the hillsides. Gould Farm, the oldest therapeutic community residence in the country, is located in Monterey. Many of the farms in this gorgeous valley are prospering under the hands of wealthy owners. When property does come on the market, it brings a substantial price.

MOUNT WASHINGTON

Down in the lowest westerly corner of the county, high in the Taconic Range, Mount Washington is the second smallest town in the state. The state's second highest mountain, Mount Everett, is nearby, as are scenic Bash Bish Falls. The town was settled by Dutch from the Hudson Valley in the late 1600s. By the 1800s a secluded section of town within spitting distance of the New York border had become a refuge for rogues, ruffians, and fugitives from that state escaping the law. Frustrated in their unsuccessful attempts to end the lawlessness, the community decided to give that part of the town to New York State. Talk about ways to skin a cat!

NEW MARLBOROUGH

Another picturesque town, New Marlborough encompasses four hamlets, whose signs you will see along the road: Clayton, Hartsville, Mill River, and Southfield. New Marlborough was established by the legislature in 1735 to help guard the trail that was then the only route between the Berkshires and Boston via the Connecticut River Valley. Settlers farmed and ran grist and cider mills. Three paper mills and factories producing boxes and buggy whips also provided jobs. The town's early meetinghouse on the green now houses the New Marlborough Arts Center, which features art shows, concerts, and readings by noted musicians, writers, and actors throughout the year. Today the Buggy Whip Factory in Southfield houses a group antiques shop and related businesses.

OTIS

A relatively peaceful town, Otis becomes a booming community in summer. More than two-thirds of the homes in town are owned by "summer people." Otis encompasses 38.02 square miles, but 1,439 acres of that are underwater, covered by lakes and ponds. Otis Reservoir is the largest body of water in the county. Those who are here in winter enjoy skiing and snowboarding at Otis Ridge. The Otis Poultry Farm is known for its excellent chicken potpies, sold in stores around the county. For entrepreneurship, you can't top the farm's success at selling its "Chicken Gickem" to gardeners, who value it as compost.

SANDISFIELD

Practically in Connecticut, Sandisfield, also called New Boston, was a boomtown in the 1800s. Located on the main stage route to the east, it had six taverns, an equal number of churches, nine doctors, and three lawyers. It also had, unique to the area, a synagogue that served the Jewish families who emigrated to the town from New York in a small back-to-the-land movement led by Solomon Polloch, a tailor. Bypassed by the railroad, the town's population slowly dropped, leaving its 30,000 acres of woods to the hunters. There are at least six dams in town, creating lakes and ponds popular for fishing and boating. Grover Cleveland was once fined $10 for possession of an undersized bass taken from Gilder Pond. Now more than half the homes in town are vacation retreats. The Sandisfield Arts Center hosts interesting events throughout the year.

SHEFFIELD

Sheffield was "bought" from the Mahican Indians in 1724. It became the county seat when Berkshire County was incorporated in 1761 but soon lost that title to Lenox. The town's boundaries have changed nine times during its history. Many of the early homes still exist, converted to galleries, inns—and more antiques shops. Sheffield Pottery is based here, as is Sheffield Plastics, now a division of Bayer Corporation. The Sheffield Historical Society maintains seven historic structures and sponsors talks of interest throughout the year. The county's only covered bridge is located off the main highway, but you have to watch carefully for the directional sign. The original 1854 wooden truss bridge was painstakingly restored after vandals torched it in 1994. Sheffield marble was used in the Washington Monument.

STOCKBRIDGE

Several main roads and dozens of small ones converge in Stockbridge, and traffic usually crawls through town under the watchful eyes of tourists enjoying the view from the porch of the venerable Red Lion Inn. Fiercely independent, Stockbridge prides itself on looking much the same as it did when Norman Rockwell portrayed his idealistic view of life in America. In December the town re-creates Rockwell's painting of *Christmas in Stockbridge,* old cars and all. In 1853 the first village improvement association in the country was founded here. Still going strong, the Laurel Hill Association was organized by Mary Hopkins, who challenged her neighbors to help make Stockbridge the jewel of the Berkshires. They planted trees, built fences, cared for the roads and cemeteries, painted their houses, and planted flowers everywhere. Clipped grass and hedges framed lawns devoid of trash, dead leaves, or fallen twigs. They bought up a right-of-way to force a trolley to go around the town. No wonder they are still mad about the scar wrought on the town by the construction of the Massachusetts Turnpike. There is no turnpike exit here, and residents vow there never will be. Historic sites include Daniel Chester French's home, Chesterwood; the Mission House Museum and Gardens; and Naumkeag, a fully furnished mansion with elaborate gardens. The Berkshire Theatre Festival has been bringing showbiz to the boards since 1928. On the outskirts of town are the Berkshire Botanical Gardens and the Norman Rockwell Museum. Smaller historic towns nearby include Interlaken and Glendale. Interlaken is the home of IS183, an innovative art school with ties to MASS MoCA.

TYRINGHAM

As it was in the 19th century, Tyringham is a seasonal home to many wealthy and famous residents and visitors. The town is divided into two sections: Tyringham Valley and Goose Pond, which consists mostly of summer homes. Adding to the dreamlike quality of life in this untouched rural community with its large estates and sprawling farms is a strange house with a thatched roof that was built in the 1920s by sculptor Sir Henry Hudson Kirson. Originally called the Witch House, it is now known as Santarella. Although more known for their community in Hancock, the Shakers also established a settlement in Tyringham in 1792. At its zenith the community on Jerusalem Road housed more than 200 Shakers. Five buildings are still standing.

WEST STOCKBRIDGE

Once a center for mining and shipping iron ore and marble, West Stockbridge had little going for it until the 1970s, when a developer bought up the center of town and spruced it up. It now houses interesting shops, galleries, and restaurants, including one of only two in the county specializing in Vietnamese cooking. Exit 1 of the Mass Pike is located here. Westbound traffic can exit but can't get back on, the only such restriction on the entire turnpike.

Central Berkshire

PITTSFIELD

Named for British Prime Minister William Pitt, Pittsfield was founded in 1761. The fast waters of the Housatonic and the flat open land attracted industry and agriculture, and Pittsfield flourished. Incorporated as a city in 1801, Pittsfield became the county seat in 1868. By the turn of that century the city was bustling with every trade imaginable. The railroad ran through the middle; all roads converged there, and the city truly was the hub of commerce. In the 1920s Stanley Electric, which would later become General Electric, began turning out power transformers, a product that sustained GE and the local workforce until the 1980s, when the plant was closed. During World War II more than 10,000 persons worked at "the GE." After the Korean War returning engineers and others spawned a building boom in the city and its bedroom communities, with split-level ranch houses sprouting up everywhere. Population peaked then but has been steadily declining ever since. The city suffered another blow in the 1980s when the county's first enclosed shopping mall opened in neighboring Lanesborough. A third-generation department store closed, leaving a huge gap in the city's North Street shopping district. Other shops closed as traffic diminished. But the city is working hard to recover from the losses of the past. Special events are scheduled throughout the year, and new businesses and eateries are moving in. The 250-acre former GE site is being developed into a combination recreational facility and industrial park, and financial incentives are being offered to companies considering moving here. The largest employer now is Berkshire Health Systems, which operates three hospitals and a group of nursing homes. GE still maintains a presence with its plastics division, and there are a large number of plastic molding companies. Other large employers include General Dynamics and Interprint, an international firm that prints decor papers for the laminate industry. A number of organizations offer job and business training. Berkshire Community College and the chamber of commerce have teamed up to encourage high school students to pursue careers in technology. As the county seat, Pittsfield is home to several courts located in imposing 19th-century buildings. A new juvenile court and a state-of-the-art jail complete the judicial system, also a source of employment.

Travelers might notice in the Accommodations chapter how few listings there are for Pittsfield. That is due in part to the fact that Pittsfield is largely a residential area. Except for the Crowne Plaza in the center of the city and a New Ramada Inn on U.S. Highway 20, most of the motels are located along U.S. 7 south of the city. That crowded strip is referred to locally as the Pittsfield-Lenox Road and despite their proximity to Pittsfield, many of the motels located there will have Lenox addresses.

Pittsfield is blessed with a number of parks, public lakes, and a small reasonably priced ski area. The Berkshire Atheneum is a comprehensive library with large local history and genealogy departments. The Berkshire Museum is located here, as is Herman Melville's home, Arrowhead. West of Pittsfield lies Hancock Shaker Village, described more fully in the Attractions chapter. Yes, it's really in Hancock, although references usually say Pittsfield!

HANCOCK

Hancock is really unusual. A long town bordering New York State, it is impossible to travel from one end to the other without leaving Massachusetts—or going the long way around through neighboring towns. That is because a mountain cuts it in half. There are two separate fire departments, one for each end. Children in northern Hancock go to school in Williamstown after leaving their modern version of a one-room elementary school. Children in the south end go to school in Richmond, Pittsfield, and even New York, depending on busing. Some consider Hancock a North County town, while others think of it as being in Central Berkshire—

both are correct. Hancock is also a town of contrasts. At the southern end is Hancock Shaker Village, a monument to the sect that believed in celibacy; at the other end, far off in the woods, is Berkshire Vista Resort, the only nudist camp in the area. Aided by the property value of Jiminy Peak Resort, Hancock has the lowest tax rate in the county. It promises to go even lower as a 400-unit time-share resort nears completion.

RICHMOND

This rural community runs along the New York border, with Pittsfield at the north and West Stockbridge at the south. The town's scenic beauty and rural ambience are protected by progressive and strong zoning bylaws that help protect the acres of farmland and orchards. Remnants of an iron-smelting furnace can be found off the beaten path. Richmond has had its own civic association since 1947, as well as a land trust and historical society. The town is named for a British nobleman who spoke on behalf of the colonists during the American Revolution.

LANESBOROUGH

One of the first towns in the county to be settled, Lanesborough was originally called New Framingham. Local heroes include Josh Billings, who gained fame in the 1800s as a Will Rogers sort of observer of the human condition. His home and birthplace was burned down in 1962 by the owner, who was protesting a property tax increase. Lanesborough and Pittsfield share Pontoosuc Lake, one of the largest in the county and popular for boating in summer and fishing year-round. The Pittsfield Y has a marina on the lake, where it offers sailing lessons. Lanesborough has not one but two miniature golf courses as well as a full-size public course and a driving range. One of the two roads leading to the summit of Mount Greylock is located here. If you don't want to go all the way to the top, you can stop at the visitor center to view the valley stretching below. The town is also home to Balance Rock State Park, where a giant triangular boulder is poised on its tip, appearing to be delicately balancing on top of another rock. You can only imagine how many testosterone-fueled young men have tried to topple this oddity of nature. Colored glass from a glassworks in the Berkshire Village section of town is in many a Tiffany window. The 90-store Berkshire Mall is the town's largest employer. The southern terminus of the recently built Ashuwillticook Rail Trail is located near the mall entrance.

NEW ASHFORD

Lanesborough's neighbor to the north is New Ashford, a sparsely populated town due in large part to its rugged terrain. After women won the right to vote, the first woman in the country to do so cast her ballot in New Ashford. All the town's residents voted at the same time in the presidential election so that the town would have the honor of being the first in the nation to report the results. In an effort to beat others to the story, the *Evening Berkshire Eagle* took everyone in town to dinner and polled them on the spot. Unfortunately for the paper, two changed their minds, and the headline proclaiming the winner the next day was wrong! Until recently, Brodie Mountain Ski Resort was the town's only employer. However, the area has been sold and is going to be developed into a time-share resort.

One of the few remaining natural springs still open to the public is located in the Berkshire Village section of Lanesborough, off MA 8. Feel free to fill a jug or thermos. The water's pure as can be and tastes great!

DALTON

East of Pittsfield lies Dalton, home of Crane & Co., maker of the paper used in U.S. currency. A small museum at the main office depicts the history of papermaking. The powerful Crane family was active in politics. Zenas, who founded the Berkshire Museum in Pittsfield, was a state senator and leader of the Republican Party. Winthrop Murray Crane served as governor and a U.S. senator. Although their mansions are no longer in the family, the largesse of the Crane family lives on in the gifts made to the town: the library, a large park, and a community center that offers programs for young and old. With all the activities for young people, Dalton is an idyllic town in which to raise a family. A very active Council on Aging runs programs for seniors, many of whom live in elderly housing complexes. Baseball is a major sport in Dalton, which has generated several famous players, including Jeff Reardon and former Red Sox manager Dan Duquette, who now runs a sports camp in the neighboring town of Hinsdale. The Crane mills, the Byron Weston paper mills, and other businesses related to the paper industry are still the main employers in town.

HINSDALE

Except for some operating gravel pits, Hinsdale is now largely residential. But in the 1800s the town was as industrialized as others situated along the Housatonic River. One of the last mills in business made cloth for the army during World War I. Early residents included post rider Israel Bissell, who gained fame for riding from Watertown through Connecticut and on to Pennsylvania in four days and six hours to carry the call to arms after the battles of Lexington and Concord. A section of town is named Bissellville in his honor, and a number of his descendants still live in the area. Home to several summer camps, the town also draws summer residents to seasonal homes bordering beautiful Ashmere Lake. Bass Ridge Golf Course is another attraction. In the 1990s residents gained national notoriety for their fight against a huge regional landfill proposed by a Brooklyn developer. They were successful, and today the land the developers sought is protected by law from further development.

PERU

Peru and Hinsdale were originally one town called Partridgefield until 1804, when Hinsdale became a separate town. Residents then decided to change the name to Peru to honor that South American nation, although it is not clear why. Sparsely populated, Peru is the highest town in the state. During World War II, a plane carrying troops crashed in fog in Peru State Forest, killing all aboard. A monument erected by residents marks the spot. Peru has experienced growth in the past few years because it is one of the few places left in the area with large parcels of land that can be developed into building lots.

WASHINGTON

Another spread-out community, Washington nevertheless has a strong community feeling, as evidenced by the popular town park constructed by volunteers—a nice place to let the kids out of the car to run around! Don't be surprised to run into Arlo Guthrie, who has a home here. The town got off to a bad start back in 1757 when a scoundrel from Sheffield sold the land on which the town would be established to investors. Three years later the purchasers learned that the seller had pulled a scam. The local Indians had never given up the land in the first place, and the investors had to buy it again from them. In 1896 Secretary of the Navy William Whitney purchased 11,000 acres on which he built a large home and started a game preserve stocked with moose, elk, deer, buffalo, angora sheep, and pheasants. He had 55 gamekeepers on his payroll. After his death the animals were collected and sold to the Bronx Zoo in New York; the land is now part of October Mountain State Forest.

WINDSOR

Heading east out of Dalton on Massachusetts Highway 9 brings you to Windsor. High in the hills, this tiny windswept town has a strong community spirit and a dandy little museum. Detailed dioramas created by a local artist depict Windsor's past and may be seen by calling the phone number on the door. The general store and post office is a pit stop in winter for snowmobilers traversing the hills. Excellent trails for cross-country skiing are located at Notchview. Turnips, pumpkins, and Christmas trees are cash crops here.

North County

ADAMS

The birthplace of Susan B. Anthony, Adams is steeped in history and has maintained much of its past. Incorporated in 1778, Adams has a rich industrial history reflected in the town's handsomely preserved downtown and 19th-century brick mill buildings. A must-see is the public library, recently refurbished for its centennial. A statue of William McKinley stands guard near the library, commemorating a visit by the president in 1899. Quakers settled here and helped establish the town as a progressive farming village. An early meetinghouse has been preserved and is opened for special occasions. Several waves of European immigrants swept into Adams during the 19th century to work in the mills. The town still has a large Polish population. Many writers visited Adams during its boom days, including Nathaniel Hawthorne, Oliver Wendell Holmes, Herman Melville, and Henry Thoreau. A huge limestone quarry still operates, owned by Specialty Minerals, an offshoot of Pfizer Corp., and tours are available. Many of the mills are gone, but some have been converted to housing. The largest was torn down after a fire, and the land is now the site of a business park. The bulk of Mount Greylock is located in Adams but you can't get there from here. The only access roads are in Lanesborough and North Adams.

CHESHIRE

A neighbor to Adams and its partner in a regional school system, Cheshire is one of the few communities where dairying continues on a large scale. Its sprawling flatlands are ideal for cattle grazing, and the town became a dairying center early on. In 1801 every dairyman in town supplied curds to produce a 1,235-pound cheese as a gift to President Thomas Jefferson. This monumental offering—it was 4 feet wide and 18 inches high—was hauled to the Hudson River, where it made its way by barge to Washington, D.C. This part of Cheshire's past is memorialized by a cement replica of the giant cheese press displayed in the town's center. Early industries included a glass factory that was one of the first in the state to develop plate glass. The forges, mills, and tanneries are gone now, and aside from the operating dairy and beef cattle spreads, Cheshire is primarily residential. The Appalachian Trail dips into Cheshire, making the town post office a popular drop for hikers. Showers and the chance to spend a night off the trail are offered by a local church. The Ashuwillticook Rail Trail also passes through Cheshire, and a new park has been developed near the trail at the southern end of Cheshire Lake, a popular spot for fishing and, when possible, snowmobile races.

NORTH ADAMS

The county's other city, North Adams is riding the crest of renewal with the opening of the world-class Massachusetts Museum of Contemporary Art (MASS MoCA). Once teetering on the brink of oblivion, the city is now bustling with activity. New businesses are moving in, restaurants are opening, and Victorian homes perched on the steep hills that surround the city are being restored. A hotel purchased at a foreclosure sale in the 1980s is now a busy Holiday Inn. Empty mills, once the white elephants of the city, are seeing new life as business incubators and artists' studios. One has been converted into the perfect place to raise shiitake mushrooms. The owners of the Red Lion Inn in Stockbridge have renovated a row of sleazy frame row houses into an upscale inn called the Porches, complete with a pool and spa! The Massachusetts College of Liberal Arts and North Adams Regional Hospital are large employers.

The city was originally a remote outpost called Fort Massachusetts. Heritage State Park contains a small museum that documents its history, including the building of the Hoosac Tunnel. The city is renovating its 1930s movie house and sprucing up other buildings as part of its renaissance. Events held during the year include an annual beach party when one of the main streets is closed to traffic, tons of sand are hauled in, and kids are encouraged to build sand castles and otherwise enjoy a once-a-year seaside setting. While MASS MoCA gets most of the press, North Adams has other art-related ventures, including the Contemporary Artists Center on the outskirts of town. This complex offers artists a residency program and a chance to work on an oversized paper press. Shows are held through the year. Another feature is the futuristic Dark Ride, a computer-programmed vehicle that takes the occupant through a virtual art installation.

CLARKSBURG

In the 1800s Clarksburg was a booming mill town with a tannery, a woolen mill, limekilns, and lumbering providing employment for hundreds. Between 1861 and 1869 three powder mills produced $36,000 worth of black gunpowder. That industry ceased after one of the mills exploded. In 1850 Nathaniel Hawthorne passed through the area and reportedly got ideas for his story "Ethan Brand" after observing workers at the limekilns. There is no industry here today, and the town is basically a bedroom community for North Adams. Clarksburg State Forest and Clarksburg State Park offer year-round recreation. The Appalachian Trail passes through here.

FLORIDA AND SAVOY

These isolated and windswept towns high in the mountains east of North Adams thrived during the construction of the Hoosac Tunnel. Today they are sparsely populated with a few operating farms. Both towns are known for their breathtaking views and excellent fishing. Travelers will be amused by Florida's welcome sign, which sports a snowplow and a palm tree. Savoy got off to a rocky start in 1762, when it was one of several parcels auctioned off by the state to raise money. After seeing the place, the buyer demanded a refund, saying the land was not as advertised. Today the state owns 11,366 acres of forest and parkland in Savoy. Another 4,000 acres are protected by the federal government and other agencies. Snowmobiling through these woods is popular.

WILLIAMSTOWN

The Village Beautiful was incorporated in 1765. It was named for Colonel Ephraim Williams Jr., who had commanded nearby Fort Massachusetts for several years and was killed in 1775 in a battle at Lake George, New York. A member of a famous and powerful family, Williams provided in his will for a free school that later became Williams College, now one of North County's major employers. In summer the college hosts a film festival and the Emmy Award–winning Williamstown Theatre Festival. The world-renowned Clark Art Institute also sponsors concerts, speakers, and plays. The former curator of the college art museum, Thomas Krens, is now head of the Guggenheim and was the catalyst for MASS MoCA in North Adams.

Businesses in town include art galleries, clothing shops, an eclectic music store, and a number of restaurants. Two public golf courses are a draw. A movie theater that almost went under in the 1980s survived with public support and now shows art films as well as popular hits. There are a number of inns and motels, plus the 124-room Williams Inn, but events at Williams often pack them all to the hilt.

Want to learn more about the area's geology? The Berkshire Museum's natural history department has lots of information plus a display of local minerals.

HISTORY

Long before the Berkshires were "discovered" by the colonists, the Mahican Indians tilled the rich floodplain, trapped in the woods, and fished the waters in the Housatonic River Valley. The first European to set foot here was Major John Talcott, who in 1676 fought one of the last battles in King Philip's War, defeating a band of raiding Narragansett Indians near what later became Great Barrington. By the early 1700s the Native American population had shrunk, and in 1724 the Indians sold the land they owned from Sheffield to Stockbridge to speculators from the East. Remaining from their time here are the names of rivers and lakes, including Pontoosuc, Konkapot, Umpachenee, and Hoosuc, although some of the spellings have changed.

Bit by bit, settlers were moving in from the Pioneer Valley to the east, the Hudson River Valley to the west, and Connecticut to the south. The first important settlement was missionary John Sergeant's outpost in Stockbridge. Established in 1739, it was supported by Christians from as far away as England. (For more about this and the relationship between religion and the development of the Berkshires, see the Worship chapter.) In 1744 the "Great Road" between Boston and Albany was opened. Passing through Great Barrington, the access spurred growth in the relatively flat southern part of the region, moving slowly northward along the river valley toward Pittsfield.

But the northern reaches, with glowering Mount Greylock, were remote and foreboding. Even the Mahicans avoided the area except for occasional hunting forays. The Mohawks, from whom the Mahicans had split, traveled through the north from New York State to reach the Deerfield River to the east and the rich Connecticut River beyond. With the French and Indian War brewing, fears of invasion from Canada via this northern passage grew. After scouting the area—and also noting the abundance of undeveloped land—Captain William Williams and his nephew, Ephraim Williams Jr., determined that a river crossing at the narrowest point in the Hoosic Valley would be an ideal place to build a fort to hold off warring Indians. Thus was Fort Massachusetts constructed, which led the way to the development of the northern region. Ephraim was later killed in a battle in New York State, but he left a will stipulating that most of his money be used to establish a school, which later became Williams College, and that the town of West Hoosuck be renamed Williamstown. He also decreed that the town remain part of Massachusetts, solidifying that portion of the border between New York and the new settlement. After the French and Indian War ended, the region was considered safe from attack. In 1761 the royal governor formally established Berkshire County, which until then had been part of neighboring Hampshire County. Great Barrington was declared the county seat, a designation that later moved to Lenox and finally to Pittsfield.

Early settlers in the north, seeking refuge from the oppressive government to the east, found rock-strewn and heavily wooded land that was a challenge to clear and farm. Yet they overcame these obstacles, and slowly the villages we now know evolved. The government dictated how these new towns were to be built. Each had a center, or common, as a main focal point for the meetinghouse and school. Streets were then laid out in a grid, as the land permitted, and lots were drawn up. Each house was to be large—precise measurements were given—but enough land was to be left open so that each could have its own garden. Some instructions, drawn up by people who had never visited the area and never would, even detailed what crops to grow. Perhaps that is where today's resistance to edicts from Boston got its roots!

Whether the remoteness, the terrain, or the general character of the settlers created an attitude of independence and feistiness, Berkshire residents were the first to rebel against the British and to oppose slavery. The first "sit-in" in the nation took place in Great Barrington in 1774, when about 1,500 angry Berkshire farmers surrounded the courthouse, preventing the royal judges from meeting. The year before, the Sheffield Declaration had been drawn up by a group of townsfolk and lawyers meeting in Colonel John Ashley's home. This early petition of grievances against British rule stated for the first time that all men are created free and equal. Many from the Berkshires served during the Revolutionary War, including some of the Mahicans. One contingent joined the Green Mountain Boys from Vermont and went on to capture Fort Ticonderoga. British cannons, taken from the fort by General Henry Knox, were hauled across the Berkshire hills along what is now Massachusetts Highway 23 to Boston, where they were used by General Washington to drive out the redcoats in 1776. Berkshire soldiers took part in battles in Bennington, Vermont; Saratoga, New York; and other decisive campaigns. Some of the Continental troops were armed with weapons created in area forges and clothed with leather goods from a commissary in Richmond.

The Revolution was followed by an economic depression. Many of those who had fought in the war began losing their homes and businesses to foreclosures and were being thrown into debtors' prisons. In 1786 angry Berkshire residents joined Daniel Shay's Rebellion, closing courthouses and releasing debtors from jail. Many were killed or captured during a failed attempt to take an arsenal in Springfield. Several battles between these rebels and government forces took place in the county, the last being near Sheffield. Basically a war of classes, the uprising caused many to see the need for a stronger federal government and helped lead to the adoption of the U.S. Constitution.

Berkshire residents had already played a major part in the adoption of the state constitution in 1780. This document was the first official declaration of equality and freedom for all and became the model for the U.S. Constitution. The state constitution led to the separation of church and state and to the abolition of slavery. Colonel Ashley's slave, Mumbet, was the first to seek her freedom under the new constitution. After being abused by Ashley's wife, Mumbet ran away. The colonel went to court to get his "property" back, but the judge ruled that she was a free woman under the new constitution. Mumbet changed her name to Elizabeth Freeman and became a servant for the prominent Sedgwick family of Stockbridge. (Thomas Sedgwick had supported Mumbet's case.) Catherine Sedgwick's book, *A New England Tale,* was published in 1822.

By the early 1800s, poor farmers were moving west and industry was moving into the area. Acres of woodland were cut to make charcoal to fuel the more than 40 blast furnaces in operation in the Housatonic River Valley, turning iron and limestone into utensils, armaments, and tools. Berkshire marble was being quarried, destined for important municipal structures in the new country. The Crane paper mill in Dalton began production, making U.S. currency then as it does now. Rivers and streams were dammed to make power for the textile, paper, and sawmills that began to dot the landscape. By the end of the 1800s, 75 percent of the woodland had been stripped bare. When the Civil War broke out, Berkshire men, including many African Americans, answered the call, with 6,000 joining the Union Army. The textile mills turned out cloth for uniforms and blankets. Iron from North Adams was used to build the ironclad ship *Monitor,* and the Richmond foundry cast train wheels and guns. The Berkshire economy was booming.

While industry was having a visual and economic impact on the Berkshires, less noticeable was the attraction of the area to

CLOSE-UP

Tracing the Past

Genealogists and historians from around the country, professional and amateur, have found that Berkshire County is rich in research resources. As is true throughout New England, each city or town clerk is required to keep records of births, marriages, and deaths. Most have retained records going back to the incorporation of their municipality and most, with some notice, are willing to help those seeking their family roots. City and town halls also hold local tax and property records. Most town libraries have a few family histories, town histories, or other useful materials, and many churches have records of their members going back into the 18th century. Property ownership can be traced back to original land grants through the three registries of deeds in the county. Two major repositories of research are located in Pittsfield: the Silvio O. Conte National Archives and Records Center and the Local History and Genealogy Department at the Berkshire Athenaeum. And remember, every town in the Berkshires has a historical commission, and many maintain collections of various sizes. To connect with those not listed here, call the appropriate town hall for information. All are listed in the white pages, but hours are limited in the really small towns.

The Silvio O. Conte National Archives and Records Administration
10 Conte Drive, Pittsfield
(413) 445–6885
www.archives.gov

Named for longtime Congressman Silvio O. Conte, these archives for the Northeast region are located on Dan Fox Drive, off U.S. Highway 7 just south of the city. This mammoth repository is unlike any other national archive in that it contains not only regional information but also data from federal records located around the country. Material includes national census records from 1790 through 1930, military records, pension and land warrant records, and naturalization records for Massachusetts, New York, and Pennsylvania starting with 1906. Passenger arrival records from several East Coast ports and numerous records relating to Native and African Americans are also found here. The volunteers who work here are friendly, knowledgeable, and helpful.

The Berkshire Athenaeum (local history room)
1 Wendell Avenue, Pittsfield
(413) 499–9486

The Berkshire Athenaeum, Pittsfield's main library, is located near Park Square on Wendell Avenue across from the Berkshire Superior Court House. The local history department's collection of town histories, vital records, and other research material is the most comprehensive in the county. With help from the Berkshire Family History Association, the Athenaeum also has built one of the finest collections available pertaining to New England family history. The collection includes early material from Rhode Island as well as Massachusetts, Connecticut, and Vermont. There is some data on adjacent New York counties, French Canada, and other areas that New Englanders came from or went to. The collection includes some 21,000 books, a half dozen large cabinets full of microfilm and microfiche, and several CD–ROM workstations. A very skilled staff is always on hand to help but does not have the time to do the actual research for you.

The Berkshire Family History Association
P.O. Box 1437, Pittsfield 01202
(No phone)

If you are unable to do your own research, you may write to the Berkshire Family History Association, whose members will do it for you. The BFHA has published more than 400 indexes to previously unindexed local and family histories, along with a guide to current and ancient cemeteries throughout the Berkshires and numerous other genealogical resources, including a quarterly newsletter.

The Berkshire Historical Society
780 Holmes Road, Pittsfield
(413) 442-1793
www.berkshirehistory.org

The Berkshire Historical Society is located in Herman Melville's Arrowhead, a National Historic Landmark, which it also maintains. The society oversees the Margaret H. Hall Local History Library and Archives and maintains a collection of more than 4,500 local history artifacts. The Hall Library contains over 200 cubic feet of manuscripts, 170 linear feet of books, 150 maps and atlases, 350 oral history tapes, and 14,000 photographic images. Letters, journals, government records, newspapers, and directories dating from the early 18th century to the present can be found here. The archives are available by appointment for public use for a fee of $2.00. Members of the society are not charged. Research inquiries may be addressed to the Archivist at 780 Holmes Road or be submitted to the society's e-mail address under the subject "Archives." The first half hour of research is free; $15 per hour is charged after that.

OTHER RESOURCES

Southern Berkshire Register of Deeds
334 Main Street, Great Barrington
(413) 528-0146

Central Berkshire Register of Deeds
44 Bank Row, Pittsfield
(413) 443-7438

North Berkshire Register of Deeds
65 Park Street, Adams
(413) 743-0035

The Adams Historical Society
Adams Library
92 Park Street, Adams
(413) 743-8345

The Dalton Historical Commission
Dalton Town Hall
462 Main Street, Dalton
(413) 684-1472

The Lenox Historical Society
P.O. Box 1856, Lenox 01240

The North Adams Historical Society
P.O. Box 333, North Adams 01247-0333
(413) 664-4700

The North Adams Public Library
Church Street, North Adams
(413) 662-3133

Sheffield Historical Society
159-161 Main Street, P.O. Box 747, Sheffield 01257
(413) 229-2694
www.sheffieldhistory.org

The Stockbridge Library Association Historical Collections
Main Street, Stockbridge
(413) 298-5501

The Williamstown House of Local History
195 Main Street, Williamstown
(413) 458-2160

Williams College Chapin Library of Rare Books and Manuscripts
Stetson Hall
26 Hopkins Hall Drive
P.O. Box 426, Williamstown 01267
(413) 597-2462
www.williams.edu

writers and artists. William Cullen Bryant, Samuel Gray Ward, Herman Melville, Nathaniel Hawthorne, Oliver Wendell Holmes Sr., Edith Wharton—even Henry Wadsworth Longfellow—found inspiration for their work in the Berkshire hills. Artists Thomas Cole, Frederic Church, John Kensett, and Asher B. Durand captured on canvas the beauty of the Housatonic River Valley. Sculptor Daniel Chester French created the Lincoln monument in his Stockbridge studio. Henry Hudson Kitson sculpted the *Pilgrim Maid* for Plymouth and the *Minute Man* for Lexington. Later came Norman Rockwell, Alexander Calder, Jason Johns, and Eric Sloane. Artists, sculptors, potters, glassblowers, and writers continue to produce their work here, much of it shown nationally. Inventors who worked here and left their marks on the world included William Stanley (the transformer); Stephen Dudley George (the first electric trolley and the electric elevator); and Frank Sprague (the first successful trolley line). These were the ancestors of General Electric and Sprague Electric, major employers in the county until they closed their plants in the 1980s.

The wealthy discovered the Berkshires in the late 1800s, choosing to build ostentatious estates they called "cottages" to house their families, guests, and burgeoning staffs. The top architects and landscape designers of the period were hired for these can-you-top-this projects. In 1880 Lenox had 33 estates. By the turn of the 20th century there were 75. Many of these sprawling mansions now are protected historic museums, as are the homes and studios of many of the artists. As millionaires, political leaders, and social climbers followed the Carnegies and others to the Berkshires, the rich took over with their horse shows, croquet matches, and hunt clubs. Garden parties prevailed, and the summer ended with a parade of carriages, or tubs, decorated with flowers—a tradition that continues in Lenox today.

The 20th century saw the Berkshires develop into a cultural mecca that now draws millions each year. Newly built roads and improved rail lines brought the touring public. Theaters opened, Tanglewood and Jacob's Pillow Dance Festival were born, museums expanded, and other venues opened. Even during the Depression, improvements were made on the highway system by workers employed through the Civilian Conservation Corps (CCC). Parks were opened, skiing expanded, and the four-season resort was born.

In the 21st century, efforts are under way to replace closed manufacturing plants with new industries and expand the area as a tourist destination. But as steeped in history as the area is, it will always have one foot in the past as it embraces the future. Above all, there is still the peace to be found snowshoeing through the woods, hiking the trails on Mount Greylock, fishing the lakes and ponds, or simply watching the sun set beyond the Berkshire hills.

GETTING HERE, GETTING AROUND

GETTING HERE

By Highway

The Berkshires are a few hours away from all metropolitan centers in the Northeast thanks to the interstate highway system. In fact, the construction of the Massachusetts Turnpike, or I-90, ensured the region's future as a tourist destination. The "Pike" has two exits in Berkshire County. Exit 1 in West Stockbridge is a bit of a maverick. It is the only interchange on the Pike that is an entrance only for eastbound traffic. Travelers from New York State bound for the Berkshires have to drive to exit 2 in Lee to get off. This was probably done to keep eastbound truck traffic from entering West Stockbridge. Westbound traffic has no such restriction. See Getting Around to find out what local roads to take once you leave the turnpike. Some travelers from the west leave I-90 in Nassau, New York, and take U.S. Highway 20 to reach the Central Berkshire area.

Several parkways and freeways lead to the Berkshires from the metropolitan New York area. The New York Thruway, or I-87, connects with I-90 in Albany. A major truck route, the Thruway is fast if a bit frantic. Less fast paced is the scenic if somewhat boring Taconic State Parkway. Large trucks are banned, but watch out for deer. There are several ways to reach the county from the Taconic. New York/Massachusetts Highway 23 leads to Great Barrington; while New York/Massachusetts Highway 295 and U.S. Highway 20 connect with Central Berkshire. Another north-south route to and from New York is New York Highway 22, which travels through many picturesque small towns and rural vistas as it wends its way north from Brewster. It takes about the same time as the Taconic, if you don't get stuck behind a truck full of hay or a school bus, and connects with all the highways mentioned above.

Folks coming from central or southern Connecticut usually use I-91, which passes Hartford's Bradley International Airport on its way through the Connecticut River Valley to Canada. It connects with I-90 in Springfield and is about an hour from Lee. There are no tolls between Springfield and the Berkshire exits. U.S. Highway 7 and Connecticut Highway 8 continue on into Berkshire County on their way to Vermont.

Many travelers heading to North County from the eastern part of the state prefer scenic Massachusetts Highway 2, also called the Mohawk Trail. The former Native American path was paved in 1914 specifically to bring tourists through the northern part of the state. There are still a few gift shops with tepees and totem poles, reminiscent of roadside stands that were prolific in the '30s and '40s. Passing through historic towns, MA 2 snakes through valleys and gorges where sparkling rivers flow. Entering the hills of western Massachusetts, the road twists and turns as it climbs and descends the hills, with awesome views along the way. Commenting on the contrasts along the way, Nathaniel Hawthorne wrote: "The mountains diversified the scene with sunshine and shadow, and glory and gloom." The descent into North Adams includes a scary hairpin turn, and drivers are well advised to heed warnings to slow down and test their brakes as the road traverses the mountains. MA 2 continues on through Williamstown to New York State, winding through more mountains until it descends into Troy and beyond. North County resi-

Despite its urbanization, Berkshire County is pretty rural. Keep an eye out for coyotes, foxes, moose, deer, bears, and other critters when driving around.

dents usually take that route to get to the airport in Albany.

ROADS IN A NUTSHELL

From the Albany, New York, area: Follow I-90 (Massachusetts Turnpike) east. For Central and Northern Berkshire take exit 11, Nassau, New York, and U.S. 20 east. For Southern Berkshire take exit 2 in Lee.

From Eastern Massachusetts: Follow I-90 west to exit 2 in Lee or exit 1 in West Stockbridge, or take MA 2 from Somerville to North Adams.

From the Hartford, Connecticut, area: Take I-91 north to I-90 west to exit 2 in Lee.

From Western Connecticut: Follow U.S. 7 or CT/MA Highway 8 north.

From New Jersey, New York City, and Long Island: Follow any of the parkways north to I-87 north to I-90 east to exit 2 in Lee.

From the Taconic State Parkway: For Central Berkshire take NY/MA 295 east to Massachusetts Highway 41 north to U.S. 20 east. For North Berkshire continue to U.S. 7 north. For South Berkshire take NY/MA 23 east.

DISTANCE GUIDE

(Miles are approximate to Pittsfield—and don't forget those mountains when estimating the time!)

Albany, New York	36 miles
Boston, Massachusetts	120 miles
Buffalo, New York	338 miles
Cape Cod, Massachusetts	220 miles
Hartford, Connecticut	84 miles
Manchester, New Hampshire	169 miles
Newport, Rhode Island	187 miles
New York City	150 miles
Philadelphia, Pennsylvania	258 miles
Providence, Rhode Island	150 miles
Portland, Maine	248 miles
Springfield, Massachusetts	52 miles
Toronto, Canada	400 miles
Washington, D.C.	392 miles

By Rail

Before the Massachusetts Turnpike was built, trains brought vacationers to the Berkshires. Today only one train provides passenger service directly to the county. Amtrak's Lake Shore Limited makes one run a day from Chicago to Boston and back, stopping in Pittsfield each way. The nearest train stations are about an hour or so away in New York State. Amtrak's commuter trains between Manhattan's Penn Station and Rensselaer, New York, run often with a scenic if expensive trip along the Hudson River. Most folks prefer using the Hudson, New York, stop—about an hour from South and Central County. The restored Hudson railroad station is comfortable; if you have time to kill, there are interesting shops and galleries plus excellent restaurants all along Warren Street, the main thoroughfare. Rensselaer is handier for those in North County but has little else going for it. Metro-North runs trains from Grand Central by a different route and recently extended its line to Wassaic, which is about an hour from Great Barrington on local roads. The Metro-North fare is about half that of Amtrak's Hudson River run. Both take about two hours, but Metro-North makes lots of stops while Amtrak doesn't.

RAIL LINES

Amtrak
(800) 872-7245
www.amtrak.com

Metro-North (Metropolitan Transportation Authority)
(212) 532-4900 (New York), (800) 638-7646
www.mta.nyc.ny.us.mnr

By Bus

Several bus companies serve the area, with stops in Great Barrington, Lee, Lenox, Pittsfield, and Williamstown and on into Bennington, Vermont, depending on the line. Information about all companies is available at the Pittsfield Bus Terminal. The city of Pittsfield, with the help of a $10 million federal grant, is building a new transportation center downtown on Columbus Avenue that will replace the present rather shabby bus terminal a few blocks away and the present Amtrak station, a tiny Plexiglas affair. Local buses operated by the Berkshire Regional Transit Authority will link with this terminal in an effort to increase the use of public transportation.

Pittsfield Bus Terminal
57 South Church Street, Pittsfield
(413) 442-4451, (800) 751-8800

LOCAL BUS SERVICE

Berkshire Regional Transit Authority
Downing Industrial Park
67 Downing Parkway, Pittsfield
(413) 499-2782

INTERSTATE BUS COMPANIES

Bonanza Bus Lines
(888) 751-8800
www.bonanzabus.com

Peter Pan Bus Lines
(800) 343-9999
www.peterpanbus.com

Greyhound/Trailways
(800) 231-2222
www.greyhound.com

By Plane

Albany, New York, and Bradley in Hartford, Connecticut, are the nearest airports, each being an hour or so away. That beats the three-hour drive from the New York airports. Boston's Logan Airport is a bit closer, but then there's the Big Dig to drive through. A park-and-ride service in Framingham is handier than going all the way into the city. Some folks fly into and out of the Providence airport to take advantage of cheaper fares, but the drive is a killer! If you don't have anyone to meet you or take you to the airport, there are limousine services and car rental agencies here and at all the airports. Of course if you happen to own your own plane or want to charter one, there are three small airports in the county at your disposal. Pittsfield Municipal Airport can handle corporate jets, while Great Barrington and North Adams are limited to single- and multiple-engine planes. Charter service and scenic flights can be arranged at all three airports.

CHARTER SERVICES AT LOCAL AIRPORTS

Berkshire Aviation Enterprises
Great Barrington Airport
North Egremont Road (Massachusetts Highway 71), Great Barrington
(413) 528-1010

Lyon Aviation
Pittsfield Municipal Airport
832 Tamarack Road, Pittsfield
(413) 443-6700

Esposito Flying Service
Harriman Airport
MA 2, North Adams
(413) 663-3330

Limousine and Taxi Services

SOUTH COUNTY

AA Taxi & Livery Services
AA Transport Car Service
195 State Road, Great Barrington
(413) 528-6778, (877) 528-3906

Abbott's Limousine & Livery Service
Greylock Street, Lee
(413) 243-1645, (413) 637-4431 (Lenox number), (800) 551-5509
www.abbottslimo.com

Berkshire Limousine Service
Berkshire Taxi
140 Housatonic Street, Lenox
(413) 637-2011

Driving Service
Egremont
(413) 528-9053

Lenox Taxi & Limousine
8 Fairview Street, Lenox
(413) 637-3014

Old's Limousine Service
Lee
(413) 243-2272, (800) 287-6537

Park Taxi Service
US 20, Lee
(413) 243-0020

Taxico
974 South Main Street, Great Barrington
(413) 528-0911

Tobi's Limousine Service
Lenox
(413) 637-1224

CENTRAL BERKSHIRE

A-1 Airport Limousine Service
10 Pleasant Street, Pittsfield
(413) 443-7111

Classic Coach Limousine
Pittsfield
(413) 448-2256

The Limo Connection
Pittsfield
(800) 924-7067

Rainbow Taxi
10 Pleasant Street, Pittsfield
(413) 499-4300

Transport the People Inc.
10 Pleasant Street, Pittsfield
(413) 443-7111

NORTH COUNTY

A-1 Airport Limousine Service
362 State Road, North Adams
(413) 664-3200

American Cab Co.
420 Curran Highway (MA 8), North Adams
(413) 662-2000

Berkshire Livery Service
141 Veazie Street, North Adams
(413) 662-2609, (800) 298-2609

Berkshire World Travel
59 Main Street, North Adams
(413) 663-7646

Transport the People Inc.
362 State Road, North Adams
(413) 664-3200

Veteran's Taxi
376 State Road, North Adams
(413) 663-8300, (413) 663-6284

BASED ELSEWHERE

Airport Car Service
180 Spring Street, Springfield
(800) 516-9616

Dove Limousine
Chicopee
(800) 342-0030
www.dove-limo.com

Michael's Limousine Service
Ludlow
(800) 533-8470
www.michaels-limo.com

Royale Limousine
Rensselaer, New York
(518) 286-4444
www.royalelimousineservice.com

Springfield Airport and Limousine Service
7 Farragut, Springfield
(413) 732-0127

Local Car Rental Companies

SOUTH COUNTY

Pete's Chrysler-Plymouth-Subaru-Kia
398 Stockbridge Road (US 7), Great Barrington
(413) 528-0848

RW's Inc.
Massachusetts Highway 102, Lee
(413) 243-0946

CENTRAL BERKSHIRE

Affordable Car Rentals
689 East Street, Pittsfield
(413) 445-5795

Enterprise Rent-A-Car
558 East Street, Pittsfield
(413) 443-6699, (800) 325-8007

Hertz
51 Center Street, Pittsfield
(413) 499-4153

National Car Rental
745 East Street, Pittsfield
(413) 442-4200

Pete's Chrysler-Plymouth-Subaru-Kia
689 East Street, Pittsfield
(413) 445-5795

NORTH COUNTY

Affordable Sales & Rental
100 Union Street, North Adams
(413) 663-3777

Enterprise Rent-A-Car
303 State Street, North Adams
(413) 664-7620, (800) 325-8007

i

Remember to stop when a school bus's red lights are flashing. To avoid getting stuck behind school buses, take a coffee break between 2:00 and 3:00 P.M., when school lets out.

GETTING AROUND

Faced with mountains and rivers to negotiate, colonists in the 1700s followed the trails laid out by the Native Americans who lived here. Stagecoach lines were developed, which became highways and byways. Today there are still only two ways to get from South to North County: US 7 and MA 8. MA 8 on the east side of the county winds through the less populated towns until it reaches Dalton and Pittsfield, where it continues on to North Adams. Busy US 7 runs up the west side of the county from Ashley Falls at the Connecticut border to Williamstown at the Vermont border. It passes through all the towns on the west side of Berkshire County except Ashley Falls and Lenox, where bypasses were built to reduce the crush of traffic. Efforts to build a similar bypass around Pittsfield have met with resistance for decades, resulting in a grinding halt in the center of that city, where you encounter the challenge of negotiating Park Square, which is really an oval. The signs don't help much, so plan ahead and try to remain calm as you maneuver to the lane you need.

You might think that the turnpike interchanges would connect with US 7 and MA 8. Welcome to the Berkshires. Neither route does, and if the residents of Stockbridge and Becket have their way, they never will! So after leaving the Pike in Lee, travelers seeking US 7 have to take either US 20 north through Lee or MA 102 west to Stockbridge. To get to MA 8 you have to backtrack on US 20. The intersection where MA 102 and US 20 converge at the Lee exit is a melange of traffic lights and merges that locals refer to as the Thousand Islands. The state highway department is trying to straighten out this maze, so watch for construction.

To get to US 7 from exit 1 in West Stockbridge, the motorist must take either MA 102 to Stockbridge or Massachusetts Highway 41 north where it connects with US 20, which leads to Pittsfield. Confused? Sorry, but the signs don't help much either. For instance, in Pittsfield US 20 merges with southbound US 7, and signs lead you to think they both go to the turnpike. But after the merged highways pass Lenox, they split, with US 7 veering off to the right to Stockbridge and US 20 going to Lee. Judging by the tire marks on the road, this split catches many a driver in the wrong lane!

The main east-west routes in South County are Massachusetts Highway 23, MA 102, and US 20. MA 23 begins at the New York border and runs through Great Barrington until it heads east to Otis and beyond. As mentioned above, MA 102 goes from West Stockbridge to Lee. US 20 continues on toward Becket, ending eventually in Boston. Some who have the time prefer to take US 20 instead of the turnpike, since it passes through scenic countryside and interesting towns.

In Central Berkshire, after going halfway around Park Square, US 7 continues north to Williamstown. But getting to MA 8 from the west side of town means traversing through Pittsfield on either East Street or Tyler Street to a five-road intersection known locally as Coltsville. Major shopping centers are located here. MA 8 heading east brings you to Dalton, where it connects with Massachusetts Highway 9. MA 9 is a popular alternative to taking the turnpike, especially if you are heading to Northampton and Amherst. MA 8 north leads to North Adams through Lanesborough, Cheshire, and Adams.

Until the late 1980s, MA 2 in North County was the only other cross-county road. But when the Berkshire Mall was built in Lanesborough, a major two-lane "driveway" was constructed to bring shoppers from US 7 to the mall on MA 8. This road with its gorgeous views soon became the major alternative to driving through Pittsfield for commuters and truckers alike. Now more than 10 years old, the road is slated for a major reconstruction.

Seat belts are mandatory for adults; however, a vehicle may not be stopped by police for that reason alone. If a car is stopped for another reason, any adults not wearing their seat belts can be issued a citation. Seat belts are mandatory for children under age 12, and car seats are required for infants and toddlers up to 2 years old. Vehicles may be stopped and a citation issued if an officer observes a violation of those laws.

Be wary of black ice, a treacherous phenomenon that occurs under certain circumstances. Black ice usually forms when a warm front moves in and rain falls on road surfaces that are below freezing. The moisture freezes in a thin glaze, and while the surface may simply look wet, it could instead be slick ice. Black ice can also be formed when the temperature drops suddenly, as at dusk, and dampness on the roads freezes.

Byways, Shortcuts, and Vistas

Most of the smaller roads in the county eventually bring you back to civilization, so don't be afraid to wander off the beaten path for some back road sightseeing. But to be on the safe side, bring along a compass and always have the Insiders' Guide handy to check the maps. Exploring is not advised in spring, when dirt roads turn to mud.

While the major highways offer some great scenery, some of the best views in the area are on side roads. In South County, some of the nicest can be found along Lenox Mountain Road, which runs from Massachusetts Highway 183 by Tanglewood to MA 41 in either Richmond or West Stockbridge, depending on which fork you take. Also in Lenox, Undermountain Road offers a fine view of Stockbridge Bowl and the valley around it. This recently repaved road also passes some spectacular homes and is a good shortcut from the center of Lenox to Tanglewood—but don't tell anybody. For a lovely view of the Tyringham Valley, take Tyringham Road off MA 102 in Lee. Stunning views from Mount Everett are only for the intrepid—the road to the summit is closed to automobiles until it can be repaired. The road to Bash Bish Falls in Mount Washington is also closed but it is slated for a major reconstruction.

In Central Berkshire, the road that winds through Pittsfield State Forest rewards the patient driver with great views and is especially beautiful in spring, when hundreds of azalea bushes are in bloom. There are wonderful views from the top of Berkshire Mall Drive, but there are no places to pull over to enjoy them at leisure. However, Partridge Road, which the mall road passes over, does have a shoulder on which to park while taking in the grand view of Mount Greylock and Hoosac Valley stretching northward. Partridge Road runs between Crane Avenue in Pittsfield and Summer Street in Lanesborough. Also in Lanesborough off MA 8 is Gulf Road, which runs through boulder-strewn Wizard's Glen to Dalton. This narrow one-lane dirt road is closed in winter and should only be traveled slowly with caution and, preferably, a four-wheel-drive vehicle. But the tumbled rocks and dark woods it passes through are mysterious, as though indeed created by a wizard.

Heading to North County, nice scenery can be found in Cheshire. Wells Road off MA 8 passes through a broad valley before joining Massachusetts Highway 116. A sharp right turn at that juncture will bring you to Stafford Hill Road. At its highest point, off the road to the right, is a monument erected on the site of the town's first settlement. It was here that Colonel Stafford issued the call to arms for members of the then New Providence Greys for the Battle of Bennington in 1777. Driving back to MA 116, you cannot help wondering what life was like back then, when full-growth trees covered the land that now lies open. Another fine view can be found on Henry Wood Road, off MA 116 to the left. This road passes through a prizewinning farm and eventually connects with East Road in Adams.

i

Don't look for a body of water at the end of Harbour Road in Cheshire. The name comes from Cheshire's reputation as a safe harbor for runaway slaves coming north along the Underground Railroad.

East Road is one of two alternatives to MA 8 in Adams, and each gives a different view of Mount Greylock. From East Road the mountain serves as a backdrop to the town in the valley. Fully visible is the scope of the limestone quarry operated by Specialty Minerals. The "steppes" are man-made tiers built and planted to reclaim land that has been stripped in the mining operation. This shortcut to North Adams also passes some of the few remaining farms in town. On the other side of Adams is West Road. The access road to Greylock Glen is off West Road. The glen is an area near the base of the mountain that the town and state have been trying to develop into a tourist draw for years. Currently there is a place to park while having a picnic, hiking, mountain biking, or snowmobiling with the mountain looming above. The town of Adams can be seen in a panoramic view of the valley below. For a spectacular view of North Adams and the Hoosac Valley take MA 2 up the west slope of the Hoosac Mountain Range and park at the observation deck at the top of the hill.

One of the most popular views of Mount Greylock is found on US 7 as it heads toward Williamstown. If there was ever a spot that cries out for a rest area, this is it. Oddly there is only a shoulder to pull off on while admiring the valley below and the mountains beyond. Of course the best view in the county is that from the top of Mount Greylock and from the two access roads: Notch Road in North Adams and Rockwell Road in Lanesborough. Both roads are slated for major reconstruction over the next two years, so check with the Department of Environmental Management's regional office at (413) 442-8928 to be sure they are open.

Another fine view in Williamstown can be found on a Stratton Road, a dirt road shortcut between Green River and Adams Roads, where the Orchards Inn is located. It's not easy to describe, but if you can figure it out, it's worth it. Green River Road, which is really Massachusetts Highway 43, runs through the valley from the Store at Five Corners on US 7. It passes Mount Hope Farm and several fine estates before entering the town proper. There it becomes Water Street and connects with MA 2. About midway between US 7 and MA 2 on the right is a sign for Blair Road. Blair leads up a hill to a breathtaking pinnacle from which you can view the valley and all Williamstown. Blair turns left and becomes Stratton Road, which is dirt until it reaches the populated area near Adams Road.

Aside from the standard signs that designate U.S., state, and county roads, you might notice small brown or blue directional signs along the way. The brown signs generally refer to state-owned attractions such as state parks managed by the Department of Environmental Management, as well as some nonprofit tourist draws. Blue directional signs denote commercial places of interest to tourists and cover everything from shopping malls to resorts. Blue signs also point the way to agricultural ventures such as farm stands, as well as historic sites and some cultural venues. Speed limits are fairly well posted, but beware of sudden reductions—and local constabulary waiting to catch you if you don't slow down.

If all this is intimidating, there are several local tour companies, including one that offers off-road sight-seeing. (See also the list above of limousines and taxis for hire.) And don't forget the local bus company for an inexpensive way to see the county.

Berkshire Regional Transit Authority
Downing Industrial Park
67 Downing Parkway, Pittsfield
(413) 499-2782

LOCAL TOUR COMPANIES

Animactions Unlimited
88 Henry Avenue, Pittsfield
(413) 448-2115
www.animactionsunlimited.com

Berkshire Sightseeing and Backroad Tour Co.
46 Elmview Terrace, Pittsfield
(413) 442-1249
www.berkshiresightseeing.com

Berkshire Tour Company
86 Sampson Parkway, Pittsfield
(413) 443-5778

Berkshire Travel Group
39 Willis Street, Pittsfield
(413) 443-9188, (800) 833-4883

Berkshire Woods Off Road Tours
11 Old Stockbridge Road, Lenox
(413) 637-8878
www.BerkshireWoodsTours.com

Greylock Discovery Tours
P.O. Box 2231, Lenox 01240
(413) 637-4442
www.greylocktours.com

Bicycling through the Berkshires

The Massachusetts Highway Department has prepared a Berkshire Bike Touring

Biking Tips

- Wear a helmet!
- Make sure your bike is properly adjusted.
- Always check brakes before riding.
- Wear clothing that will make you easy to see.
- If riding at night, use lights and reflectors and wear reflective clothing.
- Watch out for obstacles.
- Stay to the right.
- Check for traffic at intersections and driveways.
- Obey traffic laws.
- Secure quick-release wheels.
- Carry water with you, especially in warm weather.

map showing various routes through the county. The routes, originally laid out in a project in the 1930s, zigzag between towns and use mostly back roads that the average bicyclist can enjoy. The lay of the land, ease of travel, and nearness to towns and cultural centers were all taken into consideration when choosing these routes. However, most of the roads do not have marked bike lanes, and the department warns folks to be extremely careful on them. The exception is Pittsfield, where a bike route is marked with signs and bike lanes are marked on some roads. A really safe route is the recently opened Ashuwillticook Rail Trail, a paved path constructed by the state on a defunct rail line. The trail parallels MA 8 and runs 11 miles from Lanesborough to Adams. There are comfort stations at the Lanesborough end and in Cheshire, about midway. Supporters of this trail hope that eventually it will extend north to North Adams and south through Pittsfield and beyond.

The bike touring map is available at state parks, from bicycling organizations, and on the Internet; all outlets are listed below. The Berkshire Bike Path Council is a nonprofit membership organization promoting bike path development in Berkshire County. The Berkshire Cycling Association offers information and arranges group rides. More on biking can be found in the Recreation and State Parks chapters. Shops that sell or rent bikes can be found in the Shopping chapter under Specialty Stores.

INFORMATION SOURCES

The Berkshire Bike Path Council
55 South Mountain Road, Pittsfield
(413) 442-5223
www.berkshirebikepath.org

Berkshire Cycling Association
24 Alba Avenue, Pittsfield
(413) 499-0462
www.berkshirecycling.org

Berkshire Visitors Bureau
Berkshire Common, Pittsfield
(413) 443-9186, (800) 237-5747
www.berkshire.org

Department of Environmental Management
Regional Headquarters and Visitor Center
740 South Street, Pittsfield
(413) 442-8928
www.massparks.org

Massachusetts Bicycle Coalition
59 Temple Place, Boston
(617) 542-2453
www.massbike.org

MassHighway
www.state.ma.us/mhd

ACCOMMODATIONS 

Accommodations in the Berkshires range from some of the top hotels in the country to rustic bunk rooms and everything in between, including a clothing-optional resort. The discerning traveler who wants a fireplace, whirlpool tub, and other amenities will find them offered at many levels. Just as proliferate are simple rooms in private homes, made available just for the summer. Bed-and-breakfasts offer all kinds of accommodations from swanky to simple and in all price ranges. So many are furnished with antiques, it's a wonder there are any old things left for the retail world to buy. Generally, B&Bs are not able to accept folks who use wheelchairs or walkers although there are some exceptions. Most also do not accept children under age 12 unless the entire place is booked by the family. Most do this out of concern for other guests, although, again, there are exceptions. The nice thing about a B&B is the chance to talk with the owners, who usually have interesting stories to tell about how they ended up in the Berkshires and the history of their homes. Most of the rooms in B&Bs are in the owners' home, but some are in separate buildings for those who prefer to keep to themselves. B&B owners apparently love to cook and some go all out to fix a sumptuous repast in the morning. B&Bs with four rooms or more are required to comply with local building, health, and safety codes, including double exits, smoke detectors, and inspections.

Motels are handy for those traveling with children and folks who can't handle physical barriers. Practically all the older motels in the county have been refurbished in the past decade and offer the latest amenities, including whirlpool tubs and wheelchair-accessible rooms and bathrooms. Several are brand new. Most motels provide irons and ironing boards, hair dryers, and coffeemakers. Some also offer small refrigerators and microwave ovens, and many have swimming pools and exercise rooms. Generally breakfast is a simple affair, but most motels are near restaurants for those who want to eat hearty. Motels will be found on the main highways: U.S. Highways 7 and 20 and Massachusetts Highway 23 in South and Central County; US 7 and Massachusetts Highways 2 and 8 in North County.

On a larger scale, there are resorts offering all kinds of four-season recreational activities. Many of these and the larger inns are especially suited to conferences, business meetings, and weddings. Lenox and Stockbridge, with all their Great Estates, are full of inns whose owners have saved these huge "cottages" from deterioration or, worse, demolition. Two of the top-rated hotels in the country are in Lenox: Wheatleigh and Blantyre. The latter is furnished with antiques. The owners of Wheatleigh took a different approach, choosing a contemporary look with a European feel.

Motels, inns, and B&Bs are listed by areas of the county and then by town alphabetically. Resorts and campgrounds with cabins, tenting areas, and setups for RVs are listed alphabetically. All the larger places and some of the smaller ones take major credit cards. Unless stated otherwise, most charge $10 for an additional guest in a room. A few places take pets for various one-time charges.

Thanks to the Internet, shopping for lodging is not as much a pig-in-a-poke as it used to be. Most places post photos of their rooms, common areas, and grounds and

---

i ***Some places round up the 9.7 percent room tax to 10 percent, applying the difference to "service."***

---

private detailed information about rates and policies. The Berkshire Visitors Bureau lists members at www.berkshires.org, or you can call (413) 743-4500 or (800) 743-4500. Other sources include Berkshire Lodgings Association at (888) 298-4760, (413) 298-4760, or www.berkshirelodgings.com. Chambers of commerce are included in our listings where applicable.

PRICE CODE

Some rates might fall outside these categories on either the high or low side, but generally these represent the one-night charge for two adults on a peak weekend like Fourth of July or Labor Day. You will notice a wide range of prices at some places because many offer a wide range of accommodations, from basic rooms to suites. Rates do not include the 9.7 percent room tax or other charges.

$	**Less than $100**
$$	**$100–$199**
$$$	**$200–$299**
$$$$	**$300–$450**
$$$$$	**More than $450**

SOUTH COUNTY

Great Barrington

All kinds of accommodations can be found in Great Barrington and its environs. Many are listed with the Southern Berkshire Chamber of Commerce, which has an office at 40 Railroad Street. The phone number is (413) 528-4284, and their Web site is www.greatbarrington.org. The chamber operates a lodging hot line at (800) 269-4825 or (413) 528-4006. In season, volunteers staff an information booth at 362 Main Street.

Barrington Court Motel **$–$$$**
400 Stockbridge Road (US 7)
(413) 528-2340
A fixture on US 7 for 35-some years, the Barrington Court Motel has been completely renovated and now offers four suites, two with Jacuzzis. There are 25 units in the two-story building, with a variety of bed arrangements. Some rooms are adjoining, handy for traveling families. Other amenities include a laundry facility and an in-ground pool and a playground at the rear of the motel, which is set well back from the road. Some rooms are available for smokers; pets are allowed for a $10 charge. A simple continental breakfast is available in the office lobby, and there are many restaurants within walking distance.

Briarcliff Inn **$–$$**
506 Stockbridge Road (US 7)
(413) 528-3000
Sunny Patel took over this older motel in 1998 and has been improving it ever since. Each of the 16 spotless redecorated rooms is outfitted with either a king or two double beds, two Purotel air cleaners, and a small refrigerator. Microwave ovens are available on request. There are some rooms for smokers. Pets are welcome, but charges vary; owners are encouraged to inquire. A basic continental breakfast is provided in the new office area. The motel is set way back from the road, and the ample grounds are filled with flowers in season and feature topiaries that Patel himself has trained.

Christine's Bed & Breakfast and Tea Room **$$**
325 North Plain Road (Massachusetts Highway 41)
(413) 274-6149, (800) 536-1186
www.christinesinn.com
Folks who stay in one of the four rooms at Christine Kelsy's B&B are in for a treat. The woman loves to bake, cook, and entertain and has been pampering her guests since she opened in 1987. She also has a flair for interior decorating, which shows in the guest rooms in the two-story wing adjacent to the 1780 farmhouse she and her husband, Steve, have called home since 1973. The house itself, with its exposed hand-hewn beams, welcomes

guests with a sitting room furnished with family heirlooms and comfortable chairs. In chilly weather, the wood-burning stove will be going. Guests may help themselves to cordials provided in a small bar. A wraparound porch, partially glassed in, is used for breakfast and afternoon tea. A collector of teapots, Christine has shelf after shelf filled with pots and tea sets, many sent to her by guests.

From the porch folks have a view of the spacious grounds filled with around 4,000 color-coordinated perennials that bloom from spring through fall with Tom Ball Mountain as a backdrop. From her professional kitchen, Christine brings forth sumptuous breakfasts plus treats that she often leaves in a basket in the entryway to be taken by anyone who stops by. A descendant of great bakers, Christine studied at the Culinary Institute in New York State but favors recipes handed down for generations, which she will share if pressed. Fresh fruit is always served and sherbet is added in summer. Specialties include French toast Crème Brûlée, crepes with Key lime sauce, and pecan pancakes. Breakfast is served hot from the stove to guests at their nicely set tables. Christine always asks guests when they book if they have any special dietary needs so that she can plan ahead.

Although there are two guest rooms on the ground floor, they are not appropriate for folks who use wheelchairs or walkers. One room has a gas fireplace and its own porch. The other two rooms are on the second floor of the wing. All have private baths, queen beds, country decor with antique furnishings, television sets and phones, and comfortable chairs for relaxing. Robes and "comfort baskets" are provided in every room. The largest of the four, called the Family Room, also has a sofa bed and may be rented by folks with a pet. The B&B is 3 miles north of Great Barrington and 5 miles south of West Stockbridge and is open year-round. Specials and ski packages are available. Arrangements may be made for groups to come for tea and sandwiches and, of course, pastries.

Days Inn **$-$$**
372 Main Street (US 7)
(413) 528-3150

This two-story motel in downtown Great Barrington became a Days Inn in 1998 after a complete renovation. There are 63 rooms outfitted with a king or two double beds. Three are wheelchair-accessible, including bathrooms. Two rooms are for smokers. Occupancy is limited to three adults, with a $10 charge for the third occupant, or two adults and two children. Cribs are available. A continental breakfast is served in the lobby. The motel is within walking distance of entertainment, shops and restaurants along Main, Railroad, and Castle Streets.

Holiday Inn Express **$$-$$$**
415 Stockbridge Road (US 7)
(413) 528-1810
www.hiexpressnewengland.com

New to Great Barrington in 2003, Holiday Inn Express has 58 rooms on two floors, including 16 suites outfitted with fireplaces and whirlpool tubs. Four rooms are completely wheelchair-accessible. All rooms have phones with dataports and high-speed Internet access. Folks traveling on business will find a complete center for their use, including a copier, printer, fax machine, and Internet connection with e-mail. Amenities include an indoor swimming pool, spa whirlpool, fitness center, and carpeted lounge with a fireplace and large-screen television set. The complimentary continental breakfast buffet is served in the lounge. For snack attacks, there is a bank of vending machines en route to the pool.

Monument Mountain Motel **$-$$**
249 Stockbridge Road (US 7)
(413) 528-3272
www.monumentmountainmotel.com

A swimming pool, basketball and tennis courts, horseshoes, a playground, and nature trails that lead to the Housatonic River are the bonuses guests are entitled to at this renovated older motel. There are 18 smoke-free rooms, including some connecting family units. Pets are permitted for a $10 fee. Owner Vijay Mahida offers a basic continental breakfast in the office, which is in an early house on the property. For those with bigger appetites in the morning, Friendly's Restaurant is right across the street. Mahida also is building a larger two-story motel at the rear of the property.

Mountain View Motel **$-$$**
304 State Road (MA 23)
(413) 528-0250
www.mountainviewmotel.net
Set way back from the highway, the Mountain View Motel is on the eastern outskirts of Great Barrington, near Butternut ski area. Also an older motel, the Mountain View was completely renovated in 1999. There are 17 spacious rooms, including several suites plus a one-bedroom apartment—or "house," as the manager calls it—with a full kitchen, living room, two television sets, and a Jacuzzi. Many of the rooms have sofa beds and microwaves; all have refrigerators. There are various bed arrangements, and two rooms are available for smokers. A basic continental breakfast is available in the office, where Kiwi, a green parrot, lives. Pets are allowed for a $10 to $25 fee.

Seekonk Pines Inn **$$-$$$**
142 Seekonk Cross Road (at MA 23)
(413) 528-4192
www.seekonkpines.com
An inn since 1978, Seekonk Pines has been operated by the Lefkowitz family since 1996. But the property harks back to 1832, when the first home was built. A succession of owners since then have changed and enlarged the original building, but much still remains of the early structure. The inn has six guest rooms with private baths, including a downstairs one for folks who don't want to climb steps. All are comfortably furnished with antiques, appropriate reproductions, and collectibles arranged tastefully by Roberta and Rita Lefkowitz. Some rooms have queen-size beds, others double.

Guests may gather in the common room, where there is a fireplace and a color television plus books and games. Children, who are welcome here, will find lots of things to occupy their time plus a table of their own, where they can have breakfast or play. Grown-ups will be served ever-changing breakfasts that include seasonal fruits, breads, and hot entrees at the large dining table. The spacious grounds include an in-ground pool, picnic table, and paths for biking or walking. The family even has a few bikes for guests to use if they didn't bring their own. Other amenities include a guest pantry, where they can keep things in the fridge or prepare a cup of tea or coffee. Iced tea is provided in summer; hot cider in winter. There is a guest telephone in the entry. A studio apartment with a kitchen also may be rented.

The Wainwright Inn **$$-$$$**
518 South Main Street
(413) 528-2062
www.wainwrightinn.com
The Wainwright Inn began life in 1766 as the Troy Tavern and Inn and served as a fort and colonial armory during the Revolutionary War. It became the home of statesman and legislator David Wainwright in 1790. A lot happened to the house after that, all of which innkeeper Marja Tepper Grader will gladly share with interested guests. She and her husband bought the home and completely renovated it, opening their B&B in 2000. There are nine rooms, including two suites. Two rooms have working fireplaces, including a suite on the ground floor designed for wheelchair use. All have private baths and either queen- or king-size beds. There are no phones in the rooms, but there is one in a lounge on the second floor. The lounge also has a television set and a place to set up a laptop computer. Marja's taste and skill at decorating are evident in the furnishings. All the windows have different treatments. Antiques abound, including many of Marja's own collections. On the landing to the second floor, guests are treated to a display of feathered

antique hats. Port, sherry, and wine are served in the front room, which has a piano and period furnishings.

The place is spotless, which Marja blames on her Dutch background. Her European background also shows in her cooking, which she takes seriously. Early risers will be greeted with pots of coffee or tea and the baked goodie of the day set out on the sideboard in the dining room, which has a huge bay window facing south. Between 8:00 and 9:30 A.M., Marja prepares a full breakfast in her commercial kitchen and serves it to guests seated at one of five tables covered with lace cloths. The menu might include French toast, fancy pancakes, a soufflé, eggs Benedict, or a specialty dish of ham, cheese, and potatoes along with fresh fruit, yogurt, granola, and other cereals. She is happy to comply with dietary requirements. Depending on age, children are welcome; roll-away beds are available. The inn, which has a large wraparound porch, is a few blocks south of the main shopping area but within walking distance for the energetic.

Lee

Located at exit 2 off the Massachusetts Turnpike (I-90), Lee has an abundance of motels, bed-and-breakfasts, and guest houses, some of which are described below. The Lee Chamber of Commerce maintains an information center at 3 Park Place that is open seasonally. Information also may be obtained by calling (413) 243-0852 or visiting the Web sites: www.leechamber.org or www.leelodging.org.

Applegate B&B **$$-$$$**
279 West Park Street
(413) 243-4451, (800) 691-9012
www.applegateinn.com

Built in the 1920s as a summer home, this imposing Georgian mansion is now a B&B offering guests luxurious accommodations in six rooms and four suites. After passing through the iron gate at the entrance, guests are led to the imposing entry via a circular drive. The main house is furnished with Oriental carpets, antiques, and quality reproductions. In the living room, guests have access to a library and a baby grand piano. Wine and cheese are served here each evening, often by the fire in the fireplace. A classic video library, games, and puzzles are available in the sun parlor, where there is a television and VCR. Breakfast is served by candlelight in the dining room, where there is another fireplace. Each table is graced with an antique silver candelabra, bone china, crystal stemware, and flowers.

A curved stairway leads to the guest rooms upstairs. All have private baths and air-conditioning, a crystal decanter containing brandy, and a box of chocolates. Four rooms have fireplaces, including two suites that also have wet bars, television sets, VCRs, and CD players along with other amenities. Luxury suites are located in a renovated carriage house, where amenities include fireplaces, whirlpool tubs, wet bars, and private patios. For longer stays, a cottage with two bedrooms with queen-size beds, whirlpool tub, living room, kitchen, coffee bar, dining area, and private deck may be rented. Situated on six acres, Applegate is surrounded with mature apple trees, rose gardens, perennial beds, towering pines, and manicured lawns. A screened porch overlooks the pool. Bicycles are on hand for guests, and a nine-hole golf course with two tennis courts is across the road. Children over age 12 are welcome. There is a $30 charge for an extra person in a room.

Aunti M's Bed & Breakfast **$-$$**
60 Laurel Street
(413) 243-3201
www.auntimsbnb.com

Aunti M is really Michelle Celentano, who has been offering New England hospitality in her refurbished Victorian home since 1992. Her five rooms, named for her nieces and nephews, are furnished with canopy, brass, or Empire beds and antique furnishings that exude charm and warmth. One room has a private bath; the others share two baths. All have air conditioners. There are two comfortably furnished common rooms and a parlor. Guests are served an elaborate breakfast in the dining room at a lace-covered table set with china, crystal, and silver. The menu du jour might include seasonal fruits, Belgian crepes, waffles, or a frittata. There are always hot homemade breads, muffins, and granola—or hot oatmeal if it's that kind of day. The attention to detail is noteworthy. Aunti M has two dogs that are not allowed near the guests' rooms. The house is on the right as you head up the Laurel Street hill. Look for the big heart-shaped sign and, if it's summer, lots of hanging baskets filled with flowers. Open year-round.

Best Value Inn $-$$
980 Pleasant Street (Massachusetts Highway 102)
(413) 243-0501
www.bestvalueinn.com

This older motel being renovated by the owner is one of two Best Value franchises in the state. The 26 rooms in the double-decker building include a suite with a whirlpool tub and king-size bed, available by advance request. There is a $10.00 charge for an extra person; roll-away cots are available for $6.00. A two-night minimum stay is required on weekends in July and August. A continental breakfast is provided in the office. For reservations call the motel directly or Best Value at (888) 315-2378. MA 102 runs between Lee and Stockbridge.

Best Western Black Swan $-$$$
435 Laurel Street (US 7/20)
(413) 243-2799, (800) 528-1234, (800) 876-7926 (reservations)

Located on the shore of Laurel Lake off US 20, the Best Western Black Swan has 52 rooms, including two that are completely wheelchair-accessible. The two-story complex was recently refurbished. All rooms are reached by carpeted center halls. Lakeside rooms have decks, and nine rooms have been remodeled to include whirlpool tubs and fireplaces along with elegant furnishings such as canopy and four-poster beds. Smoking is allowed in some rooms. During summer, guests may use the outdoor pool or rent one of several kinds of boats docked at the hotel. Fishing is encouraged year-round. During the week, a free hot breakfast is included in the rate. On weekends there is a charge for the breakfast buffet served in the Bombay Bar & Grill. Aside from the very American breakfast, the restaurant serves cuisine from various regions of India and Asia. Best Western suggests calling (800) 876-7926 to make reservations.

i

Be prepared for a three-night minimum stay requirement during the height of the season, especially on major holiday weekends.

Chambery Inn $-$$$
199 Main Street
(413) 243-2221, (800) 537-4321
www.berkshireinns.com

What would the nuns think! This wonderful B&B, once the Berkshire's first parochial school, was headed for demolition until owners Joe and Lynne Toole moved it, set it back from the busy street, and painstakingly turned it into a unique guest house. Still retaining its high ceilings, blackboards, and boys' and girls' staircases, the schoolhouse has nine spacious suites offering varying degrees of luxury. Tastefully decorated in subdued colors, each room has its own personality. Six suites, with 8-foot high windows, have canopy beds, whirlpool baths, dataports, and sitting areas with gas fireplaces. One room has a two-person Jacuzzi, a fireplace, and large-screen television set. There are two "standard" rooms, one of which is entirely wheelchair-accessible.

Luxury abounds. Breakfasts of assorted breads baked on the premises, hot and cold cereals, fruit, and beverages are delivered to each room in a large wicker basket. While many of the old fixtures have been retained—like the drinking fountain in the hallway—such modern amenities as state-of-the-art plumbing and air-conditioning have been installed. This European-style hotel is a treat for the eyes, the spirit, and the body. The Tooles also own the Yankee Inn on US 7/20 between Pittsfield and Lee, and guests at the Chambery may use the pool and other amenities there. The Chambery is open year-round. Children over age 16 are welcome. There is a minimum-stay requirement of two nights on weekends off-season and three nights in season. There are specials during the week and off-season.

Devonfield **$-$$$**
85 Stockbridge Road
(413) 243-3298, (800) 664-0880
www.devonfield.com

The gracious living of bygone days is alive and well at Devonfield, a Federal-style home built in 1837 and restored by owners Pamela and Jim Loring. With its spacious lawns and traditionally furnished rooms, the inn has the feel of an English country estate. Accommodations are offered in six rooms, three suites, and a separate guest house. Common areas include the living room with a library, stereo, and fireplace; a cozy television room; and the dining room, where full breakfasts are served. Specialties of the house include harvest pancakes, apple cinnamon French toast, eggs Benedict, and homemade yogurt. The Lorings are both sixth-generation Lee residents, certainly a rarity among B&B owners in the county. They are well versed in the history of the town as well as the inn, which at one time hosted Queen Wilhelmina of the Netherlands, her daughter, Juliana, and her granddaughters. The couple will even give back-road tours in their 1931 Model A.

All rooms have cable television, full private baths, and air-conditioning. Guests will find brandy and chocolates in their rooms and a pantry available for their use. Some rooms have whirlpool baths and fireplaces. Most expensive is the cottage, which has a kitchen, full living room, Jacuzzi, and king-size bed. A penthouse suite offers a two-person Jacuzzi, full living room, kitchenette, and queen-size bed. There is a $35 charge for an extra person in a room. Pam owns a gift shop in town, and guests receive a 15 percent discount on purchases. The inn is on 29 acres 2 miles outside town and is across the way from a nine-hole public golf course. Amenities include an outdoor pool and a tennis court. Winter packages are available.

The Inn at Laurel Lake **$-$$**
615 Laurel Street (US 20)
(413) 243-9749
www.LaurelLakeInn.com

This landmark inn was on its uppers when Tom Fusco purchased it in 1996 and began to turn it into the welcoming bed-and-breakfast it now is. All 19 rooms have been redecorated and furnished with comfortable antiques. Two can be turned into a connecting suite. Private bathrooms have been added to all but two of the rooms. Pleasant common areas on the first floor include a library with a large-screen television set and a music room with a piano and, would you believe, 1,000 record albums of classical music left by the previous owner. Groupings of comfortable sofas and chairs provide several sitting areas to relax in. A deck overlooks the lake and grassy beach, where boats are docked for use by guests. Also at the beach are a rope swing and swing set for children, who are welcome to stay in one of three rooms. Also on the property is a tennis court. The roof of the wraparound porch serves as a balcony for rooms facing the lake, which of course cost more. An elegant buffet breakfast that includes sweet breads or muffins, granola, yogurt, a meat of some sort, French toast, or maybe a soufflé is served in the pleasant dining room furnished with five tables and plenty of chairs. There are two family cats on the premises. Guests with pets should inquire whether they would be welcome. The inn is open year-round.

Laurel Hill Motel **$$**
200 Laurel Street (US 20)
(413) 243-0813, (413) 243-9929
High on a hill off the highway, this motel has 23 rooms recently refurbished by owner Mukesh Desai. Several have kitchenettes. Smoking is allowed in two rooms. There is a charge of $5.00 or $10.00 for an extra person, at the owner's discretion. Amenities include an in-ground pool and a basic continental breakfast served in the office.

Morgan House Inn **$-$$**
33 Main Street
(413) 243-3661
www.MorganHouseInn.com
Since 1855 the Morgan House has been providing food and lodging for travelers. Where the stagecoach once stopped, buses for Springfield and beyond now take on and deposit passengers. Wesley and Kim Bookstaver are the latest in a long succession of hosts at this historic inn, having bought it in 1998. Of the 11 rooms on 2 floors, 6 have private baths. All have been redecorated with appropriately colonial colors and decor, including canopy beds in some rooms. All have small refrigerators; some have television sets. A full breakfast is provided on weekends in season. Midweek, rates include an American continental breakfast with a menu that varies seasonally. The inn's restaurant serves lunch and dinner, mixing chef's cuisine with traditional New England fare. A tavern next to the dining room offers lighter fare and is open later than the restaurant. Hours and days closed vary throughout the year, so call ahead. Rates are the same year-round.

The Parsonage on the Green B&B **$-$$**
20 Park Place
(413) 243-4364
www.bbhost.com/parsonageonthegreen
Guests at this conveniently located B&B will feel as though they are coming home to visit family. The home is beautifully furnished with antiques, photographs, and mementos that are all family heirlooms that owners Don and Barbara Mahony happily share. Escapees from Long Island, New York, the couple bought the historic parsonage in 1996. While it is in downtown Lee, the 1851 home is sheltered from the busy street by the First Congregational Church next door, known for having the highest wooden steeple in New England. The Mahonys offer four guest rooms with private baths and queen-size beds. Robes, fresh flowers, and Catherine's Chocolates will be found in each. Guests may congregate in the sitting room, where there is a fireplace, or the library, where, aside from plenty of books, they will find games, brochures, and menus from area restaurants. A log containing previous guests' comments about those restaurants makes for very interesting reading! If desired, coffee will be brought to your room to help you get going in the morning.

Breakfast is served in the dining room, where the table is set with candles, flowers, and fine china. Barbara does the cooking and usually serves homemade granola or another cold cereal, fresh fruit, some kind of baked goodie and a hot dish such as a soufflé or baked omelette. If apprised, she will consider dietary needs and will even bake cakes for special occasions. In summer a side porch offers a pleasant retreat. Golfers might want to ask Don, a retired engineer, to share his tips. As a former teacher, Barbara also has much to share. Children age 12 and older are welcome.

Pilgrim Inn **$-$$$**
165 Housatonic Street (US 20)
(413) 243-1328, (888) 537-5476
www.pilgriminn.net
The Pilgrim Inn is really three separate buildings set around a large in-ground swimming pool. A total of 24 units are located in two double-decker buildings. All have been recently redecorated by owner Ben Patel and include minirefrigerators. There is one totally wheelchair-accessible room and one partially adapted to special needs. In 2001 Patel purchased and reconfigured a residence next to the motel into a 10-room inn. All rooms there have been

outfitted with Evergreen air purifiers, water filters, and shower massages; one is a luxury suite with a two-person Jacuzzi. A coin-operated washer and dryer are located near the office. There is no charge for children under age 16 if staying in the same room. Otherwise, extra persons pay $10. A basic continental breakfast is provided in the spacious lobby.

Super 8 Motel **$-$$$**
170 Housatonic Street (US 20)
(413) 243-0143, (800) 800-8000
www.super8.com
An older motel that had deteriorated over the years, this Super 8 has been completely renovated by new owner Ben Patel, who also owns the Pilgrim Inn across the street. All 49 rooms have been redone, including new carpeting. One room is totally wheelchair-accessible; all have minifridges. Smoking is permitted in some rooms. A continental breakfast is provided in a common area, where guests can sit and read their free copies of *USA Today.* Amenities include a swimming pool.

Lenox

Accommodations in Lenox range from the sublime to the pedestrian. The epicenter of high society in the late 1800s, the town is full of former estates that now serve as inns and hotels. There also are countless old homes that have been converted to B&Bs. Some have several rooms, others only one or two. Then there are the motels along US 7, which range from local family ownership to national chains. The Lenox Chamber of Commerce, at 5 Walker Street, publishes a brochure and maintains a Web site (www.lenox.org) listing most area accommodations. Their phone number is (413) 637-0041.

Reservations in the Tanglewood area start coming in fast in March, right after tickets for the concert series go on sale.

Apple Tree Inn and Restaurant **$$-$$$$**
19 Richmond Mountain Road
(413) 637-1477
www.appletree-inn.com
Apple Tree Inn sits high on a hill in a Victorian mansion just off Massachusetts Highway 183 near Tanglewood's main gate. There are 10 cozy rooms and 3 suites reached by various hallways and levels with lots of nooks and crannies. All rooms have private baths. The odd shapes of some of the rooms have led to some interesting arrangements of the antique furnishings. Some rooms have fireplaces that burn Duraflame logs provided by the hosts and porches with great views of the Stockbridge Bowl valley. Also on the 22-acre property is a lodge with 21 motel-type rooms that rent for less than those in the inn. Smoking is permitted except in the dining room and other public gathering areas. There is a heated pool and tennis courts. The inn specializes in wedding parties and banquets and is open year-round. The restaurant is open daily in July and August, as is an adjoining deck with a panoramic view. Off-season the restaurant is open on weekends.

Birchwood Inn B&B **$$-$$$**
7 Hubbard Street
(413) 637-2600, (800) 524-1646
www.birchwood-inn.com
Since 1767 the Birchwood Inn has been welcoming travelers. Listed on the National Register of Historic Places and furnished with antiques, the inn has 11 rooms, including a suite, for a variety of rates. All are beautifully decorated with antiques and collectibles and can be viewed on the inn's excellent Web site, which also offers a very clear breakdown of the rather complex rate schedule. All rooms have air-conditioning, telephones with modem connections, and private baths. Spacious deluxe suites are on the second floor of the inn. Each has a wood-burning fireplace, featherbed, sitting area, television, and private bath with luxurious robes. Other rooms are on the third floor. Guests also may choose from rooms with

various amenities in the renovated 1885 carriage house adjacent to the inn.

A full gourmet breakfast, served at individual tables in the dining room, and afternoon tea are included in the rates. Guests are welcome to avail themselves of the books, magazines, and games in the library of this elegant mansion. Set back from the road across from the Church-on-the-Hill on Main Street and accesses to Kennedy Park, the inn is surrounded with stately oaks and towering pines. While the feel is secluded, the inn is a short walk from the shops, restaurants, and galleries in town. Innkeeper Ellen Gutman Chenaux welcomes children over age 12. There is a $25 charge for an extra person in a room.

Blantyre **$$$$–$$$$$**
16 Blantyre Road
(413) 637–3556
www.blantyre.com

Saved from demolition by the Fitzpatrick family, Blantyre was originally built in 1902 to replicate a Scottish manor, the ancestral home of wealthy businessman Robert Paterson's wife. Completely restored, Blantyre has been rated by Condé Nast and Zagat among the top hotels in the country and has earned a five-star rating from Mobil. The ivy-covered walls and multiple turrets are but a clue to the amazing interior of the main mansion, where guests will dine or lounge about in the Great Hall.

Jane Fitzpatrick and her daughter, Ann, oversaw the decorating in the entire place, including the outbuildings. There are eight romantically decorated guest bedrooms and suites on the second floor of the mansion. Antiques abound, and each room has its own personality, expressed through a variety of lush fabrics, carpets, color schemes, and wall coverings. All have private baths and king- or queen-size beds; some have fireplaces. Accessory furnishings include comfortable chairs, writing desks, window seats, and couches to curl up on.

A short distance from the main house are four private cottages with rooms as special as those in the mansion. Two cottages connect, nice for a large group. Sitting room, kitchenettes, whirlpool tubs, and fireplaces are some of the amenities found in various room combinations. More rooms are available in a restored and reconfigured carriage house; among the 12 rooms here are 3 loft suites. Blantyre lends itself to weddings and other large family gatherings but is open only from May through October. The grounds include a pool with a sauna and Jacuzzi, tennis and croquet courts, and shuffleboard. Golfers are welcome to stroll across the way to Cranwell's award-winning course.

While the accommodations are spectacular, the dining is even more amazing. Blantyre's New French cuisine has earned all kinds of awards (see the Restaurants chapter). Breakfast, however, is only for guests—and what a breakfast it is. Aside from the fruits, cereals, and other offerings, hot dishes might include a country breakfast plate of Irish bacon, tomatoes, potato cake, and Monterey chêvre; a three-egg omelette with Monterey chêvre and wild mushrooms; a caramelized onion, spinach, and red pepper tart topped with scrambled eggs and a chive sauce; or baked French toast with roasted apples, raspberries, and mascarpone with warm maple syrup.

Guests who choose to have dinner in the mansion are expected to dress appropriately. If you don't feel like getting gussied up, meals can be brought to your room. The staff also prepares picnics to take to Tanglewood, Jacob's Pillow, or other outdoor venues. Before dinner, champagne and canapés are served on the covered terrace overlooking the croquet lawn and wine is available for sampling in the music room. Those who go out after dinner may have coffee and dessert or an assortment of cheeses when they return, served in front of the fireplace, with a harpist providing background music. Rates vary depending on the accommodations chosen. Blantyre Road runs between US 20 and Walker Street.

Candlelight Inn **$$**
35 Walker Street
(413) 637-1555, (800) 428-0580
www.candlelightinn-lenox.com

Located on the corner of Walker and Church Streets in downtown Lenox, the Candlelight Inn offers eight charming rooms with private baths. Operated by Rebecca Hedgecock and her daughter, Arian Wen, since 1988, the inn was originally built by the Bishop family in 1885 as their private residence. It later became a boarding house and during the 1940s and 1950s housed the young Turks who were working at GE in Pittsfield. Many now come back to the inn with their wives, who they wined and dined as dates back then. The guest rooms are on the second and third floor and are furnished with antiques and an assortment of bed sizes. Many of the private baths have their original sinks and other fixtures, which have been updated. Hedgecock believes that her guests should leave their work behind them when they vacation, so there are no phones or television sets in the rooms. However, for those who simply can't do without it, a set is located in a pleasant lounge on the second floor. The rooms on the third floor are nestled under the eaves, creating a cozy feeling. A continental breakfast of baked goods, fruit, cereals, and hard-boiled eggs is provided on the windowed porch at the front of the inn.

Dinner is served in the dining room year-round. In summer, lunch also is offered and, weather permitting, may be enjoyed on the lawn where the chef cooks to order on the grill. The dining areas are wheelchair-accessible but the guest rooms are not. There is a large parking lot off Church Street for diners and guests. Rates vary depending on the day of the week, the season, and the room. There is a three-night minimum on summer weekends.

The Cornell Inn **$$-$$$**
203 Main Street
(413) 637-0562, (800) 637-0562
www.cornellinn.com

An inn since the early 1980s, the Cornell Inn is really three buildings—two homes and a converted carriage house—offering various accommodations in a total of 28 rooms. Two are completely wheelchair-accessible and also have visual fire alarms for the hearing impaired. Most rooms have queen-size beds. Suites that can sleep up to four persons have fireplaces; two have full kitchen facilities. Eleven rooms have minibars, 19 have whirlpool tubs, and 20 have fireplaces. Food and spirits are served in the main building, which has an attractive common area with a fireplace. A skylighted bar furnished with funky antiques offers a pleasant place to gather before or after going out for the evening. On summer weekends, sushi, chicken wings, or other nibbles are provided there. The light and airy dining room opens onto the deck, where tables are set up in summertime, offering a view of the waterfall that tumbles into the koi pond. Local newspapers are provided and the copious complimentary breakfast includes an array of fruits and baked goods and such hot entrees as baked eggs, stuffed French toast, or cranberry fritters. Innkeepers Billie and Doug McLaughlin have owned the Cornell since 1998. A tiered Victorian cast-iron fountain and seasonal flowers grace the property, which abuts 600-acre public Kennedy Park with its miles of hiking and cross-country skiing trails.

The Gables Inn **$$-$$$**
81 Walker Street
(413) 637-3416, (800) 382-9401
www.gableslenox.com

Innkeepers Mary and Frank Newton brought this classic Queen Anne "cottage" back to its original elegance and offer 17 rooms or suites to guests. Amenities include telephones, cable television, air-conditioning and, in some rooms, fireplaces. Period furnishings and the Newtons' own collections of art, rare documents, and books are scattered throughout. Theater buffs will appreciate looking through memorabilia collected by Frank, a former producer. Fans of Edith Wharton can sleep in the room she slept in when this was her family home. The grounds include a heated indoor pool, tennis court, and landscaped garden. Breads and pastries, fresh fruit, coffee, and juice are served in the breakfast room each morning. Children over age 12 are welcome. Additional guests in a room will be charged $20.

Garden Gables Inn **$$-$$$**
135 Main Street
(413) 637-0193
www.lenoxinn.com

Garden Gables began life as Butternut Cottage, a small three-gabled English-style home built in 1780. After a succession of owners, the building was moved back from the road to its present location in 1905 by Caroline Katherine "Kate" Carey, who changed the name to Gusty Gables. She undertook extensive renovations, including adding a wing, installing an elevator, and building a 72-foot-long in-ground concrete swimming pool. A first for Berkshire County, the pool is still used by guests.

A remarkable woman of means, Miss Carey built bird- and dollhouses, raised and exhibited prize horses, and established a home for aged women and a nursing home that she endowed heavily in her will. She left her home to the Episcopal Church, which sold it in 1947 to a couple who ran a guest house and changed the name to Garden Gables. More of the fascinating past of the property can be found in a history prepared for the current owners, Mario and Lynn Mekinda, who purchased Garden Gables in 1988. Since then, they have completely redecorated the 14 rooms in the inn and an additional 4 rooms in a separate cottage that is open only in summer.

All rooms have private baths and thermostats to control the central air-conditioning. Some have fireplaces, porches, and whirlpool tubs, and all are decorated with American country furniture. The living room, with fireplace and piano, is in the original cottage and retains much of the 18th-century hardware. The dining room, where the bountiful hot breakfast buffet is served, is furnished with English antiques, and the table is set with blue-and-white china. Complimentary sherry is served in the evenings. Children over age 13 are welcome. There is a $39 charge for additional persons in a room. The inn is on five landscaped acres and is near all downtown shops and restaurants.

Gateways Inn & Restaurant **$$$-$$$$**
51 Walker Street
(413) 637-2532
www.gatewaysinn.com

Gateways Inn was built in 1912 as the summer "cottage" of Harley Proctor, an executive of Proctor & Gamble. It had been an inn when Fabrizio and Rosemary Macdonald Chiariello bought it in 1996 and reopened it after an extensive renovation. Their award-winning restaurant (see the Restaurants chapter) serves breakfast and dinner to the public daily. In summer, lunch also is served. La Terraza is open nightly for light meals and drinks. Breakfast, which is included in the room rate, includes a spread on the sideboard of the elegant dining room plus two different entrees each day, which might be an omelette, pumpkin waffles, or oven-baked puff pancakes with apple cream sauce.

The inn itself has 11 rooms plus a suite, all with private baths, air-conditioning, television sets, and telephones. There are fireplaces in all but one room and the suite has two! Beds are either queen- or king-size. The rooms are beautifully appointed with antiques or appropriate reproductions. Each has a different personality, but in most there is a decidedly European feel. Lush carpets cover the floors, and fine fabrics abound. Mirrors are hung with ribbons, and crocheted canopies cover the four-poster beds. In the Battenberg Room all the window treatments, the bedding, and the canopy are of Battenberg lace. Appointments are tastefully simple. The Arthur Fiedler Suite has a large living room and bedroom separated by French doors. The bathroom contains the original marble corner sink plus a large whirlpool tub. Children over age 12 are welcome. Rates vary depending on the season and room.

Hampton Terrace Bed & Breakfast $$
91 Walker Street
(413) 637–1773, (800) 203–0656
www.hamptonterrace.com

The Hampton Terrace, built in 1897, has had a varied past. At one time it was the scene of what were considered rather scandalous social events where "actresses" gathered and smoking and drinking were allowed—much to the delight of nonconformist Edith Wharton, who lived nearby. The house moved from that era to a more subdued life until becoming an inn in 1937. In 1999 it was purchased by Stan and Susan Rosen, who upgraded the main house and redecorated it with a 1930s feel. The five guest rooms have private baths, some retaining the old claw-foot tubs with modern additions. They are furnished with king- or queen-size beds, and some have fireplaces or spa tubs. Six additional guest rooms in the modernized Carriage House feature fireplaces, whirlpool baths, vintage decor, and king or queen beds. The common area has a fireplace and is furnished with 1950s vintage leather furniture. CD players and television sets with VCRs are in all rooms. Breakfast is included.

Kemble Inn $$–$$$
2 Kemble Street
(413) 637–4113, (800) 353–4113
www.kembleinn.com

This stately inn was built as a "summer cottage" in 1881 by Frederick T. Frelinghuysen, Secretary of State to President Chester Arthur. Like many estates of the Gilded Age, this one had its ups and downs until it was purchased by Richard and Linda Reardon a few years ago. After completely renovating the building and adding bathrooms, they opened their luxurious B&B. Frelinghuysen, whose home copies a style popular 100 years earlier, would surely approve. The large welcoming foyer, with its graceful stairway to the second floor, is furnished with period elegance. The breakfast room, the dining table surrounded by fancy Sheraton-type chairs, offers views of the valley and mountains beyond, a view that can also be enjoyed from a back veranda in summer. There are 14 romantic guest rooms on three floors with private baths, telephones, color television, and central air-conditioning. Some have marble fireplaces and whirlpool tubs. Most have queen- or king-size beds; four-posters abound. Two rooms are on the first floor and are wheelchair-accessible. The most romantic room is named for actress Fannie Kemble, for whom the street also is named. On the second floor, the room features a spacious bathroom, marble fireplaces, a carved four-poster, and a Jacuzzi. A carriage house on the estate with three bedrooms also is available by the month in July and August only.

Children over age 12 are welcome. Rates are reduced $35 to $50 during October and even more from November to mid-June. Kemble Inn is within walking distance of Shakespeare & Company and shops and restaurants.

Rookwood Inn $$–$$$$
11 Old Stockbridge Road
(413) 637–9750, (800) 223–9750
www.rookwoodinn.com

Stephen Lesser and Amy Lindner-Lesser are the present stewards of this romantically decorated inn, which has had quite a history. The basic building started out several blocks away as a tavern, built in 1825 when Lenox was the county seat. Refreshments and lodging were provided for the judges and lawyers who worked in the courthouses. In the 1880s it was moved to its present location behind the Town Hall, a hop away from the main intersection in town, and a Victorian front was added. Tenants included secretaries for the wealthy owners of the "cottages" being built at that time. When that era ended, the home was a family getaway until World War II, when it was sold. It has been a B&B under various ownership ever since, with the Lessers taking the baton in 1996. Both bring previous experience in the field to the Rookwood, as evidenced in the Victorian decor and amenities offered.

Guests have their choice of 19 rooms, including a suite on the first floor and 7 rooms cleverly arranged amid the gables and turrets of the third floor. All have private bathrooms. Five rooms have fireplaces. King, queen, and twin beds are offered, and several rooms have sitting areas. Television sets and telephones are optional. Steve, an accomplished trained chef, prepares breakfasts that always include an entree such as quiche, frittata, or French toast made with French bread. Cereals, fruits, yogurt, and breads also are served. Menus are heart-healthy and seldom include meat. Dietary needs will be honored with advance notice. Children are welcome and babysitting can be arranged.

Seven Hills Country Inn & Restaurant **$$-$$$$**
40 Plunkett Street
(413) 637-0060, (800) 869-6518
www.sevenhillsinn.com

Just down the road from Edith Wharton's Mount is the former Shipton Court estate, now the home of Seven Hills Inn & Restaurant. The Tudor-style mansion lends itself beautifully to elegant dining, musical soirees, parties, weddings, and other social occasions. Hand-carved fireplaces, elaborate moldings, leaded-glass windows, and plush furnishings add to the romantic feel of the place. The inn looks out over terraced lawns and gardens, which may be viewed in summer by guests dining on the patio or in winter from the warmth of the dining room where a fireplace blazes.

Guests have a choice of 15 rooms in the Manor House, each decorated in a different theme appropriate to the period. All have private baths, phones, air-conditioning, cable television, and other amenities. Also available are 37 rooms in the two-story Terrace House and 6 rooms in the Carriage House, including 3 that are completely wheelchair-accessible. All have private baths and the same conveniences as listed above. In addition, rooms in the Carriage House have fireplaces, jet tubs, and kitchenettes. There is no charge for children under age five. The inn's restaurant is known for fine dining. Breakfast is included in room rates and the inn offers a modified American plan that also includes dinner.

Stonover Farm Bed & Breakfast **$$$-$$$$$**
169 Undermountain Road
(413) 637-9100
www.stonoverfarm.com

Although only open since 2002, Stonover Farm has already joined some heady company, having been named a grand award winner for 2004 by Andrew Harper's *Hideaway Report.* Previous winners include Wheatleigh and Blantyre. Owners Tom and Suky Werman have no idea who visited them from the respected travel publication and were totally surprised by the award. The couple bought the former Parsons estate, with its turreted and shingled 1890 mansion and barn, in 2001 and spent a year renovating it to accommodate their dream B&B. Now the main house, where the Wermans live, has three luxurious suites available year-round. Each has a sitting room, slate and marble bath with the latest fittings, queen- or king-size bed with super-thick mattress and high-end linens, radio/CD player, and state-of-the-art entertainment center. CDs and DVDs are available in the library downstairs, where guests also will find a lounge and conservatory. The suites are decorated in soft tones and natural fabrics with a mix of contemporary and antique furniture, as well as interesting works of art. Guests may enjoy breakfast, cooked to order by Tom, in the dining room or on the stone patio. Also available is a completely redone former henhouse that is now called Rock Cottage. Spaciously laid out on one floor are a fully equipped kitchen, king bedroom with luxury bath, and a large living/dining area with fireplace. Tucked up under the eaves of a gable above the kitchen is another bedroom fitted with twin beds, ideal for two children. Guests in the cottage may come to the main house for breakfast if they wish. Wine and cheese are served in the afternoon and will be brought to the cottage if guests so desire. Tom is a former music producer and the walls of his office are filled with covers from some pretty famous groups. Suky is a teacher and also represents several artists whose ceramics and other works are displayed throughout the main house. All rooms have telephones with voice mail and, at Tom's insistence, there are no charges for long distance calls. He also managed to get the phone company to run a high-speed line to the property to provide fast Internet service and has set up a computer station for guests to use. The grounds include wonderful rock formations, open fields, woods, and a duck pond. All utility lines are buried, adding to the peaceful feeling of the place. And Tanglewood is about 0.5 mile away. There is a three-night minimum stay requirement in July and August. From November through June, rates are reduced by $100 for the suites and by $125 for the cottage. The charge for an additional person in a suite is $50.

The Village Inn **$$–$$$**
16 Church Street
(413) 637–0020, (800) 253–0917
www.villageinn-lenox.com

Since 1771 the Village Inn has been providing rest and sustenance to travelers. But it took Clifford Rudisill and Ray Wilson to bring it into the 21st century. They spent 20 years modernizing the inn while preserving its colonial furnishings and ambience. The stenciled wallpapers and Oriental rugs in the public rooms complement the maple floors and simple Federal architecture. All 32 rooms have air-conditioning, telephones with voice mail, television sets with VCRs, CD players, FM clock radios, and private baths. An extensive lending library of videos is available.

The rooms are presented in three categories: superior, standard, and economy. The differences are the size of the room and the amenities, which the rates reflect accordingly. All superior and most standard rooms have whirlpool tubs, and beds range from queen to king or two twins. Economy rooms are smaller and have either queen or full beds and 20-inch television sets, compared with 25-inch sets in the other rooms. All levels are unique in decor. Some have four-poster beds with lace canopies; all are furnished with country antiques and reproductions. Some have fireplaces. There is a wheelchair-accessible room on the first floor and a two-bedroom suite that includes a living/dining area and kitchenette.

Breakfast is included in the room rate. A full breakfast is served in summer and fall and on all weekends; a continental breakfast is served midweek in winter and spring. The full breakfast includes hot dishes such as Belgian waffles, omelettes, and eggs Benedict. Afternoon tea with scones and clotted cream and desserts are served on Saturday afternoon. Late-night snacks are available in a tavern in the basement.

Wheatleigh **$$$$$**
Hawthorne Road
(413) 637–0610
www.wheatleigh.com

Cited as one of the most sophisticated hotels in the country, Wheatleigh is the ultimate in understated elegance, superb service, and fine food. As one would expect, all this comes at a cost. But the experience is worth it. The minute you enter the estate, the stage is set. The drive winds around through the lawns and towering trees until reaching a pair of pillars topped with ornate wrought-iron lamps. Beyond is a glorious fountain and the mansion itself, built in 1893 by financier and real estate tycoon Henry H. Cook as a wedding gift for his daughter. Materials and artisans were imported from Italy to execute the design based on a 16th-century palazzo.

Slowly falling into disrepair, Wheatleigh was rescued in the 1980s by Susan and Linfield Simon. Aside from restoring the building and grounds, the couple embarked on a complete interior renovation in 1998. The result is a remarkable blend of contemporary design and Old

World craftsmanship. On entering the great hall, guests are immediately struck by the detailed moldings, white against the putty-colored walls; the incredible hand-carved terra-cotta fireplace; and polished parquet floors.

The furnishings are simple in design, subtle in color: mustard, olive, sage, and other earth tones. Much of the furniture is custom-designed. Ahead, beyond the grand piano, is the lounge, where casual chairs and sofas are arranged and music plays softly through speakers hidden behind the wall covering. Full-length windows give view to the terrace, grounds, and Berkshire landscape. To the right, the grand staircase passes a pair of delicately crafted Tiffany windows on its way to the second floor, where open balconies give view to the proceedings below. The place has the aura of a magnificent stage set waiting for the cast to take its place. The international staff is unobtrusive and can converse in many languages. Many are students in hotel management schools abroad who are here for internships of varying lengths. In season, as many as 100 work at Wheatleigh.

There are 19 guest rooms, including one that is completely wheelchair-accessible. Most expensive is a private two-story suite in the former aviary. Separate from the mansion but connected by a covered walkway, the suite has a sitting room on the first floor that opens onto a terrace. A glass-enclosed spiral staircase leads to the bedroom and exceptional bathroom on the second floor. Next expensive is a first-floor suite with views of the grounds and a glass enclosed sitting room that opens onto a terrace. There are seven "junior" suites, all with fireplaces, special architectural details, high ceilings, king-size beds, comfortable sitting areas, elegant bathrooms, and beautiful views. Six deluxe rooms also have king-size beds, and two have fireplaces. Three smaller rooms have queen-size beds. Least expensive is a tiny room on the second floor. Down a few steps, the room has a full bath and a double bed snuggled between the walls of a dormer. All rooms have cable television, VCRs, CD players, and portable phones and are decorated in the same contemporary style as the common areas of the mansion. Orchids in vivid colors can be found in most rooms, an unexpected contrast to the elegant simplicity and muted tones of the walls and fabrics.

Breakfast (not included in the rate) is served to guests only in a glassed-in portico with views of the terrace and landscape beyond, one of two that extend from the rear of the mansion. The menu offers specialties like soufflé omelettes with salmon, wild mushrooms, goat cheese, or caviar; buttermilk pancakes with a compote of wild Maine blueberries; or house-made brioche French toast with spiced apple marmalade and toasted walnuts. A French breakfast of croissant, pain au chocolat, and French baguette with Echirre butter, juice, and hot beverage is around $19. The waitstaff is most obliging in translating the French. Pastries, cereals, poached eggs, and meats also can be ordered. A 20 percent service charge is added unless otherwise requested. Lunch and dinner are open to the public. Lunch is served in the library, dinner in the mirrored dining room and the portico. Room service is available around the clock. (The award-winning French cuisine is described more fully in the Restaurants chapter.)

Aside from strolling the beautiful grounds, originally designed by Frederick Law Olmsted, guests also may enjoy a fitness room, massage room, heated outdoor pool, and tennis courts. The entire inn may be rented for weddings, and lucky is the bride who descends that staircase to the great hall below. Business meetings, private parties, and other special events also may be booked. Children over age 12 are welcome. Wheatleigh has been featured in the *New York Times Magazine*, *Town & Country*, the *Wine Spectator*, and *Departures*. Following the renovation, *Vogue Germany* selected Wheatleigh as its "Hotel of the Month" and *Condé Nast Johansens* named it Most Outstanding Hotel for 2002 in North America. After a worldwide competition, *Interior Design* gave Wheatleigh its award for hotel renovation of 2002. And Andrew Harper selected Wheatleigh as Hotel of the Year Grand Award Winner in his *Hideaway Report,* also in 2002. The hotel is off MA 183 near Tanglewood's Hawthorne Road entrance.

Summer is the peak tourist period, with foliage season a close second, and rates vary accordingly. Best buys are midweek and off-season, but lots of places offer specials year-round.

PITTSFIELD ROAD MOTELS

The following motels are located on the US 7/20 strip between Lenox and Pittsfield, also known as Pittsfield Road.

Days Inn **$-$$**
194 Pittsfield Road
(413) 637-3560, (800) 329-7466
www.daysinn.com
Formerly a Super 8, this motel has been upgraded and renovated to meet Days Inn standards. The 59 rooms have been redecorated and are now equipped with amenities, including dataports and voice mail. The charge for an extra person is $5.00. Cribs and cots are available. The self-serve complimentary continental breakfast is provided in a pleasant nook off the newly tiled lobby.

Howard Johnson Express Inn **$-$$**
462 Pittsfield Road
www.hojo.com
Built in 1996, this double-decker inn has 44 spacious rooms, including several with whirlpool tubs. Some rooms are completely wheelchair-accessible. Amenities include a sauna and an outdoor pool. Business travelers will find a corporate desk. Guests receive complimentary copies of *USA Today* and a continental breakfast. There is a $5.00 charge for additional guests in a room. Cots and cribs are available for a charge of $15 and $10, respectively. Some special deals can be found on the Web site.

Lenox Inn **$-$$**
525 Pittsfield Road
(413) 449-5618
www.thelenoxinn.com
This older motel has been completely refurbished by new owners Bob and Debbie Patel. There are 18 newly decorated rooms with a king or two full-size beds and private baths. An in-ground pool behind the motel offers respite in summer. A small continental breakfast is offered on summer weekends. The rest of the time, guests are directed to a coffee shop next door or to any of several restaurants nearby. Pets may be welcome with the owners' permission. There is a charge of $10 for a third person in a room but no charge for children under age 10.

Quality Inn **$-$$**
130 Pittsfield Road
(413) 637-4244
www.qualityinn-berkshires.net
Located on a hill overlooking US 7, the Quality Inn was recently renovated. There are 120 rooms with king or double beds. Some rooms are wheelchair-accessible, but bathrooms are standard. The grounds include a swimming pool and two tennis courts. A basic complimentary continental breakfast is offered. Nearly all rooms are smoke-free. There are meeting rooms capable of holding up to 200 people for conferences, receptions, or trade shows. Rates are discounted Sunday through Thursday during non-special event times.

The Yankee Inn **$-$$$**
461 Pittsfield Road
(413) 499-3700, (800) 835-2364
www.Berkshireinns.com
Once a small roadside motel, The Yankee Inn has grown to become a three-building complex with outdoor and indoor swimming pools, Jacuzzis, a fitness room, and other up-to-date amenities. Purchased in 1996 by Joe and Lynn Toole, a local couple who also own the Chambery Inn in

Lee, the inn was renovated and expanded three years later and now has 96 new or redecorated rooms with a variety of bed arrangements. There are fireplaces in 22 of the rooms and an elevator to take guests to the second floor of the new addition. A deluxe corner room, suitable for honeymooners, is furnished with a romantic canopied king-size bed, fireplace, and Jacuzzi. Three rooms are completely wheelchair-accessible. The facility is smoke-free except for rooms that may be rented in one of the smaller buildings.

An expanded continental breakfast is served in the lounge, where cocktails are available on weekends. Two conference rooms may be booked for up to 50 persons and arrangements made for catered meals. Ski packages and dining certificates are available. The inn is located on seven acres with walking paths and a pond and has a three-diamond rating from AAA.

Wagon Wheel Motel **$-$$**
646 Pittsfield Road
(413) 445-4532
www.bestberkshirehotel.com

Looking at this motel from the outside, you'd never guess that two rooms had Jacuzzis, including one that is heart shaped. A holdover from older tourist days, the Wagon Wheel still sports its funky shutters and a life-size horse that has been poised in front of an old buggy for years. But inside all is new, redecorated by owner Neil Patel, who bought it in 1992. The 18 rooms offer king, queen, or two double beds for reasonable rates. Smoking is allowed in some rooms. Guests can count on a doughnut and coffee in the morning, but those who want more will want to head to one of the nearby restaurants.

Sheffield

B&B at Howden Farm **$-$$**
303 Rannapo Road
(413) 229-8481
www.howdenfarm.com

Howden Farm is both a bed-and-breakfast and a working 250-acre farm known especially for the heirloom pumpkins the family grows. Guests are welcome to enjoy the land, which in winter is open for cross-country skiing. Other activities include hiking, canoeing on the Housatonic River, and biking. Fall is pumpkin-picking time. Raspberries, sweet corn, and other crops often end up on the breakfast table along with eggs fresh from the henhouse. There are four guest rooms in the 1830s Greek Revival farmhouse. Three have queen-size beds, and one has twin beds. Two have private baths and two share a bath, but those have sinks in their rooms. All have views of the fields and mountains, are furnished with antiques, and have individually controlled heat and air conditioning and cable television.

Breakfast is served in the dining room at a country table surrounded with plank-seat chairs. Juice, seasonal fresh fruit, freshly ground coffee or a pot of tea, and a muffin, scone, or other baked good will start off the meal. The main course might be French toast, an egg-cheese casserole, or even a large pancake with fruit compote. Nestled in the river valley, Howden Farm is on Rannapo Road, off US 7A, 1.7 miles south of the village of Sheffield. It can also be reached via Ashley Falls. Rates remain the same year-round.

Berkshire 1802 House **$$**
48 South Main Street
(413) 229-2612
www.berkshire1802.com

Nancy Hunter-Young and Rich Kowarek pride themselves on the breakfasts they serve at their seven-room B&B. Freshly baked muffins and breads, fresh fruits, gourmet coffee and teas, juices, and cereals are offered daily. But it's the hot entrees that would make anyone get out of bed. How about blueberry-orange or ricotta pancakes; a frittata with apples, turkey bacon, and sage Derby cheese or one filled with zucchini, fresh oregano, baby bella mushrooms, and Asiago; or baked eggs with sun-dried tomatoes, wild mushrooms, and Brie? All this is served on fine china in the spacious dining room or, in nice weather, on the porch. The 200-year-old home sits on almost two acres of manicured lawn and gardens, where the couple have their own vegetable garden. Afternoon refreshments are served on the lawn or porch or in the parlor, which has a fireplace, books, music, and a television set. Five of the appropriately furnished guest rooms have private baths; two share a bath. Four rooms have queen-size beds; the others have full-size beds. Children age 12 and up are welcome. There is a $25 charge for a third person in a room. Futons are available.

Broken Hill Manor **$$**
771 West Road
(877) 535-6159
www.BrokenHillManor.com

This elegant Edwardian manor set atop Broken Hill is reached by a very long, narrow driveway that some might find intimidating. But the house is worth the trip. Innkeepers Mike Farmer and Gaetan LaChance spent four years restoring the rambling 1900 home to its former glory and clearly had a grand time furnishing it. The house sits in a clearing on 12 acres surrounded by woods filled with wildlife, gardens, and paths for cross-country skiing and walking. Once inside, the eye is dazzled by the eclectic mix of fantastic furnishings collected from around the world. Comfortable chairs are everywhere, especially around the large fireplace in the great room, where a piano, chess tables, and shelves full of books invite relaxation. In summer, porches and terraces offer places to relax and read or breathe in the mountain air and listen to the birds. Mike and Gaetan, an architect and former singer with the Oratorio Society at Carnegie Hall, are opera fans and have named each of their eight guest rooms for a famous operatic heroine and furnished it appropriately. All have roomy private baths and CD players with, of course, lots of opera recordings.

Mike, who has traveled to more than 50 countries, is the chef and has created a professional kitchen in which he prepares hot breakfasts daily. On Sunday he adds waffles, cinnamon pancakes, or, revealing his heritage, English bread pudding. A great place to escape from reality, Broken Hill Manor is off MA 23, a few miles east of Great Barrington. Rates remain the same year-round.

Race Brook Lodge **$$-$$$**
864 South Undermountain Road (MA 41)
(413) 229-2916
www.rblodge.com

Folks who don't particularly care for four-poster beds, floral print wallpaper, and colonial decor will find Race Brook Lodge a refreshing alternative. In fact, owner David Rothstein prides himself on having "No Chintz!" in his 32 rooms. Instead, guests will find lots of exposed beams, wide plank floors, and wood paneling. Instead of ruffled duvets they will find straightforward Hudson Bay blankets, simple quilts, eclectic artwork, and earth-tone carpets. The lodge itself is a restored 200-year-old post-and-beam barn along Race Brook at the base of the Taconic Range.

Guests can gather in the common room, enjoy a wine bar, and have a complimentary hearty country breakfast served buffet style. Guest rooms are tucked here and there on three levels offering king, queen, or double beds, some in connecting suites. Rooms also are available on a weekly basis in a bungalow with a large studio/dining area, eat-in kitchen, and a queen and two twin beds. Two cottages with four large bedrooms are suitable for families. All rooms have private baths and air-conditioning but no phones or television sets, by design. Phones, a television, a fax machine, and Internet ports are available in a meeting barn on the premises—especially handy for companies that hold meetings, workshops, and retreats here. Historic Stagecoach Tavern near the lodge offers fine and casual dining. There is a swimming pool on the property.

A great place for hikers, the lodge is near Race Brook Falls, the Appalachian Trail, and Mount Race. Skiing is available at nearby Butternut and Catamount ski areas, and the Housatonic and Konkapot Rivers offer opportunities to canoe or fish. Family rates include two children under age 12. There is a $10 charge for additional persons. Dogs are allowed in certain quarters for a per-stay charge of $25 for one, $40 for two. MA 41 runs between Salisbury, Connecticut, and MA 23 in South Egremont, Massachusetts.

South Egremont

The Egremont Inn **$$**
10 Old Sheffield Road
(413) 528-2111, (800) 859-1780
www.egremontinn.com

The historic Egremont Inn has 20 guest rooms furnished with antiques, four-poster beds, and wallpaper in 18th-century patterns. In summer, maroon awnings dress up the wraparound porch and second-story veranda, adding a touch of elegance to this 1700s structure, which has been enlarged over the years. On the first floor are three separate sitting rooms, five fireplaces, a public restaurant, and a tavern. There are no television sets in the guest rooms, but there is one to share in one of the sitting rooms. The entire inn is air-conditioned during summer. The guest rooms are on the second and third floors. Each has a telephone and a private bathroom with facilities ranging from claw-foot tubs to stall showers and whirlpool baths. Bed sizes also vary. Eight rooms of varying sizes have queen-size beds, and some rooms are large enough for one or two additional persons. There is an additional charge of $20 per person, regardless of age. Five rooms, ranging from midsize to a large loft, have either twin beds or kings. For families there are connecting rooms that are large enough to accommodate cots or cribs, which are available. Six of the smallest to midsize rooms have double beds. One has a whirlpool bath.

Located near Catamount and Butternut ski areas, the inn offers discounted lift tickets. In summer, guests may enjoy the outdoor pool and tennis courts. The restaurant is known for its outstanding American cuisine (see the Restaurants chapter) and is open for dinner Wednesday through Sunday. Meals are served in the tavern and dining room by fireside in season and by candlelight year-round. Live entertainment is featured on Thursday and Saturday nights. A continental breakfast is served during the week and a full breakfast on weekends. Rates vary depending on room size, season, and day of the week. A Registered National Historic Place, the inn is just off MA 23 in the village, a National Historic District.

Stockbridge

The Stockbridge Chamber of Commerce at 3 Elm Street lists all accommodations in Stockbridge as well as some in surrounding towns and operates a lodging hot line at (866) 626-5327. The chamber phone number is (413) 298-5200 and the Web site is www.stockbridgechamber.org.

Arbor Rose B&B **$$**
8 Yale Hill Road
(413) 298-4744
www.arborrose.com

Yale Hill was once the manufacturing hub of Stockbridge, with five mills catching the water from Kampoosa Brook. Today the Hill is a residential area of gracious homes, including that of Christina Alsop, which she and her family operate as Arbor Rose B&B. The Alsop property also includes a pond and the last vestige of that era: the Comstock sawmill, which also is available for guests. Dips in the pond are encouraged. Four rooms have been created in the old post-and-beam mill plus an efficiency apartment, which can be rented for longer periods. There are three guest rooms in the main house, where breakfast is served in the Shaker-style dining room. Guests may gather in the front parlor, where in

CLOSE-UP

The Red Lion Inn

Quintessentially New England, the Red Lion Inn has been accommodating travelers since 1773, although it was not nearly as big then as it is now. The Inn has had several names and configurations through the years, but a red lion has always graced its sign and the name has been used since around 1900. George Washington didn't sleep here, but Presidents Cleveland, McKinley, Teddy Roosevelt, Coolidge, and FDR have, along with a slew of writers, actors, and other famous personages. Former state senator Jack Fitzpatrick and his wife, Jane, have owned the inn since 1968. An inveterate collector of antiques, Jane has continued to add to the collections of a previous owner, Mrs. Charles Plumb, who scoured the countryside for furnishings back in the 1860s and 1870s when she and her husband ran the inn. The collection was miraculously saved when a fire in 1896 nearly destroyed the inn, and Mrs. Plumb's china and furniture are still part of the furnishings. The rebuilt hotel opened the next year and was run by the Treadway family for more than 90 years. The building was virtually unchanged until the early 1960s when private baths were added in the south wing and a swimming pool was installed.

Today the inn, with its grand front porch, has 108 rooms in various configurations. Each is carefully furnished in the New England tradition yet is modernized with cable television, air-conditioning and telephones. Some suites have VCRs and small refrigerators. There are all sorts of arrangements of beds. Some two-bedroom suites are connected by a common bathroom, others have private baths. Two suites for wheelchair use are located on the ground floor on the west side of the inn, where the wheelchair access and parking lot for the inn itself is situated. There are no elevators in the inn, so those who don't want to climb a lot of stairs might want to make sure their room is located on the lower floor. Guests can avail themselves of the Red Lion Inn's formal dining room, where contemporary regional meals are served three times a day. Casual fare may be had in Widow Bingham's Tavern or the

winter a Franklin wood stove adds to the coziness. All rooms have king- or queen-size four-poster beds, air-conditioning, private baths, and television sets and are furnished with antiques and country decor. Some have gas fireplaces, connect with each other, or have extra beds.

Families are welcome and should discuss what rooms will best suit their needs. A winter package that includes skiing at Butternut is available. During the week, breakfast includes a beverage, fruit (from the garden when available), homemade granola or other cereal, and a baked goodie. On weekends a hot entree is added. Yale Hill Road meets MA 102 at the Berkshire Theatre Festival, which is across the way from Arbor Rose. Downtown, where there are public tennis courts, is a 0.5-mile walk. By the way, an arbor at the front walk is covered with roses in summer, thus the name of the B&B.

Lion's Den, which also offers entertainment nightly. The inn has several rooms that can be reserved for meetings, conferences, and special dinners. The flagship Country Curtains store is located here, as is the Red Lion Inn Gift Shop, described in the Shopping chapter. Prices for accommodations vary widely, and some packages are available.

The inn is not the only building resurrected by the Fitzpatricks. Their daughter, Nancy, was instrumental in refurbishing the Victorian mill houses in North Adams that are now the Porches Inn. The family also owns Blantyre in Lenox as well as several buildings around Stockbridge that have been adapted to accommodate guests:

- **Meadowlark,** the studio of sculptor Daniel Chester French at Chesterwood, his summer estate. Two bedrooms, a spacious, lofty living room, kitchen, and bath are available from May through October by special arrangement with the National Trust for Historic Preservation, which owns Chesterwood.
- **The Firehouse** is furnished with a king-size bed, two bathrooms, including one with a double whirlpool bath and large shower, large living room, full kitchen, and a boardroom or dining room with seating for 10 to 15.
- **The O'Brien House** offers three suites and two regular-size guest rooms with queen or twin beds. Two suites have efficiency kitchens.
- **Stafford House** is a lovely old village residence popular for small weddings. The formal living room still retains its fine moldings and graceful staircase. There are three romantic suites with queen beds and several bathrooms plus sitting rooms.
- **2 Maple Street** has a large suite with an old-fashioned knotty pine kitchen on the first floor plus two bedrooms with separate sitting rooms and porches upstairs.

But the Red Lion remains the family's signature piece. Beautifully furnished, professionally run, and always welcoming, the inn is awash in flowers in summer, when folks sit in rockers on the porch or enjoy meals on the back patio. At Christmastime the place is aglow with decorations. The Red Lion sign still welcomes travelers as it did 100 years ago. The inn is located at 30 Main Street in Stockbridge. Call (413) 298-5545 or visit www.redlioninn.com for more information.

Conroy's B&B **$-$$$**
US 7
(413) 298-4990, (888) 298-4990
www.conroysinn.com

Jim and Joanne Conroy came here from California for a visit and never went back. Instead they bought three acres off US 7 north of town, restored the 1830s brick Federal home, and opened their B&B in 1992. They offer five rooms in the main house and three more in a restored barn, where an apartment also is available. All are furnished with antiques and decorated in a pleasant country style. The original hardwood floors and other architectural features are shown off to their best. The main house has a common sitting area and dining room, where Joanne serves a hearty breakfast of fresh-baked bread and muffins, homemade granola, fresh fruit, yogurt, juice, hard-boiled eggs, coffee, and tea, all prepared in her spacious country kitchen.

The bedrooms in the main house are outfitted with king, queen, or double beds. Three share a bathroom. The two rooms with private baths also have fireplaces. The rooms in the barn have private baths and decks or patios. One room has a queen-size bed. The others have king-size beds, one of which can be configured into two twins. The apartment suite has a television set and Jacuzzi, a full kitchen, private bath, and a sofa bed in the spacious living room. Snuggled under the eaves is a loft with a queen-size bed, from which one can view the stars through skylights in the roof. Most rooms have air conditioners.

Rates vary depending on the room chosen. A cot may be rented for $25. There is a charge of $25 for a third person in the apartment, which rents for $250 to $300 from mid-May through November 1 when it is closed for the winter.

Stockbridge Inn **$$$-$$$$**
US 7
(413) 298-3337
www.stockbridgeinn.com
The Georgian-style mansion that is now the Stockbridge Inn was built as a private residence in 1906 and restored in 1982 as a bed-and-breakfast. In 1995 Alice and Len Schiller purchased the inn and moved to Stockbridge from their home in Maplewood, New Jersey. Since then they have built a four-suite cottage and a "barn," offering a total of 16 rooms with assorted decor and amenities. All rooms have VCRs and CD players, and guests may choose tapes or CDs from the library in the main house. Robes, sherry, and personal care items are provided in all rooms. The suites in the Cottage House are decorated in international motifs. Two have 6-foot whirlpool baths, and all have king-size beds. Twin beds may be arranged here and in the mansion, which has eight rooms. The rooms in the Barn are decorated in themes honoring Shakespeare, Edith Wharton, Norman Rockwell, and the Shakers. Several suites have gas fireplaces, as does one room in the main house. Other amenities include an outdoor pool and a fully equipped exercise room. Appointments may be made with a masseuse.

Located on 12 acres off US 7 north of town, the inn has a three-star Mobil rating and a three-diamond AAA rating and has been featured in several travel magazines. Prices vary, depending on the accommodations, and off-season packages are available, but all rates include a full gourmet breakfast by candlelight in the dining room of the mansion. Len's favorites include lemon-cottage cheese pancakes and apple-walnut pancakes. A butler's pantry is open for ice, tea, coffee, and hot chocolate, and complimentary wine and cheese is served nightly in the living room by the fire in winter or on the porch in summer.

CENTRAL BERKSHIRE

Dalton

The Dalton House Bed & Breakfast **$$**
955 Main Street (MA 8)
(413) 684-3854
www.thedaltonhouse.com
Bernice and Gary Turetsky have been offering country charm with in-town convenience at their bed-and-breakfast for more than 20 years. Between their historic home and an adjoining carriage house, they have 11 rooms with private baths, cozily furnished with antiques and reproductions, most with a country feel. The exception is the Crane Room, a suite recently decorated with a more formal motif. The main house, built by a Hessian soldier in 1810, contains five rooms upstairs. A common area, where the huge early beams are revealed, provides a comfortable place to relax in front of the stone fireplace. Antiques, including a china cabinet filled with a collection of saltcellars, are everywhere. A continental "plus" breakfast is served in a cheerful room fitted with chairs and tables. All phones have dataports, and there is a computer station with Internet access in the main house. A former greenhouse converted

into a walkway connects the main house with the carriage house at the rear, in which there are four rooms and three spacious suites.

Although you can't tell from the street, Dalton House is located on two acres that have been landscaped with perennial gardens and stone walkways. A gazebo, hammock, and in-ground pool add to the luxury. There also is a large deck off the common room. Children over the age of eight are welcome. There is a charge of $15 for an additional person in a room. Ground-floor rooms have walk-in showers. The Dalton House is located near Crane & Company and the Wahconah Country Club and caters to businesspeople as well as vacationers.

Lanesborough

There are four moderately priced motels on US 7 in Lanesborough, five minutes north of Pittsfield. They provide in-room coffeemakers but do not offer continental breakfasts. There are several restaurants nearby.

Lanesborough Motel **$-$$**
110 North Main Street

Lamppost Motel
219 North Main Street
(413) 442-6717
Both of these older motels have been owned and operated by Manny Patel since 1990. There are 10 rooms in each with king- or full-size beds, some with refrigerators and microwaves. Smoking is allowed in some rooms. The Lanesborough Motel has a heated in-ground pool, which guests from either property may use. There is no charge for additional persons in a room.

Mt. View Motel **$-$$**
499 South Main Street
(413) 442-1009
The Mt. View Motel has six large rooms furnished with a king or two double beds and small refrigerators. In addition, there are four small freestanding cabins, three with efficiency kitchens. There is a $7.00 charge for additional adults. Children are welcome and are encouraged to play on the grounds, where picnic tables are set up. Pets and smoking are allowed in some rooms. Also an older motel that has been redecorated, Mt. View has been owned by Hasmukh Patel (no relation to Manny) since 1993.

Many attractions have arrangements with innkeepers and motel owners for discounted admissions or reduced-price tickets.

Weathervane **$-$$**
475 South Main Street
(413) 443-3230
Raj Shah has owned the Weathervane since 1989 and has upgraded it, furnishing the 12 rooms with king or two double beds. All have standard amenities; three have kitchenettes. Pets and smoking are allowed in some rooms. There is no minimum-stay requirement. Young children are free; other additional persons may be charged $5.00.

Pittsfield

All major highways in the Berkshires lead to Pittsfield, the county's center. The city also is near a small airport, is a stop on Conrail's Lakeshore Limited, and is served by several interstate bus companies. Additional lodging may be found online at www.berkshirechamber.com or by calling the chamber of commerce at (413) 499-4000.

Berkshire Inn **$-$$**
150 West Housatonic Street (US 20)
(413) 443-3000, (800) 443-0633
Located in town on the west side of Pittsfield, this motel has 34 nightly rooms plus

five that are rented on an adjusted weekly rental. Built in the late 1950s, the Berkshire Inn was completely remodeled in 1999. There are smoking and nonsmoking rooms, some with dataports. All have private bathrooms. Basic continental fare is provided in the office. There is an in-ground swimming pool. Special packages are offered for skiers as well as for those attending weddings or funerals. The motel sits on a hill off the highway near the center of town and is located at the corner of Beech Grove Avenue.

Comfort Inn **$–$$**
1055 South Street (US 7/20)
(413) 443–4714
www.comfortinn.com/hotel/MA011

Located on the Pittsfield/Lenox line, this Comfort Inn was built in 1998. Off the highway on a hill away from traffic noise, the inn has 58 rooms on three floors with carpeted corridors reached by elevator. All rooms are completely wheelchair-accessible, including bathrooms, a boon for disabled travelers, and six have fireplaces. A deluxe breakfast buffet, including hot and cold cereals, yogurt, and assorted muffins and bagels is provided in a pleasant area with five tables off the main lobby. Other amenities include a lounge, a fitness center, and complimentary copies of *USA Today.* There is no charge for children or cribs. Roll-away beds may be rented for $10.

Crowne Plaza Hotel **$$**
One West Street
(413) 499–2000, (800) 227–6963
www.berkshirecrowne.com

The tallest building in Pittsfield, this hotel was built during the days of urban renewal. Locals dubbed it the Tiltin' Hilton—the tower that rises above the city appears, through an optical illusion, to have a slight slant. Crowne Plaza Hotels and Resorts took over the hotel in 1998 and has completely renovated it. There are 179 rooms furnished with king, queen, or two double beds. There is a floor for smokers, and several rooms, including baths, are completely wheelchair-accessible. In-room amenities include dataports, PlayStations, and movies. Pets are permitted for a $25 fee. At certain times there are minimum-stay requirements, so it is best to inquire.

Breakfast, lunch, and dinner are served in Dewey's restaurant and lounge. Room service is available. Muddy McGee's on the ground level serves appetizers, sandwiches, and other pub fare. The hotel has a ballroom, meeting rooms, and a banquet hall. Guests may take a swim in the heated pool and avail themselves of the Jacuzzi, sauna, fitness center, and game room. The Crowne Plaza is located in downtown Pittsfield near shops, restaurants, the Berkshire Museum, and other historic buildings. The hotel has an attached parking garage and a gift shop.

Ramada Inn & Suites **$–$$$**
1350 West Housatonic Street (US 20 West)
(413) 442–8714, (800) 272–6232
www.the.ramada.com/pittsfield13538

Newly constructed in 2001, this Ramada Inn has 59 rooms with a variety of bed arrangements, including executive suites with pull-out couches and kitchenettes. There also are 10 two-bedroom suites with kitchenettes. Several rooms and suites have fireplaces. Travelers with nonservice pets may call the management to see if they will be allowed for an additional charge. There is no charge for additional persons in a room. An extensive continental breakfast is available in a nine-table dining area. There is a meeting room, and all rooms have dataports. Valet laundry and dry-cleaning service is available.

Pittsfield Travelodge **$**
16 Cheshire Road (MA 8)
(413) 443–5661, (800) 578–7878
www.pittsfieldtravelodge.com

There are 47 newly decorated rooms in this renovated two-story Travelodge located on the east side of Pittsfield near GE Plastics, General Dynamics, and several large shopping centers. Smoking is permitted in some rooms, and guests receive a complimentary copy of *USA Today*. Ground-floor rooms are wheelchair-accessible, but bathrooms are not. A restaurant next door that looks suspiciously like an IHOP is in fact a very good Indian restaurant called Sangeet, but for breakfast you have to go across the street to McDonald's, Friendly's, or Kelly's Diner.

Thaddeus Clapp House B&B $$–$$$
74 Wendell Avenue
(413) 499–6840, (888) 499–6840
www.clapphouse.com

This historic 1871 mansion has been turned into an upscale bed-and-breakfast by three innkeepers: Rebecca Smith and Robert Chok, each of whom operated B&Bs in California, and Smith's sister, Kathy McCave. The house is named for the wealthy owner of a textile mill who built it. Completely restored, the four-story inn is listed on the National Register of Historic Places and retains many of its original fixtures. There are eight roomy guest suites with formal living or sitting rooms, period furniture, Oriental carpets, fireplaces, private baths with whirlpools or soaking tubs, and all the other amenities you would expect. A full breakfast is served in the dining room, which was once the Clapps' drawing room. Afternoon tea is served daily on the front porch or in the drawing room. Located in downtown Pittsfield's historic district, the inn is within walking distance of the Berkshire Museum and other attractions. Although new to the area, the innkeepers have jumped right into local activities, opening the house for tours and letting a local group of actors create an 1870s musicale on the premises.

Yankee Suites Extended Stay $$$
20 West Housatonic Street (US 20)
(800) 835–2364

Yankee Suites are located in a former apartment complex that was completely renovated in 2002 and converted into 26 suites outfitted with king, queen, or two double beds, sleeper sofas, full kitchenettes, and living rooms. Laundry facilities are on the premises. Dataports connected to high-speed Internet service and 27-inch television sets are in each suite. Rates range from $2,250 to $2,950 a month, although corporate rates may be negotiated separately. Reservations for summer should be made by May.

Washington

Bucksteep Manor $–$$
885 Washington Mountain Road
(413) 623–5535, (800) 645–2825
www.bucksteepmanor.com

Built in the 1890s, Bucksteep Manor is the centerpiece of this former estate situated on nearly 400 acres of woodlands on the top of Washington Mountain. Built in the Tudor style, the manor has eight rooms with three shared baths and a common lounge. The dining room can seat 50 and is used for complimentary breakfasts and Saturday night dinners. A tavern there is open for light lunches and snacks. In the evening guests may purchase drinks and bottles of wine to go with dinner. More rustic in style are two cottages with a total of 14 rooms, each having a private bath. Many of the rooms have inner adjoining doors, handy for families or large parties. Rates vary, but all include breakfast. A turn-of-the-20th-century carriage house has been converted into a private hall suitable for private parties of up to 150 people. There are two restrooms, a rustic yet elegant lobby, and a large room with a stone fireplace, full bar, and dance floor.

With all its outbuildings and the manor itself, Bucksteep is particularly suited to reunions and weddings. The property has 20 miles of trails known for great cross-country skiing and snowshoeing. In summer the trails are open for hiking or mountain biking, and there is a pool and tennis courts. Skis, bikes, and snowshoes may be rented on-site. Bucksteep is adjacent to October Mountain State Forest and is half a mile from the Appalachian Trail. Washington Mountain Road may be reached from MA 8 or from Dalton Division Road in east Pittsfield.

NORTH COUNTY

Cheshire

Harbour House Inn B&B **$$–$$$**
725 North Street (MA 8)
(413) 743–8959
www.harbourhouseinn.com

One of only a few places to stay along this other north-south route, Harbour House bed-and-breakfast offers six rooms plus a two-room suite in a historic 18th-century Georgian home in the foothills of Mount Greylock. Five of the rooms have queen-size beds, and one has twin beds that can be reconfigured to a king. A suite has two bedrooms and a sitting area plus a balcony. From the romantically decorated rooms, guests can view rolling farmlands or manicured lawns and flowering gardens on the two-acre property. The common area includes a library, fireplace, sitting areas, and French doors that open out onto a large front porch and side veranda. Guests are welcome to gather around the baby grand piano in the music room.

Innkeepers Eva and Sam Amuso offer a bountiful breakfast in the dining room or on the veranda, with a menu that incorporates seasonal local ingredients. Homemade granola, jams, muffins, and breads may be accompanied by omelettes with a choice of fillings or such treats as eggs Benedict, poached eggs in crepe cups, challah French toast with glazed apples, or pumpkin waffles with honey-roasted pears. The inn may be rented for weddings, meetings, retreats, or other special events and is open year-round. It has a three-diamond rating from AAA. The Appalachian Trail and the paved Ashuwillticook Rail Trail are nearby. Although located on the east side of the county, the inn is within 30 to 40 minutes of all major tourist attractions.

Hancock

Jiminy Peak, Vacation Village, and Bentley Brook dominate the accommodations in Hancock. All are described later in this chapter: Jiminy Peak in "Resorts and Conference Centers" and the others in "Time-Shares and Condos."

Hancock Inn B&B **$–$$**
102 Main Street (Old Massachusetts Highway 43)
(413) 738–5873
www.thehancockinn.com

Located near Jiminy Peak Resort, the Hancock Inn has six romantically decorated rooms with private baths. One is a suite with a queen-size bed and living room area and is the only room with a television set. The other rooms have twin or full-size beds. All are furnished with antiques. Innkeepers Joe and Gail Mullady serve a complimentary hearty country breakfast with interesting wraps, egg dishes, pancakes, breads, and seasonal fruits. Tea and wine are served in the afternoon. Older children are welcome.

Jericho Valley Inn **$–$$**
2541 Hancock Road (MA 43)
(413) 458–9511, (800) 537–4246
www.jerichovalleyinn.com

The Jericho Valley Inn has been described by the *Boston Globe* as one of the "best bargains in the Berkshires." Located between Jiminy Peak Resort to the south and Williamstown to the north, the inn is situated on 350 acres on quiet MA 43, which runs from New York State to the center of Williamstown. Owned and operated by Ed and Julie Hanify, the inn has a three-diamond rating from AAA. There are 25 rooms, including one-, two-, and three-bedroom suites and cottages outfitted with full kitchens and living rooms with fireplaces. The cottages rent for around $200 and up. Aside from hiking trails on the property, there is an outdoor heated pool. A two-night minimum is required on weekends year-round, but there is no charge for children. Pets are allowed. The complimentary continental breakfast is served in a pleasant area off the main office furnished with tables and chairs. Although the inn is located in Hancock, the mailing address is in Williamstown. Rates are the same year-round.

New Ashford

EconoLodge **$-$$**
US 7
(413) 458-5945, (800) 277-0001

Located halfway between Pittsfield and Williamstown, this motel offers standard fare at reasonable prices that remain the same all year. There are 41 rooms, some on a second tier, which offer either two double or two queen beds. Shampoo, hair dryers, and coffeemakers are available by request at the front desk. Lower level rooms are wheelchair-accessible, but bathrooms are standard. Smoking is permitted in some rooms. There is no minimum stay, and package deals for lift tickets at nearby Jiminy Peak Ski Resort may be arranged. The grounds include a heated outdoor pool and a tennis court. The property also includes two chalets with fireplaces and kitchenettes, which may be rented for $100 to $300 a day depending on the length of stay. A complimentary continental breakfast is served in a former but no longer operating luncheonette on the premises. The former Springs Restaurant across the road, once a family-owned landmark, has been open off and on with a succession of operators. The motel does not have its own Web site, but information can be found on the Internet through a variety of sources.

North Adams

As the city becomes more of a tourist destination, there will surely be more places to stay. But right now, these are it. However, neighboring Williamstown has many B&Bs and motels, some of which are listed under that town.

Holiday Inn Berkshires **$-$$**
40 Main Street
(413) 663-6500, (800) HOLIDAY
www.holidayinnberkshires.com

Centrally located near the junction of Massachusetts Highways 2 and 8 in downtown North Adams, this 86-room hotel adheres to Holiday Inn standards and offers some amenities of its own. Built in the heyday of urban renewal, the inn suffered along with the rest of the city when the major employer, Sprague Electric, pulled out. The seven-story hotel loomed empty and dark until it was bought at auction by owner Sandy Plumb in the 1980s. Gambling that the newly proposed Massachusetts Museum of Contemporary Art would revive the city, Plumb began renovating the inn, a project that was completed in 2002.

New from the homey room decor to the Jacuzzi, the hotel offers one floor for smokers and several wheelchair-accessible rooms, including bathrooms. Single rooms contain one king-size bed; doubles have two queens. Except for peak times, like foliage and college graduations, when reservations should be made four to five months ahead, there is no minimum-stay requirement.

Steeples, a smoke-free 70-seat restaurant named for the many church spires that soar above the city, serves lunch and dinner. A continental breakfast consisting of fresh baked goods, fruit, and other fare is offered from 6:00 to 11:00 A.M. in a cafe located off the main dining room. The breakfast is not included in the room rate, but children under age 12 may partake at no charge and discounts are available through a special "B&B" rate. In nice weather, a deck overlooking the action on Main Street is opened and often features live music on weekends. A fully stocked bar is located off the dining room. Decor includes a Victorian pump organ and an oak confessional booth converted to a wine cabinet.

A fully equipped fitness center located in the basement is free to guests and open to the public through memberships. An indoor heated swimming pool, Jacuzzi, sauna, and steam room complete the offerings. Although family oriented, the inn also caters to businesspeople, with dataports in every room and a separate business center with a library, computer with free high-speed Internet access, and other office equipment. Frequent users who join the Priority Club earn air miles and are entitled to a free newspaper and a discount coupon for breakfast. The spacious lobby is decorated with photographs recalling North Adams's industrial past. Several businesses, including a real estate broker, lease space on the main and second floors. A meeting room that can hold up to 110 persons may be rented for small or large conferences and receptions. A parking lot is adjacent to the hotel.

Jae's Inn **$$**
1111 South State Road (MA 8)
(413) 664-0105
www.jaesinn.com

Boston restauranteur Jae Chung has completely renovated this 1890s former inn, adding a spa, tennis court, heated swimming pool, basketball court, bar, and restaurant offering Asian cuisine. Decorated with a warm, inviting country look are 11 air-conditioned guest rooms, each with a whirlpool bathtub, fireplace, and flat-screen television with DVD player. The spa, which is open to the public by appointment, features massage tables, a sauna, and a full range of beauty services and body treatments. The health club has a treadmill, Stair Master, and universal weight system. Pets are accepted with a one-time charge of $20. Roll-away beds may be rented for $20 per night. Rates are the same year-round. The inn is located on 11 acres off MA 8 about 10 minutes south of the city. Other cultural attractions are within an hour's drive. A continental breakfast is served in the restaurant, which is open to the public for lunch and dinner and is described more fully in the Restaurants chapter. Chung operates cafes in the Boston area and recently bought Le Jardin in Williamstown, with plans to renovate it and continue its operation as an inn and French restaurant.

The Porches Inn **$$-$$$$**
231 River Street
(413) 664-0400
www.porches.com

No less amazing than the conversion of the sprawling Sprague complex into the Massachusetts Museum of Contemporary Art is the renovation of six identical but dilapidated Victorian mill houses behind it on River Street into what is now known as the Porches Inn. Only open since 2001, the Porches has already been named one of the top 100 hotels in the world by Condé Nast's *Tatler.* And no wonder. Although rundown and housing some of the city's poorest residents, the clapboard and shingled houses were structurally sound and their slate roofs basically intact. It took the imagination of Nancy Fitzpatrick, whose parents own the Red Lion Inn in Stockbridge, coupled with the vision of local architect Ann McCallum and backing from a Williams alum, to restore the houses and turn them into a marvelous concoction of subtle colors and architectural gingerbread all connected by one long porch. The interior is a mix of contemporary and antique furnishings, kitsch, and collectibles displayed in brightly colored rooms that must be unique in the annals of hotel decor. The restoration is recorded in a pictorial book about the Porches sold at the Inn and at MASS MoCA. The arty Web site gives a good idea of the work involved and the amazing results. The six now-connected buildings house 46 rooms broken into a variety of arrangements. Two are fully wheelchair-accessible. Standard rooms offer king or queen beds with private baths. Some have their own porches, as do junior suites that include a queen bed and private bath with whirlpool tub. Two-bedroom suites are on two levels and are available with queen or king beds, two baths with whirlpool tubs and a living room equipped with a sofa bed. Some rooms are equipped with kitchenettes. Additional guests are charged $20. Amenities include a free newspaper and a complimentary European breakfast served in a dining room furnished with Mission oak or delivered to your room in a lunch bucket if desired. The fare includes cheese, yogurt, fresh breads and croissants, fruit, hard-boiled eggs, and beverages.

Despite the knickknacks and leather chairs that abound, the inn is kid-friendly and offers PlayStations that can be used in a guest's room or in Building 7, a separate house that has been converted into a state-of-the-art meeting room complete with a 60-inch plasma screen TV. Rooms are equipped with DVD players (there is a DVD library on-site), high-speed Internet access, and dual phone lines. The Board Room, located in the reception building, is outfitted with slate blackboards and can accommodate up to 15 persons for conferences. A hot tub and year-round heated outdoor pool, sauna, and fitness room complete the amenities. The Porches also is listed in *Condé Nast Traveler*'s 2002 Hot List of the "32 coolest new hotels in the world" and is included in the *Historic Hotels of America*. One of the more expensive places to stay in North County, the Porches is worth a visit just to see what can be done with flair and imagination—and $6 million!

Redwood Motel **$**
915–919 State Road (MA 2)
(413) 664–4351

At the other end of the spectrum, the Redwood Motel offers a no-frills place to sleep. Originally the site of tourist cabins run by the current owner's parents, the property was cleared and the motel built in the 1960s. There are 18 rooms, 12 with two double beds and 6 with one double. There are no amenities, but credit cards are accepted. The charge for an extra person is $5.00 or $10.00, depending on the season.

Williamstown

The availability of rooms in Williamstown is closely tied to events at Williams College and foliage season, so it definitely pays to plan ahead. For a complete list of accommodations, contact the Williamstown Chamber of Commerce at (413) 458–9077 or P.O. Box 357, Williamstown 01267. Their Web address is www.williamstownchamber.com.

Berkshire Hills Motel **$–$$**
US 7
(413) 458–3950, (800) 388–9677
www.berkshirehillsmotel.com

Located on US 7 south of Williamstown near the junction of MA 2 from New York State, the Berkshire Hills Motel offers rooms in front or in back, where guests can fall asleep to the rushing—or babbling—of Hemlock Brook. In summer the grounds are filled with flowering gardens and nestled among the trees along the brook are a gazebo and various arrangements of chairs and benches. A bridge crosses to the 45- by 20-foot heated pool. In winter there are ski packages, and guests can gather by the fireplace in the homey main office, where books are available in a small library. Mark and Jill Harris, who have backgrounds in corporate hotel management, purchased the motel in 1997. All rooms are nonsmoking; some are wheelchair-accessible but the bathrooms are standard. The complimentary cold breakfast buffet is served in a large airy corner dining room that can seat 30 persons at round oak tables. The extensive offerings include bagels, muffins, a wide variety of cereals, fruits, and beverages.

i

If you're planning to stay in or around Williamstown, make sure there are no major events scheduled at Williams College, such as graduation or alumni weekend, which make it nearly impossible to find a room.

An attached deck can seat another 25 guests. There are 21 rooms furnished with king, queen, or two double beds. There is no charge for children under age 10. Potential guests are asked to check about minimum-stay requirements, which vary depending on other bookings.

Chimney Mirror Motel **$-$$**
295 Main Street (MA 2)
(413) 458-5202

This attractive no-frills motel has 18 rooms mostly with full or king-size beds. It is not wheelchair-accessible but does allow pets in a couple of the rooms. Some rooms also are available for smokers. In season a standard continental breakfast is served. There is no charge for extra persons in a room.

1896 House Country Inn & Motels **$$-$$$**
US 7
(413) 458-1896, (888) 999-1896
www.1896house.com

Three kinds of accommodations in different price ranges are offered at this 17-acre complex centered around a historic 1896 landmark barn. The lower level of the barn itself, called "Barnside," contains six luxury suites, each decorated in a different style with period and furnishings handpicked by owners Suzanne Morelle and Denise Richer, who are frequently seen at local auctions. Early American, French Provincial, Georgian, and other styles are reflected in the king-size four-poster beds, appointments, linens, carpets, floral arrangements, paintings and prints, and specially selected wall coverings and fabrics. All rooms have fireplaces, refrigerators, dual whirlpool baths and stand-up showers, DVD/CD players, and upscale amenities. One suite is entirely wheelchair-accessible, including the shower. Guests are served creative three-course breakfasts by candlelight in a separate intimate dining room adjacent to the suites. Each suite is entered off a large porch furnished with rockers and Adirondack chairs.

Rooms in two motels on the property, "Brookside" and "Pondside," also have individual decorating styles. Brookside is down off the road on the east side of US 7 and is reached by a bridge over babbling Hemlock Brook. Most rooms there have two double beds and are decorated with Cushman maple furniture in a country style. Guests may enjoy a generous continental breakfast in their room, in the gazebo, or at a patio table. Flower gardens, footbridges, and lots of places to sit are found on the expansive grounds along the brook.

Across the highway on the west side is the more economical Pondside. Rooms there are decorated in a more simple Cape Cod style and have one queen bed. In addition, there are several special suites in Brookside and Pondside. There is no charge for children under age eight. Cots, cribs, or refrigerators for the motel rooms may be rented for $10 a day.

A two-night minimum stay is required on weekends in season, on holidays, and when there are special events in the area. Rooms are less midseason (April to June 29) and even less in the off-seasons (January 1 to March 31 and October 26 to December 31). Prices also vary depending on the days of the week booked. The pricing symbol above represents the rate for a Friday and Saturday in one of the luxury suites in season. Rates for standard rooms in Brookside and Pondside are about $100 less in season. The charge for an additional person is $25 in a luxury suite, $10 in the motels.

Four Acres Motel **$-$$**
213 Main Street (MA 2)
(413) 458-8158
www.fouracresmotel.com

Built in the 1960s, the Four Acres Motel was recently purchased from longtime owners Bill and Judy Lyon by Navin Shah, who also owns the Howard Johnson Express Inn in Lenox. The complex has 31 rooms on two levels and includes two rooms for smokers and two that are wheelchair-accessible but with regular bathrooms. The majority of the rooms have two double beds, but seven have one queen bed and one has a king-size bed. There is an efficiency unit with a queen-size bed, a sofa bed, and a full kitchen. Cribs or cots are available. The grounds include a swimming pool, garden picnic area, shuffleboard, and a quiet walking trail, and there is a room with a hot tub. The rate includes a continental breakfast with homemade muffins, fresh fruit, juices, and hot beverages. The Four Acres Restaurant located next door is under separate ownership. Lunch and dinner are served there daily except Sunday.

Green Valley Motel $-$$
1214 Simonds Road (US 7)
(413) 458-3864

Right smack on the Vermont border, this reasonably priced two-level motel has no minimum-stay requirement. There is a $5.00 charge for an additional person but no charge for children under age 10. Amenities include a swimming pool and picnic tables. A complimentary continental breakfast is served in the office. Dogs are allowed for an additional charge of $5.00. There are 18 rooms furnished with two double beds. One room is set aside for smokers.

Maple Terrace Motel $-$$
555 Main Street (MA 2)
(413) 458-9677
www.mapleterrace.com

Although Maple Terrace is right on the highway, the 15 large multiwindowed motel rooms are located at the rear and are backed by almost three acres of open land, giving a country atmosphere to this conveniently located establishment. In summer, lush gardens abound and guests are welcome to use the heated swimming pool, picnic tables, and charcoal grills. Children are welcome and have their own play area. A ski package is available in winter. A weekend getaway package is also offered.

Rooms have queen-size or two extra-long double beds. All rooms have dataports, VCRs, and refrigerators; are nonsmoking; and are not wheelchair-accessible. Additional adult guests are $10.00, teenagers are $7.00, and children under age 12 are free. There is a deluxe room with a king-size bed, fireplace, microwave, and refrigerator. There are also two spacious apartments with full kitchens that rent from $115 to $140 a night. They are located in the Federal home where the office is located and where owners Kjell and Ann Truedsson live. Retired from the Cunard Line, Kjell Truedsson has decorated the office with models of ocean liners and pictures of shipmates, an odd thing to come upon in landlocked Williamstown. The complimentary breakfast includes a homemade baked good, juices, and hot beverages, including hot chocolate.

Northside Motel $
45 North Street (US 7)
(413) 458-8107
www.northsidemotel.com

The Northside Motel is owned and operated by Fred Nagy, whose parents began the business in 1957, and his wife, Linda. There are 30 rooms, most with two beds and some with queen. Some rooms also have refrigerators, and there are two for smokers. There is an outdoor pool and a swing set for children. There is no additional charge for children under age 10, and cribs and cots are available. A complimentary continental breakfast of bagels, cereal, juice, and hot beverages is served in the coffee shop from June through October. Beverages, including hot chocolate are served year-round. The motel, conveniently located near Williams College and the Adams Memorial Theater, is open all year except for the owners' vacation in December.

The Orchards $$-$$$
206 Adams Road
(413) 458-9611, (800) 225-1517
www.orchardshotel.com

This highly rated inn is located between MA 2 and Adams Road, which runs parallel to the highway. The oddly opulent entrances are guarded by huge stone walls and iron gates topped with an elaborate crest. The brick-paved entry to the main lobby is off Adams Road. Two-story pale-pink stucco buildings surround a landscaped courtyard with a pool and a terrace that is used for alfresco dining in season. There are 49 rooms furnished with English country antiques, each in a different decor. Spacious sitting areas, fluffy robes, and imported soaps and gels complete the amenities. Singles have king-size beds; doubles have two double beds. There is a $30 charge for a third person, but there is no charge for children under age 12.

The inn was built in the 1980s, but the business failed and later was sold at auction. A previous owner completely renovated the inn in 1985, and Sayed Saleh has been the proprietor since 1991. Although the complex looks a little out of place for New England, it does offer a relief from all that white clapboard and guests are treated like royalty. The carpeted living room next to the reception desk on the main floor has a piano and a fireplace surrounded with black marble and oak. A crystal chandelier hangs from the ceiling, flanked by two brass ones. This luxurious space is used for afternoon tea, when finger sandwiches and pastries are served to guests. The well-trained staff comes from all over the world, offering patrons a chance to engage in interesting conversation if they so desire. Except for two guest rooms, the entire complex is smoke-free. There are two wheelchair-accessible rooms with appropriately outfitted bathrooms. Breakfast is not included in the rate but is available in the 75-seat AAA four-diamond restaurant located in the lower level of the inn. A lounge with a stone fireplace provides a comfortable spot for drinks before dinner or after skiing or a night out.

The hotel is a member of Preferred Hotels & Resorts, an accrediting association that grades members on certain criteria. The association has awarded the Orchards its top rating and in 2003 named Saleh Hotelier of the Year. Other accolades have come from *Yankee Magazine,* which rated it one of the top 500 inns in New England in 2001, the *New York Times,* and *Forbes* and *Gourmet* magazines.

The Villager Motel **$**
953 Simonds Road (US 7 North)
(413) 458-4046
www.williamstownvillager.com

Recently remodeled, the Villager has 13 rooms with windows front and back that are either pine paneled or decorated in warm colors. The motel is set back from the road on two acres, giving guests a country atmosphere. A continental breakfast of orange juice, English muffins, raisin bread, cereals, and fresh fruit is included in the reasonable rate. There is no charge for children under age 14. Playpens, portacribs, and cots are available. There are two rooms for smokers and two for pets, but guests are advised to call ahead to see if they are available.

The Williams Inn **$$-$$$**
On-the-Green
(413) 458-9371, (800) 828-0133
www.williamsinn.com

The Williams Inn is the granddaddy of accommodations in Williamstown. Located across from Field Park where US 7 and MA 2 converge, the three-story inn has 125 rooms, including a new wing with 6 rooms designed for complete accessibility and several suites with fireplaces and Jacuzzis. The 28-year-old inn is a traditional favorite for Williams alumni, and the hotel management is eager to accommodate the needs of that aging population. Smoking and pets, other than working animals, are not allowed in the new wing. Rooms in the main hotel are furnished in colonial-style decor on the elegant side but are being refurbished bit by bit. Most have two double beds, but there are some with king-size beds. Smoking is allowed in some rooms, and pets are permitted in certain rooms for a $10 fee. The spacious lobby has a large fireplace surrounded with comfortable seating. There also is a fireplace in the main dining room, where meals are served daily from 7:00 A.M. to 9:30 P.M., 10:00 P.M. on weekends. The menu includes classic New England dishes as well as continental cuisine and children's dishes. On Sunday a lavish brunch is served from 11:30 A.M. to 2:00 P.M. Reservations are a good idea, especially during graduation and alumni weekends. Dress is casual.

A late menu including desserts is available in the adjoining tavern, where live music can be heard on Friday and Saturday nights year-round. In July and August local talent performs cabaret-style on Sunday and Monday evenings. There is an indoor heated swimming pool with hot tub and saunas. Buses for New York and other areas stop at the inn, a convenience for Williams students and others. Because of its location near Williams College, availability of rooms is closely tied to events there. Package plans that include meals are available. The charge for an additional person is $15. There is no charge for children under age 14.

The Willows Motel **$-$$**
480 Main Street (MA 2)
(413) 458-5768
www.willowsmotel.com

Recently completely renovated, the Willows' 16 rooms have Shaker-style furnishings and attractive country decor. Full or queen beds are available. Amenities include a heated swimming pool and dataports and refrigerators in the rooms. A VCR is available on request. A continental breakfast with seasonal fare is served in a pleasant dining area. Several restaurants are nearby. There is no charge for children under age 12. A two-night minimum stay is required on weekends during July, August, and October.

RESORTS AND CONFERENCE CENTERS

Berkshire Vista Resort **$**
Kittle Road, Hancock
(413) 738-5154
www.berkshirevista.com

The Berkshires do indeed have something for everyone, including this resort and campground that caters to those for whom "social nudity is the norm." Located at the end of scenic Kittle Road, the resort serves members of the American Association for Nude Recreation as well as newcomers to the world of social and recreational nudism. Accommodations and rates vary. Members of the AANR pay $600 for the season. Guests may bring in their own RVs or rent one of several already on the property, including small campers complete with full baths and kitchenettes. Trailer or RV sites include water and electricity, with optional telephone hookups. Tent sites are available, and there is a motel with 20 rooms that rent for $50 a night.

A 1771 farmhouse on the property has been converted to a seven-room inn that is available to groups for from $75 to $90 per person, depending on the season. Day visitors are charged $20 to $35. Amenities include a large hot tub, solar-heated swimming pool, sauna, children's playground, a clubhouse with a restaurant and bar, laundry facilities, hiking trails and shuffleboard, volleyball and tennis courts, plus a court for pétanque, a lawn game popular abroad. A large recreation room is equipped with table tennis and pool tables.

Special events include entertainers on the large sunning lawn, dances with a DJ every weekend, live bands, a strawberry festival, country fair days, Christmas in July, Halloween in August, and Thanksgiving in October. Berkshire Vista is open May through October, but special arrangements may be made for winter rentals at the inn. Kittle Road is a picturesque dirt road off MA 43.

Canyon Ranch in the Berkshires **$$$$$***
165 Kemble Street, Lenox
(413) 637-4400, (800) 326-7080
www.canyonranch.com

Canyon Ranch's Berkshire resort, located in the former Bellefontaine estate, is the height of luxurious pampering. The surroundings are elegant. Add to this the nutritious gourmet meals and wide array of body and skin treatments and health and fitness programs for men and women, and you can see why *Gourmet, Travel & Leisure,* and *Condé Nast Traveler* magazines have high praises for this resort. Guests can set their own goals and design their own packages, but they might have a hard time deciding what to do. There are around 40 complimentary fitness classes each day plus more than 225 programs and services to choose from, including private health and fitness consultations with a team of more than 60 professional experts. There are lectures, workshops, and cooking demonstrations as well as such seasonal activities as skiing and snowshoeing, kayaking and canoeing, and hiking and biking. Guests may play golf at nearby Cranwell Resort. Transportation from nearby airports can be arranged.

The resort has 126 New England–style rooms and offers deluxe or luxury accommodations. Deluxe rooms have king or two double beds, a sitting area, and a vanity. Luxury suites have king or two twin beds, an adjoining living room, washer and dryer, minifridge, and two bathrooms. All meals are included in rates. Although the focus is on nutritious dining, the menus are far from boring and even include lobster, chowder, pizza, and cheesecake. Guests are asked to refrain from using cell phones in fitness classes and the dining room, at the pool, or on hikes or bike rides. Canyon Ranch in Tucson is the mother ship for this deluxe resort, which explains the not-very-Berkshire name. Prices are determined by the length of stay and season. (*Rates are for three-or four-night packages and include all meals and spa services.)

Cranwell Resort, Spa and Golf Club **$$$$–$$$$$**
55 Lee Road (US 20), Lenox
(413) 637–1364, (800) 272–6935
www.cranwell.com

Cranwell's 81 guest rooms and 26 suites are as varied as the facilities for recreation and dining, described more fully in those chapters. Rooms are available in the main mansion of this restored 19th-century estate as well as several smaller buildings. The mansion—with its great hall, elegant dining room, and more casual lounge—is furnished in the grand style of the period, and the rooms are decorated accordingly. Founders Cottage, near the 18-hole championship golf course and *Golf Digest* school and pool area, has 27 deluxe rooms, including some that adjoin. All have whirlpool tubs and balconies or terraces. Founders Cottage is linked by an underground tunnel to the state-of-the-art spa, where there is a heated pool and fitness center.

Historic Beecher's Cottage has some of the largest rooms on the property. Still retaining their character and design, they are decorated in a contemporary style. A restored carriage house next to the mansion connects with the spa by a glass-enclosed walkway, as does Olmsted Manor. Named for landscape architect Frederick Law Olmsted, who designed the original gardens at Cranwell, the manor has 10 rooms and 2 suites and houses the front desk, gift shop, and concierge desk. Suites in another "cottage" are available with an assortment of amenities, including wet bars or galley kitchens, refrigerators and ranges, and terraces or balconies. Especially suited for families, the bedrooms here have king-size beds and the living rooms have queen-size sofa beds.

Rates are broken down into the following categories: deluxe (queen beds and the least expensive), superior (king or double), luxury (suites in the cottages), and, most expensive, suites in the mansion.

The off-season runs from November 1 through April 30, and rates are reduced across the board by about $100. Smoking rooms are available on request, but smoking is prohibited in all common and dining areas. There is no charge for children under age 12 when sharing a room. Cots may be rented for $20 a night. Additional adults in a room will be charged $50. The 380-acre resort has received the AAA four-diamond award and is a member of

---

i

Cancellation policies differ, but many places will give a refund if they can rebook the room.

Historic Hotels of America. Cranwell hosts conferences and large groups and is available for weddings.

Eastover Resort & Conference Center **$$-$$$**
450 East Street, Lenox
(413) 637-0625, (800) 822-2386
www.eastover.com

Eastover has been owned by members of the Bisacca family for more than 50 years and is known locally for the herd of buffalo that roam the 1,000-acre former estate as well as the extensive Civil War memorabilia collection assembled by its founder. Accommodations are offered in the Georgian mansion and a number of accessory buildings. The family describes the rooms as "country basic." About half the rooms do not have telephones, and none have television sets or air-conditioning, although there are fans. For those who simply must have TV, there is a set in the mansion library and one in the lounge. Accommodations range from dormitory rooms to one-bedroom suites, and rates and bed configurations vary accordingly. Baths may be private, semiprivate, or shared by several rooms. The resort does not have a liquor license, but guests may bring their own.

Recreational facilities at the four-season resort include indoor and outdoor pools; miniature golf and a putting green; five clay tennis courts; skeet shooting; trails for hiking, horseback riding, and mountain biking; a softball diamond and courts for volleyball, basketball, badminton, horseshoes, and shuffleboard; 20 kilometers of cross-country skiing trails; and a toboggan run. Safaris and hayrides, scavenger hunts, and a host of lawn games also are offered. Lessons in cross-country skiing, tennis, archery, and driving golf balls are offered at no additional charge. Mountain bikes, horses, and cross-country skis may be rented. There's also a sauna and fitness center and a kid's camp. While the resort is family oriented, it does host special weeks and weekends for couples and singles that include entertainment and planned activities. Guests under the age of 25 are not accepted during those times. "Theme" weekends featuring murder mysteries, October Fest, Halloween, and other events are held throughout the year. Rates are for families and include three meals a day and access to all activities and facilities. Children's rates are graduated, with no charge for those under age three. Guests may ski free at Bousquet Ski Area in Pittsfield. If all this sounds like too much activity, doing nothing at all is both allowed and encouraged.

Jiminy Peak **$$$$-$$$$$**
37 Corey Road, Hancock
(413) 738-5500
www.jiminypeak.com

A four-season resort, Jiminy Peak offers 105 suites in the Country Inn and a number of condominiums that can be rented. Each comfortably furnished suite has a fireplace, a master bedroom with king-size bed, a living room with a queen-size sofa bed, a fully equipped kitchen, and a bath with separate vanity areas. Cable television and VCRs are provided. Amenities at the inn include a heated outdoor pool, Jacuzzi, exercise room, and lounge. Two- and three-bedroom condominiums that can accommodate up to eight persons also are available for various rates. Meals—not included in the rates—are served at Christiansen's Tavern in the base area, the Founders' Grille in the Country Inn, or at Hendricks Summit Lodge at the top of the mountain. Groceries, a deli with gourmet dishes, coffee, pastries, and other essentials are sold at the Country Store. The Village Center includes a new children's center, a welcome center, and a coffee shop.

The resort offers all kinds of specials, including reduced midweek and early- and late-season rates. Some specials include lift tickets in skiing season. Jiminy has 40 trails, including 18 that are lighted, and eight lifts plus a half-pipe for snowboarders. Lessons and rentals are available. Snowboarding and tubing also are run by Jiminy at nearby Brodie Mountain in New Ashford. Summer attractions include an alpine slide, miniature golf, mountain biking, and tennis. All recreational activities are described more fully in the Recreation and Kidstuff chapters.

The Seven Stones **$-$$**
103 Lake Buel Road, Great Barrington
(413) 528-9007, (877) 786-6307
www.thesevenstones.com

The Seven Stones is an unusual rustic retreat whose owners believe that camp isn't just for kids. Located on 85 acres on the shore of pristine Lake Buel, the resort replicates the best of the camp experience for adults who want to relive those days—or who never experienced them in the first place. The resort can provide lodging for groups of 25 to 100 persons and is particularly suited to reunions, weddings, and corporate gatherings. Children are welcome, including teams, clubs, and other youth organizations. Rooms are available in cabins and cottages outfitted mostly with single or bunk beds. The exception is the "Honeymoon Suite," a one-bedroom cottage for two that has a queen-size bed and a sitting area. Bunks are set up in communal rooms or in a cabin with separate bedrooms and two shared bathrooms. One bunkhouse is wheelchair-accessible, including the bathroom. More private are cottages, with kitchens and living areas and two or four bedrooms with two single beds in each. Folks also may set up their own tents on the grounds. The main lodge has a large recreation hall with a stage, fireplace, television set, and library. Table tennis and pool tables and a jukebox are located in the game room. A screened-in porch that can seat 120 persons is used for meetings or meals, which are included with lodging, along with linens, bedding, and towels. A mirrored meeting room capable of seating 150, a fitness center, a canteen, a laundry room, and a computer room round out the facilities.

Recreational opportunities include the lakefront beach, where a volleyball court is set up, a heated pool with Jacuzzi, a ropes course, and boats for canoeing, kayaking, or sailing. There are courts for tennis, basketball, and badminton as well as soccer, softball, and football fields; all equipment is available. The Appalachian Trail passes through the property, and there are other trails for hiking. Guided hikes, mountain biking, overnight camping, and waterskiing can be arranged. Three meals are served daily, either on the porch or in the dining hall. Vegetarian and other special dietary needs will be honored on request. There is a flat per-person charge, but rates depend on the kind of lodging chosen. Seven Stones is open May through October.

TIME-SHARES AND CONDOS

Bentley Brook **$-$$$$**
1 Corey Road, Hancock
(413) 738-8600
www.efairfield.com

Recently built, Bentley Brook is owned and operated by Fairfield Resorts, a subsidiary of Cendant Corporation, which also owns Resort Condominiums International (RCI), a time-share exchange company. Units at Bentley Brook vary in size and amenities. They are sold as time-shares but also are rented on a hotel basis. The complex is next door to Jiminy Peak resort.

Oak 'N' Spruce
190 Meadow Street, South Lee
(413) 243-3500
www.silverleaf.com

This older sprawling complex is owned by Silverleaf Resorts, which sells condominiums and time-shares ranging from $8,000 to $33,500. The resort includes a par-3 executive golf course, health club and fitness center, two indoor heated pools, an Olympic-size outdoor pool, cross-country ski trails, basketball and tennis courts, and facilities for other activities. Amenities and fees are subject to change without notice and unit floor plans vary as do prices, rates, and contracts. Time-shares and condos also are sold on the Internet through a number of sources.

The Ponds at Foxhollow **$$-$$$$**
US 7, Lenox
(413) 637-1469
www.pondsatfoxhollow.com

Once the estate of George Westinghouse and later a private girls school, the Ponds at Foxhollow now offers 48 condominiums that can be rented for various lengths of time throughout the year. Acquired in 1977, the grounds include Foxhollow Inn and Conference Center, now a spiritualist retreat, and a clubhouse built in 1989. Condominium units are available with one or two bedrooms. All overlook one of the scenic ponds on the 200-acre grounds and include a fireplace, television, stereo, and VCR. Each unit includes a master bedroom with a queen-size bed, a master bathroom with a whirlpool tub, a fully equipped kitchen, a dining area, a living area with a double sleeper sofa, and a deck. The two-bedroom units have a loft sitting room and a second bathroom. Portacribs and full-size cribs are available at no additional charge, and a list of local babysitters is maintained.

Facilities include a library and a state-of-the-art business office with a computer, laser-jet color printer, high-speed Internet access, fax, and telephone. Amenities include indoor and outdoor swimming pools, tennis and basketball courts, a playground, and rowboats and canoes for use on-site. The grounds offer trails to walk, hike, bike, or cross-country ski. The clubhouse is equipped with a hot tub, sauna, locker rooms with showers, and an exercise room with state-of-the-art Stairmasters, treadmills, weights, and stationary bicycles. Tennis rackets and other sporting equipment are kept at the clubhouse, where free use may be arranged. Rates depend on the size of the unit, the season, days of the week, and length of stay. Rentals are highest from late June through early September and late December through early January. They are less from early January to early March and late May to late June and lowest from early March to late May and early November through late December. Rates are proportionately higher on weekends and lowest midweek. Timeshares are handled through Interval at (413) 637-4040 or IVS Realty at (508) 790-7911. The latter firm is based in Hyannis.

Vacation Village
Brodie Mountain Road, Hancock
(413) 236-5885, (413) 637-9555

Located across the way from Jiminy Peak, Vacation Village is owned by Patriot Resorts of Fort Lauderdale, Florida. Being built in stages, Vacation Village will eventually consist of 148 two-story connected town houses clustered atop a hill. The phone numbers listed above are for the two locations in the county where Patriot has offices to meet prospective timeshare buyers. The first location is in Lanesborough on US 7. The second is in the Lenox Shops on US 7 in Lenox. Timeshares cost about $7,500 to $45,000 for one week. Patriot also has started construction of a 300-suite, $18 million hotel on the outskirts of Pittsfield off US 7.

CAMPGROUNDS

Campgrounds are an economical alternative to other kinds of lodging in the Berkshires. In fact, many folks, particularly in pricey South County, rent out their homes for the summer and move into an RV for the duration. Tourists considering a private campground should ask about the maximum allowable length for an RV and the kind of power supplied, as this varies from place to place.

Berkshire Vista Nudist Resort
Kittle Road, Hancock
(413) 738-5154, (413) 232-7860

See the "Resorts and Conference Centers" section of this chapter for information about this unusual campground/resort.

Bonnie Brae Cabins & Campsites **$**
198 Broadway, Pittsfield
(413) 442-3754

Located on a hill at the end of a residential street off US 7 as it passes Pontoosuc

Lake, Bonnie Brae has 48 sites with trailer or RV hookups that rent for $27 a night for two adults. Children over age 13 are an additional $4.00; age 12 and under are $1.00. The weekly rate is $163; monthly, $499. Cabins rent for $50 to $75, and on-site trailers rent for $65 to $80 a night or $1,900 a year, with four-month occupancy. There are showers, a coin-op laundry, a swimming pool, and a dumping station. Open May 1 to October 15. Owners LaMar and Laurie Smith do not accept checks or credit cards.

Bonny Rigg Campground **$**
US 20 and MA 8, Becket
(413) 623-5366
www.bonnyriggcampground.com

Open year-round, the Bonny Rigg Campground is run by a member association. About half the 210 sites on the property are occupied by members, but the rest are available for various rates. Tent sites with or without power, RV hookups, and trailers are available by the day, week, or month. Arrangements can be made to leave campers on-site year-round. Sites with power rent for $25 a night, $150 a week, $600 a month. Tent sites without power go for $20, $120, and $480. Trailers may be rented for $60 a night. Facilities include a large lodge that is heated in the winter, including bathrooms and a kitchen. The lodge has a television set and a game room with video games and is used for special events such as dances and potluck suppers throughout the summer. There are four comfort stations with free hot showers and two dump stations. Arrangements may be made for on-site pumping. Amenities include a camp store, snack bar, pool, and pavilion; courts for shuffleboard, boccie, and volleyball; and a playground, horseshoes pit, and kid's pond. Trails on the property are open for hiking and snowmobiling, and there is a stream for fishing. There is no charge for additional guests. Bonny Rigg is located at the corner of US 20 and MA 8.

Hidden Valley Campground **$**
15 Scott Road, Lanesborough
(413) 447-9419, (877) 392-2267
www.hiddenvalleycampground.net

Open year-round, Hidden Valley Campground is indeed hidden. It's on a dirt road off the road to Mount Greylock, which is off US 7. There are signs to follow, but you need to pay attention. However, the campground is worth the effort. Scattered through 44 wooded acres are 19 tent sites and 90 RV sites. The base day rate for RV sites with electricity and water is $23 for four occupants. A rental for the summer season (May 15 to October 15) is $1,350. For an additional $200, the owner may store your vehicle for the winter. Winter rental (November 1 to April 30) is $995. Tent sites rent for $18; each site has been cleaned of rocks and roots and has a 5-inch layer of sand for a comfortable floor. Owners Michael and Rose DiLego purchased the campground in 1999 and have been improving it ever since. A new swimming pool, a play area with new equipment, a camp store, and spotless coin-operated laundry facilities and showers are among the amenities. Firewood, propane, ice, snacks, and RV supplies are for sale. DiLego also offers full-service RV repairs. There is a pumping station as well as a "honey" truck. A large recreation hall has table tennis, several table games such as foosball and air hockey, a large-screen television set, and a large stone fireplace. For campers who feel like socializing, there is entertainment every Saturday night from the Fourth of July through Columbus Day weekend. Kids enjoy fishing in a nearby pond, and there are often get-togethers around a bonfire. Credit cards and checks are accepted.

Historic Valley Campground **$**
Windsor Lake Road, North Adams
(413) 662-3198

Historic Valley Campground is located at Windsor Lake, a remarkably beautiful area right in the city that is owned and operated by the city of North Adams parks department. The campground has 100 sites nestled in the woods, with five right on the lakeshore. Sites with electricity and water for tents or RVs are $25 a night. Tent sites with no electricity are $20. Sites in wilderness areas with no water or electricity rent for $12, and waterfront sites are $30 a night. Amenities include heated bathrooms with free showers, a dumping station, a pavilion that is used for activities and may be rented for large picnics, a playground, and an arcade. Ice, wood, and some staples may be purchased at the small store. Boats and canoes may be rented. The campground is open from May 15 to October 15 and management always has the coffee pot on. The lake and campground are high in the hills and may be reached from MA 2 east of the city. No credit cards accepted.

Laurel Ridge Camping Area $
40 Old Blandford Road, East Otis
(413) 298-4804, (800) 538-2267

Large, flat, wooded sites are offered at Laurel Ridge, located off MA 23. There are 16 tent sites that rent for $22 a day and 92 RV sites with water and electricity for a day rate of $25. A "safari field" may be rented for group camping. Amenities include a recreation hall with an arcade and planned activities, a 30- by 60-foot swimming pool, coin-operated showers, a coin-operated drier, and a camp store. RV supplies and propane are available. The campground is open May 15 to Columbus Day.

Mountain View Campground $
MA 8, Otis
(413) 269-8928

Mountain View opens on April 1 and closes on November 1. There are 50 RV sites with full hookups and five tent sites available for $25 a night or $1,835 for the season. A recreation hall, planned activities, a pool, and a recreation field are among the amenities. The campground is 6 miles south of Otis Center and 7 miles north of New Boston. No credit cards accepted.

Prospect Lake Park $
50 Prospect Lake Road, North Egremont
(413) 528-4158, (877) 860-4757
www.prospectlakepark.com

Open the first weekend in May through October 15, Prospect Lake Park is set along 2,000 feet of wooded lakeshore and offers 140 shaded or sunny campsites plus cabin accommodations.

Some sites are right on the shore; many offer views of the water. All have picnic tables and fire rings. All but two have water and electricity, and sewer connections are available. Rates are based on two adults and vary depending on the site. Waterfront sites and all those with electricity, water, and sewer service are $29 a day or $174 a week. A site with just water and electricity is $25, or $150 a week. There is a two-night minimum on weekends. Monthly and seasonal rates may be arranged. Seven furnished rustic cabins with full kitchens and baths are rented by the week in July and August for $385, $435, or $485, depending on the size. At other times, a three-night minimum stay is required. The charge for additional adults is $6.00 each; children, $1.50. Pets with proper papers are allowed at all but the cabins for a daily fee of $1.00. Recreational opportunities abound, with two beaches and a dock with rental boats and courts for tennis, basketball, volleyball, and horseshoes. Picnics by the lake can be set out in a pine grove near a children's playground. Scheduled activities in the recreation hall include bingo, dances, potlucks, live music, and pancake breakfasts. There is a snack bar and a camp store. The campground itself dates back 100 years, but modern amenities include free hot showers, flush toilets, and a laundry. Prospect Lake Road runs off Massachusetts Highway 71, which connects with MA 23 just west of Great Barrington.

Shady Pines Campground $
547 Loop Road, Savoy
(413) 743-2694
www.shadypinescampground.com

With 150 sites, Shady Pines is almost like a small town. In fact, it is laid out with street names and has a store, a package store, and a bar with a full liquor license. A happening place, Shady Pines is open year-round. Owners Bill and Edna Daniels even publish a schedule of events, which run from record hops to dances with polka bands. Once a month, pancakes and French toast are served; in October an early Thanksgiving dinner is held. High in the hills of Savoy, the park is a great place for stargazing. For more than 10 years, the Rockland, New York, Astronomy Club has been gathering at the end of July to hold a star party! While there is plenty for adults to do, children aren't forgotten. A fenced playground, a swimming pool, a horseshoe pit, a ball field, and a game room in the recreation hall offer plenty for them to do. Pizza and snacks are sold on Saturday night and holidays. Sites are spread through 45 wooded acres of pine and spruce and 20 acres of open fields plus a 10-acre safari field. Each site has a picnic table, fireplace, water, and electricity. Amenities include flush toilets, hot showers, a coin-operated laundry, heated comfort stations with showers, two dumping stations, and a pavilion. Pets are allowed if kept leashed. Sites rent for $24 a day for two adults. Additional family members or guests are charged $3.00 if they're over age 15 and $2.00 if they're between ages 7 and 14. Little ones are free. Weekly rentals are $130, $400 monthly. Seasonal rates are $1,300 for summer and $550 for winter, plus additional charges for utilities. The Danielses also rent cabins for $50 a day or $275 a week and trailers for $80 a day, $500 for the week. Located as it is near Savoy Mountain and Savoy State Park, Shady Pines is a popular place for snowmobilers and cross-country skiers to stay in winter. In summer the park invites hiking, fishing, mountain biking, and boating.

Summit Hill Campground **$**
Summit Hill Road, Washington
(413) 623-5761
Way off MA 8 up in the hills of Washington, Summit Hill Campground has 106 sites in open fields and wooded areas. The base rate is $22 for two adults. RV parts and supplies are on-site as is a basic needs store, firewood, propane, and ice. Amenities include a swimming pool, planned activities, community potluck suppers and activities in the recreation hall. Nature trails, horseshoes, volleyball and a sports court round out the offerings. Summit Hill is open from May 1 through October 31.

STATE CAMPING AREAS

The following state forests provide campsites. Fees run from $6.00 for a site with limited services to $35.00 for a three-room cabin. With the exception of Beartown and Savoy State Forests, state camping areas are closed from October until May. For more information about each area, see the chapter on Parks or view the Department of Environmental Management Web site at www.massparks.org.

Beartown State Forest
(413) 528-0904
Beartown State Forest has 12 campsites that are open year-round. Picnic tables and fireplaces are provided, but toilets are primitive. October to April, sites are available on a first-come, first-served basis. Campers are advised to call ahead before departure to check winter weather conditions.

Clarksburg State Park
(413) 664-8345 (in season), (413) 442-8928 (mid-October to mid-April)
Clarksburg has 44 campsites, flush toilets, showers, picnic tables, and fireplaces. Open Memorial Day to Columbus Day.

Mount Greylock State Reservation
(413) 499-4262
The regular camping season on Mount Greylock runs from mid-April through mid-October. There are 34 individual campsites, 5 group sites that can accom-

modate up to 25 persons each, plus 5 backpacker shelters. There are no showers, and toilets are primitive. Picnic tables and fireplaces are provided.

October Mountain
(413) 243-1778
Open Memorial Day to Columbus Day, October Mountain has 46 campsites. Amenities include flush toilets, showers, picnic tables, and fireplaces. A dumping station is available.

Pittsfield State Forest
(413) 442-8992
There are 31 campsites with flush and primitive toilets at Pittsfield State Forest. Picnic tables and fireplaces are available, but there are no facilities for showers. Group campsites that can accommodate up to 20 or 50 persons may be reserved. The camping season is Memorial Day to Columbus Day.

Savoy Mountain State Forest
(413) 664-9567 (summer),
(413) 663-8469 (year-round)
Savoy State Forest has four cabins that may be rented by reservation year-round. Each cabin can accommodate up to four persons. No tenting is allowed during winter. Memorial Day to Columbus Day, there are 45 sites available, plus one group site that can accommodate up to 30 persons. There are flush toilets, showers, picnic tables, and fireplaces at the park. Reservations for cabins may be made by calling (877) 422-6762.

Tolland State Forest
(413) 269-6002
Partially located in Otis, Tolland State Forest has 92 campsites. Amenities include flush toilets, showers, picnic tables, and fireplaces. A dumping station is available. Open Memorial Day to Columbus Day.

Windsor State Forest
(413) 684-0948, (413) 442-8928 (mid-October to mid-April)
There are 24 campsites plus one group site that can accommodate up to 25 persons; reservations are required. There are no showers, and toilets are primitive. Water, fireplaces, and picnic tables are provided. Open Memorial Day to Labor Day.

RESTAURANTS 

As the saying goes, a rising tide lifts all boats, and in the case of restaurants in the Berkshires, the proof is in the pudding—so to speak. Not so long ago, there were only a few places to dine out where the food was interesting, the menu creative, and the ingredients locally grown and chemical-free. Now, however, there are plenty of places from one end of the county to the other where discerning diners can enjoy all of those niceties, albeit at a price. Part of the improvement can be attributed to the sophisticated tastes of tourists and second-home owners who are accustomed to eating out in high-quality restaurants. As the demand has grown, so has the number of places catering to such tastes—much to the joy of locals who also enjoy contemporary cuisine. At the same time, many local chefs have become involved in the "slow food" movement and in using organic ingredients. This has resulted in a happy partnership with local growers and breeders through an organization known as "Berkshire Grown" (described more fully in the Farms and Gardens chapter). Through this group, chefs have been able to obtain locally raised free-range chicken, squab, duck, and other products. Prizewinning cheeses, handmade pasta, and organic vegetables appear in many dishes at member restaurants that display the Berkshire Grown logo. And even though the Berkshires are several hours from the coast, fresh seafood is brought in daily. Chefs say that one of their most popular dishes is seared tuna, with seared scallops a close second. Aside from these "pure" restaurants, there are many family-owned places that offer basic good food at reasonable prices. Some have been feeding locals and tourists for years. But most of these also have been forced to improve the quality and variety of their offerings as the dining public has become more sophisticated. In other words, it's darn hard to get a bad meal in the Berkshires.

Restaurants are listed here by region and then alphabetically by town. By far the greatest number are in South County. With around 50 restaurants, Great Barrington reigns as the eating-out capital. The largest concentration is in the center of town along Castle, Railroad, and Main Streets. Other clusters are located north and south of town along U.S. Highway 7. The cosmopolitan flavor of Great Barrington is reflected in the variety of restaurants found here: Asian, Italian, Hispanic, Scandinavian, Mediterranean, upscale continental, and traditional American cuisine are all represented in various settings, at a wide range of prices, and with varying degrees of service. Although smaller, Lenox also has many fine restaurants in town plus a number of eateries along US 7 north to Pittsfield. Choices for dining in Pittsfield include small family-run neighborhood places, chains like Old Country Buffet and Applebee's, lots of pizzerias and Chinese restaurants, and some gems noted for above-average dining. The multicultural population in Williamstown has given rise to a number of ethnic restaurants there. And the advent of MASS MoCA in North Adams has generated a number of interesting places to dine. The listings below are far from totally inclusive. Instead, they are intended to give a broad representation of the kinds of restaurants in the county. Do not dismiss those that have been omitted. It's simply a matter of space. Unless noted otherwise, all are wheelchair-accessible. Restrooms, however, might not be. If it really matters, a call ahead might be in order. Unless stated otherwise, all restaurants listed here accept credit cards. One other thing: Many restaurants serve only dinner. Those that serve both lunch and dinner often close for a break in between. Restaurants that serve breakfast and lunch are open until about 2:00 P.M. After midnight, it's pretty much Dunkin' Donuts or a convenience store, so plan ahead!

PRICE CODE

Except for restaurants that offer prix fixe menus, the price code represents the general range of a dinner entree for two persons. Obviously, adding wine, appetizers, dessert, and other goodies will cause the bill to rise accordingly. Lunches are proportionately less. Naturally, prices are subject to change.

$	**$10–$30**
$$	**$31–$50**
$$$	**$51–$65**
$$$$	**Prix fixe**

SOUTH COUNTY

Great Barrington

Aegean Breeze **$$**
327 Stockbridge Road (US 7)
(413) 528-4001

As the name implies, traditional Greek dishes are the mainstay of this restaurant. Seafood reigns supreme and is offered in many forms, from hot or cold appetizers to whole fish broiled on a charcoal grill with herbs, olive oil, and lemon. If you don't want to deal with the bone, the staff will take care of that in the kitchen. Some of the seafood is imported from Greece, including lavraki and sardines. Moussaka, spanakopita, lamb kabobs, and other dishes round out the menu. Manager Yannis Bonikos brings experience managing Greek and Mediterranean restaurants in Manhattan. The wine list is broad, the surroundings are pleasant, the chairs are very comfortable, and the Greek music is pleasantly soft in the background. This is a nice place to take a group to share dishes, especially the appetizers. Next door to the restaurant is a Greek grocery and deli with all kinds of goodies. Aegean Breeze is open daily for lunch and dinner, with a break in between.

__There is a 5 percent meals tax in Massachusetts, and it is applied to takeout as well as dine-in.__

ARMI@GreatBarrington **$**
485 Main Street (US 7)
(413) 528-3296
www.armi-at-greatbarrington.com

Owners Armi and Armand Saiia have 25 years of experience in the hospitality and restaurant business—she as the owner of a restaurant in Lake Tahoe and manager of restaurants and caterers in Manhattan and Connecticut and he as a cook in several New York restaurants. Also a sculptor, Armand designed the restaurant's hip interior. The menu focuses on a global cuisine and includes tapas, pasta, seafood, wood-smoked pizza, rotisserie poultry, and lots of vegetarian dishes. Desserts include homemade ice cream, vegan chocolate cake, and their own version of s'mores. Appetizers include unusual presentations of old standbys like a Thai curry shrimp cocktail or mini grilled-fish tacos. A wide range of entrees includes old-fashioned mac-and-cheese, paella, enchiladas, and grilled vegetable ragout with polenta. There's also a raw bar. Children will find lots of things to eat from the economical kid's menu. Located at the junction of US 7 and Massachusetts Highway 23 at the south end of town, the restaurant serves lunch and dinner daily in season but switches to a bar menu after 9:00 P.M., when nightly entertainment takes over.

Baba Louie's **$**
286 Main Street
(413) 528-8100

Not to start a pizza war, but a lot of people think that Baba Louie's wood-fired pizza is the best around, largely because of the crust. It's an exclusive handmade sourdough concocted with fresh stone-ground organic wheat, water, and sea salt. No baker's yeast is ever used. A wheat-free San Francisco version made with organic spelt berries also is available. In addition, the toppings are unusual. Combinations include the Dolce Vita (tomato sauce, wilted spinach, mozzarella, California figs, Gorgonzola, prosciutto and Parmesan cheese topped with infused rosemary oil); the Isabella Pizzarella (roasted sweet potatoes and parsnips, caramelized onions, garlic, fresh mozzarella, and shaved fennel drizzled with reduced balsamic vinegar and topped with Parmesan), or the spicy Abbondante BBQ Chicken garnished with red onions, fresh mozzarella, smoked Gouda, oregano, and Parmesan. For those who feel creative, there is a list of 28 ingredients to choose from that can be added to the basic Queen Margherita. A large pizza is 14 inches; a small is 10 inches. Baba Louie's also is known for creative salads and homemade soups plus fresh pasta dishes that change nightly. Beverages include select beers and wines plus organic coffee and teas, Scottish Highland Springs Sparkling Water, and assorted upscale sodas. Open for lunch and dinner, Baba Louie's is small and very popular, so expect to wait for a table. Takeout is available, and orders can be picked up at a window off the atrium in the walkway between Main Street and the parking lot at the rear.

Barrington Brewery Pub and Restaurant **$**
US 7
(312) 528-8282
www.barringtonbrewery.com

Interesting beers brewed on the premises, soup and sandwich specials, really good onion rings, and other hearty pub food are the mainstay at the Barrington Brewery. In summer you can dine on the patio. In winter nothing beats sitting near that nice warm stove with a cup of cheddar ale soup or a bowl of chili (beef or vegetarian), a sampling of sausages, and a bottle of Berkshire Blond Ale. The rustic interior adds to the illusion of having just walked into an English pub. Hearty appetizers include the hearty Plowman's Lunch (sausage, cheese, chutney, and country bread) or a plate of wings done just right. Burgers, salads, and sandwiches are under $10. Entrees, served after 5:00 P.M., include shepherd's pie, steak and mushroom pie, ribs, stir-fry, and crab cakes. The coffee is good and the desserts yummy. Owners Gary Happ and Andrew Mankin each has his own areas of expertise. Happ is an experienced restauranteur; Mankin is the brewer. He maintains the seven-barrel stainless-steel system that looms near the bar in full view of the restaurant. Customers can buy half-gallon growlers of their favorite Barrington Brewery beer to take home, poured straight from the tap. The beer is also sold off premises under the Berkshire Mountain Brewers label. Specialty beers and wine also are available. Darts and two pool tables complete the pub atmosphere. Open daily, Barrington Brewery is located in the Jenifer House Commons across from the Holiday Inn.

Bizen Restaurant and Sushi Bar **$$**
17 Railroad Street
(413) 528-4343

The authentic Japanese cuisine served at Bizen has gotten rave reviews from many a publication, including the *New York Times* and the *Boston Globe.* The diverse menu includes soups, salads, and various fish, tofu, and vegetable dishes, some prepared on the robata charcoal grill and all made with high-quality organic ingredients as much as possible. The sushi and sashimi are as good as one might expect. The adventurous diner will find many interesting things to try, and the knowledgeable staff can recommend a suitable beverage from around 20 estate sakes or 6 Japanese beers on tap. Single-malt scotches and single-barrel bourbons also are available. The restaurant is divided into several sections. Left of the entrance and down a few steps is the bar, which has about six stools plus several small tables crammed close together. The fast-food version of Japanese food—dumplings and other nibbles—are prepared here. A small area to the right of the entrance is cozy and quieter than the rest of the place, where more chairs and tables are set up. In the middle of it all, the sushi chef holds forth in the center of the polished bar, where customers can watch him do his thing. For a special treat, reserve one of three tatami rooms, take your shoes off, and play emperor. Shoji screens, straw mats, and the minimalist interior complete the illusion. Owner Michael Marcus is a potter whose love of Japanese ceramics led to the founding of Bizen. Teaming up with chef Hideo Furukawa, he furnished the restaurant with the traditional Japanese wares he makes at Joyous Spring Pottery in Monterey. The restaurant took off. Unfortunately, so did the pottery—in the hands of customers! So much of his expensive work was disappearing, he switched to mostly commercially produced pottery that is compatible with the authentic food and atmosphere. Bizen is open daily for lunch and dinner, with a break in between. Reservations are strongly suggested, but you might be able to squeeze in somewhere, especially if you go late for lunch or early for dinner. The restaurant has a ramp entrance, but those in wheelchairs or with walkers might want to mention when they make a reservation that they will need room to navigate and will not be able to sit in the bar area.

Fulfilling a long-time dream, Marcus recently opened an authentic Japanese teahouse next door to his restaurant. Called Bizen Kaiseki, the teahouse is entered via a stone-paved path that leads past six private tearooms, each enclosed by shoji doors. Marcus will happily explain the significance of the surroundings and the tea ceremony, which is meant to precede a many-course meal. Marcus has employed two Kaiseki chefs for his new venture. The prix fixe menu ranges from $40 per person for six dishes to $150 per person for eleven.

Castle Street Cafe **$$**
10 Castle Street
(413) 528-5244
www.castlestreetcafe.com

Owner/chef Michael Ballon has earned a reputation for serving up tasty Franco-American dishes with a great degree of reliability. And the wine list has been rated excellent by *Wine Spectator* magazine since 1994. The cafe is nicely divided into a dining room and the Celestial Bar (see the Nightlife chapter), where meals may be ordered from the full menu or from a smaller bar menu, which is mainly appetizers. Diners who don't appreciate jazz or other entertainment with their dinner will want to stay on the dining room side. Ballon uses fresh local ingredients like Monterey chèvre in his salads or shiitake mushrooms from North Adams in his soups or sauces. Entrees featuring duck, chicken, seafood, and vegetables are concocted with interesting seasonings and sauces. Expect unusual combinations, such as calves liver with glazed pearl onions and a caramelized onion sauce. The menu also includes pastas and burgers. Open for dinner and late night daily.

Helsinki Tea Company **$$**
284 Main Street
(413) 528-3394
www.clubhelsinkiweb.com

The minute you walk into Helsinki, with its funky interior and oddball furnishings, you can tell you are in for something different. And the eclectic menu confirms your initial reaction. Scandinavian/Russian dishes like borscht, blintzes, gravlax, and latkes share billing with organic chicken-apple bratwurst, vegetarian chili in a tortilla bowl, and quesadilla of the day with triple lemon salsa. Daily specials feature pasta, seafood, or the whim of the cook, who holds forth in a tiny kitchen open to the dining room. Interesting side dishes, really good bread, and a classy assortment of teas and wines complete the picture. In winter the fireplace exudes warmth and adds to the atmosphere. The menu also is available in the adjacent Club Helsinki, which features music nearly every night, some of it big-time names. Not visible from Main Street, Helsinki is entered via a walkway that connects the street with a large parking lot, where the Triplex movie theater is located.

La Choza **$**
284 Main Street
(413) 528-6380

La Choza specializes in really big burritos that you can create yourself as you order at the counter. Fillings include rice and beans, chicken, beef, chorizo, and mushrooms. Extras from which to choose include guacamole, salsa, peppers, onions, jalapeños, cilantro, black olives, and roasted corn and chipotle salsa. A variety of hot sauces are available. Specialties include the Vegan Deluxe, a really messy concoction of portobello mushrooms with lettuce, tomato, scallions, peppers, onions, salsa, black olives, and cilantro. Tacos, nachos, and overstuffed quesadillas also are on the menu. La Choza is open from noon to late night. It's all takeout, but there are some picnic tables nearby in the atrium where La Choza is located. Owner Seth Gambino also has a place in Pittsfield, where entertainment is offered on weekends.

Martin's **$$**
49 Railroad Street
(413) 528-5455

Martin's is known for having above-average meals—and with good reason. Owner Martin Lewis used to be a chef at some of the finer hotels in Manhattan. He left the big city and opened his eatery at the top of Railroad Street in 1988. Open daily for breakfast and lunch, Martin's prices are moderate, but his menu reads like those of some of his tonier neighbors. He cooks from scratch and uses fresh local ingredients as much as possible. Breakfast specialties served through the lunch hour include omelettes filled with smoked salmon and cream cheese, potato and onion, Brie, feta, salsa, and hot pepper or mozzarella and tomato. You also can create an omelette from a copious list of extras. Daily specials might include eggs Benedict with a real hollandaise sauce or pear pancakes. Popular items include the Tower Bagel (smoked salmon, cream cheese, tomato, and red onion), Egg McMartin (two fried eggs, cheese, and a choice of meat on a bagel), and Berkshire Potatoes & Eggs (scrambled together with onions). Martin makes his own granola, which he sells in bags, and for dieters offers a scooped-out bagel with nonfat cottage cheese and tomatoes. Vegetarian dishes on the menu include scrambled tofu and vegetables and an avocado melt with Monterey Jack on sourdough bread. For meat-eaters, there's a terrific turkey, Brie, green apple, and red onion sandwich on farmer's bread. Martin roasts his own chicken and turkey and makes his soups from scratch. Beverages include organic teas, flavored coffees, several kinds of beers, and house wines. You can even get a Bloody Mary or a mimosa. Martin's is kid-friendly; there are crayons at all the tables, and the walls are full of placemats decorated by industrious youngsters. The restaurant can seat 50 persons and is wheelchair-accessible, but the restroom is in the basement.

The Neighborhood Diner **$**
282 Main Street
(413) 528-8226

The Neighborhood Diner serves lunch, dinner, and breakfast all day at what owner Pierre Cum says are the lowest prices in town. However, what you save in money will be gained in calories. This is the kind of place that makes it impossible to stick to a diet. Aside from standard diner fare, Cum's breakfast menu includes homemade muffins and pancakes that change with the season. Fall brings apple or pumpkin pancakes. In summer expect blueberries, raspberries, and other fruits. Daily lunch and dinner specials include homemade soups and such interesting dishes as grilled mozzarella with pepperoni on a pita. The battered onion rings are huge and the fries piled high. Black and white tiles on the floor and around the counter, plus giant renditions of eggs, hamburgers, and the like on the walls are reminiscent of the 1950s. A seat at the counter includes taking in the banter from the open kitchen. Booths and tables can seat up to 60 persons. Open daily, the Neighborhood Diner is entered through the atrium that runs between Main Street and a large parking lot at the rear.

Pearl's **$$**
47 Railroad Street
(413) 528-7767
The chrome and black leather Corbusier chairs and minimalist interior say "New York" but the food is Berkshire-based, with much of it locally grown or raised. The menu features steaks, chops, and fish, and the wine list is an award-winner. Brunch is served on weekends. The owner also operates Bistro Zinc in Lenox.

Shiro **$$**
105 Stockbridge Road (US 7/U.S. Highway 20)
(413) 528-1898
Traditional Japanese dishes nicely presented are served here for lunch and dinner. More than 20 varieties of sushi are on the menu, plus sashimi, hand rolls, and fresh fish rolls. Unusual rolls include a shiitake mushroom roll (smoked salmon, eel, and avocado with mushrooms inside and out) and the Lobster Tempura Roll (lobster, scallion inside and out, with avocado and caviar). Seafood, meats, and vegetables prepared on the hibachi plus soups and tempura round out the list. Among the many specialties are the hearty Ishi Kari Nabe (a miso broth with scallops, shrimp, salmon, fish cake, and vegetables) and pork or chicken katsu, breaded and deep fried in tonkatsu sauce. The atmosphere is pleasingly Japanese and there is a full bar.

Sweet Peas and Petunias **$**
325 Stockbridge Road (US 7)
(413) 528-7786
With around 35 sandwich combinations and a host of breakfast specials, sweet peas and petunias are just about the only things not on the menu at Christine Koldys's fully accessible restaurant. For breakfast there are omelettes, waffles, biscuits and gravy, French toast made with challah, huevos rancheros, and fancy flapjacks. Specialties include Poached Pillows (eggs) served on an English muffin over such combinations as the Francais (mushrooms, roasted garlic, chèvre, and caramelized onion) or the Russian Princess (smoked salmon, dill sour cream, and red onion). The mind-boggling lunch menu comes out around noon, and newcomers will need time to study it. Grilled chicken, turkey, roast beef, Virginia ham, albacore tuna, and vegetables in creative combinations can be ordered as wraps or on multigrain bread. Interesting concoctions include turkey, carrot, golden raisins, spicy pecans, and red leaf lettuce with honey-Dijon mayo; another combo mixes jasmine rice, peach chutney, yogurt, red onion, and curried veggies with or without grilled chicken. Then there's the prizewinning vegetarian chili, homemade soups and quiches, and individual pizzas. The menus are by the door and the food is ordered at the counter, where it can be picked up when ready. Signs remind customers that WE ARE NOT A FAST FOOD RESTAURANT and PATIENCE IS A VIRTUE. Beverages include flavored coffees and lattes, fruit smoothies, and Italian sodas. Koldys started in the restaurant business with a bakery in Housatonic and moved to US 7 around 1991. A teacher by profession, she obviously likes to feed the mind as well as the body. Trivial Pursuit cards are set out on the tables and the eat-at counter, where an assortment of puzzles to entangle also are on hand. The decor includes paintings by family and friends plus huge Chinese kites hanging from the ceiling. Don't miss the unisex bathroom, where the walls feature a mural and a poem by her son. In summer Sweet Peas and Petunias is open daily and meals can be enjoyed out on the deck. In winter the restaurant is closed on Wednesday.

Verdura **$$**
44 Railroad Street
(413) 528-8969
www.verdura.net

The Venetian plaster walls, polished mahogany furnishings, flickering beeswax candles, and soft music at Verdura set the stage for a gastronomic trip to Italy. Owners Bill Webber, who is the chef, and Jean Louishen are dedicated to using only the freshest seasonal and organic ingredients and to preparing them in the country Italian manner. The pasta is fresh, made in-house, and the seafood and meat dishes might be prepared in the wood-fired oven or grilled over the coals. Wine may be chosen from an award-winning list. Warm, crusty bread and a dish of first-pressed extra-virgin olive oil is the first thing placed on the table. Then comes the difficult job of choosing from the tantalizing antipasti displayed on a sideboard or listed on the menu. Verdura is a good place to go with a group to sample everything. Depending on the season, first-course dishes might include pan-seared foie gras with roasted fruit, bruschetta and truffled balsamic jus, or a small duck comfit pizza with caramelized onions and mozzarella. Also listed will be a rustic soup and interesting salads. For entrees, the menu might include prosciutto-wrapped brook trout with white beans, leeks, Swiss chard, and almond caper brown butter; wood-charred beef tenderloin with potato, smoked onions, greens, truffle butter, and a balsamic reduction with olive oil; or a slow-braised lamb shank with rosemary polenta, citrus, kalamata olives, and jus. Webber, who used to be the chef at Wheatleigh, recently expanded into a space next door at 47 Railroad Street, opening Due Enoteca, a wine bar and cafe. Patrons may choose something from the extensive list of wines, sherries, and martinis while waiting for a table in Verdura or settle in for a while and enjoy a menu of interesting tapas. Lunch also is served, with the menu a cross between Barcelona and northern Italy. There's entertainment on weekends. The phone number for Due Enoteca is (413) 664-9165. Both are open evenings, but Verdura is closed on Wednesday and Due Enoteca is closed on Monday.

Many restaurants add the gratuity to the bill. However, there is no consistency in the amount of gratuity or number in the party. Some restaurants include it for parties of six, others for eight, and some add it no matter how many are at the table. Don't forget to check your bill—unless you want to leave a tip twice!

Housatonic

Jacks Grill **$$**
Main Street
(413) 274-1000
www.jacksgrill.com

Billed as "a footloose subsidiary of the Red Lion Inn," Jacks is indeed a Fitzpatrick family endeavor. As if to give a clue to its unusual nature, there is no apostrophe in the name and no "e" on the end of "grill." Jacks is open May through October, and the menu is filled with such "Mom food" as pot roast, meat loaf, mac-and-cheese, chicken potpie, and of course jiggly red Jell-O for dessert. The mashed potatoes are piled high, the applesauce deliberately lumpy. Family-style dishes for four include spaghetti with meatballs and sausage. Aside from burgers and hot sandwiches, the menu also has some less traditional items, such as gazpacho, which can be ordered with a shot of Cuervo Gold tequila added, or grilled salmon with black bean and charred corn salsa. There is an extensive list of wines at all prices and a good selection of beers. Kids can order from a menu that includes chicken fingers and fish "fins"; on Wednesday, if they're under age 12 they can eat for free. Check out the zany Web site for all kinds of tidbits about the restaurant, the town, and the folks involved in running this eatery, which has earned a mention in Zagat's. Open for dinner only from Mother's Day (naturally) through October, Jacks will book parties in the off-season.

Lee

Bombay Bar & Grill **$$**
435 Laurel Street (US 7/20)
(413) 243-6731
www.fineindiandining.com
Not your average Indian restaurant, the Bombay Bar & Grill has an extensive lunch and dinner menu with dishes from many regions of India and Asia. The restaurant is located next to the Best Western Black Swan Inn on Laurel Lake, and diners can enjoy the view from a deck or atrium. The comprehensive menu offers a number of signature dishes. Along with the samosas and tempura on the appetizer list are San Choy Bau (a mixture of flavored minced chicken in a lettuce wrap) and Ragara (spiced potato patties layered with onion, chickpeas, yogurt, and tamarind chutney). Tandoori dishes include Tabac Maz, browned lamb chops marinated in white pepper, coriander, and mint and baked in the traditional clay oven. There are at least eight other lamb dishes plus nine seafood specialties, a dozen chicken entrees, and a dozen vegetarian specialties. And that's not counting the rice and noodle dishes that can be prepared with a number of additions. Curries include a Malaysian dish in which chicken is sautéed with mango, green and red pepper, and carrots in a spicy mango sauce. For the less adventurous, there is the ubiquitous General Tso's chicken. The wine and beer list is impressive, and there is a full bar for cocktails and mixed drinks. On Sunday a mind-boggling buffet is served. Open daily, the Bombay is the kind of place to bring a large group of like-minded friends so that everyone gets to try lots of things at one sitting. Spice Root in Williamstown is owned by the same family.

From Ketchup to Caviar **$$**
150 Main Street
(413) 243-6397
www.fromketchuptocaviar.com
If you order the Black Angus burger with Yukon Gold and sweet potato fries, you will get an individual-size bottle of Heinz ketchup. But heaven forbid you put that on anything else on the French-American menu at this fine restaurant—chefs Christian Urbain, whose wife, Lynne, will seat you, and Franck Tessier will probably come flying out of the kitchen! Appetizers include escargots; pâté; frog legs Provençal; mussels steamed with white wine, garlic, shallots, and fresh herbs; and martini-cured gravlax with Absolut citron vinaigrette—no ketchup here. Entrees such as sautéed grouper with champagne-flavored sauerkraut, honey-lacquered chicken breast with mushroom mashed potatoes and a rosemary and lavender sauce, Peking Duck with a rutabaga puree and raspberry vinegar sauce—with ketchup? Not hardly. This fine restaurant also does catering, and the menu reflects the level of quality you might expect for a special event. The restaurant itself is pleasantly divided into dining areas—small rooms with a few tables—which cuts down on the noise and creates an intimate atmosphere appropriate for this kind of dining. A comprehensive selection of wines is available. Despite all that, dress is casual. A former Italian restaurant, the place is still being redecorated, but the sunny yellow corner room is a good start. Open for dinner daily in summer; check hours the rest of the year.

Morgan House Inn **$**
33 Main Street
(413) 243-3661
www.MorganHouseInn.com
The Morgan House has been providing food and lodging for travelers since 1855. The dining room still conveys the feeling of those days with its wide plank floors, high-backed benches, Windsor chairs, and pewter wares arranged on the dish shelf that tops the dark aged paneling. Guests

at the inn have included Grover Cleveland, Ulysses S. Grant, and George Bernard Shaw. Racoon banquets were held for a while during annual visits by Rob Titus, the archaeologist who opened King Tut's tomb and who enjoyed hunting the critters. Diners will not find racoon on the menu, but they will find reliable comfort food like roast turkey dinner, meat loaf, and other basic New England fare. But the menu also includes more up-to-date items, such as portobella mushroom terrine, veal and eggplant Marsala, or blackened Atlantic salmon. A kid-friendly menu includes grilled-cheese sandwiches and pasta. Lunch and dinner are served daily from Memorial Day through December. January through Easter, the restaurant is closed on Monday, serving lunch only on Tuesday and lunch and dinner the rest of the week. The tavern, adjacent to the main dining room, offers lighter fare and late-night snacks during the season but is closed January to Easter.

Sullivan Station Restaurant $$
Railroad Street
(413) 243-2082
www.berkshireweb.com

Train buffs especially will enjoy having lunch or dinner in this 1893 New York, New Haven & Hartford Railroad station, painstakingly restored in 1980 by Dan Sullivan and Marilyn Kelly, who now owns and operates the place on her own. In the 10-month process, all the woodwork, including every board of wainscoting, was removed and hand-stripped, revealing the beauty of the wood. The former waiting room is now the dining room. Noticeable at once is one table, off in a nook across from the entrance, that is unusually high. A closer look reveals the reason: The tabletop rests on top of the old iron safe, its doors decorated with Hudson River paintings. The scenes were discovered when black paint was carefully removed during the restoration. Displayed on the walls are photos, schedules, and other railroad memorabilia. Model and toy trains are everywhere, including the fully stocked bar, where a train runs around the room on a track suspended just below the ceiling. In summer, folks can sit out on the deck. And for those who want a special treat, there's a completely outfitted caboose available by reservation for up to six persons. Meals are brought to the caboose, which has a television set to occupy the kids or watch a sporting event. While rail traffic has certainly decreased since the 1890s, trains still run by the station, including the Berkshire Scenic Railway's 1920s passenger cars, which make a stop here on their trips between Lenox and Stockbridge in season. (See the Attractions chapter for more about that.) But enough about the trains.

The menu focuses on traditional fare prepared from scratch with local ingredients as much as possible. Soups, hot or cold sandwiches and burgers, salads, quiche, seafood, and steak are offered for lunch along with seasonal specials. Dinner choices include chicken or veal topped with spinach, melted Swiss, and raspberry sauce; baked or grilled seafood; ribs and chops; and pasta. Homemade desserts are prepared with eggs from the Otis Poultry Farm and milk and cream from High Lawn Farm. There is a children's menu. Lunches are about half the price of dinner entrees. An 18 percent gratuity will be added to the check for parties of five or more. From May 1 to January 1 Sullivan Station is open daily for lunch and dinner. From January 1 to April 30 the Station is closed on Monday and Tuesday, lunch only is served Wednesday through Sunday, and dinner is served on Friday and Saturday nights. Reservations are suggested.

Sweet Basil Grille $$
1575 Pleasant Street (Massachusetts Highway 102)
(413) 243-1114
www.berkshireweb.com

Chef Rick Penna and his wife, Lynn, moved their Sweet Basil Grille from Lenox to Lee more than five years ago. The 19th-century brick building in which they are located has dining areas on the first and second floors. Crisp white curtains at the windows, exposed beams, cream-colored walls, and contrasting woodwork create a pleasant atmosphere for casual dining. Northern Italian dishes cooked to order are the Pennas' forte, and they have developed a following of locals as well as shoppers from all over who come for dinner after a hard day at the nearby Prime Outlets. Interesting appetizers include cream of roasted garlic soup and artichokes, broccoli, and sausage sautéed in spices and wine with a marina sauce and then baked with mozzarella. Entrees feature vegetables, veal, seafood, chicken, or beef prepared with a variety of seasonings and sauces and served with a choice of pasta. Sweet Basil Grille also is the name of one of the restaurant's specialties, an often-ordered dish of veal sautéed with garlic, onions, and fresh basil and simmered in a sauce of wine and fresh tomatoes. Pollo Carbonara—seasoned chicken sautéed with bacon and mushrooms served over penne with a cream sauce—also is popular. Tempting desserts like the chocolate tart with raspberry preserves and tiramasu are made in-house. There is a children's menu, and parties are welcome. An 18 percent gratuity may be added to the check for parties of six or more. There are a couple of low steps at the entrance. When making a reservation, diners who use walkers or wheelchairs should mention that they want one of the ground-floor tables. The restaurant has a full bar and is open for dinner daily in season, closed Monday after Labor Day.

Lenox

Bistro Zinc **$$$**
56 Church Street
(413) 637-8800

When Charles Schultz and Jason Macioge opened their French-style bistro in 1998, eyes rolled. Until then, no one had spent the millions they did on a restaurant in the Berkshires. Most were in historic homes, refurbished storefronts, or country farmhouses with simple interiors. Those that chose a more contemporary look did so with a lot less money. By and large, the flashy, sleek eateries more common to Manhattan or California had not yet taken off here. But Zinc hit Lenox running and hasn't stopped since. While some locals find the place pretentious, the haute cuisine and city-style ambience have made Zinc a popular place for lunch and dinner, with reservations needed for the latter year-round.

The bar has become a favorite late-night gathering place. The walls are full of art by Carol Schultz, Charles's wife, who also displays work by her favorite photographers. The airy dining room seats around 50 persons at tables that are pretty close together. The menu changes seasonally, with local products featured as often as possible. Popular are the duck comfit, steak au poivre, the grilled Angus sirloin, and pan-seared rare sushi-grade tuna. The salad menu might include roasted seasoned eggplant, baby spinach, and roasted red and yellow peppers topped with crisps of baked Parmesan cheese. For an appetizer, how about grilled semiboneless quail stuffed with prosciutto and fresh mozzarella served over fried green tomatoes with baby arugula tossed in a balsamic vinaigrette and glaze. Schultz also owns Pearl's in Great Barrington.

Blantyre **$$$$**
16 Blantyre Road
(413) 637-3556
www.blantyre.com

Impeccably restored by the Fitzpatrick family, Blantyre is now one of the finest inns in the county, right up there with Wheatleigh. Unfortunately it is open only from May to November. The surroundings are elegant, creating the illusion that it is still 1904, when the first party was held at this Gilded Age "cottage." Dinner is served in the main house, where the tables are set with sterling, fine china, and crystal, and guests are expected to dress appropriately—that is, jacket and tie, gentlemen.

Don't want to take time for a full lunch? Pick up some homemade soup or a hearty sandwich and side at the deli at Loeb's Foodtown on the corner of Main and Housatonic Streets and take it across the street to the park, where there are lots of benches for an impromptu picnic.

The gentle music of the harp emulates from the music room. Dinner is preceded by canapes and champagne on the covered terrace or in the parlor. Blantyre's wine selection has received the Award of Excellence from the *Wine Spectator*. The cuisine is contemporary French, using regional products, and the three-course prix fixe menu lists many choices. Appetizers might include Scallops and Parsnips a la James Beard (the scallops are seared and served with a trio of honey-roasted crisp and pureed parsnips with a truffle dressing) or seared foie gras with caramelized pickled pears, toasted brioche, and natural jus. Among the fall entrees are pan-seared Arctic char with crab cake, roasted artichokes, and a red wine lemon thyme sauce and breast of pheasant with sweet potatoes, honey-glazed turnips, and a foie gras chestnut jus. Folks also may choose from a five-course "tasting" sampler that includes a cheese plate and dessert. Lunch is served in July and August. As with dinner, the menu includes a soup, which may be served hot or cold depending on the weather, and a fish dish as the chef chooses. Other choices might include a wild mushroom linguine with Parmesan cheese and basil puree or the interesting combination of mango, avocado, and lobster in a timbale with citrus dressing and an herb salad. The desserts, of course, are heaven-sent. Expensive? You bet. But it's worth every penny, especially for a very special occasion. For a virtual visit, check out the excellent and informative Web site.

Cafe Lucia **$$**
80 Church Street
(413) 637-2640

Jim Lucie and Nadie Agalla have been serving fine Italian cuisine at Cafe Lucia for more than 20 years. Diners may enjoy their meals on the tent-covered deck, out in the garden, in a few booths by the open kitchen, or in the refreshingly quiet, intimate dining room. Before dinner, drinks may be ordered from the full bar or the wine list, which has earned the Award of Excellence from the *Wine Spectator* for several years. The menu is full of interesting combinations made with fresh local ingredients as often as possible. Antipasti include carpaccio (thinly sliced raw beef topped with arugula and shaved Reggiano Parmesan cheese); sweet soppressata (Tuscan-style salami with arugula, Calabrese olives, and Pecorino Romano); a sautéed medley of wild and domestic mushrooms atop grilled cookie cutter–shaped semolina gnocchi; and chicken livers sautéed with Marsala wine, tomato, onion, pancetta, and fresh sage. Pasta dishes, with a variety of sauces, include a ragout of rabbit and wild mushrooms with egg fettuccini, a seafood medley over linguine, and rigatoni with sausages from Esposito's in Brooklyn. The house specialty is melt-in-your-mouth osso buco con risotto with a rich veggie-filled sauce. The pan-seared tuna and tender grilled breast of duck with brandied fruit sauce also are especially tasty. Specials are offered daily. Espresso and a dessert from an unusual and tempting list finish the meal off in style. Reservations are highly recommended. Cafe Lucia is open daily in season and closed Sunday and Monday off-season.

Candlelight Inn **$$**
35 Walker Street
(413) 637-1555
www.candlelightinn-lenox.com

Diners have their choice of four separate dining rooms, including a windowed porch that overlooks the street. All are furnished in a style appropriate for this 1885 inn. Each table has its own pewter candlestick. The continental cuisine includes appetizers like house-cured gravlax (salmon dressed in a lemon-dill vinaigrette) and smoked trout on an apple, celery root, and potato pancake garnished with horseradish whipped cream. Entrees include a pasta of the evening, several fresh seafood dishes, and the chef's specialty—crisp semiboneless duckling served with a mandarin orange demiglaze. The tavern with its well-stocked bar is a popular meeting place before dinner or after attending a cultural event in town. Lunch is served in summer and, weather permitting, may be enjoyed on the spacious lawn, where tables and umbrellas are set up and the chef cooks to order on a large barbeque grill. Innkeeper Rebecca Hedgecock welcomes private parties and often books small weddings and rehearsal dinners.

Church Street Cafe **$$**
65 Church Street
(413) 637-2745
www.churchstreetcafe.biz

Partners Linda and Allan Forman and Clayton Hambrick opened the Church Street Cafe in 1981 with nine tables and a beer and wine license. As space opened up, they expanded bit by bit. Today they own the building, which they have completely remodeled, have a full liquor license, and can serve lunch or dinner to 90 hungry folks. There are three dining rooms plus an ample covered deck. The interior reflects the owners' interest in art, and works by local artists are always on display. The food is presented artistically, too. Dedicated to serving locally produced products, the cafe prepares ethnic, vegetarian, and regional dishes with seasonal fresh ingredients. The extensive wine list has been cited by the *Wine Spectator* three years in a row. Favorite dishes for lunch in summer include an antipasto platter of salami, smoked duck breast, local cheese, and eggplant caponata with warm peasant bread and olive oil. Local cheese also is featured in an appetizer platter, which with soup and a salad makes for a dandy lunch. Dinner entrees include grilled steak, pork, lamb, and seafood prepared in a variety of ways. What could be better on a cold, dreary day than the Seafood Big Bowl, a rustic Mediterranean broth with shrimp, scallops, calamari, mussels, lobster, and crab claw served with grilled bread and Romanesco sauce? An 18 percent gratuity is added for parties of six or more. In season, Church Street Cafe is open daily for lunch and dinner, with a break in between. From October to June it is closed Sunday and Monday.

Cranwell **$$$**
55 Lee Road (US 20)
(413) 637-1364, (800) 272-6935
www.cranwell.com

Cranwell offers several venues for dining, the most elegant of these in the main mansion that is the centerpiece of this sprawling resort. Dinners are served in the Wyndhurst Room and the Music Room, both romantically furnished to suit the Tudor decor. A creative and elaborate dinner menu as well as a simpler grill menu is available in both. Breakfast, including a Sunday brunch, is served to guests as well as the public in the Music Room. Casual lunch or dinner is served in Sloane's Tavern, adjacent to the golf course. Then there's the cafe next to the newly opened spa, where nutritious lunches are geared toward those watching their grams and calories. Spa selections, as these diet-conscious dishes are called, also are included in the other menus, so there's really no excuse for going off your diet—except pure indulgence.

All this is overseen by executive chef Carl DeLuce, a member of the prestigious Chains des Rottisseurs, and chef de cuisine Christopher Bonnivier. Cranwell's wine selections have received the Award for Excellence from the *Wine Spectator.* Breakfast includes an abundant buffet with made-to-order omelettes as well as an a la carte menu.

The lunch menu at Sloane's Tavern includes soup, sandwiches, salads, and hamburgers and other grilled entrees. During summer, meals are served on the expansive terrace that overlooks the golf course. Refreshments also are served poolside. The Wyndhurst menu offers interesting appetizers like caramelized onion and fennel tart and white miso and fish soup. You might find tuna tartare, seared soft-shell crabs, roasted hapu-apu, or organic duck comfit. All are served with creative sides and sauces. A fresh pasta dish also is available. Desserts include a five-spice Italian-style cheesecake with caramelized apples, blackberry jam, and blackberry coulis or the Cranwell Apple Tart served with brandied caramel sauce and house-made vanilla ice cream. For those spa folks, there is a raspberry orange cake with a berry coulis and seasonal sorbet with a mere 250 calories and two grams of fat. Reservations are suggested for dinner in the mansion and are required for the Spa Cafe. All venues are open daily.

Gateways Inn & Restaurant **$$**
51 Walker Street
(413) 637-2532
www.gatewaysinn.com

Gateways Inn was built in 1912 as the summer "cottage" of Harley Proctor, an executive of Proctor & Gamble. It had been an inn when Fabrizio and Rosemary Macdonald Chiariello bought it in 1996 and reopened it after an extensive renovation. Entering the inn, you immediately notice the grand staircase sweeping up to the second floor. Then comes the period mahogany bar and terrace room, or lounge. La Terrazza is stocked with 98 selections of single-malt Scotch whiskey, 44 grappas, and other award-winning wines and spirits. You may enjoy light meals or cocktails in the lounge or proceed to the main dining room, which is entered through beveled-glass doors. The gracious interior includes antique Italian and European prints hanging on deep terra-cotta walls and tables covered with linen cloths and set with silver candlesticks and fresh flowers. Classical or modern music plays softly in the background, adding to the elegance.

The cuisine focuses on creative contemporary American dishes using fresh local ingredients as much as possible. Year-round favorites include wood-roasted Maine lobster and pan-seared organic duck breast. The lounge menu might offer prosciutto and roasted peach salad with Black Mission figs, toasted almonds, and pomegranate molasses; an assortment of grilled panini; or tempura soft-shell crab with a tomato and basil marmalade. On holidays a three-course prix fixe menu is offered. The lounge and restaurant are open daily for dinner in July and August and closed on Monday from Labor Day to July 1. Lunch is served on weekends in season. Breakfast is served every day for the convenience of the guests but also for the lucky public. Augmenting a continental spread on the sideboard, two entrees are served each day. Depending on the chef's whim, they might include goat cheese omelette, pumpkin waffles, or oven-baked puff pancakes with apple cream sauce. With most meals a delightful surprise, or amuse, will be brought to the table, which is a treat for the diner but also allows the chef more time to prepare the next course. The restaurant also is noted for the picnics it prepares to take to Tanglewood.

Lenox Coffee **$**
512 Main Street
(413) 637-1606

A pleasant place to rest your bones, have a chat, or sit and read the paper, Lenox Coffee sells coffee from the Barrington Coffee Roasting Company prepared in a number of ways, along with fine loose teas and fruit drinks. For accompaniments there are pound cake and several kinds of biscotti and cookies. The sunny yellow decor adds to the feeling of resuscitation. Lenox Coffee is open Monday through Saturday year-round, with reduced hours in the off-season. The coffeehouse is located off Main Street in one of several small houses clustered in the center of the block between Main and Church Streets.

Spigalina **$$**
80 Main Street
(413) 637-4455
www.berkshireweb.com/dining

Chef-owner Lina Paccaud and her husband, Serge, opened Spigalina in 1997 with the goal of providing a pleasant place to enjoy conversation and good food with a Mediterranean flavor. The menu is small by some standards, but each dish is special. Appetizers might include grilled vegetable timbale or a phyllo tartlet with shrimp and tomato. By popular demand, the restaurant's signature dish is crispy kataifi—a salad topped with goat cheese wrapped in crisp, shredded phyllo dough topped with cranberries and toasted nuts. Seafood, chicken, beef, lamb, or pork is usually marinated using European ingredients that reflect tastes from Italy, Greece, southern France, Spain, or Morocco. Depending on the season, you might find Spanish seafood stew, paella Valenciana, or grilled free-range chicken breast marinated in Moroccan preserved lemon and herbs and served with vegetables, mashed potatoes, and a tarragon chicken sauce. Serge, who trained in Lucern, Switzerland, is the dessert chef. Lina, whose parents are Sicilian, grew up in the Albany area and studied at the Culinary Institute in Hyde Park. The restaurant has a full bar, including select wines. Parking is available at the rear, where the wheelchair ramp is located. Reservations are recommended for seating in the comfortable and welcoming dining room, which holds around 70 persons. In summer another 30 persons can be seated on the porch on a first-come basis. Spigalina is open for dinner every night from May through November and closed December through April.

Wheatleigh **$$-$$$$**
Hawthorne Road
(413) 637-0610
www.wheatleigh.com

For those who don't normally move in such circles, dining at Wheatleigh is an experience worth saving up for. The setting is beautiful, the service impeccable, and the French cuisine first-rate. Lunch and dinner are served by reservation. The library of this elegantly restored mansion is where lunch is served Monday through Saturday. A la carte dinners also are served here nightly. The tables are an unusual mix of brass and wood, designed and built by Nicholas Mongiardi, a nationally known Lenox furniture maker. Seating is available on back-to-back banquettes or comfy dark green leather chairs. The tables are set with military precision, everything lined up just so by the European staff, many of whom are interns from culinary and hospitality schools abroad. The prix fixe lunch menu offers a choice of a sandwich, salad, or entree, and one dessert. All also may be ordered a la carte. Choices might include a Gruyêre tart with Applewood-smoked bacon and baby spinach, house-smoked salmon with mesclun greens and local chèvre, or the ulitmate treat—poached Maine lobster with tat soi, mizuna, and roasted beets. The food is presented simply on pure-white contemporary china at all meals.

The menu for dinner in the library is a la carte, as opposed to the prix fixe menu offered in the main dining rooms. You might begin with Maine mussels in miso broth, foie gras terrine, or the house specialty—and a favorite with diners—soup, soup, soup, and soup, a presentation of four different soups served in demitasse cups. For high-on-the-hog living, California-estate Osetra caviar also is available, priced by the ounce. Entrees might include braised lamb shank, grilled Black Angus tenderloin, house-made fettuccini with baby artichokes and wild mushrooms, or a fish of the day. Vegetables and a starch are extra and may be chosen from several options. Desserts include a seasonal fruit tart, Key lime pie, and a tasting of sorbets or ice creams. Dinner also is served in a glassed-in portico with views of the terrace and landscape beyond and a more formal dining room, furnished with Chippendale chairs. In the latter, a wall-size mirror reflects the ornately carved fireplace and the views through the floor-to-ceiling windows unfettered by mullions or other obstructions. Twenty tables in all are covered with white linen and set with the same precision as those in the library. The prix fixe menu changes nightly, with choices to be made from selections offered in four courses. Entrements from the chef will be brought to the table along the way. An imaginative vegetarian menu is available. Candlelight, views of the grounds, elegant table settings, unobtrusive staff, a visit from the chef—all add up to a meal "fit for a prince," as the *New York Times* declared. A 20 percent gratuity is added unless otherwise requested.

New Marlborough

The Old Inn on the Green & Gedney Farm **$$$**
Massachusetts Highway 57
(413) 229-3131
www.oldinn.com

Situated in the historic village of New Marlborough, the Old Inn on the Green has been racking up awards and accolades since Leslie Miller, a pastry chef of note, and her husband, Bradford Wagstaff, opened it in 1983. In fact Zagat's gave it a rarely earned top rating. Lit only by candles year-round, the 1760 inn exudes colonial charm. The dining rooms are furnished with worn Windsor chairs and mahogany tavern tables, and each has a fireplace. The candles—the owners go through around 1,400 a month—burn in candlesticks on the tables and in iron chandeliers and wall sconces. Contrary to popular belief, the inn does have electricity. It's just that the owners have decided to maintain an ambience befitting the architectural details and historical significance of this graceful landmark.

In summer, meals are served on the garden terrace under a graceful white canopy, overlooking a large colonial flower and herb garden with New Marlborough's historic church in the background. Then there's the cuisine. Executive chef Peter Platt formerly reigned at Wheatleigh and is well versed in perfect preparation and presentation. Appetizers on the a la carte menu, which changes often, might include a gateau of citrus-marinated Scottish salmon with Meyer lemon crème fraîche and a microgreens salad on toasted brioche or seared breast of Hudson Valley squab with a wild mushroom ravioli and herb-infused game consommé. A popular entree year-round is roast tenderloin of Black Angus beef. In summer the menu might include grilled loin of line-caught bluefin tuna with banana fingerling potato salad with a shallot comfit and Kalamata olive coulis. On Saturday night a varying four-course prix fixe meal is offered. Selected estate wines bottled in France, California, and Italy complete the meal. The Old Inn serves dinner every night but Tuesday from July 1 through Columbus Day. In winter it also is closed on Monday. Gedney Farm, also operated by Miller and Wagstaff, is often booked for wedding parties.

South Egremont

The Egremont Inn **$$**
10 Old Sheffield Road
(413) 528-2111, (800) 859-1780
www.egremontinn.com

Just off MA 23 in the historic village of South Egremont, the Egremont Inn offers a sophisticated menu served in the formal dining room or casual dining in the tavern. In fall and winter the fireplace burns. In summer, dinners are served on the porch that wraps around the wonderfully kept old inn. Innkeepers and restaurateurs Steve and Karen Waller opened the inn in 1996 and have earned kudos for their meals and awards for their wines. The cuisine combines the classic American background of chef Jonathan Taufman with the Italian heritage and continental approach of chef Vanessa Cortesi. Dishes are creatively prepared with fresh local ingredients. The formal dinner menu includes interesting appetizers such as spring vegetable risotto (with a hint of lemongrass) and crispy fried scallops, also available on the tavern menu. Intriguing entrees include grilled leg of venison finished with a juniper berry sauce, grilled swordfish with mango salsa, grilled loin lamb chops, and pan-roasted halibut with escarole and sautéed scallops over tagliatelle. The tavern menu offers a Caesar salad with or without grilled chicken or shrimp, fish-and-chips, pan-fried trout encrusted with blue cornmeal, and the classic InnBurger with a variety of toppings. The restaurant is open Wednesday through Sunday year-round. Live jazz is performed on Saturday nights; on Thursday it's acoustic music. The inn's Web site includes a recipe which, when last checked, featured sautéed Brussel sprouts, of all things. And they sounded terrific!

John Andrews **$$$**
224 Hillsdale Road (MA 23)
(413) 528-3469
If it weren't for the contemporary orange monoliths with "JA" written in script on them, you might zip right by this fine restaurant. The house in which is it located is dark green and fairly unassuming. The interior is simple, a blend of contemporary and country. The plaster walls, finished in soft Italian colors, often feature work by local artists. But the "New American" cuisine served within is known throughout the county for its excellence, and folks drive from all over to get there. The menu changes all the time, depending on what's available locally along with the whim of head chef Dan Smith, who has owned the place with his wife, Susan Bianchi-Smith, since 1990. Susan describes her husband as a purist who is devoted to slow food and the use of unadulterated ingredients. His signature dish features breast of heirloom French Pelkin duck served with crisp duck comfit, mashed potatoes, and braised greens. Also popular are fettuccine with wild mushrooms and seared sea scallops, served sometimes with a risotto of wild rice and wheat berries, fresh asparagus, and arugula oil. All pastas and breads are made on the premises. In summer there is seating on the terrace at the rear, which overlooks the gardens and landscaping on the four-acre property. In winter the fireplace is lit, adding to the romantic coziness. There is a small bar and lounge with a separate bar menu during the week. Appropriate wines are available for dinner. The restaurant can seat around 60 persons, including the terrace, and tends to be pretty hectic on weekends in July and August, when it is open for dinner every night. The rest of the year, it is closed on Wednesday. Incidently, John Andrews is the name of Susan's grandfather, who once owned the property.

The Old Mill **$$**
53 Main Street (MA 23)
(413) 528-1421
Chef Terry Moore has been the caretaker of this restored 1797 gristmill and blacksmith's shop since 1978. While he has preserved the original floors, double-sided fireplace, and wood beams in the historic mill, he has added an elegant touch by covering the tables with linen cloths appropriate for the cuisine he offers. The menu of new and traditional American dishes includes roast Portland cod with lobster sauce and mashed Yukon Gold potatoes along with such classics as calves liver, rack of lamb, and steak. For dessert there's profiteroles au chocolat. The restaurant can seat around 75 persons and has a small bar. It is open nightly for dinner from Memorial Day through Columbus Day. Off-season the Old Mill is closed on Monday.

Stockbridge

Michael's Restaurant & Pub **$**
3 Elm Street
(413) 298-3530
Northern Italian dishes and American favorites dominate the menu at Michael Abdella's restaurant, established in 1981. Lunch and dinner are served daily in the front dining room, which looks out onto busy Elm Street, or the more casual bar and lounge at the rear of the building. The lunch menu includes soups, salads, burg-

ers, fried seafood, wraps, and specialty sandwiches. Popular dinner entrees, served from 4:30 to 9:00 P.M., include grilled chicken carbonara, veal Genovese, mussels Fra Diavolo, baked red snapper, and an assortment of ravioli. The pub menu includes wings, nachos, wraps, skins, burgers, and sandwiches. The bar and lounge are a popular gathering place for the younger crowd at night, when only the pub menu is available. (See the Nightlife chapter.)

Red Lion Inn **$$$**
30 Main Street
(413) 298–5545
www.redlioninn.com

Folks who dine at the landmark Red Lion Inn have several options open to them, depending on the season and occasion. The main dining room is large and elegant, and although ties and jackets are no longer required, diners are expected to dress appropriately. Open every day of the year for breakfast, lunch, and dinner, the dining room is perfect for special occasions and romantic evenings. Antiques abound, the tables are set with flowers and candles, and the seasonal menu is full of traditional New England dishes with a contemporary touch at the hand of executive chef Douglas Luf. The Red Lion Inn's clam chowder is so popular it has been canned and can be purchased at the inn's gift shop or online. Classics on the dinner menu include roast turkey with cornbread stuffing and prime rib served with a hot popover. Less traditional are dishes like caramelized sea scallops or sautéed trout with wild mushroom ragout, cranberries, and toasted walnuts. Desserts include the Red Lion Inn's notoriously good apple pie, as well as carrot cake and crème brûlée.

A suitable dinner wine may be chosen from the award-winning list of more than 200 selections. After dinner, a port, cognac, single-malt Scotch, or one of several international coffees may be enjoyed. You can almost see the ladies moving off to the drawing room while the gentlemen head off to the billiard room, cigars at the ready. Today, however, there are no billiards—and cigars are definitely not allowed. More casual are the Lion's Den, downstairs, and cozy Widow Bingham's Tavern. The Lion's Den features entertainment and a varied bar menu (more about that in Nightlife). The tavern, with its dark paneling and wide-plank floors, is a nice hideaway to enjoy soups, sandwiches, or salads. In summer, lunch, cocktails, dinner, or a late-night snack in the courtyard amid thousands of blooming impatiens is a most pleasant experience. The main dining room and tavern are wheelchair-accessible via an entrance around the corner on the west side of the inn. The Red Lion Inn bustles in summer and fall and on holidays, and reservations are a must.

West Stockbridge

Rouge Restaurant & Bistro **$$**
3 Center Street
(413) 232–4111

Rouge opened in 2002 and quickly became "the buzz." The ambience, menu, and young owners have succeeded in bringing a new energy to West Stockbridge. The chef is William Merelle, who studied in France and who has been cooking since he was 14. His wife, Maggie, learned about wines and beer working for a distributor. Their union has resulted in a nice blend of excellent food in a relaxed atmosphere. From the attractive red doors to the rustic-contemporary interior, the restaurant is homey and chic at the same time. Dishes in primary colors are set on bright red tables. Cane-seat chairs and pine paneling add to the cozy feeling. The place is entered through the bar, which has become a popular hangout for locals. Here you can enjoy cocktails and assorted beers and wines while nibbling tapas or enjoying a bar menu that includes french fries and baguettes with each order. The Rouge Burger is made with fontina cheese and cornichones, tomato, and onions. A plate of Scottish smoked salmon comes with capers, arugula, tomato, and avocado.

The dinner menu includes appetizers like sautéed fois gras with celery root and apple salad with raspberry sauce. Entrees, based on seasonal local products, might include such mouthwatering dishes as grilled whole trout with tomato Provençal and basmati rice, free-range oven-crisped lemon chicken with stir-fried asparagus and roasted fingerling potatoes, or sautéed chanterelle mushrooms, asparagus, and spinach with shredded potato cake and balsamic shallot sauce. The yummy desserts are big enough to share. With its low ceilings, the place does tend to be noisy. In summer there are tables on the deck at the rear. Rouge is open evenings Wednesday through Sunday. Reservations for dinner are a must.

Trúc Orient Express **$$**
3 Harris Street
(413) 232-4204

Diners at this Vietnamese restaurant will find lots of interesting dishes on the menu prepared with flavors ranging from subtle to spicy. Starters include several kinds of soup, as well as appetizers ranging from traditional spring rolls to marinated beef wrapped with fresh mint leaves. Entrees feature beef, pork, chicken, and seafood prepared in a variety of ways. Unusual dishes include fresh sea scallops sautéed with spiced fresh orange juice and a hearty concoction of sautéed fish with scallions and peanuts flavored with dill and other herbs served with rice vermicelli and shrimp sauce. The latter is a hearty dish, particularly enjoyable on a cold day when the fireplace in the main dining room is flickering away. A long list of vegetarian dishes includes tofu sautéed with various ingredients or served as a stew in a clay pot.

With its wide polished floorboards, trickling fountain, pale orange walls, abundance of plants, and Oriental decor, the restaurant has a relaxed feel, even though more than 100 persons can be seated in the various alcoves. Adjacent to the restaurant is a small shop where silks, lacquered goods, and other Asian items are sold. In summer there is dining on the deck, unless it has been turned into a Vietnamese bazaar, where even more furnishings from Asia are sold. The family left Vietnam in the 1970s and came to West Stockbridge via Hartford, Connecticut, where other family members had settled. The restaurant opened in 1979 and has been popular ever since. In summer lunch and dinner are served every day. In winter it's dinner only, and the family takes a day off on Tuesday. Reservations for dinner are a good idea during the busy season.

CENTRAL BERKSHIRE

Lanesborough

Bob's Country Kitchen **$**
42 South Main Street (US 7)
(413) 499-3934

Open daily, Bob's is known for reasonably priced home-cooked meals, breakfast served all day, and daily specials that are filling and cheap. Workers, seniors, families, and tourists love this place, and on Sunday the line often stretches out the door. The restaurant itself started life as a roadside stand called Dopey's (for one of those dwarfs). Until recently it was owned by Bob Oparowski, who changed the name, added the Polish crest to the sign, and put kapusta, golomki, and kielbasa on the menu. New owner Peter McQuire has completely refurbished the interior but has kept both the sign and the Polish dishes. The menu is full of basic meat-and-potato dishes plus stuffed sole and chicken cacciatore. The Chuck Wagon Casserole (macaroni and ground beef) and beef stew are favorites. Most important, the long hot dogs that made the place famous are still cooked on the grill and served on a buttered and grilled roll. Homemade soups and desserts, good coffee, a kid's menu, and a senior-citizen discount add to the place's popularity. Seats are available in booths, at tables, or at the counter.

Matt Reilly's Pub & Restaurant $
750 South Main Street (US 7)
(413) 447-9780
Located on the shore of Lake Pontoosuc, Matt Reilly's is popular in summer, when the deck is open, and in winter, when the lake is frozen and snowmobilers gather to warm up. Seafood is the specialty. The lobster salad is real lobster; the fried clams and scallops are tender and sweet. The menu also has lots of interesting salads, soups, and main courses along with the usual burgers and other bar fare. The french-fried sweet potatoes are terrific. Open daily, the restaurant is now run by Joe Reilly, whose father founded the business, and his son, Shaun.

Ye Olde Forge $
125 North Main Street
(413) 442-6797
Yes, there was once a forge here, memorialized by the horseshoes and other implements that decorate the rustic interior. But the Forge is known now for its incredible selection of beers, award-winning wings (the plaques are hanging on the walls), and the above-average menu. The front half is divided into the popular bar (with two TVs) and a well-ventilated dining section for smokers. The rear is nonsmoking and in summer opens out onto the deck. Aside from burgers and other pub fare, the cooked-to-order menu includes daily specials concocted by owner Kirk Grippo, a former chef at Williams College, and his capable staff. Unique appetizers include spinach, mushrooms, and cheese warmed in a light flour tortilla served with a dipping sauce flavored with smoked jalapeños and lime. The regular menu includes such tasty dishes as grilled garlic rosemary steak; étouffée (a spicy Cajun blend of seafood and sausage); the Neptune bread bowl filled with shrimp sautéed with tomatoes, wine, butter, and herbs; and St. Louis ribs. Daily specials always include seafood and pasta dishes, plus items like braised chicken in Brooklyn Brown Ale with veggies and hazelnuts or braised pork with a demiglaze of Sinebrychoff Porter and roasted garlic served with fried leeks. While the food is good, the beer's the thing. There are around 200 brews, including ciders and ales, on hand with seasonal specials. Folks who want to try them all (not at one sitting) may join the Beer Club. Those who try 50 brews within a calendar year are honored with a personalized pewter mug, which will be hung above the bar. Perhaps more important, they will be entitled to draft pints at mug prices. Those who try another 50 beers in the next year will earn a plaque. A friendly, relaxed place, the Forge is popular with a broad cross-section of customers, including locals, skiers, summer tourists, professional folks, and young people. The parking lot is at the rear. The entrance there is up a flight of stairs, but there is a handicapped parking place by the front door off US 7. The Forge is open daily for dinner and beer-sampling year-round.

Pittsfield

Cafe Reva $
238 Tyler Street
(413) 442-6161
From the outside, you would never guess that the cook in this hole-in-the-wall studied at Le Cordon Bleu and is a former executive chef at one of the area's better resorts. But that's the background of Aura Whitman, who serves up interesting breakfasts and lunches every day but Tuesday. From the huevos rancheros to the potato salad, nothing is run-of-the-mill. Whitman uses seasonings that surprise the palate, and the moderately priced food is nicely presented. Breakfasts are mind-boggling. Aside from the egg and meat dishes, there are pancakes and waffles that can be enhanced with such toppings as caramelized bananas with brown sugar and pecans, fresh berries in season, or the ultimate: vanilla ice cream with whipped cream and caramel sauce. And the French toast made with three slices of batter-dipped challah stuffed

with apples and sweetened cream cheese is out of this world.

Breakfast is served until the midafternoon closing. As for lunch, the ample salad of mixed greens, apples, Gorgonzola, toasted pecans, and house vinaigrette would cost much more at a more elegant venue. Reuben fanciers declare Whitman's the best. For vegetarians, the portobello "burger" with sautéed onions, roasted peppers, and cheddar cheese is a messy winner, as is the tomato-basil wrap with roasted vegetables and cheddar cheese. And most of these dishes are around $5.00! Whitman also makes the desserts, a skill she honed while studying in France. She named her restaurant for her daughter, whom she can spend more time with now that she has her own place. The place is small, with seating for about 35 persons at the counter or tables. Avoid rush hour if you want to get seated and served quickly. The street entrance, located between a welder and a locksmith, is up a few steps, but there is a rear parking lot with an entrance that is only one small step up. Whitman also caters. Tyler Street runs off First Street (US 7) and eventually turns into Dalton Avenue.

Court Square Breakfast & Deli **$**
95 East Street
(413) 442-9896

As the name indicates, this family-operated eatery is across the street from the county courthouse and near Park Square. David and Deborah Flynn opened the place in 1993 and created a stir when they became the first restaurant in the city to go smoke-free. Rather than losing customers, they found the step made them more popular. Now most places either limit smoking to certain areas or ban it altogether. Used to dealing with lawyers and other professionals in a hurry, the staff is on the ball, and food is served promptly. They do a big lunch business, with orders faxed in and either delivered around town or picked up. Muffins and soups are made from scratch, as are some daily specials. Hearty breakfasts, served through lunchtime, include apple, blueberry, or strawberry pancakes and eggs with a variety of meats, including kielbasa, linguicia, and corned beef hash. Nova Scotia lox is available with a bagel or lightly scrambled with eggs and onions. Sandwiches include grilled specialties like the unusual combination of sharp cheddar cheese and onion on pumpernickel bread or the Court Square Monte Cristo with ham, turkey, and Swiss cheese on thick-cut egg bread and Russian dressing. Catering to the upscale tastes of some of the clientele, herbal tea, chai, Nantucket Nectars, and Starbucks lattes and cappuccino are available. But the place also is popular with regular folks, who often sit at the counter with a cup of regular coffee. Decorated with country kitsch, Court Square has ample seating in booths or at tables. Open daily. Cash only, please.

Elizabeth's **$$**
1264 East Street
(413) 448-8244

Poetry—in word and in cooking—abounds at Elizabeth's, where chef-owner Tom Ellas reigns supreme. Self-taught, Ellas loves good food. In search of a more creative life, he walked away from his job as a court officer in 1986 and opened his dream restaurant in an unassuming house in the industrial section of the city. He named it for his wife, who keeps the place spotless. His eclectic menu, exuberant descriptions, and nonconformist approach to running an eatery soon attracted a dedicated following. He can seat 40 persons, and although he has never advertised, reservations are definitely a good idea. The first floor is half kitchen, completely open and surrounded with shelves holding canned goods, cookbooks, and utensils. There are a few tables here, but the bulk are upstairs. Although many of the dishes involve pasta, he proudly notes there is not a can of tomato paste in the place. He uses Dececo pasta and thinks of it as a blank canvas, a vehicle for the flavorings and ingredients to be added.

The menu includes baked butterfly pasta with Gorgonzola and baby spinach, Lizzie's Four Cheese Lasagna with baby spinach and caramelized onion, and Lynn's Ballerina Sauce, a mix of fresh tomatoes and caramelized onion with a hint of garlic and sweet basil "as light as a baby's smile." From France comes baked eggplant Provençal, with roasted wild mushrooms, tomato, caramelized onion, baby spinach, two cheeses, and herbs. Added daily are a soup, which might have taken three days to prepare, and two nonpasta specials using recipes from around the world. The salad—a mix of greens with fresh veggies, seasonal fruits, and cheeses with a balsamic vinaigrette dressing—is served in a large bowl, which is how it was served when Tom was growing up. The salad was not something to be consumed while waiting for dinner but stayed on the table throughout the meal to be enjoyed at leisure. It takes restraint not to fill up on the salad or the warm organic sourdough bread. Appetizers include bagna coada, which he describes as "a robust marriage of anchovy, garlic, olive oil, and sweet butter . . . that could make a Republican smile." His chicken liver pâté is made with black currants and apple brandy. Beverages include selected wines and beers. The dessert list is small but always features various cheesecakes made by the Newsheet Nuns of Cambridge, New York. Elizabeth's is open for dinner Wednesday through Sunday in summer, Tuesday through Saturday the rest of the year. Tom takes cash, checks, and IOUs (really!) but no credit cards.

The Highland $
100 Fenn Street
(413) 442-2457

The Highland has been on Fenn Street next to City Hall since 1936. And except for the fact that the Arace family recently started taking credit cards, it has changed little in all those years. The walls are lined with pictures of baseball teams and favorite players. The "cocktail lounge" between the two dining rooms usually has some pols sitting around solving the city's problems or GE retirees reminiscing about the days when most of the city worked at the now-gone plant. The booths and counter are filled with regulars who probably know the menu by heart but peruse it anyway. And the waitresses probably know what the regulars are going to order but wait patiently for their decision. The food is made from scratch daily and is by all standards a bargain. You can get a meatball sandwich for under $3.00. Meat loaf, liver and onions, chicken Parmesan, deep-fried scallops, the turkey platter, and other comfort food are among the favorites. But the spaghetti is by far the Highland's claim to fame. No penne or ziti or angel hair pasta here—just regular spaghetti and homemade sauce. Depending on what gets added (meatballs, sausage, chicken livers, etc.), the price runs from $5.00 to $7.00 and includes a salad, bread, and a glass of house wine. Prices are seldom raised. At $12, steak is the highest priced item on the menu. For a slice of Pittsfield life, the Highland is the place to go—except on Monday, when it is closed.

House of India $
261 North Street
(413) 443-3262

Authentic dishes from the north and south of India are prepared to order at the chef-owned House of India. Specialties include chicken, seafood, and lamb prepared in a traditional charcoal-fired clay oven called a tandoor. Traditional breads also are baked in the tandoor. Starters include lentil garlic, coconut, and mulligatawny soups, samosas (turnovers filled with vegetables or lamb), and pekoras (vegetables or cheese dipped in a chickpea batter and deep fried). Chicken, lamb, or fish may be ordered as a curry or in various combinations and sauces. The diner will be asked how spicy the dish should be. There are numerous vegetable and rice dishes, relishes, and beverages, including rich yogurt drinks and a thick mango shake. For dessert there's saffron ice cream and rice pudding with cardamom flavoring. The lunch buffet, served Monday through Saturday, is a great way to sample various dishes, many not on the regular menu. Jaswant Singh Bhangu and Paramjit Singh Chanal have owned the restaurant since 1994, moving to the current location in 1997. They also have a restaurant in Worcester.

Kim's Dragon Restaurant $$
1231 West Housatonic Street (US 20)
(413) 442-5594

Formerly the owner of a restaurant in Saigon, Kim Van Huynh suffered imprisonment during the Vietnam War before he and his young family were able to escape and come here with help from some Berkshire residents. With encouragement from his newfound friends, he opened the Dragon in a tiny former diner on US 20 in 1983 and was an instant hit. Fans include Arlo Guthrie, who praised Kim's traditional blend of French-Asian cooking, a tribute that is still printed on the back of Kim's menus. The food has never changed. Incredibly, it is still all cooked to order by Kim's wife, Thuong Huynh, who uses all fresh ingredients, herbs, and spices. The crispy spring rolls filled with delicately flavored vegetables are about 6 inches long and are uncommonly good. At $5.00 for two, they also are an amazing bargain. Soups include interesting blends of crabmeat and vegetables, salmon and rice, or lemongrass with chicken or shrimp. Entrees feature sautéed chicken, pork, beef, seafood, or vegetables served with various sauces and flavorings. The curry is rich and creamy, the Vietnamese pancake light and crammed with vegetables, and the marinated beef tender and tasty. Specialties include several squid dishes, chargrilled pork, chicken, or beef in black bean sauce, Saigon fried rice (nothing like the heavy greasy kind served in some Chinese restaurants), and crispy fish served with sautéed fresh vegetables and nuoc nam sauce. There also are a number of rice noodle dishes and, of course, traditional Pad Thai. Aside from an assortment of international beers and a select list of wines, beverages include thick Vietnamese coffee and jasmine tea. Around 80 persons can be seated at tables or in booths. The place tends to be packed during the season and can get pretty noisy, but all dishes can be prepared for takeout, which is a good way to beat the crowds.

Kneebones Steakhouse $$
5 Cheshire Road (Massachusetts Highway 8)
Allendale Shopping Center
(413) 442-9537

As one would expect, steak in all its glory is the specialty here. But also on the menu are ribs, pasta (including lobster ravioli), seafood—grilled, broiled, and deep-fried; and surf-and-turf combination platters. The lunch menu includes soups and salads, wraps, a host of appetizers, and a long list of sandwiches, including grilled yellowfin tuna, grilled portobella, and the classic Reuben. Owner Kelly Genzabella likes to greet customers herself, usually from behind the large oak bar, and chef Jason Murphy prepares everything to order. The main dining area can seat 120 persons. Kneebones opened in 2001. Lunch and dinner are served every day but Monday.

Mazzeo's Ristorante $$
7 Winter Street
(413) 448-2095

Fine Italian food without a lot of carrying on has been served by the Mazzeo family since 1988. Homemade pastas are the specialty, but the menu also has lots of interesting fish, chicken, veal, and beef dishes. Grilled sirloin may be ordered in several ways, including marinated with Dijon mustard, herbs, cognac, and a shallot wine sauce. Some folks like to sit at the well-stocked bar, where they can order from a bar menu. The Italian atmosphere is enhanced by a large mural on the dining room wall. First-timers might have trouble finding Mazzeo's. It's amid a maze of little streets on the city's east side and partially hidden by a huge billboard. If you're coming from the south, take East Street; turn at Wendy's onto Fourth Street and follow it until you see the billboard. Mazzeo's also can be reached from Tyler Street by turning at the car wash onto Brown and making a left at the end of the street. The restaurant is closed on Monday and Tuesday. A large hall on the second floor may be reserved for private functions.

Trattoria Rustica **$$$**
75 North Street
(413) 499-1192

Not long after Davide Monzo finished creating Trattoria Il Vesuvio in Lenox, he decided to bring Antichi Saport (old taste) to Pittsfield. Originally from Pompeii, Monzo has been here for 30 years, but his love of all things Italian drove him to re-create old Italy in the space he occupies in the basement of a refurbished building between North and McKay Streets. The mailing address is 75 North Street but the entrance to the restaurant is on McKay Street, which runs parallel to North. He exposed the stone, brick, and wood; installed a wood-fired oven; and trained his international staff in Italian so that they would pronounce the items on the menu correctly and enhance the illusion by using Italian phrases when interacting with customers. The cuisine is from coastal Italy, and Monzo uses simple ingredients prepared with the old, simple methods. Every morning he bakes the bread and starts roasting, baking, and stewing the dishes that will be served that night.

The menu varies seasonally and nightly. Antipasti might include calamari al Ferri (grilled calamari dressed with lemon, garlic, and parsley coulis), am pepata e cozze (steamed mussels with white wine, garlic, fresh grape tomato, and parsley), or caprese (homemade mozzarella, vine-ripened tomatoes with fresh basil, sea salt, and extra-virgin olive oil). Pastas, imported from Italy and prepared to order, might be tossed with olives, capers, basil, anchovies, tomatoes, and garlic or mixed with seafood and fresh herbs and spices. Entrees are served with vegetables and polenta prepared fresh each day in traditional combinations and served at room temperature after their flavors have blended. There is always a nightly fish dish that varies, plus salmon, poultry, or game prepared in the brick oven along with dishes featuring pork, veal, and lamb. A select list offers regional Italian wines. A 20 percent gratuity is added for parties of six or more. The main entrance is down a few steps but there is a wheelchair-accessible entrance off the corridor to the left, which is the McKay Street entrance. In summer, meals are served in a courtyard at the rear of the restaurant. A sign outside the entrance advises that UPSCALE BUSINESS CASUAL attire is expected and thankfully prohibits the use of cell phones. Rustica has seating for up to 56 persons. Reservations are a good idea. Closed on Tuesday.

Zucchinis **$**
1331 North Street (MA 7)
(413) 442-2777

Italian food with flair is featured at Zucchinis, recently opened by two experienced restauranteurs, Lynne and Michael Soldato. This upscale family eatery just south of the Pontoosuc Lake dam on the corner of Keeler Street offers seating in the lounge or main dining room, where the booths along the wall all have flat-screen TVs. The menu is packed with unusual adaptations of old standbys. Pizza combinations, available in 10- or 14-inch pies, include Gorgonzola, pecan, and pears with olive oil and garlic; bacon with spinach and roasted red peppers; and Thai chicken with peanut sauce, scallions, red peppers, and broccoli. Or you can choose from a long list of toppings to add to the basic Margherita. Chicken and veal Marsala, Parmigiana, or Française (battered and sautéed), grilled Teriyaki salmon, and steak au poivre also are on the dinner menu. Pasta dishes include a combination of grilled zucchini, portobella mushrooms, sun-dried tomatoes, and broccoli; and artichoke, chicken and spinach. Sandwiches, strombolis, calzones, and burgers round out the menu.

The Soldato family operates popular Mario's restaurant "over the mountain" in New Lebanon, New York, where Michael is manager. Lynne has worked in the business since she was 14 and has managed several local restaurants. The pair renovated the brick building they now occupy, redecorating inside and out and enlarging and paving the parking lot at the rear off Keeler Street. In summer there's even a real zucchini patch by the building. The main entrance off the parking lot is at the top of a long flight of stairs, but there is a wheelchair-accessible entrance up near the highway. Zucchinis is open for lunch and dinner every day but Monday. It's extremely popular, so reservations are suggested. A large banquet room on the lower level is available for private parties.

NORTH COUNTY

Adams

Red Carpet $
69 Park Street (MA 8)
(413) 743-9781

The Red Carpet has been an Adams landmark since 1927, when it was called Clifford's Ranch. When the Haddad family took over in 1950, it was called the Park Street Lunch. They changed the name to the Red Carpet and have been serving reasonably priced family-oriented meals ever since. Favorites include fresh-battered fish and fries, which often draws a line outside the door on Friday in this predominately Catholic community. Soups and pies are homemade, and specials, depending on the whim of cook and former town official George Haddad, are prepared daily. These might include lasagna or stuffed chicken breasts. Photos of locals decorate the walls, reinforcing the small town atmosphere of the place. A counter in the rear of the restaurant is popular for singles, and the ample booths invite families or large groups. The Red Carpet is the only restaurant in Adams that serves breakfast every day. Lunch is served Monday through Saturday and dinner Tuesday through Saturday.

Cheshire

Country Charm $
5 State Road (MA 8)
(413) 743-1445

It's hard to miss the Country Charm. There's a big chicken on the roof. It's even been featured in one of cartoonist Bill Griffith's *Zippy* strips. Back in the 1950s, when such roadside art reached its peak, the restaurant was a small drive-up called the Chicken Coop, later becoming the Chicken Stop. When the Gaylord family took it over in 1971, they expanded the building and turned it into a full restaurant but decided to leave the chicken. "It was too cool to get rid of," says current chef and manager Trent Gaylord. The menu is full of moderately priced homemade family favorites, but the oversize prime rib—served on Friday and Saturday nights—is the most popular. And, yes, they still do chicken, only it is "broasted." Senior citizens particularly seem to favor the Country Charm, and the place is usually packed on Sunday after church lets out. There are three pine-paneled dining rooms, each with a fireplace. The tables are set with paper placemats, and the atmosphere is casual and friendly. Wine, beer, and mixed drinks are available, and

Reservations are a necessity in season and recommended off-season. If you're planning to attend a performance, let the staff know, especially if dining in one of the chef-owned restaurants where food is cooked to order. And allow time to enjoy those meals. They are not meant to be rushed through!

there is a kid's menu. Reservations are seldom required, as there is room for 280 persons. The Country Charm is closed on Monday and Tuesday.

Lakeside Restaurant & Catering $
287 South State Road (MA 8)
(413) 743-7399
Although he has only been running the Lakeside since 1997, owner-chef Jason Bouchard has grown the restaurant from a ho-hum eatery to a destination for locals and others looking for good food at reasonable prices. In fact, he has done so well that he recently invested in a complete makeover of the place. Slate floors, contemporary lighting and furnishings, ample booths, and a separate area with a bar have brought the old place into the 21st century. Situated across from Cheshire Lake, with the Ashuwillticook Trail nearby, the restaurant attracts all sorts of folks. Locals are greeted by name by the staff, which has worked here for years. Breakfast, served until noon, includes an old standby that most other restaurants seem to have forgotten: creamed chipped beef on toast. With picnic tables on-site or benches across the way by the lake or on the trail, take-out meals are popular. While the menu is fairly standard, the preparation is not. Most fans agree that Bouchard's fish-and-chips is the best around. Lightly battered with no hint of grease, the fish flakes into tender morsels when touched. Boucher attributes that to the freshness of the seafood he buys. On weekends he really cuts loose, with specials running from simple but perfectly grilled filet mignon with a wild mushroom gravy to lobster ravioli with a basil Alfredo sauce. Boucher had been doing so much off-premises catering that he decided to save his energy—and benefit from the bar bill—by adding a room just for special events. Capable of seating 100 persons, the room has a dance floor and is entered through French doors off the bar. All through the restaurant, with seating for 115, the decor is pleasant; The lake is visible from some seats by the front windows. The family-oriented Lakeside is open daily year-round for breakfast, lunch, and dinner.

New Ashford

Mill on the Floss $$$
US 7
(413) 458-9123
For more than 30 years, the Mill on the Floss has been the place to go for French country cuisine presented with gracious simplicity. Copper pots hang from hand-hewn beams, with the open kitchen beyond. The comfortable country furnishings belie the elegance of the meal, which will be wheeled to the table on a cart by the waitstaff, a tradition started by the previous owners in the 1950s. Back then, the specialty was classic French cooking, and one of their staff was the late Maurice Champagne, whose background was in continental cuisine. In 1970 Champagne and his wife, Jane, bought the restaurant, did some restoration to the 1700 wing that houses the bar, renovated the house that was added later, and put in a new kitchen. Their menu has evolved over the years, combining the best of the two schools. The food is prepared simply—no heavy sauces, no architectural spectacles, just the freshest ingredients, local when possible. The menu always lists around 10 appetizers, including soups, salads, escargot, chicken liver pate, and crab cake Dijonnaise, which also may be ordered as an entree. Other main dishes include roast duckling a l'orange, tournedos bearnaise, crispy cod or other fish with a chowder sauce, free-range chicken breast Paillard, and roast pork tenderloin with braised red cabbage. The Champagnes are famous for the sweetbreads "au beurre noir," a dish seldom seen on menus around here. The couple's daughter, Suzanne, herself an experienced cook, is now the chef, having taken over after her father died in 2000.

Although the restaurant conveys all the atmosphere of the old mill, the original one was destroyed in the 1950s when the state widened US 7. The bridge off the highway that leads to the restaurant passes over the Green River, near the spot where the mill once stood. Included on *Bon Appetit*'s "Best of the Berkshires" list, the restaurant seats around 80. Reservations are suggested. Mill on the Floss is closed on Monday and for occasional owner vacations.

North Adams

Appalachian Bean Cafe $
67 Main Street
(413) 663-7543
The "Bean" opened in 1996 and has become popular for both breakfast and lunch. Full breakfasts, including pancakes and French toast plus bagels, muffins, and other goodies, are available until the lunch menu kicks in. Then it's homemade soups, salads, wraps, sandwiches, and specials like chili or shepherd's pie. Orders are placed at the counter and brought to the table. Club chairs and sofas around the spacious cafe offer a retreat from the work-a-day world. Desserts are yummy and the coffee really good. The "Bean" is open every day.

Brewhaha $
20 Marshall Street
(413) 664-2020
Half a block from MASS MoCA, this interesting cross between a coffeehouse and a California eatery offers muffins, croissants, and pastries; wraps, sandwiches, and soups; and light breakfast and lunch fare, including frittatas and a remarkable fish chowder, all prepared on the premises with fresh natural ingredients. The eclectic menu always includes vegetarian dishes and comfort food, reflecting chef Barry Garton's 10-year stint at a far-from-average diner he and his wife, Nancy, operated in nearby Adams. Brewhaha carries illy espressos and three kinds of organic coffee, along with a wide range of teas, lattes, mochas, and other beverages, including fruit smoothies and other fruit drinks. Brewhaha is open daily except Wednesday.

Dora's $$
34 Holden Street
(413) 664-9449
The decor at Dora's is as eclectic as the menu. High ceilings, bare brick walls, floor lamps here and there to supplement the lighting, lace curtains at the high windows, and interesting artwork provide the ambience. Copper pots hang from a rack above the counter by the open kitchen, where chef-owner Andreas Karampatsos and his staff cook to order. On a busy night, the copious waitstaff zips back and forth from the pickup counter like a well-choreographed ballet. The reasonably priced menu reflects the chef's Mediterranean background, with some side trips. Some of the more flamboyant dishes include filet of sole sautéed with bananas and almonds and glazed with brandy, flaming Majorcan duck with orange-raspberry sauce, and steak au poivre flamed with cognac at the table. The baked stuff shrimp is filled with the chef's signature seasoned breadcrumbs and crabmeat stuffing. Vegetarians will be intrigued by Mango Tango, which features tofu marinated in ginger and garlic sautéed with fresh seasonal vegetables, toasted nuts, and mango. Interesting pasta dishes include Maria's frutta di mare (shrimp, scallops, mussels, and clams sautéed in white wine and with garlic, lemon, and parsley over linguini) and pasta fungi (portobella, crimini, shiitake, and button mushrooms sautéed with garlic and finished with a rich brandy-infused cream sauce over fettuccini). The restaurant has an extensive wine list and well-stocked liquor cabinet. Although fairly new to North Adams, the family is an old hand at the restaurant business, having operated the Taconic Restaurant in Williamstown for 20 years. Dora's is open for dinner Wednesday through Sunday.

Eleven $$$
MASS MoCA
Marshall Street
(413) 662-2004
Eleven is called Eleven because it is in Building 11 in the Massachusetts Museum

of Contemporary Art complex. You walk right by it on the way into the museum. Decidedly upscale, Eleven's decor is sparse and modern, the sleek all-white interior broken only by mushroom-color banquettes, fluorescent panels, charcoal-gray chairs, pale turquoise floor, and a few works of art on the walls. Wine by the glass or bottle and mixed drinks are served from a curved white bar with contemporary stools for six. Alfresco dining takes place in the adjoining courtyard, where brushed-metal chairs and plastic tables are set about. The contemporary American menu also is sparse but features select dishes like tuna au poivre on braised French lentils with lemon pickle. Fresh local produce is featured in season. Lunch and dinner are served, with a break in between, Monday through Saturday, with later hours on Friday and Saturday nights. Eleven is owned by Nancy Thomas, who also owns Mezze in Williamstown.

Freightyard Restaurant & Pub **$**
Western Gateway Heritage State Park
MA 8
(413) 663-6547

Located in a restored freight barn in this former railroad center, the Freightyard serves satisfying meals in a friendly, comfortable atmosphere. The large U-shaped bar, with a toy train suspended above, is ringed by tables. In winter a fire blazes in the fireplace. In summer there's dining outside on the patio. Aside from steak, ribs, seafood, pasta, salads, and soups, the place is known for its sizzling fajitas and really grande nachos. Upstairs, a copious all-you-can-eat lunch buffet is spread out on weekdays. Sunday, brunch is served. The Freightyard is open every day and is a handy place to go for a drink and late-night snack after attending something at MoCA. The park complex is off MA 8, and there is parking under the bridge or in a lot across the tracks.

Gramercy Bistro **$$**
24 Marshall Street
(413) 663-5300

An intimate restaurant with a French-Asian flair, Gramercy Bistro is owned by chef Alexander Smith, who has around 25 years' experience in the business. Although the bistro has only been open since 2001, his creative dishes have attracted quite a following. Due to popular demand, his seared scallops and sesame-seared tuna are always on the menu. While he likes to prepare seafood in a variety of ways, he also enjoys working up dishes using venison, bison, and other game and always has an interesting vegetarian dish on the menu. He adds to his basic menu as the seasons change—or when the mood strikes him. Smith prepares everything from scratch except the bread, which he buys from a local bakery because he lacks the space to bake his own. The wine list is extensive, with around 120 labels. Dinner is served Wednesday through Monday, with later hours on the weekend. On Saturday and Sunday, Smith serves brunch until 1:00 P.M. featuring omelettes, Benedicts, pancakes, and other goodies. The restaurant is closed on Tuesday. With seating for 34 persons, reservations are highly recommended.

Hickory Bill's **$**
20 Holden Street
(413) 663-6665

Authentic Texas barbecue is Hickory Bill's forte. This is not the greasy, sloppy stuff cooked over coals that most folks think of as barbecue. This is pork, beef, or chicken rubbed with seasonings and dry-roasted slowly in a wood-fired cooker installed at the back of Bill's restaurant. Made by Oyler specifically for barbecuing, this giant oven with slowly rotating racks is a larger version of the traveling smoker that Bill takes on his catering jobs. Originally from Oklahoma, William C. Ross Jr. learned how to do authentic Texas barbecue from a transplanted Texan who lives in Becket. He started catering in Pittsfield in 1984 and moved around a lot before settling at his present Holden Street address.

The walls are papered with testimonials praising his barbecue, which has been served at many a high-powered gathering in the Berkshires. Beef brisket, pork butt, and ribs (Chicago and St. Louis cut) are perfectly cooked. He serves them with hot or mild sauces but advises tasting before embellishing. Side dishes include baked beans seasoned with fancy brisket, sautéed onions and peppers, and cooked for a bit in the smoker; collard greens seasoned with ham hocks, onions, turnip roots, jalapeños, and vinegar; and warm Mexican cornbread. For dessert there's sweet potato pie and fruit cobblers. Wearing his signature straw hat, Bill holds forth behind the counter, where he laments the difficulty in keeping help. Those who do hang in have a rare chance to learn about opera, the blues, classics from the 1950s, and Bill's general philosophy of life. Open for lunch through dinner, Bill takes orders for buckets of ribs or chicken. He is closed on Sunday and Monday.

Jack's Hot Dog Stand **$**
12 Eagle Street
(413) 664-9006
www.jackshotdogstand.com

It's only hot dogs and hamburgers, but Jack's is a part of North Adams's history that goes back to 1900s, when Jafros Levanos came here from Greece through the sponsorship of a Greek family in Adams. Like many other immigrants, he changed his name and became Jack. He opened his tiny restaurant on Eagle Street in 1917, dedicated to serving the working class with fresh, affordable food. By 1920 he was able to buy his landlord's building. He made it through the Depression with a huge stack of IOUs. As things improved, those he had helped repaid him by continuing to patronize his place. His son took over in the 1980s. Today his grandson runs Jack's and takes pleasure in the locals who bring in their children while recalling when they were first plunked on one of the 12 stools, their legs dangling in the air. The hot dogs and burgers are still cooked on the original grills and the buns steamed in the original steamer. The cutting board, where onions and peppers have been chopped for years, has a well-worn dip. For many years Jack's has run a hot dog–eating contest, largely supported by students at the local college. The record, 54, was set in the 1940s. Jack's is open lunch through dinner every day but Sunday.

Jae's Inn **$$**
1111 South State Street (MA 8)
(413) 664-0100

Jae Chung brought "Asian fusion" cuisine to North County when he opened his inn and restaurant on MA 8. Open for lunch and dinner daily, Jae's international menu features dishes from Japan, China, Thailand, and Korea prepared in a multitude of ways with interesting flavors. Chung has several restaurants in the Boston area. He recently purchased and renovated the inn, decorating it in what might be called contemporary country. The main dining room, with arty lighting and paintings on the colorful walls, runs along the eastern side of the inn and is all windows. When it's crowded, the low ceiling magnifies the noise so it's hard to carry on a conversation—but then you might be too busy eating to talk. There are two smaller dining areas, and you also can order at the bar. Open daily.

Linda's Cafe **$**
178 Union Street (MA 2/8)
(413) 663-8003

Places like Linda's Cafe used to be all over North Adams, serving mill workers and their families plain home-cooked food at reasonable prices. Now that the city has gone upscale, Linda Lefaver's little restaurant may be the last place in town to get a plain grilled-cheese sandwich. No panini or foccacia here—just white bread from the supermarket with squares of American cheese grilled by the short order cook right behind the counter. The soups and specials are homemade, the salad plates forthright, and the servings ample. Breakfast is served until closing, around 2:00 P.M. The homemade hash is a favorite, as are pancakes, strawberry or plain, which are at least 10 inches across and served with a huge dollop of margarine melting on the top. Decorated with red-and-white checked curtains and lots of artificial flowers, Linda's is homey and cheery. Her clientele is still mostly local folks, but tourists are missing out on seeing a disappearing bit of Americana if they don't have a meal here. Open every day, the cafe is on MA 2 on the east side of town, just across from the Windsor Mill.

Williamstown

Arugula $
25 Spring Street
(413) 458-2152

Argentinian and Latin American dishes are the focus of this restaurant owned by Marta Ferrarina, who makes all the specialties herself, including polenta and dulce de leche, a thick sweetened-milk dessert. Fresh ingredients from local suppliers are used as much as possible and are tantalizingly visible at the working counter. Customers order at the cash register and are served at their tables unless they are taking out. Although the place is small, there is ample seating along a counter or at tables with a contemporary look. The menu includes burritos, large and small, empanadas, and quesadillas with or without salads and soup. Panini, or hot pressed sandwiches, include a popular Cuban specialty of marinated pork and ham with Swiss cheese and the vegetarian "Nicolas" consisting of lightly breaded eggplant with tomato, cucumber, olives, avocado, and fresh mozzarella cheese. The Milanese de pollo plateo (seasoned chicken breast, breaded and lightly fried) may be ordered as an entree with rice and beans and a side salad or on panini. A favorite among customers is the tortilla Espanola, a homemade potato and onion frittata prepared with Swiss cheese, also served with rice and beans and a salad. Fresh fruit smoothies, or "jugos," are tasty accompaniments. Other beverages include hot white chocolate, Cuban espresso, and Argentinian tea. Folks who like to do their own Argentinian and Latin American cooking will be pleased to find a small grocery section, where hard-to-get ingredients are for sale. The place is popular with students and tourists as well as transplanted Latinos from the Berkshires and beyond. Open for lunch and dinner, with a break in between, Arugula is closed on Monday. No credit cards accepted.

Chef's Hat $
905 Simmonds Road (US 7)
(413) 458-5120

The Chef's Hat has been around for more than 30 years, and the latest owner, Amy Pudvar, continues the tradition of serving family fare at reasonable prices. The breakfast menu (served until the afternoon closing) includes a walloping serving of French toast made with French bread prepared in a variety of ways. Apple cinnamon is especially good. Other favorites include the homemade muffins, pancakes, corned beef hash, and assorted omelettes. Homemade soups are featured for lunch, with a special every weekday. The beef stew and beer-battered fresh fish fry are popular. Pine-paneled and homey, the Chef's Hat is closed on Monday. Seating for around 60 persons includes 9 stools at the counter. The building is not wheelchair-accessible, but folks with walkers seem to be able to manage the steps. Credit cards are not accepted.

Mezze Bistro & Bar $$
16 Water Street (Massachusetts Highway 43)
(413) 458-0123

Mezze's is a popular gathering spot at night, but it also is a great place to have dinner. An avowed "foodie," owner Nancy Thomas knows how to stock a bar and find a good chef. The menu is small, usually featuring a few select appetizers and six or seven entrees that change seasonally. Local produce picked the day it is to be cooked is used as much as possible. A signature dish of Chef James Tracy—and one that is usually on the menu year-round—is roasted scallops with cauliflower puree and roasted hen-in-the-woods mushrooms with a truffles vinaigrette. Tracy also prepares a unique dish using a heritage pig bred in nearby New York State that is cured in maple syrup, adding to the remarkable flavor and aroma. One of his most popular appetizers is a combination of spaghetti squash prepared with an apple-curry lobster broth on which is placed half a roasted lobster, cut lengthwise. Depending on the season, the dessert menu might offer a fig and Belletoile cheese tart with a port sauce, concord grape sorbet served with coconut macaroons, a lemon meringue filled with lemon curd and topped with raspberries and candied lemon, or a maple pot de crème.

In contrast to the slick design of Eleven at MASS MoCA, which Thomas also owns, Mezze is comfortably uncluttered with bare brick walls and mahogany chairs at cloth-covered tables on polished bare floors. Banquettes line the walls on the bar side. At first glance the bar appears sparsely stocked, but a closer look shows an eclectic array of brandies, cognacs, and specialty wines that change seasonally. Thomas sometimes likes to feature certain liquors, like an assortment of vodkas. Occasionally there is entertainment on weekends. A deck off the bar side is next to a rambling garden of wildflowers and ornamental plantings in front of the restaurant. Reservations for dinner are requested. Late-night drop-ins can take their chances but might find the place quite crowded after a show at the theater or other major event. Mezze is open every day.

Pappa Charlie's Deli $
28 Spring Street
(413) 458-5969

If you aren't familiar with the sandwich board at Pappa Charlie's, allow an extra 10 minutes or so to study the list. It wasn't long after the place opened in 1976 that a tradition was born: Stars appearing at the Williamstown Theatre Festival were asked to concoct a sandwich that would bear their name. Today, there are 57 hot or cold sandwiches bearing the names of such headliners as Blythe Danner (tuna, sprouts, tomatoes, Swiss cheese, avocado, mayo on whole wheat), Gene Shalit (hot corned beef, melted Swiss, and sauerkraut), and Joanne Woodward (peanut butter, jam, raisins, bananas on whole wheat). Other creations are by Maria Tucci, Mary Tyler Moore, Richard Chamberlain, Bo Derek, Gwyneth Paltrow, Christopher Reeve, Gilda Radner, Bebe Rebozo, and on and on! Aside from sandwiches, the deli serves homemade soups, chili, potato knishes, and a variety of salads. For breakfast you can choose from eight kinds of bagels with all sorts of toppings, omelettes, or a breakfast sandwich of bacon, egg, and cheese on a bagel. Frozen yogurt, ice cream, milk shakes, floats, and pie and cookies round out the menu. The theater theme is carried out with posters and photos of stars on the walls. Customers who know what they are doing can call ahead and pick up their orders to go or eat on the premises at a counter or in one of the booths. Pappa Charlie's is open all day, every day. No credit cards accepted.

The Purple Pub $
8 Bank Street
(413) 458-3306

The Purple Pub is a favorite hangout for college students and returning locals, who get together for beer, a little comfort food, and a mother figure in the form of Mary Michel, who has ruled the roost since 1973. The place is small, considering the customer base, and only has a few tables and booths to augment the bar stools. The walls and beams are covered with license plates from all over the world, sent by fans or donated by students leaving the area. (The owners have learned not to question ownership.) The full bar is secondary to the assortment of beers available at six antique taps or by the bottle. In summer, when the student population vanishes, young people from the Williamstown Theatre Festival pick up the slack. In addition, townies and tourists alike have found the Pub a good place to get a reasonably priced home-cooked lunch or supper with some chit-chat with Mary or one of the other regulars thrown in.

Don't let the disposable tableware fool you. The food is good. Burgers, sandwiches, wraps, chili, soup, and daily and seasonal specials are offered, depending on the whim of the cook who likes to experiment. In nice weather, you can sit out on the patio at tables with umbrellas. The nightlife is as varied as the menu but often focuses on the sport of the season, which can be viewed on one of several television sets. After years of chasing students who wrote bad checks, the Pub happily takes credit cards, which are now common currency among college kids. It also is handily located near an ATM. By the way, purple is the official Williams College color, hence the name. Located just off Spring Street, the pub is open every day.

Spice Root **$$**
23 Spring Street
(413) 458-5200
www.fineindiandining.com

Spice Root is the sister restaurant of the Bombay Bar and Grill in Lee. The sunny interior proved such a hit that the owners decided to redecorate the older Lee restaurant in the same colors. And the brightly decorated pottery, admired by many a diner, is now being sold—and at quite reasonable prices! The menu is similar to the Bombay Grill but focuses more on modern adaptations of country recipes. Breads include a really yummy fruit-and-nut nan filled with paneer cheese. Entrees include traditional curries and tandoori specialties; fish, chicken, or lamb grilled, roasted, or sautéed with an assortment of vegetables and herbs in a variety of sauces, plus a wide range of vegetarian dishes. Dishes from cosmopolitan Bombay include Manchurian dumplings, hakka noodles, and fried rice with a ginger soy kick.

For a dining adventure, especially nice for large groups, throw yourself on the mercy of the management and let them just bring it on. The Sunday brunch offers a chance to sample various dishes. Lunches include the popular kathi rolls, Indian-style wraps filled with cheese, meat, or fish sautéed with onions, peppers, and cabbage. The restaurant makes up a variety of lunch boxes to go. The full bar includes an international selection of wine and beer. Open for lunch and dinner daily.

Taconic Restaurant **$$**
1161 Cold Spring Road (US 7/MA 2)
(413) 458-9499
www.taconicrestaurant.com

The Taconic has been at the juncture of US 7 and MA 2 in south Williamstown for more than 60 years. When it first opened, the highways were a lot narrower and the Taconic was a lot smaller. Now a landmark at this major intersection, the Taconic has a dining room that can seat around 125 persons, a lounge that holds about 60, and a banquet facility capable of seating 250. Popular for wedding receptions, meetings, and large parties as well as intimate dinners by candlelight, the Taconic has a varied menu with lots of choices prepared by executive chef Jimmy Guiden who with his wife, Deborah, has owned the restaurant since 1998. A lounge with a full bar offers a pleasant place to wait for a table, but reservations are suggested. Appetizers of interest include smoked trout with a horseradish sauce and capers and crab cakes with a basil aoli. Popular entrees among the regulars are the steak au poivre flamed at tableside; veal Oscar with a scrumptious crabmeat sauce, chicken Vermont, a house specialty prepared with Vermont cheddar, apples, and maple syrup; and grilled mahi-mahi. Children's portions are available. An 18 percent gratuity is added for parties of eight or more.

The couple's Web site includes a reminder service for important occasions and offers online specials. A newsletter with recipes also is available. The building is wheelchair-accessible, but one section of the dining room is down a few steps, something to keep in mind when making a reservation. The lower level has a fireplace, pleasant for winter dining. Except for Christmas Eve, the Taconic is open every evening year-round for dinner. On Sunday the restaurant opens at noon.

Thai Garden **$$**
27 Spring Street
(413) 458-0004

Open for lunch and dinner every day, Thai Garden prepares authentic cuisine promptly and attractively. One of several owned by the management, Thai Garden has already earned mention in Zagat's. The restaurant has two sections, each capable of seating around 30 persons, and is popular with large groups, which the staff seems to be able to serve as fast as it does a table for two.

The menu features a huge range of dishes from appetizers to traditional desserts. Soups, salads, rice and noodle dishes, vegetarian and seafood dishes, and house specialties with a variety of seasonings and sauces are offered. Curries are served in small ceramic pots kept warm over candles. Kob Kunh recommends a green curry for seafood and says red curry goes with just about anything. The Thai Melon Curry with shrimp is especially tasty. Mixed with the coconut milk sauce are winter melon, pumpkin, green and yellow squash, and bell peppers. Customers seem to favor Pad Thai—the famous dish of rice noodles stir-fried with chicken, shrimp, or vegetables, bean sprouts, Thai turnips, scallions, and egg topped with crushed peanuts. Duck is prepared in a number of ways, including the popular Bangkok duck, where the roasted bird is sliced and deboned and topped with a ginger sauce. Steamed salmon filet topped with ginger, scallions, and mushrooms in a ginger sauce is another favorite. Beverages include imported and domestic beers, Thai iced coffee or tea, and house wines. If there's room for dessert, try the ginger or coconut ice cream, Thai custard, or fried banana and honey. Yum! There is a minimum charge of $12 for credit cards.

Water Street Grill & Tavern **$**
123 Water Street (MA 43)
(413) 458-2175

The tavern side of the Water Street Grill is one of the few places you can get something to eat late at night in Williamstown, sometimes with entertainment thrown in. With its mahogany bar and indoor waterfall, the tavern is a casual place to enjoy seafood, ribs, steaks, and burgers. The Grill features fresh seafood, steaks, ribs, and fajitas in a cozy dining room with a fireplace. There is live acoustic music on Friday and Saturday nights in the tavern. Lunch and dinner are served daily, and a lunch buffet is served Monday through Friday.

Some restaurants have seasonal liquor licenses, which means they may not serve beer or wine at certain times of the year. However, you may be able to bring your own.

The Williams Inn **$$**
On-the-Green
(413) 458-9371, (800) 828-0133
www.williamsinn.com

With 125 rooms, the Williams Inn is often booked with folks attending events or conferences at Williams College, so the dining room is often crowded, making reservations a must. Meals are served from 7:00 A.M. to 9:30 P.M., 10:00 P.M. on weekends, and may be taken in the large dining room, which has a fireplace, or on the terrace. Dress is casual, and there is a children's menu. The grown-ups' menu includes continental cuisine as well as classic New England dishes. Aside from the usual breakfast offerings, one may order eggs Idaho (potato shells topped with grilled ham and two poached eggs), the Cold River (smoked salmon and dill omelette), or the Nordsman (English muffins topped with shaved ham and turkey, scrambled eggs, cheddar cheese, bacon, and scallions).

The Williams is popular among locals as a nice place to treat a friend to lunch.

Along with clam chowder and chicken potpie, the menu offers some interesting dishes like lobster frittata (lobster, asparagus, scallions, garlic, onion, tomato, and angel hair pasta mixed with egg and baked with cheese) or salmon semiramis (salmon filet dipped in egg, Parmesan cheese, and capers sautéed with saffron and served with tomato horseradish sauce). Favorites on the dinner menu include the liver and onions tart, Yankee pot roast, and Shaker chicken with apple rings. A 15 percent gratuity is charged for parties over six. On Sunday a lavish brunch is served from 11:30 A.M. to 2:30 P.M. The charge is $20 per person, and reservations are strongly recommended. For those in the breakfast mode, there are such cooked-to-order items as Belgian waffles, raspberry blintzes, choose-your-filling omelettes, an assortment of meats, plus lots of fresh-baked breads, muffins, rolls, and bagels. On the lunch side, the tables are laden with seafood and all sorts of roasts, salads, soups, vegetables, and of course, desserts. Self-control is difficult. A late-night menu including desserts is available in the adjoining tavern, where there is entertainment on weekends.

Yasmin's **$$$**
The Orchards Hotel
222 Adams Road
(413) 458–9611, (800) 225–1517
www.orchardshotel.com

As one would expect, Yasmin's reflects the high standards of the award-winning Orchards Hotel. Breakfast, lunch, and dinner are elegantly served in the dining room or, in season, in the courtyard. Tables are beautifully set with gleaming crystal, fresh flowers, and imported china, and the staff is professionally trained. The menu varies depending on the chefs who are brought from Europe on an 18-month rotation, resulting in New England cuisine with a continental touch.

A recent dinner menu featured foie gras mille-feuille on an herbed garden salad and potato-salmon roll with caviar and asparagus salad among the appetizers. Entrees included quails stuffed with sweet potatoes and cashews with mango-chili chutney, roasted sea bass on an apple-spinach risotto with 12-year-old balsamico, and mustard-crusted rack of lamb with roasted vegetables and a mushroom-stuffed potato. For lunch, soup and one of the interesting salads might be sufficient. If not, there are several sandwiches and entrees, including the pasta du jour, pineapple crab cakes with mango-chili chutney, or skewered beef tenderloin and shrimp with bell pepper cream. Luscious pastries, sorbets, and chef's specialties are available and may be enjoyed upstairs in what has been compared with the drawing room of an English country home. Breakfast or brunch offers old standbys like eggs Benedict and Belgian waffles, along with assorted fruits, warm breads and pastries, and eggs prepared with a variety of meats or seafood.

The Orchards' wine list is reputed to be one of the best in the state, offering renowned wines from Australia, Austria, California, Chile, and Germany. Hotelier Sayed Saleh has a private collection stored in a subterranean climate-controlled cellar that he will happily share by appointment in a private tasting room. Stored on the racks are wines by such fabled vineyards as Chateaux Latour (1955 through 1971), Chateaux Mouton Rothschild (1961 through 1992), Chateaux Lafite Rothschild (1947 through 1978) and others. Connoisseurs may arrange to have either a brief sample before dining or spend an evening exploring the collection.

FARMS AND GARDENS

While the cultural events in the area are much ballyhooed—and with good reason—agriculture and horticulture are important components of life in the Berkshires. Although farming has declined here as it has nationally, there still are many small working farms in the county. As pressure mounts to sell their land, many families have branched out into tourist-based activities to supplement their incomes. Pancake breakfasts, petting zoos, and pumpkin-picking bring folks to farms they might otherwise ignore, bringing in extra dollars. Others are finding a niche in raising organic produce, livestock, and dairy products. Their customers include chefs and others who value the taste and purity of unadulterated, chemical-free food.

Another agricultural endeavor undertaken by many owners of large acreage is the raising and selling of Christmas trees. Granted, it's not for everyone, but there is something special about tromping through the snow, picking out your very own tree, either cutting it yourself or letting the grower cut it, and hauling it home on the roof of your rig. Kids enjoy this outing, especially if it is followed by a cup of hot chocolate. These growers often advertise in local papers or simply put signs out when the time comes. Some growers specialize in flowers, supplying florists or selling their own bedding plants and cut flowers. Many beautiful public gardens can be found around the county. The ones included in this chapter are noted for their expertise and historic importance. Others can be found in the Attractions and Parks chapters.

Bartlett's Orchard
575 Swamp Road, Richmond
(413) 698-2559
www.Bartlettsorchard.com

On entering Bartlett's market, you can't help but notice the large painting on the wall of the fruit that has sustained this hardworking family since 1947. Back then, Francis and Betty Bartlett and his parents, A. J. and Sophie, started their orchard on 52 acres. Today the fourth generation is involved in tending, packing, and shipping 17 varieties of apples. The family also runs the market, which is a small part of the football field-size complex where the apples are stored. The orchard on Lenox Mountain—such a treat in the springtime when the trees are filled with pink and white blossoms—yields an average crop of 20,000 bushels a year. By the time fall comes, apples are stacked everywhere. Rows of weathered boxes wait for their contents to be stored in the Crisp-Aire cooler behind the big oak door in the back of the store. Shelves are stacked with white shopping bags filled to the brim with apples. And then there's the cider—and the doughnuts, muffins, and other treats to go with the cider. The family sells mixes for their baked goods along with their own jams, jellies, and condiments, maple products from Vermont, honey, and fudge. The Bartletts, being pretty hip folks, also sell gourmet coffee, hot sauces, chips, vinegars and oils, cheeses, and other specialty food items. On their Web site you can order gift packs that combine apples with jams, syrup, cheese, or other products plus a special breakfast assortment that includes pancake mix, coffee beans, and syrup. The

CLOSE-UP

The Goodness of Local Produce

Berkshire Grown is a collaborative of producers, consumers, and other supporters of the regional agriculture and food industry. This nonprofit organization works with participating farms to better market their products while preserving open land and the rural lifestyle. The collaborative grew out of a similar organization that was started in Boston by chefs wanting to give their customers quality food while supporting local agriculture. In Berkshire County more than 65 farms dedicated to raising organic produce, livestock, and dairy products belong to Berkshire Grown. Many sell the fruits of their labors at farmers' markets and at participating stores that display the organization's logo. They also supply restaurants and inns dedicated to serving these local products, which also display the logo.

Berkshire Grown also sponsors several events throughout the year designed to make the public more aware of the importance of supporting local farms and the restaurants that use their products. In early spring many top-of-the-line restaurants offer special meals at a discount, often introducing locals as well as tourists to their menus for the first time. In fall the area's top chefs prepare a Harvest Dinner from typical fall crops; tickets are sold. The collaborative also includes some cooperative farms, where members buy shares of the farm's crops in spring and harvest them as they are ready. Without such support, most farmers could not afford to grow their organic vegetables or maintain organically fed herds. Berkshire Grown's Web site lists participating farms as well as member restaurants and activities it sponsors through the year. The group also publishes a brochure with a map showing the locations of all participating members. Write to Berkshire Grown at P.O. Box 983, Great Barrington, MA 01230 for more information. Call (413) 528-0041 or visit www.berkshiregrown.org.

store is open daily year-round. The orchard is open for picking by the public Labor Day to Columbus Day.

Berkshire Botanical Garden
At the corner of Massachusetts Highways 102 and 183, Stockbridge
(413) 298-3926
www.berkshirebotanical.org

Of all the beautiful gardens at the Berkshire Botanical Garden, the Herb Garden is perhaps the best known. It was one of the first gardens to be planted when what was then called the Berkshire Garden Center opened in 1934. The center grew from an idea posed by the Lenox Garden Club. A coalition of local gardening enthusiasts, horticulturists, and others got together and organized the center as a place people could visit to see, study, and receive advice on growing regional flowers and plants. With little funds to start the center, commercial growers were asked to donate seeds, which were started in the greenhouses of Bellefontaine, a former estate that is now Canyon Ranch. Two commercial nurseries donated roses, and the New York Botanic Garden gave day lilies to get the place off the ground.

The Herb Garden was the special project of Mrs. Edward F. Belches, a major supporter who was well versed in culinary herbs. A terraced slope was constructed and planted with about 90 herbs, including those used for medicinal purposes. For the homeowner with a small yard, Mrs. Belches designed a small plot planted with a basic assortment of 10 useful herbs. Mints and scented geraniums completed the variety. An old garage was turned into the Herb House, where reference and cookbooks were available and demonstrations on herb drying and other techniques held. Herbal tea was prepared in a small kitchen and is still served there. The Herb House also is still used for workshops and demonstrations. The garden also has been featured in magazines and used as an illustration in herb books and seed catalogs. In the 1980s and 1990s, the stonework in the garden was restored and the garden redesigned and replanted in keeping with its original purpose. A bee garden, lemon garden, and all-season color garden were added. The Herb Garden continues to be one of the biggest draws at the Botanical Garden. It is tended by associates, and the organic herb products are sold at the gift shop. During its history, the center has exhibited and won prizes at flower shows in Boston and New York. For the New York International Flower Show's golden anniversary, the centerpiece of the display was a rustic building built of weathered barn doors and shingles from an old pump house on the Housatonic. For a while this country shed became the signature of the center's exhibits. Occasionally, vegetables have been the focus—especially during World War II, when Victory Gardens were featured, and in the 1970s, when there was renewed interest in homegrown vegetables. At that time, the solar greenhouse was constructed to demonstrate how to grow beautiful vegetables in cold weather. Grass trials have been conducted with the University of Massachusetts.

In the 1980s the grounds were made wheelchair-accessible and programs developed for designing barrier-free gardens. A program in horticultural therapy also was developed. It was not until 1981 that the garden finally had to charge admission to cover costs that had previously been supported by memberships. Courses, workshops, lectures, and special events are held throughout the year to support the educational programs the garden runs. Annually, local artists exhibit sculpture throughout the grounds. Aside from the Herb Garden, the garden offers intimate landscapes with annual and perennial gardens, ornamental vegetables, pond and rock gardens, a rose garden, groves of trees and shrubs, and a woodland preserve with an interpretive trail. The greenhouses include displays of tropical plants and succulents. In all, about 2,500 varieties of plants are represented. The gardens are open daily May through October. The greenhouses and administrative offices are open year-round.

---

i

If native wildflowers are your interest, local authors Phyllis Pryzby and Joseph G. Strauch have written handy paperback books on the subject. The books are sold in bookstores and sporting goods shops around the county.

Chenail's Produce Market
481 Luce Road, Williamstown
(413) 458-4910

Winthrop Chenail's grandfather started this 550-acre farm in 1913. Today the family harvests corn, tomatoes, cucumbers, pumpkins, and whatever else they can manage. Some say Chenail corn is the best in the area. At one time the family kept 100 cows, but they no longer have a dairy herd. Instead they are breeding heifers and sell hay and silage. Cousin Dick Chenail and his family operate Chenail's Farm Fresh Products on U.S. Highway 7 just north of town (413-458-4737) where they sell plants, flowers, fruit, vegetables, holiday and lawn decorations, and outdoor furniture.

Green River Farms
2480 Green River Road (Massachusetts Highway 43), Williamstown
(413) 458-2470
www.greenriverfarms.com

The Green River runs through this 300-acre farm in the valley on MA 43 in south Williamstown, hence the name. About 75 acres are tilled for vegetables, which are sold to area restaurants and to Williams College. The farm runs along a broad hillside that abuts US 7, looking east toward Mount Greylock, where an orchard, vegetables, and other crops are planted. The scene is a favorite with photographers and artists, who pull off the highway to capture the view. The farm is owned by former real estate developer Harry Patten and has been placed in the state's Agricultural Preservation Restriction program, which protects it as farmland forever. Livestock is also raised here. Seasonal plants and holiday decorations are sold from the greenhouse. Free-range, all-natural meats and poultry are available in a farm store run by Mazzeo's Meat Center, a Pittsfield-based gourmet meat supplier that also sells through Guido's specialty markets in Pittsfield and Great Barrington.

Hancock Shaker Village
U.S. Highway 20 at the junction of Massachusetts Highway 41
P.O. Box 927
Pittsfield 01202
(413) 443-0188
www.hancockshakervillage.org

The gardens, orchards, and farm at Hancock Shaker Village continue the agricultural and horticultural traditions begun by the Shaker sect in the 19th century. The Shakers were well known for their 19th- and early-20th-century medicinal herb and garden seed industries. Communities devoted many acres to herb cultivation and raising produce for seed. They processed herbs and prepared tonics, tablets, and other medicinal preparations for sale to the "World" and are credited with inventing seed packets, which they sold to farmers and gardeners. The village's demonstration herb garden contains around 90 of the more than 300 varieties of plants listed by the Shakers in the 1873 *Druggists' Handbook of Pure Botanic Preparations,* including hollyhocks, belladonna, asparagus, hops, native ginger, chicory, dandelions, wormseed, black cohosh, basil, poppies, horseradish, and pennyroyal. Staff also maintain two heirloom vegetable gardens that contain plant varieties dating back to the 1830s, some quite rare. The 1843 *Shaker Gardeners' Manual* is still used as a source for cultivation techniques, including what is now called organic gardening. Seeds are saved and shared with others interested in preserving heirloom vegetables. The Shakers' interest in agricultural experimentation and technology made their farms models of efficiency and innovation. Their yields were bountiful, supplying their communities and providing a source of income. Dairy herds were maintained by the Hancock Shakers well into the 20th century. The ingenious round stone barn they built could hold more than 50 cows and is a marvel of efficiency. In cooperation with the New England Heritage Breeds Conservancy, the village raises several historic breeds of livestock once found on the Shaker farm, including shorthorn cattle, Merino sheep, and Silver-laced Wyandotte and Dominique chickens. Oxen and historic equipment are used to work the farm and gardens. Special events that focus on farm life at the village are held throughout the year. The complex is open daily from Memorial Day weekend through late October, and visitors may wander through the various buildings on their own if they

desire. Through winter and early spring, guided tours through selected buildings and galleries are offered. Call for tour times. A gift shop and seasonal cafe are on the premises. There is an admission charge except for children.

High Lawn Farm
535 Summer Street, Lee
(413) 243-0672
www.highlawn-farm.com
In 2000 Highlawn Farm celebrated 100 years of continuous ownership and operation by one extended family. The Jersey dairy herd dates to at least 1918, with official production records continuous from 1923. The lineage of certain families in the current herd can be traced back 15 generations. High Lawn milk products, processed at the farm, are delivered twice a week to more than 1,000 residential customers, 100 restaurants, and 35 stores. The farm is off US 7, and tours can be arranged by appointment.

Holiday Farm
Holiday Cottage Road, Dalton
(413) 684-0444
www.holidayfarm.com
Located off Massachusetts Highway 9 east of Dalton, Holiday Farm is operated by Dickens Crane, who chose stewardship of the land over being involved with the family's paper mill. The farm offers weekly mountain bike races, educational programs for all ages, and a community garden where members share in the work and the organic produce. Diversified products include maple syrup and pumpkins. A cottage on the property can be rented.

Ioka Valley Farm
Massachusetts Highway 43, Hancock
(413) 738-5915
www.taconic.net/IokaValleyFarm
The Leab family has been running Ioka Valley Farm since 1936, when Robert and Dorothy Leab drove 13 head of cattle over Brodie Mountain from Lanesborough and settled in Hancock. Named from an Indian word meaning "beautiful," the farm prospered through the family's hard work and Robert's use of scientific advances in farming. Their son, Don, his wife, Judy, and their three children are now working the farm, continuing the traditions of soil conservation and innovation. As dairying became less profitable, the family sold their herd and diversified into producing strawberries, pumpkins, Christmas trees, maple syrup, and forage for horses and cattle. They have converted one barn, called Calf-A, into a restaurant of sorts where in sugaring season the family serves up pancakes, French toast, and waffles with their own syrup. In fall families are welcome to pick their own pumpkins and Indian corn and enjoy hayrides, making their way through the spooky hay tunnel or making soft-sculpture scarecrows. Children are encouraged to feed, pet, and view the farm animals in Uncle Don's Barnyard, play with the work machines in the sand box, and "milk" Molly, the mechanical cow. At Christmas, trees and decorations are for sale.

In an interesting bit of cross-merchandising, the Bookloft in Great Barrington holds an annual "Independent Bookstores Support Independent Farms" week in August featuring books on sustainable agriculture, farming, using seasonal foods, and related topics along with special events.

Lakeview Orchard
94 Old Cheshire Road, Lanesborough
(413) 448-6009
David and Judy Jurczak started planting apple trees in 1996, shortly after they bought what had been open pasture on this back road to Cheshire. Four years later they picked their first harvest. Today they have around 4,000 apple trees that yield 21 different varieties. They also have around 300 cherry trees (sweet and tart), some 200 peach trees, and another 500 of various other fruits, including apricots,

pears, and plums. Folks can begin picking fruit in spring when the sweet cherries are in, followed by raspberries and then a continuous bounty right through fall. Aside from the "you-pick" part of their business, they run a brisk business in their farm stand, where they sell seasonal produce and where a bevy of cooks bake pies, doughnuts, turnovers, and other goodies from scratch. They also sell their own cider, jams, jellies, and pickles plus honey and syrup from neighboring farms and Cabot cheddar cheese from Vermont. Aside from selling retail, the couple supply several area shops. The stand is open Friday only in May and June. Beginning in July they are open every day until the day before Thanksgiving, when they take a rest—before going out to start their winter pruning. Old Cheshire Road is off Summer Street, which runs between US 7 and Massachusetts Highway 8.

---

i ***Root Orchards on MA 183 in Great Barrington runs a native plant project, selling all kinds of native perennials, ground covers, ferns, vines, and shrubs.***

Moon in the Pond Organic Farm
816 Barnum Street, Sheffield
(413) 229-3092

Dominic Palumbo's love of cooking has led him to become one of the area's leading sources of organically raised heritage-breed livestock. Sometime in the 1980s he began to think about where the food he was cooking and eating was coming from and what was being done to it. So in 1990, utilizing a background in horticulture, he founded his farm, starting out with chemical-free vegetables. Around the same time he started learning about the movement to preserve the dwindling breeds of livestock that once had been the mainstay of America's diet. Soon he added a small flock of laying hens. Today he has around 20 Scottish Highland cattle, 20 or so Dorset sheep, 3 Large Black pigs, Narragansett turkeys, and Pilgrim geese along with pigeons (which appear on menus as squab). These descendants of livestock brought here in the 18th and 19th centuries have quite different textures and much better flavor than the mass-produced meats sold over the counter, breeders like Palumbo assert. In the early days of this resurgence, gentlemen farmers maintained the breeds, since there was little demand in the marketplace for them. But as awareness has grown—and as chefs increasingly want to use heritage breeds in their restaurants—the demand is rising. And that is a good thing, says Palumbo. These breeds were intended to provide food, and as more are slaughtered more can be raised, keeping the breed strong. Aside from supplying restaurants, he sells retail at his farm by appointment. He is also happy to give tours, also by appointment. Barnum Street is off Salisbury Road, which can be reached by taking Berkshire School Road off US 7.

The Mount
3 Plunkett Street, Lenox
(413) 637-1899
www.edithwharton.org

Gardening was one of writer Edith Wharton's passions, and when she built her dream house in Lenox in 1902, the gardens were one of her top priorities. An authority on European landscape design, Wharton, who wrote many books on gardens and architecture, divided her gardens into sections like the rooms in a house. She created a walled Italian garden with a rustic rock pile fountain and installed a French flower garden filled with petunias, phlox, snapdragons, stocks, penstemon, and hollyhocks, which she described as "an oriental carpet floating in the sun . . ." A dolphin-head fountain graced the garden with other architectural elements. Grass steps led down through her rock garden, a most unusual design for the area.

In all, Wharton had three acres of gardens filled with thousands of perennials,

shrubs, and native ferns she collected herself. The 42-room mansion, its terraces, and formal gardens were a great joy to her. She entertained, gardened, wrote, and generally enjoyed life at what she called her first real home. Sadly, Wharton was unable to spend all her days there as she had hoped. Her husband became ill, and she left the palatial mansion, which was eventually sold. As the burden of keeping up the colossal "cottages" in the Berkshires began to wear on the wealthy who owned them, they fell into disrepair, the Mount and its magnificent gardens among them.

A concerted effort to save the estate began in 1980, when the nonprofit group Edith Wharton Restoration Inc. was created. Now, nearly $9 million later, the mansion has been restored, and work on the interior is ongoing. The overgrown gardens, including the dolphin-head fountain and other features, have been 90 percent restored at a cost of $2 million. The Mount is in the process of raising an endowment to replant and maintain thousands of perennials in Wharton's French garden. A National Historic Landmark, the Mount is open daily from May to October by admission. Visitors may wander through the gardens and decorated rooms or enjoy lunch on the terrace where Wharton entertained her friends. A bookstore is stocked with works by Wharton, including rare and out-of-print editions as well as books by others on literature, architecture, interior design, and of course gardening.

Otis Poultry Farm
1570 North Main Road (MA 8), Otis
(413) 269-4438, (800) 286-2690
www.otispoultry.com

Steven and Andy Pyenson are the third generation to run the Otis Poultry Farm, started by their grandparents in 1904. They use no pesticides or herbicides, raise free-range chickens, and proclaim they are "The Home of the Custom Laid Egg." Their tasty chicken and turkey potpies—with or without peas and carrots—are sold at the farm and at stores around the county and can be ordered in frozen packs over the Internet. They also bake and sell their own pies, "corn" rye bread, and challah and package their own candy, including homemade fudge. They also carry sugar-free fudge, candy, cookies, and pies. Wine, gourmet foods, local cheeses and spreads, maple products, and gifts also are sold at the store, which is open daily. And in the spirit of waste not—want not, they sell "Chicken Gickem," a terrific compost for your garden.

---

i

The Trustees of Reservations, based in Stockbridge, maintain a number of beautiful gardens around the county, including magnificent ones at the Naumkeag estate. If you're planning to visit many gardens, become a member and save money.

Rawson Brook Farm
New Marlborough Road, Monterey
(413) 528-2138

Owner Susan Sellew started selling her Monterey Chèvre in 1983 and now markets about 450 pounds of goat cheese each week. She has won several first-place awards in the herbed fresh goat cheese categories at American Cheese Society competitions. In 1992 Monterey Chèvre with chives and garlic won "Best Fresh Goat Cheese" at a national competition held by the National Dairy Goat Association Product Committee. Her customers include Zabar's in New York, Grill 23 in Boston, a large number of Bread and Circus/Whole Foods markets in Massachusetts, plus a number of local restaurants and specialty food stores. The cheese also can be bought at the farm, which is off Massachusetts Highway 23 and is open year-round.

Taft Farms
119 Park Square (corner of MA 183 and Division Street), Great Barrington
(413) 528-3161, (800) 528-1015
www.taftfarms.com

CLOSE-UP

Farmers' Markets

- **Berkshire Area Farmers' Market** is located in Pittsfield in the Allendale Shopping Center on MA 8. It is open on Wednesday and Saturday mornings from early May to the end of October. Fruits and vegetables, baked goods, honey and maple syrup, bedding and vegetable plants, perennials, and shrubs are sold.
- **Great Barrington Farmers' Market** sets up in the parking lot at the historic railroad station at the corner of Castle Street and Taconic Avenue behind the Town Hall on Saturday morning from early May to the end of October. Products include organic and conventional vegetables, cut flowers, fruit, dairy products, bread, pasta, soups, prepared foods, bedding plants, container gardens, and soaps. Special events include a Spring Greens Fest, Strawberry Shortcake Extravaganza, and tastings.
- **Lee Farmers' Market** is held at the gazebo in River Park opposite the post office on Saturday morning from early May through October.
- **North Adams Farmers' Market** is open on Saturday morning from mid-July through late September and is located in the municipal parking lot across from MASS MoCA.
- **Sheffield Farmers' Market** is open on Friday afternoon from Mother's Day to early October. It is located at the Old Parish Church on US 7 in downtown Sheffield. Products for sale include produce, baked goods, pasta, cut flowers, perennials, soap, honey, maple syrup, and bedding plants. Special events include craft fairs, a children's day, and an apple squeeze.
- **Williamstown Farmers' Market** is located at the south end of Spring Street on Saturday morning from Memorial Day through October.

The Taft family has been farming in Great Barrington since 1945 and has established a reputation for fine plants, produce, meats, and, more recently, upscale takeout made on the premises from all natural ingredients. Dan and Martha Taft reared three children on the farm, and their grandchildren are now part of the workforce. Beginning right after the end of December, when the Christmas trees, wreaths, and other decorations grown and assembled at the farm are all gone, the seeds are started for the flowers and plants that will take over the place in spring. From spring on, the store blossoms with planted containers, hanging baskets, and flats of flowers and vegetable plants, more than 75 percent of which have been grown on-site. As the season progresses, vegetables from the farm will fill the bins, replacing the squash and root vegetables sold through winter. Soon seasonal fruits will join the largesse. The family supplies many local restaurants and also freezes fruits and vegetables to use in the soups, entrees, and pastries sold daily at the store for takeout or eating in.

Martha Taft has been making and selling family favorites for years, but recently a new cook joined the kitchen—a gourmet chef who along the way sang backup for Little Anthony and the Imperials and who

taught John Travolta how to dance for *Saturday Night Fever.* Now entrees include Asian sautées, balsamic chicken (free-range from the farm, of course), chili chicken tamale pie, mushroom and barley soup, pizza (crust made with Taft grown and milled whole wheat), and other goodies. The bakery sells pies, cookies, scones, cakes, and breads baked with Taft grains. And of course there are jellies and condiments for sale. The family even puts out a newspaper! There probably are people who have moved here just to be near Taft Farms.

i

When the zucchini glut hits, the Great Barrington Farmers' Market holds a "Zucchini Pandemonium" with recipes, games, and a "guess the weight" table.

Windy Hill Farm
US 7, Great Barrington
(413) 298-3217

Back in 1987, Judy and Dennis Mareb put in an apple orchard on part of 76 acres off US 7—and Windy Hill Farm was born. Soon they branched out into shade and specimen trees and added a garden shop and seasonal plants, growing by leaps and bounds. Today there are 25 employees, and Windy Hill is recognized as one of the foremost nurseries in the area, so much so that Martha Stewart featured it twice. A favorite place for landscapers, professional and otherwise, Windy Hill has plants and trees nobody else does. Their assortment of lilacs, hardy rose bushes, and other perennial shrubs is amazing. Dwarf, rare, and unusual conifers, including some of the more exotic weeping trees that have become popular, can be found here along with hard-to-find fruit and shade trees and a huge assortment of annuals and perennials. The garden and gift shop are fully stocked with tools, books, pots, and planters, and the employees are knowledgeable and helpful. Unusual garden furniture and decorative accessories are also around the grounds. The apple orchard is still there, bigger than ever, with varieties that start yielding fruit in July, if Mother Nature cooperates. The pick-your-own operation includes berries in season. Holiday decorations include gourds and pumpkins at Halloween and boxwood trees, quality ribbons, roping, trees, centerpieces, and wreathes at Christmas. Windy Hill is open April 1 through December 24, except for Easter, Memorial Day, and the Fourth of July.

NIGHTLIFE 

What to do at night? Well, if you discount the cultural events—and that's saying a lot—there is the popular music scene. Not so long ago, if you wanted to hear good jazz, world music, or other interesting stuff you had to head over the hill to the Iron Horse in Northampton. But now several clubs, bars, restaurants, lounges—whatever they call themselves—have live music ranging from amateurs to nationally known acts. A few offer entertainment all week long, including open-mic nights, but most bring in the bands on the weekend. Coffeehouses have been popping up, offering an alcohol-free alternative venue for live music. Local bands vary from really good to really bad. Some are cover bands, playing other people's music, while others play original work. Some local musicians have national reputations and often open for big acts when they come here. Musicians often play in lots of different groups, and the names change often to protect the innocent. Bluegrass, jazz, reggae, blues, folk, country western, rock—there is probably a group playing something somewhere every weekend. To find out who and where, you have to rely on listings in the local media (see that chapter) or fliers posted in likely places. The Web site www.iBerkshires.com runs a calendar of events. Smaller places that can't afford to advertise in the newspapers run ads in the *Yankee Shopper,* which is distributed free around the county. Most folks sort of shop around until they find their niche. The following list is by no means comprehensive but gives an assortment of places to consider.

SOUTH COUNTY

ARMI@GreatBarrington
485 Main Street, Great Barrington
(413) 528-3296
www.armi-at-greatbarrington.com

There's on-stage entertainment and dancing every night at Armi's. Monday is open-mic night, and Tuesday is usually dedicated to tapas (interesting appetizer-type nibbles) and tango. Acts run the gamut from classic rock to blues and everything in between. A full restaurant, Armi's serves lunch and dinner daily (see the Restaurants chapter). After the dinner hour, the tables are removed from the center of the small dining room, and the show goes on around 9:00 P.M. (Light fare is still available.) The owners are dedicated to giving local musicians a chance and often pair them with name bands or singers as a learning experience. The sound system is top-notch, and don't be surprised to see a Grammy winner at this hip gathering place. The colorful Web site lists all performances and the cover charge, if any. Armi's is located on the east side of U.S. Highway 7 across from the Massachusetts Highway 23 intersection south of town.

Castle Street Cafe
10 Castle Street, Great Barrington
(413) 528-5244
www.castlestreetcafe.com

Jazz is the main fare at Castle Street Cafe, although sometimes a local bluegrass or R&B group will take the stage. During July and August there's music every night except Tuesday, when the cafe is closed. Off-season, entertainment is offered on most weekends. There is never a cover charge. The groups set up on the bar side of this spacious restaurant, interestingly decorated with contemporary glass lighting from Fellerman & Raabe glass artists in Sheffield. Their work also is displayed as part of the decor in the other half of the place, which is for dining only. The food here is nicely prepared by owner-chef Michael Ballon and is available from a full menu, which is also served in the bar along with an abbreviated bar menu. The bar is stocked with a good assortment of ales and wines, and the tables and chairs are shoved aside to make room for dancing. Art and photos by local artists add to the eclectic decor.

Club Helsinki
284 Main Street, Great Barrington
(413) 528-3394
www.clubhelsinkiweb.com
The local music scene hasn't been the same since Deborah McDowell and Marc Shaffer opened Club Helsinki next to their restaurant of the same name a few years ago. Acts small and big, unknown and famous, have been brought to Great Barrington by this duo dedicated to booking "artists who improve the world through their music and who make our lives and our community a more vibrant place to be." Vibrant is right! The range of multicultural music available at Club Helsinki is incredible: zydeco, acoustic folk, punk mambo, bluegrass, Afro-reggae, Afro-Cuban, klezmer, an Appalachian string band—and on and on—with open-mic nights thrown in. The Tom Tom Club, Olu Dara, Guy Davis, Mose Allison, the Holmes Brothers, Burning Spear, Hamiet Bluiett, Soulive, the Blind Boys of Alabama, and John Scofield are among the musicians who have played the Helsinki—and more than once! Occasionally the Mahaiwe Theatre nearby has been booked for appearances by such big draws as Michelle Shocked, Richie Havens, and Doc Watson. The club itself, adjacent to the restaurant the couple runs, is small and reservations are a must, especially if you are planning to have dinner there instead of in the restaurant. There is usually a cover charge, which varies depending on the act. The Helsinki Web site lists all upcoming acts, with pictures and descriptions of the musicians.

Berkshire Blues Cafe
Massachusetts Highway 102, Lee
(413) 441-1257
Formerly a VFW hall, the Berkshire Blues Cafe has one of the largest dance floors around. Tables with seating for 200 persons surround the 30- by 30-foot area in front of the large stage. An outdoor porch can hold another 100 persons. Steaks, burgers, and other dishes are available. New owners Glenn Larson and Shelley Connors try to focus on bringing in blues bands from the region but other music is offered as well. The cafe is open Thursday, which is open-mic night, through Saturday. The cover charge varies.

Cranwell Resort
55 Lee Road (U.S. Highway 20), Lenox
(413) 637-1364
www.cranwell.com
Since 1994 The News in Revue has summered at Cranwell, offering timely satire nightly while guests relax in lounge chairs, sipping wine or having one of Cranwell's sumptuous desserts. The award-winning troupe uses the day's events for its material, and anyone or anything is fair game. "Between Iraq and a Hard Place," the title for one series, gives you an idea of what you are in for. The 90-minute show is performed cabaret-style, with wine, beer, coffee, and desserts available for purchase. Show patrons who have dinner at either 5:30 or 6:00 P.M. are entitled to preferred seating at the 8:30 P.M. show. The troupe is based in Connecticut, and tickets can be purchased before the season starts through its Web site: www.newsinrevue.com. A dinner/show combination price is available through Cranwell, which also handles dinner reservations. The show is performed every night in July and August except Wednesday.

Seven Hills Inn & Restaurant
40 Plunkett Street, Lenox
(413) 637-0060
"Music in the grand style of a salon setting" is how this summer concert series at Seven Hills is described. Vocal and instrumental soloists and groups with international reputations perform classical or popular music, including baroque, jazz, swing, opera, flamenco, and show tunes. Tickets are $20 for the concert alone or $55, including dinner. Other packages are available. The show itself, called Stockbridge Summer Music, has been offered at Seven Hills since 1985. It is managed by an outside company, which can be reached for information or reservations at (413) 443-1138 or on the Internet at www.baygo.com/ssms. Seven Hills is a mansion that is now an inn with romantic surroundings, including lush decor and terraced gardens. Concerts take place in July and August on Monday and Tuesday plus occasional other dates. This is one of the few places you might want to dress up for. Plunkett Street is off US 7, and Seven Hills is next to the Mount.

Although "dressing up" is warranted for some occasions, casual dress rules in the Berkshires. The exceptions are dinners, balls, or other special events and dining at the more elegant restaurants. Some folks dress for up for theater or classical concerts and parties, but just as many don't. Usually, you can't go wrong either way. No one will stare.

Zinc
56 Church Street, Lenox
(413) 637-8800
This upscale bistro has a separate bar in a glassed-in area where diners can enjoy music provided by the knowledgeable bartenders who bring in their own mix tapes and CDs. A popular gathering place for the 25- to 35-year-old crowd, Zinc's classic French bistro menu is available to those in the bar until 10:00 P.M., when the place turns casual. Open until 1:00 A.M., the bar seats around 20 persons; 35 to 40 can sit at tables that are quite close together. The decor is contemporary. Occasionally there is live entertainment.

Dreamaway Lodge
1432 County Road, Becket
(413) 623-8725
A former speakeasy, the Dreamaway Lodge is a grandly fanciful music club, bar, and restaurant in a remote corner of the Becket hills. Well worth the journey, this Berkshire treasure, once run by a family of Gypsies, is a favorite with locals and celebrities, including dancers from nearby Jacob's Pillow Dance Festival. A cheerfully weird and often crowded ramshackle roadhouse, the place is stuffed with kitsch—mismatched china, an orgone box, mementos of visits from Liberace and Bob Dylan, among unlikely others. It's all a very "Berkshires" combination of high art and low camp: The Boston Symphony meets Arlo Guthrie (a regular) meets John Waters. Hours are irregular, so call to find out what's happening and when. It's off Massachusetts Highway 8, but you might want to call for directions—some folks have never managed to find it.

Lion's Den
Red Lion Inn
30 Main Street, Stockbridge
(413) 298-5545
www.lionsdenpub.com
The Lion's Den provides entertainment nightly year-around from about 9:30 P.M. to 1:00 A.M. There is no cover charge. Music varies from folk to alternative and classic rock and everything in between. The Den is a cozy place for casual dining as well as late-night hanging out. It opens at noon summer through fall, 4:00 P.M. in winter and spring. Food, prepared by the Red Lion Inn's chefs and priced just high enough to keep out the riffraff, is served until 10:00 P.M. The menu features soups, salads, burgers, and a variety of interesting entrees and desserts plus daily home-style specials. The bar carries a number of

good beers, bottled and draft, a broad assortment of single-malt whiskies, award-winning wines, after-dinner drinks, and spiked coffees. Young people under age 21 are not welcome after 10:00 P.M. The Den is in the basement of the inn, seven steps down from street level.

CENTRAL BERKSHIRE

Club Red
17 Wendell Avenue Extension, Pittsfield
(413) 443-7900

Located off East Street in the basement of the Wendell House Apartments, formerly the Allen Hotel, Club Red is not your average bar. Entertainment is offered three nights a week, with a different theme each night. Thursday is retro dance party night, Friday is Latino night with salsa and similar music, and Saturday is alternative lifestyles night with dancing to a DJ. The owners of Club Red also run Zachary's, a restaurant located on the right as you enter the basement. Zachary's has a cocktail lounge where music videos or other entertainment is featured on Wednesday night. The lounge is open every night except Monday and Tuesday and bar snacks are available. Club Red is open Thursday through Saturday year-round; the cover charge ranges from $3.00 to $5.00.

Common Grounds Coffeehouse
First United Methodist Church
55 Fenn Street, Pittsfield
(413) 499-0866

On the first Friday of the month, the church's dining room is turned into a coffeehouse and various folk artists come to perform. The transformation includes special lighting and cloth-covered tables with candles. Coffee, teas, and other nonalcoholic beverages and special desserts are sold. Doors open an hour before the show, usually at 7:00 P.M. Ticket prices vary depending on the performer. Children pay less.

GEAA
303 Crane Avenue, Pittsfield
(413) 442-3585

The GEAA (General Electric Athletic Association) is a popular hangout for singles. A

CLOSE-UP 

Coalition Alternatives

Although most places in the county are fairly liberal, Club Red is just about the only nightspot that offers regularly scheduled events specifically for gays. To find out what else is happening in the gay and lesbian world, call the Berkshire Stonewall Community Coalition (BSCC) at (413) 243-8484 or check out their Web site at www.berkshirestonewall.org. The coalition holds a three-day festival each year and sponsors other activities. BSCC is a nonprofit organization that represents the gay, lesbian, bisexual, and transgendered community. Members include representatives or interested individuals from several local organizations, including WildWomenSports; Parents, Families and Friends of Lesbians and Gays (PFLAG); B-Glad at the Massachusetts College of Liberal Arts in North Adams; Simon's Rock College; the Berkshire Community College Committee on Diversity; and the Williams College MultiCultural Center in Williamstown.

The legal drinking age in Massachusetts is 21. Until recently, stores were not allowed to sell alcoholic beverages on Sunday. The legislature has changed that and store owners who obtain permits from their local officials may, if they choose, sell alcoholic beverages on Sunday, but only after 12 noon.

holdover from the days when GE was the biggest employer in town, the GEAA is now privately owned, but the name has lived on. Various local bands play, mostly on weekends. The place has a large dance floor, offers the usual bar fare, and allows smoking. Adjacent to an 18-hole golf course, the GEAA also is a handy watering hole for golfers.

La Cocina
140 Wahconah Street, Pittsfield
(413) 499-6363
www.lacocina.net

A favorite nightspot for years, La Cocina was beginning to show its age until Mark Massana bought it and refurbished the dining room downstairs and the pub upstairs. The pub is where the action is, with music every night. Sunday night it's music from the '70s and '80s. Acoustic music reigns on Monday, hometown bands take the stage on Tuesday, and Wednesday is open-mic night. Thursday through Saturday, bands from all over play. A cover charge applies for those nights, running around $5.00. There's room for dancing. Two dartboards provide diversion, unless the teams are using them. Smoking is permitted but is hardly noticeable; there is an excellent air filtering system. Wahconah Street runs between US 7 at the north and North Street at the south, coming out by Berkshire Medical Center.

JB's Lounge
191 East Housatonic Street, Dalton
(413) 684-9741

Also known as JB's Brew & Cue, this offbeat establishment offers just that: beer and billiards. Located in a home on East Housatonic, the place might be missed if it weren't for the big Budweiser sign in the front. The lounge is up a few steps from the parking lot, located at the rear. There are six billiard tables plus a jukebox and dartboards. Eight- and nine-ball leagues take over from about 7:00 to 9:00 P.M. The lounge is open Monday through Saturday from 4:00 P.M. until closing, which might be 1:00 A.M., depending on owner John Boyle's mood. Smoking is definitely allowed. There are no fancy drinks at the bar. Just beer and the usual bags of chips or other packaged snacks. But the place has character and some folks just love it.

Ozzie's Steak & Seafood
450 Housatonic Street, Dalton
(413) 684-1782

Located in an old stone railroad station about 8 feet from the railroad tracks, Ozzie's offers music and dancing from 10:00 P.M. to 1:00 A.M. Tuesday through Saturday from mid-June through the third week of August. A live band is always booked for Saturday night, with DJs filling in on the other nights. The music is aimed at a younger crowd, especially on Tuesday night, when the place is flooded with counselors from nearby summer camps. There is a $4.00 cover charge. The restaurant itself is open Wednesday through Saturday from 4:00 to 8:30 P.M., when the tables and chairs are shoved aside to clear the dance floor. An adjacent bar remains open. The menu offers standard restaurant fare from lobster to pasta. The restaurant is wheelchair-accessible, includes a large wraparound deck, some of which is enclosed, and is decorated with toy trains and other railroad memorabilia. There are two lofts upstairs, one with booths and the other outfitted with a pool table available for use after the dinner hour. The bar and restaurant remain open through the winter from 4:00 to 9:00 P.M. on Wednesday and Thursday and from 4:00 P.M. to 1:30 A.M.

on Friday and Saturday. Music on Saturday night continues.

Red Devil Lounge
75 North Street, Pittsfield
(413) 448-6100
Owner Seth Gambino offers reasonably priced Southwest comestibles and eclectic live music in this, his second restaurant in the county. Although the address is North Street, the entrance to the Red Devil Lounge is on McKay Street, which runs parallel to and behind North Street and is accessed by either Depot or West Street. Gambino is catering to an audience in the 21- to 40-year-old range, offering a mix of folk, jazz, rock, blues, and more performed by regional bands, mostly on weekends. The stage is ample and the sound system rated high by musicians who play there. Gambino's other restaurant, LaChoza Burrito in Great Barrington, does not offer music. But both have really great, really big burritos made with all fresh ingredients to order. The lounge also offers soups, salads, and entrees.

NORTH COUNTY

Gringo's & the Club Next Door
1669 Curran Highway (MA 8), North Adams
(413) 663-8552
The Club Next Door is indeed next door to Gringo's, basically a Tex-Mex restaurant with American standbys like steak, chicken, and so on. Not a spot for intimate conversation, the club is a huge room with a large dance floor. Music on weekends is usually provided by a DJ, but occasionally there is live music. The crowd is generally in the 21- to 30-year-old range. The cover charge varies. There is karaoke in the restaurant on Friday night. Owner David Nicholas recently took over Bounti-fare, another restaurant on MA 8, and is planning to offer entertainment on weekends there, too.

Joga Cafe
23 Eagle Street, North Adams
(413) 664-0126
Interesting food, unique beers and wines, and a California atmosphere make Joga a trendy nightspot. Thursday is open-mic night. On Friday and Saturday, featured bands play jazz, blues, funk, or reggae. Occasionally a party band will be brought in and tables shoved aside for dancing. There is usually a $5.00 cover charge. You can get a good martini from the bar, which has a nice selection of beers, wines, and single malts. Smoking is allowed outside on the patio. A popular gathering place for dot.comers and professionals, Joga is one of the cosmopolitan places to open since the advent of MoCA.

---

i

Finding a place to smoke in the Berkshires is getting pretty complicated. Lee, Lenox, and Stockbridge have banned smoking in restaurants and bars completely. Other towns allow smoking in well-ventilated separate areas. The legislature has considered a statewide smoking ban, which some would welcome to level the playing field. Stores are not allowed to sell cigarettes to anyone under age 18 and clerks are required to check licenses.

Key West Lounge
159 State Street, North Adams
(413) 663-5055
Popular with older folks during the day and a younger crowd at night, Key West has been a favorite hangout for locals since 1986. Aside from live music on Friday and open-mic on Thursday, patrons can play pool, watch the latest sporting events on the large-screen TV, or get into philosophical discussions with Spanky, the bartender, who has never heard of PC. Key West personifies the North Adams that some fear might eventually be lost if the city becomes gentrified.

Papyri Books
49 Main Street, North Adams
(413) 662-2099
www.papyribooks.com

Papyri always has something interesting going on, including poetry slams, acoustic jams, and song swaps. Events are listed on the Web site or in the media.

Railway Cafe
St. John's Parish Hall
59 Summer Street
P.O. Box 225
North Adams 01247
(413) 664-6393
www.fusf.org/railwaycafe
An alternative to the bar scene, the nonprofit Railway Cafe is run by volunteers and has been offering live music on weekends since 2002. Performances are listed on their Web site. Tickets are $10 with a reservation or $12 at the door. Profits are distributed to local charities. Summer Street is off Ashland Street, at the North Adams Post Office. There's ample parking nearby in the former Kmart parking lot.

The Orchards
Adams Road (at Massachusetts Highway 2 East), Williamstown
(413) 458-9611
A pianist plays tunes from the '30s and '40s in Yasmin's Lounge at the Orchards every Friday and Saturday night year-round. The lounge has a full bar, and light fare may be ordered. In winter a fire blazes in the big stone fireplace, adding to the cozy atmosphere. There is no cover charge. The lounge is on the ground level of the inn and may be entered from the lower parking lot off MA 2.

Williams Inn
On-the-Green
US 7, Williamstown
(413) 458-9371
Pianists, soloists, and blues or jazz bands can be heard at the Williams Inn in the tavern on Friday and Saturday after 8:30 P.M. year-round. In July and August a cabaret with local talent is added on Sunday and Monday nights. The tavern has a late-night menu, including desserts.

SOMETHING COMPLETELY DIFFERENT

Ballroom Dancing

A number of groups get together for ballroom dancing, the oldest being Votre Soiree, which has been in existence for more than 75 years. Dances with live bands are held at different locations. Leadership changes often, but a contact person is Joyce Boschen at (413) 684-0735. She also can lead you to other groups.

Contradancing

Similar to square dancing, contradancing is a popular nighttime activity held at various places around the county. Michael Faber organizes dances at places like the Lenox Community Center and other suitably spacious halls. He also contracts for a fiddler and a caller, who teaches the steps and calls them out as the dance progresses. There usually is a charge of around $7.00 to cover expenses. Kids pay less. By the time the dance is done, everyone will have danced with everyone else. Faber can be reached for information at www.lenoxcontradance.com. Contradancing is popular throughout the region, especially in the Northampton area, and information about dances all over can be found at www.thedancegypsy.com.

Stargazing

Hopkins Observatory
Williams College
Main Street, Williamstown
(413) 597-2188
www.williams.edu/Astronomy/Hopkins/bottom/html
The Milham Planetarium in the Hopkins Observatory presents planetarium shows rain or shine at 8:30 on Friday night during

the academic year and on Tuesday and Thursday in July and part of August. Seating is limited and reservations are highly recommended, especially in summer. If the weather is clear, observers often are allowed to tour the observatory located atop the Thompson physics and astronomy laboratory and view the sky through the college's 24-inch telescope. The Mehlin Museum of Astronomy, also located here, often features special exhibits showing views captured by various telescopes, including the Chandra X-Ray and the Hubble, as well as the results of other space explorations. The museum collection includes several astronomical telescopes and clocks dating back to the mid-1800s, several meteorites, and other exhibits of astronomical interest. Although it has been moved from its original location, the Hopkins Observatory is the oldest in the nation. The first was built during the 1830s at the direction of Professor Albert Hopkins, who went to England in search of an astronomical apparatus for the school and founded the observatory. The observatory is located in the Berkshire quadrangle on the south side of MA 2. Limited parking is available in front of the Williams College Museum of Art next door. Much more can be found across the street behind Thompson Memorial Chapel. Large groups may request special showings.

SHOPPING

The variety and quality of merchandise available in the Berkshires is truly mind-boggling. Designer clothes, the latest in kitchenwares, eclectic antiques, exotic imports, sophisticated jewelry, quality home furnishings, the latest trends in gifts and accessories—all are here. The largest collection of independently owned shops whose owners strive for quality and individuality is in Lenox and Great Barrington. The markets there are driven by second-home owners, upscale tourists, and discerning residents. But there are nifty shops from one end of the county to the other. And locals are perfectly prepared to drive from one end of the county to the other to find the perfect whatever. In fact, shopping can be a great outing with a good dinner or lunch thrown in. But if time is a factor, the distances can be frustrating.

Speaking of frustration, many shops display rather off-putting signs declaring that they have no public restroom. One can sympathize, since their restrooms are usually entered through storerooms or business offices that they don't want folks poking around in. As a public service, tips on "where to go" are included where possible. As with other chapters, this one is divided into South, Central, and North County. You will note the abundance of antiques shops in South County. In addition to the proximity to the Connecticut and New York markets, the early homes along U.S. Highway 7 and Massachusetts Highway 23 make wonderful showcases in which to display antiques. Galleries are listed in the Arts and Culture chapter, sporting goods in Recreation, and toy stores and other child-centered businesses in Kidstuff.

i ***Public restrooms are located in the Town Hall on Main Street at Castle (closed on weekends and Wednesday), the chamber office (open daily in summer, Wednesday through Sunday off-season), and the Mason Public Library at 231 Main Street, across from the post office (Monday through Saturday, with varying hours).***

SOUTH COUNTY

Great Barrington

Great Barrington bustles with business year-round but is even busier in the tourist season. Although there are shops from one end of town to the other, the majority are in the center on Main and Railroad Streets. Some people think that the only parking places are along those streets or in the most visible lots right off Railroad. These folks can be spotted cruising slowly around and around the block, waiting for something to open up. In fact, there are many public parking lots in the downtown area, although some are only open to general use after the businesses that own them are closed. And there is a two-hour parking limit no matter where you park, which is expecting a lot from the browsing—or dining—public. The chamber of commerce publishes a map showing the parking lots. It is available at the chamber's information booth at 362 Main Street and other places around town. Also check out www.greatbarrington.org for more information.

ANTIQUES

Elise Abrams Antiques
11 Stockbridge Road (US 7)
(413) 528-3201
www.eliseabrams.com

In business since 1988, Elise Abrams specializes in fine antiques for dining largely from the 19th and early 20th centuries. Stemware and china are arranged by color or design in tall showcases that ring the floor. Furniture runs the gamut from country to formal, with cupboards, china closets, and sideboards plus tables of all sizes on which are displayed table settings, serving pieces, and accessories. Decanters, centerpieces, candelabra, tureens, and silver serving pieces abound. Abrams also carries linens and art glass, for which she has a passion. The shop is open daily.

Asian Antiques
199 Stockbridge Road (US 7)
(413) 528-5091
A native of Stockbridge, Bill Talbot went from being a biologist to becoming the largest importer of Asian artifacts on the East Coast. He started bringing in Asian sculpture, furniture, and architectural components 20 years ago, opening his shop in a warehouse on US 7 in 1992. His customers include museums, decorators, movie houses in search of props, and gift shops and galleries here and abroad. If he doesn't have it and can't get it, he will have it made. The huge stock comes from Indonesia, Japan, China, Korea, and elsewhere. He imports architectural relics from Buddhist temples, including elaborately carved teak walls and ancient doorways. The yard outside his shop is filled with Buddhas and other statuary in all kinds of material. Need a rickshaw? He usually has several. Entire structures often are set up outside. A Javanese family home or an intricately carved raised shed made for storing rice might end up as a playhouse or contemplative retreat on a large estate. Stock arrives monthly, and the shop itself is crammed with all kinds of furniture, new and old, including elaborate beds, chests, trunks, mirrors, and screens. Kimonos, pillows, and other silk goods are displayed throughout, along with kites, masks, gongs, china, lighting—you name it. And he is planning to expand so that he can add a gallery for paintings and other art. The shop is open every day but Tuesday in season. Off-season it also is closed on Sunday.

Country Dining Room Antiques
178 Main Street (US 7)
(413) 528-5050
www.countrydiningroomantiq.com
China, silver, glassware, dining furniture, and decorative accessories are displayed on two floors in Sheila Chefetz's shop, which opened in 1989. She also carries custom linens and candle shades. Chefetz is the author of two books on the art of setting the table: *Antiques for the Table* and *Modern Antiques for the Table*. Located in the oldest house on Main Street, with parking at the rear, the shop is open daily.

The Emporium Antique Center
319 Main Street (US 7)
(413) 528-1660
More than 20 dealers display their wares in this group shop in the center of town. Dealers include Steve Kahn's Antique and Estate Jewelry (413-528-9550) and Toobi Ltd., specialists in art glass and jewelry. Others carry sterling silver, furniture, estate linens, and collectibles. The shop is open daily Memorial Day through December and closed on Tuesday and Wednesday from January through May.

Great Barrington Antiques Center
964 South Main Street (US 7)
(413) 644-8848
www.greatbarringtonantiquescenter.com
Around 50 dealers are set up on one floor in this group shop south of town. Stock ranges from formal to country, early to late, and includes Oriental rugs, prints, folk art, decorative accessories, paintings, and lighting plus showcases filled with quality merchandise. The center is open daily except in the off-season, when it is closed on Wednesday.

Paul and Susan Kleinwald Antiques
578 South Main Street
(413) 528-4252
The Kleinwalds specialize in American, English, and Continental furnishing from the 18th and early 19th centuries. In business since 1976, they are known for having

high-style furniture, both formal and country, and for the period appointments they carry. Gilded mirrors, paintings, silver and porcelain from England and abroad, and other decorative accessories are attractively displayed in their pleasant showroom. Paul is trained in traditional cabinetmaking and restoration and says he has literally taken apart more than 1,000 pieces of furniture and put them back together, which gives him a greater understanding of construction and finishes used by early craftsmen. He also appraises antiques for estates and insurance purposes. You might notice the restored '41 Chevy pickup truck parked in front of the shop, which Paul has driven since he first started in business. He also is a banjo and guitar player of note, having recorded with Arlo Guthrie. The shop is usually open Thursday through Monday, but a call is advisable just to be sure.

Le Perigord Antiques
964 South Main Street (US 7)
(413) 528-6777
French furnishings from the 1600s through the 1960s are imported by Martine and Jeff Roberts. The stock includes leather club chairs, mirrors, garden and architectural pieces, pottery, and decorative accessories. Open weekends, weekdays by chance or appointment.

McTeigue & McClelland Jewelers
964 South Main Street (US 7)
(413) 528-6262
www.mc2jewels.com
Although they have a Web site to show their work, Walter McTeigue and Tim McClelland do not sell over the Internet—they believe their antique and contemporary collections are best viewed firsthand. A fourth-generation jeweler, McTeigue specializes in diamonds, precious stones, and estate jewelry. McClelland's field is design and fabrication, modeled after the elaborate jewelry crafted around 1900. Both were in the wholesale trade in New York. The gallery also features jewelry by other artists. Open Tuesday through Saturday (closed in March), the gallery is located in a little yellow house about a half mile south of town center.

Mullin-Jones Antiquities
525 South Main Street
(413) 528-4871
Patrice Mullin has been importing French antiques since 1986. Furniture from country to formal includes armoires, buffets, library and china cupboards, dining tables, chairs, and desks. Accessories include mirrors and chandeliers. She also carries French ceramics and other small items. Open most days; always closed on Tuesday.

APPAREL

Barrington Outfitters
289 Main Street
(413) 528-0021
www.gbshoes.com
Barrington Outfitters sells shoes, shoes, and more shoes—even through their Web site. They carry mostly "EuroComfort" brands like Ecco, Birkenstock, Naot, Santana, Stegmann, Doc Martens, Lowa, UGG, and Kamik as well as Neos overshoes and Atlas snowshoes. Plus they have outerwear and such seasonal furnishings as hammocks and outdoor furniture. It's a very interesting mix of stuff, including formal attire. Open daily.

Church Street Trading Company
4 Railroad Street
(413) 528-6120
Sportswear, outerwear, and household furnishings share space in this eclectic shop. Sweaters, scarves, jewelry, and accessories are neatly displayed. Owner Bob Rush will even part with the antique props around the place—for a price. Open daily.

Gatsby's
25 Railroad Street
(413) 528-9455
Another eclectic gathering of merchandise can be found at Gatsby's. You can find shoes by Dansko, Clarks, Arche, Merrell, Birks, Teva, and others. Clothes, including designs by Eileen Fisher and Flax and

sportswear by Danskin and Speedo share space with trendy garb that attracts the younger set. Here also are wicker and leather furniture, curtains, throws, pillows, bamboo blinds, futons, bedding, and tons of accessories. Open daily.

Jack's Country Squire Shop
316 Main Street
(413) 528-1390

Owner David Pevzner's grandfather began this business by driving a truck around to local farms, selling clothing and other necessities. In 1947 he opened his first shop in Lee. In 1970 the Great Barrington store opened. Pevzner and his wife, Susan, still carry basic outerwear and jeans, but there's a lot more here than that. The basement is crammed with footwear for all ages, including Skechers, Dunham, Merrell, New Balance, Rockport, Nike, and Adidas. Athletic gear, kids' raincoats, all kinds of socks and slippers, plus waterproof clogs and boots fill the racks and shelves. The main floor is devoted to clothing for men and women, including a full range of Levi's plus clothing by Haggar, Enro, Sorel, Woolrich, Timberland, and others. There also are gloves, hats, scarves, backpacks, and accessories. Although most of the stock is casual, blazers and formal wear also are carried. Open daily.

T. P. Saddleblanket & Trading Co.
287 Main Street
(413) 528-6500

Hudson Bay meets New Mexico in this unusual shop on the corner of Railroad Street. The trading-post atmosphere is aided by a great collection of props, including fishing gear, antlers, tack, and old signs. Stock includes Native American–style blankets, pillows, jackets, and wraps plus turquoise and silver jewelry, beaded belts, moccasins, leather and suede jackets and vests, plaid shirts, and other garb with a country air. Vintage cowboy boots along with new ones by Tony Lama, Double H, and Don Post are carried. The basement is full of interesting items, including brightly colored enamel "camp" cookware, Claus Porto soaps, and an assortment of hot sauces and salsas. Pillows and blankets in Hudson Bay designs are piled on a rustic bed made of oak by an artist in New Mexico. Like many of the props, the bed is for sale. The shop is owned by Great Barrington residents Jack and Tasha Polizzi. A designer, Tasha's sportswear collection is sold here and in shops around the country. Open daily.

i

The sales tax in Massachusetts is 5 percent. Clothing and items shipped out of state are exempt.

HOME FURNISHINGS

The Chef's Shop
31 Railroad Street
(413) 528-0135, (800) 237-5284
www.TheChefsShop.net

The Chef's Shop caters to professional chefs and hobbyists who want the best. Everything for the kitchen can be found here, from serious cookware by Cephalon, All-Clad, KitchenAid, and Le Creuset to handy gadgets by Oxo and Zyliss. You'll also find knives by Wusthof, Lamson, and Henckel's, teapots by Bodum, coffeemakers by Kemps, and stainless steel products by Nissan. Whether you are setting up a commercial-looking contemporary kitchen or one where color and texture are important, the look can be achieved here. Table linens and ceramic dinnerware in plain white or California-pottery hues, woodenware and flatware, and aprons, cookbooks, and accessories are laid out in a wing off the main shop. A complete kitchen is set up in the rear of the shop, where classes are taught throughout the year. Local chefs, cookware representatives, caterers, and cookbook authors share their recipes and knowledge with students, who are entitled to a discount on merchandise they pick out that day. Classes run around $35. The enthusiastic owner of the shop is Robert Navarino, who started in Lenox in 1991 and moved to Great Barrington in 1994. The shop is open every day.

La Pace
313 Main Street
(413) 528-1888

With her extensive high-end stock, Betsy Lee Workman can outfit a bathroom or bedroom with everything but the fixtures and furniture. In business since 1997, Workman carries the best in linens and accessories imported from France, Portugal, and Italy, where her grandparents live. For the bedroom there are 500-thread-count Egyptian cotton sheets by several firms, including Anichini, Mastro Raphael, Frette, and Sferra. Pillows include hypoallergenic down by Dom Ogallala and others by Downright. Throws, pillows, duvets, and coverlets in lush fabrics by Anichini and Peacock Alley abound. Tabletop decor by Anichini also is featured. Workman also carries sleep- and loungewear by Pluto and slippers by Amy Jo Gladstone. For the bath there are lush Egyptian cotton towels and facecloths by Anichini and Abyss in a wide range of hues. Workman's sense of humor is reflected in some amusing products she carries, including all kinds of yellow duckies, silly soaps by Bathology, and bath sets by Kuckoo embroidered with stick people, dinosaurs, and other unlikely motifs. Bath mats and scatter rugs by Habidecor come in a wide range of colors and will remain soft even after years of laundering. They and lots of other products can be custom-ordered. Bath accessories include marble soap dishes, toothbrush holders, and other appointments by Digs LaBrazel and elegant soaps by Baronessa Cali and Gianna Rose Atalia. And for sheer luxury there are frilly pillows to cushion your neck while lounging in the tub. La Pace is open every day June to January. Winter hours vary, so a call is advised if you're traveling a distance.

Mistral's
11 Railroad Street
(413) 528-1618
www.mistrals.com

You can save a trip to Provence by shopping at Mistral's, where linens, tableware, furniture, and other products from France are displayed on three floors. Owner Lise Bouillon is French Canadian but spent years visiting relatives in Provence. She realized that many folks had trouble carrying or shipping the country ceramics and other products they admired there, so in 1994 she opened her own importing business. She makes three trips a year to France, searching out the furnishings she brings back for her shop. The main floor is filled with tables and cupboards bursting with colorful pottery and table linens. She carries flatware by Sabre and steak knives by Laguiole. Fine papers and leather goods from Italy also are displayed here. The second floor is dedicated to the bed and bath, with luscious tapestry pillows, wool shawls, fine linens, accessories, and sleepwear. She also carries lotions, creams, and other products by L'Occitane. In the basement, photographs, prints, and original artwork are for sale. This also is where sale items may be found. Open daily year-round.

Out of Hand
81 North Main Street (US 7)
(413) 528-3791

Katherine Shanahan's shop is one of those places where you can spend hours and still not have seen everything. It is a fun place to shop for gifts, home furnishings, and women's clothing imported from India. Skirts, jackets, tops, and loungewear in batik and other handmade materials are arranged in one corner of the place. In another are truly hundreds of baskets in all shapes and sizes. Then there are the throws, pillows, rugs, rice-paper lamps, runners, quilts, curtains, tableclothes, china, tableware, bamboo blinds and mats, pottery, bedspreads, mirrors, and glassware from sources in India, Provence, Guatemala, Peru, Ecuador, China, Mexico, and other countries. Soaps, candles, jewelry, and purses also are sold. For special occasions there are paper lanterns, piñatas, greeting cards, wrapping paper, and silly gifts. For kids there are specialty items, including mugs, Dover Books, and collector dolls representing great musicians that are handmade by a Brooklyn group called the Unemployed Philosophers' Guild. In business for more than 30 years, Shanahan likes to buy from co-ops and other out-of-the-mainstream suppliers. Remarkably, everything is clearly priced and, considering the number of items, that is a heroic feat. Out of Hand is in a large building that sits below highway level and is tricky to get into and out of. Open daily year-round, it is definitely worth the hassle.

OTHER SHOPS OF INTEREST

The Bookloft
Barrington Plaza
US 7
(413) 528-1521
www.thebookloft.com

Erik Wilska opened the Bookloft in 1974 and has set a record as the oldest continuously owned independent bookstore in the Berkshires. The store carries new and used books, magazines, journals, and fine note cards and has a large children's book section. Many of the knowledgeable and enthusiastic employees are full-time and are dedicated to helping customers find what they are looking for, thus developing a loyal following. A member and officer of the New England Booksellers Association, Wilska also sells through the Internet out-of-print, secondhand, and rare books from an off-site location on Main Street in Stockbridge. Called Found at the Bookloft, the depository is open to the public only on Saturday. Wilska holds book-signings and other events at the Bookloft and cosponsors cross-promotional author events with the public libraries in Sheffield and Stockbridge. The Bookloft is open every day.

Catherine's Chocolate Shop
260 Stockbridge Road
(413) 528-6052
www.catherineschocolates.com

Hand-dipped chocolates with more fillings than you can imagine have been produced at Catherine's in Great Barrington since 1958 with recipes handed down through the family, which at one time had seven chocolate shops in the New York area. A visit to Catherine's is a treat for the senses. Case after case is filled with their specialties: hand-dipped creams, fruits, and nuts; favorites like truffles, fudge, peanut butter smoothies, and butter crunch; plus nonpareils, caramels, chocolate-dipped ginger, and, in season, chocolate-dipped strawberries. Each miniature is identified with a mark, eliminating the need to nibble to find out what's inside. Prepackaged assortments are available in the shop and are pictured and described on the Web site. Assortments also may be made up to order. Novelties such as chocolate violins or corporate logos also may be ordered. Naturally, Catherine's is a favorite place to shop for Valentine's Day, Easter, Halloween, and Christmas. In addition to the chocolates, there is marzipan and brittle, plus licorice, fruit slices, jelly beans, mints, nuts, and sugar-free confections. Catherine's is open daily.

Crystal Essence
39 Railroad Street
(413) 528-2595
www.crystalessence.com

Since opening in 1985, Mark and Adrienne Cohen have earned a reputation among tourists and locals for having an incredibly well-stocked and versatile store. Visitors are struck immediately by the almost overwhelming display of crystals and minerals. Incense and oils, Native American carvings, statuary, cards, and hundreds of other items fill the shop. Clothing with an international flavor includes ethnic as well as fashionable designs and accessories. Yoga clothing and supplies also are carried here. The jewelry selection is eclectic and expansive. The shop also has a large nontraditional book section focusing on spirituality, personal growth, relationships, meditation, astrology, nutrition, aromatherapy, parenting, and education plus a children's section. Also available are books in Spanish and books and music on

CDs, cassettes, and videotape. A number of tabletop fountains are displayed along with a unique fountain that runs on ultrasound, diffusing a mist that can be scented with oil. Tarot readings, classes in drumming, and other workshops are offered for a fee. Open daily year-round.

Farshaw's Bookshop
13 Railroad Street
(413) 528-1890

Michael and Helen Selzer's shop is crammed from top to bottom with books. The stock varies depending on what collections come and go, but there are generally 6,000 to 7,000 titles on hand, with another 10,000 to 15,000 waiting to be brought in. First editions, signed or otherwise, and antiquarian books are featured. Collections of photography and original artwork come and go, too. Although the couple do not have a Web site, they did found Bibliofind, one of the first rare book Web sites, which is now owned by Amazon.com. The shop is open on Friday, Saturday, and Sunday in June, July, August, and November. In December they plan to open every day but recommend calling to be sure.

Guido's Fresh Marketplace
760 South Main Street (US 7)
(413) 528-9255
www.guidosfreshmarketplace.com

Like the mother ship in Pittsfield, Guido's is a group shop of food. The produce department is expansive, with just about everything fresh, organic, and local as much as possible. Mazzeo's Meat Center carries all-natural free-range poultry and livestock, much of it local, as well as unusual cuts, marinated meats, and specialty sausages. As in the Pittsfield store, there is a floral department, seafood section, bakery, and dairy and cheese department. There are tons of gourmet canned, jarred, and bottled goodies, plus wines, beer, and unusual sodas, dried grains, nuts and fruits; and sushi. The delicatessen is run by a local caterer. Open daily, Guido's is owned by brothers Chris and Matthew Masiero, who also own the Pittsfield store.

Locke, Stock and Barrel
US 7
(413) 528-0800

This is not a moving company. Rather, it is Locke Larkin's incredible gourmet grocery and wine shop, established in 1968 by his grandfather. Larkin calls his place the United Nations of Food and seems as awed by his stock as the "foodies" who discover him. Indeed, products from around the world can be found here—and in depth. There is a revolving stock of around 180 artisan-made cheeses and 40 to 50 kinds of extra-virgin olive oils. Hot sauce? How about 130 to 140 labels, some rather risqué and politically incorrect. Among the honeys are varieties from Tasmania, France, and Spain. The specialty vinegars include hard-to-find Saba from Japan. There are spices from Ethiopia and Bengal; jams, jellies, and preserves of exquisite quality; Slitti bulk chocolate from Italy; Jack 'n' Ollie chips from England; four shelves of chutneys; cultured butter from France and Italy; and special coffees and teas, including one from Asia that is picked by monkeys. Locke travels the world to find the rare and unusual but is also checked out by purveyors who want to be sure he is worthy of handling their product. More mundane but just as special are dried legumes, fruits and nuts, pastas, and flours (including the best cornmeal for polenta). He also has a reputation as a fine wine merchant. Nutritional supplements, vitamins, and natural cosmetics also are stocked. The shop is open Monday through Saturday year-round.

Tune Street
294 Main Street
(413) 258-4999

Tune Street sells CDs ranging from classical to folk but has a reputation for having the best selection of blues around. In business for more than 10 years, the shop also carries DVDs and a formidable stock of the latest flat-screen television sets, DVD players, home entertainment systems, speakers, and related equipment. There are comfortable nooks for listening and viewing prospective purchases. Open daily.

Jennifer House Commons

Located north of town across from the Holiday Inn at 404 Stockbridge Road (US 7), this historic marketplace with its attractive complex of frame buildings is a source for art, antiques, home furnishings, and musical instruments plus good meals at reasonable prices. Most shops are open daily, but hours vary.

The **Berkshire Art Gallery** (413-528-2690) is located in the red building on the right as you enter the complex parking lot. Owner John H. Wood specializes in art from the 19th and 20th centuries by artists who achieved success in their lifetimes but whose work has been undervalued—in other words, sleepers in the art world. Many trained at prestigious academies or schools and were associated with noted art colonies. Also here are works by contemporary artists, including many Berkshire painters. The gallery is open on weekends or by appointment.

Located in a small house at the rear of the complex, **Carriage House Antiques** (413-528-6045) is run by the Schutz family, which has been in the Berkshires for 50 years and has been working with wood all that time. The present generation, Erik and Barbara Schutz and their son, Erik O. F. Schutz, are carrying on the tradition. The elder Schutz sells restored furniture ready to go, while the son makes reproductions of hard-to-find pieces like harvest tables, cupboards to fit a certain space, and copies of chairs to complete a set. The family also buys and sells clocks.

Coffman's Antiques Market (413-529-9282; www.coffmansantiques. com) specializes in country antiques and decorative accessories from about 90 dealers who rent space from Don and Joyce Coffman in this yellow house at the back of the Commons. Furniture, including some formal pieces, all kinds of pottery and china, textiles, prints, paintings, tools, toys, and other collector's items are displayed on three floors. Most of the stock is pre-1940. There also is a section devoted to new books on antiques and collectibles.

The **Music Store** (413-528-2460), located on the second floor of the red building on the right of the complex, sells and repairs instruments and arranges lessons. Also here are music and gifts and accessories with a musical motif.

Olde—An Antiques Market (413-528-1840) is located in a green house on the left of the Commons parking lot. Joan and Howard Basis, who have been in the business for more than 20 years, rent space on two floors to around 50 dealers. While some furniture can be found here, most of the stock is a mix of small collectibles, both formal and country, including costume jewelry, Depression and other glass, china, books, maps, ephemera, linens, and decorative accessories, largely from the 20th century. The shop is open daily.

Wingate Limited (413-644-9960) offers custom-designed furniture, including reproductions, and interior design services.

White Knight Records
288 Main Street
(413) 528-9466
If vinyl's your thing, this is the place to go. Boxes and boxes of oldies line the floors and fill the shelves and bins. Racks of CDs and cassettes, used and new, also abound. Owner Ron White has a reputation for having unusual, hard-to-find, or obscure recordings—and if he doesn't have it, he will get it. He also sells posters and accessories. His slogan says it all: "Your cure for the angst of the modern world." Open daily.

Lee

Ben's
68 Main Street
(413) 243-0242
Shoes and clothing for men, women, and children are the meat and potatoes of Ben's. Pajamas, underwear, rain wear, work clothes, including Levi's, shirts, and other garb by Woolrich are offered with little fanfare. The shoes are lined up along the wall in their boxes, but don't be fooled by the humble appearance. The brands are good ones: Clarks, Hi-Tec, Chippewa, Dansko, and others. A basic store for basic needs, Ben's is open Monday through Saturday year-round, adding Sunday in the weeks before Christmas.

Berkshire Record Outlet
461 Pleasant Street (Massachusetts Highway 102)
(413) 243-4080
www.berkshirerecordoutlet.com
Joe Eckstein's Record Outlet is known among hobbyists and hard-core collectors as the place to get really good hard-to-find classical CDs at bargain prices. In business for 30 years, Eckstein searches out music deleted from record company catalogs (called cutouts in the industry), which he sells mostly on the Internet. Aside from classical music, he carries some better "pop" tunes and jazz as well as remaindered DVDs, books, and some vinyl. Most are in his database on the Web, but customers might find some not-yet-listed items when they browse the bins. He professes to be less knowledgeable than his customers, although some would debate that. Some of his finds come from abroad, where he travels often. Ironically, a lot of his sales are to overseas customers, so much of his stock ends up back in Europe or Japan. He buys in bulk and tries to sell everything at prices that are at least 50 percent less than those at other retail shops handling closeouts. His friends joke that he is the Lohman's of CDs. Most of the year he is open only on Saturday, adding Monday through Friday at the height of the tourist season.

Pamela Loring Gifts and Interiors
151 Main Street
(413) 243-2689
www.pamelaloringgifts.com
Pamela Loring Gifts and Interiors is located in a 165-year-old house on Main Street purchased in 1998 from the heirs of the previous owners, who had lived there since 1901, and lovingly restored by Pam and her husband, Jim. A year later Pam moved her gift shop to the refurbished house, which had gone from a dreary brown to a bright yellow with cheery green shutters. Pam's shop was already a destination for folks looking for just the right gift, but the new location really showed off her taste and style in decorating and has attracted even more customers. Pam is known for her great assortment of personalized stationery, birth announcements, and invitations. Customers are greeted by the friendly staff and the scent of seasonal candles and potpourri. Soothing background music plays as you browse through the nooks and crannies bursting with decorative accessories and personal-care products. There is a large assortment of affordable rugs, lamps, frames, pictures, and small furniture. Pam carries products by more than 150 vendors, including Crabtree & Evelyn, Vera Bradley, Camille Beckman, Toland, Santa Barbara, and Russ Berrie. There are jams and jellies by

Stonewall Kitchen, Beanie Babies by Ty, placemats and coasters by Pimpernel, tablewares by Portmeirion, and Christmas and home decor by Midwest. Gift baskets can be made up, and gift wrapping is offered. Consultation is available for brides-to-be who want to set up a registry. The shop is open daily.

Prime Outlets at Lee
50 Water Street (U.S. Highway 20)
(413) 243-8186
www.primeoutlets.com
Prime Outlets is located on a hill overlooking exit 2 of the Massachusetts Turnpike. The "village" of around 65 designer outlets includes Mikasa, Eddie Bauer, Polo Ralph Lauren, Geoffrey Beene, Liz Claiborne, K-B Toys, Corningware, Pfaltzgraff, Gap, Coach, and Etienne Aigner plus a food court—and restrooms! On Saturday and Sunday from Memorial Day through Labor Day, a "trolley" bus provides free transportation from the center to downtown Lee and Stockbridge with stops along the way. The schedule may be obtained from the Berkshire Regional Transit Authority at (800) 292-2782.

Serendipity Sweets
66 Main Street
(413) 243-4321
Kim Hunt has been sweetening life in Lee with her own confections since 1999. Chocolate in the form of truffles, creams, bark, and butter and peanut butter crunch are her specialties. She also sells gummies, jelly beans, and other sweets and makes up gift baskets. The shop is open Monday through Saturday.

Lenox

Lenox is a great place to shop. The stores in town are concentrated in a few blocks, so no matter where you park, the area can easily be walked. Others are found along US 7 north to the Pittsfield line. In town there often is a musical chairs of sorts as shops often move from location to location as other spaces open up. The chamber of commerce is very active and sponsors events designed to set cash registers ringing while customers have a good time. Call (413) 637-3646, or visit www.lenox.org. There is a public restroom there and at the Town Hall.

ANTIQUES

Charles L. Flint Antiques
52 Housatonic Street
(413) 637-1634
A native of Lenox, Charles Flint has been dealing in art and antiques for more than 35 years. His recently constructed shop off Church Street is a fitting showcase for the select stock of early American furniture and accessories he carries. American and European paintings, weathervanes, checkerboards, and whimsical folk art from the 18th and 19th centuries are displayed with lots of space around them to fully appreciate their form and finish. Flint has spent years learning about early blown and molded glass, especially bottles, and many fine pieces are displayed in the windows, the light accenting their rich colors. A former director of the Mount Lebanon Shaker Village Museum, Flint is known for his expertise in Shaker furniture, baskets, and other articles and always has at least a few examples of the sect's work on hand. A member of the New England Appraisers Association, Flint has authenticated pieces for a number of local museums, including the Norman Rockwell Museum. He also sells original work by Rockwell. Flint is known for his extensive collection of research material, including art references and Berkshire County history books and early maps and is more than willing to share his library and knowledge. Active in town affairs, he is president of the Lenox Historical Society. The shop is open every day.

Past & Future
63 Church Street
(413) 637-2225
Small collectibles are Marcy Cohen's forte, and her shop is crammed with hundreds of

things for the discerning collector. One whole showcase is full of lady's accessories such as scent bottles, powder boxes, and dresser accouterments. Another features medical items, while yet another houses all kinds of inkwells and desk accessories. Victorian tableware, flatware, napkin rings, and knife rests abound. Cohen has been in business since 1990, selling in Lenox since 1995. The shop is open daily from June through Labor Day and on weekends or by chance the rest of the year.

Stone's Throw Antiques
51 Church Street
(413) 637-2733

Sydelle Shapiro has been buying and selling antiques since 1985, specializing primarily in 19th-century American, English, and European furnishings with some 18th-century pieces when she can find them. She especially likes light-colored English furniture made of yew. Large assortments of glass, English porcelain, silver, and period accessories neatly arranged in cabinets or on furniture fill the spacious, well-lit shop. Small pieces include inkwells and pillboxes. She also carries mirrors, frames, and prints, which display nicely on the citron yellow or dark green walls. Stone's Throw is open daily from May through October 30 and is closed on Tuesday and Wednesday in the off-season.

APPAREL

Casablanca
21 Housatonic Street
(413) 637-2680

The minute you walk into Casablanca you know you are not going to find run-of-the-mill clothing. With its high ceilings, exposed beams, and gallery lighting, the building itself is a unique blend of city and country—and so is the clothing. Hip, cool, upscale, but far from "trendy," Casablanca has things you can be sure you won't see on everybody else. Owners Tony Chojnowski and Paul Hutchinson focus on avant-garde design, unusual textures, and interesting color combinations in selecting the clothes they sell, and they have been coming up with ahead-of-their-time finds for 20 or so years. Men's wear includes finely crafted shirts and sweaters in subtle colors; sport coats and trousers, dress and casual; T-shirts and even underwear in sizes ranging from medium to XXL. For women there are many limited-edition dresses and separates, dressy blouses and camisoles, sweaters and hats, as well as cocktail wear for black-tie occasions in sizes 2 to 16. The shop also carries a line of costume jewelry and sunglasses. The owners also have a shoe store at 44B Housatonic Street, called Shooz, that carries designer footwear in sizes 5 to 11 for women and 8 to 13 for men. Handbags and golf shoes also are sold there. Casablanca and Shooz are open daily.

Cottage of Lenox
439 Pittsfield Road (US 7)
(413) 443-5900

Cottage of Lenox is the sister—or rather, daughter—branch of the Cottage in Pittsfield. The copious stock includes Bennington Pottery, Belleek and Portemeirion English ceramics, and other tablewares, including linens and placemats. Colonial candles, Caspari paper goods, greeting cards, and gift wrappings plus seasonal decorations, including Christmas ornaments also can be found here. The women's clothing section includes designs by Putmayo, Woolrich, and Trousers plus a large assortment of Vera Bradley products. A section for babies and young children includes clothing, A. A. Milne books, Groovy Girls, and cuddly stuffed critters by Flip Flops. The shop also serves as an outlet for Catherine's Chocolates of Great Barrington. While manager Lora Kozlowski, whose mother owns the Pittsfield Cottage, does not carry the full line of chocolates, she can order any she does not have on hand. The shop is open Monday through Saturday year-round.

Evviva
22 Walker Street
(413) 637-9875

Women looking for impeccable tailoring,

unusual designs, and understated elegance will appreciate the apparel selected by Evviva's owner, Gabrielle Boege Berlet, and her partner, Nancy Fitzpatrick. Since 1987 Berlet has been searching the trade shows in Los Angeles and New York for designs that reflect her taste and criteria and bringing them to Lenox. Lines that are always in stock include Agi Brooks, Harari, Caroline Rose, and the Crea Collection from Italy. Sizes generally range from 2 to 14. Styles tend to be dressy yet adventurous in color, fabric, and design. All are hung on padded velvet hangers. There is always a selection of custom jewelry, including a line crafted by a local artist in silver, plus a collection of Bakelite designs reminiscent of the 1930s and 1940s. Handbags for evening or day use, including a line made in France, gloves, hats, scarves, and other accessories are on hand to complete an outfit. Summer or winter, Evviva is the place to look for elegant casual wear or something unique for a dressy occasion. The shopping experience is enhanced by the spacious dressing rooms, which are well lit, with comfortable furnishings and large mirrors. Evviva is open daily.

Glad Rags
66 Church Street
(413) 637-0088

Glad Rags has been selling fun jewelry and casual wear for women since 1970. Fans know that the stock changes every two weeks in summer and once a month in winter. Fashions by Eileen Fisher and ISDA are popular items as are all-cotton, machine-washable, tumble-dry BJK sweaters in a great array of colors. The buyers are admitted sock addicts, which accounts for the large assortment in stock. The shop is known for having great accessories and a friendly, easygoing staff that doesn't take itself too seriously, apparently a recipe for success. Glad Rags is open daily from April through December and is closed for a winter break January through March.

Purple Plume
35 Church Street
(413) 637-3442
www.purpleplume.com

The Purple Plume has defied categorization since it opened in 1981. You just never know what you are going to find. Granted, more than half the shop is filled with women's clothing, handcrafted jewelry, and accessories. But then there are the greeting cards, gifts, glassware, candles, Camille Beckman lotions and creams, plus items that come and go with the seasons. The clothing ranges from formal to sportswear in a wide range of sizes. While some area shops tend to carry more subdued clothing, the Purple Plume is full of bright colors, zippy patterns, and interesting textures in a full range of sizes. The stock includes novelty sweaters with fancy embellishments or seasonal designs and appliquéd and beaded jackets by Sandy Starkman and ensembles and separates by Roni, Wildwoman, and others. Also here are dresses for formal events like weddings or casual affairs on the lawn. Scarves by August Silk, accessories and jewelry by Zad, plus designs by Plum Trader, Holly Hyashi, and Monsoon also are carried. And there's always a sale section. Purple Plume is open every day April through December and Thursday through Sunday January through March.

Mary Stuart Collections
69 Church Street
(413) 637-0340

The fine assortments of perfumes, soaps, jewelry, silver, writing papers, and feminine attire found here could save you a trip to Bergdorf Goodman. In fact, that is the intention of owners MaryJane Emmet and Judith Gordon, who have been serving the discerning second-home owner and upscale visitor for more than 20 years. Frothy children's wear, silver baby cups, and similar gifts for newborns and young ones will surely grab any granny shopping for a present. Cashmere sweaters for those unexpectedly chilly Berkshire nights and gowns and robes for the unplanned overnight also can be found here. The shop is open daily year-round.

Talbots
46 Walker Street
(413) 637-3576
www.talbots.com
Talbots began selling classic sportswear in Hingham in 1947 and started its catalog business the following year. Today Talbots has more than 850 shops in the United States plus more in Canada and England, and the catalog business is available on the Internet. The specialty shop in Lenox opened in 1964 and carries clothing for women who appreciate the timeless styles. Sizes on the floor include misses 3 to 18 and petites 2 to 16. If an item is not in stock in the size needed, it can be ordered through the customer service phone in the shop, with three-day delivery. The store is open daily.

Tanglewool
28 Walker Street
(413) 637-0900
Aline Sosne opened Tanglewool in Lenox in 1981. Back then she carried fine yarns, ran knitting classes, and sold finished work. Responding to her customers' suggestions, she added accessories. As different shops opened up, she moved from one to another—seven times in all. Enlarging her stock and changing her focus as she went, she finally evolved into her present retail shop, featuring fine sweaters and other fashions imported from abroad. Now she makes two buying trips a year to Europe, bringing back hand-knit sweaters and other goodies from England, Italy, France, and Spain. She carries designs by Brunello Cucinelli, Malo, Patricia Roberts, Eskandar, Jane Wheeler, Marion Foale, Issey Miyake, and others. While the stock is mostly sweaters and scarves in gorgeous colors, you can also find jeans by Cambio, outerwear, bathing suits in season, and perfumes, candles, soaps, and other products by Diptyque. Fine imported leather handbags and other accessories also can be found here. Open daily.

Weaver's Fancy
65 Church Street
(413) 637-2013
Even on the grayest of days, Katherine Pincus's shop off Church Street is ablaze with vibrant colors. Lush scarves, cocoons, sweaters, tunics, and vests made with natural fibers and dyes and handwoven in original designs fill the shop. About half the work is by Pincus, who works at home or sometimes at a loom in the shop, weaving scarves in stunning color combinations. Other one-of-a-kind garments are from a variety of local and farther-afield artists, including Gail Robinson, a Maine resident known for the delicate floral and bamboo patterns she hand-paints on silk. Felt hats by G. G. Kingston of Housatonic also are sold here. Pincus also weaves window curtains in a variety of patterns by special order. The shop is open daily in July and August and on Friday and Saturday the rest of the year.

OTHER SHOPS OF INTEREST

B. Mango & Bird
74 Main Street
(413) 637-2611, (888) 262-6461
Decorative and useful items for the home and garden on an ever-changing basis can be found at this shop, crammed to the hilt with interesting things. Owners Kathryn McGinley and Paul Leney pride themselves on picking out things for the shop that they like. Most times, what you see is what they have, and they tend not to reorder once an item sells out. There will always be some kind of table linens, unusual note papers and cards, and whimsical decorations like giant daisies or watering cans in primary colors, along with china and pottery, light fixtures, personal care products, candlesticks, frames, imported rugs, and sushi and tea sets. In summer a deck and patio at the rear of the shop are filled with garden furniture, birdbaths, decorative planters, and sculpture. In business since 1993, the couple also handle one-of-a-kind vintage furniture from overseas, chosen for its individuality and character. The music you hear while browsing is sold at

the counter. The shop is open daily from April to January and Wednesday through Saturday from January to April.

The Bookstore
11 Housatonic Street
(413) 637-3390
For a small store, the Bookstore packs a lot in. The selection is top-notch, hand-picked by Matt Tannenbaum, who has owned the shop since 1976. Aside from a great assortment of books for children and young adults, the stock includes books by local and regional writers plus poetry, literature, and special interests, including music, theater, and cooking. Many are published by small presses outside the mainstream. Books on tape and postcards also are carried. Tannenbaum and his helpers are friendly and knowledgeable, making the Bookstore a comfortable place to hunt for something special. Author parties, book-signings, and other events are held throughout the year. The shop is open Monday through Saturday and a few hours on Sunday.

Different Drummer's Kitchen
374 Pittsfield Road (US 7)
(413) 637-0606
A trip to Different Drummer could make you throw out everything in your kitchen and start over. For the table there is sleek pottery from Lindt-Stymeist Craftworks, the brightly-colored cook-and-serve pottery by the French firm of Emile Henry, stoneware by Monroe (Maine) Saltworks Pottery, and flatware by Rowoco. Glassware includes elegant wine goblets and martini sets. For cooks who want the best, there are small appliances by Cuisinart and Waring Pro plus serious cookware by Berndes, All-Clad, Le Creuset, and Lodge Cast Iron. Woodenware includes a large selection of bowls, cutting boards, and utensils. There are coffeemakers by Capresso and Chemex, which you might be surprised to learn is made in Pittsfield. There are gadgets and implements galore by Zyliss and Oxo, professional metal baking pans by LaForme and silicone ones by Kitchen Zone, and knives by Kasumi, Wusthof, and Global plus an assortment of sharpeners and chef's knife bags. While there are a lot of exotic products here, Different Drummer also stocks the mundane, including dish drainers, Pyrex, dish towels, aprons, and potholders plus a large section of mops, brooms, and other cleaning aids. Picnic sets, including backpacks and wheeled carriers, implements for grilling, wall and ceiling racks for pots and pans, even portable serving carts and work tops are here. Owned by the Meisberger family, Different Drummer has been supplying cooks and chefs with the exotic and the ordinary for more than 20 years. They also have shops at Thorne's in Northampton and Styvesant Plaza in Albany. The Lenox shop is open every day.

Villager Gifts
68 Main Street
(413) 637-9866
It's always Christmas at Villager Gifts, although you will have to go downstairs to find it. The basement is a winter wonderland packed with Christmas items all year. At least a dozen Christmas trees are lit and decorated, often with changing themes. One might be filled with snowmen, another with glittering ornaments or pet-oriented decorations. Collectible lines include villages by Dept. 56, figures by Byers and SnowBabies, manger pieces by Fontanini, Ice Cube People by Midwest, and elves by Zims. The amazing stock includes an assortment of elaborate music boxes, snowmen in all kinds of sizes and materials, and tree ornaments of all sorts. The main floor of the shop has ever-changing stock depending on the season, but there are always greeting cards, wrapping papers, journals, baby books, plush toys, boxes of all sorts, wind chimes, afghans, pottery, Colonial Candles of Cape Cod, and silk-screened replicas of famous stained-glass panels by Glassmasters plus Caspari paper products and lotions and creams by Camille Beckman. Jim Terry, who owns the shop with his wife, Nancy Hall, also does custom framing in one cor-

The Lenox Shops

Until recently, this attractive shopping center on US 7 was all but empty, victim of an exodus of specialty stores that moved to Prime Outlets in Lee when that complex opened. But a new owner has injected life into the place, bringing in new tenants, including those listed below. Shop hours and days open vary.

Bare Furniture—Unpainted furniture; (413) 637-5050.
Berkshire Soaps—Locally made natural soaps, essences, and candles; (413) 637-0641.
Chocolate Springs—Gourmet baked goods and beverages; (413) 637-9820.
Crossing Borders—Decorative accessories for the home and garden; (413) 637-2666.
Lenox Antique Center—a group shop that has space for around 80 dealers; (413) 637-9700.
Lenox Sportscards & Games—Gaming and sports collectibles, Magic and Yu-gi-oh tournaments; (413) 637-3243.
Love Dog Cafe & Apothecary—Breakfast and lunch; (413) 637-8022, herbal apothecary; (413) 637-4633.
Pine Cone Hill—Outlet for this firm's line of bedding, quilts, and other soft goods and decorative items for the home; (413) 637-8962.
Yesteryears—Supplies for making scrapbooks and greeting cards, papers, writing implements, stickers; (413) 637-5060.

ner. Prints for sale include photographs of Berkshire scenes by John Bedard. The shop is open daily.

R. W. Wise, Goldsmiths
81 Church Street
(413) 637-1589
www.polygon.net/~rwwise

Richard Wise travels around the world gathering gemstones for the fine jewelry crafted at his Lenox shop. The author of *Secrets of the Gem Trade,* Wise has been designing and creating jewelry in Lenox for 25 years. About two-thirds of his elegantly presented stock is handcrafted on the premises using techniques handed down from master to apprentice for hundreds of years. Colored gemstones and pearls are a specialty, and pieces are custom-designed for clients after serious consultation. Aside from his own work, Wise, a graduate gemologist, exhibits pieces crafted by other contemporary designers as well as selected antique and estate pieces presented in attractive, well-lit showcases. Between the soothing decor and the well-chosen background music, a visit to this attractive shop is a reward in itself. The shop is open daily in July and August and Tuesday through Saturday from September 1 through June 30.

Mill River

David M. Weiss Antiques
15 Mill River-Great Barrington Road
(413) 229-2716
www.davidmweiss.com

David Weiss's parents and grandparents were antiques dealers, and he is carrying on the tradition with his shop, which he opened in 1982. He focuses on 18th- and 19th-century American furniture, landscape paintings, portraits, and decorative accessories, examples of which may be seen on his Web site. He is open by appointment.

Sheffield

Bradford Galleries
US 7
(413) 229-3279
www.bradfordauctions.com

Rare book and ephemera auctions are held at Bradford Galleries five times a year. Auctioneer Robert Emberlin also runs monthly sales featuring antiques and other furnishings and accessories. There are always things to poke through that are for sale in an addition to the gallery, which is open every day.

Corner House Antiques
US 7
(413) 229-6627

This is the place to look for wicker. Thomas and Kathleen Tetro have been specializing in 19th- and early-20th-century wicker since 1977. They also carry panel and leaded-glass lamps and bamboo along with accessories of the period and are open most days.

Cupboards and Roses
296 South Main Street (US 7)
(413) 229-3070
www.cupboardsandroses.com

Edith Gilson opened her shop in 1989 and quickly established herself as a leading source for painted furniture from Europe and Scandinavia. The 18th- and 19th-century cupboards, chests, and armoirs she finds have been featured in *Architectural Digest, Better Homes and Gardens,* and *Country Living.* Most were made by country craftsmen who, lacking the fine woods available in the cities, used lesser woods that they then camouflaged with elaborate false graining, flowers, rural scenes, or geometric designs that almost seem contemporary. Many are dated and some contain family names, since they often were given as wedding presents. As works of art, they fit well in either country homes or city apartments. Accessories include decorated pottery, paintings, and Mora tall-case clocks from Sweden. Open daily.

Dovetail Antiques
440 Sheffield Road (US 7)
(413) 229-2628

American clocks from the 18th, 19th, and early 20th century are David and Judith Steindler's specialty. All are sold with a one-year guarantee. In business since 1975, the couple also carry country furniture, mostly in original finish or paint, plus stoneware, redware, spongeware, and other early accessories. Closed Tuesday, but appointments may be made.

Good & Hutchinson
US 7
(413) 229-8832, (413) 258-4555

David Good and Robert Hutchinson have been in the antiques business since 1948, which has to be some kind of record. Known for quality merchandise, they specialize in 18th- and 19th-century furnishings, including Chinese export porcelain, American, English, and Continental furniture, paintings, brass accessories, and lamps. Members of the Art and Antiques Dealers League of America, they exhibit at the better antiques shows. The shop is open every day but Tuesday from June through October and by appointment or chance the rest of the year.

Tracy Goodnow Art & Antiques
576 Sheffield Plain (US 7)
(413) 229-6045
www.tracygoodnow.com

American painted country furniture and folk art, especially on canvas or paper, are Tracy Goodnow's specialty. Two other dealers also display here. Kathy Immerman, who owns Kuttner Antiques, (413-229-2955), and Sally and Samuel Herrup (413-229-0424). Immerman specializes in

When shopping for gifts, don't forget the museums and nonprofit organizations like the Berkshire Botanical Garden. Out-of-the-ordinary items can be found in their gift shops, plus the profits go toward supporting these institutions.

early English and American country and formal furniture, paintings, accessories, folk art, and porcelain. The Herrups carry formal and country American furniture, folk art including portraits, and European decorative arts, including ceramics, metalwork, and sculpture. The shop is open every day but Tuesday and by appointment.

Great Finds Antiques & Arts Marketplace
1840 North Main Street
(413) 528-8059
www.egreatfinds.com
Peter and Lisa Schneyer run this shop, which has around 40 dealers selling collectibles, furniture, books, prints, jewelry, and other items of interest. Also on the premises is Outer Edge Frames and Gallery. Open daily year-round.

Hill House Antiques
276 South Undermountain Road
(Massachusetts Highway 41)
(413) 229-2374
Beverly Dahl and Edward Surjan carry early-20th-century decorative arts, including Mission furniture (old and new), art pottery and tiles, textiles, lighting, and accessories from here and abroad, along with clocks and pre-1960 rotary dial phones. The shop is open Friday through Monday from May through December, weekends or by appointment the rest of the year.

Painted Porch Antiques
102 South Main Street (US 7)
(413) 229-2700
www.paintedporch.com
Carol and Larry Solomon display their early French and English country furniture in their 1815 colonial home and barn. They specialize in cherry, pine, and painted armoires, tables, chairs, cupboards and servers, and selected decorative accessories from the 18th, 19th, and early 20th centuries. The shop is open Thursday through Monday or by appointment.

Bruce A. Sikora
549 Sheffield Plain (US 7)
(413) 229-6049 (shop), (413) 274-6049
Bruce Sikora deals in landscape and marine paintings, American and English furniture, plus English candlesticks and glass, English and Dutch delftware, and German stoneware. The shop is open Friday through Sunday or by chance or appointment.

South Egremont

Geffner/Schatzky Antiques
MA 23
(413) 528-0057
The focus here is on the unusual. Architectural elements and garden pieces are featured, along with decorative furniture and accessories and vintage jewelry. Open Friday through Monday and at other times by chance or appointment.

Red Barn Antiques
MA 23
(413) 528-3230
John and Mary Walther are known for their large stock of lighting fixtures and lamps. Kerosene, gas, and early electric lights—restored if necessary—are always on hand, along with furniture, glass, and accessories. They also have a repair and restoration service, do fine metal polishing, and arrange for silver plating. Open daily.

Elliott and Grace Snyder Antiques
37 Undermountain Road (MA 41)
(413) 528-3581
Open by chance or appointment, the Snyders carry early American furniture, period lighting, paintings, and folk art. They also are known for their textiles, including hooked rugs, samplers, and needlework pictures.

The Splendid Peasant
MA 23 at Sheffield Road
(413) 528-5755
www.splendidpeasant.com
American folk art, 19th-century weathervanes, game boards, paintings, sculpture, and early American furniture are among the antiques carried by Martin and Kitty

Jacobs. Pieces are displayed in gallery-like settings in two buildings overlooking a stream. The shop is open daily from May through December and Friday through Monday the rest of the year or by appointment.

Southfield

The Buggy Whip Factory
Main Street
(413) 229-3576
The rambling floors of this former buggy whip factory are filled with antiques and collectibles shown by around 90 dealers. Stock ranges from country to formal, with some dealers focusing on architectural pieces, kitchenware, tools, china, sterling, glassware, jewelry, and books. There is a cafe on the premises. Open daily in season; closed Tuesday and Wednesday January through April.

Stockbridge

Country Curtains
Red Lion Inn
Main Street
(413) 298-5565
www.ccretail.com
The flagship store for nationally known Country Curtains is at the back of the Red Lion Inn, which is to be expected since this is where the famous line was designed by inn-owner Jane Fitzpatrick. Featured here are hundreds of ready-made window treatments along with the rods and hardware to hang them. Also here are rugs, pillows, bedding, lamps, and decorative accessories for the home. The shop is open daily but hours vary, so a call might be in order if you're coming from a distance. Curtains and sample swatches also may be ordered through the Web site.

Greystone Gardens
The Mews
(413) 298-0113
www.greystonegardens.com
Romantic and frilly, Greystone Gardens in the Mews next to the Red Lion Inn is the second shop opened by the owner of Greystone Gardens in Pittsfield. Managed by partner Carla Lund, the shop opened in 1995 and is filled with examples of the same fine one-of-a-kind vintage and antique clothing, scented soaps and oils, flowers, and appurtenances typical of a lady's boudoir that are available in Pittsfield and described more fully in the write-up for that flagship store. The Mews shop is open daily from Memorial Day through fall and Thursday through Monday the rest of the year.

Heirlooms
The Mews
(413) 298-4436
Nancy Stoll has sold contemporary, vintage, and antique estate jewelry for 30 years in a glittering jewel box of a shop in the Mews next to the Red Lion Inn. The stock, recently purchased from a previous owner, runs the gamut from literally hundreds of affordable earrings, including the clip-on kind, to necklaces, rings, and the like dazzling with gemstones. One-of-a-kind pieces in reasonably priced amber share space with designer creations from the '50s, '60s, and '70s. Stoll also carries a line of jewelry that re-creates in miniature architectural features from historic homes ranging from Monticello to Frank Lloyd Wright's home, each with a history of the structure from which the design was taken. Interesting gift items include wares from Turkey in Byzantine designs. The shop is open daily in season and weekends or by appointment in winter.

Nora Martin
8 Elm Street
(413) 298-4840
Raised in the business, Nora Martin opened her Stockbridge shop in 2002. Furniture from all periods is the focus, and the floor is crammed with desks, armoirs, chests of drawers, and tables large and small. There also are many accessories and collectibles displayed in showcases and on the shelves. Estate jewelry, ceramics, glassware, and

linens are always in stock. Later collectibles, comics, sheet music, country items, and other finds are stashed in a back room that is fun to poke around. Nora is closed on Tuesday in season and Monday and Tuesday off season. She also has a shop in Pittsfield on Tyler Street.

Red Lion Inn Gift Shop
30 Main Street
(413) 298-5545
www.redlioninn.com
Gourmet foods, including the Red Lion Inn's own clam chowder, jams, and jellies are but a small part of the varied stock found in the inn's gift shop. Also here are jewelry, pajamas, soaps, perfumes, scarves, shawls, and books. A children's section carries books, games, and toys, including some terrific teddy bears. Gift packages featuring the inn's chowder and other products are available. You also will find a huge selection of teapots as well as packages of the inn's own tea. The stock includes lamps, decorative accessories, and unique Christmas and other holiday decorations. Open daily.

Vlada Boutique
Elm Street
(413) 298-3656
Vlada Rouseff's eclectic boutique is high on the list of places local women go when they want something special for themselves or someone else. The clothing, selected with an eye for quality, texture, and color, is suitable for important business meetings, casual affairs that require something nice, formal occasions, or just hanging out. Every nook and cranny is filled. Tops, skirts, slacks, dresses, and jackets hang on the racks or are suspended along the walls. Brands include Eileen Fisher, Flax, Cut Loose, and Christy Allen. There is always a huge assortment of sweaters and scarves in luscious colors and in a wide range of prices. Jewelry, footwear, purses, and shoes round out the stock. Vlada's also carries zany greeting cards, political commentaries, music, wrapping paper, gag gifts, and silly trinkets. Open daily.

West Stockbridge

West Stockbridge has two shopping areas. One is along Main Street, or Massachusetts Highway 102. The other is a cluster of galleries, restaurants, and shops on Harris and Depot Streets. These can be reached from Main Street by a pedestrian bridge over the river or by car from MA 102 via Depot Street. There is a public restroom at the Depot Street parking lot that is wheelchair-accessible.

Charles H. Baldwin & Sons
One Center Street
(413) 232-7785
www.baldwinextracts.com
Charles H. Baldwin and his father, H. M. Baldwin, began making and selling extracts in 1888. Charles sold their flavorings from a wagon, traveling all over the Northeast. Today the fifth generation is running the business, and their famous extracts are sold over the Internet. Earl Baldwin Moffat and his wife, Jackie, follow the mantra of the founders: "Never tamper with the recipe or use inferior beans." Indeed, they still use the original recipe to produce what most say is the best vanilla extract you can buy. Walking into the rambling, crowded former carriage shop on Center Street is like walking into the past. The beans, the process, and the equipment are the same as those first used by the elder Baldwins. Bourbon vanilla beans imported from Madagascar are placed in a large copper percolator, where their essence is extracted. The extract is then aged in oak barrels more than 100 years old that sit along the wall. The final product is bottled and labeled on the premises.

But vanilla is not the only extract sold here. Pure anise, lemon, orange, spearmint, peppermint, and almond extracts also are available. The firm also sells imitation flavors, including raspberry, root beer, and black walnut. In the 1920s, in response to requests for a good-tasting syrup that could sell for less than pure maple syrup, the firm developed Baldwin's Table Syrup.

The blend of pure maple and cane sugar syrups contains no preservatives, artificial color, or flavor and has a following of fans who prefer it over pure maple. In addition to all sizes of bottled extracts and flavorings, the shelves are full of other Baldwin products: Worcestershire sauce, walnuts in maple syrup, vanilla vinaigrette, even the whole Madagascar vanilla beans they prefer. Personal care products include bay rum, witch hazel, rose water, also with glycerine, and locally made soaps. Baldwin's even sells their own wood stove polish. One section of the store contains baking ingredients, handy if the recipes the Baldwins hand out bring on the urge. Curries and other spices, oils, and vinegars also are for sale. As if that wasn't enough, the store is chock-full of old-timey things like corncob pipes and reproductions of silly 1950s toys. Even if you don't give a hoot about vanilla, the store is worth a visit. And you might care a lot about vanilla by the time you leave. Open daily.

La Bruschetta Food & Wine To Go
1 Harris Street
(413) 232-7141
www.LBfoodandwine.com
Fine wines and gourmet food for takeout are sold daily at La Bruschetta, an outgrowth of a restaurant by the same name opened by Cathy Ligenza in 1992. After nine successful years—including rave reviews and numerous awards from the *Wine Spectator*—Ligenza and partner Danny May decided to change the restaurant part to takeout only while maintaining their well-stocked retail wine shop. The move has been successful with locals as well as weekend visitors stopping in for interesting ratatouille, soups, chowders, stews, gourmet pizza, and main dishes like rotisserie duckling and chicken plus desserts and other goodies. Items are priced by the pint or pound. For instance, osso buco goes for around $13 a pound. The exception is half a roasted duckling, which will cost around $10. La Bruschetta will do catering in the sense that they will cook the food for a party, but someone has to pick it up. La Bruschetta is closed Monday.

Sawyer's Antiques
1 Depot Street
(413) 232-7062
www.sawyerantiques.com
Edward S. Sawyer has been dealing in antiques since the 1970s. He and his son, Scott, run estate sales and also sell at the Shaker Mill on the corner of Depot Street and MA 102. Here you can find early silver, collectible glass, frames, furniture, and who knows what. The place is packed with interesting things. The structure itself is a historic building. Originally built in 1805, the gristmill was briefly owned by the Tyringham Shakers before being bought in 1867 by what was to become a long line of private owners. A member of the American Society of Appraisers, the elder Sawyer, with his son, also appraises estates, donations, collections, and items for insurance purposes. The number to call for appraisals is (413) 443-5908. The Shaker Mill is usually open daily in summer, other times by appointment.

CENTRAL BERKSHIRE

Lanesborough

Berkshire Mall
Massachusetts Highway 8
(413) 445-4400
The county's only enclosed shopping mall is anchored by Sears, JCPenney, and Filene's. Around 70 other tenants include Old Navy, Eddie Bauer, Klein's All Sports, Wilson Suede and Leather, K-B Toys, Waldenbooks, Limited, Jonathan Reid, and Footlocker plus a food court, a restaurant, and a 10-screen cinema. The mall also can be accessed from US 7 via Berkshire Mall Drive just over the Pittsfield line.

By law, shops cannot open on Sunday until noon—except during the pre-Christmas shopping season.

Berkshire Pendleton
US 7
(413) 443-6822, (888) 443-1432
Since 1971 this shop has been the sole source in the area for Pendleton woolens. Year-round you can find outerwear, sportswear, suits, and separates for men and women made by this famous Oregon company. The shop also carries Pendleton's brightly colored wool and cotton-blend blankets decorated with traditional or adapted Native American designs. There are usually around 350 examples on hand, and some are always displayed on the porch outside the shop. Classic and novelty sweaters in washable wool for men and women are neatly arranged in the post-and-beam building reminiscent of a trading post. Also here are suits and separates in Pendleton's classic tartans. In addition to the copious stock on the ground floor, there is a basement full of bargains with price reductions ranging from 40 to 70 percent. Open daily, the shop is north of town.

Second Life Books
55 Quarry Road
(413) 447-8010
www.secondlifebooks.com
Established by Russell and Martha Freedman in 1972, Second Life Books buys and sells rare and antiquarian books by appointment in an 18th-century farmhouse at the foot of Mount Greylock. The emphasis is on woman's studies, Americana, agriculture and horticulture, and English, American, and Continental literature from the 16th century to the present. Catalogs are available by mail or on the Internet, and appraisals can be arranged. The Freedmans are members of the Antiquarian Booksellers Association of America and the International League of Antiquarian Booksellers.

Pittsfield

Barnes & Noble
555 Hubbard Avenue
(413) 496-9051
Barnes & Noble is located in a free-standing building in the Berkshire Crossing shopping center on the east side of Pittsfield, off Dalton Avenue, or MA 8. Aside from the usual assortment of titles, this branch has a large collection of Berkshire writers and Berkshire County-related material. The magazine section is all-encompassing; special-interest newspapers also are carried here. There is a Starbucks coffee shop where you can sit and study possible purchases while nibbling goodies, plus other areas around the store where you can sit and read. Other businesses in the center include Pier 1, Wal-Mart, Home Depot, Staples, Michael's Crafts, and Fashion Bug. All are open daily.

Berkshire Hills Coins & Estate Jewelry
222 Elm Street
(413) 499-1400
Peter Karpenski has been in the coin business for more than 30 years. He specializes in collectible coins, estate gold and costume jewelry, sterling items, pocket watches, and diamonds plus an assortment of furniture and accessories. The shop is open Monday through Saturday.

The Cottage Store
31 South Street
(413) 447-9643
The Cottage Store carries stock similar to the Cottage in Lenox, including women's and children's apparel and accessories, gifts, greeting cards, jewelry, and home furnishings. Table linens, china, glassware, flatware, and accessories can be found here. The shop is an outlet for Bennington Pottery, which is made from Sheffield clay. Seasonal items run from picnic sets to Christmas decorations. Clothing for women is suitable for business, casual gatherings, or dressy occasions. While the shop has been a fixture on Park Square for more than 25 years, it has been owned by Bobbie Dus since 1998. Her daughter, Lora Kozlowski, manages it and the Lenox shop.

Dierdre's
75 North Street
(413) 499-9959

Dierdre Tovia has the largest selection of formal evening wear and wedding gowns in the area, filling a niche she perceived when she opened her store in 2000. The racks are filled with glittery gowns and dressy ensembles in all sizes. While many of her customers are seeking something dressy for a holiday ball or special event locally, a large percentage are shopping for gowns to wear on cruises or to attend events out of the area. Her stock includes hats, scarves, jewelry, handbags, and just about anything you might need to complete the effect. Weddings are a large part of her business. She has more than 300 wedding gowns in stock and can provide clothing for the entire wedding party, including a frilly dress for the flower girl, gowns for attendants, and a dress for the mother of the bride. She also has tuxedos and shirts, dyes shoes, and does alterations. She even carries gifts for the members of the wedding. In short, she is a one-stop shopping center for wedding parties, particularly handy for young people who have moved away from the area and are returning here to be married. Her shop also is one that high school girls check out when looking for a prom gown, and mothers often bring in their daughters for something special to wear to a dance with Dad. Although she intended to focus only on social occasions when she opened the shop, she has responded to requests from local professional women looking for business suits and sportswear on the dressy side. She carries sweaters in a range of styles from classic to beaded and sequined. Labels that may be found here include David Brook, Sigrid Olsen, City Girl, and Albert Nipon. She likes to carry lines by unusual designers to maintain an eclectic mix of merchandise. Dierdre's is open every day.

Fontaine's Auction Gallery
1485 West Housatonic Street (US 20)
(413) 448-8928
www.fontaineauction.com

John Fontaine has been in the auction business since the 1970s. He is known for his specialty sales, particularly of Victorian furniture and art glass lamps, and holds other sales throughout the year.

Greystone Gardens
436 North Street
(413) 442-9291
www.greystonegardens.com

Lynda Meyer moved up from Manhattan to open her dream store in 1980 and has been offering her customers an escape from the present ever since. Lush fabrics, romantic accessories, jewelry, collectibles, and clothing from as far back as she can find are crammed into the shop. A large men's department features shirts, formal wear, and accessories, including a mélange of hats, jewelry, scarves, books, and leather journals. Aside from the huge collection of women's antique and vintage clothing and accessories, there is a special wedding salon full of items for that special day, including antique, vintage, and replica gowns and headpieces; guest books and wedding favors. Some popular but hard-to-find items in both men's and women's wear are being reproduced in painstaking detail. Lines of soaps, oils, perfumes, lotions, and silk flower arrangements add to the romantic feel of the place. You feel pampered just walking through the door. A great place to find unusual gifts and attire, Greystone Gardens is open Monday through Saturday.

Guido's Fresh Marketplace
US 7 at Dan Fox Drive
(413) 442-9912
www.guidosfreshmarketplace.com

Five different purveyors are under the roof at Guido's, which started out as a small roadside stand with a reputation for fresh vegetables and fruits at reasonable prices. The family moved down the road to the present location in the 1980s and continued to sell fresh, organic fruits and vegetables. But soon there were additions, and now there is Michael Mazzeo's meat section, which carries free-range livestock and poultry, unusual cuts, marinated dishes, and specialty sausages; Masse's

Seafood, which offers salads and a wide range of fresh fish; Berger's Bakery and Deli, where you can get prepared main courses and appetizers, desserts, and breads; and Bella Flora cut flowers and arrangements. There also is a section of serve-yourself dried fruits, nuts, and grains; beer, wine, and unusual sodas; gourmet items; cheeses; fresh pasta and sauces; sushi prepared on-site; and local products like maple syrup and honey. There are usually a few plates full of seasonal samples sitting around to nibble while you shop, and cooking demonstrations often are held. A small gift section has greeting cards, candles, and books. Chris and Matthew Masiero, owners of Guidos, are planning another move a couple of miles down the road to the Lenox Shops complex. Until then, they are open daily, as is their sister store in Great Barrington.

Haddad's
12 Bank Row
(413) 443-4747

The Haddad family has been selling carpets and Oriental rugs in Pittsfield since 1895, the last 45 years or so at the shop on Park Square. Three floors at the shop are chock-full of stock, including antique rugs by Kashan, Bohkaras, and Tabriz as well as Caucasian rugs. New carpets include handwork from Iran, China, Afghanistan, India, and Turkey and machine-made Couristan rugs from Belgium. High-end designer wall-to-wall carpeting also is available here, as are window treatments, linoleum, and trims. Remnants, laminate flooring, economy Orientals, and roll goods are offered at the family's warehouse on Park Street. Installation may be arranged. The firm also is the only one in the county that cleans rugs by washing. The shop and the warehouse are open Monday through Saturday.

Pittsfield Precious Metals
93 First Street
(413) 443-3613
www.lujohns.com

John and Luisa Economou deal in antique, estate, and contemporary jewelry, diamonds and precious stones, coins, and pocket and wristwatches. They also carry sterling silver, porcelain, art glass, and quality collectibles and decorative accessories. John also holds auctions at a gallery in Lee and offers services for the liquidation of estates. The shop is open Monday through Saturday.

Paul Rich & Sons
242 North Street
(413) 443-6467, (800) 723-7424
www.paulrich.com

Paul Rich started out with one shop on North Street in 1983. Today the shop takes up half the block with four connecting stores filled with fine furniture and accessories displayed in complete settings for every room in the house. Styles available in a wide array of woods, treatments, and finishes include American, European, country, Shaker, Arts & Crafts, Traditional, and Contemporary by Thomasville, Harden, Henredon, Drexel Heritage, Hickory Chair, Woodmark, Ralph Lauren, Nichols & Stone, and Lexington, among others. There is a large selection of rugs, including hand-knotted Orientals from India, Pakistan, Turkey, and Tibet plus all-wool Oriental rugs and broadloom carpets by Karastan. Beds, mattresses, and bargains from other departments are located in the basement. The firm also sells leather furniture suitable for home or office and can provide design services for space planning and style and fabric coordination. Outdoor furniture in aluminum, cast aluminum, wrought iron, teak, wicker, and rattan by makers including Barlow, Tyrie, Lloyd Flanders, Lane Weathermaster, and Summer Classics is sold in season. Bargains are offered at sales throughout the year. The shop is open daily year-round.

Ronnie's Motorclothes
501 Wahconah Street
(413) 443-0638 ext. 18
www.ronnies.com

Ronnie's Motorclothes has the largest selection of leathers and other riding gear in the county. Harley riders from near and far make it a point to shop at Ronnie's, which also sells and services motorcycles, ATVs, and snowmobiles. Everything from scarves to helmets—even stuff for little kids—is here. Much bears the Harley insignia, but also in stock are apparel and gear by Fox, Polaris, HJC, and Oneil. The shop is open Monday through Saturday.

Steven Valenti Clothing for Men
157 North Street
(413) 443-2569

As a young man, Steven Valenti worked in several local men's shops before deciding to open his own store in 1983. The others are long gone, but Valenti has carved out a niche for himself by focusing on quality merchandise and offering services to his customer that others might consider way beyond the call of duty. He has been known to take an assortment of clothing to a house-bound customer and deals with last-minute shoppers with aplomb. If a man who has spilled something down his front before an important meeting calls in need of a shirt in a hurry, Valenti will select an appropriate one and deliver it ironed. Now, that's customer service. The stock ranges from silk pajamas and cashmere sweaters to casual cotton shirts and every-day pants. Depending on the maker, sizes run from 36 to 4XL, including some talls. Brands include Scott Barber, Jhane Barnes, Ralph Lauren, Tallia, Cohen, Calvin Klein, Hanes, and Dockers. He also carries Cole Haan shoes. Outerwear includes cashmere overcoats, rainwear, leather jackets, hats, and gloves. Colognes include Acqua di Gio by Armani and Royall Bay Rum. While this is the place to get something special, you also can pick up underwear, socks, belts, and other accessories. Valenti sells and rents formal wear and insists on perfect fits. He will arrange to deliver and pick up attire for wedding parties that might be staying at a local resort, eliminating the last-minute scramble for out-of-towners. Valenti's is open Monday through Saturday and stays open later on Thursday night. The shop is closed on Sunday except for the four preceding Christmas. Gift wrapping is available.

Wood Brothers
Allendale Shopping Center
MA 8
(413) 447-7478

Lennox and Fletcher Wood opened their music store on Pittsfield's North Street in 1880. As they developed their niche, they became the first in the county to own a delivery truck. Their forward-looking approach kept the business alive through the Depression and other ups and downs for around 80 years until the last member of the family sold to the present owners in the 1960s. Around 20 years later, a branch store was opened in the basement of the Allendale Shopping Center. This eventually led to a consolidation and a move to the present location on the ground floor in a huge space crammed with nearly everything relating to music and music-making. Lennox and Fletcher would be in shock if they could see it. Around 200 guitars—acoustic, electric, and otherwise—hang from the ceiling. Violins and other stringed instruments line the walls. The floor is crammed with speakers, amplifiers, sound boards, lighting equipment, mixing consoles, keyboards, pianos, and percussion instruments. Every kind of accessory is available. The walls carry the banners of such brand names as Fender, Yamaha, Jackson, Taylor, and Kawai. The store serves the needs of the large number of talented musicians in the area plus disc jockeys, karaoke fans, and students. The staff counters Internet and catalog sales with knowledge and personal service. The largest stock of sheet music in the area is found here, and special orders can be filled through a computerized service and printed out on the spot. Instruction books, CDs that augment Suzuki lessons, video and audio educational aides, and rental instruments are available for students of all ages. The shop also buys and sells new and used CDs and tapes, many of which are outside the mainstream. Lessons for percussion or stringed instruments may be arranged with any of six instructors. Wood Brothers is open every day but Sunday, plus Thursday, Friday, and Saturday nights. They even have kazoos.

Yours, Mine & Ours
136–140 South Street
(413) 443-5260
Mary Donohue usually has something interesting out on the sidewalk in front of her shop, which she calls a "resale boutique." Collectibles and furniture are spread through the first and second floors of three connected shops. Filling in the gaps are Stonewall Kitchen jellies and other gourmet foods, CBK accessories, American Girl books, and Caswell Massey personal care products. Donohue also runs estate sales. The shop is open Monday through Saturday, and there is a large parking lot at the rear, around the corner off US 20.

NORTH COUNTY

Adams

The Interior Alternative
3 Hoosac Street
(413) 743-1986
Hip decorators, professional or otherwise, head to this historic warehouse off MA 8 for bargains in fabrics, wallpapers, linens, and notions. Hundreds of seconds and closeouts of fabrics by Waverly and other designers are lined up row after row, bolt after bolt. Decorative prints, sheers, damasks, and tapestries suitable for upholstery, slipcovers, curtains, and drapes abound. There are bins of remnants and piles of decorative trimmings, including braiding, tassels, fringe, and cord. Discontinued wallpaper and borders can be purchased at bargain prices. Just be sure you buy enough—there might not be any more if you have to go back. Pillows, comforters, bedspreads, and other bedding are displayed on the second floor along with rugs. There is a custom sewing service for small projects. Interior Alternative does not have its own Web site, but shoppers can check out Waverly.com; if they see a fabric they like, they can call the shop to see if it is in stock. The shop is closed on Sunday.

Cheshire

Winter Brook Farm Antiques
450 North State Road (MA 8)
(413) 743-2177
www.winterbrookfarm.com
Gene Gebarowski deals mostly in furniture. He also is a good source for reproduction hardware and brass polishes. Open Monday through Friday, the shop is down off the road, where there is room for parking. You can also park off the highway and walk down, if so inclined.

North Adams

Galadriel's
105 Main Street
(413) 664-0026
Comfortable free-flowing garments made of natural fibers with an international flair make up the bulk of the stock at this shop named for the Elven Lady of Lorien in *Lord of the Rings*. Owner Joann Burdick searches for things from all over the world, with an eye to quality workmanship and earth-friendly materials that can be sold at a reasonable price. These goals result in an interesting mix of styles and fabrics from Guatemala, India, and elsewhere. Separates made of hemp share space with cut-velvet shawls, beaded tops, and gorgeous silk scarves. Former hippies will feel at home here, as will college kids and women looking for something different to spice up their wardrobe. Interesting handbags, jewelry, and other accessories can be found here, too. Generally open Tuesday through Saturday, but call if you're coming from a distance, just in case.

Papyri Books
49 Main Street
(413) 662-2099
www.papyribooks.com
An independent, locally owned bookstore, Papyri holds poetry slams and readings throughout the year. Every April the store celebrates National Poetry Month by arranging special appearances by such notable poets as Richard Wilbur and Billy Collins. Events are publicized and listed on the Web site. Owner Karen Kane also brings in local musicians for casual concerts and supports local artists by showing their work. Thousands of quality used books in all categories plus selected new titles, particularly those written by local authors or about the area, fill the shelves. Cards and journals also are for sale. This is a friendly shop. Customers are welcome to have a free cup of coffee or tea and settle into one of the comfy chairs to read or chat. Papyri is open daily.

Skiddoo
36 Eagle Street
(413) 664-8007
Paige Carter specializes in "stuff" from the 1950s through the 1970s. Folks looking for retro-clothing will love this place. There's lots of polyester for both men and women. She also carries vintage furniture, housewares, and collectibles. Her hours vary, so a call is in order.

Tala's Quilt Shop
Heritage State Park, Building 12
MA 8
(413) 664-8200
www.talasquiltshop.com
Serious quilters from all over come to Tala Neathawk's shop for their materials, knowing that with more than 3,500 bolts to choose from, they will find just the fabric they are looking for. In the running as one of the top-10 quilting shops in the country, Tala's carries 100 percent cotton, flannel, and wool by Baum, Thimbleberries, P&B, and Moda, among others. Row after row of brightly colored bolts fill the shop, stacked on the shelves or displayed in and on antique racks and carts salvaged from the old Arnold Print Works textile plant (which is now MASS MoCA). Piles of "fat quarters"—ensembles of pre-cut squares—are everywhere. The shop itself is in one of the restored buildings in this former freight yard off MA 8. The mellow, polished floorboards and Tala's collections of sewing machines, baskets, needle cases, pincushions, and other memorabilia add to the 1890s aura of the shop. Patterns, books, thread, notions, filling—everything you need for making a quilt is here. In addition, Tala and four of her five employees teach quilting at every level. Quilting has come into its own as an art form, and the work of quilters from around the area is shown annually at Berkshire Community College. The shop is open every day.

Williamstown

The Cottage
24 Water Street
(413) 458-4305
Once part of the Cottage stores in Pittsfield and Lenox, this Cottage is now independently owned by Amy Bryan, who has stocked the place with an amazing assortment of gifts, unusual glass and ceramics for the table, clothing, toys, home furnishings, stationery, and personal care products. A recent mother, she also carries clothes and gifts for babies and toddlers. There are piles of stuffed animals everywhere and a select assortment of playthings for little ones. For parties there are candles, paper products by Caspari, table linens, and seasonal holiday decorations. She even carries a full line of teas by the Republic of Tea—and the teapots to make it in. For the home—or dorm room—there are lamps, picture frames, and scatter rugs. Women's clothing, generally in sizes small through large, is mostly casual but can be dressed up with any number of accessories. Brightly colored bags by Vera Bradley are always in stock. Personal products include full lines by Burt's Bees, Crabtree & Evelyn, Cooks, and Caldrea.

Once the perfect gift has been found—which is a pretty sure bet—the wrapping paper and snappy card to go with it is here, too. The shop is open daily.

Library Antiques
70 Spring Street
(413) 458-3436
www.libraryantiques.com
Edward Fauteux opened Library Antiques in 1993 and has been a popular source for antiques, decorative accessories, and jewelry ever since. American and European antiques from estates or auctions include a large assortment of sterling items plus interesting boxes, candlesticks, and inkwells. Interesting furniture, paintings and prints, and architectural pieces also are here. New items include greeting cards and notepapers, candles, gift items, and hand-knit alpaca sweaters for men. Fauteux also goes to China twice a year and imports containers filled with furniture and architectural elements, smalls, and decorative accessories. Those, along with paintings by Chinese artist He Feng, are sold at LiAsia Gallery across the street. The phone there is (413) 458-1600. Items at both shops can be viewed on the Web site listed above. Both stores are open daily.

Saddleback Antiques Center
1395 Cold Spring Road (US 7)
(413) 458-5852
Owner Dan Rhodes opened this eclectic shop in 1993. Period furniture, Victoriana, stoneware, porcelain, folk art, paintings, and Civil War items are among the collections for sale here. The shop is open daily.

The Store at Five Corners
6 New Ashford Road (US 7)
(413) 458-3176
The Store at Five Corners began life as Sloan's Tavern in 1769. An inn and stop on the Pony Express line, the historic building has been operating continuously with one business or another ever since. The latest stewards, Tom Masone and Meddy and Jeff Woodyard, picked up the baton in 1998 and have established themselves as purveyors of fine wines and gourmet foods to eat in or take out. Made from scratch with seasonal ingredients are desserts, soups, quiche, salads, and entrees like barbecued chicken, grilled salmon, osso buco, beef stir-fry, or tenderloin and pork roasts. They also make excellent sandwiches, which can be eaten in an enclosed porch or, in summer, on the deck or at picnic tables by the Green River. Picnics may be ordered to take to Tanglewood or other outdoor venues. The store also stocks a wide selection of candies and chocolates, including their own fudge plus gourmet jams, jellies, and condiments. A favorite item is Sloan's Tavern mustard, created by a local resident. Gift baskets featuring New England products may be ordered. The family also operates a store at Jiminy Peak resort that carries similar products. Although a lot is upscale, locals can count on getting a newspaper and other basics of life. The five corners are created by the intersection of Massachusetts Highway 43, US 7, and Sloan Road. The store is open daily.

Toonerville Trolley
131 Water Street
(413) 458-5229
In 1976 Hal March loaded up a truck with records and started driving around to colleges in the area selling music to students. Two years later he decided to give up his "Toonerville Trolley" and settle in Williamstown, applying the name of his truck to the store on Water Street where he has been ever since. The small shop is crammed with thousands of new and used CDs and tapes and collectible vinyl records. Although he has everything from classical to world music, including best-sellers, Hal is most known for having obscure and esoteric recordings, including imports, with jazz being his strong suit. He also sells used records on the Internet at www.recordcollectorsabyss.com. The staff at this independent store is extremely knowledgeable, thanks largely to Hal's willingness to share his expertise. "Tooner" is open Monday through Saturday year-

round, with Sunday added during summer and in December.

Water Street Books
26 Water Street
(413) 458-8071

Water Street Books is the official textbook store for Williams College students and is affiliated with Follett Higher Education Group. But it also is a general bookstore with a huge stock of books in every category imaginable. With carpeted floors, bare brick walls, and painted murals, you might think the place was a coffeehouse were it not for the rows and rows of polished mahogany stacks laden with volumes of all sorts. An extensive biography section, a large assortment of poetry from mainstream to extreme, anthologies, and depth in history and philosophy make this store a cut above the average. Also featured are works by Williams faculty. Bestsellers are offered at 30 percent off. Literary journals and magazines are sold here as well as notebooks and journals yet to be filled. The staff cares about what they sell, and they know their stuff. Requests are welcome. A wing off the main floor houses the inviting children's section, where books are displayed in small areas on kid-height shelves. Hanging mobiles and light blue walls decorated with trees and birds add to the friendly feeling. Water Street Books is open Monday through Saturday year-round and on Sunday from June to January.

The Women's Exchange
277 Cole Avenue
(413) 458-5853

Some folks will be unhappy to see this great shop listed in the Insiders' Guide. They probably would like to keep it all to themselves. But, hey—that's what this book is all about. And for quality clothing at reasonable prices, the Women's Exchange can't be beat. Since 1957 the Exchange has accepted clothing on consignment from—or donated by—residents, many of whom have a taste for designer clothes, name brands, and fine fabrics. You can find real sleepers among the racks and leave with top-quality attire. Any guilt you feel can be assuaged by remembering that the Exchange was founded by a visiting nurse with a purpose: to raise funds for health care in the community. Over the years it has provided financial support to North Adams Regional Hospital, including a donation of $50,000 for improvements to the emergency department. Funds also have been given to the Visiting Nurse Association & Hospice of Northern Berkshire to provide free care. Aside from carrying all kinds of clothing and accessories for men, women, children, and babies, the shop often has drapes and bedding, lamps, furniture, toys, glassware, household items, small appliances, exercise equipment, and furniture, much of it displayed in a separate building at the rear of the shop. Many an antiques dealer has been seen checking out the stock. The Exchange is open Tuesday through Saturday—but don't tell anybody.

Zanna
41 Spring Street
(413) 458-9858, (800) 773-9858
www.zanna.com

Zanna has been meeting the fashion needs of women of all ages and sizes since 1971. High school kids, college students, and professional women are among the clientele who have established relationships with the helpful and supportive staff, who also come in all ages and sizes. Regular shoppers eagerly await Thursday, when new items arrive. Zanna's carries junior through plus sizes and fights dressing room anguish with the motto "You are perfect just the way you are." Formal and casual fashions include designs by Eileen Fisher, Cut Loose, Sigrid Olsen, Staples, CP Shades, Gertie's, and others. The shop also carries shoes by Dansko and Arche. Accessories include a wide range of jewelry, fancy and plain, as well as scarves, purses, and socks. And there is always something tempting on the sale rack. Zanna's is open every day. The shop also has branches in Amherst and Northampton.

ATTRACTIONS 

Considering what a small area Berkshire County is—947.14 square miles—it is truly amazing how many attractions there are. From one end of the county to the other, there are venues for the performing arts and museums large and small, many with international reputations. The attractions listed below are more or less the cream of the crop—the "must see" places, depending on your interests. They are listed alphabetically, rather than geographically, as they are major destinations. Many more attractions will be found in the Parks and Arts and Culture chapters.

While you're running around checking out the big draws, don't forget to notice the scenery. Take time to smell the flowers—and the new-mown hay. Try to imagine the days when the first settlers came over the mountains from the east to this rich, rock-strewn land and how the Mahicans lived before they were driven west. Envision the days when the rich discovered Lenox and Stockbridge, building their huge estates, playing croquet on the lawns, hunting foxes, and boating on the lakes. Think of the days when trains changed the landscape, bringing socialites from New York and opening up North Adams to the rest of the country.

Consider the vision of people like Serge Koussevitsky, who turned the Tanglewood estate into a summer learning experience for young musicians; Tina Packer, who founded Shakespeare & Company to share the deeper messages of the Bard's works with young and old; Ted Shawn, driven to change dance in America; and Thomas Krens and the small band of believers who changed an abandoned mill complex in North Adams into a world-class museum of contemporary art. And think also of those generous and forward-thinking families and individuals who preserved the landscape by giving their land to various trusts and organizations, of the collectors who decided to share their possessions with the public, and the hundreds who have worked to preserve historic landmarks that would otherwise have been lost.

Arrowhead
780 Holmes Road, Pittsfield
(413) 442-1793
www.mobydick.org

This unassuming farmhouse was the home of writer Herman Melville and his family from 1850 to 1863. An established writer by then, Melville sought respite from the hectic life in New York and bought the 18th-century home to have a quieter place to work. Three of his four children were born here. He named the place Arrowhead after finding artifacts while tilling the soil. During the 12 years he lived here, he developed close friendships with other Berkshire writers, including Nathaniel Hawthorne, Oliver Wendell Holmes, and Catherine Maria Sedgwick, and wrote a number of books, including *Moby Dick,* as well as a collection of short stories. He and his family returned to New York in 1863, but Arrowhead remained in the Melville family until 1927, when it was used as a private residence. It was purchased in 1975 by the Berkshire County Historical Society, which opened it to the public as a museum.

Visitors may stroll the 44-acre property, through which a nature trail winds, and view the panoramic vistas that Melville reveled in. Guided tours of the furnished house are conducted. The society also has protected the north meadow, preserving the view of Mount Greylock to the north that was a major inspiration to Melville, particularly for *Moby Dick.* A Registered National Historic Landmark, Arrowhead is open Memorial Day weekend through October 31. A fee is charged. The phone number listed above may be called for winter hours and membership information. For those interested in more research on Melville, the Berkshire Athenaeum in Pittsfield (413-499-9486) has a very large collection of his work, including original manuscripts and correspondence as well as family portraits, pictures, and other memorabilia. Aptly named the Melville Room, it is open whenever the library is. Special materials housed in a vault may be used by appointment.

Colonel John Ashley House
Cooper Hill Road, Ashley Falls
(413) 298-3239
www.thetrustees.org

This house, built in 1735 by 25-year-old Colonel John Ashley for his Dutch bride, Hannah Hogeboom, is the oldest in Berkshire County. But its age and period furnishings are not its only claim to fame. The Ashley home was the center of social, economic, and political life in South County. Several years before the Declaration of Independence was signed, a group gathered in the upstairs study and drafted a petition against British tyranny and a manifesto for individual rights. Called the Sheffield Declaration, it was published in 1773. The cause for the abolition of slavery in America gained ground after a state court ruled in 1781 that under the new state constitution the Ashleys' slave, Elizabeth "Mumbet" Freeman, should be freed. The house, near the remarkable Bartholomew's Cobble Nature and Visitor Center, is listed on the National Register of Historic Places and has been a property of the Trustees since 1972. The home is off Rannapo Road, reached by U.S. Highway 7A south of Sheffield. It is open Memorial Day weekend to Columbus Day on weekends and Monday holidays. A 45-minute house tour is offered. There is a modest admission fee.

Berkshire Botanical Garden
Intersection of Massachusetts Highways 102 and 183, Stockbridge
(413) 298-3926
www.berkshirebotanical.org

The Berkshire Botanical Garden was founded in 1934 to provide a place for visitors to enjoy beautiful public gardens and to provide instruction on the kinds of plants, flowers, fruits, and vegetables best suited to growing in the region. Since then, the gardens have been expanded in size and variety and the educational programs for adults and children have grown. Located on 15 donated acres, the garden now enhances the grounds through the summer by displaying sculpture by local artists. Staff visit schools throughout the tristate area to nurture children's interest in nature and to teach about the importance of caring for the environment. Busloads of school children also visit the center, where they may plant seedlings to take back with them. Adults can learn about garden design, flower arranging, herb gardening, and other topics through courses taught throughout the year for varying fees.

Volunteer herb associates tend the renowned herb gardens and produce jellies, vinegar, dressings, mustard, and other organic products that are sold in the visitor center along with gardening books, greeting cards, select tools, and gifts for all ages. The garden researches and tests new varieties of perennials, annuals, and vegetables. Community events include a plant sale in May, an antiques or arts and crafts show in mid-July, a flower show in early August and, continuing a tradition established in 1934, the Harvest Festival on the first weekend in October. In December seasonal decorations and gifts may be found at the Holiday Marketplace. A nonprofit educational institution, the garden is open May through October and is supported by memberships, donations, and fees charged for some classes and special events. There is no charge for children under age 12.

Berkshire Museum
39 South Street, Pittsfield
(413) 443-7171
www.berkshiremuseum.org

Between the bright red banners that flank the entrance and "Wally," the life-size stegosaurus munching away in the garden, you can tell right away that the Berkshire Museum is no stodgy collection of dusty artifacts. Between ever-changing exhibits and educational programs, the museum continues to enrich the community the way its founder intended. Dalton paper maker and philanthropist Zenas Crane established the museum in 1903, and it continues to be the only museum in western Massachusetts combining art, natural science, and history. From the fine art and ancient civilization galleries to the stick-your-hand-in aquarium, the Berkshire Museum has something from all ages for all ages. Adults might admire the amazing colors in classical Greek and Roman jewelry and glass and appreciate the fine collections of silver, paintings, and sculpture, while kids will be fascinated with the rocks that glow flourescent at the push of a button or the mummy that reposes under glass in the ancient civilizations gallery. Exhibits relating to the Berkshires include native birds and mammals. One of the finest collections of Hudson River School landscapes in the Northeast can be seen here. And then there's the gallery lined with vintage refrigerator doors decorated with work by children.

The museum sponsors lectures, performances, and films, shown in the 291-seat air-conditioned theater. An annual favorite is the Festival of Trees just before Christmas when the museum is filled with trees decorated by local businesses and individuals. (More about the galleries will be found in the Arts and Culture chapter. Offerings for children, of which there are many, will be found in Kidstuff.) The museum is open every day. The admission charge varies depending on age but is free to children under age three and to members. The museum is located in the center of Pittsfield and is wheelchair-accessible, with appropriate parking spaces at the side of the building. Other parking is available on the street, if you're lucky, or in nearby parking garages.

If you go to the Berkshire Museum on your birthday, there is no admission charge, no matter how old you are.

Bidwell House Museum
Art School Road, Monterey
(413) 528-6888
www.bidwellhousemuseum.org

If early American furnishings make you drool, prepare to keep a handkerchief handy when you tour the Bidwell House. Set amid 196 acres of fields, woodlands, and period gardens is a beautifully proportioned Georgian saltbox built around 1750 for the Reverend Adonijah Bidwell, who came to preach to the pioneer settlers. Additions were added in 1790 and 1836 by the Reverend's son and grandson. Completely preserved, the buildings contain extremely fine examples of hand-carved wall panels and unique door details. A massive center chimney services four fireplaces, three with open hearths, plus two beehive ovens. Cupboards and shelves are filled with an extensive assortment of pewter, earthenware, and china, including Delft, redware, and slipware. Early samplers, paintings, and mirrors hang on the walls, and linsey-woolsey coverlets and patchwork quilts are displayed on the beds. Fine furniture and accessories of the period abound along with rare lighting devices, hand tools, and other utensils. The collection is said to be one of the finest in the county. The agricultural heritage of New England is also preserved here with heirloom vegetable and herb gardens containing varieties dating back to their original planting.

The grounds include several 19th-century outbuildings and the ruins of several barns available for exploration. Hiking trails and footpaths wind through the forest. The nonprofit museum is privately operated, supported by memberships, contributions, and bequests and a modest admission charge. It is open Memorial Day to late October. The museum is at the end of Art School Road off Tyringham Road,

CLOSE-UP

The Trustees of Reservations

The Trustees of Reservations is one of the oldest conservation organizations in the nation, having been empowered by the state legislature in 1891 to acquire and maintain publicly accessible properties across Massachusetts. Landscape architect Charles Eliot, a protégé of Frederick Law Olmsted, is credited with forming the organization with other visionaries who were concerned by the dramatic loss of open space in the Boston area as urban development spread. The nonprofit organization's board is made up of voluntary trustees. The properties—or reservations—they protect include beaches, forests, meadows, mountains, farms, gardens, and historic homes from Cape Cod to the New York border, more than 80 in all. Collectively, these landscapes and properties tell the story of the cultural and natural history of Massachusetts.

The organization relies for support on contributions, grants, endowments, receipts from attendance at properties or special events, and memberships. Annual dues begin at $40 ($30 for seniors) and rise depending on the level of contribution desired. Members receive free or reduced admission at all properties, so if you are planning to visit several reservations you have a chance to save money while doing a good deed. Members also receive mailings of special events held throughout the year at various properties. Most of the properties in Berkshire County are open to the public, but hours and rules vary. Details are available on the Web site at www.thetrustees.org or the Western Regional Office, The Mission House, Sergeant Street, Stockbridge, MA 01262-0792. Call (413) 298-3239 for information.

- Bartholomew's Cobble—296 acres, Ashley Falls
- The Colonel John Ashley House—Ashley Falls
- Field Farm—316 acres, Williamstown
- McLennan Reservation—594 acres, Tyringham and Otis
- The Mission House—Stockbridge
- Monument Mountain—503 acres, Great Barrington
- Naumkeag—46 acres, Stockbridge
- Notchview—3,108 acres, Windsor
- Questing—407 acres, New Marlborough
- Tyringham Cobble—206 acres, Tyringham
- The William Cullen Bryant Homestead—195 acres, Cummington

which runs north from Massachusetts Highway 23 in Monterey or south from MA 102 in Lee.

The William Cullen Bryant Homestead
297 Bryant Road, Cummington
(413) 734-2244
www.thetrustees.org

Just outside Berkshire County, this pastoral estate was the boyhood home of William Cullen Bryant, one of America's foremost 19th-century poets. A National Historic Landmark, the property was purchased in 1789 by Bryant's grandfather. The homestead and its surrounding countryside inspired much of young Bryant's poetry, including "The Rivulet" and "To a Waterfowl." After a law career in Great Barrington, Bryant moved to New York City to become editor and publisher of the *New York Evening Post,* where he served for 50 years. His family sold the Homestead in 1835. Thirty years later Bryant repurchased it as a summer retreat and converted it from a center-stair colonial to a Victorian cottage. Among the orchards, maple groves, and old-growth forests are trees almost 200 years old. Footpaths and carriage roads wind through the property, allowing for moderate hiking. The home is furnished with colonial and Victorian pieces from Bryant and his ancestors as well as memorabilia Bryant collected during his travels to Europe and Asia.

Largely unchanged for more than 159 years, the 195-acre property was given to the Trustees of Reservations with an endowment by Minna Godwin Goddard in 1927. Additional land was purchased in 1981 with funds given by Mrs. Winthrop M. Crane III. Around 970 acres of actively managed farm and forest land that surround the property are protected from development by the Trustees in conjunction with the state's Agricultural Preservation Restriction Program. A museum shop in the visitor center is one of a few places to find complete volumes of Bryant's poetry, last published in 1947. While these books are not part of the Homestead's collection, some with elegant bindings date to the 19th century. Biographies and memoirs and maple syrup from trees on the property are also available. The grounds are open year-round from sunrise to sunset. The house is open for guided tours Friday through Sunday and on Monday holidays from the last weekend in June through Labor Day and Saturday, Sunday, and Monday through Columbus Day. There is a nominal admission charge. A craft festival is held in July. Cummington is on Massachusetts Highway 9 east of Windsor. The Homestead is off Massachusetts Highway 112, which meets MA 9 near the William Cullen Bryant Public Library.

Chesterwood
4 Williamsville Road
P.O. Box 827, Stockbridge 01262
(413) 298-3579
www.chesterwood.org

Chesterwood is a 122-acre estate that was the summer home and workplace of sculptor Daniel Chester French, most remembered for his statue of the seated Lincoln for the Memorial in Washington, D.C., and *The Minuteman* in Concord. Working models for these and other works are displayed in his former studio, the museum gallery, home, and gardens.

French sought respite from the hurly-burly world of New York by working at his Berkshire retreat. He carefully planned his estate to satisfy different needs: formal gardens and spacious lawns for elegant receptions and parties; broad porches for dining with a spectacular view of the peaceful mountains; and cloistered garden nooks for tranquility. However, peace was difficult for the noted sculptor to attain. Frequent visitors, models, assistants, and clients made the trek to his studio. He then built a second studio in a cool, quite secluded space on the grounds, which he found more conducive to the concentration needed for his work. Today that studio, called Meadowlark, may be rented through the Red Lion Inn for weekend getaways in season. The grounds also are available for photo sessions, weddings, and corporate meetings. A national trust, the museum is open daily May through October. Special events held at other times throughout the year include Christmas at Chesterwood.

Sterling and Francine Clark Art Institute
225 South Street, Williamstown
(413) 458-2318
www.clarkart.edu

At first glance, the Clark Art Institute, with its marble columns and Grecian facade, looks like some kind of temple. And that is just what its founders considered it: a temple of art. In its galleries and those of a later addition are the acquisitions of a remarkable couple for whom collecting art was a shared passion. Sterling Clark was the grandson of Edward Clark, partner of Isaac Singer of sewing machine fame. Aside from receiving a sizable fortune from his grandfather, he inherited his grandfather's love of art. Clark studied at Yale and served in the army before settling in Paris, where he began his collection. While there he met former actress Francine Clary; they married in 1919. Together they amassed what is considered one of the finest collections of European and American paintings and sculpture, prints, and drawings; English silver and porcelain; and early photographs. But the couple's passion was French Impressionism, and they purchased many works by Renoir, Monet, and Degas, acquisitions that are the heart of the Clark collection. They moved to Williamstown and established the Sterling and Francine Clark Art Institute in 1950 (it opened to the public in 1955). Together they designed the building that houses their collection and beneath whose front steps they both are buried.

Surrounded by 140 acres of expansive lawns, meadows, and walking trails, the Clark opened to the public in 1955. But the collections are only part of it. In conjunction with Williams College, the Clark is also dedicated to being a center for research and higher education. Throughout the year, the Clark sponsors lectures, concerts, films, and special exhibitions for the public as well as students of all ages. The Clark also houses one of the finest art reference libraries in the world. As it approaches its 50th anniversary, the Clark has embarked on an ambitious plan to redesign the campus, expand the facilities for its academic and public programs, and reconfigure its galleries to broaden the ways in which visitors experience works of art. Prize-winning architect Tadao Ando of Osaka, Japan, and Massachusetts landscape architects Reed Hilderbrand Associates have been engaged to design the project, which will fully integrate all the buildings while preserving the idyllic setting. Much of the project will be partially underground, topped with a one-acre reflecting pool. Plans include expanding the present museum shop and restaurant. The Williamstown Art Conservation Center now located on the campus will be moving to a new site on US 7 south of Williamstown when construction begins. The Clark is open daily in July and August. Except for President's Day, Memorial Day, Labor Day, and Columbus Day, it is closed on Monday the rest of the year. The admission charge for adults, which may vary depending on exhibits, is waived November through May. There is no charge for persons age 18 and under or students with identification. The galleries, library, cafe, restrooms, and auditorium are fully accessible. The museum is located on South Street, a right turn at Field Park where US 7 and Massachusetts Highway 2 converge.

The Frelinghuysen Morris House & Studio
92 Hawthorne Street, Lenox
(413) 637-0166
www.frelinghuysen.org

If 18th- and 19th-century Americana is not your cup of tea, this might be the place for you. Amidst the colonial houses and outrageous "cottages" of Lenox is a concrete and glass structure of Bauhaus design filled with abstract art from the 1930s and beyond. It is the home and studio of George L. K. Morris and Suzy Frelinghuysen, prolific artists who were at the leading edge of the national and international art scene at that time. George L. K. Morris was born in 1905 to a wealthy and prominent American family. After his education at Groton and Yale, Morris traveled to Paris with his cousin, artist and collector A. E. Gallatin, where he met Picasso, Braque, and Brancusi. Two years later he returned to study in the studio of Fernand Léger and Amédée Ozenfant. In 1930 he built his studio on the grounds of his parents' 46-acre estate in Lenox. Based on a design by Le Corbusier, the studio was the first of that genre to be built in New England. Morris made more trips to Europe in the 1930s to collect European abstract art, often from artists he knew. In the process he met Suzy Frelinghuysen, daughter of a

CLOSE-UP

The Berkshire Cottages

There are as many theories about why the rich and powerful came to the Berkshires as there are estates they left behind. There was the natural beauty, captured by artists who had fallen in love with the area earlier. Then there was the nearness to New York City, the center of all their financial and political wheelings and dealings and their complex social lives. The Berkshires had already attracted the literati. The land was unspoiled by the industrial development that had created all those fortunes. And it was cheap—$50 an acre, although that quickly escalated to $1,000 when the locals caught on. It might have been that the rich had to have someplace to go "between seasons." They went to Newport for the ocean in June and July, to Saratoga in August for the horses and to take the waters, and to New York for the theater in November. The Berkshires fit neatly between Saratoga and New York—and there was the splendor of fall foliage. In any event, and it's not clear who came first, one by one they built their elaborate hideaways.

There were rules, probably unwritten, about how these "cottages" were to look. The homes had to have no fewer than 20 rooms and had to sit on at least 30 acres. Their architecture mimicked that of the wealthy in England, France, and Italy, sometimes combining all three. Their gardens were laid out by the best names in the business. By the turn of the 20th century there were 75 estates in Lenox, another 25 or so in Stockbridge, considered by the elite to be a less desirable location. They were built on hills with commanding views, at the ends of long drives or, if close to the road, well screened from the nosy by high walls and plantings. One of these cottages, Shadow Brook, was described by one resident as "a great leviathan laying curled on the hilltop; lit up at night, it looked like a great ship afloat."

Although it is not clear exactly why they came here, we do know why they left: The Great Depression and two world wars took their toll. Society, as it had been dictated at the turn of the 20th century, was unraveling. Soon everyone had a car, everyone could eat ice cream. Bit by bit, some of the cottages disappeared. Shadow Brook, the

wealthy and politically prominent New Jersey family. The glamorous couple married in 1935 and spent their time between a Paris town house, a 14-room apartment on Sutton Place in Manhattan, and Morris's Lenox studio. Although born of the upper crust, the two were irreverent to say the least and were once removed, albeit temporarily, from the Social Register for listing their dog.

Privately tutored in art and music, Frelinghuysen practiced both. Morris encouraged her art, and she was quite successful, becoming the first woman artist to have a painting placed in the permanent collection of Gallatin's Museum of Living Art in New York. But her main interest was music, and after World War II she auditioned for the New York City Opera, singing under the name Suzy Morris. Her highly success-

Edith Wharton's "The Mount." THE MOUNT/DAVID ANDERSEN

largest of all, burned to the ground in the 1950s. Many of the others have burned or have been lost to the wrecking ball. Of those that remain, about one-fourth are still private homes. Some have become resorts, like Canyon Ranch, Cranwell, and Seven Hills. Wheatleigh is an inn, and Orelton has become the Gateways Inn and Restaurant. Several became part of the complex at Tanglewood. Some are educational or therapeutic institutions, like High Point. Others, like Naumkeag and the Mount, are preserved for all to see. The Gilded Age that made Lenox the seat of aristocracy for a while was a fascinating period that the Ventfort Hall Association hopes to memorialize in its museum. For those interested in learning more, *The Berkshire Cottages: A Vanishing Era* by Carole Owens is a must. It is available in most book stores and was used as a source here.

ful career ended after she became ill with bronchitis, and she returned to painting full-time. By then the couple had enlarged their Lenox residence, building a Bauhaus-inspired home onto the studio. They incorporated frescoes into the walls and filled their home with Cubist and other abstract works of their own and others of the period they championed. Morris died in 1975 after a car crash in Stockbridge. Frelinghuysen died 13 years later. Their home is still filled with the dramatic murals, paintings, and sculptures they collected and furnishings of the period. It is open to the public Thursday through Sunday in summer, through Saturday in fall, with tours given on the hour. The house is a 10-minute walk through the woods from the parking area off Hawthorne Street. A shuttle also is available.

Hancock Shaker Village
U.S. Highway 20 at the junction of Massachusetts Highway 41
P.O. Box 927, Pittsfield 01202
(413) 443-0188
www.hancockshakervillage.org

Forty-some years ago, this Shaker community was all but abandoned, its fields and gardens overgrown, its beautifully constructed buildings in disrepair. Silence filled the rooms where the industrious Shakers once sorted and packaged their herbs and seeds, wove textiles and baskets, and crafted furnishings for themselves and "the world." It took the foresight and caring of Amy Bess Miller and her family to save the settlement from extinction and, through years of fund-raising and grants, bring it to the restored gem it is today. Preserved for all to enjoy and marvel at are 20 original buildings, including the ingenious round stone barn. The gardens flourish, sheep and cattle graze, and interpreters are on hand to explain the history of this celibate sect, which has all but died out. At their peak, the Shakers had 19 communities in New England, New York, Ohio, Kentucky, and Indiana. The Shakers believed in equality, pacifism, and a dedication to creating a heaven on earth. Putting their "hand to work and hearts to God," the Shakers created a community based in spirituality and rich in practicality and ingenuity.

Hancock, called the City of Peace, was home to the members of this communal religious society from 1783 until 1960, when it officially moved toward becoming an outdoor historical museum. Now suppers with authentic dishes, sheepshearing, timber framing, ice harvesting, plowing, and other hands-on activities for all ages are held throughout the year, keeping the Shaker way of life alive. The collections housed here are known throughout the world for their beauty of scale, craftsmanship, and sparse yet functional design. The art and music of the Shakers are also celebrated here. Located on the west side of Pittsfield, Hancock Shaker Village is open year-round. The complex is open daily Memorial Day weekend through late October, and visitors may wander through the various buildings on their own if they desire. Winter and early spring, guided tours through selected buildings and galleries are offered. Call for tour times. A gift shop and seasonal cafe are on the premises. There is an admission charge except for children under age 12. Special annual events include a topflight crafts show in July and an antiques show in August, both held in and around the round stone barn.

Jacob's Pillow Dance Festival
358 George Carter Road, Becket
(413) 637-1322
www.jacobspillow.org

Jacob's Pillow was originally a family farm at the crest of a stagecoach road that zigzagged through the mountains on its circuitous route between Albany and Boston. Viewed from the bottom of the hill, the road, locals felt, resembled the rungs of a ladder and, being Biblical New Englanders, they named it Jacob's Ladder. Today that road is US 20. On the rock-strewn Carter farm there were many boulders, but one in particular reminded the family of the rock pillow described in Genesis on which Jacob rested his head. Thus came the name Jacob's Pillow.

That was in 1790. Fast-forward to 1930, when modern dance pioneer Ted Shawn bought the farm as a retreat. At that time, Shawn and his wife, Ruth St. Denis, were America's leading couple of the dance. Their Denishawn Company eschewed traditional European ballet, instead popularizing a revolutionary dance form rooted in theatrical and ethnic traditions. But a year after buying the farm, their partnership ended. A few years later Shawn decided to act on a long-held desire to legitimize dance in America as an honorable career for men. He recruited eight men, including Denishawn dancer Barton Mumaw and several physical education students from a men's school in Springfield, and formed his new company. Intent on challenging the "sissy" image of men in dance, he forged a new, boldly muscular style celebrating such manly images as Pawnee braves, toiling sharecroppers, and union machinists. When they weren't dancing, they built structures still used at the Pillow today. To promote their work—and eat—the group started giving public "Tea Lecture Demonstrations," which gradually became so popular that by the end of summer, they were turning people away. For the next seven years, Shawn and his Men Dancers toured throughout the country as well as Canada, Cuba, and England and continued the summer programs at the Pillow. By the time World War II broke out, Shawn felt his troupe had succeeded in changing the image of male dancers. His mission accomplished, Shawn disbanded the group, and the dancers joined the armed forces.

Professionally successful, Shawn still was economically in trouble. He leased the property to dance teacher Mary Washington Ball, who produced the Berkshire Hills Dance Festival in 1940 and who is credited with beginning the diverse programming that has become the Pillow's hallmark. However, the summer was a financial disaster. The following year Shawn leased the Pillow to British ballet stars Alicia Markova and Anton Dolin. Their International Dance Festival was so successful that local supporters formed the Jacob's Pillow Dance Festival Committee and raised $50,000 to buy the property. They built a theater, the first specifically designed for dance, that blended in with the rest of the farm and made Shawn director in 1942. Despite gas and tire rationing, audiences came any way they could to attend the wide array of programs. For 30 years the festival continued successfully until Shawn's death at 81. A succession of directors followed, each leaving his or her mark and with varying success. Along the way, new studios were constructed, programs added, and innovations encouraged.

The grounds have been landscaped and the public is welcome to stroll around, see works in progress, and enjoy picnics or meals from the cafe or pub. Young dancers from around the country are encouraged to apply for the summer programs conducted by world-renowned performers. And the Pillow has teamed up with MASS MoCA to present various programs throughout the year. Recently celebrating its 70th anniversary, Jacob's Pillow remains true to Ted Shawn's vision of presenting and preserving an unparalleled variety of dance forms, a diversity unique among American dance festivals. For its contribution to cultural life in America, Jacob's Pillow was named in 2001 to the National Register of Historic Places. Open June through August, the Pillow is located off US 20 about 8 miles from Lee.

MASS MoCA
87 Marshall Street, North Adams
(413) 663-8548
www.massmoca.org

Fifty years ago, life in North Adams all but centered around 87 Marshall Street, where thousands churned out electronic components for Sprague Electric Company. The streets were flooded with workers heading home in the afternoon. People checked their watches by the chiming clock tower; shops and restaurants flourished. The city of North Adams was a thriving blue-collar town—and then the bottom fell out. Succumbing to the foreign market, Sprague closed up and left town, resulting in unemployment, closed stores, and empty eateries. The clock stopped chiming, and a feeling of desolation set in. Then along came this flaky idea of turning the empty complex—24 buildings on 13 acres—into a museum. Crazy, right? Not really, it turned out. After an infusion of $18 million in state money matched by $8 million in private funds, the Massachusetts Museum of Contemporary Art opened in 1999. And not only did it flourish but it also has become one of the top museums of its kind, with an international reputation.

Fusing visual and performing arts on all kinds of levels, MASS MoCA, as it is nicknamed, has generated interest in the art world from coast to coast. Locally it has caused residents to ignore snowstorms—and the distance from South County—to get to films, dance performances, concerts, and exhibits. And the once dead downtown is filled with fluttering flags, opening businesses and, above all, hope. Once again, 87 Marshall Street is the hub of life in North Adams. Amazing! Not that everyone appreciates the art. A canvas painted flawlessly in one solid color or small houses depicting the 13 Stations of the Cross ending with a life-size upside-down Jesus might not turn everyone on. But even if you don't "get" the art, the complex is worth a visit. Bricks and beams have been left as found, multiple layers of paint and all. Cavernous galleries with polished floors and airy ceilings have become a work of art themselves. The buildings, dating back to the 1800s when textiles were decorated by Arnold Print & Dye Works, have proved to be wonderful showcases for the stark and large works by contemporary artists.

The possibilities of turning all that space into galleries first gained the attention of Thomas Krens, then director of the Williams College Museum of Art. Now with the Guggenheim, Krens knew that there were few spaces in the country that could display the huge works done by some of today's artists. With the backing of chief cheerleader Mayor John Barrett III, local businesspeople, and just plain folk, the idea grew into an economic development plan. After years of fund-raising and near-deaths, the project was eventually funded by the state. After the museum opened, a huge fund-raising ball was held to celebrate. Parking lots were jammed with cars, and folks in formal gowns and tuxedos strolled the streets. Suddenly North Adams looked like SoHo. Since then, programming has expanded through partnerships with the Clark Art Institute, the Williams College Museum of Art, the Williamstown Jazz, Film, and Theatre Festivals, and Jacob's Pillow. From the upside-down maple trees that hang in the courtyard to the clock in the tower that chimes with new sounds, MASS MoCA is thought-provoking, stimulating, and full of excitement. And it isn't even finished. Eventually the buildings will be linked by covered bridges and elevated walkways resembling a small medieval city. In addition, catering to the needs of high-tech businesses in the complex, a fiber-optic network will be installed throughout.

MoCA is so much more than a multi-disciplinary center for the visual, performing, and media arts. It provides space, tools, and time for artists, cultural institutions, and businesses to work in sculpture, theater, dance, film, digital media, and music. It is a place where the processes of creativity can be explored. It has also become an educational tool for local schools, offering Kidspace for art classes as well as family gatherings. The museum gift shop, Hardware, is full of art books and techno-gadgets. There are two restaurants—Lickety-Split in MoCA and Eleven in another building on-site. Tenants in the complex include Geekscorps, a company that aims to bring technology to developing countries; Eziba, a firm that imports exceptional products from around the world and sells them via the Internet; and Kleiser-Walczak Construction, a special effects company. A work in progress, MoCA is open daily June 1 through October 31. November through May, hours are reduced; the museum is closed on Tuesday. Tours are given hourly in season. There is an admission fee unless you are a member.

---

i

It's probably the last place you would expect to find maple syrup for sale, but it's available in the MASS MoCA gift shop. The label features the upside-down maple trees that are suspended high above the courtyard outside the museum entrance. The installation by artist Natalie Jeremijenko is called "Tree Logic" and yes, the branches are turning up toward the sky.

The Mission House and Gardens
19 Main Street (MA 102), Stockbridge
(413) 298-3239
www.thetrustees.org

Following ministerial studies at Yale, the Reverend John Sergeant moved to what was to become Stockbridge to establish a mission for the Mahicans. He lived in a simple cabin in town until he married Abigail Williams in 1739 and built the Mission House on Prospect Hill. During his tenure, Sergeant learned the language of the Mahicans and frequently invited them into his home for study. Around 1926 Miss Mabel Choate had the home carefully disassembled, moved to its present location on Main Street, near the site of Sergeant's log cabin, and restored it. The most prominent feature of the otherwise simple structure is the ornate front entrance carved in the Connecticut River Valley style. The house contains an outstanding collection of simple 18th-century furnishings, more humble than those found in the Reverend Adonijah Bidwell's home in Monterey.

The Colonial Revival garden was designed by landscape architect Fletcher Steele over five years. It features a dooryard garden of circular brick paths enclosed by a tidewater cypress fence. A kitchen garden divided by graveled walkways contains 100 herbs, perennials, and annuals that had culinary or medicinal value to early colonists. A replica of an old cobbler shop serves as the entrance to the property. A grape arbor in the Well Courtyard behind the Mission House leads to a small Native American museum that tells the story of the Mahicans. The property is managed by the Trustees of Reservations, whose regional office is located in a red barn on the premises. A National Historic Landmark, the Mission House is open Memorial Day weekend to Columbus Day. A nominal admission fee is charged, which includes tours of the house and gardens led every 45 minutes. The house is located on the corner of Main and Sergeant Streets just west of the US 7 intersection.

The Mount
3 Plunkett Street, Lenox
(413) 637-1899
www.edithwharton.org

Author Edith Wharton visited Lenox several times at the turn of the 20th century, the heyday of the Gilded Cottages, and fell in love with the place. In 1902 she bought 113 acres that overlooked Laurel Lake for $40,600 and embarked on creating her dream house. The mansion and gardens would reflect the principles outlined in her influential book *The Decoration of Houses,* written in 1897. Architect Ogden Codman Jr. was coauthor, and Wharton enlisted his services in building the 42-room terraced mansion where she would entertain, garden, write, and seek refuge.

Beautifully proportioned, the estate is considered an icon of American architecture. A 17th-century Palladian-style English country house with classical French and Italian influences was the inspiration for the main house, which was built at a cost of $57,619. The gatehouse and stable of Georgian Revival style cost an additional $25,710. In a little more than a year, Wharton moved into what she called "my first real home." She named the place after her great-grandfather's home and lived there for more than 10 years, during which, according to her autobiography, "I lived and gardened and wrote contentedly and should doubtless have ended my days there had not a grave change in my husband's health made the burden of the property too heavy." Wharton moved to France in 1911, where she died on the eve of World War II.

One of America's greatest writers, Wharton penned more than 40 books in 40 years, including works on architecture, gardens, interior design, and travel. Essentially self-educated, she was the first woman awarded the Pulitzer Prize for Fiction, an honorary Doctorate of Letters from Yale University, and full membership in the American Academy of Arts and Letters. After Wharton left the Mount, the

Parking in the center of Stockbridge at the height of the season is extremely limited, so wherever you find a legal space, grab it and walk.

estate and its magnificent gardens fell into disrepair. A concerted effort to save the estate began in 1980 when the nonprofit group, Edith Wharton Restoration Inc., was created. Now, nearly $9 million later, the mansion has been restored. Work on the interior is ongoing, with Wharton's bedroom the first to be returned to the way it was when she wrote there. Other rooms were decorated by name designers for the centennial celebration. The gardens Wharton designed are 90 percent restored after an expenditure of more than $2 million.

A National Historic Landmark, the Mount is one of a few that honor a woman and the only monument to Wharton's remarkable life. Visitors may wander through the gardens and decorated rooms or enjoy lunch on the terrace where Wharton entertained her friends. A bookstore is stocked with works by Wharton, including rare and out-of-print editions as well as books by others on literature, architecture, interior design, and gardening. The Mount is open daily May through November. The terrace is open for lunch mid-June through August and fall weekends, weather permitting. Admission charges vary, but there is none for children under age 12 accompanied by an adult. The Mount also sponsors a lecture series through the season.

Naumkeag
Prospect Hill Road, Stockbridge
(413) 298-3239
www.thetrustees.org

Designed by Sanford White in 1885, this 26-room mansion is crammed with furniture, ceramics, rugs, tapestries, and artwork collected from America, Europe, and the Far East. But if Joseph Hodges Choate had had his way, it would not have been built here. A prominent New York attorney who was ambassador to England at the turn of the 20th century, Choate wanted to retire to his boyhood home in Salem. His family, however, disagreed, and the 40-acre site in Stockbridge was apparently a compromise. Possibly in an effort to soothe Choate's feelings, the place was named Naumkeag, the Native American name for Salem. Choate's friend Charles F. McKim was the original architect, but he turned the project over to his young and promising partner, Stanford White. The house is probably the last to represent the shingled English cottage style, as White was moving toward a more classical yet whimsical style incorporating brick turrets, leaded-glass windows, and mortar embedded with broken glass. The remarkable gardens also had two architects. Initially Frederick Lay Olmsted laid them out, but a dispute erupted over the cost; Nathaniel Barrett of Boston finished the project. When Choate's daughter inherited the place, she hired landscape architect Fletcher Steele to redo the gardens, which in a way are even more remarkable than the house.

Surrounded by 40 acres of woodland, meadow, and pasture that stretch to the Housatonic River are 8 acres of terraced gardens and landscaped grounds divided into "rooms" or themes. The Rose Garden offers a heady and profuse mix of color and fragrance when in bloom. Other settings include the Afternoon Garden, the Chinese pagoda and Linden Walk, the brick-walled Chinese Garden replete with stone Buddhas and carved lions and dogs, and the topiary of the Evergreen Garden. The most famous feature—and most photographed—is the hillside where towering white birches frame a series of deep blue fountain pools flanked by four flights of white-railed steps.

Miss Choate, who was instrumental in moving and restoring the Mission House, left Naumkeag and an endowment to the Trustees of Reservations, who manage it today. The property is open with an admission charge daily from Memorial Day weekend to Columbus Day. Guided house tours last around 45 minutes. Naumkeag hosts an annual Garden Party in July, a Farm Day in August, and other special events. Prospect Hill Road veers to the left off Pine Street, which begins at the intersection of US 7 and MA 102 near the Red Lion Inn. Naumkeag is one of several spectacular mansions along Prospect Hill Road.

The Norman Rockwell Museum
MA 183, Stockbridge
(413) 298-4100
www.nrm.org

Illustrator Norman Rockwell's national appeal makes this museum a major stop on any visit to the Berkshires. Built in the late 1990s at a cost of $4.4 million, this white clapboard building with its slate gables and fieldstone terraces is a fitting showcase for Rockwell's work, displayed in spacious, well-lit galleries. Center stage is reserved for his famous Four Freedoms, painted in 1943 after President Franklin Roosevelt's address to Congress. Rockwell's interpretations of *Freedom of Speech, Freedom to Worship, Freedom from Want,* and *Freedom from Fear,* published in four consecutive issues of the *Saturday Evening Post,* were enormously popular. The works toured the United States in an exhibition that was jointly sponsored by the *Post* and the U.S. Treasury Department and, through the sale of war bonds, raised more than $130 million for the war effort.

At the time Rockwell painted the Four Freedoms, his studio was in Arlington, Vermont, which was completely destroyed in a fire that same year. He lost many paintings plus his collection of historical costumes and props. Ten years later he moved to Stockbridge. Rockwell loved Stockbridge and often used local folks in his paintings. His portrayal of *Christmas on Main Street in Stockbridge* continues to be a popular work, and the town reenacts the setting every year, old cars and all. In 1973 Rockwell established a trust to preserve his artistic legacy by placing his works in the custodianship of the Old Corner House Stockbridge Historical Museum, which later became the Norman Rockwell Museum at Stockbridge. His studio, which he added to the trust in 1976, remained in a carriage house behind the family home on US 7 until it and its contents were moved to the new museum, along with the collections at the Old Corner House. The studio is open to the public May through October. In 1977 Rockwell received the nation's highest civilian honor, the Presidential Medal of Freedom, for his "vivid and affectionate portraits of our country." He died at his home in Stockbridge on November 8, 1978, at the age of 84.

In addition to Rockwell's work, the museum exhibits the work of other illustrators of various periods.

Exhibits of Rockwell's work change frequently, focusing on different aspects of his career. The museum, designed by architect Robert A. M. Stern, is located on MA 183, off MA 102 on the outskirts of Stockbridge. Sculptures by Rockwell's son, Peter, grace the expansive lawns and gardens on the grounds, which overlook the Housatonic River. The museum is open daily, including Monday holidays, May through October. November through April, hours are reduced, so call to check. Admission fee varies; admission is free with membership.

Many a marriage proposal has been "popped" at the Norman Rockwell Museum in front of the artist's rendition of a young man on bended knee doing just that.

Shakespeare & Company
77 Kemble Street, Lenox
(413) 637-1199, (413) 637-3353 (box office)
www.shakespeare.org

A theater is more than a theater, said artistic director Tina Packer on the 25th anniversary of her visionary Shakespeare & Company. And Shakespeare & Company is more than Shakespeare. It is heading toward becoming the world's first Shakespeare Center for Performance and Studies. It already is more than performances, although the season is packed with more plays than you can shake a stick at. It is a training ground, an educational center, a source for research, and a group dedicated to perpetuating the Elizabethan ideals of inquiry, balance, and harmony. With internationally acclaimed Packer at the helm, the company is committed to exploring Shakespeare's plays and connecting them to life experiences.

Packer founded Shakespeare & Company in 1978, and it has grown to become one of the largest Shakespeare Festivals in North America. Born in England, Packer journeyed to the United States in the early '70s with the idea of creating and running a company that merged the spoken word of British actors with the physical body of American actors. Reinvigorating her sense of what Elizabethan theater and acting constituted, Tina secured residency at the Mount, novelist Edith Wharton's beautiful turn-of-the-20th-century estate. Shakespeare was performed in the woods, on the grounds, off the balcony, in the Stable—it was a remarkable adventure for theatergoers and performers.

As efforts to restore the Mount grew, Shakespeare & Company became more of a liability than a welcome guest, so Packer searched for a new home. In 1999 the company took a huge step into the future by moving to the 63-acre estate on Kemble Street that it now occupies. One of many buildings on the property was renovated into Founders Theatre, where 422 seats are arranged on two levels and three sides of the stage for intimate performances. Spring Lawn, a 1904 "cottage" on the property, next to the Kemble Inn, has been adapted to become a theater, with 101 seats in an elegant salon. But the most ambitious part of the project is yet to come: the re-creation of an Elizabethan village complete with a historically accurate replica of the Rose Theatre, where Shakespeare's plays were first performed. To that end, the theater footprint has been laid out on the grounds and covered with a tent. A simple stage and bleacher seating have been constructed and a pit area set aside for lawn chairs and blankets. With these three venues, a variety of plays is offered each season.

The company also is home to one of the largest theater-in-education programs in the Northeast. Over half a million students each year take part in socially responsive and educationally challenging performances, workshops, and residencies throughout the country. The program is recognized as an innovative leader in the field of integrating the arts into the national school curriculum. Shakespeare & Company also features one of the most extensive actor training programs by a regional theater in the country. Professionals from all over the world come to train with the company in monthlong intensive workshops. Training in method, text analysis, movement, fight, dance, and clown, plus Packer's own singular exercises, are combined to explore the relationship between actor and audience. Eventually, Shakespeare & Company hopes to offer year-round programming in the Berkshires, including performances, education, actor and teacher training, seminars, workshops, lectures, broadcasting and recording services, as well as accommodations. Re-creating the Rose Playhouse reflects the company's passionate mission statement: "to perform as the Elizabethans did—in love with poetry, physical prowess and the mysteries of the universe." The theater season runs from May through December, with the heaviest schedule in summer. The grounds are open for strolling and picnicking daily.

Tanglewood
297 West Street (MA 183), Lenox
(413) 637–5165 (June through September), (617) 266–1492 (winter)
www.bso.org

Of the many concert venues in the area, Tanglewood is at the top of the list. If you don't go at least once, you haven't "done" the Berkshires. The summer home of the Boston Symphony Orchestra, Tanglewood is a 500-acre former estate with spacious grounds, towering trees, formal gardens, three concert halls, and buildings that house rehearsal studios. From the end of June through Labor Day weekend, world-famous conductors, soloists, and musicians perform a wide variety of music for audiences who often buy their tickets in March when the program is announced. While public concerts are the mainstay of Tanglewood, these artists also share their talents with students who spend the summer in Lenox through the Boston University Tan-

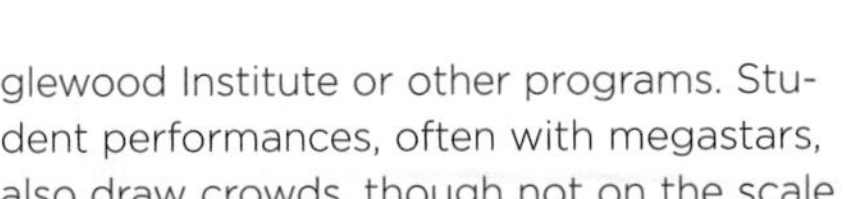

glewood Institute or other programs. Student performances, often with megastars, also draw crowds, though not on the scale of the regular concert schedule.

Most major concerts are held in the open-sided auditorium called the Shed, built in 1938 when BSO conductor Serge Koussevitsky created the then Berkshire Music Center as a place for young performers and composers to study with experienced musicians. On summer nights the lush and spacious lawn in front of the Shed is filled with concertgoers who enjoy the program under the stars. In what has become a ritual of summer, many come early to picnic on the grounds, some with candelabra, fresh flowers, linens, china, and crystal stemware; others with a bucket of Kentucky Fried Chicken.

Chamber music, smaller ensembles, and soloists often perform in the inspirational Ozawa Hall. The grounds are open for free strolling year-round or up to an hour before concerts. If you are lucky, you might stumble across an impromptu rehearsal. Formal rehearsals are open to the public for reduced fees on Saturday morning. A gift shop and cafeteria also are on the grounds. Ticket prices vary depending on seating, the program, and other factors. For more on Tanglewood and other concert venues, see the Arts and Culture chapter.

Ventfort Hall
104 Walker Street, Lenox
(413) 637-3206
www.gildedage.org

In 1994 Ventfort Hall was empty and desolate and slated for demolition. Today it is being restored and in the process of becoming a Museum of the Gilded Age—that period around 1900 when the rich discovered the Berkshires. Ventfort Hall was built in 1893 for Sarah Spencer Morgan—sister of J. P.—and her distant cousin and husband, George. It was designed by architects Rotch & Tilden.

Located in the center of Lenox, the Elizabethan Revival mansion presents a somber and formidable facade of brick and Longmeadow redstone. The interior is dominated

Checking out the can-you-top-this picnic spreads on the lawn at Tanglewood and people-watching are great ways to pass the time before the concert starts.

by a Great Hall and main staircase. The ground-floor rooms are filled with stained glass, elaborate plaster ceilings, and extensive and varied wood paneling and architectural detail. The house was privately owned until 1947, when a succession of organizations took it over. It served from time to time as a ballet camp and a property owned by the religious organization, The Bible Speaks. By the 1970s it had fallen into disrepair and the property was eyed as the site for a nursing home, with the mansion to be torn down. In 1994, fearful of the loss of such an important symbol of the Berkshire Cottage period, a group of citizens formed the nonprofit Ventfort Hall Association. Board members and supporters worked from day one to rescue the property, and on June 13, 1997, with the help of many private donations and loans, including one from the National Trust for Historic Preservation, the organization bought the site. Now, even as restoration continues, the mansion is open for tours and has become a venue for lectures, theatrical and musical events, and special exhibits relating to the period. Programs will center around the changes that occurred to American life, industry, and society during the late 19th century. If the mansion looks familiar to you, you might have seen it in the movie *Cider House Rules*, where it depicted an orphanage. Ventfort Hall is open daily Memorial Day through October 31 and on weekends from November 1 to the end of May, with tours given on the hour.

Western Gateway Heritage State Park
9 Furnace Street, North Adams
(413) 663-6312
www.massparks.org

This state-backed urban park commemorates the building of the Hoosac Tunnel, a monumental task that took 24 years and the lives of 196 workers before it was completed in 1875. Built at a cost of $21,241,842, the tunnel was the longest at that time and is considered one of the greatest engineering feats of the 19th century. Still in use, the tunnel turned once-isolated North Adams into a gateway to the west. Artifacts, photographs, and exhibits at the park demonstrate the dangerous and controversial work that went into boring through almost 5 miles of solid rock. An audiovisual presentation takes visitors back in time, where the sounds of dripping water, pickaxes against stone, explosions, and debates re-create the hardships and heroism of the tunnel's construction. Located in a former freight yard next to the still-operating railroad, the exhibit is housed in one of several beautifully restored buildings that were once used to store freight and commodities. The complex, surrounding a cobblestone courtyard, is listed on the National Register of Historic Places.

Concerts, walking tours, arts and crafts, and environmental education are offered regularly to the public in programs held here throughout the year. The gallery often features work by area artists. A model railroad portrays North Adams at the turn of the 20th century. A restaurant and a gift shop are in other buildings. The visitor center is open every day except Thanksgiving, Christmas, and New Year's Day. Admission and parking are free. The park is located off Massachusetts Highway 8 at the southern entrance to the city, near the Holiday Inn. Plans are under way to replace an aging bridge at that location, so watch for construction and directional signs.

Williams College Museum of Art
Main Street (Massachusetts Highway 2), Williamstown
www.williams.edu

The Williams College Museum of Art is located on a rise off Main Street, or MA 2, amid several other college buildings. Just look for the bronze and granite eyeballs peering from the earth. Or better yet, look for the graceful brick octagon designed in 1846 as the college's first library by Thomas S. Tefft. Now home to the museum's collection of 11,000 works, the structure was expanded with additions in 1983 and 1986 designed by internationally renowned architect Charles Moore. The original building is linked by a dramatic three-story atrium to a four-story addition, connecting the college's art department and an auditorium with the museum's 14 galleries above.

The Williams College Museum of Art collection spans several centuries with works from around the world, including 17th-century Chinese painting and calligraphy, African art, American art from the 18th century to the present, European art, and art of other world cultures. In addition to displaying works from the permanent collection, the museum procures loan exhibitions from other collections. The Prendergast Archive and Study Center, founded in 1990, is a resource for works by American modernists Maurice and Charles Prendergast and their contemporaries. The museum has more than 400 works by the Prendergast brothers. The collection of European sculpture, painting, prints, and photographs from the medieval period to the present includes devotional art, Spanish and Northern Baroque painting, and graphic arts from Dürer to Picasso. Modern art from 1900 to 1945 is represented by almost 1,000 works. Pieces by post-1945 artists include works by Willem De Kooning, Robert Rauschenberg, and Andy Warhol. A gift shop offers a unique selection of art-related products highlighting the permanent collection as well as traveling exhibitions.

The museum is open Tuesday through Sunday. Except for Memorial Day, Labor Day, and Columbus Day, it is closed on Monday. There is no admission charge. The museum is reached by a semicircular driveway with limited parking, but there are parking lots in the area. By the way, the eyeballs, which light up, are by American artist Louise Bourgeois, who created them in 2001 for the museum's 75th anniversary.

ARTS AND CULTURE

The Berkshire Visitors Bureau describes the area as America's Premier Cultural Resort—and considering the choices available, they are right on! While the major museums are open year-round and various venues offer theater, dance, and music off-season, the peak is reached in July and August. Summer stock brings big-name performers to the boards. The woods of Jacob's Pillow throb with music and dance. The Boston Symphony brings Tanglewood to life after a dormant winter, and returning musicians join retirees in the area to perform chamber music at a number of locations. This chapter focuses on classical music. Popular music is listed in the Nightlife chapter.

Art in all its forms can be viewed from one end of Berkshire County to the other. There are museums of world renown as well as less publicized exhibits to be ferreted out in the small towns. The performing and visual arts often comingle in joint programs, particularly at MASS MoCA, so film festivals and movie theaters are included in this chapter.

The works of contemporary artists are shown in galleries and at shows. Sundry potters, glassblowers, sculptors, weavers, cabinetmakers, and metalworkers keep old skills alive, often adding their own contemporary twist.

PERFORMING ARTS

Dance

Albany Berkshire Ballet
51 North Street, Pittsfield
(413) 445-5382
www.berkshireballet.org

The Albany Berkshire Ballet is nationally recognized for its versatility and excellence in performing both classical and contemporary dance works. The company was founded in 1960 by artistic director Madeline Cantarella Culpo as an outgrowth of her school, the Cantarella School of Dance, located in Pittsfield. Originally known as the Berkshire Ballet Guild and later as the Berkshire Civic Ballet, it was originally intended as a performance outlet for the school's advanced students, who soon pushed the company toward becoming a full-time professional troupe. Renamed the Berkshire Ballet in 1975, the company performed throughout the Northeast and Canada. In 1989 the company expanded again by establishing a partnership with the Albany (New York) Ballet, resulting in its present name.

The company's classical repertoire includes works by some of ballet's greatest choreographers, including Igor Youskevitch, Michel Fokine, and Antony Tudor. Full-length performances have included *Giselle, Cinderella, Coppelia, Romeo and Juliet, A Midsummer Night's Dream,* and the perennial favorite, *The Nutcracker.* The company supports newly emerging artists and does not shy away from contemporary works, having performed pieces choreographed by Phillip Jerry, Saecko Ichinohe, Mary Giannone Talmi, Ginger Thatcher, Bill T. Jones, Charles Moulton, Daryl Gray, and others. Alumni have gone on to perform with companies around the country, including the American Ballet Theater, Boston Ballet, and the Joffrey.

In 1993 Culpo choreographed the *Rockwell Suite,* which the company performed at the grand opening of the Norman Rockwell Museum in Stockbridge. Other local performances have been given at Jacob's Pillow, where the company opened the 46th season with *Coppelia,* and the Sterling and Clark Art Institute in Williamstown for the opening of a Degas art exhibit. The company also has performed at the Riverside Dance Festival in New York. The Ballet also offers performances, residencies, and educational programs to schools and nonprofit organizations. Most regular performances are held at the Koussevitsky Arts Center at Berkshire Community College on outer West Street in Pittsfield.

Jacob's Pillow Dance Festival
George Carter Road (off U.S. Highway 20), Lee
(413) 243-0745
www.jacobspillow.org

The setting is rural, bucolic, rustic, and picturesque. The dancing is daring, exciting, and invigorating. It's Jacob's Pillow, the country's oldest dance festival, started in 1933 by the legendary Ted Shawn. Since then an unprecedented roster of debuts, world premieres, and emerging, master, and downright extraordinary artists have studied, created, taught, and performed at the Pillow. For its contribution to the country's cultural experience, Jacob's Pillow has been named a National Historic Landmark. The international festival of dance brings performers from around the world to the Berkshires along with the nation's top troupes and dancers. And since the opening of MASS MoCA, Jacob's Pillow has brought many of these performers to North Adams, melding dance with art and technology. A recent visit by the Mark Morris Dance Group spilled over into an appearance at Tanglewood, where they performed "Falling Down Stairs," a collaboration on Bach's Suite no. 3 with Yo-Yo Ma.

The eclectic programming has included the work of such diverse choreographers as Twyla Tharp, Lionel Hoche, and MeMe BaNjO; Maria Page's Flamenco Republic; Robert Battle's Battleworks; and Nacho Duato's new troupe, CND2. Imagine seeing in a barn in the woods of Berkshire County the likes of the Aspen Santa Fe Ballet, Merce Cunningham, Batoto Yetu, a company of young dancers from Harlem keeping alive the spirit of African culture and folklore, Irma Omerzo from Croatia, and the Jo Stromgren Company from Norway. And there's more.

The free Inside/Out series, held Wednesday through Saturday at 6:30 P.M., offers informal, informative, and entertaining dance showings on the outdoor stage. Preshow talks about performances or with scholars and artists also are free. Materials from the Pillow Archives are exhibited in Blake's Barn, and there is even a chance to observe classes. Food is available at the Pillow Cafe, a full-service restaurant where reservations are required; the Pillow Pub for casual fare and picnic takeout or aftershow gatherings around the bar; and the Tea Garden, where, contrary to their muscular image, Ted Shawn's Men Dancers served tea to patrons at the first Pillow performances in the 1930s. Despite the cosmopolitan programming, the friendly down-home traditions started by Shawn on "the farm" continue. The Pillow remains true to Shawn's vision: to present and preserve an unparalleled variety of dance. Jacob's Pillow is off US 20, east of Lee.

i

Jacob's Pillow Dance Festival sponsors a free Community Day in August and offers discounted tickets to young people for some performances throughout the season.

Music

Aston Magna Festival
323 Main Street, Great Barrington
(413) 528-3595, (800) 875-7156
www.astonmagna.org

Since 1972 the Aston Magna Foundation for Music and the Humanities has been bringing baroque and classical music performed on period instruments to the Berkshires. The annual summer festival is the oldest in America devoted to interpreting the music of the past with historically correct instruments and performances. The concert series is under the direction of violinist Daniel Stepner, currently first violinist of the Lydian String Quartet. Depending on the program, concerts feature baroque violins, oboe, bass, flute, and cello as well as the harpsichord and viola da gamba, all played by distinguished musicians who have immersed themselves in the periods of the composers they interpret. The foundation's goal is to reach a larger public for authentically interpreted and performed works through performances, recordings, and workshops. To that end, children ages 6 to 12 are welcome, and up to two children per adult ticket are admitted at no charge. Concerts are performed at 6:00 P.M. on five consecutive Saturdays in July and the first week of August at St. James' Episcopal Church at the Corner of Main Street and Taconic Avenue. The series also is presented on Friday evening at Bard College in Annandale-on-Hudson, New York.

Berkshire Choral Festival
245 North Undermountain Road (Massachusetts Highway 41), Sheffield
(413) 229-8526, (413) 229-1999 (box office)
www.berkshirechoral.org

For those who enjoy performing or listening to choral music, the Berkshire Choral Festival presents a rare opportunity to enjoy both. Around 225 amateur singers from all walks of life come here to spend their "vacation" totally immersed in studying and performing a great choral work. They live at the Berkshire School, leased for the summer, and work with professionals in the field. They top off their stay with a concert, usually performed with the Springfield Symphony, and often with a name soloist. There are five classes offered, which means five concerts. Hearing 225 voices honed to perfection presenting such glorious works as Orf's *Carmina Burana,* Bach's *St. Matthew's Passion,* or Beethoven's *Missa Solemnis* is a treat not to be missed.

Founded as a nonprofit educational institution in 1982, the Berkshire Choral Festival presented a challenging new way to learn and sing choral music with topflight conductors and staff. Participants are allowed time off for tours of the area or recreation. The festival also holds classes in Santa Fe, New Mexico; Canterbury, England; and Salzburg, Austria. Berkshire School is located on North Undermountain Road, or MA 41, which runs between Massachusetts Highway 23 west of Great Barrington and U.S. Highway 7 in Sheffield.

Berkshire Concert Choir
250 Summer Street, Lee
(413) 243-2140

A community choir for more than 25 years, the Berkshire Concert Choir gives two major performances a year: a spring concert, usually given at Tanglewood's Ozawa Hall, and a Christmas concert, usually performed in a church. There are between 55 and 70 members from around the area. Some have been with the group since the beginning. The choir tackles serious work. In 1995 the choir performed Mendelssohn's *Elijah* at Ozawa Hall. The concert was memorable, a reviewer recalled, because a shaft of sunlight fell on the choir as it sang the triumphant final hymn. The group celebrated its 25th anniversary in 2003 with a concert at Ozawa, where the program included Beethoven's Mass in C. A community orchestra accompanies the choir. Soloists sometimes include guests. Tickets are reasonably priced to encourage folks to attend who might otherwise not be able to afford a concert at Ozawa Hall.

Berkshire Highlanders
P.O. Box 1023, Pittsfield 01201
(413) 447-7050

Dressed in full regalia, the Berkshire Highlanders Celtic pipe band is a familiar fixture in Berkshire County parades. Formed in 1976 the band also plays at Scottish festivals and Highland games and at various other events, including performances at Tanglewood. Around 25 members practice every Wednesday night year-round, either at South Congregational Church or the Banknorth parking lot, weather permitting.

Berkshire Opera Company
297 North Street, Pittsfield
(413) 442-9955
www.berkshireopera.org

Berkshire Opera Company was founded in 1985 by Rex Hearn to fill a conspicuous gap in the performing arts offerings in the Berkshires. While symphonic and chamber music, theater, and dance were offered at various cultural venues through the summer, the company was first to bring professional, fully staged opera to the Berkshires and continues today to be the only professional opera company performing in Massachusetts during the summer. A transplanted Englishman, Hearn envisioned the company as an American Glyndebourne, opening with an early curtain time and following the first act with a lengthy picnic break. However, a few rainy evenings and the lack of suitable picnic grounds soon led to the adoption of a traditional performance schedule.

The company's first home was in the now demolished chapel at Cranwell in Lenox. Its first production was Handel's *Acis and Galatea.* The production featured Berkshire resident Maureen O'Flynn, who has since gone on to become an internationally acclaimed soprano and who still appears in productions here. During its first 16 years, the company presented two fully staged operas during July and August while wandering the Berkshires in search of a permanent home. For its first seven seasons, the repertoire consisted of comic operas, primarily from the Baroque or Classical periods. A production of Britten's *The Rape of Lucretia* in 1992 was acclaimed by a *New York Times* reviewer who wrote: "Just up the road from Tanglewood, the Berkshire Opera Company performs miracles."

i ***Half-price tickets for performances at participating venues are offered in July and August at the visitor centers in Great Barrington, Pittsfield, and Adams. Available tickets are released through ½Tix on the afternoon of the performance (or morning, if it's a matinee).***

After finding a home at the Berkshire Community College's Koussevitsky Arts Center in 1997, Berkshire Opera expanded its offerings to four productions. A staging of Gian Carlo Menotti's *The Consul* won critical acclaim and was recorded on the Newport Classic label, the first commercial recording ever made of that work. Two years later the company collaborated with Edith Wharton Restoration to present *Summer,* an original opera by Stephen Paulus based on Wharton's novel of the same name. On September 21, 2000, Berkshire Opera Company purchased the historic Mahaiwe Theatre in Great Barrington and launched a $15 million capital campaign to restore the Mahaiwe to its original 1905 grandeur. But the events of September 11 of the following year and the subsequent economic downturn severely affected the company's restoration efforts, and in January 2003 they sold the theater to the Mahaiwe Performing Arts Center, a newly formed not-for-profit organization that is continuing the restoration.

Now located back in Pittsfield, the company will continue to mount productions at various locations, including the Mahaiwe, the stage at BCC, and Chapin Hall at Williams College, as well as expanding programming through the rest of the year and increasing outreach to the community. Despite its bumpy ride, the Berkshire Opera Company continues to fill the gap in the county's performing arts menu.

Berkshire Lyric Theatre
P.O. Box 347, Pittsfield 01201
(413) 499-0258
www.berkshirelyric.org

For local folks who enjoy singing on a professional level, the Berkshire Lyric Theatre has been the group to join since 1963. Director Robert P. Blafield founded the community organization to provide a variety of forums in which singers and instrumentalists interested in choral music can come together, learn, practice, and perform. The organization also offers scholarships for deserving vocal and instrumental students. Blafield studied opera at the

Juilliard School of Music and was a choral conductor and voice teacher in Manhattan. The Berkshire Lyric Theatre comprises the full concert chorus, a smaller Camerata Ensemble, and the Blafield Children's Chorus. Performances are given fall through spring at a variety of venues, including the Berkshire Museum, St. James' Church in Great Barrington, Trinity Church in Lenox, and St. Stephen's in Pittsfield. Programs have included *Brigadoon, Carousel,* and Gilbert and Sullivan as well as choral works by Handel, Mozart, Bach, and Brahms. The organization also sponsors innovative musical educational events in area schools.

Berkshire Music School
30 Wendell Avenue, Pittsfield
(413) 442-1411

Founded in 1940 the Berkshire Music School (formerly the Pittsfield Community Music School) is a place for young and old to discover and develop their musical interests and talents.

Toddlers to senior citizens, tin ears as well as prodigies, are encouraged to study the instrument of their choice. A faculty of 30 experienced professionals teach as well as perform with and without students at concerts throughout the year. The Linden Trio is the faculty's ensemble-in-residence. The school also sponsors a community orchestra, Synkrony, which auditions students and adult amateurs and joins them with professionals for practice one evening a week, presenting at least two concerts annually. Chamber music groups are organized each year, meeting with a coach for 10-week sessions and performing for the community when ready.

The school's mission is to provide quality education and musical opportunities to all Berkshire County residents. More than 450 students are enrolled in various classes, with some earning college credits through a cooperative program with Berkshire Community College. The school also designs and implements curricula, workshops, and concerts for schools, day-care centers, nursing homes, and other agencies. All students participate in an annual two-day Music Marathon that raises funds for scholarships, awarded on a needs basis. Wendell Avenue is in the historic district of the city, just off Park Square.

Close Encounters with Music
P.O. Box 34
Great Barrington 01230
(518) 392-6677, (800) 843-0778
www.cewm.org

Another one of those "off-season" goodies, Close Encounters with Music offers contemporary and classical chamber music performed by distinguished musicians with a twist—commentary and discussion about the work that's being performed. This unusual combination is the brainchild of director and cellist Yehuda Nanani. No slouch, Nanani studied with Pablo Casals and is Professor of Cello at the University of Cincinnati (Ohio) College, Conservatory of Music. He presents master classes internationally in conjunction with concert tours. He also presents his Close Encounters with Music series in Scottsdale, Arizona, and south Florida, including Miami and Fort Lauderdale. The performances—entertaining as well as educational—are given here from fall through spring, mostly at St. James Church in Great Barrington. An annual Thanksgiving weekend concert is held in collaboration with the Norman Rockwell Museum in Stockbridge, and a spring concert is given at Ozawa Hall at Tanglewood. A Close Encounters' Children's Concert is held at Searles Castle in Great Barrington.

Eagles Band
75 South Church Street, Pittsfield
(413) 443-9709

Founded in 1936 the Eagles Band is the official band of the city of Pittsfield. It comprises professional, amateur, and student musicians from the Berkshires, Pioneer Valley, New York, and Connecticut. The marching band participates in parades and gives concerts at city parks and other locations in summer. Members also play in a jazz ensemble and wind symphony.

The Guthrie Center
4 Van Deusenville Road, Housatonic
(413) 528–1955
www.guthriecenter.org

Local and global traditions of folk and acoustic music are kept alive at the Guthrie Center, housed in the former home of Alice Brock of Alice's Restaurant fame. Now owned by Arlo Guthrie, who made Alice a nationally known figure in his song about an ill-fated trip to the Stockbridge dump, the center is named for his parents, Woody and Marjorie Guthrie, and is dedicated to their ideals of global understanding while preserving cultural traditions. The church itself was originally built as the St. James Chapel in 1829. It was enlarged in 1866 and renamed Trinity Church. Ray and Alice Brock bought the property in 1964 and made it their home until the early '70s. It is where "The Alice's Restaurant Massacree" was conceived and where the movie *Alice's Restaurant* was filmed. After several changes of ownership, Arlo Guthrie purchased the church and established the interfaith center as a place for cultural and educational exchange. Aside from concerts, the center hosts various community programs and events sponsored by the nonprofit educational Guthrie Foundation, formed to help preserve traditional music, stories, medicine, dance, and spiritual practices. The concert series and other events are posted on the Web site.

Music & More in the Meetinghouse
Massachusetts Highway 57,
New Marlborough
(413) 229–3126

Attending an event at the Meetinghouse in New Marlborough is a triple treat. First, there is the 200-year-old church that is now the Meetinghouse and the perfectly preserved village green where it sits. Picturesque is too weak a word to describe the beauty of this village. The Meetinghouse itself is a prime example of the elegant simplicity of early New England architecture. The original interior is shown off at its best when the light slants through the windows in late afternoon, when Music & More programs are presented. Then there's the series itself. Started by Harold Lewin in 1991, Music & More features renowned musicians, actors, and writers, depending on the program. Chamber music, literary discussions, exhibits, and/or films are presented in the ever-changing series held on five afternoons beginning in late August through fall. The time, 4:30 to 6:00 P.M., was chosen to allow people to have dinner afterward, which brings us to the third bonus: dinner by candlelight at the Old Inn on the Green, one of only a few Berkshire restaurants to receive Zagat's top rating. An afternoon at Music & More offers a chance to treat the eyes, ears, and tastebuds while taking a step back in time.

South Mountain Concerts
US 7/20
P.O. Box 23
Pittsfield 01201
(413) 442–2106

Concerts of chamber music played by some of the top string quartets in the business have been presented at South Mountain since 1918, when the intimate South Mountain Concert Hall was founded by Mrs. Elizabeth Sprague Coolidge. Located off US 7/20 in a wooded glen, the hall is listed on the National Register of Historic Buildings. The acoustics are renowned for their quality, especially for chamber music. Internationally known artists who have appeared here include Leonard Bernstein, Leontyne Price, Rudolf Serkin, and the Beaux Arts Trio. String quartets that have played here include the Emerson, Guarneri, Juilliard, and Tokyo ensembles. The series of five concerts is presented on Sunday in September and the first week of October. The South Mountain Association also brings chamber music into the public schools in the county through its Young Audiences Concerts. As the name implies, the hall is located on the side of a mountain just south of Pittsfield and is reached by a walk from the parking lot on hilly and uneven terrain. Patrons who have difficulty walking may be dropped off and picked up close to the hall, but drivers will be asked to return to one of the lots.

Stockbridge Chamber Concerts
Searles Castle
389 Main Street, Great Barrington
Mail: 68 Kenilworth Street, Pittsfield 01201
(413) 442-7711

This ensemble performs a series of concerts at Searles Castle in Great Barrington throughout the summer. The group was originally formed in 1975 by Elizabeth Hagenah, who had been hosting musicians from the Boston Symphony in private concerts at her home. Participants are principals and members of the BSO, members of Boston University's School for the Arts, and other distinguished musicians—all of whom are colleagues and friends of Mrs. Hagenah and her husband, William, both accomplished and noted musicians. Aside from concerts, the group sponsors a program for young highly gifted musicians, who are given the chance to be coached by and play with professional musicians.

Over the years many of the world's top performers have appeared in the series, which was performed in various locations until finding a permanent home at Searles Castle in 1989. The group also gives a Christmas Concert for families at Searles and has performed at other locations around the county, including the Berkshire Museum and the Mount. One year, Boston Pops conductor Keith Lockhart read the only children's story written by Norman Rockwell accompanied by music commissioned for the Stockbridge Chamber Concerts by Seymour Barab. Resident artists include Betty Wilson Long and Bernard Krainis. Recent programming included works by Prokofiev, Beethoven, Mozart, Bach, and Mendelssohn.

Tanglewood
297 West Street (Massachusetts Highway 183), Lenox
(413) 637-5165 (in season), (617) 266-1492
www.bso.org

Back in 1934 a group of musicians from the New York Philharmonic came from Manhattan by bus, stayed in local hotels, and put on a concert series. A great success, it was repeated the following year. But the next year, that group bowed out and in their place came Serge Koussevitzky and the Boston Symphony. They put on three concerts under a tent on a single August weekend, drawing nearly 15,000 people. Later that year the Tappan family gave their Tanglewood estate on the Stockbridge-Lenox line to the BSO for a permanent summer home. A drenching thunderstorm led to an impromptu fund-raising effort to replace the tent with a more weatherproof structure. Architect Eliel Saarinen and Stockbridge engineer Joseph Franz designed the pavilion, now known as the Shed, and it was open for business in 1938. As the series grew, Koussevitzky and the BSO formulated the idea for a school for young musicians, and the Berkshire Music Center was established. It opened in 1940 with Randall Thompson's moving "Alleluia," composed for the occasion. The unaccompanied choral piece has been performed at the opening of the school every year since. More buildings were added to the complex, with the latest being the $10 million Ozawa Hall, an architectural and acoustical masterpiece

You don't have to wait until the night of the concert to get lawn tickets for Tanglewood. Buy them anytime, even that morning. Then you can walk right by that long line at the box office. But don't forget to allow time for traffic, especially if it's one of the blockbuster events.

that is used for chamber music and smaller group performances. A smaller theater is used for student performances. Today the sprawling complex with its gardens and walkways is an internationally known performance center, attracting more than 300,000 patrons in a season.

But one can only wonder what Koussevitzky would say if he could read today's Tanglewood program. Of course it is still the summer home of the Boston Symphony. Yes, the great works of Beethoven, Mozart, and the rest are still performed by the biggest names in the world of classical music. And certainly, young musicians and singers continue to come from all over to the Music Center to hone their talents with the finest in their fields. But a radio show? Jazz? Blues? Dance? Opera? Motown? Yes, all that and more are now part of Tanglewood's ever-changing eclectic programming. The season opens in late June, but the schedule is announced in March, and seats sell fast. Recently the big opener was a James Taylor concert. That backed up traffic for miles! A recent Fourth of July event featured the Supremes and the Spinners in a Motown extravaganza that climaxed with fireworks. Garrison Keillor and his *Prairie Home Companion* radio broadcast have become an annual event. And the daylong Tanglewood-on-Parade continues to pack 'em in. The program always concludes with a rock 'em sock 'em performance of Tchaikovsky's "1812 Overture" complete with live cannons and fireworks over Stockbridge Bowl. Programs combining music and dance recently brought together the Mark Morris Dance Group and Yo-Yo Ma. And of course the Boston Pops make a couple of appearances. The last three days of the season are dedicated to the Jazz Festival, which recently featured Wynton Marsalis and other noted artists.

Whatever Koussevitzky may think of the programming, the success of the music center can be seen in the graduates who have gone on to be greats in the classical music world, including Leonard Bernstein, Seiji Ozawa, and Zubin Mehta. Around 20 percent of the members of America's major orchestras are Music Center alumni. Today's students perform almost daily, and their concerts are often free. Unfortunately, the rest is not. Prices vary depending on the performer or the event. The spacious lawn is the least expensive and is a favorite spot for preconcert picnics. Inside seats for a regular performance are most expensive up front, naturally, with the last row, barely under the roof, the cheapest. If there is a downside to Tanglewood, it is the mass exodus that occurs at the end of every event. Smart folks will relax a little longer on the lawn while they let the rest fight it out. Despite that, Tanglewood is an experience that can't really be described. Live music, great performers, aspiring young musicians, starlit skies, gorgeous surroundings—all a gift from Serge Koussevitsky and those early supporters of music under a tent in the country.

Williams College Department of Music
54 Chapin Hall Drive, Williamstown
www.williams.edu/music

One of the advantages of having one of the country's top liberal arts colleges right in your own backyard is the variety and quality of music available through the Williams College Department of Music. The college offers more than 100 concerts and recitals throughout the academic year, always open to the public and, with very few exceptions, at no charge. Most are held in Chapin Hall, the grand old concert hall at the center of the campus, or in the Brooks-Rogers Recital Hall in Bernhard Music Center, added to the side of Chapin in 1979.

In addition to highlighting student and faculty talent, the college brings many visiting artists and internationally acclaimed ensembles to Williamstown, including the Takacs String Quartet, Boston Musica Viva, Lydia Artymiw, JanDeGaetani, Top Brass of the Royal Concertgebouw Orchestra, Sweet Honey in the Rock, the Count Basie Orchestra, and Habib Koite and other world music groups, many hosted through the Thompson Concert Series.

Performances are given throughout the school year by the Berkshire Symphony Orchestra, composed of both students and professional musicians, the Concert and Chamber Choirs, the Jazz Ensemble, both large and small groups, Symphonic Winds, Kusika, and Zambezi Marimbas. The Williams Chamber Players, comprising faculty, adjuncts, and occasional guest artists, give a series of four or five performances annually, highlighting a variety of combinations of instruments. One recent concert piece required an organ and was therefore held in the nearby First Congregational Church.

The Handbell Choir, Student Symphony, Brass Ensemble, Woodwind Chamber Music, and String Chamber Music ensembles also provide strong outlets for student musicians and variety for the listening public. A series of more informal studio recitals offer students studying an instrument an opportunity to try out a work in progress in front of an audience. These are often late-afternoon recitals, whereas most concerts are at 8:00 P.M. September through May. During spring, a Sunday afternoon series of Artworks at the Clark Art Institute features accomplished Williams College students performing in one of the galleries, also free and open to the public. In addition, the public is welcome to attend at no charge lectures in Bernhard Music Center by musical scholars, composers, and others.

A more recent tradition is the annual Williamstown Jazz Festival, usually held in April. This is a four-to five-day festival of big bands, small groups, traditional and modern jazz, dancers, film, and gospel singers from far and near. The collegiate jazzfest also brings about 12 college jazz bands from the New England area to play for one another and two adjudicators who are experts in their field and who give feedback to the groups. Often the visiting students will stay for informal jam sessions at area restaurants following the major festival concerts. Collaboration with the Williamstown Chamber of Commerce, MASS MoCA, Clark Art Institute, St. John's Church, and the Williams Dance Program make the Jazz Festival and other programs accessible to a wide audience.

JUST NEXT DOOR

Falcon Ridge Folk Festival
Long Hill Farm
Hillsdale, New York
(800) 364-0366
www.falconridge.com

The Falcon Ridge Folk Festival has been bringing music and dancing to this farm off New York Highway 23 since 1988. Late in July, more than 40 acts perform on four different stages, including an intimate workshop stage and an 8,000-square-foot wooden dance floor under a tent. Advance tickets go on sale in February. The schedule is usually announced in May and refined as the festival nears. Camping is available on the property. Information may be obtained from the Web site or through the business office at 74 Modley Road, Sharon, CT 06069.

Music Mountain Summer Music Festival
Music Mountain Road
Falls Village, Connecticut
(860) 824-7126
www.musicmountain.org

Founded in 1930, Music Mountain presents jazz, chamber, and baroque concerts performed by nationally known musicians-in-residence and guest artists. The 132-acre campus with its gardens and historic Gordon Hall is listed on the National Register of Historic Places. Music Mountain Road is off US 7 and Connecticut Highway 63.

Tannery Pond Concerts
Darrow Road (off US 20)
New Lebanon, New York
(413) 443-1696, (888) 820-1696

This summer concert series is held at Darrow School on the grounds of the former Mount Lebanon Shaker community.

Theater

Barrington Stage Company
Consolati Performing Arts Center
Mount Everett Regional High School
Berkshire School Road (MA 41), Sheffield
(413) 528-8888
www.barringtonstageco.org

Founded in 1995 with artistic director Julianne Boyd at the helm, Barrington Stage Company (BSC) started off with a bang by winning the Elliot Norton/Boston Theatre Critics Award for its production of *The Diary of Anne Frank.* Two years later, BSC won two Elliot Norton/Boston Theatre Critics awards and four Outer Critics Awards for its production of *Cabaret,* which moved to Boston and played an extended run at the Hasty Pudding Theatre. BSC's production of Stephen Sondheim's *Company* was described by Alvin Klein of the *New York Times* as "revelatory" and "the most emotionally centered *Company* of all." Barrington Stage annually produces three MainStage productions, two Stage II productions dedicated primarily to emerging artists, a Youth Theatre Production, and a New Works Festival. A recent addition is StudioSpace, which will present intimate productions, cabarets, and staged readings throughout the year. To broaden its audience, BSC often takes to local roads, bringing productions to various appropriate sites around the county.

Not your average theater company, BSC's mission is twofold: to produce and develop top-notch professional theater and to develop a local audience by establishing a strong community relationship with area residents. To that end, Barrington Stage has from day one offered a state-licensed nursery for children 2 to 8 years old, free tickets for students age 13 and younger, and half-price tickets for students 14 and older. BSC's Youth Theatre Production, in which local teenagers work with a professional director and choreographer, plays for two weeks in Sheffield and then moves to Springside Park in Pittsfield for two weeks. BSC also initiated a theater program for at-risk youth that led to the formation of the Railroad Street Youth Project and a galvanizing production of Erik Bogosian's *Suburbia.* A Playwright Mentoring Project also was established, bringing together professional artists and at-risk high school-age youngsters to create an original stage piece. The result was *Dancing on Thin Ice,* created and written entirely by the young people in the program. The BSC production toured local schools, garnering state attention as well as a segment on National Public Radio.

BSC spearheaded the opening of a half-price ticket booth in Great Barrington. In collaboration with the Southern Berkshire Chamber of Commerce, the Berkshire Visitors Bureau, and many cultural organizations throughout Berkshire County, half-price tickets and discount offers are made available to performing arts organizations and nonperforming cultural organizations. Any remaining tickets are made available to the public on the day of the performance or exhibit on a first-come, first-served basis.

Berkshire Theatre Festival
6 East Main Street (Massachusetts Highway 102), Stockbridge
(413) 298-5536, (413) 298-5576 (box office)
www.berkshiretheatre.org

The Berkshire Theatre Festival has been entertaining audiences for more than 75 years, thanks to the foresight of Mabel Choate, daughter of Ambassador Joseph H. Choate who built Naumkeag as a summer "cottage" at around the turn of the 20th century. The ambassador was a partner in the building of the Stockbridge Casino, which opened in 1888. The gracious building was designed and built by Stanford White and for years was the hub of social and cultural life in Stockbridge. After the Stockbridge Golf Club opened, the casino's popularity fell. By the late 1920s, the building was so dilapidated there was talk of tearing it down. Enter Miss Choate, the wealthiest woman in

Stockbridge, who bought the casino and then sold it for $1.00 to a group of entrepreneurs who called themselves the Three Arts Society. Members included Walter Clark, a partner of J. P. Morgan; editor Frank Crowninshield; drama critic Walter Pritchard Eaton; sculptor Daniel Chester French; and pioneer psychiatrist Austen Riggs. They moved the building to its present location and remodeled and expanded the interior by adding a stage and seating for 415. Reborn as the Berkshire Playhouse, the theater opened on June 2, 1928. Nearly 40 years later, the Society sold the Playhouse, and the name was changed to the Berkshire Theatre Festival.

Today Stanford White's building, now known as the Main Stage, sports a new balcony and seats and is listed on the National Register of Historic Places as well as being a member of the National Trust. In 1996 BTF built the 122-seat Unicorn Theatre to provide a place for emerging actors, directors, and playwrights to test their wings. BTF also operates the 9.5-acre Lavan Center up the road, which houses summer apprentices and interns. The BTF also runs residency programs in local schools for children in grades 4 though 6 and a summer residency program for performing arts students ages 18 to 25. That group produces two plays that are seen by more than 10,000 young people in July and August.

But summer stock is the meat and potatoes of the BTF, and it has been a groundbreaking leader since it opened. Major works by nearly every American playwright, including Tennessee Williams, Eugene O'Neill, and Thornton Wilder, have been produced here. Wilder himself played in the productions of his plays *Our Town* and *The Skin of Our Teeth.* Performers over the years have included Ethel Barrymore, Frank Buxton, Buster Keaton, Ruth Gordon, John D. Seymour, Anne Bancroft, Katharine Hepburn, Joanne Woodward—and on and on. Blending old standards with new works, BTF presents productions with name actors from Memorial Day weekend through Labor Day weekend at both the Main Stage and the Unicorn Theatre. Some productions are offered at other locations in the county. The theaters are located at the intersection of US 7 and MA 102 at the bottom of Yale Hill.

Main Street Stage
57 Main Street, North Adams
(413) 663-3240
www.mainstreetstage.com

"Theater with a conscience" is how those involved with Main Street Stage describe their mission. The works this small company performs on its storefront stage range from published pieces to original plays by local writers. All have a common thread in that they serve as models for successful living. Lest that sound boring, be assured their performances are far from that. Bringing live theater to downtown North Adams is in itself an admirable goal. The small venue in which they perform brings the audience into the work, whether it be somber or silly. The menu includes comedies, dramas, and thrillers aimed at involving the audience and the actors in the theatrical experience. The company, also known as Trova Theatre Arts Inc., is always on the lookout for volunteers, actors, directors, musicians, artists, technicians, and "just all-around cool people" to work with. Improvisation is encouraged, especially through a resident team called RBIT! (Royal Berkshire Improvizational Troupe), which performs regularly.

Shakespeare & Company
70 Kemble Street, Lenox
(413) 637-3353
www.shakespeare.org

Shakespeare & Company's ambitious programming begins in May and ends in December, if you don't count all the productions that take place in local schools the rest of the year through the company's educational component. Twelve plays—not all of them by the Bard—are mounted and presented in a rotation. The company also links up with other cultural institutions in the county, including MASS MoCA, the Clark Art Institute, Tanglewood, and

Jacob's Pillow for special events and is responsible for turning on hundreds of kids to Shakespeare through its in-school programs and annual school festival. All this from artistic director Tina Packer's drive and dedication to live theater and Shakespeare's continuing contribution to it.

Having passed the 25-year mark in its history, Shakespeare & Company has definitely become a fixture on the Berkshire theatrical scene. Productions featuring name actors and known works share the stages with new plays and aspiring thespians, all in the name of keeping live theater alive, relevant, and thought-provoking. To Packer, theater is the pathway to understanding one another. Ambition, power, lust, death, and love can be dissected and inspected through the stage. And in Packer's view, no one explores those human conditions better than Shakespeare. Theater that does not challenge, raise questions, provoke discussion, and promote the greater good is not doing its job, in Packer's view, and the productions that are mounted are aimed at generating those responses.

In taking on the sprawling property in Lenox and turning it into the Shakespeare Center for Performance and Studies, the company has provided three venues: Founder's Theatre, with 466 seats, either box or armless cushion-backed benches, that surround the stage on three sides; Spring Lawn Theatre, 99 seats in the original and elegant salon of a 1904 mansion; and the Rose Footprint Theatre, a simple stage with bleacher seating under a tent. The latter is the first step in an ambitious plan to re-create the 1587 theater where Shakespeare's plays were first performed. Eventually the playhouse will be surrounded by its own Elizabethan Village. Plans also call for the construction of an outdoor Greek theater, a Shakespeare library, walking paths, and picnic areas, some of which are already in place. Prices vary depending on seating, venue, and production. Some things are even free. Kemble Street is in Lenox proper; the campus is within walking distance of town center.

Town Players of Pittsfield Inc.
P.O. Box 765, Pittsfield 01201
(413) 443-9279
www.berkshire.net/townplayers

A community theater group, the Town Players have been entertaining Berkshire residents since 1910. The group puts on three productions a season in the Robert M. Boland Theatre at Berkshire Community College's Koussevitsky Arts Center. Although the theater is capable of seating 450, seats can be arranged in smaller configurations to suit the production. The Town Players reorganized in 1916 as the Pittsfield Theatrical Company, performing throughout New England until 1920, when they reformed as the Colonial Players. Productions were then mounted mostly in Pittsfield at the Colonial Theatre. In 1921 the group reincorporated under their original name. Except for the 1940s, when most of the members were active in the war effort, productions have continued ever since. In 1958 Town Players bought the former St. John's Temperance Hall, an 1881 building at 148 Lebanon Avenue, to use as a production rehearsal hall. Recent productions have included *Moon over Buffalo* and a female version of *The Odd Couple.* The group holds auditions for the community prior to productions.

Williamstown Theatre Festival
1000 Main Street (Massachusetts Highway 2), Williamstown
(413) 597-3399, (413) 597-3400 (box office)
www.WTFestival.org

Since it was founded in 1955, the Williamstown Theatre Festival has staged nearly 500 full productions of plays and musicals, along with countless workshops, readings, and special events. In 2002 the Williamstown Theatre Festival became the first summer theater to receive the Regional Theatre Tony Award for its proven continuous level of artistic achievement contributing to the growth of theater nationally. The list of WTF alumni reads like a Who's Who of film, television, and stage. Local residents have gotten pretty blasé about bumping into famous stars on the streets of Williamstown. Many WTF productions have transferred to Broadway and Off Broadway and to regional theaters around the nation. In addition, many of the festival's training programs have given nearly 200 aspiring artists and managers a chance to study acting or serve as interns with professional designers, directors, and administrators.

Productions are given from mid-June through late August in buildings owned by Williams College and used by students and others for performances and presentations during the school year. The college has undertaken a $50 million project that includes a 234-space parking deck and that expands theater seating. The 550-seat Main Stage in the Adams Memorial Theatre and the more intimate Nikos Stage will be augmented by a new state-of-the-art 200-seat CenterStage, designed to be a flexible and innovative teaching theater. WTF productions generally run for two weeks only, and tickets go fast when the program is announced in April.

In keeping with its mission to bring theater to a broader audience, the Festival's Free Theatre has been presenting plays and fables to families at no charge in nearby Buxton Field. Productions take place at twilight, and patrons are encouraged to bring picnics, creating an informal, convivial atmosphere. The festival also operates a number of programs designed to attract and assist young writers and actors from neighboring North Adams who might not normally experience live theater. The lead program, the Greylock Theatre Project, is a replication of New York City's 52nd Street Project, a nationally renowned organization recognized for its inventive acting programs for inner-city children. Other programs have been added, but all culminate in free public performances for hundreds of people in which the imagination and commitment of the individual child is celebrated. The Greylock Theatre Project receives corporate sponsorship, private contributions, and generous donations of goods and services from local area merchants and residents. Another effort to reach young people is Kids' Night, held on the first Friday evening of each of the festival's five Main Stage productions. Under the program, youths 18 and under who purchase a ticket receive a free one for their parent or guardian.

OTHER THEATER IN THE AREA

While not in Berkshire County, the following nearby companies also offer live performances in summer.

Mac-Haydn Theatre
New York Highway 203
Chatham, New York
(518) 392-9292
www.machaydntheatre.org
Professional musical productions are given in the theater-in-the-round May through September. Performances are followed by a cabaret, with refreshments and songs by young musicians.

miniature theatre of Chester
15 Middlefield Street, Chester
(413) 354-7770, (413) 354-7771 (box office after June 1)
www.miniaturetheatre.org
New and established plays have been presented by professional Equity actors at the miniature theatre since 1989. Performances in the Chester Town Hall are given Wednesday through Saturday at 8:00 P.M. with matinees on Thursday and Sunday at 2:00 P.M.

StageWorks
North Pointe Cultural Arts Center
New York Highway 9
Kinderhook, New York
(518) 822-9667
www.stageworkstheater.org
Classic and new plays are presented April to September.

The Theatre Barn
US 20
New Lebanon, New York
(518) 794-8989
www.theatrebarn.com
Broadway musicals and plays are performed by professional actors Thursday

CLOSE-UP

Three Classics

Berkshire County has not one but three historic theaters, all in various stages of restoration: the Mahaiwe (pronounced *ma-hay-wee*) in Great Barrington, the Colonial in Pittsfield, and the Mohawk in North Adams.

In Great Barrington efforts are under way to upgrade the opera house/music hall/movie theater, which has been in continuous operation since it was built in 1905. After a succession of owners and operators, Hoyts, an international cinema chain, bought the 650-seat Mahaiwe in the 1980s but decided a few years later that it was not a paying proposition. After a community campaign, Hoyts kept the theater open and allowed local folks, including the Berkshire Opera, to book concerts and other activities. But the relationship was tenuous at best, and the Opera, fearing it would lose its venue, bought the theater from Hoyts in 2000. The company planned to undertake a full restoration, but fundraising sagged after 9/11, there were changes within the Opera itself, the time commitment to book the place year-round was daunting, and the company soon realized it was in over its head. That's when the nonprofit Mahaiwe Performing Arts Center was formed. They bought the theater from the Opera and are continuing plans to bring the structurally sound building into compliance with present codes. That will include making the restrooms and the theater fully accessible, upgrading the stage equipment, installing new seats, and restoring the marquee. The project received a federal grant through the "Save America's Treasures" program, but other funds are being sought from the public. When the renovations are completed, the backers hope to offer a variety of programs for the community, ranging from opera (yes, the Berkshire Opera will return) to live theater, and to provide a venue for young people to stage and perform their own works.

Hillary Clinton visited the Colonial Theatre in Pittsfield and rightly declared it an architectural gem. She gave the city a Save America's Treasures grant to the tune of $400,000. More elaborate than

and Friday at 8:00 P.M., Saturday at 5:00 and 8:30 P.M., and Sunday at 2:00 and 7:00 P.M. mid-June through October.

VISUAL ARTS

Film

Berkshire Mall
Massachusetts Highway 8, Lanesborough
(413) 499–2558
The latest releases are shown on 10 screens with digital sound at the Berkshire Mall. Formerly owned by Hoyts Cinemas, the theaters are now operated by Regal Cinemas. The seats are comfy, with cupholders and lots of legroom. The theaters are located off the food court.

Images Cinema
50 Spring Street, Williamstown
(413) 458–1039, (413) 458–5612 (movie information)
www.imagescinema.org
This historic single-screen cinema is the only year-round, nonprofit, independent film house in the Berkshires. It survives in large part because of a dedicated group of supporters, who buy tax-deductible

the other two historic theaters, the Colonial was built in 1903 with a design by noted theater architect J. B. McElfatrick. Of the 350 theaters he designed—66 in New York City alone—the Colonial is one of only a dozen still standing. It has been called one of the greatest acoustical houses in the world, largely because of the soundboard hidden in a mural depicting the arts and the curved interior architecture—design signatures of McElfatrick. In its days as a music hall, the 1,200-seat theater hosted such greats as Sarah Bernhardt, Douglas Fairbanks, Pavlova, John Philip Sousa, and the Ziegfield Follies. It closed in 1934 but reopened three years later as a movie house, which it remained until 1952, when it was purchased by George Miller for his paint, wallpaper, and artists' supply business. Incredibly, Miller did not touch the interior but instead put in a drop ceiling and partitions that for years hid and protected the ornate balconies, murals, and stage. He did remove the ticket booth and seats and covered the sloping floor to make it level. Occasionally a sharp-eyed customer would notice that there were some very ornate columns placed in a semicircle near the checkout counter and Miller would delight in revealing the secrets hidden behind the partitions. After much negotiating, Miller's son sold the theater to the city and relocated the business. Now Pittsfield has undertaken the task of bringing the theater back to its original splendor. Located on South Street, the Colonial will serve as the centerpiece for plans to create a new entrance to the city, information booth and all. Until reconstruction starts, tours of the theater are available. It's worth a peek, but if you can't see it in person, there are pictures and more information on the Web site: www.colonialtheatre.org.

The Mohawk in North Adams is in for a longer haul. Built in 1938 as a Loew's movie house, the Mohawk is really two buildings that ended up being owned by two different people. After much negotiating, the city now owns both and plans to restore the theater as a community resource. The roof has been repaired, halting damage from leaks, and the marquee has been repaired. Lit up at night, it adds an air of gaiety and expectation to Main Street. The classic Art Deco interior is fairly well preserved, but much work is needed to bring the building up to code. Plans are on hold for now, but in this city of miracles you can be sure the Mohawk will someday be open for business.

memberships at various levels. The fare is varied, running from foreign and American independent films to new Hollywood releases. The popcorn is good, and the seats are plush. Incentives to members include half-price admission, discounts at a local restaurant, a monthly program by mail or Internet, and other goodies, depending on the membership level.

Little Cinema at the Berkshire Museum
39 South Street, Pittsfield
(413) 443–7171
www.berkshiremuseum.org

Open May through September, the Berkshire Museum's Little Cinema shows contemporary American, foreign, and independent movies in a 300-seat theater equipped with Surround Sound. Films are shown every night at 8:00 P.M. until September, when the showings are Thursday through Sunday. There are 2:00 P.M. matinees throughout the season. A five-film "movie buff" special may be purchased.

MASS MoCA
87 Marshall Street, North Adams
(413) 662–2111
www.massmoca.org

As part of its multifaceted programming,

MASS MoCA shows films, often accompanied by live music—and more—on its state-of-the-art screens. If the weather is good, films are shown outside in the courtyard on a three-story-high screen. In inclement weather they are shown inside in the Hunter Theater, no slouch of a venue either, or in the comfy lounge. Sometimes, the classics are shown on their own, as in a recent screening of *Rebel Without a Cause*. But *Apocalypse Now* outdoors on the huge screen with vivid digital sound undoubtedly added another dimension to the viewing. For the showing of *Creature From the Black Lagoon*, the sound was killed, and the Jazz Passengers provided live music and made up their own dialogue as the film rolled on the big screen. Not your ordinary movie theater, but then it's MoCA. What did you expect?

North Adams Cinema
MA 8, North Adams
(413) 663-5873
Also operated by Regal Cinemas, the North Adams Cinema has six screens. It is located in a shopping plaza south of the city on MA 8 and often has smaller audiences than the Berkshire Mall.

The Triplex Cinema Theater
70 Railroad Street, Great Barrington
(413) 528-8885
www.thetriplex.com
The Triplex's three state-of-the-art Surround Sound theaters offer patrons a comfortable, relaxed venue to watch both blockbuster hits from major studios as well as critically acclaimed independent films. The theater opens its doors at off hours for special events, shows, and films especially geared to children. Recently the theater showed all the films nominated for the "Best Picture" Oscar. The courtyard outside the theater regularly exhibits sculpture, and the inner lobby often doubles as a gallery for local artists.

Williamstown Film Festival
P.O. Box 81, Williamstown 01267
(413) 458-9900 (tickets)
www.williamstownfilmfest.com
A recent addition to the arts in North County, the Williamstown Film Festival shows innovative, independent films over a 10-day period at the end of October. The nonprofit festival was founded in 1998 by a group of local residents and graduates of Williams College to honor America's film past with classics; to explore the present with panels, seminars, and interaction between audiences and those involved in independent filmmaking; and to look into the future by examining the new technologies being used in filmmaking. Partnerships with the Clark Art Institute and MASS MoCA have been formed, and the number of independent films being shown has increased, as have the numbers of writers and actors participating in question and answer sessions after the screenings. As the festival has grown, so has its reputation, gaining the attention of *Variety, Boston Magazine,* and others who have commented on the intimate nature of the viewings when compared with big festivals like Sundance. The Web site gives detailed information about the films to be shown.

Art Centers

Becket Arts Center
MA 8, Becket
(413) 623-6635
The Becket Arts Center of the Hilltowns is located in an 1855 schoolhouse in the center of town on MA 8. Shows are mounted in two galleries. Concerts, lectures, and workshops in art, writing, and crafts are offered. Classes for children, either free or modestly priced, are offered in painting and drawing, sculpture, music, drama, and dance. The center is open June 30 through Labor Day from 10:00 A.M. to 4:00 P.M. daily except Tuesday.

Berkshire Artisans
28 Renne Avenue, Pittsfield
(413) 499-9348
www.berkshireweb.com/artisans
Berkshire Artisans is a community arts center in downtown Pittsfield that offers work space for artists, gallery space for exhibits, a performance area, and instruction. The work of regional and local artists and craftspeople are exhibited in the spacious first-floor gallery on a rotating basis. Painting, sculpture, photography, and fiber art in a variety of media, styles, and genres are shown throughout the year. The public is invited free of charge to all gallery openings, where refreshments are served to the accompaniment of live piano music. Free performances and readings by local musicians, dancers, actors, and poets are presented, usually announced in the local media.

Artists affiliated with the center have painted a series of public murals on buildings around Pittsfield. Signs around the city point to these murals, which can be seen on a walking tour from the Artisans building. The most readily visible murals are a depiction of a firefighter painted on the side of the Pittsfield Fire Department on Columbus Avenue and a mural depicting various events recalled by Vietnam veterans, which is on the side of a building on First Street. Berkshire Artisans rents studios to artists, maintains a slide registry of exhibitors, and assists artists with grant applications and referrals. The gallery and office are open Monday through Friday and by appointment on Saturday. The center was founded by Kitty Lichtenstein, who continues to support it through the Lichtenstein Foundation for Music and Art. Other support comes from the city of Pittsfield, national and state grants, and The Friends of the Berkshire Artisans.

Contemporary Artists Center & Gallery (CAC)
189 Beaver Street (MA 8), North Adams
(413) 663-9555
www.thecac.org
Located in historic Beaver Mill, the nonprofit CAC predates MoCA by almost 10 years. It was started by artist Eric Rudd as a place for artists to immerse themselves in their work in spacious studios, to interact with other artists, and to recharge and grow through residencies and workshops. The CAC owns the largest hydraulic press available to artists in New England. Dubbed the "Monster," the press has a bed measuring 5 feet by 10 feet, with total pressure of 800,000 pounds. The print facilities also contain smaller hydraulic presses, a Brandt etching press, and a silkscreen table. The hydraulic presses are used by sculptors and painters as well as printmakers. Other facilities include a darkroom, a wood shop and sculpture studio, and general studio space for mixed-media and monotype printmaking and other techniques. The 130,000-square-foot brick mill is situated on 27 acres of woodland adjoining Natural Bridge State Park. The large industrial studios and galleries have high ceilings, enormous windows, and ample room for painting, printmaking, sculpture, drawing, mixed media, and large-scale site-specific installations. CAC studios are open 24 hours a day year-round to resident artists. Shows are held throughout the year. The center itself is closed during the winter. A schedule of events can be found at the Web site.

Dark Ride Project
189 Beaver Street, North Adams
(413) 664-9550, (800) 689-0978
www.darkrideproject.org
Located in the north wing of the Beaver Mill, this unique exhibition is the work of artist Eric Rudd, who uses nontraditional technology and materials to broaden and heighten the experience of viewing art. The "Dark Ride" takes place in a computer-programmed vehicle called a sensory integrator that takes the viewer on a 10-minute visual trip through art installations created by Rudd using space-age materials and other technology. Dark Ride is open in summer Wednesday through Saturday afternoons and on weekend afternoons in fall.

Another installation by Rudd can be viewed in a former church on Summer Street in downtown North Adams. Called *A Chapel for Humanity,* the sculptural epic includes more than 150 life-size figures and 250 low-relief ceiling figures that took 10 years to complete. After September 11, 2001, Rudd created an homage to the victims consisting of figures floating above an ash-colored terrain. The work fuses traditional and contemporary art and offers both an art experience and a place for meditation. The construction is located in the former Unitarian-Universalist Church built in 1893. Summer Street is off Ashland Street, where the North Adams Post Office is located. It is open Wednesday through Sunday afternoons in summer and weekends in fall or by appointment.

IS183
13 Willard Hill Road, Stockbridge
(413) 298-5252
www.IS183.org

IS183, formerly the Interlaken School of Art, is dedicated to providing access to studio-based art for persons of all ages, means, and abilities. Classes are taught by professional working artists from the region and around the country. Based in a historic school off MA 183, IS183 offers classes in ceramics, fiber arts, painting, and drawing. Fees are charged but tuition assistance is available in the form of work-exchange opportunities and partial scholarships. Classes, artist lectures, workshops, summer programs for young artists, gallery shows, and intensive studies are offered year-round. The nonprofit community-based school is located in the historic village of Interlaken, a section of Stockbridge through which MA 183 passes. Willard Hill Road is off Trask Road, which connects with MA 183.

Sandisfield Arts Center
Hammertown Road, Sandisfield
(413) 258-3309, (413) 258-4904
www.berkshireweb.com/sandisfieldarts

The Sandisfield Arts Center is the oldest public building still standing in Sandisfield. Originally built by Baptists in 1839 as a meetinghouse, the Federal-style building later became a synagogue. Vacant for years, it was rescued by the Sandisfield Arts & Restoration Committee, which was founded in 1995 to restore the historic structure and transform it into a community arts center. With its original decor and marvelous acoustics, the center is an inviting venue for art shows, concerts, and educational events.

Sheffield Art League
Main Street (US 7), Sheffield
www.sheffieldart.com

The Sheffield Art League is a nonprofit association of artists of all levels of skill and experience working in all media and is dedicated to furthering the development and appreciation of fine arts in the Berkshires. Open to dues-paying artists and nonartist supporting members, the league sponsors workshops, demonstrations, lec-

The Association of Housatonic Artists

Gallery owners and artisans in the tiny but avant-garde town of Housatonic have banded together to sponsor town-wide shows and events throughout the year. One activity involved dispensing sunflower seeds to any resident who wanted some, with the hope that the entire town would be awash in sunflowers at the end of summer. Other events include an art walk around town. Members are listed under galleries; check the media for activities.

tures, and activities throughout the year and awards significant scholarships to high school seniors after holding a competition. The league also holds a juried show in July and member shows in August and at the Berkshire Botanical Garden on Columbus Day weekend. The summer shows are usually held at Dewey Hall on US 7 and are open daily except Tuesday. The organization also selects an artist-of-the-month, whose works are then shown at the Banknorth branch at 271 Main Street in Great Barrington.

Galleries

GREAT BARRINGTON

Habatat Galleries
117 State Road (US 7/MA 23)
(413) 528-9123
www.habatatgalleries.com
Located in a beautifully remodeled barn overlooking the Housatonic River, Habatat in Great Barrington is the latest gallery opened by Linda Boone, who has been having a love affair with glass since the late '60s. Her first gallery opened in Michigan in 1971. The focus back then was on traditional fine arts plus what were considered new art forms: photography, clay, fiber, art furniture, and glass. As interest in glass art grew, so did Boone's excitement about this up-and-coming art form. By 1983 she began to concentrate completely on artists working in glass.

The gallery has held invitational glass shows every year since and now represents more than 60 of the most significant and creative artists in the field of contemporary glass, including Dan Dailey, Joseph Pagano, Kari Russell-Pool, Peter Powning, and Jon Kuhn. Boone and her family now have two galleries in Michigan, one in Chicago, one in Boca Raton, Florida, and this latest one in Great Barrington. The pieces displayed here are awesome examples of the versatility of glass as a medium: flame-worked threads woven in an intricate, delicate filigree, glass embraced by cast iron or bronze, glittering chips of color suspended in perfectly polished cubes, soaring shafts of light, and whimsical constructions. If you are not a glass collector, a visit to Habatat could be the beginning of a new love. The gallery here is open daily except Wednesday from Memorial Day through fall.

Gallery hours vary widely so call ahead if coming from a distance.

S. K. H. Gallery
48 Castle Street
(413) 528-3300
www.SamKasten.com
The initials stand for Sam Kasten, Handweaver, which explains the giant looms set up in this high-end gallery located in the former waiting room of the Great Barrington railroad station. Kasten has been weaving rugs and fabrics dyed to order for 30 years. His work, sought after by New York designers and architects, has been featured in *Architectural Digest* and *Interior Design*. The founder of the former Interlaken School of Art, now IS183, Kasten decided to open the gallery to feature work by other artists working in ceramics, stoneware, Raku, metal, and fibers. Here also are paintings by known and emerging American and European artists. Exhibitors are chosen carefully and their works displayed in spacious surroundings, allowing the viewer to imagine how a piece will look in his or her home. Prospective clients also are able to view Kasten's textiles and discuss custom orders for rugs, upholstery, or hangings. While much of the work shown here is upscale, less-expensive items like handwoven scarves can be found.

You are apt to find things here that no one else in the area has. The gallery is open Thursday through Monday from spring through fall, with four different shows held during the year. This part of Castle Street is off Taconic Avenue, which meets Main Street at St. James Church. It also can be reached by walking through an underpass west of the Mahaiwe Theater, which is on the other part of Castle Street between the railroad and Main Street. In season, the farmers' market sets up in front of the train station. And, yes, a train still runs by but does not stop here.

Bobbie Lefenfeld Gallery
50 Castle Street
(413) 528-6007
Across the parking lot from the S. K. H. gallery, ceramic artist Bobbie Lefenfeld shows her earthy and imaginative work. Also featured are the works of artists from Kathmandu, imported by her husband, Howard Lefenfeld. The gold- and silver-leafed ceramics by artist Michael Wainwright also can be found here, along with changing exhibits of works by other contemporary artists and artisans. The gallery is open January through March by chance or appointment and daily the rest of the year, if possible.

HOUSATONIC

Claymania
214 Pleasant Street
(413) 274-9915
A working studio as well as a gallery, Claymania provides the equipment and moral support for anyone interested in learning how to decorate functional pottery pieces at a nominal cost. Plain bisque objects like bowls, mugs, and plates are sold; and paints, brushes, instruction, hand-holding glazing, and firing are included in the price, which ranges from $5.00 to $10.00 or so. The glazes are safe and washable. The gallery section of the studio offers finished pieces for sale. Children, accompanied by an adult, are welcome. Claymania is owned by Karen Woolis, an artist in her own right, whose work is sold here and in other galleries around the Berkshires. A great place to discover and nurture latent artistic talents, Claymania is open year-round Wednesday through Sunday. Special after-hours events include soirees on the first Monday of the month, often with music, wine, and cheese; "Ladies Night" on Wednesday; and senior discount night on Thursday.

Fox-Martin Fine Art Gallery &
1100 Main Street (MA 183)
(413) 274-1249
The ampersand is an important part of Belle Fox-Martin's gallery name, and if you visit you will see why. A self-taught artist, Fox-Martin likes to represent artists outside the loop. You will not find traditional landscapes here. Rather, you might find works she has gleaned from assorted artists who create art with a variety of themes and media and who are not accustomed to having their work shown in galleries. She has had shows of art by teenagers, art with Christian or Judaic themes—even a show that featured paintings of chairs as interpreted by a number of artists. Fox-Martin's gallery is open only on Saturday from mid-June through September, but she is happy to make appointments for other times.

Front Street Gallery
129 Front Street
(413) 274-6607
The Front Street Gallery is artist Kate Knapp's studio, and it is packed with her work. Occasionally she holds shows for other artists. The gallery is open on Saturday, if she isn't doing a show, or by appointment.

Great Barrington Pottery
391 North Plain Road (MA 41)
(413) 274-6259
www.gtbarringtonpottery.com
The pottery made by Richard Bennett is the result of 28 years of study in the Far East and West. Made of Georgian red clay, shaped by hand, and glazed with Japanese feldspar and rice straw ash, each unique piece possesses a timeless quality. Cups, plates, bowls, and tea and sake sets for use or display are fired in a traditional wood-burning brick kiln built by Bennett and his Japanese master. Bennett offers workshops and two-year apprenticeships

to those wanting to learn this ancient art. Also sold at the pottery are silk flower arrangements to complement specially designed vases. An ancient tea ceremony is performed every afternoon on the property, which is open daily. The landscaped gardens add to the illusion of being transported to 14th-century Japan. Bennett also has showrooms in Ireland and Japan.

Tokonoma Gallery & Framing Studio
402 Park Street (MA 183)
(413) 274-1166
A small but dynamic gallery, Tokonoma specializes in functional and decorative contemporary glass, pottery, fabrics, jewelry, and furniture as well as a diverse collection of fine art by regional and internationally recognized artists in shows throughout the year. The gallery also offers museum-quality framing. A Peace Garden next to the periwinkle-blue building that houses the gallery contains sculpture designed to inspire thoughts and feelings about peace through contemplation of the artists' works. The gallery is open year-round Thursday through Sunday.

LENOX

Concepts of Art
65 Church Street
(413) 637-4845
www.LenoxJudaica.com
Concepts of Art specializes in Judaica and is owned by Lynda Hagerstrom, who has a similar gallery in North Miami, Florida. Founded in 1992, the Lenox shop specializes in designs created by gifted Jewish artists from America, Canada, and Israel and has the largest collection of Judaica in the area. Art, jewelry, home furnishings, greeting cards, books, and music suitable for gifts for all Jewish holidays and occasions can be found in profusion here. The gallery/shop is open year-round, including all Christian holidays, but is closed for brief periods around the important Jewish holidays. Hagerstrom also owns the Wit Gallery on Church Street.

DeVries Fine Art Inc.
17 Franklin Street
(413) 637-3462
www.andrewdevries.com
Whether large or small, the flowing, graceful, dancing forms that sculptor Andrew DeVries creates give bronze an ethereal quality. Known and collected internationally, DeVries now shows his work in Lenox, where some of his larger works are displayed on the green at the corner of Franklin and Main Streets. His gallery is located three doors down on Franklin Street. Along with his sculpture, the gallery shows prints and other art works by DeVries. The works of other artists are also displayed. The gallery is open on weekends in spring and daily in the summer season. Appointments may be made January through March. DeVries is an artist-in-residence at Chesterwood, where he demonstrates bronze casting on certain weekends through the summer, weather permitting. Chesterwood may be contacted for information or check the sculptor's Web site for dates.

B. J. Faulkner Gallery
48 Main Street
(413) 637-2958
www.bjfaulkner.com
Bonnie Jeanne (B. J.) Faulkner's colorful and imaginative interpretations of Berkshire scenes and European villages as well as images from her days as an opera and cabaret singer exude whimsey, romance, elegance, and charm. Primarily self-taught, Faulkner works in oils and watercolors creating a fanciful, bright image with a French flair that brings joy to the viewer. She also sells giclee reproductions of her originals. The gallery, open since 1995, is in one of several small buildings off Main Street in the center of Lenox; open weekends year-round.

The Ferrin Gallery
69 Church Street
(413) 637-4414
www.FerrinGallery.com

Leslie Ferrin has been representing contemporary ceramic artists for more than 20 years, beginning with P!NCH, her first gallery in Northampton, Massachusetts. Works large and small are displayed here—some elegant, others humorous. Exhibits, with accompanying openings, change often, but you can be sure there will always be unusual teapots somewhere in the place, as Ferrin has been fascinated with that symbol of comfort for years. In fact, she has written a book on the subject called *Teapots Transformed: Exploration of an Object.* Ferrin participates in the SOFA show in New York. Her gallery is open Thursday through Saturday from May to July and Labor Day through October; open daily July and August.

Tom Fiorini
63 Church Street
(413) 243-0636
www.tomfiorini.com

Artist Tom Fiorini describes his work as "junk with a personality." Using found materials, Fiorini has been creating sculptures of animals, birds, and imaginary critters as well as furniture and abstract forms for 25 years. Hubcaps, pitchforks, faucet handles, car bumpers—anything is likely to end up as part of something from Fiorini's imagination. He also creates whimsical shapes and artistic creations with a chainsaw. His studio is in Becket (the phone number listed above), but his work is displayed year-round in this garden behind 63-65 Church Street. He is usually around on weekends, but when he isn't, the owner of Concepts of Art at 65 Church Street serves as his agent. Fiorini's work is also displayed at the Tokonoma Gallery in Housatonic and Bits and Pieces in Sheffield.

Hoadley Gallery
21 Church Street
(413) 637-2814

The Hoadley Gallery specializes in work by contemporary artists working in various media, including ceramics, glass, wood, metal, and fabric. Watercolors, oils, collages, and constructions share space with interesting furnishings for the home, fine handcrafted jewelry, and wearable art. In addition to a wide spectrum of work, the gallery features pottery made by Thomas Hoadley in the Japanese nerikomi technique, where layered clay of various colors is rolled and then cut to reveal interesting patterns. His work is in several museum and private collections, including the White House. Aside from his larger pieces, Hoadley has created a line of porcelain jewelry made with the same materials and techniques, which he calls Kenwood Porcelain. The jewelry is carried at the gallery and also may be viewed at www.kenwoodporcelain.com. The gallery is open daily March through January. Evening hours are extended in July and August. January through March, the gallery is closed Tuesday through Thursday.

The Lenox Gallery of Fine Art
69 Church Street
(413) 637-2276

The work of more than 30 artists is represented in this spacious two-floor gallery, owned by Jerome Connoy since 1994. Sculpture, ceramics, and fine art by continuously working artists within a 75-mile radius of Lenox are featured permanently or on a rotating basis. Although the first floor is full of many fine works, the second floor is the main gallery. Here, representational paintings, drawings, watercolors, and sculpture are displayed in six airy and spacious connecting rooms. Connoy likes to help develop local talent and often shows the work of promising young artists that are ready to step up. The overall theme of the gallery is to show beauty expressed in a wide variety of ways. Located in the courtyard off Church Street, the entrance to the gallery includes an anteroom that offers a preview of the work to be found inside. November 1 to June 1 the gallery is open Friday, Saturday, and Sunday. In June and from Labor Day to the end of October, Thursday is added. In July and August, the gallery is open Thursday through Tuesday.

Lydia Mongiardo
51 Church Street
(413) 274-6975

Lydia Mongiardo's gallery features furnishings designed in the French Art Deco style by her husband, Nicholas, who has been restoring furniture made by the greats of that period for more than 25 years. Mongiardo's work, which has garnered a write-up in *Architectural Digest,* includes lamps, tables, chairs, and screens unique in shape and finished in ice-smooth organic lacquer. His decorative arts studio is in the Monument Mills in Housatonic. Examples of his work may be viewed at www.nicholasmongiardo inc.com. Also in Lydia's gallery are accessories and other apparel designed by Shaftsbury, Vermont, artist MaryJane; slip-decorated pottery by Lauren Mundy; jewelry crafted in Zurich; and paintings by Carlo Domeniconi. The gallery is open daily from late spring through fall.

R. W. Wise, Goldsmiths
81 Church Street
(413) 637-1589
www.polygon.net/~rwwise

Jewelry designed by gemologist Richard Wise and other contemporary artists is attractively displayed in this shop/gallery. The author of *Secrets of the Gem Trade,* Wise has been designing and creating jewelry in Lenox for 25 years. About two-thirds of his elegantly presented stock is handcrafted on the premises using techniques handed down from master to apprentice for hundreds of years. Colored gemstones and pearls are a specialty, and pieces are custom-designed for clients after serious consultation. Between the soothing decor and the well-chosen background music, a visit is a reward in itself. The gallery/shop is open daily in July and August and Tuesday through Saturday September 1 through June 30.

The Wit Gallery
27 Church Street
(413) 637-8808

Furniture with complex marquetry inlay by Silas Kopf, kinetic sculpture by Rein Triefeld, incredible majolica pieces by George Alexander, and sculpture chiseled from glass by Henry Richardson are among the works of artists presented here. Bronzes by Walter Horak and Chris Cairns, blown glass by Barry Entner, and stone sculpture by Paul Braun also are always on display, along with oil paintings by classically trained artist Eleana Fleurova and amusing bar scenes by Harry McCormick. Also here are photographs by Ormond Giglie, creator of *Models in the Window*. Other artists are featured in changing exhibits. The gallery is open daily Memorial Day through October.

World's Best Imported Chocolate & Art
4 Housatonic Street
(413) 637-9114, (800) 244-9120
www.photographyeditions.com

Yes, you can buy both at this little gallery, where former *National Geographic* photographer Charles Steinhacker and artist Linda Clayton display their work—and their selections of chocolates from around the world. Originals and giclee reproductions of Steinhacker's scenic photographs and Clayton's mixed-media drawings are available in limited editions in various sizes. The chocolates are from various chocolatiers around the country as well as Belgium and France. Fudge from a California chocolatier who makes his own rice paper wrapping is also on hand. Gift boxes may be assembled or purchased ready-made. Also for sale are sauces and chocolate bars, along with tins and baskets suitable for filling with chocolates for gifts. The shop is open daily May through October 30.

MONTEREY

Grenadier Pottery
12 Tyringham Road
(413) 528-9973

Potter Ellen Grenadier creates her own pottery at her Monterey studio and welcomes visitors, who can view all stages of creation from wet clay to gallery setting. Sushi sets, plates, casseroles, platters, lanterns, bowls, and other tableware in rich, natural colors are for sale here as well as at other galleries in the area, including Tokonoma in Housatonic. Grenadier also gives private lessons. Although she is usually at the studio, she recommends a call if you're coming from a distance.

NORTH ADAMS

Eziba
46 Eagle Street
(413) 664-6888
www.eziba.com

The work of skilled artisans from around the world can be found online or at Eziba's shop on Eagle Street. The stock changes often, and bargains can be found at the shop, which features jewelry and decorative items for the home. Eziba is based at MASS MoCA. Eagle Street is off the junction of MA 2 and MA 8 in downtown North Adams. The shop is open daily.

PITTSFIELD

Empty Set Project Space
150 South Street
(518) 781-3899

This second-floor gallery, located at the corner of South and West Housatonic Streets, features changing exhibits by young and upcoming artists working in a variety of mediums. Permanent displays show the photography of Monika Pizzichemi and paintings and collages by Michael McKay, both owners of the gallery. Their home phone is listed above. Dedicated to showing unusual work, including performance pieces, the pair are also political activists and use the windows that face the street to display clever, caustic, and/or sarcastic comments on a variety of topics. The entrance is on South Street, where parking is prohibited, but there is a parking lot around the corner behind the building. The gallery is open on weekends.

Pasko Frame & Gift Gallery
243 North Street
(413) 442-2680

Landscapes by local artist Walter Pasko are exhibited here along with the work of other local artists. The gallery also features work by popular artist P. Buckley Moss. Custom framing and ready-made frames are available. The shop is open Monday through Saturday.

The Storefront Artist Project
All along North Street

A recent phenomenon, this project pairs artists in need of short-term large studio spaces with local building owners who have vacant storefronts on North Street. The spaces are donated, until rented, and the artists work in full view of the public behind the large windows, which are also used for display. Those involved in the project, which has no main address, occasionally sponsor shows involving other artists. Most of the storefront studios are located in a 4-block area on the west side of the street between Park Square and Bradford Street.

SHEFFIELD

Fellerman and Raabe Glassworks
534 South Main Street (US 7)
(413) 229-8533
www.fellerman-raabe.com

Stephen Fellerman and Clair Raabe are forever pushing the envelope as they pursue their art, which is sold at galleries in New York and elsewhere, online, and at their shop/studio on US 7. Fellerman is a hot-glass worker; Raabe is a self-taught glass carver. Their work is in private and public collections, including those at the White House, the Corning Museum of Glass, and the Chrysler Museum, as well as in public installations. Visitors to their Sheffield gallery can watch glass being blown on the hot floor or peruse pieces for sale in the brightly lit gallery. Tent sales are held occasionally, with pieces marked down from 20 percent for museum quality work to 75 percent for seconds or experimental pieces. Pieces produced in quantity but with individual variations include glass lamp shades in the iridescent Art Nouveau style, bowls, and vases in cut Cameo glass, jewelry, and perfume bottles in a variety of shapes. In fall the Pumkin Patch features hundreds of blown-glass pumpkins, each a little different, as well as Christmas ornaments. The pair also teach glassblowing and sculpture and have an intern program. From the beginning of July through fall the shop is open daily. Off-season the shop is closed on Monday.

The Loring Gallery
US 7
(413) 229-0110
www.loringgallery.com
The Loring Gallery traces its roots back to Cedarhurst, New York, where it was founded by Eve Loring in 1952. Loring focused on artists of the 1930s, including those of the WPA School of Art and a small group of abstract artists. Associate Rosemary Uffner and her husband, Arthur, purchased the Loring Gallery in 1972, adding the work of renowned and up-and-coming artists of the 1970s. Rosemary opened the Berkshire gallery in 1990, where it continues to feature fine art and sculpture by a select group of 20th-century artists. The gallery also carries original prints and posters of Henri de Toulouse-Lautrec. Shows and occasional lectures are held from late May through October. Open every day but Tuesday.

Sheffield Pottery
US 7
(413) 229-7700, (888) 774-2529
www.sheffield-pottery.com
Behind the big red barn that houses Sheffield Pottery lies the field of clay that has been supplying potters around the country with material for their work since 1941. John and Diane Cowen are the latest generation of the family to run the business. Along with their own clay, they sell other raw materials plus all the equipment needed by potters, including kilns. Their huge showroom, open daily year-round, is filled with finished work for sale by a number of potters, including Stone Soldier, Monroe Salt Works, Robert Fishman, East Knoll, Sara Burns, and John Zentner. Tableware and decorative accessories in a variety of glazes and designs in all price ranges can be found here.

STOCKBRIDGE

An American Craftsman
36 Main Street
(413) 298-0175, (800) 834-9437
www.AnAmericanCraftsman.com
The work of more than 800 artisans from around the country is sold through this ever-changing gallery owned by Richard and Joanne Rothbard. The price range is as wide as the selection—from many items for under $5.00 to thousands for a piece of sculpture. Unique accessories in all forms and materials are for sale here. Art glass, handcrafted wooden boxes and desk sets, ceramics, jewelry, furniture, lighting fixtures, and more are exhibited. While the Rothbards have been in Stockbridge only since 1997, they have been handling American crafts since the 1980s and have three galleries in Manhattan. The shop also features Rothbard's Boxology—a term he created to describe the process, philosophy, poetry, and psychology of the puzzle boxes he makes. There are thousands of variations of these intricately carved boxes that come apart piece by piece, depending on the grain of the wood, the way the wood is dissected and put back together, and the form chosen. Examples can be viewed at www.boxology.com.

The gallery is located near the Red Lion Inn and is open daily in summer. In winter the gallery is closed on Tuesday and Wednesday. The couple are in the process of expanding to a new building around the corner on US 7 and plan to open a cafe where all the furnishings and utensils will be artisan-made and for sale. Rothbard sponsors the three-day juried arts festivals held at Butternut Basin in Great Barrington over the Fourth of July and Columbus Day weekends.

Holsten Galleries
3 Elm Street
(413) 298-3044
www.holstengalleries.com

One of the top-three galleries dealing in contemporary glass sculpture in the country, the Holsten Gallery has not one but two Dale Chihuly chandeliers, along with myriad examples of this world-renowned artist's stunning work, including several paintings. Displayed on two floors are breathtaking pieces by other topflight artists, including Tom Patti, Sidney Hutter, Marvin Liposky, Dante Marioni, Christopher Ries, Lino Tagliapietra, and Steven Weinberg. Ken Holsten and his associates have been in the forefront of the development of glass as an art form and recently celebrated their 25th anniversary as a showcase for artists dedicated to that movement. Today they represent around two dozen renowned artists. The gallery is the only one in New England that always carries Chihuly's work. Holsten also exhibits at the Sculpture Objects and Functional Art (SOFA) Exposition in New York.

Tucked away behind a bank next to the Stockbridge Post Office, the gallery might be missed by the casual stroller, which would be a shame, but it has become a destination point for collectors from around the country and beyond. Parking in the small plaza where the gallery is located is tight; those in the know park behind Michael's Restaurant, if they can find a spot. Open daily year-round; hours are extended in July and August.

Origins Gallery
36 Main Street
(413) 298-0002
Contemporary stone sculpture from Zimbabwe, ceremonial tribal art from West and Central Africa, and ethnographic jewelry are featured in this gallery at the end of the Mews next to the Red Lion Inn. Owner Albert Gordon is well versed in the spiritual meanings and tribal histories of the pieces he has found and is more than happy to share his knowledge. Formerly located in Manhattan, Gordon has made at least 50 trips to Zimbabwe and other areas over the past 35 years. He and Judith Schuchalter opened Origins in 1996. Most of the stone pieces are sculpted by Shona artists in Zimbabwe from serpentine, springstone, or verdite that is polished on completion, accenting striations in the stone. The artists believe that the shapes they form are already in the stone and that they are simply cutting away the unwanted parts to reveal those shapes. The symbolism in their work often conveys harmony, peace, or family unity. Wood carvings from other areas are more related to tribal history, which the couple also will explain. For the serious collector, there are more works on display in Norman Rockwell's former studio down the block, over the Stockbridge General Store. Here also are bronzes, textiles, ceramics, and other folk art imported from around the world. The gallery is open daily in summer, weekends at other times.

TYRINGHAM

Naoussa Gallery
8 Main Road
(413) 243-0456, (413) 243-2555
Prints, mixed media, sculpture, ceramics, photography, and fiber art are beautifully displayed in changing exhibits in the post-and-beam barn that has been converted to the Naoussa Gallery by owner Ricki Cowell. The gallery is open Friday through Monday from Memorial Day through Columbus Day or by appointment.

WEST STOCKBRIDGE

Berkshire Center for Contemporary Glass
6 Harris Street
(413) 232-4666
Glass in all shapes, colors, and contemporary designs is displayed on lit shelves and in the windows of this gallery, which also houses a working glassblowing studio. About half the work is done by resident glassblowers, the rest by other artists, some of whom occasionally use the studio. Glass flowers, fish, snails, pixie balls, marbles, hummingbird feeders, and garden balls are displayed in profusion. More

serious are candlesticks, bowls, vases, decorative tiles, and works of art in blown or more complex fused glass. Imaginative metal and glass furniture completes the assortment of handcrafted furnishings available here. The glassblowers welcome observers, and on weekends, if you are older than age 10, you can make your own paperweight. The center is closed from January through March and open daily June through December. Call for hours in those in-between months.

Hoffman Pottery
103 MA 41
(413) 232-4646
www.ehoffmanpottery.com

First there are the brightly colored flags that mark her driveway. Then there's the bright red-and-yellow building in the back that is the studio and gallery. Next comes the garden, where ceramic vessels, birds, frogs, and turtles lurk among the plants and flowers. This is the world of Elaine Hoffman, who for 30 years has been making functional and decorative pottery in colors riotous as well as subdued. Her colors are multilayered, and sometimes she scratches a design through one or more of them. Once she has created a design and color combination, she produces many pieces in that pattern: plates, pitchers, teapots, candlesticks, vases, trays—too many to list. Where words fail, the Web site reigns. Occasionally Hoffman will phase out a design and create a new one in its place. She also creates ceramic sculpture, samples of which are in the garden. Check out the heads on sticks, which she says are guarding spirits. A teacher, Hoffman is open only on weekends and holidays during the school year. But come summer, she is open every day. Memorial Day to Labor Day she invites folks of all ages to come in and "paint a plate." Hoffman Pottery is on MA 41 about 10 minutes south of West Stockbridge or 30 minutes from Great Barrington. If you overshoot the driveway, you will eventually find a place to turn around. It's worth the hassle!

Train Station Gallery
6 Depot Street
(413) 232-7930

When artist Elaine Ranney and her husband, Herbert, saw this space in the beautifully renovated West Stockbridge train station, they knew immediately that it would make a great gallery. That was in 1998, and they have been showing her work and that of other artists in the light and airy space ever since. Elaine works in oils, creating joyful and colorful renditions of flowers, landscapes, and other subjects. Originally she wanted to handle work of artist friends she and her husband admired, but they keep discovering more and more artists whose work they find exemplary and interesting, often touched with humor or political commentary. Although the artists and artisans change, the groupings always include sculpture in metal and stone, jewelry, etchings, and photographs. The gallery is open daily from late June through August; Friday through Monday in April and May and September through December.

Waterside Gallery
30-32 Main Street
(413) 232-7187

The focus is on the sculpture displayed in the park next to the Williams River as well as inside at this Main Street gallery, where sculptor Jean Khalaf's studio is located. Also found here are antiques, art, jewelry, and collectibles. The shop/gallery is open daily in summer.

WILLIAMSTOWN

Beaver Pond Gallery
2993 Hancock Road (MA 43)
(413) 738-5895

Landscape artist Richard A. Heyer captures the four seasons in oils, watercolors, and prints. He also does custom framing and gives private lessons. The studio and gallery actually is located in the town of Hancock, but the mailing address is Williamstown. Call for an appointment.

The Harrison Gallery
39 Spring Street
(413) 458-1700
www.theharrisongallery.com

The Harrison Gallery is a fine-art gallery and custom framing studio. Landscapes of the Northeast are often presented in single-artist or collaborative theme shows. Sculpture and other contemporary art by emerging and established artists are presented, with a new exhibit every month. In cooperation with the Pucker Gallery of Boston, the sleek, vividly glazed pottery of Brother Thomas is exhibited. Fine handcrafted furniture is also offered. In keeping with the gallery's slogan, "Bringing Art Home," the works offered are varied and distinctive in a wide range of prices. Owners Jody Harrison Silipo and Laurie J. Thomsen earned degrees in art history from Williams and, after traveling other paths, decided to return to town to open the gallery, which is named for Silipo's father, also a Williams alum. Many of the artists whose work is shown here also are Williams graduates. The gallery offers high-quality custom framing services for both residential and commercial customers and is open daily year-round.

The Plum Gallery
112 Water Street
(413) 458-3389
www.plumgallery.com

Plum Gallery presents painting, photography, drawing, printmaking, sculpture, and ceramics by emerging and established artists in a newly restored 1922 variety store attached to a 1787 chestnut post-and-beam house. The polished wood floors and stark white walls provide a dramatic backdrop to the uncommon works displayed here. The gallery also offers prints from the Vermont Studio Center Press. Owned and directed by artist Mary E. Natalizia and her husband, photographer Nicholas Whitman, the gallery is open year-round. Call for hours, and check the Web site for changing exhibits and opening receptions.

LITERARY ENDEAVORS

The Berkshire Writers Room
28 Renne Avenue, Pittsfield
www.berkshirewritersroom.org

The Berkshire Writers Room is located in space provided by the city of Pittsfield above the Berkshire Artisans Gallery. More than 100 members meet monthly to read their work, give and receive constructive feedback, and share their passion for writing. Topics include poetry, fiction, creative nonfiction, script writing, and writing for children and young adults. The group also sponsors readings at other locations, including Barnes & Noble Booksellers in the *Berkshire Crossing* shopping center off MA 9 in east Pittsfield. The group also publishes the annual *Berkshire Review*, featuring poems, short stories, plays, and nonfiction submitted by both members and nonmembers and chosen by an editorial board for originality and literary merit. The Review is available at bookstores, museums, and libraries in the area and elsewhere.

The Bookloft
Great Barrington Plaza (US 7), Great Barrington
(413) 528-1521
www.thebookloft.com

The independently owned Bookloft sponsors various events, including appearances by authors of new books at the store and other locations. Events are listed on the Web site.

The Bookstore
11 Housatonic Street, Lenox
(413) 637-3390

Also independently owned, the Bookstore holds poetry readings and book signings throughout the year, especially focusing on local writers.

Inkberry
63 Main Street, North Adams
(413) 664-0775
www.inkberry.org

Inkberry is an independent, nonprofit organization dedicated to fostering the literary arts in and around Berkshire County. Supported by several grants, the group holds workshops for all levels of writers and sponsors a reading series that brings established writers to the community as well as promoting local talent. A writers' resource library, open to the public Wednesday through Saturday year-round, is stocked with a collection of videotapes of poets reading from their works; books on writing, publishing, and the literary life; and an archive of literary magazines. The group also sponsors tutorials and holds classes throughout the year. Times and topics vary but are listed on the Web site.

Papyri Books
49 Main Street, North Adams
www.papyribooks.com
An independent, locally owned bookstore, Papyri holds poetry slams and readings throughout the year. Every April the store celebrates National Poetry Month by arranging special appearances by such notable poets as Richard Wilbur and Billy Collins. Events are publicized and listed on the Web site.

Edith Wharton Restoration
The Mount
3 Plunkett Street, Lenox
(413) 637-1899
www.edithwharton.org
Edith Wharton Restoration, the group overseeing the return of the author's estate to its former glory, sponsors lectures throughout the year relating to Wharton's work. Sometimes lectures include tea on the veranda, a custom the writer enjoyed. A bookstore at the Mount is filled with works by Wharton, including rare and out-of-print editions as well as books by others on literature, architecture, interior design, and gardening, some of Wharton's favorite topics. Check the Web site for information about the lectures or other special readings.

MUSEUMS

Berkshire Museum
39 South Street, Pittsfield
(413) 443-7171
www.berkshiremuseum.org
The Berkshire Museum celebrated its 100th birthday in 2003 with a bang-up party, as well it should have. The only museum in western Massachusetts that combines science, history, and art, the Berkshire Museum crams a lot into three floors. The exhibits of minerals, fossils, and sea life on the first floor are especially intriguing to children (more about that in the Kidstuff chapter). The Museum Store also is located here, offering fine papers, books, and jewelry and many things for children. The museum's 300-seat theater, located across from the entrance, is used for concerts and lectures and is home to the Little Cinema, where foreign and first-run American films are shown May through September.

Twin marble staircases wind up to the second floor, where the Ancient Civilizations gallery shows fascinating artifacts, including Roman and Greek glass and the museum's resident mummy. Fine arts galleries feature sculpture from the 17th to the 20th century; portraits by such masters as John Singleton Copley, Charles Wilson Peale, and John Singer Sargent; and a fine collection of Hudson River School landscapes, including works by Albert Bierstadt, Frederick Edwin Church, and George Inness. Other galleries exhibit the Hahn Collection of Early American Silver, the Gallatin Collection of Abstract Art, and the Spalding Collection of Chinese art. The spacious Crane Room, with its high ceiling and wonderful Art Deco interior, is a fitting place to display replicas of classical statues. Receptions and special events are often held here. The subtle wood trim in the Crane Room was executed by A. Sterling Calder, whose son, Alexander, created a series of wooden toys that are now on permanent display at the museum. Galleries on the second floor also are used for changing exhibits. Recently the museum presented an exhibit of 12 masters of contemporary glass art, including works by William Morris, Dale Chihuly, and Marvin Lipofsky. Down a few stairs to the basement level is the aquarium, where the diversity of aquatic life from Berkshire ponds to coral reefs may be examined. Two touch tanks allow visitors to handle the sea stars and urchins that inhabit the tidal pools of coastal New England.

A remarkable community asset, the Berkshire Museum was a gift from Zenas Crane. It is open daily by admission. Memberships help support the museum and include free admission and discounts at the museum shop, films, and some special events. The museum is located just south of Park Square in the center of Pittsfield. Parking is available at nearby garages or on the street if you are lucky. There are handicapped parking places by the side of the museum, which is fully wheelchair-accessible.

Most historic sites and museums remain open year-round but with reduced hours in the off-season. A phone call ahead is a good idea.

Sterling and Francine Clark Art Institute
225 South Street, Williamstown
(413) 458-2303
www.clarkart.edu

The Clark, as it is affectionately called, houses the collections of a remarkable couple who bought what they liked, amassing a collection of art, furnishings, photographs, and prints that has earned an international reputation. At the top of the list is the work of the French Impressionists they both admired. By the time the Clarks opened their museum in 1955, they had 36 Renoirs plus works by others of the period, including Monet, Degas, and Matisse. The collection includes painting by the Old Masters, including Rembrandt, as well as American artists Winslow Homer, John Singer Sargent, and Frederick Remington. Also exhibited are fine examples of porcelain, silver, furniture, prints, and early photographs by masters of their crafts.

But the Clark is more than the airy and beautifully lit galleries that exhibit these collections. It also is distinguished for the depth of its research and academic programs, as well as the natural beauty of its pastoral setting. The Clark houses one of the finest art reference libraries in the world and collaborates with the Williams College graduate program of art history and operates an art conservation center.

There is always something happening at the Clark, whether it be the opening of a new exhibit, a concert on the lawn, a lecture, or a film, usually centered around a theme relating to the current exhibit. Recently a show of seascapes by J. M. W. Turner (1775-1851) prompted a host of activities, including a New England lobster bake, showings of *Mutiny on the Bounty* and *Horatio Hornblower,* lectures on the sea and related topics in art, and a British Seaside Family Day. The museum shop has an exceptional collection of art books and unique gifts. A full-service upscale restaurant is open for lunch during July and August. Delicious salads, sandwiches, baked goods, and beverages are available throughout the year at the cafe. The museum is open daily mid-June through August. Except for Monday holidays, it is closed on Monday the rest of the year. There is no admission charge off-season. South Street is off the intersection of US 7 and MA 2 at Field Park in the center of Williamstown.

Chapin Library of Rare Books & Manuscripts
Stetson Hall, Williams College
Main Street (MA 2)
(413) 597-2462

This library, which is located on the Williams College campus, contains rare literary works, including permanent displays of the original copies of the Constitution,

Bill of Rights, Declaration of Independence, and Articles of Confederation. The collection includes 50,000 rare and reference books and 40,000 manuscripts. Established by a Williams alumnus in 1923 as a resource for students and other scholars, the collection also includes illustrated books, prints, drawings, photographs, and ephemera of historical and literary importance relating to graphic and performing arts. Exhibits change throughout the year. The library is open Monday through Friday but closes for lunch at noon.

Crane Museum of Papermaking
30 South Street, Dalton
(413) 684-6481

The history of American papermaking dating back to Revolutionary times is exhibited here in one of Crane & Company's earliest buildings. Built in 1844, the historic Old Stone Mill is on the National Register of Historic Places. It is located on the banks of the Housatonic River, which supplied water to wash the rags and drive the machinery of the early Crane paper mills. The interior architecture is unusual, resembling a ship's hull. The oak beams and early lighting devices provide an appropriate backdrop for the collection, most of which is housed in glass cases. Scale models, ledger entries, and examples of currency and other papers produced by Crane & Company through the years are among the displays. The museum is located on the grounds of the Pioneer Mill on East Housatonic Street, behind the company's headquarters at the intersection of South Street and Massachusetts Highway 9. It is open afternoons Monday through Friday from June through mid-October. There is no admission fee.

The Frelinghuysen Morris House & Studio
92 Hawthorne Street, Lenox
(413) 637-0166
www.frelinghuysen.org

George L. K. Morris and Suzy Frelinghuysen were a remarkable couple at the leading edge of the national and international art scene in the 1930s. Both artists in their own right, their Bauhaus-style home—certainly not traditional in Berkshire County—is furnished with their own work as well as the works of contemporaries that they collected. Displayed as they were when the dynamic couple lived there are pieces by Picasso, Braque, Leger, and Gris. Murals, paintings, and sculpture abound in the Moderne home, which is located off Hawthorne Street. The house is open mid-June through Labor Day Thursday through Sunday. In September and October the home is open Thursday through Saturday. Hourly tours are given. If you don't want to go through the house, you can see an example of Morris's work at the recently built Morris Elementary School on West Street. In the 1960s Morris and his brothers gave the town the land on which the original elementary school was built, and Morris donated a three-piece fresco that was incorporated into the design of the school. A few years ago, the school was torn down to make room for the new building, and the mosaic mural was almost lost. But a group rescued the fresco, which is now incorporated into the wall of the new school with a plaque explaining the history.

Hancock Shaker Village
US 20, Pittsfield
(413) 443-0188, (800) 817-1137
www.hancockshakervillage.org

Aside from the gardens, livestock, and historic buildings, Hancock Village houses one of the largest and most representative collections of Shaker artifacts available to the public at an original Shaker site. Furniture, tools and equipment, household objects, textiles, manuscripts, and inspirational art reflect the important role the Shakers played in this country's social, religious, and economic life. A communal religious society, the Shakers were also entrepreneurs, selling herbs, medicines, seeds, and household furnishings to "the world." Among their ingenious inventions were machinery to sort and package seeds and herbs, a complex water system,

Nothing is open on Thanksgiving, Christmas, or New Year's Day and hours on other holidays vary. But during school vacations, like Presidents' Week, check out the museums for special programs for children.

and a unique round stone barn with cattle on an upper level, allowing for grain to be fed to all from a central shaft while waste settled below.

A celibate society, the Shakers dwindled from 19 communities in several states to none by the 1970s. The Hancock settlement, formed in the late 1700s, became a museum in 1960. The settlement had deteriorated considerably, and it has taken many years of fund-raising, grants, and hard work to restore it to its present state. Furnishings and artifacts are displayed in 95 room settings throughout the village and in exhibition galleries in the Center for Shaker Studies. Twenty original Shaker buildings spanning three centuries are open to the public. The restoration was led by the late Amy Bess and Lawrence K. Miller. A library bearing their names contains an extensive collection of historic photographs, commercial graphics, and ephemera; it is open to qualified scholars by appointment.

Now a national landmark, Hancock Village runs programs for all ages throughout the year. Rare species of livestock are maintained, and the annual spring birthing of new generations is celebrated with events for the family. Spring also brings sheep shearing, with related hands-on activities, including spinning, weaving, and dyeing of the wool. Winter activities include ice harvesting and sleigh rides. Other annual events include a crafts show, an antiques show, a country fair, and Shaker suppers. The museum is open year-round. Memorial Day weekend to late October, the complex is open for visitors to wander through the buildings on their own if they desire. Winter and early spring, guided tours through selected buildings and galleries are offered; visitors are asked to call for tour times. A gift shop and seasonal cafe are on the premises. There is an admission charge except for children under age 12.

MASS MoCA
87 Marshall Street, North Adams
(413) 662-2111
www.massmoca.org

The Massachusetts Museum of Contemporary Art, wrote a critic in the *New Yorker*, "is the damnedest place." Absolutely! First of all, the works shown in the huge mill complex that once teemed with Sprague Electric workers are hard to describe. The art is thought-provoking, sometimes scary, often amusing, occasionally perplexing, and certainly different. The galleries range from intimate to cavernous. Surprises are squirreled around the place. The clock in the tower chimes electronically, and the chime is different each time, depending on the amount of sunlight the computer gets. The upside-down trees hanging in the entryway are curving upward, showing that light has a stronger pull than gravity. Videos, computer screens, projected images, animation, graphics, light bulbs, jigsaw puzzles, electric fans blowing rows of tiny flags, a giant cheese grater—anything is fair game as a subject or a medium at MoCA. Lucky children in local schools are able to explore art with their families at Kidspace, a collaboration between the Clark, Williams College, and MoCA that's open to the public at certain times.

The museum also celebrates the creativity of today's dancers, filmmakers, playwrights, actors, and musicians through a lively mix of programming. The Phillip Glass ensemble, Mark Morris Dancers, Bill T. Jones, Joan Baez, Roseanne Cash, courtyard dance parties, rock musicals—you just never know what the season will bring! Collaborations with the Clark Art Institue and Williams College Museum of Art and Department of Music, Jacob's Pillow, and other county organizations have expanded since MoCA opened in 1999. The place reeks of creativity. The artistic urge even spread to the parking lot, where folks started decorating the light standards with their admission stickers.

What started out as a pie-in-the-sky idea has become the economic engine the proponents hoped for, with the help of state funds. Eventually all the brick and stone buildings that housed the Arnold Dye and Print Works in the 1800s will be turned into studios and work space for all kinds of projects. Businesses will be moving in to help support the upkeep and provide more jobs. The *Boston Globe* said MoCA "is a case study for urbanologists and politicians seeking to revive failing cities." The *Wall Street Journal* called MoCA "a millennial prototype. Indeed," the reviewer wrote, "I have seen the future and it is MASS MoCA." It really is "the damnedest place."

The museum is in downtown North Adams off MA 2 and MA 8. Look for the big aluminum letters on the roof. It is open June 1 through October 31. November through May, hours are reduced; the museum is closed on Tuesday. Tours are given hourly in season. There is an admission fee unless you are a member. Prices for special events vary. Check the Web for what's happening when.

Norman Rockwell Museum
9 Glendale Road, Stockbridge
(413) 298-4100
www.nrm.org

Norman Rockwell has been called the Babe Ruth of American illustrators. An icon, Rockwell chronicled life in America for nearly 60 years, from everyday occurrences to milestones in our history. How fortunate that he spent the last 25 years of his life living and working in Stockbridge. And how fortunate that he and his wife, Molly, helped to save the Old Corner House on Main Street that was about to be torn down. For that clapboard home is where the seeds for the Rockwell Museum were planted. The Rockwells worked with other residents to purchase the house, which was given to the Historical Society in 1969. Rockwell gave the society a few drawings to spice up the collection of town historical memorabilia on exhibit, and bit by bit word got out that originals of his work could be seen there. Soon his illustrations became the major draw at the Old Corner House.

Attendance swelled, and in 1973 Rockwell gave his entire collection in trust to the Historical Society. The Old Corner House became the Norman Rockwell Museum. Three years later, in failing health, Rockwell added his studio and its contents to the trust. It became apparent that the museum was outgrowing its home, so efforts began to build a proper museum. A farm on which astronaut Story Musgrave spent part of his youth was purchased, and architect Robert A. M. Stern was hired to design a new building. In 1993, 15 years after Rockwell's death at age 84, the museum—including the studio—moved to its new home on 36 acres overlooking the Housatonic River Valley.

The collection includes more than 570 drawings and paintings, including his famous Four Freedoms, and an archive of more than 100,000 photographs, letters, and mementos. A recent exhibition featured the original tearsheets of each of the 322 covers Rockwell did for the *Saturday Evening Post*. Aside from preserving Rockwell's legacy and making it available to the public, the museum is devoted to showing the works of other great illustrators, including Maxfield Parrish, J. C. Leyendecker, Rockwell Kent, and Currier and Ives. The museum also arranged for a national tour of Rockwell's work and has expanded its educational programming through events on-site and on the Internet, where a museum-designed classroom curriculum is available at www.nrm.org. The museum is open daily May through October. November through April, hours are reduced during the week. The studio is closed from November through April. A gift shop is filled with prints, collector plates, and other memorabilia, and there is a cafe on the premises. Admission is charged for visitors over age 18 unless they are members of the museum.

North Adams Museum of History and Science
Western Gateway Heritage State Park
Building 5A, North Adams
(413) 664-4700
www.geocities.com/northadamshistory

More than 25 exhibits depicting the history of North Adams are located in this renovated former coal shed. The building is a tribute to the craftsmanship of the early days of railroading, which came to the city when the Hoosac Tunnel was completed. The shed was built to store tons of coal to feed the engines that came through, and the supporting beams and masonry supports are huge. Refurbished when the state created this park to commemorate the city's railroading history, the building now has refinished floorboards and up-to-date lighting. Spread over two floors and a third floor balcony are exhibits pertaining to railroading, ballooning, and the textile and shoe industries—all major contributors to booming North Adams in the late 1800s.

Model trains lazily run around a large layout. While there are some artifacts relating to the Hoosac Tunnel, most of the history of that incredible project can be learned from exhibits in another building in the park. Displays in this museum focus on everyday life, school days, fire and police, farm life, religion, and the military. Photographs of Chinese, Welsh, Irish, Jews, and other ethnic groups record the variety of people who settled here. Architectural remnants from long-gone Victorian buildings are all around. One display re-creates the vanishing front porch, where folks used to sit and watch the world go by. A natural science center and discovery room offer hands-on opportunities for learning. The North Adams Historical Society operates the museum, which is staffed by volunteers and is open Thursday through Sunday. There is no admission charge but donations are welcome.

Williams College Museum of Art
Main Street (MA 2), Williamstown
(413) 597-2429
www.williams.edu/WCMA

The Williams College Museum of Art houses 11,000 works that span the history of art, including more than 400 works by artist brothers Maurice and Charles Prendergast. The collection emphasizes contemporary and modern art along with American art from the late 18th century to the present and the art of world cultures. Shows mounted throughout the year include an exhibition of work by Williams art students at the end of the school year. The 14 galleries are located in an 1846 two-story brick octagon that served as the college's first library and in additions constructed in the 1980s, where the art department is also situated. New and old are linked by a dramatic three-story entrance atrium, designed by internationally renowned architect Charles Moore, who also did the additions. Recently Tibetan monks constructed a mandala under the neoclassic rotunda of the original building. The three-week residency was part of a five-month multifaceted program of events relating to Tibetan art and culture.

The museum's modern and contemporary art collection is the most significant in the area and includes practically every artist of note that you can think of. Modern art from 1900 to 1945 is represented by almost 1,000 works, and there are more than 2,500 post-1945 works by American, British, and European artists and photographers too numerous to name here. The most recent additions to this extensive collection are the bronze eyes peering from the earth in front of the museum. They are by Louise Bourgeois, who created them in 2001 for the museum's 75th anniversary.

Almost 700 works represent art of world cultures. A 1993 bequest added 60 important works of Indian art to the college's already significant collection of

Rajput and Mughal paintings of the 17th to 19th centuries. There also are fine examples of 17th-century Chinese painting and calligraphy and a collection of African art. Works by John Singleton Copley, Thomas Eakins, William Harnett, Winslow Homer, Edward Hopper, William Morris Hunt, George Inness, John Frederick Kensett, John LaFarge, Georgia O'Keeffe, Benjamin West, and Grant Wood are among the 5,500 pieces in the collection of 18th- and 19th-century American art. The museum is open free of charge Tuesday through Sunday.

HISTORIC HOMES

Arrowhead
780 Holmes Road, Pittsfield
(413) 442-1793
www.mobydick.org
The Berkshire County Historical Society maintains Arrowhead, the 18th-century home of writer Herman Melville and his family from 1850 to 1863. Melville bought the property to find respite from the hectic life he was leading in New York as a successful writer. During his stay here, three of his four children were born and he developed close friendships with other Berkshire writers, including Nathaniel Hawthorne, Oliver Wendell Holmes, and Catherine Maria Sedgwick. Between working the farm and spending time with his family, he wrote a number of books, including *Moby Dick* as well as a collection of short stories. He and his family returned to New York in 1863, but Arrowhead remained in the Melville family until 1927, when it was used as a private residence. It was purchased in 1975 by the Berkshire County Historical Society, which has its offices and collections here. The 44-acre property includes a nature trail with views of the panoramic vistas that Melville reveled in. Guided tours of the furnished house are conducted. The society also has protected the north meadow, preserving the view of Mount Greylock to the north that was a major inspiration to Melville, particularly for *Moby Dick*. A Registered National Historic Landmark, Arrowhead is open Memorial Day weekend through October 31. A fee is charged. The phone number listed above may be called for winter hours and membership information.

Colonel John Ashley House
Cooper Hill Road, Ashley Falls
(413) 298-3239
www.thetrustees.org
This house, built in 1735 by 25-year-old Colonel John Ashley for his Dutch bride, Hannah Hogeboom, is said to be the oldest in Berkshire County. But its age and period furnishings are not its only claim to fame. The Ashley home was the center of social, economic, and political life in South County, where a number of historic documents were drawn up. Several years before the Declaration of Independence was signed, a group gathered in the upstairs study and drafted a petition against British tyranny and a manifesto for individual rights. Called the Sheffield Declaration, it was published in 1773. The cause for the abolition of slavery in America gained ground after a state court ruled in 1781 that under the new state constitution the Ashleys' slave, Elizabeth "Mumbet" Freeman, should be freed. The house, near the remarkable Bartholomew's Cobble Nature and Visitor Center, is listed on the National Register of Historic Places and has been a property of the Trustees of the Reservation since 1972. The home is off Rannapo Road, reached by US 7A south of Sheffield. It is open from Memorial Day weekend to Columbus Day on weekends and Monday holidays. A 45-minute house tour is offered. There is a modest admission fee.

Bidwell House Museum
100 Art School Road, Monterey
(413) 528-6888
www.bidwellhousemuseum.org
Judging by the quality of the furnishings in this house, the Reverend Adonijah Bidwell did not take a vow of poverty when he came to preach to the pioneer settlers around 1750. The beautifully proportioned

Georgian saltbox is filled with the finest examples of silver, pewter, china, and furniture of the period. The house itself is set on 196 acres of fields, woodlands, and gardens. Wings were added in 1790 and 1836 by the Reverend's son and grandson. Completely preserved, the building contains extremely fine examples of hand-carved wall panels and unique door details. A massive center chimney services four fireplaces, three with open hearths, plus two beehive ovens. Early samplers, paintings, and mirrors hang on the walls; linsey-woolsey coverlets and patchwork quilts are displayed on the beds. Fine furniture and accessories of the period abound, along with rare lighting devices, hand tools, and other utensils. The collection is said to be one of the finest in the county.

The agricultural heritage of New England is also preserved here with heirloom vegetable and herb gardens containing varieties dating back to their original planting. The grounds include several 19th-century outbuildings and the ruins of several barns available for exploration. Hiking trails and footpaths wind through the forest. The nonprofit museum is privately operated, supported by memberships, contributions and bequests, and a modest admission charge. It is open Memorial Day to late October. Bidwell House is at the end of Art School Road off Tyringham Road, which runs north from MA 23 in Monterey or south from MA 102 in Lee.

The William Cullen Bryant Homestead
297 Bryant Road, Cummington
(413) 734-2244
www.thetrustees.org

Just outside Berkshire County, this pastoral estate was the boyhood home of William Cullen Bryant, one of America's foremost 19th-century poets. A National Historic Landmark, the property was purchased in 1789 by Bryant's grandfather. The homestead and its surrounding countryside inspired much of young Bryant's poetry, including "The Rivulet" and "To a Waterfowl." After a law career in Great Barrington, Bryant moved to New York City to become editor and publisher of the *New York Evening Post*, where he reigned for 50 years. His family sold the Homestead in 1835. Thirty years later Bryant bought it back as a summer retreat and converted it from a center-stair colonial to a Victorian cottage.

Among the orchards, maple groves, and old-growth forests are trees almost 200 years old. Footpaths and carriage roads winding through the property are good for moderate hikes. The home is furnished with colonial and Victorian pieces from Bryant and his ancestors as well as memorabilia Bryant collected during his travels to Europe and Asia. Largely unchanged for more than 159 years, the 195-acre property is managed by the Trustees of Reservations. A museum shop in the visitor center is one of a few places to find complete volumes of Bryant' s poetry, last published in 1947. The grounds are open year-round from sunrise to sunset. The house is open for guided tours Friday through Sunday and on Monday holidays from the last weekend in June through Labor Day and Saturday, Sunday, and Monday through Columbus Day. There is a nominal admission charge. A craft festival is held in July.

Cummington is on MA 9 east of Windsor. The Homestead is off Massachusetts Highway 112, which meets MA 9 near the William Cullen Bryant Public Library. Look for the store with the cow on top. That's the Cummington Creamery, which sells great food and interesting crafts—and has the best bulletin board around.

Chesterwood
4 Williamsville Road, Stockbridge
(413) 298-3579
www.chesterwood.org

Chesterwood is a 122-acre estate that was the summer home and workplace of sculptor Daniel Chester French. Seeking respite from the hurly-burly world of New York, he carefully planned his Berkshire retreat to satisfy different needs: formal gardens and spacious lawns for elegant receptions and parties; broad porches for dining with a spectacular view of the peaceful mountains; and cloistered garden nooks for tranquility. However, visiting models, assistants, clients, and others interfered with his work. He built a second studio in a cool, quite secluded spot on the grounds, which he found more conducive to the concentration needed for his work. Today that studio, called Meadowlark, may be rented through the Red Lion Inn for weekend getaways in season. Working models for French's works, including the famous seated Lincoln for the Washington, D.C., memorial and *The Minuteman* in Concord, are on display in the museum gallery, home, and gardens. The museum is open daily May through October. Special events held at other times throughout the year include "Christmas at Chesterwood."

The Mission House Museum and Gardens
19 Main Street (MA 102), Stockbridge
(413) 298-3239
www.thetrustees.org

Unlike the Reverend Bidwell, the Reverend John Sergeant lived in a simple log cabin in town when he came to what was to become Stockbridge to establish a mission for the Mahicans. When he married Abigail Williams in 1739, he built a new home on Prospect Hill, but it was still a fairly plain structure. Sergeant was most revered in Stockbridge for his acceptance of the Mahicans as equals. He learned their language, invited them into his home, and learned from them as they learned from him. The house on Prospect Hill attracted the attention of benefactress Mable Choate who, around 1926, had it disassembled and reconstructed at its present location on Main Street, near the site of Sergeant's first log cabin. The house contains an outstanding collection of simple 18th-century furnishings, more humble than those found in the Reverend Bidwell's home in Monterey. The colonial gardens were designed by landscape architect Fletcher Steele, a favorite of Miss Choate's, who took more than five years to replicate the originals. The kitchen garden with its gravel walkways contains 100 herbs, perennials, and annuals that had culinary or medicinal value to early colonists. A replica of an old cobbler shop serves as the entrance to the property. A grape arbor in the Well Courtyard behind the Mission House leads to a small Native American museum that tells the story of the Mahicans. The property is managed by the Trustees of Reservations, whose regional office also is located here. The Mission House is open Memorial Day weekend to Columbus Day. A nominal admission fee is charged, which includes tours of the house and gardens led every 45 minutes. The house is located on the corner of Main and Sergeant Streets just west of the US 7 intersection. Parking in the center of Stockbridge at the height of the season is extremely limited, so wherever you find a legal space, grab it and walk.

The Mount
3 Plunkett Street, Lenox
(413) 637-1899
www.edithwharton.org

One of America's greatest writers, Edith Wharton penned more than 40 books in 40 years, including works on architecture, gardens, interior design, and travel. Wharton visited Lenox many times at the turn of the 20th century and fell in love with the place. In 1902 she bought 113 acres that overlooked Laurel Lake for $40,600 and embarked on creating her dream house. The mansion and gardens would reflect the principles outlined in her influential book *The Decoration of Houses*, written in 1897. Architect Ogden Codman Jr. was coauthor, and Wharton enlisted his services in building the 42-room terraced mansion where she would entertain, garden, and write.

Beautifully proportioned, the estate is considered an icon of American architecture. In a little more than a year Wharton moved into what she called "my first real home." She lived there for more than 10 years, gardening, writing, and entertaining until her husband became gravely ill and the property became a burden to manage.

She moved to France in 1911, where she died in 1937. After many changes in ownership, the mansion and its elegant gardens fell into disrepair. A concerted effort to save the estate began in 1980 when the nonprofit group Edith Wharton Restoration Inc. was created. Now, nearly $9 million later, the mansion has been restored and work on the interior has begun. Wharton's bedroom was one of the first to be returned to the way it was when she wrote there, sitting in bed, surrounded by her dogs and tossing papers on the floor for the help to pick up. Other rooms were decorated by name designers for the centennial celebration in 2002. The gardens she designed are 90 percent restored after an expenditure of more than $2 million. A National Historic Landmark, the Mount is one of only a few such landmarks that honor a woman and the only monument to Wharton's remarkable life. Visitors may wander through the gardens and decorated rooms or enjoy lunch on the terrace where Wharton entertained her friends. A bookstore is stocked with works by Wharton, including rare and out-of-print editions as well as books by others on literature, architecture, interior design, and gardening. The Mount is open May through November. The terrace is open for lunch mid-June through August and on fall weekends, weather permitting. Admission charges vary, but there is none for children under age 12 accompanied by an adult.

Naumkeag
Prospect Hill Road, Stockbridge
(413) 298-3239
www.thetrustees.org

Designed by Stanford White in 1885, this 26-room mansion is crammed with furniture, ceramics, rugs, tapestries, and artwork from America, Europe, and the Far East collected by Ambassador Joseph Hodges Choate and his daughter, Mable. The mansion, with its turrets and leaded-glass windows, had two architects: Charles F. McKim, a friend of the ambassador's, who turned the project over to White, a young and promising partner. The remarkable gardens had three architects. Initially Frederick Lay Olmsted laid them out, but a dispute erupted over the cost and Nathaniel Barrett of Boston finished the project. When Choate's daughter inherited the place, she hired landscape architect Fletcher Steele to redo the gardens, which in a way are even more remarkable than the house.

Surrounded by 40 acres of woodland, meadow, and pasture that stretches to the Housatonic River are eight acres of terraced gardens and landscaped grounds divided into "rooms," or themes. The Rose Garden offers a heady and profuse mix of color and fragrance when in bloom. Other settings include the Afternoon Garden, the Linden Walk, the brick-walled Chinese Garden replete with stone Buddhas and carved lions and dogs; and the topiary of the Evergreen Garden. The most famous feature—and most photographed—is the hillside where towering white birches frame a series of deep blue fountain pools flanked by four flights of white-railed steps. Miss Choate left Naumkeag and an endowment to the Trustees of Reservations, who manage it today. The property is open with an admission charge daily from Memorial Day weekend to Columbus Day. Guided house tours last around 45 minutes. Naumkeag hosts an annual Garden Party in July, a Farm Day in August, and other special events.

Prospect Hill Road veers to the left off Pine Street, which begins at the intersection of US 7 and MA 102 near the Red Lion Inn. Naumkeag is one of several spectacular mansions along Prospect Hill Road.

Ventfort Hall
104 Walker Street, Lenox
(413) 637-3206
www.gildedage.org

Located in the center of Lenox, Ventfort Hall is largely hidden from view by homes built on land that was once part of this great estate. But behind those homes along Walker Street, Ventfort Hall presents a somber and formidable facade of brick and redstone—an imposing reminder of the Gilded Age, when the rich discovered Lenox and Stockbridge and built their outlandish summer "cottages." A summer home for Sarah Spencer Morgan—sister of J. P.—and her distant cousin and husband, George, the mansion was designed by architects Rotch & Tilden and built in 1893. The house has 28 rooms, including 15 bedrooms, 13 bathrooms, and 17 fireplaces. The interior features a soaring three-story great hall and paneled wood staircase. Other rooms include an elegant salon, a paneled library, a dining room, a billiard room, and a bowling alley. When it was built, the mansion had all the latest modern amenities, including numerous ingeniously ventilated bathrooms, combined gas and electric light fixtures, an elevator, burglar alarms, and central heating. There also were several outbuildings, including two gatehouses, a carriage house/stable, and six greenhouses. Now on 11.7 acres, Ventfort Hall was originally the centerpiece of a large landscaped garden of 26 acres.

After the death of both Sarah and George Morgan, the house was rented for several years to a young widow, Margaret Vanderbilt, whose husband, Alfred Gwynne Vanderbilt, had died on the *Titanic*. In 1925 W. Roscoe and Mary Minturn Bonsal, tenants for seven years, purchased the house. They sold Ventfort Hall in 1945 to the first of a succession of owners. Over the years it served as a dormitory for Tanglewood students, a summer hotel, the Fokine Ballet Summer Camp, and housing for a religious community. By the mid-1980s Ventfort Hall was empty and desolate and slated for demolition. Fearful of the loss of such an important symbol of the Berkshire Cottage period, a group of citizens formed the nonprofit Ventfort Hall Association and raised $500,000 to purchase the property, which by then had been stripped of much of its decorative architecture. Restoration has begun, and the mansion is open for tours and special events, including lectures, theatrical and musical events, and special exhibits relating to the period. Even as work continues, the mansion is open for tours daily Memorial Day through October 31 and on weekends November 1 to the end of May, with tours given on the hour.

KIDSTUFF 

Four-season recreational opportunities, kid-friendly cultural institutions, and family-oriented businesses offer a break from routine to youngsters who live here and a treat for those just passing through. But be prepared to do a lot of driving—things are kind of spread out.

Families that hike, bike, or ski together have all kinds of public trails and paths to explore. The Ashuwillticook Trail from the Berkshire Mall in Lanesborough to the town of Adams provides a safe paved car-less path for biking, in-line skating, or cross-country skiing. State and local parks are laced with trails, and some have nature centers with fascinating exhibits. (See the Parks and Recreation chapter for more information and for places to rent equipment.) If you want to see kids' faces light up, watch their reaction when they feel that tug on the line at one of many fishing derbies sponsored in spring. Picnicking at one of the public beaches is great fun; some of those are listed below.

Most of the area's cultural venues offer activities for kids—some for fees, others for free. Shakespeare & Company runs day camps in summer, as does the Berkshire Theatre Festival, Barrington Stage Company, and Norman Rockwell Museum. Community centers and organizations like the "Y" run all kinds of programs, some only for members, others for drop-ins. Most libraries—even in the little towns—run story times and reading programs open to all at no cost. Agricultural fairs can be entertaining and educational, too, and several local farms have petting zoos and child-centered activities. For little or no money, kids can play simple games and get their faces painted at any number of fairs sponsored by churches, schools, and other groups as fund-raisers throughout the year. Bowling for little ones is no longer the frustrating thing it once was, thanks to someone's clever idea of filling in those darned gutters with bumpers that keep the ball rolling down the alley. Bowling alleys, miniature golf courses, and other family-activity centers are listed below.

Local media are the best source for finding out what's going on locally. They all have a kids section in their weekly calendars.

During the school year kids are involved with organized activities sponsored by their schools or towns, and their parents are busy driving them to all those things. Recreation committees, often with the help of local businesses, sponsor soccer, softball, football, and baseball leagues for youngsters in various age groups. Older kids might participate in golf, basketball, tennis, track, cross-country skiing, swim meets, or hockey games, depending on what is available in their community. Participants in school-based arts programs will be putting on concerts, musicals, and plays, often giving special performances for senior citizens in their districts.

Even though there is plenty going on here, you might want to check out the Day Trips chapter for more things to do. Six Flags Amusement Park in Agawam, Look Park in Northampton, and Lebanon Valley Speedway just over the border in New York State come to mind. More detailed information about parks and recreation and cultural venues will be found in their respective chapters. The list below suggests activities for kids of all ages.

Unless stated otherwise, the activities listed below cost from $5.00 to $10.00. Adult admissions to museums run around $10, plus or minus a few dollars. Students and seniors get discounts.

OUT AND ABOUT

Baker Farm Golf Center
658 South Main Street (U.S. Highway 7), Lanesborough
(413) 443-6102

Baker Farm's 18-hole miniature golf course is fun to play and a treat to see. The holes are interesting but not too hard for most youngsters. And there is lots of water to get into. At the height of the season, the course is abloom with hundreds of flowers. Open daily spring through fall.

Bartholomew's Cobble
106 Weatogue Road, Ashley Falls
(413) 229-8600

The Cobble runs programs for kids through most of the year. The best bet is to check the media and call for registration. Most activities, all related to nature, are free for kids. Adults pay a nominal fee, unless they are members of the Trustees of Reservations, which manage the property.

Berkshire Scenic Railway
Willow Creek Road, Lenox
(413) 637-2210
www.berkshirescenicrailroad.org

The Berkshire Scenic Railway recently inaugurated weekend trips between Lenox and Stockbridge in summer. A diesel locomotive and vintage standard-gauge coaches from the 1920s make the 90-minute round trip excursion from the old Lenox Station to Stockbridge. Rolling stock and another diesel engine are permanently parked at the 1903 station, which was recently restored and is now listed on the National Register of Historic Places. One coach houses a permanent exhibit that introduces visitors to the Gilded Age that brought rich tourists from New York to the area by train at the turn of the 20th century. An electronic map indicates the location of 24 "cottages" of that era. Inside the station are model railroads, railroad memorabilia, and a gift shop with railroad-related items particularly appealing to children. The car and station are open weekends and holidays from Memorial Day to Columbus Day at no charge. Lenox Station is at the east end of Housatonic Street, 1.5 miles east of US 7/20 in Lenox. The train ride costs around $12.00 for adults, $8.00 for kids. Call for times.

Bousquet Ski Area
101 Dan Fox Drive, Pittsfield
(413) 442-8316

A kid-friendly ski area, Bousquet's offers lessons and holds special races and activities throughout the winter. Snowboarding and tubing also are permitted. In summer Bousquet's becomes a center for outdoor fun for the whole family. Kids are sure to enjoy zipping down the giant water slide into the large but shallow pool, or they may choose just to float around in the water on a tube. Use of the 18-hole miniature golf course is included in the pool charge. Future Tony Stewarts can test their skills in a Grand Prix–style racing car on a road course patterned after the European Formula One circuit. For even more thrills, there's the Deval Kart, a gravity-powered racer that anyone over the age of 12 can take up the mountain on the chairlift and then ride back down on the grass. Other activities include volleyball, horseshoes, and a climbing wall. Prices vary depending on the number of activities in which you and your kids take part. Bousquet's also books Paintball parties and takes reservations for company picnics or other special events at group rates for 20 or more persons.

Buster's Entertainment Center
457 Dalton Avenue, Pittsfield
(413) 499-7500
www.bustersforfun.com

This former supermarket is a great place to take kids, especially if they are of different ages. From teens to toddlers, there is something for all to do here, even grown-ups. Clean as a whistle, smoke-free, spacious, and kid-friendly, Buster's is ideal for a rainy day or as a reward for putting up with a visit to a less interesting place. For the older set there are pool tables, video and arcade games, and physically challenging games of skill, including air hockey, hoop shoot, and football pass, and on Friday nights live music. For under $5.00, youngsters from the ages of 2 to 12 can take off their shoes and burn up energy in the Adventure Crawl—a series of in, out, up, down, and bouncy constructions. For even less, little ones age 6 and under can run around in the Blue Skies and Rainbows play area, where there are all kinds of interesting things to get involved with. There's a "two-for" price for families using both play areas, and parents of young children are expected to hang around. Tokens are sold to be used in all coin-operated amusements. Some games, like old-fashioned Skeeball, reward the player with tickets that can be accumulated and turned in for prizes.

A large fenced-off section with brightly colored tables and chairs can be rented for birthday parties for up to 10 kids. Prices vary depending on how many tokens are included in the package and what activity areas the kids will be using. Basic eats like pizza, bagels, hot dogs, fries, soda, and ice cream with toppings are available at the food counter and can be eaten inside at picnic tables for big people or low tables for little ones. There also is a take-out window and picnic tables outside. Buster's is open daily year-round.

Cove Lanes
109 Stockbridge Road (US 7), Great Barrington
(413) 528–1220

Cove Lanes caters to kids with all sorts of bowling arrangements and a double-decker indoor miniature golf course. With 24 lanes, there is usually a lane open for drop-ins. For little ones, there's bumper bowling, and for really young ones the ball can be placed on a ramp for extra mileage. Friday and Saturday nights "cosmic bowling" takes over, with strobe and black lights and disco music. There's also an arcade with a dozen or so games. The 18-hole miniature golf course is laid out in a room adjacent to the alleys. The course seems to be perpetually in summer, with brightly painted outdoor scenes on the walls and imitation flowers, trees, and a three-tiered fountain placed around the course. To get 18 holes in the place, owner Tom Hankey built a second-story deck around the perimeter. Entry and exit are gained by a winding wooden stairway. The course is interesting, with hills and sand traps. Obstacles include a race car, a castle, and a couple of dragons. Birthday parties, including cosmic bowling, can be arranged. There is a snack bar and separate enclosed lounge. Cove is open year-round. In summer, Tuesday night is designated for senior and junior leagues. The rest of the year, leagues meet on Saturday morning.

Imperial Bowl
555 Dalton Avenue, Pittsfield
(413) 443–4453

Imperial has 14 candlepin lanes that can be turned into bumper bowling for kids at a moment's notice. Owners Bob and Rosemary Ireland have been in the business since 1978 and moved to this former roller skating rink on Dalton Avenue in 1987. Rosie runs the kitchen, where wings, grilled sandwiches, fries, and specials are available at mealtimes. Birthday parties can be arranged, and group rates are available. Saturday is Family Night. A pool table provides an alternate activity. There is a lounge with a bar and a few tables separate from the bowling area, where more tables and chairs are set up. Imperial is open daily in winter. Summer hours vary, so a call ahead is a good idea.

Jiminy Peak Resort
37 Corey Road, Hancock
(413) 738–5500
www.jiminypeak.com

Winter or summer, there are plenty of things for youngsters to do at Jiminy Peak. In winter lessons are offered to a variety of ages through several programs for skiers and snowboarders. There is also a supervised playroom, available by reservation, for non-skiing kids. Jiminy also offers tubing and snowshoeing at Brodie Mountain, a short distance away on US 7 in New Ashford. In summer youngsters can try their hand at trout fishing or zoom down the mountain on a summer bobsled on the alpine slide. There is also the Euro-bungee trampoline, for big air and fancy flips, or the bouncy-bounce inflatable trampoline. Other activities include miniature golf, a rock-climbing wall, mountain bike trails, and a laser trap shoot. Prices vary depending on the number of activities you participate in. Package deals are available. Summer recreation hours (weather permitting) are 11:00 A.M. to 9:00 P.M. daily mid-June through Labor Day; weekends only mid-May to mid-June; and 11:00 A.M. to 6:00 P.M. after Labor Day weekend to the end of October. From the end of June to Columbus Day, the chairlift to the summit operates on weekends for scenic rides.

Ken's Bowl
495 Dalton Avenue, Pittsfield
(413) 499-0733

With 50 tenpin lanes, there is always an open one for bumper or regular bowling at Ken's. There's also a snack bar that serves hot dogs, pizza, burgers, and nachos. Arrangements can be made for birthday parties and group rates. During summer Ken's Bowl is open Friday through Sunday, daily in winter. Leagues meet in the fall through winter, but there is usually an open lane at night and always one during the day. For adults there is a cocktail lounge.

Mt. Greylock Bowl
Roberts Drive, North Adams
(413) 664-9715

Located off MA 2 on the west side of the city, Mt. Greylock Bowl has bumper bowling for little ones and "Rock 'n' Bowl" with disco lights and music for teens. Around since the 1960s, Mt. Greylock Bowl was purchased in 1999 by Gary Superneaux. Renovations include a new sound system and automatic scoring. Food available from a larger-than-you-would-expect menu can be eaten at the sizable counter, and there is a lounge for adults. Other amenities include a pro shop, pool table, and some arcade games. Labor Day through May, leagues meet Monday through Saturday mornings but the rest of the weekend is open. During summer, lanes are available on Wednesday and Thursday and Saturday afternoons.

HANDS ON!

Berkshire Museum
39 South Street, Pittsfield
(413) 443-7171
www.berkshiremuseum.org

If the kids groan when you say you're taking them to the Berkshire Museum, their displeasure will be short-lived. The museum reaches out to children in ever-enticing ways, beginning with the front lawn where Wally, the life-size stegosaurus, grazes. The Berkshire Backyard features flora and fauna found locally and shows how to identify animals by their tracks and birds by their calls. The Mineral Gallery includes a Geiger counter, used to detect radioactivity that occurs naturally in some minerals, and a black light that reveals the fluorescence in plain-Jane samples with the push of a button. In the Dinosaurs and Paleontology Gallery, real fossils and a "Dino Dig" let the visitor become a paleontologist. Also on the main floor—right next to the Vend-O-Mat snack dispenser—is the Refrigerator Art Gallery, where young people display their work. The Museum Store has lots of miniature dinosaurs and reptiles plus books, educational toys, games, and gizwhizzes popular with the younger set. From the dinosaur dig to the geologists' workstation, youngsters are encouraged to actively investigate nature.

In the lower level of the museum are the aquariums, ranging from 30 to 535 gallons, and assorted terrariums. Venomous lionfish, moray eels, and piranha are among the more exciting specimens displayed along with living corals, local fishes, insects, spiders, turtles, and snakes. There are two open-water tanks, one representing the sandy shore with live hermit and horseshoe crabs, scallops, and snails. A larger New England tank gives you the opportunity to examine and handle live sea stars and sea urchins without anyone yelling "don't touch that!"

On the art side, the museum recently added nine toys designed by artist Alexander Calder to its permanent displays and, of course, has created a hands-on way for kids to relate to them. They are allowed to play with reproductions of these animated toys while being encouraged to understand the mechanisms that allow the seal to balance the ball on his nose or the frog to "hop" across the floor. Two Calder mobiles also are on display. The museum sponsors programs for children year-round. From puppet shows to plays, movies to musicals, interactive exhibits to special workshops, the Berkshire Museum is far from dull.

The admission charge varies depending on age (there's none if you go on your birthday) but is free to children under age 3 and to members. Adults who are not members pay $7.50. Open year-round, the museum is located in the center of Pittsfield and is wheelchair-accessible, with appropriate parking spaces at the side of the building. Other parking is available on the street, if you're lucky, or in nearby parking garages. If everybody behaved, you all can walk down the street a couple of blocks to Ben & Jerry's and celebrate!

Berkshire Botanical Garden
Intersection of Massachusetts Highways 102 and 183, Stockbridge
(413) 298–3926
www.berkshirebotanical.org

The Berkshire Botanical Garden welcomes children with a variety of activities, beginning in April with a family celebration of Earth Day. In summer the Children's Garden opens for business, with nature explorations and garden projects to take home. Kids may dig in Peter Rabbit's Garden to see who lives there, check out the different vegetables, and see if they can find Peter's blue jacket in the corn maze. Toddlers are welcome for "Story Time in the Garden," with activities, walks, and a take-home project. At the annual Harvest Festival in October, the children's Craft Tent offers pots to paint and natural materials for designing an arrangement to go in it. Kids can get their faces painted, make a Halloween mask, or create a scarecrow doll. Call or check the Web site for dates and other events. The garden is open May through October and folks are welcome to picnic on the grounds. Children under age 12 are admitted free. Donations for the School Scholarship Fund are accepted and are used to support field trips to the garden during the school year.

Berkshire Center for Contemporary Glass
6 Harris Street, West Stockbridge
(413) 232–4666

The glassblowers at this working studio and gallery welcome rubberneckers at no charge. If you are older than age 10 and visiting on a weekend, you might even get a chance to create a glass piece of your own. The center is closed January through March and open daily June through December. Call for hours in those in-between months.

Claymania
214 Pleasant Street, Housatonic
(413) 274–9915

Youngsters are welcome to drop by this working studio, select and decorate their own pieces of pottery, leave them for glazing and firing, and pick them up later. For as little as $5.00, they can paint their own designs on piggy banks, mugs, or other simple shapes. During summer Claymania runs weeklong day programs for children ages 7 to 12, where they can create their own pieces from wet clay, learn how to make mosaic decorations, or create their own stained-glass works. Fees run around $110 a week, but some materials might be extra. Aside from the day camps, Claymania is open afternoons Wednesday through Sunday.

Sterling and Francine Clark Art Institute
225 South Street, Williamstown
(413) 458-2303
www.clarkart.edu
Band concerts, plays on the green, and family fun days are sponsored by the Clark Art Institute throughout the summer. As might be expected, participants are given the chance to work on some kind of art project, usually related to the theme of the current show at the museum. Events are often free.

Hancock Shaker Village
U.S. Highway 20, Pittsfield
(413) 443-0188, (800) 817-1137
www.hancockshakervillage.org
Even though the Shakers were celibate, their community included children who came with their families or were "adopted" by those living there. Children visiting Hancock today can learn what life was like back then by spending time in the Discovery Room, open daily Memorial Day weekend through late October. Kids can don reproduction Shaker clothing to see how they would have looked as young Shakers and try their hand at carding, spinning and weaving wool; making a basket; or weaving a chair seat—tasks children often performed. In the schoolhouse a "Shaker" teacher gives lessons in writing with a quill pen and spelling with historic letter boards and imparts instruction on how to be a good Shaker. Kids can help roll out dough or cut up vegetables in the kitchen, help make butter and cheese in the dairy, and learn about fine Shaker craftsmanship in the workshops. Working farm that it is, Hancock offers a chance for kids to feel the soft wool of the Merino sheep or learn how to hold a chicken and gather eggs. In winter they can take sleigh rides and see how ice was cut. In spring the village welcomes children to come and see the new crop of farm animals. Children are admitted free.

IS183
13 Willard Hill Road, Stockbridge
(413) 298-5252
www.IS183.org
Formerly the Interlaken School of Art, IS183 runs classes for children in various forms of art, from pottery to painting. Fees are substantial but may be reduced for those in need of financial assistance. The school also runs weeklong arts-based day camps at $25 a day per child.

MASS MoCA
87 Marshall Street, North Adams
(413) 662-2111
www.massmoca.org
Hours and activities for the public at MASS MoCA's Kidspace vary throughout the season but are listed on the Web site. When Kidspace is open, staff members guide families through the small gallery, where hands-on projects relating to the current exhibit are offered. Children under age 3 or accompanied by a member are admitted free. Kids ages 6 to 16 pay $3.00.

Norman Rockwell Museum
9 Glendale Road, Stockbridge
(413) 298-4100
www.nrm.org
Aside from special events, the Norman Rockwell Museum runs educational programs throughout the year for children and families. Most are for seven-year-olds and up. Some run for a week; others can be experienced for a day. Often geared to the museum's main exhibit at the time, activities can include painting or drawing, in-gallery discussions, storytelling, creative writing, games, and projects like toy-making or kite-designing. All are designed to introduce children to the world of art while encouraging observation and stimulating the imagination. Monthly events are listed on the Web site. Persons under age 18 are admitted free.

CENTER STAGE

Barrington Stage Company
Consolati Performing Arts Center
Mount Everett Regional High School
Berkshire School Road (Massachusetts Highway 41), Sheffield
(413) 528-8888
www.barringtonstageco.org

CLOSE-UP

Clowning Around

If your child is infatuated with the circus, this is a great summer program to consider—but you have to plan ahead. Applications for the Berkshire Community College Circus Camp are due in February. The three-week program is held at BCC's Pittsfield campus from the last week of July into August and is open to boys and girls ages 8 to 16. There is a sizable fee, but some financial aid is available on a first-come basis. Deferred payment also may be arranged. Since 1993 the camp has been giving kids a chance to learn tumbling, artistic cycling, juggling, clowning, stilt and wire walking, trapeze skills, partner acrobatics, and other skills. Older campers learn more complex acrobatics, balancing, and clowning. The history of the circus and its place in the arts, makeup, costumes, prop construction, publicity, concessions, and management are also taught. Regular day camp activities include field sports, cooperative games, and trust- and team-building activities. The whole thing climaxes with performances for the public on the last two days. For information call Berkshire Community College at (413) 499-0856. If you didn't get into the program, try to go to the grand finale! For tickets call (413) 499-4660.

Simon's Rock College of Bard in Great Barrington also runs week-long circus camps at various times. Call (413) 528-7772 for information.

Barrington Stage Company staff run a summer program called KidsAct! for youngsters ages 8 to 10, 11 to 13, and 14 to 17. Classes in a variety of theater arts are offered, and each session ends with a student-created production. All classes are taught at Mount Everett High School in Sheffield. There is a tuition charge.

Berkshire Music School
30 Wendell Avenue, Pittsfield
(413) 442-1411

The Berkshire Music School runs an assortment of programs for kids throughout the summer. All have a tuition fee running from $25 to $150, depending on the child's age and length of the program. There also might be an extra charge for materials. All programs involve music in one way or another. Art Sparks is a three-week day camp for children ages 8 through 13 that includes dance, creative writing, theater, singing, and crafts. A program for two- and three-year-olds uses music, storytelling, instruments, and movement to learn about backyard wildlife.

Berkshire Theatre Festival
6 East Main Street (MA 102), Stockbridge
(413) 298-5536
www.berkshiretheatre.org

In summer the BTF offers an acting program for kids ages 9 to 13 in half-day sessions for a negotiable fee.

Shakespeare & Company
70 Kemble Street, Lenox
(413) 637-1199
www.shakespeare.org

Shakespeare & Young Co. and Riotous Youth are day programs run by Shakespeare & Company for fees. Riotous Youth is for kids ages 7 to 15. Shakespeare and Young Co. offers training and performance experience for 16- to 20-year-olds. Check the Web site for more information or call extension 123. In addition, there are many free performances for kids at various times throughout the year.

Williamstown Theatre Festival
1000 Main Street (MA 2), Williamstown
(413) 597-3399, (413) 597-3400 (box office)
www.WTFestival.org
In a twist on "kids are free," the Williamstown Theatre Festival offers a free ticket to any parent whose child (up to age 18) purchases a ticket for a show at the Main Stage on the first Friday of the production. The WTF also sponsors free plays and fables at family events in nearby Buxton Field. Productions take place at twilight, and patrons are encouraged to bring picnics, creating an informal, convivial atmosphere. Call for information, or watch the media.

DOWN ON THE FARM

Green River Farms
2480 Green River Road (MA 43), Williamstown
(413) 458-2470
www.greenriverfarm.org
Kids can visit with farm animals, take part in various activities, or ride the pony and get their picture taken, too, at Green River Farms just off US 7 at Five Corners.

Ioka Valley Farm
Massachusetts Highway 43, Hancock
(413) 738-5915
www.taconic.net/IokaValleyFarm
Pumpkin picking, maple syrup boiling (followed by pancake eating), and Christmas tree gathering are some of the seasonal activities that go on at Ioka Valley Farm. There's also Uncle Don's Barnyard for visits with farm animals and a play area where kids can make believe they are milking Molly the cow.

Whitney Farms
Massachusetts Highway 8, Cheshire
(413) 442-4749
The Whitney family has set aside an area next to their greenhouses and market that caters to kids spring through fall. A dairy bar sells ice cream, hot dogs, and the like that can be eaten at picnic tables under a tent. Sandwiches, salads, baked goods, and beverages also are sold at the market. Animals for petting or feeding are housed in roomy roofed pens. Special events often are held with pony rides and other activities, and participants often leave with a plant of their very own. Kids can pick out their own pumpkins when the patch is ready in fall. The Ashuwillticook Bike Trail is on the other side of MA 8, and the Whitneys have installed a rack for folks to park their bikes while they have lunch or visit the animals.

WHERE TO GET STUFF

Fantasy Realms
222 Elm Street, Pittsfield
(413) 445-8809
The largest selection of new and collectible comics in the county can be found at Fantasy Realms. Owner James Arlemagne also specializes in games, gaming supplies, and cards. He is the sole source for Games Workshop miniatures. With five tables dedicated to gaming, the place is usually hopping with youngsters (and some not so young) playing out fantasy roles. The shop is open every day but Sunday and Tuesday.

The Gifted Child
72 Church Street, Lenox
(413) 637-1191
28 Railroad Street, Great Barrington
(413) 528-1395
www.thegiftedchild.net
Both branches of this shop are crammed to the hilt with stuff for kids from newborns to pre-teens. Toys include playthings by Brio, Playmobil, Wild Planet, Ravensburger, and others; books, puzzles, art sup-

plies, and games; old standbys like Etch-a-Sketch and Silly Putty; and the latest novelties. There are stickers and rubber stamps, sunglasses and journals, backpacks and umbrellas, lunch boxes and science kits. Grown-ups looking for silly gifts also might find something here. Contemporary clothing by Flapdoodles, LeTop, Sweet Potatoes, Zutano, and others are also sold here. The Gifted Child also rents cribs and high chairs by the week. The Lenox shop has a sale barn in back where half-price bargains can be found. Both shops are open year-round, but the sale barn is open only May through October.

K-B Toy Works
Allendale Shopping Center
MA 8, Pittsfield
(413) 499-6647
www.KBtoys.com

This K-B outlet in the Allendale Shopping Center carries games for Nintendo, PlayStation, XBox, and GameBoy, along with the necessary consoles, controllers, and other equipment. Seasonal toys include bicycles and helmets for the younger set, kiddie pools, rafts, beach toys, skateboards, sleds, snow tubes, and other sporting goods. Playhouses and other large play equipment are displayed in this spacious store. Popular toy lines include Sesame Street, Fisher Price, Lego, and Barbie and her accoutrements. Also here are collectible action figures, remote-control vehicles, and road-racing tracks and vehicles. The store sells family videos and DVDs and computer games and is open daily. K-B, once Kay-Bee, stands for Kaufman Brothers, two local men who founded the company. The international headquarters are located in downtown Pittsfield. There is another K-B store in the Berkshire Mall, also on MA 8, which carries similar items except for the large outdoor toys.

Matrushka Toys & Gifts
252 Main Street, Great Barrington
(413) 528-6911

Located on the second floor of an attractive yellow frame house on Main Street, Matrushka is filled with things chosen with care by owner Ruth Blair. She believes that most mass-produced toys and books fail to teach children about quality or stimulate their imagination, and she searches abroad and at U.S. toy shows to find items that reflect her philosophy. Her select stock is mostly European and is devoid of plastic. Dolls and other soft goods are made of natural fibers. Playhouses and other play furniture are made of natural wood. She also chooses the children's books she sells with care and insists that they have both excellent illustrations and good stories. She also sells inspirational, educational, and parental guidance books and unusual greeting cards, plus interesting items that make nice gifts for grown-ups as well as kids. The shop name comes from the traditional Russian wooden nesting dolls, which to Blair symbolize the importance of family and the link between generations. The shop began as a nonprofit venture to raise funds for the Waldorf School, and Blair continues to pass on the proceeds after deducting her expenses. She is closed on Sunday and Tuesday except in December, when she is open daily.

Tom's Toys
307 Main Street, Great Barrington
(413) 528-3330
www.tomstoys.com

Owner Tom Levin clearly enjoys kids, toys, and having fun. His store is packed with all the popular playthings, plus exotic brands not found elsewhere. Even though there is merchandise everywhere, there is space to move around. Items are nicely displayed, so you can see what's what. Collectors will find miniatures by Britain, Corgi, and others, Madame Alexander dolls, Breyer horses, Groovy Girls, Bendo figures, diecast vehicles by Schylling, Thomas the Tank Engine, Brio, and tons of soft stuffed friends. Aside from the great stock, the store includes a real tree filled with birds that chirp Audubon-approved calls, a playhouse to climb up into, a glow-in-the-dark section that really does, and an area filled with costumes to try on. In the basement, kids, even pretty big ones, can play with remote-controlled construction equipment made by Rokenbok. Marked-down toys live there, too. Tom, who drives around town in a Volkswagen Beetle with a big key on top, has a great Web site that even includes a game to play. The shop is open daily year-round.

Where'd You Get That!?
20A Spring Street, Williamstown
(413) 458-2206
www.wygt.com
For more than 10 years Ken and Michele Gietz have been the source in North County for interesting and different toys and gifts for all ages. The store is crammed with clever games, brainteasers, puzzles, educational and developmental toys, gag gifts, gizmos, and novelties, plus customized party favors, cards, and balloons. Popular with the college crowd, the Gietzes also cater to older folks with their Over the Hill birthday section. Full of enthusiasm, both will help you find the perfect present no matter the age of the recipient. They also host community game nights and operate a miniscience shop at the Children's Discovery Room in the North Adams Museum of History and Sciences at Heritage State Park. Open daily year-round; they also prepare packages for campers.

ORGANIZED FUN

South County

Berkshire South Regional Community Center
15 Crissey Road, Great Barrington
(413) 528-2810
www.berkshiresouth.org
New in 2002, this state-of-the-art community center is open daily and offers a multitude of opportunities for exercise and organized activities to members and drop-ins. The facility includes a six-lane, 252-yard swimming pool, a smaller warm-water pool, and a children's splash playground with water features; a gymnasium with adjustable basketball hoops, volleyball setups and indoor hockey and soccer setups; and a fitness center for kids age 14 and older. Birthday and pool parties can be arranged for children of all ages. Special activities, offered for fees that are less or nonexistent for members, include dances, craft workshops, water safety classes, gymnastics, nature study, and traditional summer camp activities. Pool and table tennis tables are available, and there is a 3-mile hiking trail on the hill behind the center. For those just passing through, the daily rate to enjoy the facility is $5.00 for children, $10.00 for adults. Kids age 12 and older can be left for day programs while parents run off to the galleries or other adult pursuits.

Lenox Community Center
65 Walker Street, Lenox
(413) 637-5530
Under the auspices of the Lenox Parks and Recreation Department, the community center provides a wide range of activities for kids of all ages. Summer activities are offered mid-June to late August and include a playground program for kids age six and older. Arts and crafts, storytelling, games, field trips, and group activities are included for a fee of $45 per child, $75 for nonresidents. Five-year-olds may enroll in a similar program for $30, $35 for nonresidents. Sports camps also are available for a wide range of fees. Call for requirements. Activities also take place during the school year.

Southern Berkshire Family Net Family Center
940 South Main Street, Great Barrington
(413) 528-0721
This organization runs play groups and activities for children birth to age six who are accompanied by their parents. Programs are offered at the center in Great Barrington and at other locations in South County, including Lenox, Otis, West Stockbridge, Sandisfield, and Sheffield. Call for information, or check the media.

Southern Berkshire YMCA
357 Main Street, Great Barrington
(413) 528-9622
The Southern Berkshire YMCA runs a variety of programs at several locations, among them a drop-off for parents who would like time for appointments or other obligations without their children in tow. The Y also runs a vacation camp in Housatonic. Call for information, or check the media.

Central Berkshire

Becket-Chimney Corners YMCA
748 Hamilton Road, Becket
(413) 623-8991
Arts, crafts, and other traditional day camp activities are offered here. Registration is required, and applications should be in by early May because the program fills quickly. Fees are $78 a week for the half-day preschool program to $137 a week for children ages 6 to 12.

The Boy's and Girl's Club of Pittsfield
16 Melville Street, Pittsfield
(413) 448-8258
www.boysandgirlsclubofpittsfield.org
The Boy's and Girl's Club of Pittsfield runs a variety of programs for urban youth from preschool through teens, with special concern for the disadvantaged. The club has a gymnasium, a swimming pool and, in winter, an ice-skating rink used for hockey, figure, and recreational skating. A game room and a teen center are used for after-school, vacation, and summer programs. The facility is also used by other organizations and clubs. The club aims to provide good role models and support for kids, especially those growing up in difficult situations. Counseling and other social services are available. Fees vary.

Dalton Community House
400 Main Street, Dalton
(413) 584-0260
A wide range of programs for children of all ages are run by the Dalton Recreation Association at the Dalton Community House and Youth Center and at town parks. Day camps for preschoolers and children from kindergarten through Grade 6 offer arts, crafts, swimming, and educational games. Sports camps help children improve their skills in basketball, baseball, and track and field. Fees vary. Membership is required for participation. Additional fees might apply.

Girls Incorporated of the Berkshires
165 East Street, Pittsfield
(413) 442-5174
Girls Inc. provides a wide range of year-round programs and services, mostly for girls but not entirely. Programs are designed to improve self-esteem and empowerment. The recently renovated facility includes a swimming pool that is busy with activities for all ages. Indoor and outdoor sports and exercise programs are offered. The organization runs day camps for girls and boys and a counselor training program at Camps Stevenson and Witawentin, located on 88 acres on Lake Onota on Pittsfield's west side. Traditional camp activities are augmented with boating and nature study. Overnights and special events take place in each session, and "camperships" are available. Girls Inc. also runs day and after-school child-care programs and provides support for women who need temporary child care due to emergencies.

Pittsfield YMCA
292 North Street, Pittsfield
(413) 499-7650
The Pittsfield Y runs day camps at Ponterril Outdoor Center, its facility off Pontoosuc Lake. Family memberships to Ponterril also are available for around $200 for the summer season, which includes use of the swimming pool and other facilities. Monthly rates also are available.

North County

Northern Berkshire YMCA
Brickyard Court, North Adams
(413) 663-6529
The Northern Berkshire Y runs a variety of summer day camps, many geared toward sports. Fees vary, and registration is required. The Y also runs after-school programs, including swimming, which is handy for kids who go to the elementary school next door.

Williamstown Youth Center
270 Cole Avenue, Williamstown
(413) 458-5925
www.williamstownyouthcenter.org
The nonprofit Williamstown Youth Center runs recreational programs and activities throughout the year for youths in Grades 1 though 12. Small and large groups are supervised by professional staff. In summer, trips, outings, cookouts, and other activities are included during one-week sessions at $65 a week. Call for information if the Web site isn't current.

DAY AND SUMMER CAMPS

Berkshire Country Day School
Brook Farm Campus
MA 183, Lenox
(413) 637-0755
www.berkshirecountryday.org
Berkshire Country Day School's summer camp is a traditional day camp in nine one-week sessions for children ages 3 through 10. All camp activities are held on the school's 27-acre campus. Activities are geared to the appropriate age group, but all include hikes or nature walks around the campus and swimming in the pond on the property. Fun is mixed with developing skills and creative expression while learning the value of cooperation. Arts and crafts, theater, music, dance, sports, and field activities are included in the program. Rates vary depending on age and whether the camper is taking part in a full- or half-day program.

Camp Fox Hill
Berkshire West Athletic Club
11 Dan Fox Drive, Pittsfield
(413) 499-4600
Arts and crafts, tennis and/or swimming lessons, theme days and field trips to nearby Bousquet are included in the week's activities at this all-day camp for around $120 a week.

Camp Half Moon
Massachusetts Highway 57, Monterey
(413) 528-0940
This large camp on Lake Buel offers traditional arts and sports electives in one-week day sessions for children ages 3 to 15 for around $300 a week.

Camp Mohawk
Old Cheshire Road, Lanesborough
(413) 499-3902
The third generation is running this day camp, which has been operating for 55 years. Located on Cheshire Lake, the camp offers water-skiing and other water sports, along with traditional camp activities. Rates are around $250 for one week, $450 for two weeks, and $350 for three weeks.

CYC Summer Camps
26 Melville Street, Pittsfield
(413) 445-5469
Nature camp, Bible camp, and camps centered around sports are offered to a wide range of ages by the Catholic Youth Center. Call for fees and to register.

Flying Cloud Institute
731 Sandisfield Road, New Marlborough
(413) 229-3321
The focus here is on science and the visual and performing arts. Fees run around $200 a week.

Gymfest of the Berkshires
10 Lyman Street, Pittsfield
(413) 445-5689
Offered in conjunction with Berkshire West, this summer camp offers experience in gymnastics in half- or full-day sessions.

Moon in the Pond
816 Barnum Street, Sheffield
(413) 229-3092
The fee is around $125 a week for this arts and farm-fun day camp.

Pine Cobble School
163 Gale Road, Williamstown
(413) 458-4680
www.Pinecobble.org
Pine Cobble offers coeducational day programs in three two-week sessions for children ages 3 to 15. Campers are encouraged to design their own program from the activities offered, which include enrichment in French, Spanish, math, and English. Other activities include arts and crafts, swimming, computer lab, sports, claymation, and, for the younger set, theater arts, story time, games, cooking, and outdoor play. Rates vary depending on age and whether the camper is participating for a full or half day.

TAKE A DIP

South County

The Williams River is accessible to the public where Massachusetts Highway 23/41 crosses it a few miles west of Great Barrington. You'll know you've found it when you see the cars lined up along the highway. There is a small park in Housatonic on the river of the same name where you can take a dip and have a picnic. There's also Lake Mansfield in Great Barrington and Laurel Lake, accessible in both Lenox and Lee. Swimming is allowed at Beartown State Park in Monterey, York Lake in Sandisfield, and Tolland State Forest in Otis.

Central Berkshire

Pittsfield's two lakes, Onota and Pontoosuc, have public beaches, picnic tables, and grills. Burbank Park at Onota has restrooms, a pavilion where refreshments are sold, and a large playground. Pittsfield State Forest has swimming areas and picnic tables and grills. Although it isn't sanctioned, it is hard to visit Wahconah Falls in Dalton and not get in the water, especially on a really hot day. East of Dalton in Windsor off Massachusetts Highway 9 to the north is Windsor Jambs State Park, also reachable from the north via MA 8A. Farther along MA 9, in Cummington, the Westfield River is a popular place for swimming, including one spot often frequented by those who prefer not to wear bathing suits.

North County

Windsor Pond in North Adams offers respite in the city with a pleasant park and wide beach. Swimming also is allowed in Savoy State Forest, off MA 2 east of North Adams, and Clarksburg State Park, on Middle Road off MA 8 north of the city.

ANNUAL EVENTS 

It's sort of a secret, but in many ways the kind of life that Norman Rockwell preserved in paint still thrives in the Berkshires. Stripped of the glamor and hubbub of summer's cultural glut, life revolves around celebrations of history, family, community, and the ever-changing gifts of the seasons. Depending on the town they live in—and what goes on there—locals mark their calendars for such events as the fire department's annual cookout, the Memorial Day parade, the Founder's Day celebration, the town picnic, or other community activities. On a larger scale, the city of Pittsfield's Fourth of July parade draws folks from all over, as does the Fall Foliage Festival in North Adams.

As the school year progresses, families will be busy attending sporting events or performances that their children participate in. And around the holidays the Berkshire Museum will be filled with decorated Christmas trees, and the newspapers will list concerts, bazaars, and open houses at some of the historical homes. If Mother Nature cooperates, winter will bring carnivals, snowmobile races, skiing, and, for the intrepid, ice fishing. Other than that, not much happens in winter. Folks know that road conditions can make travel difficult and that planning an event is flirting with disaster. Still, the cultural venues that are open all year cross their fingers and schedule concerts and other events, hoping for the best.

Come spring, things begin to pick up. In May locals will be involved with their annual town meeting, where the budget for the coming year will be set, and elections for local officials. Mother's Day events will include benefit plant sales around the county plus the annual Women's Running Race, a 5-mile event from Berkshire Community College on West Street in Pittsfield to Park Square and back. Moms of all ages participate, some pushing their offspring in strollers. Memorial Day will be marked with parades and services at cemeteries and monuments in Pittsfield, North Adams, and most towns. And farmers' markets around the county open for the season (see the Agriculture chapter). In June locals will be busy with high school graduations while Williamstown and North Adams brace for families coming for graduations, at Williams College and the Massachusetts College of Liberal Arts. In South County, folks will be gathering for graduation at Simon's Rock College of Bard; in Pittsfield, associates degrees will be awarded at Berkshire Community College.

From the Fourth of July through Columbus Day, the museums, historic homes, galleries, and performing and visual arts run full tilt. Mindful of the population increase, chambers of commerce, churches, and other groups schedule street fairs, sidewalk sales, bazaars, and various fund-raisers to get in on the largesse. With the exception of holiday celebrations in December, there will be a lull between the time the last bus of leaf-peepers departs and the start of the ski season. In North Adams and Pittsfield, huge spruces donated for the season are installed and lit during community gatherings. Williamstown and Dalton decorate their main streets with luminarias for Holiday Walks that include the arrival of Santa, carol sings and other musical events, hayrides, and general festivities. Participating merchants offer discounts, hot chocolate, or other enticements. And before the season is out, you can be sure that someone somewhere in the county is going to perform *The Messiah,* often with a community sing-along. Because so many activities depend on volunteers, the list ebbs and flows as energies wane or interest revives. To keep up with what's happening, folks depend on the local media, all of which carry calendars of events or broadcast announcements of community activities. The following events are listed chronologically.

JANUARY

Notchview Ski-Fest
Notchview Reservation
Massachusetts Highway 9, Windsor
(413) 684-0148
www.thetrustees.org

Known for its excellent cross-country skiing, Notchview holds a Ski-Fest with free lessons, waxing clinics, and fun activities for all ages. A 10-kilometer freestyle race also is held. The property is one of many managed by the Trustees of the Reservations, based in Stockbridge. Entrance fees are waived for members.

Pittsfield Winter Carnival
Pittsfield Department of Parks & Recreation
874 North Street, Pittsfield
(413) 499-9343

Depending on the snow cover, the Pittsfield Recreation Department sponsors various events at city parks and locations around the county, including the Vietnam Veterans Skating Rink in North Adams and Canterbury Farm ski touring area in Becket. (See the Recreation chapter for more information.) The Winter Carnival includes a button-design contest and climaxes with the crowning of the queen. Entry fees are charged for some events.

The Pittsfield Rotary Club Auction
Pittsfield Rotary Club, Pittsfield
(413) 499-9484

Held since 1991, this annual fund-raiser takes place at the Crowne Plaza (1 West Street, Pittsfield), usually on the last Saturday of the month. An admission fee is charged. The event begins with a silent auction and goes live after an hour or so.

FEBRUARY

Hancock Shaker Village
U.S. Highway 20, Pittsfield
(413) 443-0188
www.hancockshakervillage.org

On President's Day weekend, Hancock Shaker Village offers a chance to experience life in the 19th century with sleigh rides, demonstrations of Shaker crafts and winter farm activities, and hands-on activities for children and adults, including ice harvesting. The village's 20 historic buildings, usually closed in winter, are open for self-guided visits. An entrance fee is charged.

Father-daughter dances at schools or other venues have become a popular Valentine's Day event.

Winterfest/North Adams
Mayor's Office of Tourism & Cultural Development
6 West Main Street, North Adams
(413) 664-6180

Usually held on the last weekend of February. Events include ice sculpting and a chowder cook-off to take the chill off.

MARCH

Winterfest Auction
Southern Berkshire Chamber of Commerce
40 Railroad Street, Great Barrington
(413) 528-4284
www.greatbarrington.org

The Southern Berkshire Chamber of Commerce has held a gala Winterfest Auction at the Egremont Country Club since 1995. A suggested donation at the door benefits a local cause. There is usually a theme, with appropriate food and music. Items up for sale or by drawing include trips, services, and products made or grown in the Berkshires. Proceeds from the auction benefit the chamber.

APRIL

Berkshire Chamber of Commerce Expo
75 North Street, Pittsfield
(413) 499-4000
6 West Main Street, North Adams
(413) 664-6180

Hoping to jump-start the construction season, the Berkshire Chamber of Commerce Expo showcases area businesses, including landscapers, builders, financial institutions, hardware and rental companies, real estate agents, and pool and spa businesses. Folks are enticed to take advantage of raffles, giveaways, and contests plus free technical advice from participating businesses. The location alternates each year between the Vietnam Veterans Memorial Skating Rink in North Adams and the Berkshire Mall in Lanesborough.

Hancock Shaker Village
US 20, Pittsfield
(413) 443-0188
www.hancockshakervillage.org
Hancock Shaker Village celebrates spring and the new life on the farm with a monthlong series of activities focusing on baby animals and their early development. Organized by the New England Heritage Breeds Conservancy with support from the village, various events offer families a chance to see lambs, hatching chicks, kids, piglets, and other newly arrived livestock and their moms and learn about the special bond between them. No charge for children.

Greek Pastry Sale
St. George Greek Orthodox Church
73 Bradford Street, Pittsfield
(413) 443-8113
The Saturday before Easter, folks of all religious persuasions who enjoy baklava and other Mediterranean goodies rush to the pastry sale at St. George Greek Orthodox Church, located between North and Center Streets in downtown Pittsfield. Music and special events round out the offerings.

Gay and Lesbian Berkshire Festival
Berkshire Stonewall Community Coalition, Otis
(413) 243-8484
www.berkshirestonewall.org.
The Berkshire Stonewall Community Coalition Gay and Lesbian Berkshire Festival is held at Seven Hills Country Inn (40 Plunkett Street, Lenox). The three- or four-day event features entertainers and speakers of national and local note and ends with a gala dinner and dance.

i

In spring, when the maple sap is running and steam rises from the sugaring huts, syrup festivals and pancake breakfasts will spring up all over.

Williamstown Jazz Festival
Williamstown
(800) 214-3799
www.williamstownjazz.com
The Williamstown Jazz Festival runs for several days through the last week of April. A collaboration between the Williams College departments of music and dance, MASS MoCA, and the Williamstown Chamber of Commerce, the festival features name as well as local jazz groups coupled with dances and lectures held at various locations.

Mercy Sunday
Shrine of the Divine Mercy
Eden Hill, Stockbridge
(413) 298-3691
On the last Sunday in April, thousands of devout Catholics come from all over come to worship at the Marian Helpers National Shrine of the Divine Mercy at Eden Hill in Stockbridge. Mercy Sunday commemorates Sister Faustina, a Polish nun who is believed to have received a visitation from the Lord in 1931.

MAY

Berkshire Athenaeum Book Sale
Berkshire Athenaeum
3 Wendell Avenue, Pittsfield
(413) 499-9480
Book lovers look forward to rummaging through the hundreds of volumes for sale at this two-day sale sponsored by the

The county road race season opens in April with the April Fool's Day Race, usually held in Lenox.

Friends of the Berkshire Athenaeum. The library is on the corner of East Street and Wendell Avenue.

Shaun Thornton Memorial Bicycle Race
www.berkshirecycling.org
Hundreds of cyclists take part in the Shaun Thornton Memorial Bicycle Road Race, a challenging 74-mile loop that starts at Jiminy Peak ski resort in Hancock, goes north to South Williamstown via Massachusetts Highway 43, and returns to Hancock by U.S. Highway 7.

Berkshire Botanical Garden Plant Sale
Massachusetts Highway 102, Stockbridge
(413) 298-3926
www.berkshirebotanical.org
The Berkshire Botanical Garden opens for the season with a variety of family-oriented activities and a huge plant sale where you can purchase select annuals, perennials, herbs, organic and heirloom vegetables, rock garden and woodland plants, plus choice trees and shrubs. Proceeds benefit the center. No admission charge.

Riverfest & Riverworks
Hoosic River Watershed Association
160 Water Street, Williamstown
(413) 458-2742
The Hoosic River Watershed Association celebrates the Hoosic River with Riverfest & Riverworks, a weekend of raft and pony rides, exhibits, fly-fishing, art displayed along the riverbanks, and music. Activities are based at Cole Field off Cole Avenue; a small admission fee is charged.

JUNE

Celebrate Pittsfield Street Festival
Downtown, Inc.
75 North Street, Pittsfield
(413) 443-6501
www.downtownpittsfield.com
North Street is closed for several blocks for this annual festival held on the last Saturday of June. Folks can get up close to raptors, fascinating birds of prey that include eagles and hawks. Entertainment, children's amusements, food and craft vendors, baby animals, and clowns also are featured.

The Dalton Fair
American Legion Field
MA 9, Dalton
(413) 684-0500
The Dalton Fair offers four days of rides, games, and food, plus amusements, fireworks, and maybe even a fireman's muster, where area departments compete against one another in various timed events. The fair benefits the Dalton Fire Department and is held at the American Legion Field on MA 9.

Northern Berkshire Food Festival
Mayor's Office of Tourism & Cultural Development
6 West Main Street, North Adams
(413) 664-6180
While the focus is on restaurants in North County, others also participate in this event, showing off their culinary skills while raising money for a good cause.

JULY

The Berkshire Arts Festival
Butternut Basin Ski Area
Massachusetts Highway 23, Great Barrington
(800) 834-9437
www.americancraftmarketing.com
Held on the first weekend of July on the grounds of Butternut Basin Ski Area, the

Berkshire Arts Festival brings around 200 juried artists who show their jewelry, art, decorative accessories, and other products, rain or shine. Gourmet food, demonstrations, and jazz complete the offerings at this three-day event, which also is held in October.

Look for area church folk to be baking biscuits and whipping cream for their strawberry festivals, held when these sweet berries are ready for picking.

The Pittsfield Fourth of July Parade
Pittsfield Parade Committee
Pittsfield
(413) 447-7763

Folks line up early for Pittsfield's Fourth of July Parade. The route begins at West Housatonic Street, around Park Square, and north to Wahconah Park. Participants include local fire departments dressed to the nines and various law enforcement and military units. New and antique apparatus and automobiles, huge balloons, and floats interpreting the theme of the year also are featured. Marching bands from around the Northeast are invited to participate in this donation-supported event. Some compete for prizes the night before the parade, with performances at Wahconah Park.

Shakespeare & Company
70 Kemble Street, Lenox
(413) 637-1199
www.shakespeare.org

Performers from Shakespeare & Company celebrate the Fourth of July with a reading of the Declaration of Independence at the Lenox campus.

Berkshire Charity Auto Show
Hillcrest Hospital
West Street, Pittsfield
(413) 684-4889 (Night CruZers)

This charity auto show has been held on the beautiful grounds of Hillcrest Hospital off West Street since 1985. Displayed around the lakeside campus are more than 500 vehicles in 48 classes, including antiques, street rods, muscle cars, motorcycles, and monster trucks. Prizes totaling $5,000 are awarded. The event nets around $13,000, and the proceeds are donated to charities funded through United Way. The show is sponsored by Night CruZers, a local car club whose phone number is listed above.

The Clyde Beatty/Cole Bros. Circus
Berkshire Mall, Lanesborough
(413) 445-4400

The Clyde Beatty/Cole Bros. Circus sets up at the Berkshire Mall in Lanesborough for two days, usually in the second week of July. The appearance is sponsored by the Dalton Lions Club as a fund-raiser.

Susan B. Anthony Days
Adams
Berkshire Chamber of Commerce
(413) 663-3735

The town of Adams, birthplace of 19th-century women's rights activist Susan B. Anthony, commemorates her legacy with a weekend of special events, downtown sales, and a sanctioned biathalon called the Pedal & Plod. The event consists of a 4-mile footrace and a 22-mile bike race through Adams, Cheshire, and Lanesborough.

Beach Party
Eagle Street, North Adams

Just because we're landlocked doesn't mean we can't have a beach party, as proven by local artist Eric Rudd who started this event several years ago. Eagle Street is closed to traffic, and the city highway department deposits tons of sand in the street for kids to play in. Sand castles and whatnot are created in this free-form event, usually held in the middle of the month—just for the fun of it.

Woodworkers Guild Furniture Show & Sale
Berkshire Botanical Garden
MA 102, Stockbridge
(413) 298-3926
www.berkshirebotanical.org
Thirty of the region's finest woodworkers exhibit furniture and other examples of their work at the Berkshire Botanical Garden on the last weekend of the month. The Woodworkers Guild Furniture Show & Sale is a two-day indoor event. Included in admission to the garden.

Americana Artisans Craft Show
Hancock Shaker Village
US 20, Pittsfield
(413) 443-0188
www.hancockshakervillage.org
Hancock Shaker Village hosts the Americana Artisans Craft Show toward the end of July. Managed by Marilyn Gould, the show features around 100 nationally acclaimed artisans who exhibit their best folk art, furniture, ceramics, baskets, metalware, woodenware, and other work crafted in traditional 18th- and 19th-century methods. Admission varies depending on whether you also want to explore the village.

AUGUST

Flower Show
Berkshire Botanical Garden Flower Show
MA 102, Stockbridge
(413) 298-3926
www.berkshirebotanical.org
The Berkshire Botanical Garden Flower Show, held annually since 1969, features entries in floral design, horticulture, and special children's classes that are judged prior to public viewing. The gardens are in full bloom and offer many wonderful niches to enjoy a picnic lunch after taking in the show. Included in admission to the garden.

Adams Agricultural Fair
Bowe Field, Adams
(413) 743-5281, (413) 743-9037 (fairgrounds)
The Adams Agricultural Fair kicks off the country fair season with three days of demonstrations, tractor and animal pulls, livestock shows, and exhibits. Youngsters proudly show the livestock they are rearing, including lop-eared bunnies, calves, lambs, and unusual breeds of poultry. The best produce and flowers are displayed along with canned and baked goods, with ribbons awarded to prize winners. A midway offers games of skill and chance, and live entertainment is featured throughout the three days. Local groups and outside vendors sell hot dogs, hamburgers, pizza, baked goods, ice cream, and the ever-popular fried dough. Held since 1974, the fair sets up at Bowe Field on Old Columbia Street, off Massachusetts Highway 8 north of town. Parking is free. Admission is $5.00 for adults, $1.00 for children. A three-day bargain ticket is available.

Grecian Festival
St. George Greek Orthodox Church
73 Bradford Street, Pittsfield
(413) 443-8113
Those energetic folks at St. George Greek Orthodox Church hold a two-day Grecian Festival at the church on Bradford Street, between North and Center Streets. There's lots of music, dancing, food and, of course, baklava.

Berkshire Crafts Fair
Monument Mountain Regional High School
US 7, Great Barrington
(413) 528-3346
www.berkshirecraftsfair.org
The juried Berkshire Crafts Fair has been held at Monument Mountain Regional High School since 1973. While the show and sale feature a wide range of high-quality contemporary and traditional crafts, the fair is unusual in that it is organized and run by students and staff as a fund-raiser for the school. The exhibitors set up in the air-

conditioned building, which has ample parking and is wheelchair-accessible. The fair is cited in the *Harris List of the Nation's Best Arts and Crafts Shows.*

Circus Camp Finale
Berkshire Community College
1350 West Street, Pittsfield
(413) 399-0865

Young people who have immersed themselves in learning the many arts of the circus at the Berkshire Community College Circus Camp show off their talents with a grand finale performance for the public at the end of the three-week session. The day camp begins at the end of July and accepts boys and girls ages 8 to 16 who are taught tumbling, cycling, juggling, clowning, stilt and wire walking, trapeze work, partner acrobatics, and pyramid-building. They also learn the history of the circus, how to apply makeup, and how to make costumes and props. The business end—publicity, ticket selling, concession-running, and management—also are taught and handled by the kids. Applications for the $600 course are accepted in February. Family and friends tend to gobble up the tickets for the finale as soon as the date is announced—if you're interested, don't procrastinate.

Berkshire County 4-H Fair and Horse Show
Holmes Road, Pittsfield
(413) 448-8285

The 4-H Fair is held near the end of August off Holmes Road in southeast Pittsfield. In addition to the horse show, youngsters exhibit produce, flowers, crafts, and other fruits of their labors along with animals they are rearing. A great place to take kids, the fair includes games, contests, and entertainment.

Stockbridge Summer Arts and Crafts Show
Berkshire Botanical Garden
MA 102, Stockbridge
(413) 298-5200
www.stockbridgechamber.org

The Berkshire Botanical Garden is the setting for this juried show sponsored by the Stockbridge Chamber of Commerce. More than 80 artists and crafters from New England exhibit the best examples of their work in ceramics, wood, jewelry, fine art, leather, furniture, and fiber clothing. The chamber operates a cafe during show hours that provides light refreshments. Admission to the show, held rain or shine, is included in the $3.00 parking fee.

Mayor's Downtown Celebration
Mayor's Office of Tourism & Cultural Development
West Main Street, North Adams
(413) 664-6180

The main drag is closed off for this midweek event, and folks come in droves to enjoy bands and other performers and sample food from vendors that line the street.

---

i

The city of North Adams holds First Friday events every month, weather permitting. Music, art, poetry, and readings are often featured—and stores stay open late.

SEPTEMBER

Tub Parade
Lenox Chamber of Commerce
Lenox
(413) 637-3646
www.lenox.org

Continuing a tradition that began around the turn of the 20th century, decorated horse-drawn carriages are driven through the town of Lenox in what is called the Tub Parade. The wealthy who summered in Lenox marked the end of the season—and the closing of their elaborate estates—by decorating their various carriages, known as tubs, with flowers and driving them along the main streets. Nowadays the Lenox Chamber of Commerce sponsors the event.

Josh Billings RunAground
(413) 637-6913
www.joshbillings.com

The major sporting event of the year, the Josh Billings RunAground is held on the second Sunday in September. The triathalon draws hundreds of participants who—as teams or individuals—bike, row, and run a grueling course over land and water. The event began in 1976 and bears the name of a Will Rogers–type humorist from Lanesborough who was a popular sage at the turn of the 20th century. It has evolved into the current 27-mile cycle route from Great Barrington to Stockbridge Bowl, where the race continues via canoes and kayaks to the opposite shore, 5 miles away. From there runners undertake a 10K race that ends at Tanglewood. Teams of various genders and ages compete alongside folks who undertake all three legs in Iron Man and Iron Woman categories. A party is held at the end, with live music and food and drink vendors.

Apple Squeeze
Lenox Chamber of Commerce
Downtown Lenox
(413) 637-3646
www.lenox.org

Lenox has celebrated fall with the Apple Squeeze since 1979. Vendors line the streets in the center of town selling locally made crafts, food and, of course, apples in the form of pies and cider or by the bagful. The annual firefighters' parade kicks off the two-day event, which includes hayrides, sidewalk sales, music, antique and collector cars, face-painting, and a dog show for kids plus a pie-baking contest. There's also a giant pumpkin weigh-off and a 5K race.

Founders Weekend
Lee Chamber of Commerce
(413) 243-0852
www.leechamber.org

Founded in 1778, the town of Lee celebrates the occasion with two days of sidewalk sales, displays, activities for children, and live music. The celebration begins with the Hometown Parade on Saturday of the last weekend in September. Lee's Latino population, which has grown over the past few years, spices up the festivities with music and food representing their culture. History is recalled with Civil War encampments, and Lee's various restaurants provide "A Taste of Lee," bringing favorites from their kitchens to booths set up in the town square.

Fall Motorcycle Run
Adams
(413) 743-4631 (Custom City Cycle)

Hundreds of motorcyclists gather in Adams on the last weekend of September for the Fall Run. Held since 1981, the 6-mile ride benefits the Shriner's Children's Hospital in Springfield. Participants take off from Bowe Field on MA 8 in Adams in a breathtaking roar and follow a route that ends on Massachusetts Highway 2 in Charlemont, where various biking events take place along with music and refreshments. Custom City Cycle at 26 Depot Street in Adams is the lead organizer and may be called for information at the number above.

Fall Festival
Hopkins Forest, Williamstown
(413) 458-3080
www.williams.edu

Hopkins Forest is a 2,500-acre preserve owned by Williams College and used for environmental studies. It is open to the public for the fall festival, which features woodworking demonstrations, hikes, a ropes course, and music plus activities for kids. Apple butter and cider are made on the premises.

World Suppers
Hancock Shaker Village
US 20, Pittsfield
(413) 443-0188
www.hancockshakervillage.org

The stoves in the kitchen at Hancock Shaker Village are cranked up for suppers for "the world," offered on selected weekends in fall and later in December. The menu features traditional Shaker dishes, and the hearty meals are served by candlelight in the 1830 Brick Dwelling by reservation. Shaker music follows in the Meeting Room.

Country Fair and Crafts Festival
Hancock Shaker Village
US 20, Pittsfield
(413) 443-0188
www.hancockshakervillage.org
Held on the last weekend of September, the fair focuses on the New England Heritage Breeds at the village. Held in conjunction with the Heritage Breeds Conservancy, the festival includes one of the largest heritage livestock exhibitions in the country. There is a parade of animals and lots of chances for hands-on experiences with them. The old-fashioned country fair includes activities for children plus demonstrations by traditional craftspeople, who also sell their work.

OCTOBER

Berkshire Arts Festival
Butternut Basin Ski Area
MA 23, Great Barrington
(800) 834-9437
www.americancraftmarketing.com
The Berkshire Arts Festival returns to the grounds of Butternut Basin for another three-day run. Held rain or shine, the show features 200 juried artists, who exhibit and sell their work. Demonstrations, gourmet food, and live music round out the offerings.

Fall Foliage Parade
Berkshire Chamber of Commerce
6 West Main Street, North Adams
(413) 664-6180
www.berkshirechamber.com
Thousands will flock to North Adams on the first weekend of the month for the Fall Foliage Parade. Held since 1955, the parade has grown by leaps and bounds but is still a hometown production to honor the splendor of the season. Floats, bands, veterans groups, military units, and fire departments march along MA 8 north into the city, ending on Ashland Street. Jet planes from Westover Air Force Base provide a thrill by flying over the city during the parade. The weekend starts with a children's parade downtown on Friday night. Children wear costumes and design floats, and winners are invited to march in the big parade on Sunday. An all-you-can-eat pancake breakfast is traditionally served the morning of the parade at the Fraternal Order of the Eagles on MA 8. A 5K road race also is held—not recommended for folks who catch the pancake breakfast.

Harvest Festival
Berkshire Botanical Garden
MA 102, Stockbridge
(413) 298-3926
www.berkshirebotanical.org
The garden's Harvest Festival has been held on the first weekend of October since 1934. Family-oriented rides and games are featured along with food, music, and crafts. Admission fee is by the carload.

Berkshire Quilt Festival
Berkshire Community College
1350 West Street, Pittsfield
(413) 499-4660
The work of around 180 quilters of all ages is shown at this festival. Some are for use on beds, while others reflect the growing interest in quilts as an art form and are presented as wall hangings. Special lecturers and vendors selling quilting supplies also are featured. The two-day show benefits a scholarship fund established by the Quilt Festival Committee and alumni and friends of Berkshire Community College. Admission is $5.00 for adults, $2.00 for children.

Walk for the Homeless
Construct Inc.
Great Barrington
(413) 528-1985
The Walk for the Homeless is held in Great Barrington to raise funds for Construct

Inc., a nonprofit organization dedicated to assisting the homeless and creating affordable housing. Construct sponsors the roughly 6-mile walk, which takes a different route each year. Relief stations and light refreshments are set up along the way. Those who don't want to walk the whole way can be picked up along the route. The event finishes with entertainment and homemade goodies.

Williamstown Film Festival
Williamstown
(413) 458-9700
www.williamstownfilmfest.com

The nonprofit Williamstown Film Festival shows innovative, independent films over a 10-day period beginning the end of October. The festival was founded in 1998 by a group of local residents and graduates of Williams College to honor America's film past with classics and to explore the present state of independent filmmaking. Writers, actors, directors, and others participate in question-and-answer sessions after the screenings. As the festival has grown, so has its reputation, gaining the attention of *Variety, Boston Magazine,* and others who have commented on the intimate nature of the viewings compared with big festivals like Sundance. Most of the films are shown at Images Cinema, 50 Spring Street, but some are shown at MASS MoCA and the Clark Art Museum. The Web site gives detailed information about the films that are shown; they also are listed in local media.

Ski Sale
Jiminy Peak, Hancock
(413) 738-5446

For 30 years, skiers have been taking advantage of the Hancock Volunteer Fire Department Ski Sale at Jiminy Peak ski resort on Brodie Mountain Road in Hancock. New and used downhill and cross-country ski equipment, accessories, ice skates, and clothing are sold at bargain prices, and 20 percent of the proceeds go to the fire department. It's a good time to get ready for the season, save some money, and do a good deed all at the same time. Other groups also hold used equipment sales around this time, but this is the granddaddy of them all.

BMC Follies
Berkshire Medical Center
725 North Street, Pittsfield
(413) 447-2000

The Berkshire Medical Center Follies are eagerly anticipated each year by locals who get to see their friends, coworkers, and neighbors shed their normal personas and kick up their heels for a good cause. Hundreds of volunteers put on this musical extravaganza at the end of October to benefit BMC. For three days these dedicated folks sing and dance under the leadership of a professional director, with a different theme chosen each year. Performances are given at Reid Middle School on Friday and Saturday nights, with a matinee on Sunday. Tickets—$10.00 for adults, $8.00 for children and senior citizens—are sold at the hospital gift shop, the BMC Hillcrest Campus gift shop, and at participating businesses.

Halloween Parade
Pittsfield Department of Parks and Recreation
874 North Street, Pittsfield
(413) 499-9343

This city-sponsored parade is the largest event in the area. City schools and local businesses participate with floats and other ghoulish presentations, and prizes are awarded at various levels. Haunted houses are sponsored by local groups, and many small towns hold Halloween parties at their schools or other public facilities. Trick or treating is usually held on a night designated by local officials. Folks who welcome kids leave their porch lights on.

NOVEMBER

Fall Festival of Shakespeare
Shakespeare & Company
70 Kemble Street, Lenox
(413) 637-1199; ext. 316
www.shakespeare.org

Shakespeare & Company's nationally acclaimed Fall Festival of Shakespeare culminates a two-month program involving around 400 students in nine area schools who begin working with company staff shortly after school opens. Students develop their own interpretation of Shakespeare's works and give performances of their own inimitable versions of these plays in their own schools. These young thespians then perform in a four-day marathon at the Founders' Theatre on Shakespeare & Company's Lenox campus. Each play lasts around 90 minutes, and you can be sure that the Bard would be amazed—and pleased—at these performances, usually held just before Thanksgiving. Tickets are $7.00 for each play or $25.00 for all nine, and they go fast, even though the theater holds 422 persons.

Festival of Trees
Berkshire Museum
39 South Street, Pittsfield
(413) 443-7171
www.berkshiremuseum.org

Just after Thanksgiving, the Berkshire Museum's Festival of Trees opens to the public. The galleries are filled with more than 200 creatively decorated trees, including around 60 created by area children. The festival runs through the end of December, and special programs, concerts, and workshops are held during that time.

DECEMBER

Holiday Marketplace
Berkshire Botanical Garden
Route 102, Stockbridge
(413) 298-3926
www.berkshirebotanical.org

The Berkshire Botanical Garden exhibits and sells handcrafted wreaths and holiday decorations, seasonal plants, herb products, crafts, and gift items on the first weekend of December. The three-day Holiday Marketplace is part of the Stockbridge Main Street at Christmas celebration, sponsored by the Stockbridge Chamber of Commerce since 1989. Main Street is decorated for the holidays, and Norman Rockwell's famous painting is re-created, complete with 1950s automobiles. All events are free.

PARKS

Nearly 30 percent of the land in Berkshire County is preserved for public use, protecting more than 175,000 acres while preserving nature's gifts for generations to come. Folks today are indebted to the foresight and generosity of many private landowners who have deeded their properties to the organizations that manage and keep them open for hiking, fishing, cross-country skiing, horseback riding, swimming, or just plain enjoying the scenery. There are more than 20 state parks in the area plus innumerable preserved areas administered by land trusts and other land conservation organizations. Every town has a park, some big with large playing fields, tennis courts, and other facilities; others small with just a picnic table or two, a basketball hoop and maybe a Little League field.

Most of the county's lakes and ponds are accessible to all for boating, swimming, or fishing. Most state parks allow motorized vehicles and hunting. Some provide camping areas; others are less developed. Some of these gems, like Windsor Lake in North Adams, Springside Park in Pittsfield, and Kennedy Park in Lenox, are right under your nose, yet invisible until you find them. Others, like majestic Mount Greylock and ominous Monument Mountain, rise above the landscape, enticing you to climb their heights for the breathtaking views that await. Entries are arranged alphabetically by town name. In addition to the parks, preserves, and reservations listed below, see the Recreation chapter for some special places that reward the visitor with nature at its best.

SOUTH COUNTY

Bartholomew's Cobble
Weatogue Road, Ashley Falls
(413) 229-8600
www.thetrustees.org

Located off U.S. Highway 7A near the Colonel John Ashley House, Bartholomew's Cobble has so many unique natural areas and is home to such a broad assortment of plant and wildlife that it has been deemed a National Natural Landmark. The most prominent feature of this 329-acre preserve are the cobbles, or rocky knolls, that rise above the Housatonic River. Composed mostly of limestone and marble, their alkaline soil supports an unusual array of ferns and wildflowers. The high point at Bartholomew's Cobble is Hurlburt's Hill, which rises 1,000 feet to a 20-acre upland field. Those who climb the trail to the top are rewarded with panoramic views of the Housatonic River Valley. Away from the cobbles, the landscape changes to open fields dotted with red cedars and then to forest. The reservation's numerous and varied habitats feature more than 800 species of plants and more forest types than anywhere else in Berkshire County. There are freshwater marshes and beaver ponds to explore as well as the Housatonic River itself, and the reservation is a flyway for more than 250 species of birds.

Facilities include a Natural History Museum and Visitor Center with exhibits, maps, historical information, and restrooms that are wheelchair accessible. Both are open daily from 9:00 A.M. to 5:00 P.M. except December to March, when they are closed on Sunday and Monday. There are 5 miles of trails for moderate hiking that are open all year. The property is managed by the Trustees of Reservations, which offers guided three-hour canoe tours for adults and children over age 12. Reservations are required and may be made by calling (413) 229-8600. There is a charge for exploring the cobble for those who are not members of the Trustees.

Workshops, lectures, and children's programs take place throughout the year. Volunteers occasionally gather to weed invasive plants from areas that might be overtaken, killing off native growth. You might say that Bartholomew's Cobble has been cobbled together through the years, beginning with a tract of land purchased in 1946. Since then, various individuals have bequeathed parcels and the National Park Service and the Massachusetts Historical Commission have provided funds for additional purchases.

Housatonic River Walk
195 Main Street, Great Barrington
(413) 528-3391
www.gbriverwalk.org

Hidden behind the shops and other buildings along the east side of Main Street, this public path has been laboriously created along the Housatonic River, offering respite from the hectic world beyond. Called the Housatonic River Walk, the greenway is the result of years of hard work by a dedicated corps of volunteers led by a local woman committed to resurrecting the neglected river and its abused banks. The project began in 1988 when Rachel Fletcher and a group of 16 formed the Great Barrington River Conservancy and cleaned up part of the riverbank that had been used as a dumping ground for generations. They removed 15 tons of accumulated rubbish and demolition debris from a small area behind Brooks Drug Store. A year later, 70 middle school students cleaned up the bank behind their school, removing 20 tons of debris and constructing a nature trail and canoe access.

Since then, approximately 1,600 volunteers of all ages have collected 335 tons of assorted debris and built the trail that now runs for 2,100 feet between Cottage and Bridge Streets. They stabilized banks and removed invasive plants, replacing them with native flowers, trees, and shrubs. A wooden boardwalk was constructed for one portion of the trail and benches placed along the way. Flow-forms were constructed to direct runoff and purify it before it enters the river. Most recently, a memorial garden was dedicated to civil rights leader W. E. B. DuBois, who was born nearby and who as early as 1930 decried the sad state of the river and its banks. A booklet prepared by the Conservancy explains in detail the history of the river; the work that has been done; the plantings, including their Latin names; and plans for the future. As signs along the path remind visitors, property owners have given permission for the trail to cross their land, a privilege not to be abused. The path is closed in winter.

Lake Mansfield
Great Barrington Town Parks
(413) 528-3140 (Town Hall)

A public beach with swings and a lifeguard on duty in summer is maintained by the town at this lake, located off Massachusetts Highway 41 on Christian Hill Road.

Memorial Field Park
Great Barrington Town Parks
(413) 528-3140 (Town Hall)

Located in town off Bridge Street, Memorial Park has a skateboarding bowl and is staffed in summer, when programs are run for various age groups.

Monument Mountain Reservation
U.S. Highway 7, Great Barrington
(413) 298-3239
www.thetrustees.org

Just north of town, Monument Mountain rises 1,735 feet above the southern Berkshire terrain. Established in 1899 with a gift and an endowment, the reservation has grown to 503 acres with subsequent gifts and land purchases by the Trustees of Reservations, which manages the property. With US 7 running at its base, the mountain now attracts more than 20,000 visitors a year who climb to the summit for the panoramic views. Three miles of trails, some quite steep and strenuous, lead through the forests. Small caves are hidden in the rock outcroppings, and several streams wind through the woods.

The mountain has been a source of inspiration to poets, novelists, and artists. William Cullen Bryant, who stayed in Great Barrington from 1815 to 1825, wrote "Monument Mountain," a not-very-happy lyrical poem that tells the story of a Mahican maiden whose forbidden love for her cousin led her to leap to her death from the mountain's cliffs. A rock cairn marks the spot where she supposedly is buried. Nathaniel Hawthorne and Herman Melville hiked up the mountain and, during a thunderstorm, spent several hours in a cave, where their discussions reportedly led to ideas for *Moby Dick*.

Aside from hiking and picnicking, hunting is allowed, and dogs on leashes are permitted on the trails. Visitors are also urged to bring binoculars for birdwatching and viewing the valley from the summit. The reservation is open at no charge year-round from sunrise to sunset, but caution should be the rule when hiking in winter. There are picnic tables and trail maps at the parking area off the highway.

Laurel Lake
U.S. Highway 20, Lee
(413) 243–2100 (Lee Town Hall)
www.masswildlife.org

This 170-acre lake is popular for swimming and fishing. The state Department of Fisheries and Wildlife maintains a boat launch right off US 20, just north of town. A small town park with a public beach is near the boat launch. Another public beach is maintained on the Lenox side of the lake. Laurel Lake is one of many lakes in the county formed during the Industrial Age, when water was dammed to provide mill power. Although the lake is "owned" by Lee and Lenox, the top 12 feet of water in the lake and the dam that controls it are the property of Schweitzer-Maudit, a nearby paper mill in Lee.

October Mountain State Forest
Woodland Road, Lee
(413) 243–1778
www.massparks.org

The largest state forest in Massachusetts, October Mountain encompasses 16,627 acres. Much of the land was once a private game preserve that was given to the state in the early 1900s. Today the facility includes 46 campsites, some adapted for wheelchair use. Showers are available. Trails for hiking, horseback riding, cross-country skiing, mountain biking, and off-road vehicles run through the forest along with the Appalachian Trail, where a lean-to has been constructed. One of the most scenic trails leads to Schermerhorn Gorge, a natural feature that has intrigued generations of geologists. October Mountain Reservoir and several other bodies of water are open for fishing and nonmotorized boating. Hunting is permitted, and there is a dumping station for trailers and other recreational vehicles. Many roads lead to parking areas throughout the forest that are open seasonally, but the main entrance and headquarters are located on Woodland Road off East Street in Lee.

Kennedy Park
Off US 7 and US 7A, Lenox
(413) 637–3646 (Chamber of Commerce)

Hidden off the main roads yet completely accessible to all is Kennedy Park, a 180-acre tract of land maintained by the town. The land was once part of Aspinwall, a high-end hotel built in 1902 to accommodate visitors to the area's "cottages." The hotel burned in 1931, and the property lay dormant until longtime resident John D. Kennedy and the town of Lenox obtained the land and created the park. There are now seven trails of varying degrees of difficulty groomed for cross-country skiing in winter and walks in summer. No motorized vehicles are allowed. Maps of the park may be obtained from the Lenox Chamber of Commerce and the Arcadian Shop, an outdoor specialty store on US 7, where one of the entrances is located.

Lilac Park
Main Street, Lenox
(413) 637-3646 (Chamber of Commerce)
Recently restored by the Lenox Garden Club—a member of the Garden Club of America—Lilac Park in the center of town is the focal point for many activities throughout the year. The best time to visit the park is in spring, when hundreds of lilacs in countless varieties bloom. Kids love climbing on the cannon. In December the town's Christmas tree is erected here with appropriate ceremony.

Pleasant Valley Wildlife Sanctuary
472 West Mountain Road, Lenox
(413) 637-0320
www.massaudubon.org
One of two sanctuaries operated in Berkshire County by the Massachusetts Audubon Society, Pleasant Valley encompasses 1,314 acres filled with all kinds of wildlife. Seven miles of trails, including boardwalks, wind through hardwood forest, meadows and wetlands, and along the slopes of Lenox Mountain. Beaver lodges can be observed in Yokum Brook, and the salamander migration is an annual spring event. Guided walks and tours may be arranged through the nature center on West Mountain Road. The sanctuary can be reached by West Dugway Road, just off US 7 north of Lenox. There is an admission charge, which is lower for members of MassAudubon.

Beartown State Forest
Blue Hill Road, Monterey
(413) 528-0904
www.massparks.org
This immense forest sprawls over 12,000 acres encompassing parts of Great Barrington, Stockbridge, Lee, and Monterey. The main entrance and headquarters are located on Blue Hill Road off Massachusetts Highway 23 in Monterey. Facilities include wheelchair-accessible restrooms and picnic areas. Because the forest is open year-round, there are two trail maps—one for summer and one for winter. Trails used for horseback riding and mountain biking in summer become paths for cross-country skiing and snowshoeing in winter. There are many hiking trails, including the Appalachian Trail, and some trails are multiuse. Beartown is one of the few parks where snowmobiles and some off-road vehicles are allowed, but inquiries are advised. There are 12 campsites open all year. Benedict Pond, a pristine 35-acre body of water, has a boat ramp and is popular for swimming and fishing. A pleasant 1.5-mile trail loops around the pond. Canoes, kayaks, and other nonmotorized boats are welcome.

Mount Washington State Forest
East Street, Mount Washington
(413) 528-0330
www.massparks.org
Mount Washington State Forest is the central information point for this and three other state parks located off MA 41 in the lower corner of Berkshire County bordering New York and Connecticut. The others are Mount Everett State Reservation, Bash Bish Falls State Park, and Jug End State Reservation and Wildlife Management Area. The Department of Environmental Management's Division of Forests and Parks and the state department of Fisheries and Wildlife share jurisdiction in some areas. The four parks encompass almost 6,900 incredibly scenic acres, much of it open to the public for a host of activities year-round.

The center at Mount Washington State Forest has restrooms and provides information about points of interest. Maps showing 30 miles of trails for hiking, mountain biking, horseback riding, and cross-country skiing are available. There are 15 wilderness campsites. Fishing and hunting are allowed within state regulations, and there are picnic tables and a scenic viewing area.

Bash Bish Falls State Park is right on the New York border. Forming the state's most dramatic waterfall, Bash Bish Brook rushes for 80 feet through gorges before tumbling into a pool at the base. It is reachable only by foot via several paths, some more strenuous than others. Fishing, cross-country skiing, and hunting are allowed. There are public restrooms at the parking area off Falls Road.

Jug End State Reservation and Wildlife Management Area is a former ski resort that went belly-up and was purchased by the state Department of Environmental Management and the Division of Fisheries and Wildlife. The property is used for environmental research and recreation, including cross-country skiing, hiking, hunting, and fishing. Facilities include restrooms and a scenic viewing area. The Appalachian Trail runs through the reservation and on into Mount Everett State Reservation.

Mount Everett reservation encompasses 1,356 acres crossed by several brooks and streams. While there are some trails leading from parking areas, the Appalachian Trail is the only access to some parts of the reservation. There are several campsites and a lean-to along the trail. Camping is prohibited around Race Brook Falls, just off MA 41, and Guilder Pond, a 17-acre lake popular for fishing and nonmotorized boating. Picnic tables and restrooms are available.

Questing
New Marlborough Hill Road, New Marlborough
www.thetrusteees.org

Questing is a 438-acre reservation as magical as its name. Why it was called the Questing is not clear. The farmers who came to the area in the 1700s called their settlement Leffingwell. Cellar holes and stone walls—remnants of their time here—can be found in the forests on Leffingwell Hill, where a number of trails are maintained. Questing features extensive tracts of transitional hardwood forest, pockets of wetlands, small streams, and vernal pools. In season, a 17-acre upland field of native meadow wildflowers attracts dragonflies and butterflies, including giant green darners and monarchs. The property was given to the Trustees of Reservations in 1996. It is open year-round daily from sunrise to sunset. There is no admission charge. Dogs on leashes are allowed. New Marlborough Hill is off Massachusetts Highway 57 east of Monterrey.

Tolland State Forest
Tolland Road, Otis
(413) 269-6002
www.massparks.org

Parts of the 10,305 acres that make up the Tolland State Forest lie in Sandisfield, Tolland, Otis, and Blandford, and there are entrances to the forest in all of those towns. The main entrance is off Massachusetts Highway 8 on Tolland Road via Reservoir Road in East Otis. The park headquarters there has wheelchair-accessible restrooms, and the staff offers narrative programs. Star of the forest is Otis Reservoir, a 1,065-acre man-made lake with a sandy beach and wooded lakeside picnic area. Canoes and other boats, including motorized ones, may be launched from a ramp near the southeast bay. The reservoir is stocked with bass and trout. In addition, there are several streams for fishing, including the Farmington River. Popular for camping, the forest has 93 campsites, some on a scenic lake peninsula. Camping season runs from mid-May through mid-October.

Tolland is one of the few parks that provide showers for campers. There also is a dumping station for trailers and recreational vehicles. In summer, trails are open for walking, mountain biking, off-road vehicles, and hiking. In winter, as shown on a different map, trails are open for snowmobiling and skiing. Hunting is allowed.

Sandisfield State Forest
York Lake Road, Sandisfield
(413) 229-8212 (summer), (413) 528-0904 (winter)
www.massparks.org

Almost in Connecticut, Sandisfield State Forest encompasses 7,785 acres and six lakes, ranging from 10 to 60 acres. All are stocked with trout. Canoes, kayaks, and other nonmotorized boats have to be carried to most accesses except for the largest, York Lake, where there is a ramp.

York Lake has a 300-foot sandy beach, a picnic area, and restrooms. The forest is full of trails for walking, hiking, horseback riding, and cross-country skiing. Snowmobiles are allowed and hunting in season is permitted. The main entrance is on York Lake Road, off MA 57 south of MA 23.

McLennan Reservation
Fenn Road, Tyringham
www.thetrustees.org
Round Mountain and its neighbor, Long Mountain, form the backdrop for the McLennan Reservation, nearly 500 acres of forested hills and wetlands that make up the southeastern end of the beautiful Tyringham Valley. In the saddle between these 1,500-foot elevations lies Hale Swamp, created when Camp Brook was dammed by beavers long ago. Runoff from the swamp and its adjacent hills feeds several brooks that empty into Hop Brook, which runs to the Housatonic River. While early farmers cleared much of the forest, many old tree stands remain on less accessible slopes. A 1.5-mile trail, strenuous in places, follows the graceful rises and dips of this densely forested landscape before reaching the high plateau where Hale Swamp is located. The reservation was once part of the Ashintully estate, whose gardens are located at the southern end of the valley. Open year-round from sunrise to sunset. Fenn Road is a poorly marked dirt road off Tyringham Road, called Main Road, south of Tyringham center. The entrance to the reservation is about a 0.25-mile walk from the parking area.

Tyringham Cobble
Jerusalem Road, Tyringham
www.thetrustees.org
This unique 206-acre reservation with its knobby hills might have been created by a cataclysmic geological event 500 million years ago. At least that's what geologist Daniel Clark concluded when he studied Tyringham Cobble in 1895. Finding that rock strata on top of the hill were older than those at the bottom, he deduced that the cobble had broken off a nearby mountain and flipped over with immense force.

The forested slopes of the cobble were cleared in the 1760s by pioneer farmers. Later the cobble was purchased by a growing Shaker community, whose members farmed it and pastured cattle and sheep on its northwest side. In 1876 the community left; subsequent farmers acquired the land and used it to graze their sheep and dairy cattle. When a ski run was proposed in the 1930s, a group of conservation-minded individuals calling themselves "The Cobblers" purchased the land, and in 1963 their descendants donated the property to the Trustees of Reservations. Today 2 miles of trails, a section of which is a link of the Appalachian Trail, pass over the twin knobs of the cobble, offering spectacular views of Tyringham Valley. Small trees and shrubs have taken root among dramatic rock outcrops and glacial boulders. Wildflowers, blackberries, blueberries, and wild strawberries grow in clearings and open meadows. The cobble is open to the public at no charge from sunrise to sunset. Leashed dogs are allowed. Hunting is permitted subject to state and town laws. The preserve is off Jerusalem Road, in the center of Tyringham.

Central Berkshire

Dalton Town Parks
Through the generosity of the Crane family, Dalton has four town parks and a community recreation center plus numerous trails that cross Crane lands. The largest park, Pine Grove, has a well-equipped playground for children of all ages and abilities, basketball courts, and fields for baseball games and other sports. The Community House on Main Street (413-684-0260) runs a host of programs for all ages. While many are for residents only, memberships may be purchased to use the fitness center and other facilities. A sector of Crane property known as the Boulders contains several trails, including a section of the Appalachian Trail, where a

camping area is available to hikers. Access is off Massachusetts Highway 9 or Gulf Road, a one-lane dirt road that is closed to vehicles in winter. The road and some trails pass through Wizard's Glen, a dark and slightly spooky area filled with massive boulders and tumbled trees. Although the Boulders is open to the public, the area is the main source of water for the Crane papermaking business; folks who use it are urged to be aware of the environmentally sensitive nature of the land.

Wahconah Falls State Park
MA 9, Dalton
(413) 442-8928 (Pittsfield State Forest)
www.massparks.org

Wahconah Falls State Park, off MA 9 near the Windsor line, has no facilities other than picnic tables and trails that lead down to the falls, a walk worth taking. Wahconah Brook cascades more than 80 feet in three stages, and nothing beats standing under the falls or swimming in the pool below on a 90-degree day. When the water is high, the roar of the falls can be heard a mile away. The park is reached by a dirt road which you might want to avoid in mud season.

Burbank Park at Onota Lake
Off Valentine Road, Pittsfield
(413) 499-9343 (Parks Department)

The second largest lake in the county, Onota's shores are mostly in private hands except for Burbank Park. Maintained by the city of Pittsfield, this beautiful park on the eastern shore has walking trails through wooded groves dotted with picnic tables and grills. There are two parking areas. The southern one is geared to boat owners, with ample room for trailers and a large launching ramp. A concrete pier into the lake provides lots of space for anglers. Paths lead from this section through the woods to the northern part of the park, where there is a public beach and the recently built Controy pavilion with bathhouses and wheelchair-accessible restrooms. Bathers may park in the large northern lot. Nearby are a large playground, picnic tables reserved for wheelchair use, and a paved path that runs along the shore. Fishing derbies and other activities are held here throughout the summer, when lifeguards and park police are on duty. The Berkshire Rowing and Sculling Society (BRASS) maintains a boathouse on the lake. Dogs are banned from the park, which makes walking in the woods even more enjoyable. Located on the west side of the city, Burbank Park is off Valentine Road. Dan Casey Causeway at the northern end of the lake is a popular spot for fishing and duck-watching. The causeway runs between Churchill Street and Pecks Road.

Canoe Meadows Wildlife Sanctuary
Holmes Road, Pittsfield
(413) 637-0320
www.massaudubon.org

The other property in the Berkshires managed by the Audubon Society, Canoe Meadows incredibly is only 1 mile from the center of Pittsfield, yet it teems with wildlife. Birds such as bobolinks, ospreys, and great blue herons can be seen at different times of the year. Three miles of trails wind through the sanctuary's scenic woods, fields, and wetlands and along the edge of the Housatonic River, which winds through the property. Beavers, otters, and wild turkeys are often seen during explorations of Canoe Meadows. Programs include a community garden, birding, and a day camp operated by the Pleasant Valley Wildlife Sanctuary in Lenox. Canoe Meadows is on Holmes Road. It can be reached by US 7 south of the city or via Williams or Elm Street in the city. There are no public facilities, but an admission fee is charged.

Fred Garner River Park
Pomeroy Avenue, Pittsfield
(413) 499-9343 (Parks Department)

Located on the Housatonic River, this city park provides parking for canoeists and others who want to enjoy the river from a boat. The park is on Pomeroy Avenue in southeast Pittsfield.

Pittsfield State Forest
Cascade Street, Pittsfield
(413) 442-8992
www.massparks.org

Located on the western edge of the city, Pittsfield State Forest is popular for picnicking, fishing, swimming, and just plain enjoying nature. Streams, waterfalls, and flowering shrubs abound. In June, Berry Mountain, the highest peak in the park, practically glows when 65 acres of wild azaleas are in bloom. The view from the top is wonderful, especially at sunset. Berry Pond, at 2,150 feet one of the highest natural water bodies in Massachusetts, is a great spot for fishing. Berry Pond Campground offers 13 rustic campsites on the peak. There are 18 campsites with flush toilets at Parker Brook Campground at the base of the mountain. Swimming and picnicking are permitted there and at Lulu Brook, where an earthen dam holds back the clear, cold spring water.

Thirty miles of trails run through the forest for both summer and winter use. There are bridle paths and trails for hiking. Off-road vehicles, mountain bikes, and snowmobiles are permitted on all but the Taconic Crest Trail, which runs for 35 miles from US 20 west of Pittsfield all the way north to Petersburg, New York, via Hopkins Memorial Forest in Williamstown. Pittsfield State Forest is a boon for those with physical disabilities. Tranquility Trail, near the main entrance, is paved for wheelchair use. A wheelchair-accessible picnic area with appropriately outfitted restrooms is nearby. Pavilions are popular for group picnics, but as in all state parks, alcoholic beverages are prohibited.

The main entrance to Pittsfield State Forest is on Cascade Street, off Churchill. At the northern end of the forest is Balance Rock, a 165-ton limestone boulder that rests precariously on its point on a bedrock base. The paved road to that phenomenon is off Balance Rock Road in Lanesborough and is open to vehicles May through October.

Pontoosuc Lake
Pittsfield
(413) 499-9343 (Parks Department)
www.masswildlife.org

Travelers along US 7 will come upon this jewel of a lake, framed by a hill with towering pines to the south and a view of Mount Greylock to the north. More than half the lake lies in neighboring Lanesborough, but the main access is in Pittsfield on Hancock Road, just off US 7. A boat launching ramp and a parking lot that can handle trailers are located here. Another parking area for picnickers and bathers is nearby. In winter the lake is a popular spot for ice fishing and snowmobiling. In summer the YMCA rents sailboats at its marina and boathouse off the highway.

Springside Park
874 North Street, Pittsfield
(413) 499-9343 (Parks Department)

With 231 acres, Springside is the largest park maintained by the city of Pittsfield. Centrally located off North Street, this oasis in the heart of the city is laced with trails and gardens, including the Vincent Hebert Arboretum. A living library of trees, the arboretum displays a wide diversity of trees and other plants in formal landscapes and natural settings. A greenhouse flourishes with plants grown by the Springside Greenhouse Group, whose annual sale around Mother's Day is eagerly awaited. Activities that take place throughout the year include walks focusing on birds, wallflowers, and stargazing, plus lectures, poetry readings, and concerts. Educational programs promoting environmentally sound gardening and landscaping practices are offered. The grounds include a lilac walk, butterfly and hospice gardens, and a kiosk where maps and literature are available. An 1890s mansion on the property, a former estate donated to the city, serves as headquarters for the city's parks department, which also maintains and runs recreational programs at a number of playgrounds around the city.

Notchview Reservation
MA 9, Windsor
(413) 684-0148
www.thetrustees.org
Once the estate of Arthur A. Budd and now a property of the Trustees of Reservations, Notchview is open year-round but is best known for its cross-country skiing. High in the hills, snow comes early and leaves late. Skiers are protected from harsh winds by the woods, through which about 16 miles of trails run. There also are trails along wooded roads and through open fields. In summer the trails take hikers through old orchards, open meadows, and stands of northern hardwoods. A self-guiding trail leads through a woodlot demonstrating forest management practices.

Windsor State Forest
River Road, Windsor
(413) 663-8469 (Savoy State Forest)
www.massparks.org
Windsor State Forest is known for its swimming area and cascading falls, where the Windsor Jambs Brook plunges through a 25-foot-wide gorge, with 80-foot-high perpendicular granite walls rising on either side. The popular day-use swimming area on the Westfield River offers a 100-foot sandy beach with picnic sites. There are 24 campsites and numerous trails and old roads that wind through the forest for use by equestrians, hikers, mountain bikers, cross-country skiers, and snowmobilers. Fishing and hunting are permitted. The entrance is on River Road off Massachusetts Highway 116 in Savoy, but it also can be reached by following signs off MA 9 east of Dalton. Wheelchair-accessible restrooms are located there.

NORTH COUNTY

Clarksburg State Park
Middle Road, Clarksburg
(413) 663-8469
www.massparks.org
Aside from nearly 3,500 acres of unspoiled forest, scenic Mauserts Pond is the main attraction at Clarksburg State Park. A landscaped area for day use offers pleasant surroundings for swimming and picnicking. A pavilion may be booked for group use, and there is a bathhouse. Restrooms are wheelchair-accessible. The pond is skirted by a scenic trail from which visitors can observe a variety of wild plants and animals. Nearby there are 50 well-spaced campsites with showers, including some adapted to wheelchair use. The Appalachian Trail passes through the forest, which was once home to the Mohawk Indians and is still a popular place for hunting and fishing. The park is on the Vermont state line, and trails include the first—or last—stop in the Berkshires for hikers on the AT. Both the Berkshire hills and the Green Mountains may be seen from scenic viewing areas along the trails. Nonmotorized boats are allowed, but you have to carry them in. Cross-country skiing is allowed in winter. The park is on Middle Road just off scenic MA 8 out of North Adams. There are several parking areas.

Savoy Mountain State Forest
Central Shaft Road, Florida
(413) 663-8469
www.massparks.org
Savoy Mountain State Forest encompasses 11,118 acres of land along the Hoosac Mountain Range in North Adams, Adams, Florida, and Savoy. The bulk of the land is in Savoy; in fact, the state forest takes up more than half the land in town. Nevertheless, the main entrance and headquarters are located in Florida on Central Shaft Road off MA 2. The forest is also accessible from Adams via Savoy Center Road and Savoy via Center Road off MA 116. With more than 60 miles of multiuse trails,

the forest offers four-season recreation. Spectacular natural features include Bog Pond, with its floating bog islands, and Tannery Falls, which cascades through a deep chasm, finally plunging over a precipice to a clear pool below. Much of the area was farmland that was abandoned after the Hoosac Tunnel was completed and there was no longer work for people in the area. During the 1930s the Civilian Conservation Corps (CCC) reforested this abandoned farmland with Norway and blue spruce and replaced older dams at Bog, Burnett, and Tannery Ponds. Apple trees interspersed throughout what is now a 45-site campground are the only reminder of its farming history. The remainder of the park includes the North Pond recreational day-use area and South Pond, where there are four log cabins available for rental year-round.

Summer uses include fishing, swimming, nonmotorized boating, horseback riding, and mountain biking. Off-road vehicles under 1,000 pounds are permitted. Universally accessible facilities include restrooms, campsites, cabins, picnic tables, trails, and swimming areas. Many roads through the area are closed in winter, but there are many trails open for snowmobilers and cross-country skiers. Hunting is permitted in season. Scattered throughout the forest are many historic cemeteries, another reminder of the past. Interpretive programs are offered by park staff.

Natural Bridge State Park
MA 8, North Adams
(413) 663-6392
www.massparks.org

This abandoned quarry, just off MA 8 north of the city, offers visitors a lesson in geology and, since the advent of MASS MoCA, art. While the geology is visible in the fascinating rock formations throughout the park, the art is not. In fact, it is a sound installation that can only be heard at dusk, when speakers hidden in the rocks emit eerie sounds, mingling with the evening sounds of birds, crickets, and the like. The park itself contains the only marble dam in North America, as well as an amazing natural marble arch, created centuries ago by melting glaciers. The "natural bridge" spans a brook that rushes and tumbles through a steep gorge. Paths lead to several ledges offering different views of this natural phenomenon. From 1810 to 1947, a marble quarry flourished here, producing coarse-grained white marble used in many buildings in the city. From 1950 to 1983 the quarry was operated as a privately owned tourist attraction, becoming a state park in 1985. The 42-acre site includes trails for easy walks or more energetic hiking and cross-country skiing. There are picnic tables and wheelchair-accessible restrooms.

Windsor Lake (Historic Valley Park)
Windsor Lake Road, North Adams
(413) 662-3198

Tucked away on the side of a hill on the east side of the city is this gem of a lake maintained by the City of North Adams. Pleasant beaches, picnic areas, a boat launching ramp, and a pavilion with bathhouses and restrooms are among the facilities. Historic Valley Campground, also operated by the city, is adjacent to the park. There are 100 wooded sites, most with water and electricity; modern restrooms; and hot showers. The Hoosac Tunnel can be viewed by taking a 15-minute walk from the campground. The park can be reached by taking Bradley Street off Church Street or via Kemp Avenue from MA 2 and following the campground signs.

Field Farm
Sloan Road, Williamstown
www.thetrustees.org

The 316 acres that make up Field Farm offer varied ecology and terrain, including forests, hedgerows, a swamp, marshes, meadows, fields, two streams, and a small spring-fed pond. At the north end of the farm, which has been a center of agriculture since at least 1750, is a 42-acre area called Caves Lot. Here small streams disappear into a series of underground channels and caves carved over the millennia

CLOSE-UP

Mount Greylock State Reservation

Mount Greylock Reservation encompasses 12,500 acres and is the oldest park in the state system. At 3,491 feet, the mountain itself is the highest peak in the state. The first parcel was acquired by the state in 1898. Since then additional parcels have been obtained to bring the reservation to its present size. According to history, the Mahicans who hunted in the area did not climb the mountain because they considered it sacred. The first European to do so was Jeremiah Wilbur, who in 1767 at the age of 14 set out to establish his farm. Over the course of time he cleared enough land to grow 100 tons of hay a year and tapped enough maple to produce 1,800 pounds of sugar in one season. He built a road to haul his produce to Adams, a path that eventually became part of Notch Road, one of two access roads to the summit, which is still in use. He raised cattle and sheep and harnessed the water power of Notch Brook, building a cider mill, a gristmill, and a sawmill. We can only imagine the hardships he endured as he worked the mountain that we travel and hike so easily today. His efforts might not have been recorded at all had it not been for the travels of Timothy Dwight, a retired Yale College president who toured upstate New York and New England in 1800 and published a book recording his observations in 1822. While in Williamstown he teamed up with Williams College president Ebenezer Fitch, who took him to Wilbur's spread. Together the three hiked to the summit, where they climbed trees to take in the view.

Visitors today do not have to go to such great lengths to enjoy that five-state vista, although those who are so inclined can climb an additional 100 feet to the top of the beacon known as the War Veterans Memorial Monument for the ultimate view. In 1937 the CCC built Bascom Lodge, a large stone structure at the peak that still provides meals and lodging to visitors, hikers, and campers. Blueberry pancakes served at sunrise are a treat not to be missed. The corps also paved and built guardrails on what are now the two main access roads to the summit: Notch Road from MA 2 in North Adams and Rockwell Road via North Main Street from US 7 in Lanesborough.

Although Mount Greylock is the highest peak in the reservation, there are others clustered in the area with more than 60 miles of trails for hiking, biking, and skiing. The summit and the roads to it are closed from late fall to spring but are open to snowmobiles provided there is enough snow coverage. There are 34 campsites, five group campsites, and five backpacker shelters available, many along the Appalachian Trail, which passes over the range. Wheelchair-accessible restrooms and viewing areas are provided at the summit. On the Adams side of the mountain, Greylock Glen, off West Road, has picnic areas and a swimming hole and trails for biking and hiking. Efforts to develop that area into a major economic draw for the town have been in the works for years. Even though the bulk of the mountain lies in Adams, you can't get to the summit from there—the road that Wilbur laid in the late 1700s from North Adams no longer meets its counterpart in Adams.

War memorial atop Mount Greylock. BERKSHIRE VISITORS BUREAU/A. BLAKE GARDNER

Even if the roads to the summit are closed, the park generally is open for hiking and cross-country skiing from sunrise until 30 minutes after sunset, except for snowmobiles, which are permitted to ride after dark. The visitor center on the Lanesborough side is open year-round from 9:00 A.M. to 4:00 P.M. Information on the trails and the reservation may be obtained here, and there are several interesting exhibits. The phone number is (413) 499–4262. Nature's Classroom (413–743–1591) runs Bascom Lodge, which is open mid-May to mid-October from 8:00 A.M. to 10:00 P.M. The Veterans Memorial is open daily Memorial Day to Labor Day, weekends only for the weeks preceding and following those dates. A parking fee was recently instituted at the summit, a first in the park's history. Information specifically about Mount Greylock may be obtained from the Department of Environmental Management's regional headquarters at (413) 442–8928 or www.massparks.org, or the Appalachian Mountain Club at (413) 528–6333 or www.amcberkshire.org. The Berkshire Natural Resources Council, a nonprofit conservation organization that aims to protect open space by acquiring large tracts of land through gift or purchase, has published an excellent guide and topographical map for Mount Greylock. Their office is at 20 Bank Row, Pittsfield 01201; (413) 499–0596. Their Web site is www.bnrc.net.

through limestone bedrock. There are more than 4 miles of moderate trails for hiking, cross-country skiing, and snowshoeing. There also are picnic tables and a nature center

On the property are modernist-style houses designed by Edwin Goodell and Ulrich Franzen. The Goodell house was built in 1948 for Lawrence and Eleanor Bloedel, whose family donated Field Farm to the Trustees of Reservations, which manages it now. Other properties were donated or purchased later to round out the reservation. Around the gardens and landscaped grounds are 13 sculptures, including works by Richard M. Miller and Herbert Ferber. Nine are part of a collection given by the Bloedel family to the Williams College Museum of Art. Overlooking the pond is the Folly, a shingled three-bedroom guest house designed in 1965 and furnished by Franzen, a noted modernist architect. There also is a five-room guest house that operates as a bed-and-breakfast year-round. (For more information about the guest house see the Accommodations chapter or call 413-458-3135.) Field Farm is open year-round from sunset to sundown, with no admission charge. The Folly is open for guided tours from noon to 5:00 P.M. on weekends from early June through Columbus Day for a nominal charge. Tours of the guest house are by appointment only. Sloan Road is just off Massachusetts Highway 43 near the US 7 intersection in South Williamstown.

i

The Department of Environmental Management is hoping to pave the roads that lead to the Mount Greylock summit and rebuild many of the crumbling railings and culverts the CCC installed in the 1930s. If the project moves forward, be prepared for Notch Road from MA 2 in North Adams or the access from Rockwell Road in Lanesborough to be closed from time to time. Call the visitor center (413-499-4262) for information.

Hopkins Memorial Forest
Williamstown
(413) 458-3080
www.williams.edu

The 2,500 acres that make up Hopkins Memorial Forest serve as a teaching tool as well as a community and recreational resource. Located on the eastern slopes of the Taconic Mountain Range, the forest encompasses land in bordering New York and Vermont. Once an assortment of abandoned fields, pastures, and woodlots, the land was deeded to Williams College in the 1930s. The USDA Forest Service managed the site as an experimental station from that time until the late '60s, leaving a legacy of permanent monitoring plots, historic land-use maps, stream-gauging stations, and genetic plantations. Since 1971 Hopkins Forest has been operated directly by Williams College for research and scholarly activities. In addition to now-unbroken stands of hardwoods, there are four weather stations and a field station that includes two labs, a classroom, an office, exhibit space, and networked computer facilities. A primary mission of the forest is to provide unique outdoor classroom and research experiences for Williams undergraduates, and several lab sections are routinely taught at the site. Many independent studies and honors thesis projects have been conducted at the forest. Various community events are held during the year, including a maple sugar festival and nature programs.

Margaret Lindley Park
US 7 and MA 2, Williamstown
(413) 458-3500 (Town Hall)

Margaret Lindley Park is a town park located at the junction of US 7 and MA 2 south of town. Lifeguards and changing rooms are provided. A fee is charged. No dogs, please! The Williamstown Rural Lands Foundation runs a children's nature program at the park. A number of walking trails are accessible here, including the Taconic Crest Trail.

Mountain Meadow Preserve
Williamstown
www.thetrustees.org
Mountain Meadow is a 176-acre preserve that lies along the Vermont border north of Williamstown. This protected area is teeming with wildlife, including animals large and small, reptiles, and butterflies. There are 4 miles of trails on the Williamstown side. One encircles and cuts through an upland meadow that is especially spectacular when filled with wildflowers in season. The other trail loops through the woodland and up a hill to a summit with views of Mount Greylock and the Taconic Range. Additional trails are located on the abutting Pownal, Vermont, portion of the preserve. Most of the property was a gift of Pamela B. Weatherbee, a town resident long interested in preserving the environment and protecting wildlife. The property is open from sunrise to sunset. Dogs on leashes are permitted. There are parking areas at the end of Mason Street, off US 7 north of town, or White Oaks Road, off Sand Springs Road, also off US 7. For more information call the regional office of the Trustees of Reservations in Stockbridge at (413) 298-3239 or check their Web site.

RECREATION 

The Berkshires are a year-round mecca for outdoor enthusiasts. While folks tend to divide activities into the four seasons, in reality there are two: winter—and the rest of the year. Generally, after the spring thaw myriad trails in the parks, forests, and preserves are open for hiking and walking. Mountain biking begins in earnest (hey, a little mud makes it more interesting!), and road racers are suddenly pedaling along the highways, curled over their handlebars. Fishing takes off, especially after the state has stocked the streams in late spring. If the weather cooperates, golf courses open sometime in May and local Little League and softball teams begin practicing. These activities continue into the fall, when baseball gives way to soccer and football, and hikers begin to pay attention to when hunting season starts. Come winter, the trails are taken over by cross-country skiers and snowmobilers. Shelters appear on the lakes, set up by ice fishermen determined to break the records held by previous fanatics. The ski slopes crank up, snowboarders go crazy, and suddenly it's a whole other world out there. This chapter divides recreation into those two "seasons": winter and the rest of the year. But because there's more of the rest of the year than winter (although it doesn't always seem like that!), we will lead off with activities that begin after winter ends.

These entries are arranged alphabetically and include descriptions of bowling alleys and fitness centers, which are open year-round. The biking section provides information about where to get in-line skates and skateboards. Winter activities and outfitters are grouped together at the end of the chapter.

BIKING

Mountain trails, paved highways, and rural back roads offer many opportunities for different kinds of biking in the Berkshires. There is no shortage of places to buy or rent bikes, and many are involved in racing or organizing trips. Beartown, Mount Greylock, Mount Washington, Pittsfield, and October Mountain State Forests allow mountain biking on designated trails. Maps are available at park headquarters or online at www.massparks.org. Mountain bike races are held weekly on a private course at Holiday Farm in Dalton. An $8.00 fee is charged, less for youngsters, and those who wish to enter weekend races must first be checked out on a Wednesday night. See www.holidayfarm.com for more information, or call (413) 684-0444. Jiminy Peak (www.jiminypeak.com) Resort in Hancock also offers mountain biking for experienced riders on 14 lift-served trails. Bring your own helmet, which is required, and bike. An all-day trail and lift pass is $20. Bucksteep Manor (www.bucksteep manor.com) in the town of Washington opens its 20 miles of cross-country ski trails to mountain biking. Bikes and helmets may be rented for $15 for four hours, $25 for the day.

The state highway department publishes the *Berkshire Bike Touring Map* showing the best roads for touring, with the caveat that cyclists must watch out for traffic at all times. See the Getting Around chapter for more about local roads. Detailed information about the map is available at www.massbike.org, Web site for the Massachusetts Bicycle Coalition, an organization that advocates for bicyclists. Rubel Bike Maps publishes a *Western Massachusetts Bicycle Map,* available from them at P.O. Box 411035, Cambridge 02140, or at www.bikemaps.com. The newly opened Ashuwillticook Rail Trail, described below, offers safe pedaling for 11 miles between Lanesborough and Adams. The trail also is popular with in-line skaters.

Road races are held often, many sponsored by the Berkshire Cycling Association, a grassroots bicycle racing club affiliated with the United States Cycling Federation, the National Off Road Bicycling Association, and the League of American Bicyclists. A complete list of sponsored races and other activities can be found on their Web site: www.berkshirecycling.org. Most popular for participants as well as spectators is the annual Josh Billings RunAground, a triathalon for bikers, rowers, and runners held in September. The Shaun Thornton Memorial Jiminy Peak Road Race, held in May, recently attracted 700 competitors, a record turnout for an event in the Northeast. This 74-mile loop originates at Jiminy Peak Resort in Hancock and is dedicated to the memory of one of the area's most promising racers, who died in 1993 at the age of 22. The Association also sponsors the 100-mile Mount Greylock Century Ride, described by one rider as "a nice lumpy ride" over four ascents. The Adams Chamber of Commerce sponsors a sanctioned biathalon in July called the Pedal and Plod that includes a 22-mile bike race.

South County

Arcadian Shop
91 Pittsfield Road, Lenox
(413) 637-3010, (800) 239-3391
www.arcadian.com
Knowledgeable staff; a full range of bikes, carriers, accessories, and attire; plus all kinds of information can be found at this outdoor specialty shop. Everyone here rides and has favorite places to recommend. Mountain and hybrid bikes, also called comfort bikes, are available for sale or rent. Brands include Trek, Bianchi, and Rocky Mountain. Test rides are encouraged. Staff also maintain and repair bikes, and parts are sold. Rental fees range from $35 for a full day to $100 for a week, excluding hybrids, which can be rented for $25 for up to four hours. The shop is located at one of the entrances to 500-acre Kennedy Park, where there are many trails for biking. Guide services are available by advance appointment, and inquiries are welcome. The shop also carries canoes and kayaks, hiking and camping gear, and, in winter, cross-country skis and snowshoes. They also have loads of maps, books, and guides for all kinds of outdoor recreation. Open daily.

Berkshire Bike & Blade
326 Stockbridge Road (U.S. Highway 7), Great Barrington
(413) 528-5555
www.bikeandblade.com
Located in the Great Barrington Plaza, next to Price Chopper Supermarket, Berkshire Bike & Blade carries a huge stock of bicycles, cycling-specific clothing and accessories plus in-line skates and skateboards. Owners Steffen Root and Dave Clark have been selling, renting, and servicing bikes since taking over the business in 1999, but Root's experience goes back to 1995, when he began working for the former owner. Hybrid bikes by Iron Horse and Diamondback may be rented for four hours for $20, $35 for 24 hours, including helmet and lock if needed. Deliveries within the local area may be arranged. Bicycles for sale include models by Giant, Janos, Devinci, and Santacruz. Purchasers are entitled to free complete tuneups worth about $45 for as long as they own their bike. Repairs and service for all makes are available. The stock includes all kinds of information about biking, including videos and CDs; bike racks, baby joggers, and really cool kid's tricycles. The shop also carries Roces brand in-line skates. Winter stock includes snowshoes and snowboards. Open daily year-round.

Expeditions
278 Main Street, Great Barrington
(413) 528-7737
www.skibutternut.com
Bicycles are just about the only thing not sold by Expeditions, but the shop does carry many accessories useful for recreational bikers, including helmets, sunglasses, Nixon watches, backpacks, and clothing. Skateboards and in-line skates by Salomon also are sold here.

Harland B. Foster
15 Bridge Street, Great Barrington
(413) 528-0546
Primarily known as a great hardware and tool store, Harland Foster also sells and repairs bicycles year-round. The stock includes hybrid and mountain bikes by Raleigh and Gary Fisher, children's BMX bikes, trailer bikes, jogger strollers, parts, tires, pumps, and accessories. Open Monday through Saturday.

Mean Wheels Bike Shop
57 Housatonic Street, Lenox
(413) 637-0644
www.mean-wheels.com
Cycling enthusiast Dave Drumm has been selling, servicing, and renting bikes since taking over Mean Wheels in 2000. He carries an assortment of bicycles, including Titus, Gary Fisher, Kona, and Felt. He rents hybrids for $35 a day, $29 for a half day, including helmet. The stock includes clothing and accessories, trailers, and maps. Dave likes to recommend rides to his customers and has drawn up several loops into Stockbridge, including one that takes folks past Tanglewood and the Norman Rockwell Museum on Massachusetts Highway 183. Kennedy Park also is a favorite. In summer he is closed on Sunday and Tuesday. Winter hours vary, so a call is recommended, especially if the skiing is good.

Central Berkshire

Ordinary Cycles
247 North Street, Pittsfield
(413) 442-7225
www.ordinarycycles.com
A founding sponsor of the Berkshire Cycling Association, Ordinary Cycles is owned by Thomas Martin, whose professional biking experience dates back to 1972. The shop has had several locations since opening in 1983 and is currently on North Street in downtown Pittsfield. Road, mountain, cyclocross, touring, BMX, comfort, and children's bikes are sold and serviced here. Accessories include clothing, shoes, and helmets. Located in Pittsfield's business district, the shop is open 9:30 A.M. to 5:30 P.M. Monday through Saturday in summer, Tuesday through Saturday the rest of the year, and until 8:00 P.M. every Thursday.

Plaine's Bike, Ski and Snowboard
55 West Housatonic Street (U.S. Highway 20), Pittsfield
(413) 499-0294, (888) 216-7122
www.plaines.com
Plaine's has been repairing, servicing, selling, and renting bicycles for at least 30 years. The large stock includes BMX, comfort, cruiser, freestyle, hybrid, mountain, and racing bikes plus bikes for kids. Custom bikes also can be built. Accessories, clothing, helmets, parts, trailers, and car racks are also available, as well as skateboards. Bikes rent for $18 to $25 a day, including a helmet and lock. The shop and large parking lot are on the corner of West Housatonic and Elizabeth Streets, at the Center Street traffic light. Their Web site also includes information about rides and races. Open daily.

North County

Berkshire Outfitters
169 Grove Street (Massachusetts Highway 8), Adams
(413) 743-5900
www.berkshireoutfitters.com
Located near Greylock Glen and across the way from the Ashuwillticook Rail Trail, with an access nearby, Berkshire Outfitters sells, repairs, and rents bicycles. Brands in stock include Schwinn, Iron Horse mountain bikes, KHS, and GT. Rentals run $15 for up to four hours or $19 for the day. Owner Steve Blazejewski also stocks Salomon in-line skates and roller skis, plus biking accessories, maps, and books. The shop also sells and rents kayaks and canoes and carries hiking and camping

CLOSE-UP

Ashuwillticook Rail Trail

The name is a tongue twister, but this recently opened paved trail is beautiful. Running from the Berkshire Mall in Lanesborough to the center of Adams, the 11-mile trail has developed into one of the most popular venues for outdoor activity in the county. Since opening in 2002, the 10-foot-wide path has attracted folks on bikes and in-line skates, families with baby carriages, people in wheelchairs, joggers, and walkers. In winter the snow-covered path is used for cross-country skiing. Snowmobiles are prohibited, since their treads could tear up the pavement. Aside from providing a place to bike or walk away from traffic, the trail has opened up an environmental wonderland, offering glimpses of birds and waterfowl, foxes, coyotes, and other critters. Benches along the way provide a place to rest and observe nature. Historical markers can be found along the path.

The trail parallels MA 8 between Adams and Lanesborough, passing along Cheshire Reservoir (aka Hoosac Lake) in the process and opening up new areas for shoreline fishing. There are large parking areas at the Berkshire Mall and at the Farnams Road crossing in Cheshire, where a park has been upgraded. Universally accessible comfort stations are located at both parking areas. After crossing MA 8, where extreme caution is advised, the trail runs through Cheshire, eventually following along the south branch of the Hoosic River into Adams, where a visitor center is located. The offices of the Berkshire Visitors Bureau recently moved from Pittsfield to this new center. There are additional parking areas in Cheshire on Church Street and in Adams on Harmony Street and the town parking lot off Hoosac Street. The path is lighted in populated areas.

Originally laid in 1867 by the predecessor of the Boston & Albany Railroad, the line was abandoned in 1990 after declining use by a succession of owners. Seeing the potential for recreational use of the corridor, a group of citizens organized to preserve the right-of-way. Seeking to reconnect people to local history and the natural environment, the committee chose to name the trail after the Native American word for that section of the Hoosic River. Pronounced *Ash-oo-will-ti-cook,* the name translates to "the pleasant river in between the hills." With political and local backing, the trail became a project of the state Department of Forests and Parks, which manages it with help from volunteers.

As plans for the trail were being developed, a group of bicyclists formed a nonprofit organization called the Berkshire Bike Path Council (413-442-5223). Members are dedicated to facilitating and maintaining bike path development in Berkshire County and would like to see the rail trail eventually extend through Pittsfield south to Great Barrington as well as north to North Adams. Their Web site, www.berkshirebikepath.org, provides updates on trail conditions, special events, and general information on biking in the Berkshires.

equipment and, in winter, cross-country skis. Closed Monday.

The Mountain Goat
130 Water Street, Williamstown
(413) 458-8445
The Mountain Goat sells, rents, and repairs bikes and organizes rides of varying length and skill. The Goat carries mainly Trek bikes, which can be rented for $25 for 24 hours or $15 for 4, including a helmet and lock. The select stock also includes accessories, footwear, and apparel for various seasons and activities, including lots of children's wear. Open daily.

The Spoke
279 Main Street (Massachusetts Highway 2), Williamstown
(413) 458-3456
www.thespoke.com
Paul Rinehart, coowner of the Spoke with Dave Lucznyski, has been involved with bike racing for more than 40 years as a racer, official, and coach. The Spoke organizes races as well as noncompetitive group road rides and sells road, mountain, comfort, BMX, and other bikes by Diamondback, Jamis, Bianchi, Felt, and others. The shop includes a full line of accessories, and there is a service department for repairs. Open Monday through Saturday.

Sports Corner
61 Main Street, North Adams
(413) 664-8654
Sports Corner, owned by Ron Hansen, sells and services Fuji and Marin mountain bikes, BMX and cruiser bikes, plus accessories, including trailers. The stock also includes running shoes and casual clothing. The staff recommends good places to mountain bike, which include Greylock Glen in Adams, the Taconic Crest Trail that runs between Petersburg, New York, and Pittsfield via Williamstown, and the Shady Pine Campground loop at Windsor Lake. In business since 1991, Sports Corner is open daily, but hours vary; a call might be a good idea.

BOATING

The Housatonic River is one of the most popular waterways for canoeing and kayaking, with the Williams a close second. The Berkshire Regional Planning Commission (www.berkshireplanning.org) and the Housatonic Valley Association (www.hvathewatershedgroup.org) have written a canoeing guide for both rivers that describes the flow and scenery along the way, with detailed maps that list all access points. The guide is available at outfitters and bookstores and sells for around $6.00. The Appalachian Mountain Club also has published a river guide titled *Discover the Berkshires of Massachusetts: AMC Guide to the Best Hiking, Biking, & Paddling,* available at some outfitters and from the AMC at 5 Joy Street, Boston 02108. The Berkshire Chapter of AMC, which encompasses all western Massachusetts, organizes various river trips. Check the AMC Web site, www.outdoors.org, for more information.

The Massachusetts Audubon Society (www.massaudubon.org) offers guided trips on the Housatonic River and Goose Pond in Lee. Information may be obtained from the local sanctuary in Lenox (413-637-0320). Other pleasant paddling can be found on the Hoosic River in North County, which flows from Cheshire Reservoir. Also called Hoosac Lake, the reservoir also is a good place to paddle around in. Despite its title, the *North Berkshire Outdoor Guide,* published by the Williams College Outing Club, describes good places for paddling all around the county. While Pontoosuc in Pittsfield is inviting, it's best to stick to early or late hours—motorboats, personal watercraft, and other traffic abounds during the season's peak. Many of the state parks have carry-in access to ponds and lakes. See the Parks chapter for detailed descriptions, or check the Department of Environmental Management's Web site (www.massparks.org) or call the regional office at (413) 442-8928. Some outfitters that rent kayaks and canoes can arrange for guides, and all are great sources for information. Several places to stay, including resorts, organize trips or refer guests to places to paddle.

While the Housatonic seems pretty bucolic, there are some areas that should be avoided by inexperienced paddlers and other sections that can be downright dangerous for anyone. For those who like white water, the Deerfield River next door in northern Franklin County can be pretty exciting, especially after a water release from one of the hydroelectric plants. Zoar Outdoor Outfitters in Charlemont is a leader in white-water rafting. Visit www.zoaroutdoor.com or call (413) 339-8596 or (800) 532-7483 for information. There are races in Huntington in spring when the Westfield River is rushing. Locally, a stretch of the Farmington River between Otis and Sandisfield is good for white-water paddling in spring and in the fall when the Otis Reservoir dam is opened.

Sculling is a recent addition to the ways in which you can enjoy the lakes and ponds of the area, thanks to the Berkshire Rowing and Sculling Society (BRASS). Formed in 1995 this nonprofit organization is based at Burbank Park on Onota Lake in Pittsfield, where lessons are offered for all ages and shells are available for hourly rental May through October. BRASS also sells sculls, instructs rowing teams, and sponsors a regatta in September. For more information visit www.berkshiresculling.com or call (413) 442-7769 for a brochure or to make a reservation.

Canoe and Kayak Tours

Berkshire Canoe Tours
151 Bull Hill Road, Lanesborough
(413) 442-2789

Hilary Bashara leads canoe tours from Decker's Landing on the Housatonic River in Lenox by appointment. She has 14 canoes available for use by her clients and is adding kayaks. She charges $30 per adult, $24 per child, which includes water and apples for the trip, which lasts about five hours down and back. Along the way she will point out the abundant wildlife, which often includes hawks, eagles, blue or green herons, and other river inhabitants. Hilary also leads hikes on foot in summer and on snowshoes in winter.

i

In late afternoon, westerly winds often kick up that can make lake paddling difficult if you have to head back in that direction. Also keep an eye on the sky—the weather can be quite changeable.

Greylock Discovery Tours
P.O. Box 2231, Lenox 01240
(413) 637-4442

Greylock Discovery Tours arranges outings for groups or individuals in the Berkshires and beyond. The company started out offering guided hikes but has branched out into kayaking and canoeing. Tours of cultural institutions also can be arranged. The firm specializes in developing tours for corporate outings that can include team-building experiences. Prices vary, depending on the service.

Outfitters and Boat Dealers

SOUTH COUNTY

Arcadian Shop
91 Pittsfield Road, Lenox
(413) 637-3010, (800) 239-3391
www.arcadian.com

Kayaks and canoes are sold and rented at this all-season outfitter. Rentals, including paddles and safety equipment, are $35 a day for singles, $60 for tandems. Staff offers instruction, and guide services can be arranged. Recommended trips include gliding down the Housatonic from Decker's Canoe Launch on East New

Lenox Road in Pittsfield to Wood's Pond in Lenox. Goose Pond in Lee and Stockbridge Bowl also are favorites. Staff will transport boats by arrangement. Arcadian also sells and rents bicycles and attire and supplies for hiking and backpacking and in winter sells and rents cross-country skis. Open daily.

Expeditions
276 Main Street, Great Barrington
(413) 528-7737
www.skibutternut.com/expeditions
Expeditions rents kayaks and will arrange guided tours on the Housatonic River. A single-seat kayak may be rented for $35 a day, including paddles and life vest, or $55 for a two-seater. Car-top carriers and straps are available. Kayaks also are sold. Demonstrations are held weekly on a pond at Butternut Ski Area off Massachusetts Highway 23. Owned by Butternut, Expeditions also carries hiking equipment and other recreational accessories and garb, plus maps, guides, books, and of course skis and snowboards in winter.

CENTRAL BERKSHIRE

Onota Boat Livery
463 Pecks Road, Pittsfield
(413) 442-1724
This full-service marina on Onota Lake sells and rents all kinds of boats, including pontoon boats, runabouts, sport boats, and nonmotorized boats, including canoes, rowboats, pedal boats, and one- and two-person kayaks. Nonmotorized boats may be rented for $10 an hour, $30 for four hours, and $45 for a day. Kayaks for two cost $15 an hour, $45 for four, and $60 for eight. Rates for motorized boats vary according to length, size of motor, and steering method. Rentals for pontoon boats that can hold 7, 8, or 10 persons also vary depending on the day, length of time, and size. The largest rented for a full day will cost $300. Fees include fuel and life vests. Deposits are required, some in cash, and reservations are suggested, especially for weekends. Trailers are available for sale or rent. Mercury and Honda outboard motors and Volvo and Mercruiser sterndrives are sold and serviced here. Servicing is available at other lakes in the area by appointment. Dock space can be rented and boats stored for the winter. Open daily except for Christmas, New Year's Day, and Easter. The livery is off Peck's Road, which runs along the northeastern shore of Lake Onota between Hancock Road to the north and Wahconah Street to the east.

Quirk's Marine
990 Valentine Road, Pittsfield
(413) 447-7512
Located in an old mill on the corner of Valentine and Pecks Roads, Quirk's sells and services boats and accessories, including safety equipment, lubricants, and oils. Motorboats, canoes, kayaks, and paddlers, plus tubes of all sizes and water skis are available here. Trailers and hitches also are sold. The firm also stores boats for the winter.

Tony's Berkshire Boats
483 West Housatonic Street (US 20), Pittsfield
(413) 443-6475
Tony Cera sells pontoon boats, Yamaha motors, tubes, waterboards, and skis and accessories, including really cool life jackets for kids. Boats may be rented, but only by the month. The shop, located on the outskirts of the city, is open Monday through Saturday from May through November. Call for winter hours.

Wild 'n' Wet Sport Rentals
US 7, Lanesborough
(413) 445-5211
Owner John Casey sets up shop in Lanesborough on the shore of Pontoosuc Lake, off US 7 next to Matt Reilly's Pub and Restaurant. In summer he rents canoes and kayaks, pontoon boats, paddleboats, tubes, and personal watercraft. The latter are capable of seating three and are powered by quiet four-stroke engines. They may be rented for $69 for 30 minutes or

$124 for an hour. One person may rent a canoe or kayak for two hours for $20.

Pontoon boats come in two sizes: A small one that holds 6 to 8 folks rents for $135 for two hours; the larger one, capable of holding 10 to 12, rents for $170. Paddleboats that can seat up to five persons rent for $28 for two hours. Casey also arranges for water-skiing and tube rides by reservation in the morning, when the lake is calm. He sets up shop on weekends in May and then daily from around the end of June through Labor Day, weather permitting. In winter he rents snowmobiles and leads tours. His mailing address is P.O. Box 2284, Lenox 01240.

YMCA Marina
US 7, Pittsfield
(413) 499-0694

The Pittsfield YMCA (413-499-7650) operates this marina on the eastern shore of Pontoosuc Lake just off US 7. Canoes and rowboats may be rented for $10 an hour. Sailboats, sunfish, and others may be rented for $20 to $35 an hour, depending on the craft. Membership in the YMCA is not required, but members get $5.00 off rental fees. Reservations are suggested. The Y also leases moorings at $300 for the season, which are used by private sailors, many of whom are members of the Pontoosuc Sailing Club and/or the Berkshire Community Sailing Association. Sailing lessons are offered by Richard Cote of the BCSA. He may be reached at (413) 684-3106 or through BSCA at www.rcote0.tripod.com. The association also sponsors regattas and races. The marina is open afternoons during the week and 10:00 A.M. to 6:00 P.M. on weekends, weather permitting.

NORTH COUNTY

Berkshire Outfitters
169 Grove Street (MA 8), Adams
(413) 743-5900
www.berkshireoutfitters.com

Established in 1976, Berkshire Outfitters carries recreational boats that are light, stable, and user-friendly. Canoes and kayaks, paddles, carriers, safety equipment, accessories, and information are available here from either Steve Blazejewski, whose father founded the business, or his son. The stock includes Old Town canoes, which sell for around $350, plus models from Mad River, Ranger, Perception, Seda, We-No-Nah, Boreal, and Dagger. Canoes and kayaks may be rented for $22 or $32 a day, depending on size. Berkshire Outfitters is located near Cheshire Reservoir (Hoosac Lake) and across the way from the Hoosic River, where there is a nearby launch area. Transportation to nearby Cheshire Reservoir may be arranged if you don't have a carrier. The shop also carries camping and hiking equipment, in-line skates, and bicycles, which he also rents. In winter, cross-country skis and other seasonal gear are on hand. Open every day except Monday.

BOWLING

Cove Lanes
109 Stockbridge Road (US 7), Great Barrington
(413) 528-1220

There are 24 lanes plus an indoor miniature golf course and a small arcade at Cove Lanes. Friday and Saturday nights are devoted to "cosmic bowling" with disco lighting and popular music designed to appeal to teens and young adults. There is a snack bar and separate enclosed lounge. Cove is open year-round. In summer Tuesday night is designated for senior and junior leagues. The rest of the year, leagues meet on Saturday morning.

Imperial Bowl
555 Dalton Avenue, Pittsfield
(413) 443-4453

Imperial has 14 candlepin lanes plus a pool table, a lounge with a bar, a full kitchen with homemade specials at meal times, and a dining area. Imperial is open daily in winter. Summer hours vary, so a call ahead is a good idea.

Ken's Bowl
495 Dalton Avenue, Pittsfield
(413) 499-0733
With 50 tenpin lanes, there is always an open lane at Ken's. There's also a cocktail lounge and a snack bar that serves hot dogs, pizza, burgers, and nachos. During summer Ken's Bowl is open Friday through Sunday, daily in winter. Leagues meet fall through winter, but there is usually an open lane at night and always one during the day.

Mt. Greylock Bowl
Roberts Drive, North Adams
(413) 664-9715
Located off MA 2 on the west side of the city, Mt. Greylock Bowl has a pro shop, pool table, and some arcade games. Recent renovations added a new sound system, usually used for teen "Rock 'n' Bowl" nights, and automatic scoring. Food is available from a larger-than-you-might-expect menu and can be eaten at the sizable counter or in the lounge. Labor Day through May, leagues meet Monday through Saturday morning but the rest of the weekend is open. During summer, lanes are available on Wednesday and Thursday and on Saturday afternoon.

Valley Park Bowl
1274 Curran Highway (MA 8), North Adams
(413) 664-9715
Valley Park Bowl has 18 candlepin lanes with automatic scoring, two pool tables, and about 25 arcade games, plus a lounge that serves light fare and is open late. A separate restaurant on the premises has a full menu and is open Wednesday through Saturday. September through April Valley Park is open daily, with leagues meeting every day except Saturday afternoon. However, management says there are always lanes open. In summer the place is closed Sunday through Tuesday. Call for hours for other days.

FISHING

Hundreds of rivers, streams, and lakes in the Berkshires give anglers of all abilities and styles a shot at rainbows, browns, brookies, bass, northern pike, chain pickerel, tiger muskies, and, believe it or not, salmon. There also is the usual assortment of panfish, including pumpkinseed, perch, crappies, and sunfish. The Massachusetts Department of Fisheries and Wildlife stocks many of the county's lakes, rivers, and streams. The department's Web site (www.masswildlife.org) is full of data about stocking and other topics, including creel limits and catch-and-release zones. Printed information is available at the regional office located in Pittsfield at 400 Hubbard Avenue (413-447-9789), which also sells licenses. The cost varies, depending on age, length of time, and whether the applicant is a resident or a visitor. The basic yearlong license for a resident between the ages of 18 and 65 costs $27.50. Seniors and youngsters 15 to 17 pay less. A three-day license costs $12.50. Nonresidents may obtain a three-day license for $12.50 or a yearlong one for $37.50. Licenses also may be bought at some outfitters and sporting goods shops, which are great sources of information; discount stores like Wal-Mart; and some but not all town clerks. A complete list of sources can be found on the Web site. These nonstate sources are allowed to tack on a handling fee, which can range from 50 cents to $1.50.

State parks and forests are full of great places to fish. A boat ramp fee of $5.00 is charged at state parks. Check the Parks chapter for more information or the Department of Environmental Management's Web site at www.massparks.org. Or call the DEM's regional office in Pittsfield at (413) 442-8928. Armed with topo maps and local lore, some folks like to hike along old logging roads up into the hinterlands to fish little-known spots. Others are just as happy to pull off the highway and grab some trout for supper on the way home from work. Of course everyone has his or her own favorite spot, method, bait, or lure.

You might see a fully outfitted fly-caster working a stream while a youngster nearby is hauling in the browns using corn kernels for bait. Go figure.

It would be unfair not to mention rivers known for their fine fishing that touch on or originate in the Berkshires but are largely located in adjacent counties. In North County the Deerfield passes through the town of Florida on its way east to Greenfield, where it joins the Connecticut River. Considered one of the coldest and cleanest of the waterways in western Massachusetts, the Deerfield is well stocked with rainbow, brown, and brook trout. It is also a site for Atlantic salmon restoration. The river passes through forests and gorges, and much of the bed is rock-strewn. Cleated waders and wading sticks are recommended for sure footing. There are two designated catch-and-release areas along the river, where the use of live bait is prohibited. One is between the east portal of the Hoosac Tunnel in Florida and Fife Brook in Rowe. The other is a section in Charlemont between Pelham Brook and the Mohawk Campground. The Deerfield, with its deep runs and riffles, has 10 hydroelectrical plants along its shores, and sudden water releases from dams at those locations can make this a challenging river to fish. While white-water rafters find this sudden release a thrill, it can be dangerous. If you are within earshot of one of these plants, you will hear a warning blast on a horn prior to a release. If you are farther downstream, you should pay attention to watermarks on nearby rocks; if you see the level start to rise, get out fast.

The east branch of the Westfield River originates in Savoy and continues on through Windsor and Cummington, where it flows along Massachusetts Highway 9 before heading south to Chester. There it merges with the west branch, which originates in Becket. The two then flow to Huntington, merging with the middle branch, which flows from Worthington. Be wary of another catch-and-release area along the east branch, where live bait is prohibited.

Also famous for trout fishing is the Battenkill River in southern Vermont, where Orvis was spawned, so to speak. The river can be reached and fished, canoed, or tubed in a nice day's outing.

About those salmon. They are "retired" broodstock from the Anadromous Fish Restoration Project run by the U.S. Fish & Wildlife Service at the White River National Fish Hatchery in Vermont and the Roger Reed Salmon Hatchery in Palmer. When available, salmon are being released into several lakes, including Laurel Lake and Goose Pond in Lee, Onota Lake in Pittsfield, and Windsor Pond in Windsor.

The Housatonic is the largest and longest river in the county. Its headwaters are in Hinsdale on the east and Lanesborough on the west. The two branches converge in Pittsfield, forming the main stem that flows all the way through Connecticut to Long Island Sound. Unfortunately much of the riverbed is contaminated with polychlorinated biphenyls (PCBs), a suspected carcinogen that was used in the production of transformers at the General Electric plant in Pittsfield until 1970. A $250 million cleanup of the river is under way, but for now fishing is restricted to catch-and-release, especially between the plant and Woods Pond in Lenox. For more information about this complex and extensive project being undertaken jointly by GE and the federal Environmental Protection Agency, see www.housatonic-river.com, Web site for the Housatonic River Initiative, a citizens' group actively involved in the cleanup, or the EPA's Web site at www.epa.gov/region01/ge/. In addition to the PCB warning, the state Department of Public Health has issued a statewide advisory warning pregnant women, women of childbearing age who may become pregnant, nursing mothers, and children under 12 years of age to refrain from eating freshwater fish because of possible mercury contamination. The advisory does not apply to fish stocked by the state or to farm-raised freshwater fish sold commercially. For more information visit www.mass.gov/dph and search for "fish advisory."

Despite its man-made problems, the Housatonic is a beautiful and fertile river, easily reached as it meanders through miles of farmland and wooded valleys. Hatches of mayflies and caddis are tempting treats for the vigorous trout population, which includes some sizable browns. These hardy descendants of tributary stockings run from one to three pounds, with an occasional lunker weighing up to six pounds. There are many good, easily accessible fishing spots along the river—too many to list here—but some favorites include a stretch below the Glendale Dam along MA 183 in Stockbridge and several spots along US 20 between Lee and Stockbridge.

The Housatonic Fly Fisherman's Association, based in Hamden, Connecticut, maintains a premiere trout fishery and has published a guide titled *Fishing the Housatonic River Trout Management Area* that includes a river-specific fly hatching chart, angling tips, and other information. The association's address is P.O. Box 5092, Hamden, CT 06518. Another good resource is *A Canoeing Guide for the Housatonic River in Berkshire County,* published by the Berkshire County Regional Planning Commission and the Housatonic Valley Association. Detailed maps show access points, and the text describes flow and even throws in some fishing tips. The booklet also covers the Williams River and sells at outfitters and bookstores for around $6.00.

Aside from the Housatonic, rivers known for good trout fishing in South County include the Konkapot, Green, Williams, and Farmington. The Konkapot flows out of Lake Garfield in Monterey as a small, swampy rill. Fed by Lake Buel in New Marlborough and a few streams along the way, it continues into Connecticut before returning to Massachusetts in Sheffield. Several good spots for dry fly-fishing can be found along the Clayton–Mill River Road.

The Green River flowing through Alford, Egremont, and Great Barrington has some of the best water quality in Berkshire County. It is home for many stream-born brown trout and brookies as well as stocked rainbows. The undercut banks, roots, and pools are great for the trout, but they do make for tricky fishing. One really handy access point is in Great Barrington, just a mile outside town on MA 23 West, near the intersection of Massachusetts Highway 41 South. Just park at the bridge and go fishing! Incidentally, some folks say that Alford Brook is one of the best fishing streams in Berkshire County.

The Williams River flows between Lake Mansfield in Great Barrington and Shaker Mill Pond in West Stockbridge. While much of the river travels through private property, there are several access points used by canoeists and kayakers. One is at a bridge on MA 41 in West Stockbridge. Another is at the end of Wyantenuck Street in Great Barrington at a town park known as Old Maids. The river is slow and shallow here, with several beautiful fishing spots.

The Farmington River begins in Becket and continues through Otis, Sandisfield, and Tolland before crossing into Connecticut, where it eventually forms the Colebrook Reservoir. Boggy at its headwaters, the Farmington becomes an attractive place to fish beginning in Otis, where it follows along MA 8, offering many accessible yet quiet, contemplative spots to cast a line. With lots of pools, riffles, and runs, that stretch can be waded nearly all the way to the reservoir and is well stocked with rainbows and browns. Clam and Buck Rivers, both in Sandisfield, feed into the Farmington and are both stocked with trout by the state.

Other trout-stocked waters in South County include the following brooks: Seekonk (Alford); Hubbard (Egremont); Thomas, Palmer, and West (Great Barrington); Beartown, Greenwater, and Washington Mountain (Lee); Hop (Lee and Tyringham); Rawson (Monterey); Umpachene (New Marlborough); Dimmock (Otis); Hubbard (Sheffield); Marsh (Stockbridge); and Cone and Flat Brooks in West Stockbridge.

Otis Reservoir, which covers 1,065 acres in Otis and Tolland, is the largest lake in the state. It supports a diverse fish population in its relatively shallow waters. Motorized boats are permitted, and there are two marinas at the northern end of the reservoir, where one of two public access ramps is located on Reservoir Road. The other ramp is in Tolland State Forest near the park entrance, off East Otis Road from the south or New State Forest Road, which runs from Reservoir Road. The latter is off MA 8. The fish population includes trout, smallmouth and largemouth bass, chain pickerel, northern pike, brown bullheads, white and yellow perch, tiger muskies, and salmon. Fishing for trout is good up to midsummer and picks up again in late September after fall stocking by the state. Smallmouth bass fishing is best here from May through July. Also in Otis is Benton Pond, which is stocked with trout, smallmouth bass, chain pickerel, white and yellow perch, and brown bullheads.

Laurel Lake, shared by Lee and Lenox, is best accessed off US 20, where there is a large parking area and a wide boat launch suitable for small craft. Also known as Scotch or Scotts Pond, Laurel Lake is stocked with thousands of trout in spring, with a follow-up stocking later in fall. According to a recent survey, the lake contains chain pickerel, yellow and white perch, rock bass, bluegill, pumpkinseed, black crappie, carp, brown bullhead, white sucker, rainbow smelt, and golden sucker. Salmon are stocked here when available and the lake has some deep spots where these landlocked beauties like to hang out, along with some really big trout.

Goose Pond in Lee is populated with stocked trout, large- and smallmouth bass, chain pickerel, yellow perch, and brown bullheads. In Monterey, Buel and Garfield Lakes are stocked with trout. Benedict Pond also contains largemouth bass, yellow perch, and brown bullheads. All three have public boat launches.

Thousand Acre Swamp is a 155-acre very shallow pond about 6 miles south of New Marlborough center off Massachusetts Highway 57. It is considered one of the best warm-water fishing spots in the Berkshires. With a maximum depth of just 8 feet, it is perfect for the weed beds so beloved by bass. Submerged tree stumps provide another favorite hideout, giving those seeking to hook a bass a run for their money. Chain pickerel, yellow perch, and brown bullheads can also be found here. The public access boat launch is off Hotchkiss Road, off Norfolk Road, south of the town's center; or from East Hill Road, south off MA 57.

i

Take home panfish to promote better growth rates.

Nestled in the valley, Stockbridge Bowl is a beautiful 372-acre pond, but recreational use makes fishing this lake virtually impossible during the summer months. However, the Bowl is a great spot for trout fishing during spring and fall, thanks to regular stockings by the state. The Bowl also has a population of large- and smallmouth bass, chain pickerel, yellow perch, and brown bullheads. Boats may be launched from a double concrete ramp off MA 183 on the northwestern shore, where there also is a large parking area.

Greenwater Pond in Becket is sandwiched between US 20 and the Massachusetts Turnpike and is the first Berkshire body of water travelers on the pike from the east see as they head toward the Lee exit. Unfortunately there are no ramps or parking lots, and access to its 88 acres is limited to a few spots along US 20. The pond is moderately productive, but you might snag a smallmouth bass. Because the water is cold enough for trout to survive from year to year, browns weighing around five pounds have been reported.

Central Berkshire

The east branch of the Housatonic River begins in Hinsdale and flows through Dalton to Pittsfield, offering many fine spots for fishing along the way. It is stocked by the state, and the trout are edible, unlike

CLOSE-UP

The Berkshire Fishing Club

Located in Becket is the Berkshire Fishing Club, a secluded reserve with a 125-acre lake that was created and stocked some 33 years ago. Renowned for its superior bass fishing, the lake has yielded largemouths weighing up to six pounds. Chain pickerel measuring around 33 inches and pumpkinseeds up to 8 inches in length also have been caught. It is entirely possible to snag up to nearly ten fighting fish an hour in this catch-and-release lake. The club is the brainchild of Allen Strassler, who in 1998 negotiated with the owners to lease their 850-acre wooded tract to create a completely secluded reserve for avid anglers. Open May to October, this unique resource is a mere 10 miles or so from the Lee exit on the Massachusetts Turnpike. Seasonal memberships are sold for $1,500 per family, which includes a guest plus the use of boats, fishing equipment, and enjoyment of the property for hiking, picnicking, or hanging out in the log clubhouse, where showers, satellite TV, and Internet access are available. To keep traffic to a minimum on the lake, reservations are required. Trial memberships are offered for around $250. Additional fees may be charged, depending on the kind of boat chosen. Kayaks, canoes, and flat-bottomed bass boats with motors are available. The club also offers spinning-reel and fly-fishing classes where you will learn everything from fish biology, entomology, water reading, selecting flies, and rigging lures to casting techniques and fish handling. Fees are $75 for half a day, $150 for a full day, and include a three- to four-hour fishing excursion on the lake. For more information see the club's Web site, www.berkshirefishing. com, or call (413) 243-5761. The club's address is 398 Plumb Road, Becket, but mail is received at P.O. Box 83, Great Barrington 01230.

the fish caught south of Pittsfield, where several miles of the riverbed is polluted with no-longer-used industrial chemicals. Other good sources for trout in Hinsdale include Bennett Brook; Ashmere Lake, which also has small- and largemouth bass and yellow perch; and Plunkett Reservoir. The latter is a shallow 73-acre warm-water pond with an average depth of 10 feet and a maximum of 22 feet. It is on Plunkett Road, reached by Michael's Road off MA 8. An informal access suitable for small craft can be found here. Beyond this is a causeway, the only public fishing spot available along the built-up shore. The annual spring trout stocking makes for lively fishing into early summer. Largemouth bass also can be found here, particularly along the dam and in a cove at the north end. In Dalton trout also are stocked in Sackett and Wahconah Falls Brooks.

The west branch of the Housatonic River originates in Lanesborough, where Secum and Town Brooks, both good sources for trout, flow into Pontoosuc Lake. The outflow from the lake forms the west branch, which traverses through Pittsfield's inner city before joining with the southwest branch, which originates in Richmond and is stocked by the state. The two then converge with the east branch in south Pittsfield at Fred Garner River Park on Pomeroy Avenue, forming the main stem of the Housatonic.

Trout-stocked streams in Pittsfield include Daniel, Jacoby, Lulu Cascade, Sackett, and Smith Brooks. Onota and Pontoosuc Lakes also are stocked with trout. Onota, on the city's west side, is popular for fishing as well as boating and tends to be busy. Encompassing 617 acres, Onota's average depth is 22 feet, with a maximum of 66 feet. Aquatic vegetation is abundant in shallow spots. Burbank Park on the east side of the lake has a fishing pier that is designed for wheelchair users, a double concrete boat ramp, and a large parking lot. It can be reached by taking Valentine Road to Lakeway Drive. Another popular location for shore fishing is the Dan Casey causeway at the north end of the lake. The Causeway runs between Churchill Street and Pecks Road, and there is a wide shoulder for parking. Onota boasts an exceptional diversity of fish, including northern pike, large- and small-mouth bass, chain pickerel, and yellow perch. Stocked twice a year, trout dominate, including trophy-size natives. Salmon are stocked when they are available.

Pontoosuc Lake's 480 acres lie along US 7, half in Pittsfield and half in Lanesborough. While most of the shore is developed, there are several spots for shoreline fishing along the highway and off. In Lanesborough, folks use causeways at Bull Hill Road, off US 7, and Narragansett Avenue on the west shore. In Pittsfield there are areas around the YMCA boathouse and nearby parking lots off the highway. The shore at the southern tip of the lake near the Hancock Road dam also is a popular place. Also off Hancock Road is a sizable boat ramp with a large parking lot for vehicles with trailers. Motorized boats and personal watercraft are permitted, and the lake can get pretty busy in summer. The best times for fishing are weekdays during early morning and late afternoon. The lake is stocked with tiger muskies and trout. Lots of submerged trees and weeds make a nice habitat for bass, and some records have been set here. Chain pickerel, yellow perch, bluegills, yellow bullheads, and black crappie are abundant.

Richmond Pond is located in Richmond and Pittsfield between MA 41 and Swamp Road. Much of the shoreline of this 218-acre pond is developed with seasonal and year-round homes, but there is a public access point with a concrete ramp; a sizable parking lot on the western shore suitable for canoes, kayaks, and shallow-draft trailer boats; and an informal access on the southwestern shore. Rainbows define the fishing here, but browns and brookies also can be found along with 11 other species, including bass, chain pickerel, yellow perch, and brown bullheads. With a maximum depth of 53 feet, the pond is noted for its transparency. The state stocks Richmond Pond as well as Cone, Furnace, and Mount Lebanon Brooks.

North County

There are two rivers in North County that offer good fishing: the Hoosic and the Green (no relation to the Green River in South County). The Hoosic River has three main arteries. The south branch begins in Lanesborough on the MA 8 side of town and flows into the Cheshire Reservoir before running through Adams and on into North Adams. The north branch begins in Clarksburg and converges with the south branch in North Adams, where the main stem then flows on to Williamstown. The Hoosic eventually makes its way to the Hudson River in New York, passing through Vermont. The main stem has a good supply of stream-born brown trout but unfortunately the river suffers from past industrial pollution; from North Adams to Williamstown it's strictly catch-and-release. However, both branches are pollution free, although the south branch sometimes gets too warm as it passes through concrete flood-control chutes in Adams. Nevertheless there is plenty of good fishing along both branches, which are well-stocked with rainbows and browns that take advantage of reliable hatches of mayflies and caddis. Probably the best fishing on the Hoosic may be had between Cheshire and Adams. Anthony, Southwick, and Tophet Brooks in Adams are also stocked with trout, as are Dry, Kitchen, Penniman, Thunder, and South Brooks in Cheshire; Hudson Brook in Clarksburg; and Notch Brook and Windsor Lake in North Adams. Farther east in Savoy, Center Brook, Chickley River, and Cold River are stocked along with the east branch of the Westfield River.

On the other side of the county, the Green River presents a gorgeous stretch of lively waters with plenty of formal and informal access points along Massachusetts Highway 43 in south Williamstown. Most notable is a point just beyond a stone fence at the entrance to Mount Hope Farm, where you will find steep but negotiable stony banks and tumbling waterfalls. The river, including its west branch, spills out of the mountains from New Ashford and Hancock and is heavily stocked by the state with rainbows and browns that mingle with the stream natives. It may mess with your head, but the Green and the Hoosic Rivers both flow north. Broad, Hemlock, and Roaring Brooks in Williamstown also are stocked with trout. Some good fishing may be had in Hancock in the Kinderhook, which eventually flows to the Hudson River, and Berry Pond, both off MA 43. Jiminy Peak Resort also offers trout fishing.

Like most of the county's lakes, Cheshire Reservoir is man-made, dammed in the 1800s for industrial use. Also called Hoosac Lake, it comprises three basins covering 418 acres, two of which are excellent for fishing. Avoid the picturesque but weed-filled southern bowl (though it is fabulous for bird-watching) and concentrate on the middle and northern ponds. The northern basin has benefitted from an intensive weed-control program and has good public access off MA 8, where parking has been expanded to accommodate both anglers and persons who want to walk, bike, or in-line skate the Ashuwillticook Rail Trail. The rail trail runs along the entire eastern flank of all three basins, and some good shoreline fishing can be had, especially in the evening hours. There also is access to both the northern and middle basins from a wide causeway at Farnums Road, just off MA 8, though you may have to compete with the Canada geese that congregate there.

East of Adams off Massachusetts Highway 8A/116 is Windsor Pond, a small but fairly deep pond averaging 21 feet in depth with a maximum of 53 feet. With rainbows and brookies stocked annually in spring, it's a good trout fishery, but pressure is high through the end of May. Eleven species can be found here, including largemouth bass, chain pickerel, yellow perch, and brown bullheads. Located about 0.5 mile from the highway on Windsor Pond Road, the pond has a surfaced ramp that will accommodate shallow- to moderate-draft tailored boats. Windsor Jambs and Windsor Brooks also are trout-stocked.

i ***Best Bets for Trophy Bass: Ashmere Lake in Hinsdale; Goose Pond in Lee; Benedict Pond, Lake Buel, and Lake Garfield in Monterey; Three Mile Pond in Sheffield; and Center Pond in Becket.***

Ice Fishing

Pontoosuc Lake in Pittsfield is renowned for its large tiger muskies as well as good pike. The world record for a tiger muskie caught with a tip-up through the ice is held by local angler Jim Lambert, who hauled a 27-pounder out of Pontoosuc on the last day of December 2001. Onota Lake, also in Pittsfield, also has yielded some record-breaking pike, while Cheshire Reservoir is famous for the northern pike taken through the ice there. Laurel Lake, in Lee and Lenox, also is popular for pickerel, yellow perch, and panfish, as are Stockbridge Bowl, Richmond Pond, and Thousand Acre Swamp.

CLOSE-UP

Aquaculture in the Berkshires

The Berkshire National Fish Hatchery is located on 148 spring-fed acres that originally were the private preserve of John Sullivan Scully, an avid trout fisherman. In 1914 the reserve was donated to the government by his family and served as a hatchery until a cut in federal funds forced it to close in 1994. After several years of neglect and vandalism, it was rescued by Kenneth Bergstrom, a former commercial trout farmer who founded the Western Massachusetts Center for Sustainable Aquaculture at Hampshire College in Amherst. Working with state and federal wildlife officials and a corps of dedicated volunteers, Bergstrom revived the hatchery, which was reopened in 1999. Its mission is to make aquaculture—the cultivation of fish for food, educational, and recreational purposes—a sustainable industry.

Now overseen by a nonprofit foundation, Berkshire Hatchery has been restored and is open to the public. Informal tours of the hatch house reveal the process used to raise Atlantic salmon and rainbow and brown trout. Brood stock is contained in 10 3,500-gallon pools fed by a pristine aquifer that produces 200 gallons of chilled water per minute. Some tanks hold trout and salmon as big as your arm. Protected from the sun and predators by space age-looking domes, some 40,000 trout, the first batch to be produced since the reopening, await dispersal. Kevin Ferry, assistant director and hatchery coordinator, is working with state officials to supply Berkshire County with healthy trout from the hatchery. Some fry are participating in a study comparing a new soy-based vegetable feed with animal-based commercial products. The hatchery also offers educational programs to schools that teach fish biology, plant cell structure, pond dynamics, and water chemistry. Through this effort, a 200-gallon aquaponic tank was installed at nearby Mount Everett High School, demonstrating the relationship between fish, plants, and water. Open daily, the hatchery is on Hatchery Road, off MA 57/183 in Hartsville. Although well marked, the entrance is tricky to negotiate. It's best to drive past the entrance, turn around, and then proceed up the driveway past the domes to the visitor center. The property also includes 7 miles of beautiful hiking trails. Call (413) 528-9761 for more information about Berkshire National Fish Hatchery (240 Hatchery Road, New Marlborough 01230).

Boats and Supplies

Where there is water, there are sure to be folks selling bait. Some of the larger suppliers are listed below, along with those that sell tackle, rent equipment, service boats, or provide other fishing-related services. For more information about boat sales and rentals see Outfitters and Boat Dealers.

SOUTH COUNTY

Housatonic River Outfitters
684 South Main Street, Great Barrington
(413) 528-8811
www.dryflies.com

Housatonic River Outfitters is a full-service fly-shop, outfitter, lodging, and guide service. They carry fly-fishing equipment and tying materials, used and consigned fishing equipment, clothing, maps, and waders and can provide information on local activities and services. Their river guides have been featured in the *New York Times, Gray's Sporting Journal, Fly-Fishing Guide,* and other publications. They offer both drift-boat and wading trips and will tailor individual or larger outings to specific interests and requirements and provide up-to-the-minute information on insect activity and river conditions throughout the year. They also have a shop in Cornwall Bridge, Connecticut at 24 Kent Road. The phone there is (860) 672-1010.

RiverRun
271 Main Street, Great Barrington
(413) 528-9600
www.berkshireflyfishing.com

This Orvis outlet carries a full stock of fly-fishing equipment, including rods, reels, waders, vests, artificial bait, fly-tying materials, and pre-tied flies. They even have inflatable rafts. Also available are books, maps, and all kinds of attire, plus a selection of luggage and other travel gear. The shop offers Orvis-endorsed fly-fishing classes, slide shows, and lectures about fly-fishing and a guide service on local rivers.

J&D Marina
Reservoir Road, East Otis
(413) 269-4839

J&D Marina operates a boat ramp and docks, plus a restaurant with light fare at this north-end location on Otis Reservoir.

Miller Marine
Reservoir Road, East Otis
(413) 269-6358

Engine repair and docking are provided at this full-service marina, also located at the north end of Otis Reservoir.

CENTRAL BERKSHIRES

Dave's Sporting Goods
1164 North Street, Pittsfield
(413) 442-2960
www.davessportinggoods.com

Dave's Sporting Goods sells a full line of fishing equipment, including lures, live bait, waders, rods, reels, line, and nonmotorized boats. Dave Benham Jr., whose father founded the store some 25 years ago, is the man to talk to about bass fishing tournaments in the Berkshires and beyond. Except for some holidays, the shop is open daily year-round. It is located on the corner of Crane Avenue and North Street (which is also US 7) heading out of Pittsfield.

Dick Moon Sporting Goods
114 Fenn Street, Pittsfield
(413) 442-8281

Dick Moon's shop has been a fixture in Pittsfield since 1941. Smack in the heart of the city, it is easy to miss on congested Fenn Street, which runs between First and North Streets. But there is parking nearby, and the shop is worth the effort. It is crammed with all kinds of sporting goods, including fishing gear. But the comprehensive stock is not the only reason to stop here. Rod Moon, whose father started the business, is full of information and happy to dispense it.

Passionate about fishing in particular, Moon promotes angling on many levels, passing on pointers in casual conversation. He urges parents to learn the sport themselves as an art they can then share with and teach their kids and recommends fly-fishing for women recovering from mastectomies. He offers fly-tying classes and casting lessons, occasionally given in the parking lot across the street, and will organize guided fishing trips from simple to elaborate. Moon believes it is important to break through the mystique that has developed around fly-fishing and is decidedly not a fan of superexpensive brand-name equipment, though he does carry some to satisfy that kind of customer. He buys or takes in trade old, used, and antique equipment, including canoes and lures. In describing some of his own favorite fishing spots along the Green River in Great Barrington, Moon suspects that for him, fishing is just an excuse in the end for being there.

The shop is open year-round Tuesday through Saturday from 9:00 A.M. to 5:00 P.M. It is down the street from City Hall, next door to the Highland Restaurant, another Pittsfield fixture.

Onota Boat Livery
463 Pecks Road, Pittsfield
(413) 442-1724
Another city fixture, the Onota Boat Livery has been doing business on the shore of Onota Lake for longer than folks can remember. Current owner Tom Dailey has been running it since 1991. This full-service marina sells all kinds of boats, including pontoon boats, runabouts, sport boats, and nonmotorized boats, including canoes, rowboats, pedal boats, and one- and two-person kayaks. Nonmotorized boats may be rented for $10 an hour, $30 for four hours, and $45 for a day. Kayaks for two cost $15 an hour, $45 for four, and $60 for eight. Rates for motorized boats vary according to boat length, size of motor, and steering method. Rentals for pontoon boats that can hold 7, 8, or 10 persons also vary depending on the day, length of time, and size. The largest rented for a full day will cost $300. Fees include fuel and life vests. Deposits are required, some in cash. Reservations are suggested, especially for weekends. Dailey sells Mercury and Honda outboard motors as well as Volvo and Mercruiser sterndrives, services them and other motors, and sells and rents trailers. The firm also makes "house calls," servicing boats on other lakes in the area.

Half the large shop is devoted to boating accessories, including water skis and safety equipment; the other half is full of tackle, including lures, line, rods, reels, hooks, and other fishing paraphernalia. Pictures of prize catches adorn the walls and service desk. A sign, hanging near tubs of live bait, guarantees they will catch fish OR DIE TRYING. Dock space can be rented and boats stored for the winter, when the stock inside focuses on ice-fishing equipment.

The livery opens at 7:00 A.M. every day except Christmas, New Year's Day, and Easter. It is at the end of a dirt driveway off Peck's Road, which runs along the northeastern shore of Lake Onota between Hancock Road to the north and Wahconah Street to the east.

Porter's Sporting Goods
370 Pecks Road, Pittsfield
(413) 442-9967
Live bait and a good stock of tackle and fishing accessories are sold here year-round. In winter tip-ups, shanties, and augurs for ice fishing are added. The shop is an official weighing station and licenses are sold here. Open daily.

Quirk's Marine
990 Valentine Road, Pittsfield
(413) 447-7512
Located in an old mill on the corner of Valentine and Pecks Roads, Quirk's sells and services boats and accessories, including safety equipment, lubricants, and oils. Motorboats, canoes, kayaks, and paddlers, plus tubes of all sizes and water skis are available here. Trailers and hitches also are sold. The firm stores boats for the winter.

Tony's Berkshire Boats
483 West Housatonic Street (US 20), Pittsfield
(413) 443-6475
Tony Cera sells pontoon boats, Yamaha motors, tubes, waterboards, skis, and accessories, including really cool vests for kids. Boats may be rented but only by the month. The shop, located on the outskirts of the city, is open Monday through Saturday from May through November. Call for winter hours.

NORTH COUNTY

John's Fishing Tackle Service Center
187 Bates Road, Windsor
(413) 684-4587
www.johnsfishingtackleservicecenter.com
John Topper Sr. ties flies and sells them at his home and through his Web site, where samples with prices are pictured. He also sells lures for bass, cod, and salmon; repairs and custom-builds rods; and

respools and repairs reels. Bates Road is off MA 8A between MA 116 to the north and MA 9 to the south.

FITNESS CENTERS AND SPAS

South County

Berkshire South Regional Community Center
15 Crissey Road, Great Barrington
(413) 528-2810
www.berkshiresouth.org
This state-of-the-art recently built community center is open daily and offers a multitude of opportunities for exercise to members and drop-ins. The facility includes a six-lane 252-yard swimming pool, a smaller warm-water pool, and a children's splash playground with water features; a gymnasium with adjustable basketball hoops and volleyball, indoor hockey, and soccer setups; and a fully equipped fitness center with lockers for men, women, and families. Special activities, many for children, are offered for fees, which are less or nonexistent for members. For those just passing through, the daily rate to enjoy the facility is $5.00 for children, $10.00 for adults.

Body & Soul
40 Railroad Street, Great Barrington
(413) 528-6465
Body & Soul offers massages, including hot rock; aromatherapy treatments; and facials, manicures, pedicures, and waxing with licensed therapists in a relaxing, intimate atmosphere. Bath and body products, including the Dr. Hausckha line of skin care and makeup, are sold here. Open daily, evenings by appointment. Fees vary; packages are available.

Canyon Ranch in the Berkshires
165 Kemble Street, Lenox
(413) 637-4400, (800) 326-7080
www.canyonranch.com
Voted Best Spa by *Condé Nast Traveler* seven times, Canyon Ranch's Berkshire resort is the height of luxurious pampering. Located in the former Bellefontaine estate, the surroundings are elegant. Add to this the gourmet meals and wide array of body and skin treatments and health and fitness programs for men and women, and you can see why *Gourmet* and *Travel & Leisure* also have high praises for this resort. Guests can set their own goals and design their own packages. But they might have a hard time deciding what to do, since there are around 40 complimentary fitness classes each day plus more than 225 programs and services to choose from, including private health and fitness consultations with a team of more than 60 professional experts. In addition, there are lectures, workshops, and cooking demonstrations, plus seasonal activities like skiing and snowshoeing, kayaking and canoeing, and hiking and biking. Guests may play golf at nearby Cranwell Resort. Transportation from nearby airports may be arranged. Prices are determined by the length of stay and season. A three-night package in August runs around $2,200 per person for a double room. Canyon Ranch in Tucson is the mothership for this deluxe resort, which explains the not-very-Berkshire name.

Cranwell Resort, Spa and Golf Club
55 Lee Road (US 20), Lenox
(413) 637-1364, (800) 272-6935
www.cranwell.com
Also located in a Gilded Age mansion, Cranwell recently added a 35,000-square-foot spa to its resort, which includes an 18-hole championship golf course and *Golf Digest* School. The spa is linked to 58 of the resort's 107 guest rooms by heated, glass corridors. A 60-foot-long indoor pool is enclosed by a dramatic 20-foot-high glass wall, revealing the mountains beyond. In addition to saunas, steam rooms, and therapeutic whirlpool baths, there are 16 treatment rooms, including a spa suite, plus lounges with fireplaces and refreshment bars and a cafe for relaxing before or after treatments. Guests may

choose from more than 30 spa services, including massages, healing wraps, and organic skin and body treatments. The fitness center has the latest equipment for strength and endurance training. The spa is open to the public for day use, with prices ranging from $135 for the basic package, which includes a massage and a fitness class and use of all spa facilities, to around $300 for the ultimate package. A men's package is around $200. Prices for spa packages for hotel guests vary depending on how many nights they are staying, the kind of package they choose, and the season. A three-night midweek stay with spa services runs around $800 per person May through October. Situated on 380 acres, Cranwell also has tennis courts, open to the public for $25 an hour; an outdoor heated pool, 10 kilometers of cross-country ski trails, and three restaurants. The resort recently won the AAA Four Diamond Award.

Eden Hill Recreation Center
2 Prospect Hill Road, Stockbridge
(413) 298-1106

The Eden Hill Recreation Center is located on the grounds of the Congregation of the Marion Fathers. Offered as a community service, the center is a year-round multipurpose recreational facility featuring a wide variety of wellness and performing arts programs for adults and children of all abilities. The facility includes a three-lane 73-foot lap pool and a gymnasium. Fitness and weight training classes including aerobics and free weights are offered. Classes also are given in swimming, dance, drumming, jazz, and other performing arts. Memberships are $65 for one month or $500 for the year. Fees for drop-ins vary depending on the activity and age. Adults pay $10.00 for day use of the facility, children ages 5 to 15 pay $3.00. Classes run around $12. A special after-school performing arts program also is offered.

Essencials Day Spa
459 Pittsfield/Lenox Road (US 7), Lenox
(413) 443-0260
www.berkshirespas.com

Services at Essencials Day Spa include manicures, pedicures, hair care, facials, massages, aromatherapy infusion, wraps, body buffing, and waxing. All are offered at immaculate state-of-the-art work stations or in one of six pleasant treatment rooms. Clients may relax in a sauna before undergoing a treatment or sit by the central fireplace where herbal tea may be sipped. Fees vary depending on the type of treatment and length of time. An 80-minute gentleman's package that includes sauna, exfoliating scrub, sports massage, hand and foot massage, and minifacial is $115. For $70 you may enjoy a Swedish massage with fragrant essential oils or a European facial. A hot rock massage is $120. A manicure including a gentle hand massage is $17. Several lines of health and beauty products are sold. On-site services for wedding parties may be arranged. Essencials is open daily; evening hours vary.

The Healing Place
1 West Street, Lenox
(413) 637-1980
www.thehealingplace.com

An array of body and skin care treatments are offered at the restorative Healing Place. Yoga, facials, massages, wraps, and other relaxing treatments may be booked singly or in packages. A traditional four-hour spa package, including yoga, a facial, a massage and body polish, and the time it takes to change attire runs around $305. A one-hour facial followed by a massage costs around $160. Skin care products and dietary supplements by Dr. Hauschka are sold here along with body care products by Ahava and essential oils and soaps by several makers. These and other herbal products also are available through the firm's Web site. The Healing Place is located at the intersection of MA 183 and US 7A in the center of Lenox.

Kripalu Center for Yoga and Health
MA 183, Lenox
(413) 448-3152, (800) 741-7353
www.kripalu.org

What others seek to do with wraps, massages, and aromatherapy, Kripalu does with yoga, meditation, and healthy meals. Located in a former Jesuit monastery, Kripalu offers retreats and workshops designed to provide a getaway from everyday life while learning how to use inner focus for serenity and good health. Guests live in comparatively austere rooms but are rewarded with extraordinary views of Stockbridge Bowl and grounds that invite walks and appreciation of nature.

A typical day is filled with classes in healing arts, dance, and yoga with personal time for reading or reflection or relaxing in the sauna or whirlpools. Practitioners of yoga teach that by learning physical postures, breathing techniques, deep relaxation, and meditation, one's physical, mental, and emotional blockages begin to dissolve. Energy is freed and stress and pain are released, leading to higher levels of emotional stability, mental clarity, and physical well-being. Vegetarian meals are served at Kripalu and are included in the cost of the room. Workshops are held throughout the year, and rates vary depending on the season, program, length of stay, and accommodations chosen. There are dormitories, shared rooms, and private rooms, all priced differently depending on whether the bath is shared or private. A typical basic weekend retreat for a shared room with private bath runs around $200 per person. Tuition for a two-day beginners yoga class costs around $145 plus the cost of a room and meals. A three-day retreat for beginning meditation runs around $219 plus room and meals.

A gift shop at the center is filled with books that reflect the philosophies of homeopathic medicine, meditation, and other Eastern thought along with oils, clothing, and music. Kripalu is located at the intersection of MA 183 and Richmond Mountain Road, near the Tanglewood entrance.

Lenox Fitness Center and Spa
90 Pittsfield Road (US 7), Lenox
(413) 637-9893
www.Lenoxfitnesscenter.com

Spinning, yoga, and aerobics are among the fitness classes given here. If the weather is good, folks can choose to go for a power walk in Kennedy Park, across the highway from this new facility. Strength and cardiovascular equipment in the airy gymnasium includes treadmills, bicycles, stair machines, and a free-weight section with bars, benches, and stations. The services of a personal trainer may be contracted. Membership in the fitness center runs in three-month increments, beginning at $99 for one month. A six-month membership is $315; a year is $510 with a reduced renewal rate. The center also offers 12- and 24-visit punch cards for $96 and $144, respectively, and a daily drop-in rate of $10. Discounts are available. Healthful snacks and refreshing drinks are available. Spa services include facials and waxing, manicures and pedicures, tanning, acupuncture, and massages at various rates for men and women by appointment or walk-in. Open daily.

Michele's Salon & Day Spa
54 Stockbridge Road (US 7), Great Barrington
(413) 528-9999
www.michelessalon.com

Michele's offers a variety of packages for men, women, and teens. A full day of pampering plus a catered lunch runs around $300 and includes an exfoliating salt glow, steam shower, customized massage, facial, manicure and pedicure, hair treatment, and Aveda makeup application. A shorter visit for $195 includes a full body massage, facial, shampoo and blow-dry, and makeup application. A nice present for a new or expectant mother is offered in a $250 package that includes a therapeutic and comforting massage, facial, spa pedicure, classic manicure, shampoo, blow-dry, a makeup touch-up, and lunch. All clients receive complimentary hair and skin care products. The salon is open Monday through Saturday, with some evening hours, and Sunday by appointment.

Studio 21 Fitness Center
359 Stockbridge Road (US 7), Great Barrington
(413) 528-2148
www.studio21online.com

Studio 21 has a fully equipped fitness center with a pool and offers personal training on use of the machines. Other services include body-composition testing, flexibility assessments, diet analysis, blood pressure screening, and target heart rate calculations. Child care is available, and home fitness equipment is sold. Delivery, assembly, and home training may be arranged. Massages also are offered. The center is affiliated with Michele's Salon & Day Spa (see above), where center members receive a 10 percent discount. A host of classes are offered at various times throughout the year, including spinning, Pilates, yoga, aerobics, stress relief, and cardiovascular exercise along with lessons in belly dancing or fencing. A day pass costs $10 and punch passes are available for 10, 15, or 20 visits. Membership rates run $55 for one month, $264 for six months, or $462 for the year, with a 10 percent discount for seniors, students, and spouses. Family and weekend rates are available. Members receive two complimentary guest passes. The center is open daily, with varying hours.

Central Berkshire

Berkshire Nautilus
42 Summer Street, Pittsfield
(413) 499-1217

Located in downtown Pittsfield just off North Street, Berkshire Nautilus is a favorite with city workers. Owner Jim Ramondetta is dedicated to fitness as a way of life and works with his customers to develop programs that fit their individual needs. Members have access to more than 40 Nautilus stations for specific muscle groups and body parts; more than 40 cardiovascular machines, including treadmills, Stairmasters, rowers, exercycles, and NordicTrack skiers; an Olympic weight floor with more than 40 stations plus saunas, steam baths, and hot tubs. Showers and lockers are provided in separate facilities for men and women. Also available are personal training, massage therapy, use of a rock climbing wall, computerized diet and nutritional analysis, fitness evaluations, and babysitting. Fitness equipment for home or commercial use is sold in the Fitness Store. Memberships run around $70 for a month to $500 for the year, but discounts are available for young adults, seniors, corporate clients, couples, and families. Walk-in rates are available.

Berkshire West
100 Dan Fox Drive, Pittsfield
(413) 499-4600
www.berkshirewest.com

A multipurpose family athletic facility, Berkshire West offers a variety of aerobic, aquatic, and fitness activities and instruction. Class in aerobics, karate, ballet, and kickboxing take place on a cushioned wood floor in the aerobics center. There are always some lanes free for laps in the 30- by 60-foot swimming pool, and the Quonset-type roof is removed in summer for outdoor swimming. A kid's wading pool and hot tub complete the aquatic center. The fitness center includes Nautilus stations, free weights, a cardiovascular area, and indoor cycling. Classes, personal trainers, and consultations are offered. Four racquetball and 12 tennis courts plus a ball machine are used for various activities, including league games. An adult tennis lesson package, including equipment, eight weeks of lessons, and six of league games costs around $200. A member of the International Health and Racquet Sports Association, Berkshire West is open daily; child care is available for members by reservation. Most classes and all equipment, including the pool, tennis courts, and steam room or sauna, are available to drop-ins for a daily fee of $15 for adults, less for juniors and little ones. Memberships run $50 a month for adults or $600 for the year.

Dalton Community House
Main Street, Dalton
(413) 684-0260
The Dalton Community Recreation Association operates a fully equipped fitness center with a pool and saunas in the Community House, open by membership and to the general public by a daily rate. Classes offered include muscle tone and strength, strength training, floor and water aerobics, Pilates, and yoga, some for additional fees. A trained staff is on hand for Nautilus and free weight instruction and health and fitness education training. The director publishes a fitness newsletter through the year. An adult membership in the fitness center is $45 for a month, $215 for six months, or $320 for a year, with discounts for juniors, seniors, and couples plus $100 for pool privileges if desired. A one-time visit is $7.00, but a $60.00 punch card for the fitness center is good for 14 visits. Personal training may be arranged. The center is open daily, and hours are extended from October through May.

YMCA
292 North Street, Pittsfield
(413) 499-7650
www.pittsfieldymca.org
Membership in the Pittsfield Y includes use of the fitness center, equipped with state-of-the-art Nautilus and LifeFitness cardiovascular equipment, gymnasium, racquetball and squash courts, weight room, and the Olympic-size indoor swimming pool. In summer members also may use the facilities at the YMCA's outdoor center at Ponterril, off Pontuoosuc Lake, which includes a pool, tennis courts, basketball and volleyball courts, and picnic areas. Members also are entitled to discounts on marina boat rentals and the use of a lodge. In addition, the Y offers numerous classes and programs for youngsters and adults, some free to members, all open to nonmembers for fees.

An initial joiner fee of $60 is charged to most. Monthly fees range from around $35.00 for adults to $6.00 for youngsters under age 13 and $30.00 for seniors. Daily use by adults unaccompanied by a member run around $8.00. The Y also runs a number of social service programs, including affordable housing for low-income adults.

North County

YMCA
Brickyard Court, North Adams
(413) 663-6529
The North Adams YMCA, which operates separately from the Pittsfield Y, almost went under some years ago until Mayor John Barrett rescued it with an unusual plan. Needing to build a new elementary school, Barrett conceived of the notion to build it next to the Y, providing the organization with a built-in supply of youngsters for after-school events while finding a site for the new school that met state requirements. Now the Y is rolling along, offering members a fully equipped fitness center, heated swimming pool, basketball and racquetball courts, saunas for men and women, and a coed steam room plus classes in a host of activities. There are two levels of membership. While both include use of all facilities, the complete membership includes a personal locker. There is no joiner fee for the first three months of membership, which for an adult is $175. At the end of that period you may join for the rest of the year for $445 plus a fee of $37 for the complete program or $290 and a joiner fee of $24 for the basic program. Monthly payments are available, and some discounts are offered. There are some fees for classes, but members pay less.

GOLF

The valleys and hills of the Berkshires are the perfect setting for interesting and often-challenging golf. There are more than a dozen courses from one end of the county to the other, including several private ones not listed here and one under construction in New Ashford. As you travel north, the courses generally become more hilly, and the views from some verge on spectacular. The courses in South County tend to be more open, with gently rolling hills. All have pros on hand, and carts are available for rental at various prices. Proper golf attire is required, although some courses are more relaxed about this than others. Tournaments are held through the season, often to raise funds for local nonprofit organizations. Driving ranges and places to play miniature golf also are listed here, as is an indoor practice range open in winter.

South County

Cranwell Resort, Spa and Golf Club
55 Lee Road (US 20), Lenox
(413) 637-1364
www.cranwell.com

Cranwell Resort's 60 acres include a challenging 18-hole championship course and a state-of-the-art learning facility affiliated with *Golf Digest*. The par-70, 5,979-yard course was designed by Wayne E. Stiles and John Van Kleek in 1926 on the site of the original Berkshire Hunt Club. The course, irrigated to provide consistent play throughout the golf season, offers magnificent views, fast greens, and a demanding back nine. Ponds and streams come into play on four holes. The 8th hole, atop a plateau, offers a panoramic view of the Berkshires with Cranwell's stately 1896 Tudor mansion as the centerpiece. The 9th hole has a reputation as the toughest, offering a demanding tee shot to an elevated green.

Golfers who feel intimidated might want to head to the Golf School to brush up on their techniques. Target greens, practice bunkers, putting areas, driving fairways, chipping/pitching stations, and three practice holes are provided, all with no course traffic or other distractions. More than a practice arena, the facility is the largest of its kind in the Northeast. And you get to work with director of golf and head PGA professional David Strawn, who has been with Cranwell since 1994. The resort recently expanded its offerings across the road, where there is a three-acre driving range with 25 stations, some with mats and others with grass.

Cranwell has been named one of the top 100 courses by the *New England Journal of Golf* and one of the top 50 by *Golf Boston*. The full-service pro shop will fill and ship orders for customers and rents top-quality equipment. It is located next to Sloane's Tavern, one of four restaurants at Cranwell that offer everything from light fare to fine dining. There is also the 35,000-square-foot spa to work out the kinks and the 104-room mansion to stay in; golfing packages are available.

Greens fees vary by season, day, and time. The fee for 18 holes on a spring or fall weekday is $59, dropping to $39 after 3:00 P.M. Weekend rates are about $10 higher. June through Labor Day, fees are higher. Eighteen holes on a summer weekend will cost $99, or $53 after 4:00 P.M. Rates are for one person and include a cart. Reservations are required five days in advance, three weeks for hotel guests (who save $5.00 on greens fees). Monday and Tuesday from 4:00 to 6:00 P.M. are reserved for men's and women's leagues, respectively. And if you get thirsty, watch for the beverage cart. Cranwell is the only course in the county that offers that amenity.

Egremont Country Club
MA 23, Great Barrington
(413) 528-4222
www.EgremontCountryClub.com

The Egremont Country Club features a challenging 18-hole semiprivate course, fully stocked pro shop, and 20-station driving range. Golf lessons are available by appointment with PGA golf professional Marc Levesque. Public tee times are available up to seven days in advance. The well-maintained par-71, 6,000-yard course is surrounded by rolling hills, beautiful views, and winding streams. The course was originally laid out with nine holes in the 1930s when it was the Mount Everett Golf Club.

The most scenic hole on the expanded course is the par-4 18th. You tee off an elevated green through a chute of trees over a pond before taking on a slight uphill dogleg framed by trees. The narrow approach to the sloped green at the 3rd hole makes this 182-yard par-3 hole a challenge. The unusual arrangement of back-to-back par-5s makes the 12th and 13th holes very popular. Both are 550 yards and are reached by alternating doglegs.

A putting green with sand traps is located near the first tee. Greens fees during the week are $25 for 18 holes, $15 for 9, with a $12 twilight special. Weekends during peak season fees are $40 from 6:00 A.M. to 2:00 P.M., $28 from 2:00 to 5:00 P.M., and $15 after that. A restaurant with banquet facilities that can accommodate up to 250 serves lunch daily from 11:00 A.M. to 4:00 P.M. There also is a canopied deck and a full bar.

Greenock Country Club
West Park Street (US 20), Lee
(413) 243-3323

Views of the valley and hills around Lee await the golfer who takes on this nine-hole, par-35, 3,080-yard course. A lush, well-groomed semiprivate course with elevated greens, Greenock was designed by Donald Ross in 1927. There are several challenging holes, including two with water hazards. The par-4 5th hole is generally considered the most scenic—and the most difficult. The tee is on a hill overlooking the town down in the valley. There are two ponds to the left of the green. On this hilly but walkable course, five holes are reached through open but tree-lined shafts, and there are lots of sand traps. There is a putting/chipping practice green.

Greenock is a popular course and is often crowded. The season runs from April 1 to November 15. Reservations are always needed for weekend play and must be made on Thursday. Reservations for weekday play are required Memorial Day through Labor Day and must be made on Saturday. Greens fees for 18 holes are $28 on weekdays, $42 on weekends, all season long. A twilight special of $14 is offered weekdays after 5:00 P.M. Carts are available for $40.50 during the week, $55.00 on weekends.

The pro shop sells, rents, and repairs equipment, and there are lockers and showers at the clubhouse. Naji's restaurant "on the green" (413-243-8000) offers a full menu, including Mediterranean specialties, and is open daily from 11:00 A.M. to 9:00 P.M., Sunday from 11:00 A.M. to 4:00 P.M. A banquet hall may be rented for special occasions. Two clay tennis courts at the club may be rented for $8.00 an hour, if you are lucky. Reservations are needed at least three days ahead.

Central Berkshire

Bas Ridge Golf Course
151 Plunkett Avenue, Hinsdale
(413) 655-2605

The newest course in the county, Bas Ridge was designed by Roland Armacost and laid out in 1996 on the site of an old gravel bed. This nine-hole, par-70, 5,051-yard course has bent-grass greens, rolling banks, and an unusual layout, making for interesting play. One local golfer called Bas Ridge "the craters of the moon national golf course." Depending on what's going on, tee times may be reserved on short notice, but a week ahead is recommended for weekends. Greens fees are $10 for 9 holes, $18 for 18 holes. Carts are $10 or $15 but are included in a weekday $20 18-hole special. Other facilities include a small pro shop, a practice putting green, a bar where light snacks are sold, and a dining room that can be reserved for parties.

Described as a working man's course, Bas Ridge allows golfers to bring their own beverages onto the greens and has a relaxed dress code. It is located off MA 8 near the center of Hinsdale. The course is owned and operated by Bill Basiliere, thereby explaining the one "s" in Bas.

GEAA (General Electric Athletic Association)
303 Crane Avenue, Pittsfield
(413) 443-5746
Originally designed in the mid-1940s for General Electric employees, this nine-hole course is now independently operated by association members and is open to the public at reasonable prices. Greens fees during the week for the par-72, 6205-yard course are $11 during the week and $14 on weekends. Fees for 18 holes are $18 and $20, respectively. Carts are rented separately but are really not needed for the gently rolling terrain. About half the holes have a water hazard, and in some places overhead wires might present a challenge. The 570-yard 9th hole, with a par-5, is considered the most difficult—a pond and sloping green have to be dealt with. Tee times can be reserved from 10 days to two weeks ahead. Facilities include a full-service pro shop, a driving range, and a putting green.

Crane Avenue runs between US 7 and MA 8 in the city. As with most other Berkshire courses, there are wonderful views of the mountains, including Mount Greylock. A full-menu restaurant on the premises is open from noon to 9:00 P.M. Drinks purchased at the lounge are allowed on the course, which is open from April to Thanksgiving Day.

Pontoosuc Lake Country Club
Kirkwood Drive, Pittsfield
(413) 445-4217 (club house), (413) 445-4543 (tee times)
Laid out over 100 acres, this gem of an 18-hole course is the closest thing to Scottish links in the area, local aficionados say. Owned and operated by the Moxon family since 1925, the club's par-70, 6,224-yard course was designed by Wayne Stiles in 1939. The rolling terrain is filled with natural mounds and rocks, the fairways are bumpy, and the views are great. The par-5, 610-yard 15th hole is the longest in Berkshire County. During wet season, a brook bordered by tall, uncut grass comes into play on three holes. The 11th hole involves a shot over a pond.

Greens fees for all-day play are $17 during the week and $20 on weekends. If you want to play before 2:00 P.M. on Friday, Saturday, or Sunday, you will need a reservation, which you can make during the week. Otherwise it's come as you wish, remembering that leagues start around 4:00 P.M. Seniors get a discount, and a reduced twilight rate is available after 5:00 P.M. Carts may be rented for $21. Shirts with sleeves are required dress.

There is a putting green but no pro shop or restaurant. The clubhouse offers simple snacks and beverages for in-house consumption. It's really just all about the golf. The course is a little hard to find. Kirkwood is off Ridge, which is off Hancock Road, which is off US 7 at the Pontoosuc Lake dam.

Skyline Country Club
US 7, Lanesborough
(413) 445-5584
www.skyline-cc.com
Aptly named, this 18-hole course runs along the top of a ridge off US 7, offering stunning views of Pontoosuc Lake and the valleys on both sides. The course was originally nine holes laid out by Roland Armacost in 1963. It was expanded to 18 holes in 1994, again with Armacost's design. Now a par-71, 5,634-yard course, the rolling terrain has varied fairways and a creek that winds through a couple of links. The elevated tee at the par-3, 188-yard 5th hole is particularly scenic. The pro shop carries quite a large stock and takes in repairs. Pro golfers are Chris Tremblay and owner James Mitus. A 15-station grass tee driving range and a practice green complete the offerings.

Greens fees during the week are $22 for 18 holes, $13 for 9. On weekends and holidays fees are $25 and $15, respectively. Reservations are needed seven days ahead. Leagues play after 4:00 P.M., but because of the size of the course there is seldom a backup. Cart rental is $11.50 per person but is sometimes included in various specials. There is no dress code. The clubhouse includes a banquet room, a bar, and a restaurant that serves burgers, sandwiches, appetizers, wraps, and other grill fare from 11:00 A.M. to 9:00 P.M. Alcoholic beverages are allowed on the course if purchased on the premises.

Wahconah Country Club
20 Orchard Road, Dalton
(413) 684-1333
Another course designed by Wayne E. Stiles and John Van Kleek, Wahconah's 18 holes were laid out in 1930. The Housatonic River winds through the gently rolling property, making for a picturesque as well as challenging 6,223-yard par-71 course. In the past five years, bunkers and tees have been renovated and remodeled and the putting green expanded. All the holes are considered strong and challenging, with several water hazards and sand traps. Local golfers describe Wahconah as the second best course in the county, after Taconic in Williamstown. On the sloping back nine, the 16th hole, with a 430-yard par-4, is rated most difficult. The semiprivate club offers lessons through the pro shop and arranges for repairs by a member in the business. Greens fees are $75 on the weekend, $65 during the week. Tuesday, Wednesday, and Thursday mornings at 11:00 A.M. and afternoons at 4:00 P.M. are reserved for leagues. Members have the course to themselves on weekends until 2:00 P.M. Tee times may be reserved a week ahead for weekdays, eight days ahead for weekends. A popular location for wedding receptions and other functions, Wahconah's restaurant is open from 11:00 A.M. to 9:00 P.M. Meals also are served in the lounge or may be enjoyed outside on the new stone patio. Beverages purchased at the bar may be taken on the course.

North County

Forest Park Country Club
41 Forest Park Avenue, Adams
(413) 743-3311
Dubbed the "billy-goat course" by some, Forest Park was designed around 1900 by Alex Findley. The par-34, 2,555-yard nine-hole course is definitely hilly and presents a number of challenges. The green on the second hole (par-4, 341 yards) is on the other side of a knob, out of sight of the tee. The 5th hole presents several traps, and shots have to be maneuvered between trees to a banked green. The view of Mount Greylock and the orchards at its base are especially nice from the 8th hole. Greens fees are the same all season: $11 for 9 holes, $16 for 18. Carts may be rented for $10 or $20. A small pro shop offers gift certificates, and there is a putting/chipping practice green. Leagues take over the course Sunday morning until 11:00 A.M. and on Wednesday and Thursday at 4:00 P.M., but there is usually no waiting after 5:00 P.M. Reservations are not needed during the week, but a call ahead is recommended for weekends, just in case there is a tournament scheduled. The clubhouse is an early-20th-century "cottage" built by a prominent Adams industrialist. A lounge located there offers beverages and light snacks. Alcoholic beverages are not allowed on the course.

North Adams Country Club
641 River Road (MA 8), Clarksburg
(413) 663-7887
Located just north of North Adams between the mountains in the Clarksburg Valley, North Adams Country Club has been around since 1903. Designed by William Mitchell and Robert Orrin, the moderately rolling nine-hole course is known for its small, firm, and fast greens. Local golfers describe it as being fun but no pushover: a true old New England golf course. Water comes into play on three holes. The 4th hole, a 364-yard par-4, is the signature hole, presenting the challenge of a short dogleg leading to a short

green. Pro Jack Tosone says success requires a perfectly placed tee shot. Repairs are accepted at the fully stocked pro shop, and there is a practice putting green. Tosone offers lessons and runs golf clinics. Greens fees for nine holes are $12 on weekend mornings and weekday afternoons, $22 for an 18-hole game. At off-peak times fees are $1.00 per hole. Carts may be rented for $5.00 a person for nine holes. Leagues tee off on Monday, Tuesday, and Thursday from 4:00 to 5:00 A.M. On weekends and holidays, reservations are required one week in advance. The club has banquet facilities and a lounge with a pub menu that includes daily specials. Drinks purchased on-site may be taken on the course.

Taconic Golf Club
19 Meechum Street, Williamstown
(413) 458-3997

Steeped in tradition, the semiprivate Taconic Golf Club is considered the crème de la crème of Berkshire County's links. Designed by Wayne Stiles and John R. Van Kleek in 1926 on land owned by Williams College, the 18-hole, par-71, 6,230-yard course is the most expensive in the county. Greens fees are simple: $140 per person Tuesday through Friday, period. Members get the course the rest of the week. Tee times should be reserved a week ahead. Taconic has been the scene of many championship games, including the Massachusetts Amateur and US Senior Amateur play-offs. A plaque notes the spot where Jack Nicklaus once hit a hole-in-one.

The dress code is strict, and alcoholic beverages are not allowed on the course. The greens have been described as difficult but not overbearing, challenging but without tricks or gimmicks, straightforward and beautiful. The last three holes involve some tricky shots over water hazards but offer views south to Mount Greylock and north to Vermont. This course has stood the test of time, and local golfers say Taconic evokes a feeling of reverence, similar to being in church. The season begins when the weather allows but always ends early in November on the day after the Williams-Amherst football game. A restaurant and bar offer light refreshments until 4:00 P.M. with credit card only. The fully equipped pro shop will take cash. The course is on a side street in town near the Williams College athletic fields and can be reached by either Water Street (MA 43) or Spring Street.

Waubeeka Golf Links
137 New Ashford Road (US 7), Williamstown
(413) 458-8355

Waubeeka is on the other side of town in the South Williamstown Valley and is more relaxed than Taconic, although certainly no slouch. Framed by Mount Greylock to the east and the Taconic Range to the west, the 18-hole course is beautiful, especially in fall. And the golfing is good, too. Roland Armacost designed the par-72, 6,024-yard course in 1966. The signature hole is the 12th—a hard par-4 over water—and the view from the tee is terrific. The well-maintained greens and rolling hills present many challenges—there is a brook near, by, or through almost every hole. Facilities include a full-service pro shop, an eight-station driving range, and a practice putting green. Greens fees are $33 per person on weekdays, $42 on weekends and holidays. Reservations are required a week ahead, beginning at 7:00 A.M. Carts may be rented for $14. A good restaurant with an expansive menu rounds out the offerings. Alcoholic beverages are not allowed on the course.

Practice Ranges and Miniature Golf

Baker Farm Golf Center
658 South Main Street (US 7), Lanesborough
(413) 443-6102

Baker Farm's miniature golf course and driving range have been a fixture on US 7 since 1943. When Baker's opens, you know it's spring. The 300-yard driving range, which is lighted at night, has 13 covered stations and 15 more on adjoining grass. A practice putting green and sand trap are nearby. Buckets of balls range from $2.50 for around 25 to $8.00 for 175. Clubs may be rented. The 18-hole miniature course is challenging but not too frustrating for little ones. Many of the obstacles are funky fixtures dating back to the original layout. Others were installed in a complete renovation of the course done in the '90s. Hundreds of plants and flowers add beauty to the course, which has a waterfall, several water hazards, bridges, and a gazebo. The fee for an 18-hole game is $3.00. The driving range and miniature course are located at the intersection of US 7 and Berkshire Mall Drive. Baker's also operates a lighted 18-hole pitch 'n' putt course up the road, which is open weather permitting. Each hole is a par-3 and runs from 40 to 80 yards.

Bousquet Ski Area
101 Dan Fox Drive, Pittsfield
(413) 442-8314

In summer Bousquet offers miniature golf along with a driving range, water slides, and a pool; a climbing wall; and other activities. Prices vary depending on how many activities you take part in.

Jiminy Peak Resort
37 Corey Road, Hancock
(413) 738-5500
www.jiminypeak.com

Summer activities at Jiminy Peak include miniature golf, an alpine slide, a rock-climbing wall, and trampolines, with or without bungee cords. Prices vary. A package deal is available.

Sky Dome Golf Center
75 South Church Street, Pittsfield
(413) 442-8742

An indoor practice facility and learning center, the Sky Dome is open during winter, providing a place for golfers to keep up with their game or improve their skills. The center is operated by PGA professional Chris Tremblay, who offers lessons here during the winter and at Skyline Country Club in Lanesborough during the outdoor season. The 12,000-square-foot Sky Dome has eight individual hitting bays, two putting greens, and two short game areas. A large bucket of balls is $8.00, a small one $6.00, and access to the putting and game areas is included. Players who want to putt and chip pay only $5.00. Clubs are included, and it's a cash only business. The Sky Dome opens in December and closes around the middle of April. Hours are 10:00 A.M. to 8:00 P.M. Tuesday through Thursday, 10:00 A.M. to 5:00 P.M. Friday through Monday. The center is located in the former Schaeffer-Eaton mill on South Church Street in the center of Pittsfield.

HIKES AND WALKS

The Berkshires are laced with hundreds of trails and footpaths in parks and preserved lands, so many that it would be impossible to list all of them here. Most of the places described in this section have easy to moderately difficult trails that can be hiked or walked in a few hours. There are several good books on hiking plus maps and guides available at various sources, which you will find listed here and in the Parks chapter. Hired guides can be found through outfitters and outdoor specialty stores listed here. For something really different, check out the llama hikes!

The state allows all-terrain vehicles in Pittsfield, October Mountain, Beartown, Savoy, and Tolland State Forests, which some hikers don't like. However, if you don't mind encountering ATVs or dealing with their wear on trails, those places have many pleasant vistas and are worth visiting. The other state parks do not allow ATVs, nor are they allowed on properties managed by the Trustees of Reservations, Berkshire Natural Resources Council, and other land trusts.

South County

If you only have time for one hike, Monument Mountain in Great Barrington is the place to take it. Rising like a sentry standing guard over the valley, the mountain is composed of quartzite that has been sculpted by eons of water and ice. At the summit the exposed rock is tinged with hues of pink, yellow, gold, and orange. The trails here can be slightly difficult, but it's possible to get to Squaw Peak (the summit) and back in less than two hours. You really should try to make it all the way for the incredible views of the Taconic Range and the Catskills to the west, the Litchfield Hills to the south, Mount Greylock to the north, the Berkshire Plateau to the east, and the Housatonic River winding through the valley. In fall it is even more spectacular. The mountain teems with all kinds of wildlife and birds, heard more clearly when you get away from the noise of the highway below. Plants, shrubs, and trees of all sorts flourish here, with gnarled pines capping the summit. There are picnic tables and trail maps at the parking lot off US 7, where the jumble of boulders gives a clue to the rough life this mountain has led.

Other trail-rich areas in South County include the Yokun Ridge, which encompasses parts of south Pittsfield, Lenox, Richmond, Stockbridge, and West Stockbridge. Also worth trying are the many paths in the Pleasant Valley Wildlife Sanctuary, operated by the Audubon Society, and Kennedy Park, both in Lenox. Also in Lenox is Burbank Trail, which is actually several trails that can be entered off Reservoir or Lenox Road. The latter has a pullout called Olivia's Overlook, with a great view of Stockbridge Bowl. In Stockbridge the hike to Laura's Tower and the scramble through Ice Glen are musts. The trailhead for both begins at Memorial Bridge off Park Street in the middle of town. After a bit, the trail splits. The left branch climbs nearly 500 feet to a hill called Laura's Rest, which is topped by a metal tower. Those who climb the tower are rewarded with a spectacular view of the valley beyond. The right branch goes to Ice Glen, but you can get there from the other path, too. The trail through the glen winds through cool, dark woods before entering what is basically a crack between two small mountains. Here you thread your way through a jumble of boulders through which torchlight parades have been held on Halloween for more than a century. The path eventually leads to open land and Ice Glen Road, which connects with US 7 a bit south of Park Street.

The South Taconic Range is filled with trails running through state parks and

Tips for Safe Hiking

- Consult maps ahead of time—and take them with you.
- Tell someone your route, or leave a note in your vehicle.
- Bring plenty of water; a quart per person for a half-day hike is recommended. All those pure-looking streams probably have animal droppings in them.
- Stick to the paths. Don't take "shortcuts."
- Wear a hat and layered clothing. Temperatures can change quickly.
- Be prepared. Carry some snacks, a pocketknife, a basic first-aid kit, a flashlight, matches or a lighter, and a whistle or other noisemaker.
- Don't rely on your cell phone. There are many "dead spots" in the Berkshires.
- Wear sensible shoes.

reservations in Egremont, Sheffield, and Mount Washington, which includes the state forest of the same name. Areas with trails worth taking include Sages Ravine, Jug End Reservation, Race Brook Falls, and Mount Everett. The Taconic Range includes parts of bordering New York and Connecticut, where there are more parks and trails to explore. Other places in South County to enjoy beautiful scenery while hiking are Tyringham Cobble, the Questing in New Marlborough, Bartholomew's Cobble in Ashley Falls, and Benedict Pond in Beartown State Forest in Monterey.

For something really different, consider getting in touch with Richard Cleaver, who runs Berkshire Mountain Llama Hikes. No, you don't ride the llama. You take it for a hike through the woods. Cleaver, a biology major and amateur naturalist, also is a private hiking and touring guide. He and his llamas live in Lee near October Mountain on Hawkmeadow Farm, where he also runs a bed-and-breakfast. The llamas are haltered, experienced hikers and are at ease with humans. Gentle and intelligent, the llamas provide personable companionship on the hikes, which can last for one to three hours. Children—even very young ones—might especially enjoy this experience. They are allowed to brush, pet, and hug their companions—who might kiss them back. Guests are welcome to picnic by a pond before or after their hike. The well-maintained trails wind through the forests and hills surrounding the farm. The hikes are offered year-round, and sunset hikes are especially rewarding. Appointments are needed, and rates vary depending on how many persons and how long the hike lasts. A group of four hiking for 90 minutes would cost around $45. For more information call (413) 243-2224 or check the Web at www.bcn.net/llamahike/. The address for Hawkmeadow Farm is 322 Lander Road in Lee.

If you are thinking of taking a walk in areas where hunting is approved, be aware that deer season generally begins in October for archers and in December for muzzleloaders and shotguns. Black bears may be hunted in September as well as November. Check with Mass Wildlife for definite dates, and if you must go into the woods in late fall or early spring, be sure to wear bright colors (not white) and maybe even wear bells or a similar noisemaker.

Central Berkshire

If you don't mind the heavy traffic, there are trails and walks of varying degrees of difficulty and length in Pittsfield State Forest. Especially nice in spring and fall are the trails around Berry Pond at the summit. In the city itself, Canoe Meadows offers some nice paths to explore, as does Springside Park. West of Pittsfield in Richmond, Stevens' Glen has an ecologically conscious path that takes visitors through a delicate balance of soil, rock, plants, and water to a cascading waterfall in a narrow ravine where a viewing platform extends out over the water. Preserved through the Richmond Land Trust and the Berkshire Natural Resources Council, Stevens' Glen can be reached via Lenox Street, which runs between Lenox and Swamp Roads in West Stockbridge.

East of Pittsfield, the Appalachian Trail passes through Dalton, threading through the watershed for the Crane paper company and the mysterious woods of Wizard's Glen. Farther east, off MA 9, Notchview Reservation has trails through 3,000 acres of forest. In Peru the Dorothy Francis Rice Sanctuary on South Road has woodland trails through a 300-acre preserve managed by the New England Forestry Foundation. It can be reached off Massachusetts Highway 143. Farther south in Becket is a little known "ghost quarry" that is worth tromping through the woods to get to, although rambunctious children should be left at home. Still being developed, the Historic Becket Quarry and Forest is open to the public. Led by the Becket Land Trust, the site was bought by the townspeople for $300,000 to head off a plan by a developer to reopen the quarry for blasting and a stone-crushing plant. A parking area with an informational kiosk is located off Quarry Road, where the trail starts. To be on the safe side, take a map. After a walk of about a quarter of a mile, the first remnants of the abandoned quarry begin to appear. The place looks as though everyone just walked away on the day it closed in 1940. Trees have grown up through the rusting cables, power plant, and vehicles. One huge derrick stands above the southern rim of the quarry, which is filled with water and debris. Resist the temptation to take a swim.

North County

Mount Greylock Reservation really consists of five mountains, Mount Greylock being the highest. The others are Mount Prospect, Mount Williams, Mount Fitch, and Saddle Ball Mountain. All are crisscrossed with old logging roads and hiking trails that vary in degrees of difficulty. The Mount Greylock summit is a premier destination for visitors on foot as well as those who drive to the top by car for the five-state view. The Appalachian Trail leads here, as do many of the trails on all sides of the range. A map is a must for tackling the reservation.

The Hopper is one area that can be reached by several paths. The easiest can be found by driving MA 43 to Hopper Road in south Williamstown and following the signs. The trail follows Hopper Brook and then Money Brook, named for a band of counterfeiters who supposedly hid out here and whose spirits later haunted the surrounding woods. Another popular path that is not too difficult is the Cheshire Harbor Trail, which begins on the east slope in Adams and leads to the summit. Every year on Columbus Day about 2,000 hikers of all ages climb this trail in a daylong event called the Greylock Ramble. Kids, dogs, parents, couples, singles, and senior citizens all clamber up to the top, where they receive a certificate of accomplishment and other awards.

The Cheshire Cobble, through which the Appalachian Trail passes, is a little-explored area, probably because you have to park in town some distance away from it. Some suggest biking from there to the beginning of the trail, which leads to a rock outcropping with great views of the Hoosic River Valley and Mount Greylock. Other popular trails in North County can be found in Williamstown on Stone Hill, Bee Hill, and Pine Cobble; in Hopkins Forest; along the Taconic Trail; and at Field Farm. East of North Adams there are trails in Savoy and Windsor State Forests. North of Greylock the Appalachian Trail leads to Clarksburg State Park, where there are other paths to walk. The AT crosses into Vermont here. Less than a mile from downtown North Adams is 85-acre Cascade Park, where a path with a footbridge over Notch Brook leads to a 40-foot-high waterfall.

Trails for All-Terrain Vehicles (ATVs)

ATVs are allowed on certain trails in Pittsfield, October Mountain, Beartown, Savoy, and Tolland State Forests. For information

Hopkins Forest in Williamstown has an unusual walkway 70 feet above ground that is open to the public a few times a year, usually when there is a community festival. Reached by ladders and suspended between two platforms, the walkway stretches through the treetops for 40 feet, offering a rare view of the forest canopy and the floor from above. Not for the faint of heart or children under age 10. Williams College, which owns the forest, may be contacted for information at (413) 458-3080 or www.williams.edu.

CLOSE-UP

The Appalachian Trail

The Appalachian National Scenic Trail was the brainchild of forester Benton MacKay, a Massachusetts native who in 1921 conceived the idea of creating a footpath that would provide a continuous green corridor along the ridge of the Appalachian chain of mountains and hills. Developed by volunteers, his vision became a reality in 1937. It was designated as the first National Scenic Trail in 1968. Today the footpath runs 2,100 miles from Springer Mountain in Georgia to Mount Katahdin in Maine, and 90 miles of it are in Berkshire County. During the 1970s and 1980s, the National Park Service undertook a sometimes contentious land acquisition program to create a protected corridor for the trail. This sometimes meant purchasing land from private owners or acquiring it through other means. Now more than 99 percent of the corridor is owned and protected by federal or state governments or by rights-of-way. Volunteers still play a key part in maintaining the trail, with more than 4,000 contributing over 175,000 hours cutting brush, removing fallen trees, and often sprucing up or building shelters. The Appalachian Mountain Club is the lead organization for trail maintenance and also leads hikes.

The trail can be accessed at many points in the Berkshires, beginning in South County at Mount Everett going all the way to the Vermont border. The elevation ranges from 650 to 3,491 feet at Greylock's peak, which is the highest point in the state. Much of the trail passes through wooded hills, with several summits and ledges offering views of the surrounding terrain. There are long, flat sections atop the Berkshire Plateau and through the Housatonic Valley. Water, although not for drinking, is plentiful along the Housatonic and Hoosic Rivers and Upper Goose Pond. There are some steep ascents, but they are short-lived. Hikers can take short walks or moderate hikes if they wish. Those who choose to walk the whole trail are called thru-hikers, and there are many of them in the summer. Hikers can stay overnight in a variety of rustic lodges, cabins, shelters, and campsites along the trail. Bascom Lodge at the top of Mount Greylock is a popular stop. There also are towns along the way where thru-hikers can have their mail delivered, restock, and rest. Cheshire is one of them, and St. Mary's Church has opened its doors for years to hikers, who can take showers there or grab some sleep on a cot.

With thousands traversing the trail, the following admonition has been adopted to protect the land and plant life: "Take only photographs—leave only footprints." Detailed maps may be obtained from the National Park Service, the Appalachian Trail Conference, the regional office of the state Department of Environmental Management, or the Appalachian Mountain Club—all listed below—as well as some bookstores and outdoor specialty stores.

contact the Massachusetts Department of Environmental Management Regional Office listed below. Information may also be obtained from the Western Massachusetts ATV Association, a group of riders dedicated to trail maintenance, resource preservation, emergency response, and responsible use of the trail systems and off-road motorized trail use throughout the area. For information visit www.westernmassatv.org or write to them at P.O. Box 557, Dalton 01227.

i

A couple of miles north of the Petersburg Pass Scenic Area on MA 2, the Taconic Crest Trail leads to a phenomenon called the Snow Hole, a deep bedrock cleft where ice and snow remain, often year-round. This 90-minute hike begins at the pullout and accesses beautiful views along Shepherd's Well Trail and Brook Trail, which leads to the Snow Hole. The Taconic Hiking Club maintains these marked trails.

Sources for Information and Maps

ORGANIZATIONS

Appalachian Trail Conference
799 Washington Street
Harpers Ferry, WV 25425-0807
(304) 535-6331
www.appalachiantrail.org
or
National Park Service
www.nps.gov/appa

Appalachian Mountain Club
5 Joy Street
Boston 02108
www.outdoors.org

Berkshire Natural Resources Council
20 Bank Row
Pittsfield 01201
(413) 499-0596
www.bnrc.net

Berkshire Wildlife Sanctuaries
Massachusetts Audubon Society
472 West Mountain Road
Lenox 01240
(413) 637-0320
www.massaudubon.org

Massachusetts Department of Environmental Management
Division of Parks and Forests
Regional Office
740 South Street
Pittsfield 01201-1433
(413) 442-8928
www.massparks.org

Massachusetts Division of Fisheries and Wildlife
Regional Office
400 Hubbard Avenue
Pittsfield 01201
(413) 447-9789
www.masswildlife.org

Taconic Hiking Club
45 Hakely Street
Albany, New York 12208
(518) 482-0424

Trustees of Reservations
Western Regional Office
The Mission House
Sergeant Street
Stockbridge 01262-0792
(413) 298-3239
www.thetrustees.org

Williamstown Rural Lands Foundation
671 Cold Spring Road (US 7)
Williamstown 01267-0221
(413) 458-2494

OUTFITTERS

The Arcadian Shop
91 Pittsfield Road (US 7), Lenox
(413) 637-3010, (800) 239-3391
www.arcadian.com

Maps, books, camping gear and trail food, outerwear, and information abound here. Guide services are available. One of the entrances to the trails in Kennedy Park is located behind the shop. Outfitters for all kinds of recreation, Arcadian Shop also sells and rents bicycles, canoes and kayaks, and in winter cross-country skis and snowshoes. Open daily.

Dick Moon Sporting Goods
114 Fenn Street, Pittsfield
(413) 442-8281

This small but crammed shop has been fulfilling the needs of outdoorsmen for more than 60 years. Camping gear of all sorts plus outerwear and accessories are sold year-round. If they don't have it, you don't need it!

Expeditions
276 Main Street, Great Barrington
(413) 528-7737
www.skibutternut.com

Butternut Ski Area owns this sporting goods shop, which carries, among other things, books and maps plus equipment and outerwear for camping, hiking, and backpacking. Guided hiking tours along the Appalachian Trail and other trails may be arranged. Recommendations for pleasant hiking include Bartholomew's Cobble, Benedict Pond, the Housatonic River Walk, Monument Mountain, Ice Glen, and Laura's Tower. Open daily.

Berkshire Outfitters
169 Grove Street (MA 8), Adams
(413) 743-5900
www.berkshireoutfitters.com

Hiking boots, backpacks, and other gear along with maps are available here. Bikes, canoes, roller skis, in-line skates, cross-country skis, and other seasonal equipment is for sale; some is rented. Closed Monday.

The Mountain Goat
130 Water Street, Williamstown
(413) 458-8445

The Mountain Goat is a gathering place for weekly hikes through the summer and fall, some guided, some not. Maps, books, hiking boots, and sports apparel and outerwear also are sold here along with bicycles, which also are rented. In winter cross-country skis and snowshoes are available to buy or rent. Open daily.

BOOKS

Hikes and Walks in the Berkshire Hills

This book by local resident Lauren R. Stevens offers a comprehensive overview of trails throughout the county with directions, maps, distances, times, and degrees of difficulty. It is published by Berkshire House and is available at many bookstores and outfitters.

The North Berkshire Outdoor Guide

This four-season guide has been published by the Williams College Outing Club since 1927. Now in its ninth edition, the guide contains invaluable information and tidbits about the region. Primarily a student organization, the Outing Club also leads hikes for others. For more information visit www.williams.edu/orgs/woc or write to the club at 1004 Baxter Hall, Williams College, Williamstown 01267.

HORSEBACK RIDING

Berkshire Horseback Adventures
293 Main Street (US 7A), Lenox
(413) 637-9090

Trail rides and overnight camping trips may be arranged through Berkshire Horseback Adventures, based at Aspinwall Stables on US 7A, across from the state highway department. Trail rides are $50 an hour. Camping trips to various locations are $200 per person, including dinner and breakfast. Weekends fill up quickly in the height of the season, so plan ahead. Rides are offered spring through fall, weather and trail conditions permitting. Lessons are available at $30 an hour year-round. Horses also are boarded and trained here.

Sunny Banks Ranch
MA 8, Becket
(413) 623-5606
Folks hankering for a bit of the Old West can find it right in the Berkshires at Sunny Banks Ranch. The ranch is run by Steve Robinson, a former firefighter whose family has owned the ranch since 1906. Robinson's true love is riding and roping, a dream he pursued in rodeos for years and is now offering to kids as well as grown-ups who otherwise wouldn't have the chance to be cowboys or cowgirls. Robinson leads trail rides at $35 an hour. Although reservations aren't required, they are recommended. Some rides include breakfast or dinner at the chuck wagon on the trail. Riding lessons are $40 an hour but may be less for year-round customers. Lessons in rodeo skills for kids or adults are $50 an hour. Kids who want to just ride can do so for $25 for half an hour. Robinson trains horses and has around 27 on the property. A kids' rodeo is held every weekend in July and August. Participants pay $25, which is pooled and awarded to winners, with additional funds added by the ranch. Events include roping and bull riding. Even youngsters under age six participate, riding sheep, called mutton busting, or taking part in the calf scramble.

Undermountain Farm
400 Undermountain Road, Lenox
(413) 637-3365
Located on the back road to Tanglewood with spectacular views of the valley beyond, Undermountain Farm offers guided hourlong trail rides through Kennedy Park and other areas for $45 per person. Appointments are required and may be canceled if rain affects trail conditions. Private lessons are available year-round for $50 an hour, $25 for 30 minutes. Pony rides for children under age six also are offered at $20 for a 15-minute ride. Undermountain boards horses and has indoor and outdoor arenas.

HUNTING

With a couple of exceptions, hunting is permitted on all state-owned land within the regulations promulgated by the state Division of Fisheries and Wildlife (www.masswildlife.org). The exceptions are Mount Greylock, where hunting is prohibited at all times within a .75-mile radius of the summit and throughout the entire reservation in summer and fall, and Mount Everett, where hunting is banned all the time. Hunting is prohibited everywhere on Sunday. There are seasons for black bear, turkey, deer, pheasant, partridge, and a host of other wildlife. The regulations are complex, and a copy should be obtained by anyone not familiar with them. Copies are available at the division's regional office at 400 Hubbard Avenue in Pittsfield (413-447-9789) or on the Internet. Fees also are complex. A hunting license ranges from $27.50 for residents to $99.50 for nonresidents going after large game, $65.50 for small game. "Sporting" licenses are good for both hunting and fishing and are a bargain at $45. But they are for residents only. Licenses may be obtained at the regional office or from some town clerks and sporting goods shops, which are allowed to charge an additional handling fee.

Development has closed off much of the open land that hunters once used, and signs posting private property have proliferated along the county's rural roads. Some property owners will allow hunters to use their land, although in some cases town approval also might be needed.

Williams College opens Hopkins Forest to deer hunters for a limited period and sells up to 100 permits allowing shotgun hunters to go on the premises. The hunting is reputed to be excellent in this undeveloped area.

Out-of-state residents planning to hunt in Massachusetts had better bring enough ammunition—they can't buy any here. Massachusetts gun laws also prohibit the sale of guns to nonresidents.

Hunters also should be aware that the regulations are different in states that border Berkshire County and that they are expected to know when they cross state lines, even if they are in the woods.

The division sponsors a special three-day deer hunt for wheelchair-bound hunters. Locally the hunt takes place in Mount Washington, usually around the end of October. Friends and local sportsmen help out. Whether injured in accidents or dealing with mobility-robbing illnesses, the hunters are able to take part in an activity they otherwise might have to give up. For more information on this special session call (508) 792-7270.

Hunting Supplies

Dave's Sporting Goods
1164 North Street, Pittsfield
(413) 442-2960
www.davessportinggoods.com
Dave's Sporting Goods has the largest stock of hunting equipment and accessories in the county. Shotguns and rifles of all makes are stacked in racks and line the walls. Also here are ammunition, carrying cases, scopes, knives, maps, boots, camouflage, tree stands, and gun safes. The store also sells archery equipment, including bows by 30 different makers plus tips, arrows, and targets. Dave's is an official weighing station. Open daily.

Pat's Gun Shop
US 7, Lanesborough
(413) 499-3897
Pat King's shop is small, but his knowledge is large. His stock includes new and used rifles, ammunition, and accessories, including cleaning supplies, scopes and mounts, and gun safes. Aside from his Berkshire-based business, Pat runs a guide service with a partner in Maine that includes deer hunting, canoeing, and fishing. Closed Sunday.

Porter's Sporting Goods
370 Pecks Road, Pittsfield
(413) 442-9967
Black powder, bows, arrows, tree ladders, and other hunting gear are sold at this shop, which is open daily. Shotguns will be added when a planned expansion is completed.

ORGANIZED SPORTS

Baseball rules in summer in Berkshire County. Practically every town has a Little League, with local businesses sponsoring teams. Both North Adams and Pittsfield host professional teams with day and night games. Recently built Noel Field in North Adams also is used by youth and adult leagues. The complex includes basketball and tennis courts. In Pittsfield baseball has been played at Wahconah Park since 1892. This nostalgic old diamond with its 1950s wooden grandstand is on its way to becoming listed on the National Register of Historic Places, which supporters hope will lead to state and federal funds for preservation and restoration. Over the years, farm teams for the Red Sox and the Mets have played here. The Astros were the last major team to play at Wahconah Park, leaving it for a new stadium in Troy, New York. But county fans still had their baseball in the presence of the Berkshire Black Bears. While the park has its fans, others believe it has outlived its usefulness and will no longer attract minor league ball teams even if it is refurbished. For one thing, it is one of a few parks—if not the only park—in the country that was built with the batter's box facing west. When the sun starts to set, it shines right into the batters' eyes; all play has to stop until the sun slips behind the trees. Some find this endearing, while others most assuredly do not. A recent effort to build a new stadium in downtown Pittsfield was defeated, and that is when the Astros left town. Pittsfield also has a complex for Little League games and a large softball complex. Williams College and the Massachusetts College of Liberal Arts in North Adams field softball teams.

Local high school football games also have their supporters, and several area teams have won state championships over the years. Williams College football games attract local folks as well as college kids, and the annual Amherst game is a big draw, especially for alumni. Soccer also is popular, especially with elementary-age kids, who are signing up in droves. Hockey is popular, but participation depends on access to rinks. In North County the Vietnam Veterans Memorial Skating Rink in North Adams and Lansing Chapman Rink in Williamstown are available for skating and hockey games. In Pittsfield the Boys and Girls Club rink is used for hockey and figure and general skating. All are open to the public at certain times and are used for many children's programs.

PAINTBALL

Folks who are into this fast-growing sport have plenty of woods in which to play "Capture the Flag," including a course at Bousquet Ski Area in Pittsfield that is open during summer. "Guns" and other supplies are sold at New England Paintball Supplies at 147 Tyler Street in Pittsfield (413-442-6377) and at Dave's Sporting Goods and Porter's Sporting Goods, both also in Pittsfield and listed above in the Fishing and Hunting sections.

RUNNING

Road races and walks are held through most of the year, often as fund-raisers or as part of a holiday celebration. The annual Josh Billings RunAground, held in September, is a popular triathalon attracting hundreds of competitors. It and several other races are sponsored by the Western Massachusetts Athletic Association. Information is available on their Web site at www.runwmac.com. Other sources are local chambers of commerce and various media.

TENNIS

Several towns, including Pittsfield, Stockbridge, North Adams, and Williamstown, have municipal courts that are open to residents and, in some cases, guests at local accommodations on a first-come basis. Some resorts allow the public to use their courts for a fee. See the Accommodations chapter for more information. See also Fitness Centers for facilities that allow nonmembers to use courts for fees.

WINTER RECREATION

Some locals profess to hate winter. Many even leave to return in spring. Others can't wait for the first flakes to fall. Their reward is glistening forests, snow-covered slopes, icebound lakes, and vistas blanketed with a layer of white. As soon as the temperature drops to 28 degrees, the ski resorts start making snow. If all goes well, by Thanksgiving the trails are groomed and the ski lifts cranking. And when Mother Nature covers all those hiking and walking trails with the white stuff, runners and bikers are replaced with cross-country skiers, snowshoers, and in some places snowmobilers.

As a winter wonderland, Berkshire County offers as much in the way of outdoor enjoyment as it does in summer, much of it free or reasonably priced. Many of the trails in the parks, forests, and other preserves are open for winter use. But some trails in state parks differ in winter; it is recommended that skiers obtain a map geared to the season before heading out. These can be obtained at park headquarters, on the Web at www.massparks.org, or at the regional office in Pittsfield at 740 South Street; (413) 442-8928. (See also the Parks chapter.)

Snowmobiles are allowed on some trails in many parks. Many snowmobilers are in clubs that spend a lot of time clearing trails and instilling good rules of the road. Some of those are listed below. If snowmobiles really bug you, Mount Washington State Forest is one park where they are banned.

Skiing

Good skiing trails here include the 4-mile Ashley Hill Brook Trail. Other places to check out in South County include Beartown, Monterey, Sandisfield, and Otis State Forests. In Lenox there is wonderful Kennedy Park plus the Pleasant Valley Wildlife Sanctuary, with trails laid out by the Massachusetts Audubon Society. A fee is charged that includes a map. Bartholomew's Cobble in Ashley Falls, managed by the Trustees of Reservations, also has some good trails, the best being on the far side of Weatogue Road. A modest fee is charged, and maps are available.

The Trustees manage one of the most popular places for classic and skate cross-country skiing and snowshoeing in central Berkshire: Notchview Reservation in Windsor. High in the hills off MA 9 east of Dalton, snow comes early and leaves late at this former estate of Arthur D. Budd. There are 35 kilometers of groomed and back-country trails through woods and open fields on 3,108 acres. Skiers are advised to stick to the woods to avoid the wind and to remember that the temperature at Notchview is usually 10 degrees colder than in the valleys. Snowshoes may be rented to be used alongside, but not on, the ski trails. Some trails are set aside for folks who want to bring their dogs along. The heated Budd Visitor Center has a waxing area and offers hot chocolate and water. Along the trail there are two alpine-style warming huts. Clinics, lessons, races, and special events, like the Valentine's Day moonlight ski, occur throughout the season. Members of the Trustees ski for free. Others pay $9.00. Children ages 6 through 12 pay $2.00. Group and half-day rates are available. Trail conditions and other information may be found at www.notchview.org or by calling (413) 684-0148. For information about winter recreation on other properties owned by the Trustees, visit www.thetrustees.org.

The Audubon Society maintains Canoe Meadows on Holmes Road in Pittsfield, which is open for cross-country skiing on weekends for a small fee. Fees are waived or reduced for members of the society. Near Canoe Meadows off Williams Street is Sackett Brook Park, open to the public for free. On the other side of the city, Pittsfield State Forest has some challenging trails. Pick up a map before venturing forth. The 11-mile Ashuwillticook Rail Trail between Lanesborough and Adams is open for cross-country skiing in winter. Snowmobiles are prohibited.

State parks in northern Berkshire with good trails include Savoy State Forest and of course Mount Greylock, particularly Greylock Glen on the east side. The latter is a popular place for snowmobilers, but there are some trails just for skiing. In Williamstown the Taconic Golf Course in town, Stone Hill above the Clark Art Institute, Hopkins Forest, and Field Farm offer trails with a variety of slopes, some more challenging than others.

SOUTH COUNTY

Butternut Ski Area
MA 23, Great Barrington
(413) 528-2000
www.skibutternut.com

Butternut, with a 1,000-foot vertical drop, offers downhill and cross-country skiing, snowboarding, and tubing, plus two terrain parks outfitted with numerous tabletops, spines, kickers, rails, and assorted other hits for high-flying snowboarders and skiers. For downhill fans there are 22 trails whose slopes are covered by a 100 percent snowmaking system. There are 10 lifts. A weekend lift ticket for an adult costs $45, less for kids. Reduced rates are available at certain times, and a package that includes a lift ticket, rented equipment, and 90 minutes of lessons is available for $55. Eight kilometers of groomed cross-country trails are opened when Mother Nature provides enough cover. A trail fee of $8.00 per person is charged. The cross-country center rents skis, poles, and boots for $15.00, $9.00 for youngsters under age 12. Although there is no night skiing, there are lighted runs for tubing.

Butternut prides itself on its work with new skiers of all ages, making every effort to instill confidence and provide a pleasant experience on the slopes. If the weather cooperates, Butternut opens on the day after Thanksgiving and closes at the end of the first week in April. The ski area operates daily; the cross-country center is open Thursday through Sunday and on holidays. During summer, craft shows and music festivals are held on the grounds. Butternut owns Expeditions, an outfitter at 276 Main Street in Great Barrington, where snowshoes, snowboards, cross-country skis, and accessories are sold in season. Equipment, accessories, and attire for other outdoor activities are sold year-round. Alpine and other skis and equipment are sold at the full-service center at the ski area.

Canterbury Farm
1986 Fred Snow Road, Becket
(413) 623-0100
www.canterbury-farms.com

Canterbury Farm Ski Touring Center offers 20 kilometers of groomed and tracked ski trails that take the skier through woods and fields; by frozen brooks, beaver ponds, stone walls, and lakes. A $12 trail fee is charged. Equipment may be rented for $12. Reservations are suggested for lessons, which are available separately or through a package that includes skis for $32. Prices are less for half days and weekdays and for children or family groups of four or more. The trails are open every day except Tuesday. Skiers are welcome to warm up in the farmhouse, where soup, chili, snacks, and drinks are available. The Web site includes a map of all the trails. Canterbury Farm is off MA 8 on Fred Snow Road, just south of Becket center. Skiers coming from the Mass Pike who like back roads and shortcuts (and have good traction) might want to take Becket Road, a left off US 20/MA 8 across from the Belden Inn east of Lee. Becket Road leads to Fred Snow Road via Tyne or Leonhardt Road.

Catamount
New York Highway 23
Hillsdale, New York
(518) 325-3200

South Egremont
(413) 528-1262
www.catamountski.com

Catamount has two phone numbers because it is in two states, straddling the border between Massachusetts and New York. With an elevation of 2,000 feet and a vertical drop of 1,000 feet, Catamount has 28 trails and eight lifts, plus a base lodge and children's learning center. Half the trails are lighted, and three are set aside for slow family skiing. Snowmaking has been expanded and pumping capacity increased for better coverage. Hottest new thing on the mountain is the snowboarders' Megaplex terrain park. Separate from the skiing areas, the park features berms, rails, banks, jumps, spines, kickers, tabletops, and a 400-foot halfpipe and is lighted at night. Lessons are offered in skiing and snowboarding. Skis, boots, and poles or snowboards may be rented for $28 a day, less for juniors and wee ones. Snowblades and helmets also may be rented. There are many programs for children and a playroom for nonskiing little ones. A learn-to-ski or snowboard package that includes the equipment, lift ticket, and one lesson is $49. An adult lift ticket for a weekend day is $44. Several discounts and packages are offered, including a frequent skier card and deals with local inns. Catamount is open daily, with night skiing offered only during peak season.

Cranwell Resort
55 Lee Road (US 7/20), Lenox
(413) 637-1364, (800) 272-6935
www.cranwell.com
Cranwell runs a ski touring center with 10 kilometers of groomed trails and equipment that may be rented. An adult trail pass for a full day of skiing is $14. Snowshoes and/or skis, boots, and poles may be rented for $16. Cranwell also offers an introduction to cross-country skiing that includes lessons and equipment for $50. The trails are open daily, weather permitting.

Otis Ridge
MA 23, Otis
(413) 269-4444
www.otisridge.com
Otis Ridge Ski Area is a low-key place for kids and families to have fun at reasonable prices. There are 11 trails, including three expert ones; one chairlift; and several rope-and-bar tows. The vertical drop is 400 feet, and the area makes snow for 90 percent of the trails. There are also 6 kilometers of cross-country trails. Otis Ridge is known for its ski camp, offering lessons along with the camp experience for kids during school vacations. Otis Ridge is open daily, including some nights. Skis, poles, and boots may be rented for $15; snowboards and boots for $25. An adult lift ticket on a weekend costs $25. The area includes a lodge that serves meals and rents rooms.

CENTRAL BERKSHIRE

Bousquet Ski Area
101 Dan Fox Drive, Pittsfield
(413) 442-8316
www.bousquets.com
With an elevation of 1,875 feet and a vertical drop of 750 feet, Bousquet's might seem like small potatoes when compared with other ski areas. But the 21 trails at this kid-friendly ski area are just about evenly divided between easiest, more difficult, and difficult. The longest trail is 5,280 feet. There are two chairlifts and two surface lifts, including a "Magic Carpet" for beginners. Users of various abilities can enjoy alpine skiing, tubing, skiboarding, and snowboarding. During the week, lift tickets cost $25 for all day or $15 for night skiing on the lighted trails. Weekend prices might be more, and there are packages for groups. The area has 98 percent snowmaking capability. Snowboarders can test their skills in a terrain park and a halfpipe. The lodge includes a rental section and a child-care center. Equipment, including a complete ski package, may be rented for $18. Lessons are offered for all ages and abilities. A beginners package that includes a one-hour lesson and equipment is $55. Open daily from around Thanksgiving to March, Bousquet's is located on Dan Fox Drive off US 7 south of Pittsfield.

Bucksteep Manor Inn
885 Mount Washington Road, Washington
(413) 623-5535
www.bucksteepmanor.com
This rural turn-of-the-20th-century estate, now an inn, on top of Washington Mountain has 20 miles of trails for cross-country skiing and snowshoeing that are open to the public on weekends for a trail fee of $10. Skis, boots, and poles may be rented for $12.50. Prices are lower after 2:00 P.M.

NORTH COUNTY

Jiminy Peak
37 Corey Road, Hancock
(413) 738-5500
www.jiminypeak.com
Efforts to ski the 2,380-foot mountain that is known as Jiminy Peak began in the 1940s with a couple of trails and a rope tow. As time went on, it became the first ski resort in the area to have a chairlift. Today the multimillion-dollar complex boasts 40 trails, 18 of them lit for night skiing, and eight lifts. A newly built Village

Center houses a children's center and retail space plus two-bedroom condominiums augmenting those already on the property. A country store, tavern, restaurant, and new welcoming center round out the facilities. While there are recreational activities year-round, skiing is still the main focus at Jiminy, with snowboarding a recent addition. The trails, spread over 156 acres with a vertical rise of 1,150 feet, are graded from easiest to extremely difficult, with 93 percent snowmaking coverage. Seven trails are designated as nonspeed zones, where everyone is asked to follow the flow and avoid speeding. About 30 percent of the trails are designed for experts. The chairlifts include a new high-speed six-passenger Berkshire Express, which takes folks to the summit in five minutes. There you can access 35 trails, including the 18 that are lit at night. Also at the peak is the Hendricks Summit Lodge, with spectacular views of the surrounding terrain. Open year-round, although less in summer, the lodge is the former home of the late Bartlett Hendricks and his wife, Mary, who were early supporters of skiing and founders of the original ski area. Even after turning the resort over to present owner Brian Fairbank, the couple continued skiing well into their eighties.

Jiminy offers lessons for all ages, with a beginner package for skiing or snowboarding priced at $55, including equipment. Adults may rent skis, boots, and poles or snowboards and boots for a daily rate of $28, less for juniors. Helmets, wrist guards, and radios also may be rented. A lift ticket for eight hours on a weekend is $45 for an adult, less for seniors, juniors, and toddlers. A variety of price packages are available, including season lift tickets, a discount card, preseason bonuses, and reduced rate periods. E-coupons may be purchased online.

Jiminy Peak can be reached by either US 7 to the east or MA 43 via New York Highway 22 on the west. Jiminy also sponsors snow tubing and snowshoeing at Brodie Mountain, a short distance away on US 7 in New Ashford. But this option may be short-lived, as the property is slated to become a time-share development.

Mount Greylock Ski Club
Roaring Brook Road, Williamstown
(413) 743-5308

Good skiing at a bargain price is available to skiers who want to be involved in this unusual cooperative. In exchange for really low fees, members maintain 17 trails, which include four novice, nine intermediate, and four expert runs for downhill and cross-country skiing. Other jobs include keeping the woodstove going in the lodge, checking in members, maintaining the engines that power the two rope tows, and generally helping out, much like an extended family. The ski area is off US 7 in south Williamstown and is reached by either walking about half a mile from the parking area on Roaring Brook Road or driving up a gravel road, which is one-way until midafternoon. The area has a base altitude of 1,200 feet and a vertical drop of 500 feet and depends on natural snow. It is open weekends and holidays and sometimes during school vacations. The membership fee for a family, including children up to the age of 21, is $120 for the season. Singles and couples pay less. Information may be obtained by calling (413) 743-5308 or (413) 458-3060.

OUTSIDE THE COUNTY

Berkshire East
MA 2, Charlemont
(413) 339-6617
www.berkshireeast.com

Just over the Berkshire County border, Berkshire East offers skiing at all levels day and night, with 100 percent snowmaking capability. The area has five lifts, including a new quad, and 45 trails, about half of them described as steep and demanding for experts. With a vertical drop of 1,180 feet, some runs are more than 4,000 feet long. There's a halfpipe for snowboarders. Beginners are welcome and have an area all to themselves where lessons are given. Berkshire East is open daily, but night skiing is offered Wednesday through Saturday only. Prices are reasonable and are broken down into afternoon, night, or all-day skiing. Lift tickets for an adult for nights only run around $20. A full day ticket for an adult costs $25, $38 for a full-day on a weekend or holiday. Afternoons cost only $20 during the week, $25 on weekends. Ski equipment packages for adults may be rented all day for $25, snowboards and short skis for $30. Afternoon or evening rentals are $15. Season tickets and other special prices are available. Berkshire East is off MA 8A, just off MA 2.

Skating

Lucky are the folks who live in communities where the local fire department or recreation committee creates an outdoor skating rink. The lakes are fine for skating if they freeze before the snow falls. Otherwise, unless some kindly shore dweller clears the surface, they are too bumpy. In North County the Vietnam Veterans Memorial Skating Rink in North Adams and Lansing Chapman Rink in Williamstown are available for skating and hockey games. In Pittsfield the Boys and Girls Club rink is used for hockey and figure and general skating. All are open to the public at certain times and are used for many children's programs.

Snowmobiling

Wild 'n' Wet Tours
US 7, Lanesborough
(413) 445-5211

As soon as Pontoosuc Lake is frozen, John Casey leads two- and four-hour snowmobile tours daily from his base on the shore next to Matt Reilly's Pub and Restaurant. Casey rents snowmobiles and will lead tours over the lake through Pittsfield State Forest by various routes and back. Tours from the visitor center at Mount Greylock also can be arranged, depending on trail conditions. Prices vary depending on the number of adults and/or children and the length of the ride. One adult will pay $129 for a two-hour ride, $219 for four hours. A second adult will pay $89 or $159. Equipment, including gloves, bibs, boots, face masks, and coats may be rented individually or for a package price of $34. Reservations are required. Casey's mailing address is P.O. Box 2284, Lenox 01240.

SNOWMOBILE CLUBS

The nonprofit Snowmobile Association of Massachusetts (S.A.M.) is the lead organization for snowmobilers. The association encourages responsible snowmobiling and provides information on clubs, laws and registration, and trail conditions on its Web site (www.snowassocma.com). Local clubs are listed below. Some have their own Web sites as well.

Adams Sno-Drifters
P.O. Box 25
Adams 01220
(413) 743-2659

Meetings are held on the first and third Thursdays of the month at American Legion Post 160 in Adams. The club operates a snow phone at (413) 743-1132.

Berkshire Snow Seekers
P.O. Box 1102
Pittsfield 01202
(413) 499-2111

Meetings are held on the first and third Tuesdays of the month at the Skyline Country Club in Lanesborough.

Florida Mountaineers
P.O. Box 284
North Adams
(413) 662-2705

The club meets in Monroe Bridge at the Depot Restaurant on the first Tuesday of every month.

Knox Trail Sno-Riders Club
P.O. Box 363
East Otis 01029
(413) 269-0243
Breakfast meetings are held on the second and fourth Sundays between October and April at the Club House on Tannery Road.

Sandisfield Snowmobile Club
P.O. Box 94
Sandisfield 01255
(508) 759-5127
Meetings are held at Tuckers Restaurant on MA 8 on the second Sunday of the month and at Daffers Restaurant on MA 57 on the fourth Sunday of the month.

Savoy Kanary Kats
20 Old Dalton Road
Savoy 01256
(413) 743-1549
The Kanary Kats meet on the first Wednesday of the month at the Hilltop Restaurant in Plainfield.

Southern Berkshire Sno-Dusters
P.O. Box 393
Ashley Falls 01222
(413) 229-3578

Outfitters and Equipment Rentals

SOUTH COUNTY

Arcadian Shop
91 Pittsfield Road (US 7), Lenox
(413) 637-3010, (800) 239-3391
www.arcadian.com
During winter this outdoor specialty store sells and rents skis and snowshoes. Nordic, skating, and telemark skis are available. The daily fee to rent skis, poles, boots, and bindings runs around $11 for classic skis, $18 for skating and racing models, and $35 for a telemark package. Snowshoes rent for $11. Adjacent to Kennedy Park with its miles of groomed trails, the shop also carries a wide range of outerwear and accessories. Open daily.

Expeditions
276 Main Street, Great Barrington
(413) 528-7737
Snowshoes, snowboards, cross-country skis, accessories, and outerwear are sold at this shop run by Butternut Ski Area. Equipment, accessories, and attire for other outdoor activities are available here year-round.

Kenver Ltd.
39 Main Street, South Egremont
(413) 528-2330, (800) 342-7547
www.kenverltd.com
Located in a 250-year-old former tavern, Kenver Ltd. probably has the largest stock of winter sporting equipment, winter outerwear, and accessories around. It's all they do! The stock includes alpine skis, bindings, and boots from Volk, Atomic, Rossignol, Tecnica, and others. With snowboarding taking off there is an expanded selection of equipment, apparel, and accessories. Cross-country skis by several makers, Redfeather snowshoes, snowblades, and figure and hockey skates for kids and adults by Bauer and Nike also are sold here. Snowboards and downhill skis may be leased for the season at rates that vary depending on many factors. Located about 10 minutes from Catamount Ski Area, Kenver Ltd. is open daily from the end of September through the end of March, and shoppers are treated to a complimentary cup of coffee or cider or a nice, crisp apple. Bargain hunters look forward to the annual tent sale held in August.

CENTRAL BERKSHIRE

Plaine's Bike, Ski and Snowboard
55 West Housatonic Street (US 20), Pittsfield
(413) 499-0294, (888) 216-7122
www.plaines.com
Plaine's sells a full line of skis and snowboards, outerwear, and accessories and also rents equipment. A performance ski package or snowboard package rents for $25 a day or $150 for the season. Daily rental for skiboards is $25. Cross-country

skis rent for $10 a day. The stock includes skis by Atomic, Rossignol, Salomon, and K2. Outerwear includes outfits by Karbon and Bonfire. The shop and large parking lot are on the corner of West Housatonic and Elizabeth Streets, at the Center Street traffic light. Open daily.

Ski Fanatics
241 North Street, Pittsfield
(413) 443-3023
www.skifanatics.com
John Kirby Jr. sells and rents alpine skis, snowboards, and showshoes at his downtown shop and knows what he is talking about. A PSIA instructor, Kirby is an experienced freestyle competitor, having started as a youngster. Now the father of a young skier and snowboarder, he likes to work with kids and has several rental and lease packages geared toward their needs. Youngsters may rent skis or snowboards for $15 a day, $59 a week, or $99 for the season. He also has lease packages that allow kids to trade up at the end of the season. Adults may rent skis for $25 a day, $79 a week, or may buy a package, which includes boots, bindings, and poles for $199. Kirby also services performance skis, including shaping and waxing, and counts high school teams and ski patrol members among his customers. His stock includes Redfeather and Atlas snowshoes, Avalanche and Elevation snowboards, and Volkl, Fischer, Nordica, and Line skis, along with Tecnica, Dolomite, and Nordica boots and brand name outer- and underwear. He also leads a couple of group skiing trips out west during the season. The shop is open daily from September through April.

NORTH COUNTY

Berkshire Outfitters
169 Grove Street (MA 8), Adams
(413) 743-5900
www.berkshireoutfitters.com
Cross-country skis may be rented for $22 a day at Berkshire Outfitters, which is located near Mount Greylock. Snowboards rent for $18 for three hours or less; snowshoes are $20 for the day, $16 for three hours or less. All also are for sale along with snowtubes and accessories. Closed Monday.

The Mountain Goat
130 Water Street, Williamstown
(413) 458-8445
www.themountaingoat.com
The Mountain Goat sells and rents skis and snowshoes, along with carrying a full stock of winter gear for adults and little ones. The daily rental for cross-country skis, boots, and poles or snowshoes is $25. Additional days are $10 each. The stock includes backcountry and telemark skis. Knowledgeable staff leads snowshoe hikes at various times by announcement, usually in the *Advocate* newspaper.

Sports Corner
61 Main Street, North Adams
(413) 664-8654
Sports Corner carries snowboards, snowshoes, and accessories in winter. Snowboards by Nitro, Ride, and Elevation may be bought outright at $249 for the package or rented with an option to buy for $189. Snowshoes by Redfeather and Dion, a local maker, are available. The shop is open daily, but hours vary; a call ahead might be a good idea.

DAY TRIPS AND WEEKEND GETAWAYS

Aside from myriad offerings locally, Berkshire County is smack in the middle of an area filled with cultural activities, recreational resources, shopping centers, educational institutions, historic sites, and performing arts venues. With New York or Boston about three hours away, many folks zip into the city for flower shows, plays, museums, gallery openings, parades, sporting events, and what have you. However, for the purposes of this guide, this chapter will touch on some of the offerings that can be found in the Pioneer Valley to the east, neighboring counties in New York to the west, lower Vermont to the north, and upper Connecticut to the south. With a couple of exceptions, most of these are not more than a two-hour trip from Central Berkshire. Pertinent phone numbers and Web sites will be found throughout.

It should be noted that for some, a jaunt from Great Barrington to North Adams is considered a day trip, especially if the visit includes all the museums and galleries in North County. Those who want to pamper themselves might consider staying overnight at one of the many inns in the area, especially in the off season when bargains are offered. See the North County listings in the Accommodations chapter for more information.

THE PIONEER VALLEY

The Pioneer Valley is the section of western Massachusetts between the Vermont and Connecticut borders through which the Connecticut River flows. It was developed long before the colonists made it over the mountains to what became Berkshire County, and there are many historic sites and early settlements. Due to the number of colleges and larger communities along the river, the area offers much in the way of interesting shops and entertainment. The valley can be reached by all the major roads leading out of Berkshire County. Residents in South County often take the Mass Pike to Springfield and than I-91 north to reach this area. Or they might choose the slower but more picturesque U.S. Highway 20 out of Lee. Massachusetts Highway 9 from Dalton leads directly to the Northampton area, while Massachusetts Highway 2 in the north follows along the Vermont border. Choosing the route you want will depend on your destination and how fast you want to get there. The Greater Springfield Convention & Visitors Bureau publishes a comprehensive guide to the area. Their address is 1441 Main Street, Springfield 01103. The phone number is (413) 787-1548 and Web site is www.valleyvisitor.com.

MA 2 in the north, also called the Mohawk Trail, leads over the mountains to Greenfield and Old Deerfield. Originally a footpath used by the Mohawk Indians, the trail was paved and opened as New England's first scenic road in 1914, when motoring was becoming a form of recreation. Starting in North Adams with a wild hairpin turn, the highway winds over the mountains with impressive views and down through deep, wooded valleys until it flattens out along the Deerfield River. The ride is beautiful any time of year but especially in fall. But it is a slow two-lane road with few passing zones, and you can occasionally get stuck behind a truck. If it happens to you, relax and enjoy the scenery!

Along the way are a couple of hokey gift shops selling Indian wares. One even has a giant tepee reminiscent of tourist shops in the '40s. The town of Charlemont has a great restaurant and an early Federated Church with phenomenal acoustics. A concert series is held here annually. The Deerfield River is popular for white-water rafting, canoeing, and fishing, and several businesses in the area rent equipment or provide guides.

Shelburne Falls is worth a visit just to see the glacial potholes worn in the rocks by the river over the centuries. The town is also known for its Bridge of Flowers, an old trolley span adopted by local horticulturists, covered with earth, and planted with hundreds of species of flowers. The works of talented local artisans are sold in several interesting shops. You can watch candles being made at the Mole Hollow Candle company or glass being blown at the North River Studio. For more about what can be found along MA 2, visit www.mohawktrail.com.

MA 2 goes all the way to Waltham, but Greenfield is far enough for a day trip. Here you can visit Old Greenfield Village, check out a covered bridge that offers a splendid view of Franklin County, or climb Poet's Seat Tower for views of the Pioneer Valley, southern Vermont, and New Hampshire. MA 2 connects with I-91, a high-speed four-lane highway that runs through the valley. For a more leisurely ride take U.S. Highway 5, which parallels I-91, passing through all the towns along the river from Greenfield to Springfield. Those in a hurry usually take I-91 to reach the Amherst-Northampton area, the Holyoke Mall at Ingleside, or Springfield, where it connects with the Mass Pike.

South of Greenfield on US 5 is Old Deerfield, founded in 1669. Attractions include a children's museum and several historic early homes. The Yankee Candle Company in South Deerfield demonstrates candle-making with antique equipment. Santa is here year-round in the Bavarian Christmas Village and toy factory, and candles in every scent imaginable are for sale in the 90,000-square-foot showroom. Chandler's Restaurant on-site offers traditional New England food. The Magic Wings Butterfly Conservatory and Gardens on Greenfield Road houses hundreds of living butterflies in a glass-covered conservatory and indoor and outdoor gardens. For more information about this unusual attraction, which is open year-round, visit www.MagicWings.net or call (413) 665-2805.

The Northampton area can be reached by continuing south on US 5 or by taking I-91. Many folks in Berkshire County take MA 9 from Dalton to reach this part of the valley. Dubbed the Berkshire Trail, MA 9 passes through a number of small towns in neighboring Hampshire County. Cummington, where ballooning is a popular pastime, hosts one of four small old-fashioned agricultural fairs in western Massachusetts. The others, held within weeks of one another, are in Middlefield, Chester, and Adams. The William Cullen Bryant Homestead is located in Cummington, just off MA 9. A Crafts Festival is held here in July and in December, the fully furnished home is decorated for a Victorian Christmas, and an open house is held. Just outside Northampton, in Florence, is Look Park, given to the city in 1930 as a memorial to her husband by Fannie Burr Look. The park spans more than 150 acres and is open year-round with seasonal activities and entertainment. Features include a 5,000-square-foot water spray park with pools for kids of different ages, tennis courts, pedal and bumper boats, steam train rides, a zoo, botanical gardens, and an amphitheater where name acts perform. A day at Look Park makes for a great day trip, especially if you have kids. Visit www.lookpark.org or call (413) 584-5457 for more information.

With five colleges in the area, Northampton and Amherst are bursting with activity. The University of Massachusetts and Mount Holyoke, Hampshire, Amherst, and Smith Colleges are all within a few miles of one another. Restaurants, nightspots, and interesting shops and galleries abound, catering to the eclectic and sophisticated tastes of this large and diverse population. Northampton's shopping district is anchored by Thornes Marketplace, an old four-story department store rescued from oblivion and now filled with specialty shops, an ice-cream parlor, and an excellent restaurant. The cuisine of nearly every nationality can be found among the eateries in Northampton. They showcase their menus in the annual three-day Taste of Northampton held in August. Film and arts festivals and antiques shows also take place at various venues during the year. The restored Calvin Theater and the Academy of Music present live entertainment, foreign and domestic films, and lecturers of note, as do the colleges. Naturally there are many places to stay in the area, including the venerable Northampton Hotel. The Northampton Chamber of Commerce at 99 Pleasant Street has a full range of brochures on the city and the area. Call (413) 584-1900 or visit www.northamptonuncommon.com.

Amherst is smaller than Northampton, but the colleges located here sponsor many activities, speakers, concerts, art shows, and sporting events. The largest of these is the University of Massachusetts. MA 9 between Northampton and Amherst is loaded with shopping centers, strip malls, and other businesses while Amherst has a number of interesting specialty shops, book stores, and restaurants.

Holyoke, a city struggling to recover from the loss of industry, nevertheless hosts a number of interesting tourist attractions. It has developed one of the top children's museums in the country, located in the Holyoke Heritage State Park at 221 Appleton Street. Also there are a restored 1929 merry-go-round and the Volleyball Hall of Fame. Hours at these attractions vary, so call (413) 534-1723 or check www.state.ma.us/dem/parks/hhsp to avoid disappointment. The elevators at the Robert Barrett Fishway move more than a million migrating salmon and shad over the Holyoke Dam into the Connecticut River between the middle of May and the end of June. This amazing transfer can be witnessed Wednesday through Sunday from an observation platform or through viewing windows. Mount Tom State Reservation, off I-91, houses a museum of natural history and offers four-season recreational opportunities.

The city of Springfield has all the attractions you would expect in a major city, plus some you can't find anywhere else. The recently expanded $103 million Basketball Hall of Fame is a must for fans of the sport. Visit www.hoophall.com for more information. Also new is a park and museum in the center of Springfield dedicated to native son Theodor Seuss Geisel, aka Dr. Seuss. Located at the Springfield Library and Museums Quadrangle at 220 State Street, this whimsical memorial commemorates with monumental bronze sculptures the Lorax, Horton the elephant, and other characters from Dr. Seuss's wonderful children's books. For information visit www.catinthehat.org or www.quadrangle.org. The phone number for all the attractions at the Quadrangle, including the Museum of Fine Arts and the Smith Art Museum, is (800) 625-7738. Springfield is also the home of the Duryea Transportation Society Museum, the Indian Motorcycle Museum and Hall of Fame, and the Springfield Armory National Historic Site. The Hatikvah Holocaust Education and Resource Center, dedicated to educating the community and combating prejudice, hate, and racism, is at 1160 Dickinson Street. For information call (413) 734-7700 or visit www.hatikvah-center.org. The Springfield Civic Center hosts numerous events, concerts, and sports. The Springfield Symphony Orchestra shares Symphony Hall with the theatrical company, CityStage. Cruises on the Connecticut River via the Peter Pan Bus Company's RiverBus can be arranged at the Riverfront Park on State Street. Springfield also has a zoo, located in Forest Park, off I-91. The Eastern States Exposition complex on US 20 in West Springfield is a collection of buildings that house various shows throughout the year. The biggest attraction is the Big E in September, a 17-day extravaganza that combines agricultural exhibits and animal judging typically associated with a county fair along with entertainment, crafts, the Storrowton Village Museum, parades, rides, and international food booths.

South of Springfield in Agawam is Six Flags New England, boasting more than 160 rides, shows, and attractions. Home of the Superman Ride of Steel, this mega-amusement park also includes a new eight-acre water park. The Web site, which is for all the Six Flags parks in the country, is at www.sixflags.com. The park in Agawam is the only one in Massachusetts.

A bit beyond the scope of this chapter, but worth seeing if the sight of a soaring eagle takes your breath away, is Quabbin Reservoir. Located in Belchertown, this man-made lake was created to provide water for Boston in the 1930s. The Swift River was impounded and four towns in the valley flooded to create the 412-billion-gallon reservoir. Quabbin is one of the largest man-made reservoirs in the world devoted solely to unfiltered water supply. Parts of the reservoir are off-limits. Swimming is prohibited, but there are plenty of places to fish for lake trout, large- and smallmouth bass, and landlocked salmon. Boats may be rented, but launching areas are restricted. The area has also become a sanctuary for the bald eagle, which had all but disappeared from the area until a restoration project was undertaken. Catching a glimpse of one of these magnificent birds is something not easily forgotten. Belchertown can be reached by MA 9 out of Amherst or Massachusetts Highway 202 from Holyoke. The reservoir is managed by the Metropolitan District Commission, which operates a visitor center at the southern tip of the reservoir. The main phone number is (413) 323-7221; the Web site is www.state.ma.us/mdc/water.

US 20 from Lee, also called the Jacob's Ladder Scenic Byway, winds through the mountains of Becket all the way to Springfield and on to Boston. The area includes a number of small towns, some off the beaten path, who have joined to publicize their attractions. They have published a brochure and set up their own Web site: www.hidden-hills.com. Halfway between Becket and Springfield is Chester, a town that has fought its way back from oblivion through the determination and hard work of many dedicated volunteers. The 1841 railroad station was saved from demolition and restored and is now the focal point of an annual festival, Chester on Track. Held in May, daylong events include reenactment of a Civil War camp, a parade, live entertainment, and model trains. Exhibits educate the public about the importance of rail travel to the development of the area. The Westfield River flows along US 20, and rafting and canoeing are popular here. The miniature theatre of Chester is an Equity theater, and its productions often are acclaimed by local reviewers. For more information about Chester visit www.chestermass.com or contact the Chester Foundation at (413) 354-6570.

Located in the Becket-Chester-Middlefield area are the Keystone Arches, built in the 1840s to carry trains over the winding rivers and through the ravines. Originally there were 10 of these architectural marvels, the first stone bridges to be built in this country. That they were even built in this hilly and hard-to-reach area is a wonder in itself. No mortar was used, and the blue stone was quarried locally. Today there are only five left, and two of them are still in use. Most are reachable only by arduous and sometimes dangerous hiking. But one is visible in the Bancroft section of Middlefield, a short ride from Chester on Middlefield Road. The Skyline Trail off Massachusetts Highway 8 in Hinsdale also will take you there. A group of concerned citizens has organized to preserve the remaining arches and has created a fairly safe walking trail for those who want to see them. More information, including a map of the trail, may be obtained from the Friends of the Keystone Arches at P.O. Box 276, Huntington 01050.

NEW YORK STATE

Columbia County

i

All roads leading out of Berkshire County to the west enter New York state at one point or another. Check the map before starting out to find the best route. Columbia, Rensselaer, Albany, and Schenectady Counties are considered part of the Capital-Saratoga Region by New York tourism officials, and information about towns in the area may be found at www.capital-saratoga.com, with links to individual Web sites.

Just over the Massachusetts border on US 20 is New Lebanon, which comes to life in summer. Attractions include the Lebanon Valley Speedway (518-794-9606). Here dragsters, stock cars, funny cars, demolition derbies, and monster trucks make appearances on the dirt track throughout the season. A schedule is posted at www.lebanonvalley.com. Although now the location of Darrow School, the former Mount Lebanon Shaker Village off US 20 is open for tours in summer. The Tannery Pond Concert series and the Shaker Mountain Performing Arts Festival are also held here (518-781-0196). The Theater Barn presents aspiring actors in tried-and-true Broadway hits at moderate prices. A large number of Massachusetts license plates can usually be seen in the parking lot of the Off Track Betting parlor on US 20. A weekend day can easily be spent hitting the antiques shops and a large flea market, where some antiques can be found amid the produce, flowers, job lots, and second-hand items. There are a number of restaurants, including the Pillars and Mario's. Dinners run around $20 or so, and reservations are a must on weekends, especially at the Pillars, where they might have to be made weeks ahead. At the other end of the spectrum is Jimmy D's, where daily specials range from $6.00 to $12.00. The Hitchin'post Cafe serves breakfast and lunch daily, also for moderate prices.

About 25 minutes from New Lebanon on New York Highway 295 is Chatham, also reached by New York Highway 66. The Columbia County Fair (518-724-1846), held here over Labor Day weekend, is one of the area's longest running county fairs and offers a full roster of agricultural events and entertainment. The MacHayden Theater on New York Highway 203 (518-392-9292) presents up-and-coming actors in musicals with after-show cabarets throughout the summer. The Shaker Museum and Library in Old Chatham on New York Highway 13 (518-794-9100) has a small collection compared with the museum over the mountain in Hancock, but some might find it a more manageable way to glimpse the Shaker life.

If antiquing is your goal, you will want to head to Hudson via NY 66 or NY 9. There are around 50 shops up and down Warren Street, plus a number of galleries. Most are only open Thursday through Monday. A brochure is available from the Hudson Antiques Dealers Association by e-mailing hada@hotmail.com. Antiques shops also can be found in Hillsdale on New York Highway 23, in Nassau on US 20, in Kinderhook on NY 9H, and on many of the highways running through the area. Maps are available at participating shops. Architecturally speaking, Hudson is veritably untouched from its early days as a whaling center. Federal houses in various stages of restoration are everywhere, but Warren Street really shows them off. This main drag also has a number of excellent restaurants—Brandow's and Earth Foods come to mind. South of the city on NY 9G is Olana, an outrageous Moorish villa designed and decorated by artist Frederic Edwin Church for his own enjoyment (518-828-0135). The American Museum of Firefighting (518-828-7695) on NY 9 north of the city has an amazing collection of equipment and memorabilia.

A number of historic sites are located farther north in the village of Kinderhook, including the 18th-century furnished homes of Dutch settlers Luykas Van Alen and James Vanderpoel. Information about both is available at (518) 758-9265. Tours also are given at the retirement home of President Martin Van Buren, a national historic site (518-758-9689). Kinderhook is also the location of the Columbia County Museum (518-758-9265). Concerts and other performing arts are presented at StageWorks in the village (518-828-7843) and the North Pointe Cultural Arts Center on NY 9 (518-758-9234).

More information on all the attractions in Columbia County may be obtained from the Columbia County Chamber of Commerce at 518-828-4417 or www.columbiachamber-ny.com, the Columbia County Tourism Department at (800) 724-1846 or www.columbiacountyny.org, and the Columbia County Council on the Arts at (518) 392-3289.

The Capital Region

Farther north on the west bank of the Hudson is Albany, New York's state capital. Albany is best reached by I-90 and has much more to offer than can be listed here. Berkshire residents often take the Pike to Albany for performances at The Egg or the recently restored Majestic Theater, sporting events or concerts at the Pepsi Arena, or exhibits at the New York State Museum. Popular with children are the life-sized representations of the state's flora and fauna, complete with sounds. Re-creations of a Native American settlement and early life in New York City, including life in Harlem in the '20s, are also popular. Permanent collections include minerals, birds, and fossils. The museum recently added a World Trade Center memorial exhibit, with artifacts recovered from the site, photos, and other material. Visit www.nysm.nysed.gov for more information about the museum, or call (518) 474-5877. Fully accessible, wheelchairs and strollers are available. Admission is free, but modest donations of $2.00 per person or $5.00 per family are requested. The museum is located in the Empire State Plaza, an impressive public space created by Governor Nelson Rockefeller with more granite than you can imagine. New Yorkers vacationing in the Berkshires may want to visit this area just to see where their tax dollars have gone. Boat and auto shows and other events are held in the bowels of the plaza. Seasonal activities aboveground include the Tulip Festival in spring and the largest First Night celebration in the area.

The city sponsors various events on the waterfront, as does the Albany Heritage Visitor Center and Planetarium (518-434-0405). Check www.albany.org for more information. There are two large shopping malls near I-90 in the Albany area: Crossgates and Colonie. But for the larger selection, shoppers pay a higher sales tax than they do in Massachusetts, and it is applied to clothing, which is exempt in the Bay State.

Albany is a good candidate for a weekend getaway. A list of accommodations may be obtained from the Albany County Convention and Visitor Center at www.albany.org/VisitorsCenter or by calling (518) 434-1217 or (800) 258-3582. Accommodations range from the standard to the unusual. Rooms in name-brand motels run around $80 to more than $100 per night. Many are located near Albany International Airport. One offers rooms for the "road warrior" from $40. Restored mansions, stagecoach inns, or Victorian homes turned into B&Bs are priced around $100 a night, according to the Web site.

West of Albany is Schenectady, home of Union College and the magnificently restored Proctor's Theater. Although it is a bit of a jaunt, Berkshire residents often make the trek to Schenectady, via New York Highway 2 or I-890, for a show at Proctor's and to check out the immediate area, which is undergoing a renaissance. The theater's program is listed at www.proctors.org or by calling (518) 346-6204.

North of Albany, off I-787, is Watervliet, where the nation's first and still-operating arsenal is located. Here military history buffs and other aficionados of weaponry will find the Watervliet Arsenal Museum. Housed in the historic Iron Building, made entirely of cast-iron plates, are artillery pieces representing the history of big guns from the 1500s to the present. Open archives are available to historians, authors, genealogists, and other students of ordnance production. The grounds of the arsenal are off-limits, but the museum is open to the general public from 10:00 A.M. to 3:00 P.M. Sunday through Thursday. There is no charge, but donations to the Watervliet Arsenal Historical Society are appreciated. More about this fascinating place may be learned from its most informative Web site, www.wva.army.mil, or by calling (518) 266-5805 to speak to Curator John Swantek—a man who enjoys his work.

Across the river from Watervliet is Troy, the county seat of Rensselaer County. MA/NY 2 out of Williamstown leads over the picturesque Petersburg Pass to Troy, which is touted as the home of Uncle Sam. Built by wealthy industrialists in the 1800s, Troy is full of wonderful Victorian architecture and has been chosen as the locale for several major motion pictures. Tiffany windows abound. Concerts and other events are held at the restored Troy Saving Bank Music Hall. Troy is the home of Rensselaer Polytechnic Institute, which operates the Nanotechnology Center and the Junior Museum at 105 Eighth Street. The museum, which includes a Lally Digistar II Planetarium, offers classes to youngsters in kindergarten through eighth grade for a fee and by prearrangement, but according to the Web site, visits may be arranged. More information is available at www.junior museum.org or by calling (518) 235-2120. The city's Riverfront Park has a 1,500-foot public dock that services pleasure boats en route to the state's canal system. Troy's RiverSpark Visitor Center at 251 River Street (518-270-8667) sponsors various events on the waterfront, and river tours can be booked. A calendar of events is listed at www.troyvisitorscenter.org or www.troynet.net. General information may be obtained from Rensselaer County Tourism at (518) 270-2959 or www.capital saratoga.com.

Berkshire folks have been known to make the drive to Saratoga Springs for a dip in the mineral springs, a day at the track, or a performance at the Saratoga Performing Arts Center (SPAC). Saratoga's mineral springs and spas have attracted tourists "taking the waters" since the 1700s. The Lincoln Bath House located in 2,200-acre Saratoga Spa State Park is one option. Services include mineral baths, massages, and other pampering treatments. Berkshire County currently has no operating racetracks, so if you crave some horse racing, the Saratoga track is the nearest. It opens with a flourish in August. A Web site for tourists, as opposed to the official racing Web site, is at www.saratoga racetrack.com. The summer home of the New York City Ballet and the Philadelphia Orchestra, SPAC is sort of a combination of Tanglewood and Jacob's Pillow. Other performances include the Saratoga Chamber Music Festival, Freihofer's Jazz Festival, and Lake George Opera Festival. Their Web site is www.spac.org. If you are in South or Central Berkshire, you will want to take I-90 to I-87, also called the Northway, to Saratoga. North County folks will find taking MA/NY 2 through Troy to I-87 quicker. Filled with interesting shops and restaurants, historic Saratoga Springs is another good choice for a weekend getaway. Visit www.saratoga.com for complete information, or call the chamber of commerce at (518) 584-3255.

A visit to one of the locks along the New York State Canal system makes for an interesting day trip. The nearest locks are located along the Erie Canal between Waterford, where the Mohawk and Hudson meet, west to Rotterdam. There are 12 locks along the Champlain Canal from Troy north to Lake Champlain. Kids especially enjoy watching the water levels rise and drop as boats pass through. For more information visit www.canals.state.ny.us.

SOUTHERN VERMONT

Bennington is about 30 minutes from Williamstown via US 7. A day trip is worth taking, if only to admire the scenery, especially during foliage season, and the colonial estates in Old Bennington on Vermont Highway 9. Collections at the Bennington Museum include works by Grandma Moses and pottery and porcelain of the 18th and 19th centuries. Other attractions include the collections at the Bennington Arts Center, where contemporary sculptures whirl in the breezes, and of course the Bennington Monument commemorating the Revolutionary War battle fought there. Pottery has been made in Bennington since the late 1700s and is still being crafted at the historic Bennington Potters Yard complex on County Street off US 7 (800-205-8033). Around 16 potters make and sell their wares here alongside renowned Bennington pottery, which can be bought at the retail store along with glassware and other home furnishings. With Bennington College and Southern Vermont Community College located here, a number of shops cater to students. An assortment of galleries and shops sell antiques and contemporary crafts. Lunch or dinner at the Blue Benn Diner on US 7 is a must. Moderately priced, the diner offers standard blue plate specials along with unusual vegetarian dishes such as the Mushrooben, a delectable if messy concoction of portobello mushrooms, coleslaw, and mozzarella cheese on grilled sourdough bread. If you want a booth during the rush hours, you will probably have to wait your turn in the foyer. Seating operates on the honor system, and they don't take credit cards or checks. The Blue Benn is open daily, but closing hours vary. If you're thinking of dinner, call (802) 442-5410 to make sure they'll be open. For more information about Bennington or other attractions in southern Vermont, check out www.vtliving.com.

About 25 miles north of Bennington is Manchester Center, a town that has practically been gobbled up by outlet stores. Every major upscale brand is located here, including Baccarat, Coach, Waterford, Armani, and Brooks Brothers—all in new, freestanding, colonial-style buildings. Orvis, known around the world for its fly-fishing rods and other equipment, is based here but has branched out into clothing and home furnishings, many selling at discounted prices. This shopping mecca is jammed on holidays and weekends, so a weekday jaunt might be more enjoyable. Some of these shops have branches in the Prime Outlet complex in Lee, which is a lot closer, especially for folks in southern Berkshire. From Bennington, Manchester can be reached quickly by new US 7, but the old road, US 7A, is much more interesting. It passes Mount Equinox; through Arlington, where there are several antiques complexes and book stores, and Old Manchester, where the elegant Equinox Inn and other upscale B&Bs are located. This is also the site of Hildene, the grand summer estate of Robert Todd Lincoln. Aside from tours, annual events held here include a polo match, a classic and antique car show, and the Peony Festival. Visit www.hildene.org for more information.

Skiers not worn out in Berkshire County might want to check out the slopes at Mount Snow on the eastern side of Vermont. MA/VT 8 out of North Adams will take you there. For more information check www.mountsnow.com.

NORTHWESTERN CONNECTICUT

US 7 south from Sheffield and MA 8 from Otis lead to Litchfield County, the northern part of Connecticut that abuts the Massachusetts border. Also called the Litchfield Hills, this area is bordered by New York to the west, Hartford County to the east, and I-84 in the south. In between are 26 towns and villages located on an array of crisscrossing roads. US 7 and Connecticut Highway 8 are the main north-south highways. US 7 follows the Housatonic River, where tubing and fish-

ing are popular, and passes through many picturesque towns and parks. CT 8 takes you through Winsted and Thomaston. The whole area is full of antiques and specialty shops, restaurants, vineyards, galleries, gardens, and nature centers. Brochures published by the Litchfield Hills Visitors Bureau contain detailed maps and listings and suggested tours by foot, car, and boat. They may be obtained by writing P.O. Box 968, Litchfield 06759-0968, or by checking their Web site at www.litchfieldhills.com. The bureau's phone number is (860) 567-4506. A few of the area attractions are highlighted below.

If you are seeking action, Lime Rock Park off US 7 on Connecticut Highway 112 offers high-speed road track auto racing through the summer. Special events include the annual vintage car race, TransAm Grand Prix, the Busch North NASCAR Final, and some of the best sports car racing in the Northeast. Skip Barber's Racing School, where fantasy can become reality, operates here. Check out www.limerock.com or www.skipbarber.com for more information. If watching race cars roaring around a track is not your idea of fun, you might like to visit the corn maze at White Hollow Farm. It's open only in fall, but it's a great place to take the kids.

US 7 passes through Kent, home of the Sloane-Stanley Museum, showcasing the work of artist/author Eric Sloane and a large tool collection. Next door is the Connecticut Antique Machinery Association museum, where every so often the steam- and gas-powered behemoths are fired up and shown off. There is also a narrow-gauge railroad on the premises. For information about the Sloane museum call (860) 927-3849. The Antique Machinery Museum may be reached at (860) 927-0050. One of the state's most scenic parks is located in Kent, where a dramatic 200-foot waterfall cascades down the hills.

Hot air balloons and biplane flights are another source of adrenaline-pumping activity. Aer Blarney Balloons in Litchfield (860-567-3448) offers charter flights over the countryside year-round. Flights may be arranged for weddings, private parties, or corporate outings. Visit www.aerblarney.com for more. Preston Aviation (860-350-3662) at Candlelight Farms Airport in Sherman lets you play at being a WW I flying ace by donning helmet and goggles and feeling the wind in your face in the cockpit of a 1937 PT-17 Stearman. Their Web site is www.flytailwheel.com.

There are two amusement parks in this region. Lake Compounce Theme Park in Bristol is a trek from Berkshire County, but if you want to ride the world's top-rated wooden roller coaster, the trip is worth it. The park has 50 rides, a water park, and other attractions. CT 8 would be the better road to take to this park, which is just off I-84. The phone number is (860) 583-3300, and the Web site is www.lakecompounce.com. Even farther afield is the Quassy Amusement Park in Middlebury. This venerable park offers affordable family fun, including more than 30 rides and attractions, swimming and picnicking, a water coaster, and an arcade. Call (203) 758-2913, or visit www.quassy.com.

Litchfield is literally bursting with attractions of all sorts. There are several ways to get there, but from Berkshire County the best routes are either Connecticut Highway 63 off US 7 in South Canaan or Connecticut Highway 202 from Torrington, off CT 8. Litchfield is considered to be the finest example of a colonial town in America. Its principal streets and village green have been on the National Register of Historic Places since 1959. There are so many antiques shops in this area that the Litchfield Visitors Bureau has mapped two driving tours to take them all in, each consuming a day. Litchfield also has a Performing Arts Center where a jazz festival is held annually (www.litchfieldjazzfestival.com) and a host of nurseries and gardens, including the famous White Flower Farm. Connecticut's first established winery, the Haight Vineyard, is in historic Litchfield. It is one of several wineries on the Connecticut Wine Trail. All offer tours and tastings and special events. Haight Vineyard's phone number is

(860) 567-4045; the Web address is www.haightvineyards.com.

Nearer to Massachusetts on US 20 off CT 8 is Riverton, home of the Hitchcock Museum. Although the famed stenciled Hitchcock chairs are no longer made here, original versions and other hand-decorated antique furnishings can be seen in the Old Union Church museum. There is also a huge showroom of new Hitchcock products, many at reduced prices. Phone the factory store at (860) 379-4826 for museum hours or other information. Riverton is near Winsted, known for its architecture and the annual summer Mountain Laurel Festival.

Other rare collections may be seen at the Carousel Museum of New England (860-585-5411) and the American Clock and Watch Museum (860-583-6070), both in Bristol. The Lock Museum of America in Terryville (860-589-6359) features locks, keys, and ornate Victorian hardware.

With so much to see in Litchfield County, a weekend getaway might be in order. If you like to camp out, there are plenty of private and public sites, some on or near the Appalachian Trail. The Litchfield Visitors Bureau can provide information on accommodations ranging from quaint B&Bs to large inns and resorts. Or you might consider staying in Hartford, where there are plenty of motels and hotels. Although Hartford is almost two hours from Central Berkshire via the Mass Pike and I-91, it is worth the drive just for the collections at the Wadsworth Atheneum, to visit Mark Twain's home, or see a show at the Hartford Stage. The *Berkshire Eagle* often reviews productions shown there. For more about the Hartford area check out www.enjoyhartford.com, the Web site for the Greater Hartford Convention Center and Visitors Bureau & Tourism District.

REAL ESTATE 

Low interest rates and smaller down payments have created a demand for housing in Berkshire County that far exceeds the amount of property available. With buyers waiting in the wings and prices up by 10 to 20 percent, many real estate agents have been soliciting residents, asking them to consider taking advantage of the market and selling now. South County has traditionally been one of the most expensive areas to buy in and is one of the most volatile markets. Its proximity to New York and Boston has long made this part of the county a haven for second-home owners, many of whom end up moving here permanently. The nearness to the county's major tourist attractions also adds to the desirability. If you are willing to work on a handyman's special or drive a little farther to get to Tanglewood, there are bargains to be found, especially in the hill towns. Generally, country homes that offer spectacular views or are secluded, on water, or historic bring top dollar, no matter where they are.

Finding an average price for property in any particular area is practically impossible. For instance, in South County, properties for sale in New Marlborough run from $126,000 for a tiny two-bedroom cape to $895,000 for a historic Greek Revival on 10 acres. A five-bedroom house in a sought-after neighborhood in Great Barrington is priced at $460,000. Victorians run from $270,000 to $895,000; split level or raised ranches go for $225,000 and up. Recent sales in West Stockbridge included several homes averaging around $250,000, but then there's one for $750,000 and—whoa—a 63-acre estate for $2.25 million!

The summer rental market has always been hot, and many residents supplement their incomes by vacating their homes and renting them out for the season. With rents running anywhere from $2,500 to $30,000 a month or more, it's no wonder! And the nearer to Tanglewood, the tighter the market. You can't help but wonder if all those musicians that converge in Lenox for the Boston Symphony's summer stay will be able to find a place to stay if this keeps up. Rents for year-round apartments in Great Barrington start around $600—if you can find one—up to $2,500 and beyond. Granted, the prices listed here might seem low compared with other parts of the country. But this is Berkshire County, and there is a growing concern that the folks who make their living here may be being priced out of the housing market. Efforts are being made to fill the gap in South County by an organization in Great Barrington called Construct, which is trying to purchase buildings that can be converted to low-cost apartments, and in Central and North Berkshire by Habitat for Humanity, which helps low-income families renovate and buy homes with "sweat equity."

The market in Central Berkshire also has risen, but it is less susceptible to the wild swings that occur in South County. Moderately priced homes can be found in Pittsfield, although there are not as many in the $100,000 to $250,000 range as in the recent past. Much of the housing in the city reflects its manufacturing history. In the north end, where many textile mills operated at the turn of the 20th century, and the eastern areas around the General Electric plant, homes were built for the workers. There are remnants of the early row houses, but most are modest homes ranging from colonial styles and capes from the 1920s to ranches from the 1950s and 1960s. When these come on the market, they generally sell for around $100,000 to $200,000, much less than their counterparts in Great Barrington. Colonials from the 1970s sell for $300,000 and up. Pittsfield does have its share of more expensive properties. The southeast and west sides were considered affluent neighborhoods, and portions of them still are. Homes that sold there for around $500,000 10 years ago are reselling for $750,000. New homes being built in a recent subdivision start at $600,000. On outer West Street a large 1940s colonial went on the market for $1.1 million. Properties around Pittsfield's lakes also command good prices when they come on the market, which is not often. The spectrum runs from a waterfront ranch at $525,000 to a small cape for $450,000 and a large contemporary home with many amenities for $1.45 million.

Many of the large homes in the center of Pittsfield that were built by well-off merchants, lawyers, and other businesspeople in the late 19th and early 20th centuries have been converted to offices or multiple-family dwellings. Some formerly grand homes in the heart of the city's west side have fallen into disrepair or have been converted to multiple-family dwellings by absentee landlords. But amid those are pockets of well-kept homes whose owners are determined to turn the area around. For those willing to work on a place and weather the transition, there are many wonderful Victorian homes to be bought and refurbished in that distressed area. Another neighborhood in a similar state of transition is Morningside on the east side, where homes range from around $90,000 to $125,000. Those that need work go for much less.

Pittsfield is one of the few communities with an abundance of apartments. Many large single-family homes have been converted to apartments to house blue-collar workers. Apartments rent from $500 to $1,000 a month, depending on location and whether utilities are included. Houses rent for $800 to $2,000 a month. And no matter where the rental, it's almost impossible to find one that will allow pets.

Properties in North County run the gamut from estates in Williamstown to Victorians that need work in North Adams to modest homes in Adams. Property in Williamstown tends to be pricey. Estates aside, the average home with several bedrooms runs around $200,000 and up. Monthly rentals in Williamstown are at a premium, as they either house students during the school year or Williamstown Theater Festival personnel during the summer. The market for yearly rentals is tight, and a nice two-bedroom apartment might run around $800 a month. The same apartment in North Adams would cost around $600, but rentals are hard to find there, too.

Even though prices have risen in North Adams, bargains can still be found, although the home might need work. A house that might have sold for around $50,000 a few years ago might now cost around $100,000—still a bargain, according to one broker. Much of the housing is from the late 1800s, when the city expanded up into the steep hills. Most homes have small lots, but many offer views of the valley below. The grander Victorians were owned by the industrialists, while housing in the valley was built for the mill workers. Since the opening of MASS MoCA, many of the best Victorians have been bought up and refurbished into grand painted ladies, and parts of the city are taking on a San Francisco look. North Adams also has a large stock of apartments, but with the recent awakening of the city, they are at a premium—and rents are rising. With the focus on art, the city is becoming known at the place to be for artists. To meet that demand, one forward-looking individual is turning an empty mill into studio and living space for that market. Other developments in the area, such as the growth of dot-com businesses, are bringing in other clientele.

---

i ***Buying a fixer-upper? Before you hire a contractor, you might want to check out the Attorney General's* Consumer Guide to Home Improvement *to avoid pitfalls and disappointments. The publication is on the Internet at www.ago.state.ma.us or may be obtained by calling the AGO's publications office in Boston at (617) 727-2200, ext. 2674.***

CLOSE-UP

About Taxes

Since 1980 property taxes have been limited by state law. They cannot exceed $25 per $1,000 of the home's assessed value. In addition, municipalities are limited in the total amount of taxes that can be raised in one year unless the voters approve exceeding that limit with a special ballot vote. This is called an override, and while it is often rejected by residents, some towns have succeeded in raising their levy limit to cover expenses. Another option is called a debt exclusion, which allows towns to add certain expenses on to the tax rate—but only for a limited period of time. This method is often used to pay off bonds associated with large projects such as new schools or sewer lines and also requires a ballot vote by residents. Taxpayers in the county's 30 towns have the ability to control spending through the unique town meeting form of government, when budgets are voted on by residents annually in the spring. The mayors and city councils in North Adams and Pittsfield set the budgets for those municipalities.

The town of Hancock has one of the lowest tax rates in the county, due in large part to the high values of Jiminy Peak Resort and Patriot's Vacation Village coupled with a low town budget. The highest rates are in Dalton and Lanesborough, although as the new budget year progresses, those may change. The state Department of Revenue's division of local services publishes all the town's tax rates on their Web site: www.dls.state.ma.us.

Tax rates alone do not always reflect costs associated with living in certain communities. In some the rate includes operation of a water and/or sewer system, garbage pickup, an active recreation department, or other amenities. In others these rates might be paid separately, or the property owner might have to maintain a septic system and a well. And tax rates certainly do not reflect what you get for your money. It is not necessarily a given that a high tax rate will mean lots of services. It may mean there are few businesses to help offset the town's operating expenses, so more of the burden falls on the homeowner. Or it may mean the town is temporarily paying off an expensive project, like a new school. While the tax rate is a consideration in choosing a community in which to live, other quality-of-life factors such as schools and recreational facilities may be of more importance. A family with children living in one of the outlying towns may end up spending a lot of time driving to and fro so that their kids can socialize with others or take part in activities and recreational opportunities not available locally. A city dweller might like the convenience but dislike the lack of space. (See the Area Overview for brief descriptions of the towns in Berkshire County.)

Adams is another town where the housing reflects its history. Row houses, working-class homes, and middle-class neighborhoods grew from the mills along the river. Higher up are the grand houses of the mill owners. Adams even has a mill that was converted to apartments in the 1980s. The town has a large Polish population as reflected in block after block of neat homes with meticulous yards in the St. Stanislaus Church neighborhood. Values have escalated here, too. A property that sold for $80,000 a year ago recently brought $100,000 after some sprucing up.

For those who don't want the hassle of managing their own property, a number of developments offer condominiums. Some have their own salespeople, but many are listed with real estate agents around the county.

You can check out Berkshire County real estate on the Internet at www.realtor.com, the national Multiple Listing Service Web site operated by the Board of Realtors, a national organization with state and local chapters. Only properties listed with Realtors (with a capital *R*), who have agreed to abide by a code of ethics, may be placed on the MLS. There are more than 400 Realtors in Berkshire County and more than 1,000 associates. All are licensed through the state Department of Licensing and Registration. You might see letters such as CRS, CBR, and GRI after some folks' names. These designations mean that the broker or sales associate has taken certain courses and become a certified residential specialist, certified buyer representative, or graduate of the Realtor Institute, respectively. The Board of Realtors is continually offering courses to its members on a broad range of topics. Some offices represent buyers only, as opposed to brokers that represent buyers and sellers. Agents who have this dual representation are supposed to inform buyers that they also list property. Responsible Realtors will find the right property for the buyer, no matter whose listing it is. Some brokers specialize in rentals; others have expertise in relocation. There are many small independent agencies, while others are affiliated with larger offices or national chains such as Century 21, Coldwell Banker, or RE/MAX. There are also a number of firms that are not affiliated with the Board of Realtors. The list below highlights the bigger players and others chosen at random, all of whom are Realtors. A complete list may be obtained from the Berkshire County Board of Realtors, 194 Fenn Street, Pittsfield (413-442-8049) or by checking their Web site at www.berkshirerealtors.com.

Some agencies have their own Web sites. Homes, apartments, land, and commercial properties also are advertised in all the local media, some of which publish monthly real estate supplements. Summer rentals are usually listed with agents in January and gone by March. Winter rentals are less expensive but harder to find. The *Berkshire Eagle*, the *Berkshire Business Journal*, and the *Berkshire Record* publish real estate sales as they are recorded in local registers of deeds, as does *Banker & Tradesman*, a Boston publication.

SOUTH COUNTY

Southern Berkshire County Realtors and agencies generally handle properties in Lee, Lenox, Great Barrington, Stockbridge, Becket, Sheffield, Otis, Sandisfield, New Marlborough, Mount Washington, Egremont, Alford, Tyringham, Monterey, and surrounding towns. Those listed below are but a few of the agencies focusing on this area.

Alford Farm Realty, Inc.
248 East Road, Alford
(413) 528-4201
www.alfordfarmrealty.com

Mel and Ellen Greenberg and five others handle a wide range of residential and commercial properties and land in Berkshire, Litchfield (Connecticut), and Columbia (New York) Counties. They also carry seasonal rentals.

Apple Hill Realty
297 Main Street, Great Barrington
(413) 528-3458
www.applehillrealty.com

In business since 1978, this full-service agency specializes in properties and homes in South Berkshire from the Lenox/Tanglewood area to northern Connecticut and west to adjoining New York State. There are 10 agents with buyer and seller representation. The firm also handles summer and winter rentals.

Barnbrook Realty
62 Stockbridge Road, Great Barrington
(413) 528-4423
Broker Mary White began selling real estate for the former owners of Barnbrook Realty in 1978 and bought the agency when they retired in 1984. She and her daughter, Maureen, are certified buyer and seller representatives and handle everything from "land to castles." Recently elected president of the Berkshire County Board of Realtors, White describes her firm as "little but mighty."

Berkshire Hearth Realty
50 Dresser Avenue, Great Barrington
(413) 528-5891
One of the first brokers to represent buyers only, Marguerite DeSantis started selling real estate in 1991. Three years later she decided to work exclusively for buyers and stopped getting her own listings.

Carriage House Real Estate
208 Main Street, Lee
(413) 243-0096
www.carriagehousehomes.com
Established in 1986, Carriage House is a full-service agency that focuses on homes in the Lee area but handles other properties, including land. Broker Sheila Wood has seven associates.

Century 21/ Franklin Street Associates
31 Church Street, Lenox
(413) 637-2323
www.Century21FranklinStreet.com
This is one of several independently owned offices affiliated with Century 21. Broker Robert Romeo also has offices in Becket (888-665-7121), Pittsfield (413-445-2674), and Great Barrington (413-528-8118). The firm deals in fine homes, estates, and condominiums as well as business properties and is a member of the Commercial Investment Network.

Charlotte Isaacs Real Estate
Main Street, Stockbridge
(413) 298-3207
Charlotte R. Isaacs offers personal, professional real estate counseling for sales of residential, vacation, and commercial properties, land, and estates in Massachusetts, Connecticut, and New York.

Cohen & White Associates
47 Church Street, Lenox
(413) 637-1086
www.cohenwhiteassoc.com
This agency specializes in distinctive town and country properties and handles a limited number of seasonal upscale rentals, usually listed around the first of the year.

Corashire Realty
Corashire Road, Hartsville
(413) 528-0014
Nancy Dinan has been selling South County properties for 36 years. She and now her daughter run a full-service agency specializing in residential properties and seasonal rentals "seven days a week."

Dennis G. Welch Real Estate Ltd.
5 Walker Street, Lenox
(413) 637-1709
www.welchrealestate.com
Dennis G. Welch specializes in the marketing of "equity" in the form of condominiums, houses, and land.

Evergreen Buyer Brokers of the Berkshires
17 Housatonic Street, Lenox
(413) 637-4110
www.evergreenbuyerbrokers.com
Deane Christopolis and Barbara C. Kolodkin have been in the real estate business since 1978. In 1992 they decided to solely represent buyers.

Isgood Realty
490 Main Street, Great Barrington
(413) 528-2040
This is the main office of Isgood Realty,

which was founded in Pittsfield in 1948 by the late Isadore Goodman, dean of county Realtors. At one time Isgood's main office was in Pittsfield, with satellite offices in many towns. Many of today's brokers began by working with Isgood. Headed by Richard Krzynowek, the Great Barrington office has seven agents handling residential properties in all price ranges and condominiums, including a town house development being built by the agency.

Roberts & Associates Realty
48 Housatonic Street, Lenox
(413) 637-4200
www.berkshirehouses.com
Pamela J. Roberts opened her office in 1988, and it has grown to have 10 Realtors and a full-time office administrator. She specializes in residential and vacation homes, condominiums, investment properties, and land, representing both buyers and sellers. About half her business comes from second-home buyers. She also handles seasonal rentals. Roberts was Realtor of the Year in 2002 and has advanced real estate education and designations.

Southern Berkshire Buyer Broker
45 Walker Street, Lenox
(413) 637-1333
Henry Hagenah has been representing buyers exclusively since 1996. He handles land and homes from Dalton south. An attorney, he is able to handle legal issues for clients; as a former contractor, he is familiar with zoning issues and state regulations.

Stone House Properties
Main Street, West Stockbridge
(413) 232-4253
www.stonehouseproperties.com
Brokers Randy and Sheila Thunfors and Eileen Taft and eight associates handle residential and commercial properties and land. They are licensed in Massachusetts, Connecticut, and New York.

Wheeler & Taylor Realty Co., Inc.
333 Main Street, Great Barrington
(413) 298-3786
Main Street, Stockbridge
(413) 528-1006
www.wheelertaylor.com
The granddaddy of all South County Realtors, this office has been handling sales of country estates, vacation homes, and land since 1871. The exclusive affiliate of Sotheby's International Realty in southern Berkshire County, the office has 13 agents. President Joseph L. Carini's two full-service offices also handle commercial properties, farms, condominiums, and rentals "seven days a week." Wheeler & Taylor also sells insurance through a separate company.

CENTRAL BERKSHIRE

Brokers in Central Berkshire generally handle properties in Pittsfield, Dalton, Lanesborough, Hancock, Cheshire, Richmond, Hinsdale, Washington, Windsor, Peru, and Middlefield, but several have satellite offices in South County.

Ashmere Realty Inc.
150 Pine Cone Lane, Hinsdale
(413) 655-2624, (800) 570-0597
Broker/owner Barbara Osborne sells homes and land in Hinsdale, Becket, Peru, and other hill towns in all price ranges.

Century 21/ Perras Realty Inc.
481 Dalton Avenue, Pittsfield
(413) 442-0109
www.a-perras.com
Established in 1972, Arnold and Doreen Perras's agency has been tops in sales in Berkshire County for five consecutive years and has been ranked by Century 21 as one of the top 10 offices in New England. With a 24-member team, the agency handles all sorts of properties and recently became a principal member of the Cendant Mobility Broker Network, a provider of global mobility management

and workforce development solutions. The agency also has an office in Lee.

Coldwell Banker/Rose Real Estate
443 Dalton Avenue, Pittsfield
(413) 443-7211
www.cbrose.com
The Rose agency was founded in 1971 by Carol Rose. Her son, Jeffrey, joined in 1983. The firm handles residential, commercial, and industrial property. A major relocation specialist, the firm also is a principal in the Cendant Mobility Broker Network. There are more than 20 associates in the office, including 14 certified buyer agents. The firm also offers market analysis and consulting.

Dalton Town & Country
659 Main Street, Dalton
(413) 684-2001
www.daltontowncountryre.com
This firm focuses mainly on residential property in Dalton, where it is developing a new subdivision, but it also handles property in Pittsfield and neighboring towns. Five agents work in this full-service office.

Dayspring Realtors, Inc.
55 Church Street, Pittsfield
(413) 442-8581
www.dayspring-realtors.com
Dayspring Realtors, Inc., was founded in 1989 by Kathleen Hazelett, who now has 10 associates. Services include residential buyer and seller representation, market analysis and consulting, rentals, and property management. She is affiliated with Global Relocation.

Barb Hassan Realty
69 South Main Street, Lanesborough
(413) 447-7300
www.BarbHassanRealty.com
Broker/owner Barbara L. Davis-Hassan claims total career sales exceeding $52 million. A top saleswoman in the county for several years, she is a certified buyer and seller representative and handles mainly midrange properties in the bedroom communities around Pittsfield.

Isgood Realty—Pittsfield
100 Wendell Avenue, Pittsfield
(413) 443-4416
Until recently, this was the flagship office of Isgood Realty, founded by the late Isadore "Izzy" Goodman in 1948. The main office is now in Great Barrington (see South County listings), but the Pittsfield office remains a full-service agency with six associates headed by brokers Stephen R. Ricci and Edward N. Sloper. The agency handles residential and commercial properties and land and offers free market analysis to prospective sellers.

Liberty Realty
Albany Road (U.S. Highway 20), Pittsfield
(413) 442-8957
Pierre Joseph's firm handles property in neighboring New York State as well as the border communities in Berkshire County.

RE/MAX Integrity, Realtors
154 Elm Street, Pittsfield
(413) 443-7274, (877) 858-8121
www.algelinas.com
Al Gelinas has been in the real estate business since 1986. After working with several local brokers, he formed his own agency and became affiliated with RE/MAX Integrity in 1997. He says his sales to date top $83 million, including $9.5 million in 1999. The staff of 12 includes buyer and seller representatives. The firm sells residential and commercial property, does market analysis and consulting, works with businesses relocating employees, and manages property.

Tucker Associates
392 Merrill Road, Pittsfield
(413) 499-4760
www.Tuckerassoc.com
Richard F. Tucker Sr. founded his firm in 1957. His son, Richard F. Tucker II, is vice president and general manager. The agency has six associates. Located across the street from GE and General Dynamics, the firm has specialized in corporate relocation for those and other companies for

CLOSE-UP

Building in Massachusetts

Nearly 30 percent of the land in Berkshire County is protected from development through various restrictions designed to preserve open space. While buildable land can still be found, what is available is apt to be harder—and more expensive—to build on, partly because of regulations that did not exist 20 or so years ago. City folk sometimes forget that this is a rural area and that some towns and most outlying areas do not have sewer systems and wastewater treatment plants. That means that every house not on a sewer line has to have its own septic system. Whether you're building from scratch or purchasing an existing home, the system will have to meet current state guidelines, called Title V. If it does not, banks will not approve financing. Bringing an old system into compliance can be a costly affair, especially if the lot is small or the soil does not allow effluent to dissipate properly. These regulations are enforced by local boards of health. Approval also may be needed for additions to existing homes, and it is wise to check beforehand. That additional bedroom or bath could mean that the septic system will need to be upgraded, and it sure is better to find that out *before* the addition is built.

Aside from laws pertaining to waste disposal, Massachusetts has strict regulations regarding construction in or near wetlands, which are enforced at the local level by conservation commissions. Reputable contractors who think the land you want to build on might fall under these regulations will advise you to seek a ruling from the commission or

years. Aside from finding homes for employees new to the area, the firm handles vacation, retirement, and second homes in Williamstown and Stockbridge as well as Central Berkshire.

NORTH COUNTY

Northern Berkshire County Realtors and agents generally handle property in North Adams, Adams, Williamstown, Clarksburg, New Ashford, Savoy, and surrounding towns, including towns in southern Vermont.

Alton & Westall Real Estate
77 Water Street, Williamstown
(413) 458-8366
www.altonwestall.com

The late Philip Alton founded this firm in 1971 and was joined by Donald Westall in 1984. The agency offers fine homes, land, condominiums, and commercial properties and is the exclusive affiliate of Christies's Great Estates for Berkshire County. The office has eight associates and recently became licensed to handle properties in Vermont.

Century 21/ Harold Dupee Realtors
40 Main Street, North Adams
(413) 664-4941
Harold Dupee started selling real estate in 1965, becoming a licensed broker in 1972. He opened his own office, which is now located in the Holiday Inn in downtown North Adams, in 1986 with three other principals: Frances V. Buckley, Louis S.

their enforcing officer before finalizing your plans. You should be wary if your property abuts a river, brook, or even a stream that appears periodically. Plant growth also can indicate a wetland, and an inspection and determination by the commission might be in order. It is also important to know whether any endangered plants or creatures are on the property; the state has drawn up quite a list of those. Conservation commissions are also concerned about runoff from land under construction and may ask that an erosion barrier be installed to keep mud and muck from washing into and clogging a sensitive area. Wetlands function as nature's kidneys, purifying runoff as it seeps into the earth or runs into adjacent water. Again, it is far better to get this all straightened out before building. Fines can be levied and construction halted for violations.

Zoning bylaws are another area where folks can run afoul of local officials. These regulations vary from town to town, and some are more strict than others. Generally they regulate such things as how close to your neighbor's lot you can build, how high your fence can be, how big your building lot must be, and how much frontage is required. They may even determine whether what you want to build is allowed in your neighborhood. The building inspector is the enforcer of zoning bylaws. If your plans do not conform to the regulations, the inspector may advise you to contact the local zoning board, which can sometimes help you seek an exception to the rules. Again, this is an area to check out before construction. Many an individual has had to remove a second story, tear down an addition, or rip out a fence after neighbors complained and it was found that the construction did indeed violate the zoning bylaws.

Gagliardi, and Mary-Jane Dalmaso. The three cohost a weekly radio show about real estate. In addition, there are 15 full-time sales associates. Services include buyer and seller representation, commercial investment and industrial brokerage, and new home construction. A state certified appraiser, Dupee has served on the ethics panel of the national Appraisal Institute.

Harsch Associates
311 Main Street, Williamstown
(413) 458-5000
www.harschrealestate.com

A Williams College graduate and resident since 1967, Paul A. Harsch III is licensed in Massachusetts, Vermont, and New York and handles premier residential properties, land, businesses, commercial real estate, and new construction. Personal sales exceed $72.7 million in approximately 366 commercial and residential transactions. Harsch Associates has been involved in selling some of the region's most prestigious properties for record prices, including the former Cole Porter estate and a Williamstown estate that was, among other things, the former residence of the Shah of Iran. He is the area representative of Sotheby's International Realty and is a member of First Global Relocation Inc., a worldwide referral network.

Elizabeth Randall Realty
30 Park Street, Adams
(413) 743-7022

Broker-owner Elizabeth G. Randall has

The Home Builders Association of Western Massachusetts lists member contractors as well as a host of other building-related professionals on its Web site: www.hbawn.com.

been in the real estate business since 1976, opening her own office in 1990. A graduate of the Real Estate Institute, she works mostly with local families and specializes in property in Adams and surrounding towns. She has two associates in her office.

RCI Real Estate
10 Ashland Street, North Adams
(413) 664-7116
148 Main Street, Williamstown
(413) 458-4196
www.rci-realestate.com

Possibly the youngest broker in the county, Michael Zeppieri learned the business from his late father, who founded RCI in 1988 when Michael was 15. On his own since his father's sudden death in 1995, Michael has become one of the major players in the hot North County real estate market. He handles residential, commercial, and investment properties from high end to mobile homes, as well as rentals in both Williamstown and North Adams. A certified HUD broker, he also deals in foreclosures. There are six agents in the office.

EDUCATION AND CHILD CARE

EDUCATION

The Berkshires have been fertile ground for educators seeking to sow the seeds of knowledge since 1734, when missionary John Sergeant opened his school for Native Americans. Six years later, the first school for white settlers opened in Sheffield, with Stockbridge following suit in 1760. In 1793, through a bequest from Colonel Ephraim Williams Jr., a "free school" that later became Williams College was established in Williamstown. Lenox Academy for boys and girls opened in 1803, followed by the Pittsfield Female Academy in 1806. Other milestones include the opening of the first comprehensive high school in Pittsfield in 1844. In the early 1900s Dalton became the testing ground for progressive educational reform by allowing Helen Parkhurst to test her radical theories in what was then Dalton High School. After working with Maria Montessori, Parkhurst developed what was called the Laboratory Plan and started the Children's University School. Her new methodology replaced rote learning and rigid classes with individualized "laboratories" that allowed students and teachers to work together to create educational plans that students could follow at their own pace. In 1916, with help from Mrs. W. Murray Crane, the forward-thinking principal of Dalton High School, Earnest Jackman, encouraged Parkhurst to try out her plan in his school. Three years later Parkhurst opened the Dalton School in Manhattan. The Laboratory Plan was eventually tinkered out of existence in Dalton, but it lives on in New York City and is practiced in schools around the world.

Today the county boasts four colleges, including the avant-garde Simon's Rock College of Bard; seven private schools; and a public school system that includes more than 55 schools, some recently built or renovated. These days, however, public education in Massachusetts is in a state of flux. Between a state budget crisis, a new, controversial mandatory test, and efforts to establish a charter school in the region, educational funding is being affected on a number of fronts. As the county's public schools attempt to deal with these issues, no one knows how or if the quality of education will ultimately be affected.

The young people in the county's 30 towns and two cities are educated in a variety of arrangements. North Adams and Pittsfield and the towns of Lee and Lenox have their own K–12 systems. Most of the remaining towns belong to one of five regional districts in the county. These range from two-town mergers, as in the case of Adams and Cheshire, to multitown districts. Alford, Monterey, New Marlborough, Egremont, and Sheffield form the Southern Berkshire Regional School District. Formed in the 1950s, this was the first regional district in the county; it took more than 30 town meeting votes to get if off the ground. Great Barrington, Stockbridge, and West Stockbridge are members of the Berkshire Hills District. The Central Berkshire Regional District is largest in the state, encompassing Dalton, Peru, Windsor, Hinsdale, Washington, and Becket in Berkshire County and Cummington in neighboring Hampshire County. Otis and Sandisfield are members of the Farmington River District in neighboring Hampden County.

Most regional districts operate small elementary schools in some if not all of their member towns, merging students at the middle and high school levels. An exception is the Mount Greylock Regional

District, which serves only middle and high school students from Williamstown and Lanesborough. Williamstown's elementary school is a separate entity operated by the town; Lanesborough's elementary school is partners with Hancock, New Ashford, and Richmond in what is called a school union. The differences boil down to governance—or local control, if you wish—and funding. A regional district is governed by a school committee made up of representatives elected by the member towns, and state reimbursements go directly to the district. Reimbursements for schools not in a regional district go directly to the coffers of the towns in which they are located. Towns in a school union share administrative costs but operate independently in overseeing their elementary schools. Clarksburg, Florida, and Savoy run their elementary schools through a school union, and their students go on to middle and high school in either North Adams or Adams-Cheshire, depending on distance. Since they do not share in the operating costs of those schools, they pay tuition for the students they send.

There are two regional districts formed to provide educational alternatives. The Northern Berkshire Vocational District provides technical training in a variety of fields to students who apply from the member towns of Adams, North Adams, Clarksburg, Savoy, Florida, and Williamstown and Monroe, in neighboring Franklin County. Students from other towns may apply and may be accepted if space is available. The Southern Berkshire Educational Collaborative in Great Barrington is governed by a board made up of representatives from Lee, Lenox, and the Berkshire Hills and Southern Berkshire regional districts. Pittsfield's Taconic High School offers vocational courses and accepts students from outside the city if space is available.

The state recently enacted the Massachusetts Compulsory Assessment System, which tests students in certain grades and requires that certain criteria be met in order to graduate from high school. Schools that do not score well are labeled underperforming and can lose state aid, a punishment some find perverse. Scores are available on the Department of Education Web site: www.doe.mass.edu. But educators caution that the numbers do not reveal the whole story. And some are resisting even administering the test, saying the preparation takes away from the kind of teaching they want in their schools and unfairly penalizes poorer communities and minority students.

Another recent development is the effort by a group in North County to establish a charter school there. It would be funded in part by money taken from the attending child's local school budget. Supporters say charter schools provide a much-needed alternative for students who are not performing well in their public schools. Others say charter schools are not as innovative as they claim to be and that they are basically private schools funded with public money. At a time when state aid is being reduced, any loss in reimbursements is seen to be a threat to the regular school program. Massachusetts also recently implemented school choice, which allows students to attend schools in other districts. The sending town or district loses reimbursement for that student also.

So where are the "good" schools? The simplistic answer would be that the best schools are in areas where the residents have a strong interest in and dedication to education and where parents are involved with their children's education at an early age. For instance, it's hard to deny the influence Williams College has on the quality of education that children in Williamstown receive. On the other hand, the children in North Adams and Pittsfield are no less important to educators there, although the cities must deal with a larger population of transients and disadvantaged children. Still, the larger systems offer as much enrichment and stimulation as the smaller ones, thanks to dedicated and creative teachers and administrators.

Between all those school board seats to be filled, school improvement councils, and parent-teacher organizations, there are plenty of ways to get involved with your child's education if you are so inclined. Most of the schools welcome volunteers they can depend on to help out in the classroom, on the playground, or in other ways.

For those who eschew the public schools, alternatives include a variety of schools operated by Catholics and other Christian denominations and the Jewish community. Home schooling is also a popular alternative; more information is available at www.berkshirehomeschoolers.org.

Looking through the schools listed in the *Yellow Pages,* you will see a number of schools not listed here, including Hillcrest Educational Centers, Eagleton School, and John Dewey Academy. These residential schools specialize in working with young people who have had difficulty functioning in public schools because of developmental or emotional problems and who generally do not interact with the community.

Private Schools

Berkshire Country Day School
Massachusetts Highway 183, Lenox
(413) 637-0755
www.berkshirecountryday.org
Founded in 1946, Berkshire Country Day School is an independent coeducational day school with a faculty of 85 teachers serving children from three years of age through Grade 12. The enrollment of around 350 includes students from Berkshire and Hampshire Counties and neighboring New York. The 89-acre campus is located near Tanglewood. The school is widely known for its strong focus on academic achievement through a traditional but sophisticated curriculum, including modern languages, arts, shop, physical education, and interscholastic sports. There is strong emphasis on writing and study skills, community service, and cooperation among the students. Classes are small, with a one-to-six teacher-student ratio, and advance placement courses are offered to those in the upper grades. Parents are encouraged to be involved with the school in the classroom or serving on the governing board. Depending on the age group, tuition runs from $7,900 to around $15,000. Needs-based tuition assistance is offered.

Berkshire School
245 North Undermountain Road, Sheffield
(413) 229-1003
www.berkshireschool.org
Berkshire School was founded in 1907 in a rented building on a farm at the foot of Mount Everett by Mr. and Mrs. Seaver B. Buck. The couple, graduates of Harvard and Smith, respectively, at first devoted their new school to educating young men to the values of academic excellence, physical vigor, and high personal standards. The school began accepting girls in 1969. The strong academic curriculum is augmented with various programs in the arts and sciences. Facilities include the Dixon Observatory, which houses computer synchronized telescopes and is considered one of the best in New England. Students operate an FM-radio station, and the school is a member of the Intercollegiate Broadcasting System and is affiliated with the Associated Press wire and radio services. Music facilities include classrooms and rehearsal spaces and the 400-seat Allen Theater. During summer the facilities are taken over by the Berkshire Choral Festival, whose members perform works for the public after intensive study. Berkshire School is a nonprofit institution with an endowment of $36 million. Tuition is around $30,000 for boarding students and $20,000 for day students. Financial aid is available.

Buxton School
South Street, Williamstown
(413) 458-3919
www.buxton.williamstown.ma.us
Buxton School was founded by Ellen Geer Sangster in 1928 as a coeducational day school in Short Hills, New Jersey. In 1947 the high school was moved to Mrs. Sang-

ster's family estate in Williamstown and was formed anew as a boarding school. Today there are 17 buildings located on a 150-acre campus that overlooks the town. From its inception, Buxton has been an innovative school, devoted to experimentation and change. The student body is diverse, and life at the school is flexible, noninstitutional, and open to change. A coeducational, boarding, college-preparatory and arts school for Grades 9 through 12, Buxton houses 90 or so students in single-gender dormitories. The average class size in the upper school is seven, with a faculty-student ratio of one to five. Standard subjects are augmented with a broad range of classes in such subjects as African studies; drama, music and dance; global issues; and marine biology and oceanography. Every year the entire school plans and takes a trip to a city in the United States, where the students put on a play they have produced. The cost of the trip is included in the tuition, which runs around $30,500, including room and board, tickets for approved cultural events, athletics (including a ski pass), and all other school-sponsored activities. Committed to maintaining the diversity of its student body, the school awards needs-based financial aid.

Darrow School
110 Darrow Road
New Lebanon, New York
(518) 794-6000
www.darrowschool.com

Darrow School was founded in 1932 by a group of Shaker, community, and educational leaders, including the headmasters of Deerfield, Taft, and Hotchkiss. The school occupies 365 acres adjoining Pittsfield State Forest on the western slope of Mount Lebanon and is situated on the site of the Mount Lebanon Shaker Village, a designated National Historic Landmark The campus includes playing fields, tennis courts, extensive hiking paths, and a cross-country ski trail. Of the 24 buildings, 21 are original Shaker structures.

A new arts center recently opened, providing studio and lab spaces for fine arts programs, including photography, woodworking, and ceramics plus a public exhibition gallery. A $1.8-million environmental center includes a state-of-the-art wastewater treatment plant that is used as a learning tool in the science curriculum. The Meetinghouse, built in 1824 and remodeled in 1962, houses the library, which contains more than 15,000 volumes and a computer network. Most of the student body of around 120 live at the school in Shaker buildings converted to dormitories. A small minority attend on a daily basis. Classes are offered from ninth grade through postgraduate level and, with a full-time faculty of 27, have an average teacher-student ratio of four to one. Tuition is $15,000 for day students and $27,300 for boarders, plus other costs depending on course work. Financial assistance is available. In summer the grounds are opened for the popular Tannery Pond concert series.

Great Barrington Rudolf Steiner School
35 West Plain Road, Great Barrington
(413) 528-4015
www.rudolfsteinerschool.org

The Great Barrington Rudolf Steiner School is one of more than 1,000 Waldorf schools, a worldwide movement of independent coeducational schools founded more than 80 years ago by Rudolf Steiner. At the heart of the Waldorf philosophy is the belief that education is an art. Everything that is taught must speak to the child's experience and imagination. The coeducational day school serves around 240 students from Berkshire County, northwest Connecticut, and Columbia County in pre-kindergarten through ninth grade. The curriculum is described as unique and creative, integrating the fine and practical arts with the sciences, mathematics, literature, and cultural heritage. There are 30 full-time teachers, some of whom follow a group of students from kindergarten through eighth grade. Founded in 1971 on donated property, the school was known as Pumpkin Hollow

School, and the first kindergarten was held in an old barn. Tuition is around $10,000, and financial assistance is available.

Miss Hall's School
492 Holmes Road, Pittsfield
(413) 443-6401
www.misshalls.com
Founded in 1898 by Mira Hinsdale Hall, Miss Hall's School was one of the first girls' boarding schools established in New England. A graduate of Smith College, Mira Hall believed that girls needed a place of their own in which to learn and grow. In her 40-year tenure, she created a learning environment based on respect for the individual student, stimulating teaching, competitive spirit, intelligent supervision, and personal warmth—a philosophy that continues today.

The comprehensive four-year college preparatory curriculum includes offerings in the visual arts, music, and theater, as well as advanced-placement courses in six disciplines and an honors tier. The main building on the campus is a Georgian-style mansion built in 1923. Recently renovated, it houses laboratories, practice rooms, offices, the dining room, dormitory rooms, and faculty apartments. New facilities include an athletic center, art center, technology lab, larger library, and student center. There are around 140 culturally diverse students and a full-time faculty of 47, 17 of whom live on campus. The average class has nine students with a one-to-five teacher-student ratio. Tuition runs around $29,900 for boarding students and $17,500 for day students. Strongly committed to providing needs-based financial aid for deserving candidates, Miss Hall's awarded more than $1 million in financial aid to 42 percent of the student population in 2002. The school has an endowment of $3.5 million.

Pine Cobble School
163 Gale Road, Williamstown
(413) 458-4680
www.Pinecobble.org
An independent coeducational day school, Pine Cobble prides itself on its family atmosphere. Around 150 children are enrolled, ranging from two years, nine months, through ninth grade. Class sizes vary, but most have a faculty ratio of one to five. French is offered beginning in prekindergarten. Latin and Spanish are offered in the upper school. There is an extended day program and a strong emphasis on arts and drama. Interscholastic sports include lacrosse, field hockey, skiing, and soccer. Tuition averages around $9,000, and financial aid is available to qualifying students.

Higher Education

Berkshire Community College
1350 West Street, Pittsfield
(413) 499-4660, (800) 456-3253
www.cc.berkshire.org
Founded in 1960, Berkshire Community College is a state-supported two-year college offering associate degrees and certificates in wide a variety of courses, including those focusing on workplace training, business and industry development, health care, and the arts. Most of the 2,400 undergraduates are part-time students, with around 945 attending full-time. About 40 percent of the faculty of 167 is full-time, and the student-teacher ratio is 14 to 1. The 100-acre campus is located on a hillside on the outskirts of Pittsfield. Athletic facilities include playing fields and a large gymnasium with a pool. The Koussevitsky Arts Center theater, with 510 seats, is the largest auditorium north of Tanglewood. Aside from college functions, it is used for professional concerts and stage productions and by noted lecturers and dance troupes, including the Albany Ballet for its annual production of *The Nutcracker.*

Funding for state colleges has been reduced in the past few years and is being reviewed again, but currently tuition is calculated at $130 per credit. A full-time student who is a resident of the state will be paying around $1,236 a semester, including all fees and costs except books. Students may cross-enroll at the Massachusetts College of Liberal Arts in North Adams. Many earn their associate degrees at BCC and then go on to earn their bachelor degrees at MCLA, the University of Massachusetts in Amherst, or another four-year college. Senior citizens are eligible for waivers, as are employees and their children. Financial aid and work study programs are available. BCC runs satellite programs in downtown Pittsfield and in Great Barrington.

Massachusetts College of Liberal Arts
375 Church Street, North Adams
(413) 662–5410, (800) 292–6632
www.mcla.edu

A four-year residential, coeducational public college, the Massachusetts College of Liberal Arts (formerly North Adams State College) was founded in 1894 as North Adams Normal School. There are approximately 1,500 undergraduate students enrolled; an additional 200 part-time students take graduate, evening, and special program courses. There are around 80 full-time faculty members and 50 part-time. The student-faculty ratio is 13 to 1. As explained above, the funding for state-supported colleges is being reduced, leaving more of the costs to the students. Tuition for in-state students was around $4,000 for 2002, plus costs for housing, meal plan, books, and various fees. Located within walking distance of downtown North Adams, the complex includes three residential facilities that hold more than 1,000 students. The four-story campus center houses one of three gymnasiums, a state-of-the-art fitness center, swimming pool, dance complex, racquetball and handball courts, two cafeterias, and a counseling center, as well as the bookstore and an athletic training center. Located around the 80-acre campus for use in intercollegiate sports and recreation are softball, baseball, and soccer fields; tennis courts; and a cross-country course.

MCLA offers bachelor of arts and bachelor of science degrees in 14 undergraduate programs. Around 25 minor courses are offered. Students may cross-enroll in courses at Williams College and Berkshire Community College. Travel courses for credit are offered during school breaks, and the college participates in programs that encourage students to study abroad. Qualified students may earn credits through internships on campus and at various off-campus businesses and cultural institutions. Teacher certification in three levels may be acquired through courses at MCLA. The college also grants a master of education degree. The Office of Lifelong Learning sponsors year-round conferences and noncredit courses for children and adults. Housing is available for summer programs.

Simon's Rock College of Bard
84 Alford Road, Great Barrington
(413) 528–0771
www.simons-rock.edu

Once described as "a tiny school with big ideas," Simon's Rock is the nation's only four-year college of the liberal arts and sciences specifically designed for bright, highly motivated young persons age 15 or 16, who often find the last two years of high school a time of boredom and frustration and who are ready and eager to tackle college-level courses. The school opened in 1966, dedicated to serving this group of adolescents with academic and social programs specifically designed to meet their needs. The school was created through the philanthropy and vision of Elizabeth Blodgett Hall and her mother, Margaret Kendrick Blodgett. Mrs. Blodgett gave the land that now supports the college's main campus and established a foundation to support the construction and growth of a new educational institution on that property. An educator, Mrs. Hall created the nation's first "early college" and committed the resources of the Blodgett Foundation to realizing her vision, building and sustaining Simon's Rock through its first decades. Enrollment runs around 375 students, with a faculty of 68. Students earn associate degrees and may continue on to earn bachelor's degrees or transfer to other colleges. Each year Simon's Rock conducts a national search for 10th graders with outstanding records of academic accomplishment and community involvement and offers 20 of them full two-year scholarships. Those who earn their associate degree with excellent records may continue to study for a bachelor of arts degree at Simon's Rock at the same tuition they would pay at their state university. Tuition is around $25,000. Room, board, and a student services fee add roughly another $10,000, plus other fees that might apply.

Generous gifts through the years have expanded the rural campus and led to renovations of existing buildings and the construction of new facilities, including the $4 million Fisher Science and Academic Center and an $8.5 million athletic center. The Fisher Center houses laboratories, a greenhouse, rooms for various tutorials and seminars, and a state-of-the-art multimedia 60-seat auditorium. The athletic center includes an NCAA-size multiuse basketball court, an elevated 100-meter indoor track, and an eight-lane swimming pool. In its annual surveys of "America's Best Colleges," *U.S. News and World Report* has regularly identified Simon's Rock as one of the best regional liberal arts colleges in the country and twice ranked it first in its category. The Carnegie Foundation has identified Simon's Rock as one of the 163 most selective liberal arts colleges in the United States.

Williams College
Main Street, Williamstown
(413) 597-3131
www.williams.edu

Established in 1793 with funds bequeathed by Colonel Ephraim Williams, Williams College is a private, residential liberal arts school with graduate programs in the history of art and in development economics. From its modest beginnings, the campus has grown to encompass 450 acres in town plus 2,500 outlying acres, including Hopkins Memorial Forest. The college operates more than 98 buildings, including 41 residences or dormitories, five dining rooms, a theater used by the Williamstown Theatre Festival in summer, a Jewish religious center, and the Williams College Museum of Art (described more fully in the Museums section). The oldest operating observatory in the country is located here and is open to the public for special astronomical viewings. The college is an NCAA affiliate, and facilities for sports include a hockey rink, swimming pool, track, tennis courts, and playing fields. The annual Williams-Amherst football game is a popular event, with alumni setting up elaborate tailgate parties.

Nine libraries house 835,745 volumes plus thousands of government documents, videos, microtexts, sound recordings, and archival material. The Chapin Rare Books Library, with 52,759 volumes, is an invaluable resource. In addition, students have access to the Clark Art Institute's fine collection of reference and research materials, including 200,000 books.

There are three academic curricular divisions: humanities, sciences, and social sciences. Students may choose from 31 majors plus concentrations and special programs, and many have double majors. The student-faculty ratio is eight to one. Students actively participate with faculty in research, something nearly all the 277 professors are involved in. In 2001–02, $2,841,300 in new grants was awarded from various sources to support faculty research. An impressive number of national awards and honors have been bestowed on Williams faculty members, including a Pulitzer for poetry.

Williams became a coeducational school in 1970, and the student body of 2,000 is nearly equally divided between the genders. Students are admitted without regard to their ability to pay, but Williams is considered tough to get into. Around 24 percent of those who apply are admitted. The college is committed to meeting 100 percent of each accepted student's demonstrated financial need. Forty-four percent of the members of the class of 2006 received aid through scholarships, jobs, or loans ranging from $4,150 to $36,470. Tuition, room and board, and other fees total $33,750, which college officials say covers about half the true cost of a student's education. An endowment of just under $1 billion helps to cover the gap. *U.S. News & World Report* has ranked Williams as the top liberal arts college in the nation 11 times. *Black Enterprise* ranks Williams as the 14th best college in the country for African Americans.

CHILD CARE

Child care in Massachusetts is overseen and licensed by the state Office of Child Care Services, which is represented in Berkshire County by Resources for Child Care in Pittsfield. This agency is the place to call if you're starting from scratch to find child care. There are several options, ranging from small groups in approved homes to large centers. While the larger centers are easily found in the Yellow Pages, the small in-home family centers are not. However, they are listed by town on the Resources for Child Care Web site, listed below. There are more than 70 in-home centers in Pittsfield alone. There are three types of licensed family child-care centers in private homes. The smallest program allows for up to six children, including the provider's own child. Large family child care allows for up to 10 children with an approved assistant. The third type allows a provider with proven child-care experience to care for six preschoolers plus two school-age children.

Much of the child care here is tied into early education, such as Head Start, which offers free part-time care for children ages three to five who have disabilities or are from low-income families. Other programs are aimed at children with physical or other disabilities or are geared toward helping single parents move from welfare to work. These more formal programs differ from play groups, which are usually run by a stay-at-home parent or in child-care centers. You might be led to a home day-care arrangement by word of mouth, but it is important to check to see if the home has been inspected, the workers investigated and trained, and that other state standards have been met. Care given by grannies, aunts, or other relatives does not fall under the Office of Child Care Services. Elementary schools also offer some preschool programs, but those fall under the jurisdiction of the Department of Education. Many schools have gone to all-day kindergarten classes, a boon for working parents and a leg-up for their kids. There are many programs for youngsters at places like the YMCA or the Girls and Boys Club, but they do not accept visitors to the area. The exceptions are summer camps, which are listed in the Kidstuff chapter. Whatever the program, vacancies are hard to come by, according to those involved with child care. Waiting lists are long, so it pays to do the research early.

Sources of Information

Child Care of the Berkshires
210 West State Street
North Adams 01247
(413) 663-6593

150 North Street
Pittsfield 01201
(413) 443-0676
Based in North Adams with a satellite office in Pittsfield, this agency provides information and referrals and assists with obtaining subsidies if applicable. The agency also operates family day-care programs at several locations, including Williams College and Berkshire Community College. The Pittsfield office provides information about child care in Pittsfield and Southern Berkshire.

Family Center
940 South Street
Great Barrington 01230
(413) 528-0721
A wealth of information and services are available here. Play groups, car seat rental, clothing and toy exchanges, father's activ-

Looking for Child Care

The Office of Child Care Services suggests the following criteria when looking for child care:

- Visit programs and compare. Allow plenty of time to choose a program.
- Look for the center's license. It should be prominently displayed and means that the provider meets standards for health, safety, and education; the premises have been inspected; and the adults' backgrounds checked. Providers have been trained in CPR and first aid.
- Go in the morning, when children are most active. If the provider is very busy, but you like what you see, go back when there is time to talk.
- Watch how caregivers interact with your child and other children. There should be enough adults to work with a group and to care for individual children.
- Is there an emphasis on reading, singing, and language stimulation?
- Ask questions—and trust your instincts.

ities, referrals to area child-care providers, and parenting education are a few of them. The Family Center has a drop-in center that is open at various times.

Resources for Child Care
152 North Street, Suite 230
Pittsfield 01201
(413) 443-7830
www.qualitychildcare.org
This agency is the Berkshire County representative of the state Office of Child Care Services. Staff can provide information and referrals for family and center-based day care, financial aid, and community partnerships for working parents. Families of young children with disabilities will be assisted in finding child-care programs that will best meet their child's developmental needs while being included with other children. The agency also provides training and holds workshops for providers and lends toys and equipment to centers.

Babysitting Services

With the exception of child-care centers at most of the ski areas, babysitting services are practically nonexistent for tourists. If you are lucky, the hotel you are staying at might have the name of a tried-and-true sitter who will stay with your kids while you are out. If so, you might ask if they received training from the Red Cross, which runs courses in Pittsfield. Child-care centers at the ski resorts often accept children from ages six weeks to six years. Parents are expected to supply formula and diapers for infants. Reservations are advised at most and required at some. Most also have instructional opportunities for three-year-olds and up.

HEALTH CARE AND WELLNESS 

No one likes to think of a disaster happening away from home, but fortunate is the traveler who has a medical emergency in Berkshire County. Every town either operates or has access to ambulance service and trained emergency medical technicians or paramedics who will rush to the nearest hospital—and there are three with emergency rooms: Berkshire Medical Center in Pittsfield, Fairview Hospital in Great Barrington, and North Adams Regional. BMC is the designated trauma center for the county, and those with the most serious life-threatening injuries or illnesses will be taken there. It may be determined there that care at a more highly specialized hospital is needed. For instance, patients suffering from severe burns or head injuries may be airlifted by helicopter to Worcester, Albany, New York, or elsewhere for treatment.

Berkshire Medical Center is an affiliate of Berkshire Health Systems, the health-care giant in the county. BMC is a teaching hospital, affiliated with the University of Massachusetts Medical School. The medical staff is augmented by doctors who have completed their training but who are serving their residency requirements. BHS also owns and manages Hillcrest Hospital in Pittsfield and Fairview Hospital in Great Barrington. There is no emergency room at Hillcrest. Fairview, which serves residents and visitors to south Berkshire County, northwest Connecticut, and Columbia County, New York, does have an emergency room and is in the process of adding a walk-in center. North Adams Regional Hospital is an affiliate of Northern Berkshire Health Systems. It serves but is not limited to residents of North County, southern Vermont, and parts of neighboring New York State. Services at all are available to tourists.

Folks with non-life threatening medical problems also may go to the nearest emergency room or to any of the walk-in facilities. Naturally those in need of serious medical attention will be seen first in an emergency room, which means you might have to wait a while if your need is not urgent.

Even though you might think of the Berkshires as the boonies, these hospitals have the latest in medical technology, including on-site magnetic resonance imaging (MRI), radiation therapy, computed tomography (CAT scans), and other diagnostic tools. Many of the doctors and programs here have gained national honors for their work. For instance, Dr. Robert D. Fanelli, vice chairman of the department of surgery at BMC and assistant professor of surgery at UMass, has designed and developed four instruments that are being used nationally in minimally invasive surgery. A fifth instrument is waiting for a patent, and others are in the works. Fanelli, who is also on staff at North Adams Regional, was named one of the country's top surgeons by the Consumers' Research Council of America.

Berkshire Health Systems and Northern Berkshire Health Systems offer a number of wellness clinics through their hospitals or through the visiting nurse associations they own. Such programs focus on disease prevention and improving health by offering help with smoking cessation, weight reduction, stress reduction, and other issues. Community resource centers at all the hospitals are filled with information on disease prevention, treatment, and diagnosis, also available on their Web sites.

In addition to the services offered at or through the hospitals, residents and visitors have access to a wide range of medical expertise, as illustrated in the Yellow

Emergency Rooms and Medical Centers

Phone Numbers
All medical emergencies 911
Poison Control Center (800) 682-9211

24-hour Emergency Rooms
- Great Barrington
  Fairview Hospital, 29 Lewis Avenue; (413) 528-0790
- Pittsfield
  Berkshire Medical Center, 725 North Street; (413) 447-2834
- North Adams
  North Adams Regional Hospital, 71 Hospital Avenue; (413) 664-5256

Walk-in Centers (call for hours)
- Great Barrington
  Fairview Hospital, 29 Lewis Avenue; (413) 528-0790
- Pittsfield
  Accessible Medical Arts, 197 South Street; (413) 236-0995
  510 Medical Walk-in Center, 510 North Street (rear); (413) 499-0237
  Hillcrest Hospital, 165 Tor Court; (413) 445-9105
  Neighborhood Health Center, 510 North Street (front); (413) 447-2351

Pages of the phone book. Not that you can be sure of getting an appointment immediately. For many of these doctors, appointments are being made months ahead, and some are not taking new patients. Folks who are moving here should ask their local physician for a referral to an appropriate provider. Once you get in the loop, there is care available in just about every field of medicine. Many specialists have formed groups so that they can share office space and personnel. Oncologists, surgeons, orthopedists, and internal medicine practices are among these. In addition to standard Western medicine, a number of alternatives can be found in the county, including acupuncture, herbal medicine, massage therapists, myotherapists, hypnotherapists, and practitioners of holistic medicine.

Berkshire Health Systems
725 North Street, Pittsfield
(413) 447-2000
www.berkshirehealthsystems.org
Berkshire Health Systems is the nonprofit umbrella organization for three hospitals, four nursing homes in Berkshire County (see the Retirement chapter), and a host of other services. Their Web site is full of information, if you can stand to read the tiny green print. Find A Doctor lists physicians associated with BHS by name and specialty. BHS employs 3,500, making it the largest employer in the county. Recent revenues exceeded $231 million. At Berkshire Medical Center, 53 percent of the income was reimbursement for Medicare/Medicaid patients.

HOSPITALS AND MEDICAL CENTERS

South County

Fairview Hospital
29 Lewis Avenue, Great Barrington
(413) 528-0790
Fairview Hospital is a small nonprofit community hospital serving residents and visitors in southern Berkshire County,

northwest Connecticut, and neighboring Columbia County in New York. Fairview opened its doors in 1913, occupying two wooden buildings on a 20-acre site given to the community to establish a health-care facility. The wooden buildings were replaced with the present brick building in 1927 after a major capital campaign raised $310,000 in 10 days. Subsequent campaigns have continued to update medical equipment and bring in the latest technology. Fairview was acquired by Berkshire Health Systems in 1989.

With 24 beds, Fairview is one of the smallest hospitals in the state, yet it offers a full range of acute-care services on an inpatient and outpatient basis. Diagnostic services include laboratory testing, mammography, ultrasound, and bone densitometry. Cardiopulmonary, surgical, maternity and physical therapy services are available in addition to 24-hour emergency care. The hospital also offers ongoing community health education and support programs. Fairview is completing a $5 million renovation that includes the addition of a women's center, new operating rooms, and a walk-in center. The rehabilitation unit and radiology department also are being upgraded.

Many of the larger tourist attractions have medical staff on duty during performances who are trained to handle emergencies, often without the audience even knowing it!

Central Berkshire

Accessible Medical Arts
197 South Street, Pittsfield
(413) 236-0995

Urgent care for walk-ins is provided in this office operated by Dr. Alice Ling, who does not accept patients without insurance. Services include physical examinations for school or work and testing for various illnesses.

Berkshire Medical Center
725 North Street, Pittsfield
(413) 447-2000

Berkshire Medical Center is the anchor affiliate of Berkshire Health Systems. There are more than 300 beds in units ranging from intensive care to maternity and everything in between. BMC, and ultimately BHS, grew from the House of Mercy hospital, which opened in 1875 on the city's east side. With the capacity to care for 22 patients, it was the only such facility in the county. Mercy later moved to North Street and in 1949 built a new facility across the street, which became Pittsfield General Hospital. In the interim, St. Luke's Hospital opened on East Street, focusing on nurse training. In 1967 Pittsfield General and St. Luke's joined to form what eventually became Berkshire Medical Center. Berkshire Health Systems was formed in the 1970s as a management company. The Cancer Institute of the Berkshires was added to BMC in 1987 after a community-wide fund-raising effort. The radiation equipment in this center was recently upgraded with the addition of a linear accelerator to deliver precise radiation therapy. The BMC complex also includes a Medical Arts building, where a number of specialists and services are located.

Berkshire Health Systems has undertaken a $40 million renovation and expansion project that includes a three-story addition to Berkshire Medical Center, which will include an expanded emergency department with a total of 37 examination rooms, four ambulance bays, and a greatly enlarged waiting room. There also will be direct access from the ER to the surgical wing, which is also being expanded. Currently surgical patients are wheeled through the halls and onto the same elevators that visitors and others use. When completed, the surgical wing will have eight operating rooms plus two minor procedure rooms. A separate building is used for outpatient day surgery and minor procedure rooms. The surgery floor will be outfitted with new state-of-the-art equipment and a more private waiting room for family and friends. Laboratory services now in three different areas will be combined for greater efficiency and a new computerized records system installed that will allow physicians to access test results and other data immediately at a secure site.

As a teaching hospital affiliated with the University of Massachusetts Medical School, BMC provides training in internal medicine and offers residencies in surgery, osteopathy, and pathology. There are also schools of dentistry, medical technology, and cytotechnology, as well as undergraduate and continuing medical education. BHS also provides nursing education and emergency medical technician training to area fire departments and ambulance squads.

BMC was recently recognized by *U.S. News & World Report* as operating one of the top cardiac rehabilitation programs in the country. In addition to its surgical services and radiation therapy, BMC has dedicated stroke recovery and rehabilitation units, provides renal dialysis, treats sleep disorders, and offers mental health and substance abuse treatment in conjunction with the Department of Mental Health and Substance Abuse. Diagnostic screening is done with on-site CT scanners and MRI units, ultrasound mammography, and bone density tests. Endoscopy suites provide screening for colorectal cancer and treatments for gastrointestinal disorders.

BMC's department of psychiatry and behavioral sciences, in conjunction with the Department of Mental Health and Substance Abuse Service of the Berkshires, provides mental health care through 18 psychiatrists, nine clinical nurses, and a team of clinical psychologists, social workers, nurses, and others. The collaborative program was cited by the state Department of Public Health for its innovative approach. Alex Sabo, head of BMC's department of psychiatry, was recently honored by the American Psychiatric Association for excellence in medical education. He is an associate professor of clinical psychology at UMass and a lecturer at Harvard Medical School.

Hillcrest Hospital
165 Tor Court, Pittsfield
(413) 443-4761

The Hillcrest campus is located on the west side of Pittsfield on a hill overlooking Onota Lake. With its views of the mountains and surrounding area, the land was chosen as the site for a fort in the early development of the area. A lodge was built on the hill in 1856, operated by William Allen until his death, when his heirs sold the property to a varnish manufacturing tycoon who owned many acres around the lake. In 1907 the estate was rented to Colonel and Mrs. E. Parmalee Prentiss. She was the daughter of John D. Rockefeller. In 1908 Warren Salisbury bought the estate and a year later renamed it Tor Court. He built a columned mansion in the Colonial style that was used in summer. After his wife died, the property lay dormant until 1948 when it was sold and the mansion became Hillcrest Hospital. Berkshire Health Systems acquired Hillcrest in 1996, closing the emergency room and moving inpatient care to BMC.

Services at Hillcrest now include a primary care Family Health Center, where three doctors and two nurse practitioners practice internal medicine specializing in pediatrics and women's health. The McGee Alcoholism Treatment Center, operated in conjunction with Berkshire Mental Health/Substance Abuse, also is found here. Other services include pain management and occupational therapy. The office of International Travel Health Services is staffed by a nurse practitioner, who provides information on and can administer all legally required or medically recommended vaccines or immunizations needed for travel out of the country. Patients who use any BHS service but who do not have health insurance are offered assistance in determining eligibility for coverage under state or federal programs or free care through the Advocacy for Access office located here.

510 Medical Walk-in Center
510 North Street, Pittsfield
(413) 499-0237
This privately operated walk-in center is owned by Dr. Ellis W. Fribush and staffed by board-certified physicians who provide prompt medical care for adults and children. Full laboratory and X-ray services are on the premises. Most insurance is accepted; patients without insurance are not.

Neighborhood Health Center
510 North Street, Pittsfield
(413) 447-2351
Another satellite of BHS, the Neighborhood Health Center provides outpatient health care by attending physicians, nurse practitioners, and medical residents. Many folks use the center as their primary care provider, especially those who have limited or no health insurance. Depending on their need, walk-in patients might be directed to the BMC emergency room, seen by the next available provider, or scheduled for an appointment. State Department of Public Health clinics also are based in this facility. Tests for sexually transmitted diseases and pregnancy as well as premarital blood tests and hepatitis education, testing, and immunization may be scheduled here by calling (413) 447-2654. The Neighborhood Health Center is not to be confused with the 510 Medical Walk-in Center in the same building. That is a privately operated office, which only takes patients who have health insurance.

North County

North Adams Regional Hospital
71 Hospital Avenue, North Adams
(413) 663-3701
www.narh.org
Until 1882 there was no hospital in North County. But when the second train disaster in a month left 35 workmen badly injured or dying, citizens of North Adams took the first steps toward building one. Three hours after that second wreck, a subscription drive with a goal of $12,000 began. A 30-acre pasture on the former Estes estate high above the city was chosen as the site, and on March 2, 1885, North Adams Hospital opened with 12 beds. In 1891 a nurses' training school was opened in an effort to ensure an ongoing supply of fully trained staff to care for the growing number of patients. By 1905 the building was hopelessly overcrowded, and the first of many additions was constructed. In 1912 a nurses' residence was built on the grounds that was used for training until 1943. The "accident and emergency department" opened in 1938.

As the hospital became a more important and necessary community resource, periodic additions to the original structure continued, but by the 1950s it became clear that a new hospital would be needed. Fund-raising ensued, and in 1955 a new $1,789,183 building opened. A similar effort in the 1960s resulted in the addition of the North Wing, providing more beds and room for ancillary services. In the 1980s a new fund-raising effort with a goal of $3.5 million began, resulting in modernizing the existing facility and constructing new areas for clinical use. Since then the hospital has added a stereotactic breast biopsy unit, expanded the endoscopy suite, and added a new ambulatory care center housing around 40 physicians and health professionals and a new blood-drawing lab. A Radiologic Technology Training Center provides clinical experience for students. The two-year program is offered through an affiliation with hospitals in Springfield and Vermont.

Having come a long way from those first 12 beds, NARH now provides primary care and specialty physician services and diagnosis and treatment to residents and visitors from the northern Berkshire, southern Vermont, and eastern New York area. The emergency department treats more than 20,000 people annually. More than 2,200 surgeries are performed each year. The medical staff includes internists, family care practitioners, and a broad range of specialists. Ninety-seven percent of the medical staff is board-certified or board-eligible, meaning they have met the highest standards set by the medical profession.

Diagnostic procedures using magnetic resonance imaging, echocardiographs, nuclear medicine, mammography, and bone densitometry are available. Chemotherapy is administered at the Eileen Barrett Oncology Center and there is a computer connection to the National Cancer Institute. Maternity care and childbirth education, wellness programs, health screenings, and physical, occupational, and speech therapy are also offered. Inpatient psychiatric care is provided at the Greylock Pavilion.

Northern Berkshire Health Systems
71 Hospital Avenue, North Adams
(413) 664-5140
www.nbhealth.org

Northern Berkshire Health Systems is the nonprofit parent company of North Adams Regional Hospital. NBHS also operates Sweetwood Continuing Care Community and Sweet Brook Care Centers, both in Williamstown, Northern Berkshire Visiting Nurse Association, and Hospice of Northern Berkshire. In an effort to ensure continuing health care for the community, the corporation created REACH Community Health Foundation. This collaborative organization has two major fund-raising goals. One is to develop a $20 million endowment that will generate $1.2 million annually for education, advocacy, and treatment. The other is an annual appeal program directed toward capital improvements, staff training, and program development.

HOME CARE

Visiting nurse services are available through three agencies to qualifying patients. Sometimes these services are arranged through social workers at the hospitals or nursing homes in conjunction with Elder Services or other agencies. Private pay home care is also available.

Berkshire Visiting Nurse Association
76 South Church Street, Pittsfield
(413) 447-2862, (800) 788-2862

More than 100 years old, this organization continues to provide home care services to improve the physical and emotional well-being of its clients. Until recently the VNA operated as an independent agency. But recently the Central Berkshire operation was acquired by Berkshire Health Systems. The North County component is now part of Northern Berkshire Health Systems, based in North Adams Regional Hospital. The BVNA offers skilled nursing services, physical occupational and speech therapies, home health aides, behavioral health services, IV therapy, and mother and child services. Visiting nurses also run blood pressure clinics at various locations, including senior centers and popular stores around the county. Their community outreach programs serve more than 30,000 annually. In addition, health care professionals travel more than 250,000 miles providing more than 80,000 home visits to nearly 4,000 patients. The BVNA has more than 200 employees.

HospiceCare in the Berkshires
369 South Street, Pittsfield
(413) 443-2994

HospiceCare was formerly two volunteer hospice organizations that merged in 1990 and became Medicare-certified the following year. The agency provides information and services to terminally ill individuals at home, in skilled nursing facilities and hospitals, and their families through an interdisciplinary team of health care professionals, therapists, social workers, and physicians. A corps of around 60 volunteers provides support in many ways. They may help a patient write a life story or finish a project or provide more practical assistance by cooking or driving. Patient care includes expert pain and symptom management as well as such nonmedical services as massage therapy, stress reduction, and the use of art as a therapy. Counseling and support groups are offered for grieving adults, children, and adolescents. Aside from reimbursements for services from third-party payers, the agency relies on donations and holds fund-raisers throughout the year.

A resource guide for end of life services is available from the Massachusetts Commission on End of Life Care, which was created by the state "to improve the quality of life at the end of life." Topics covered include home care, pain management, symptom control, and others that are often faced too late to address the needs and wishes of the dying patient. The guide is available on the Internet at www.endoflifecommission.org.

Lee Regional Visiting Nurse Association
21 High Street, Lee
(413) 243-1212, (800) 427-1208
www.leeregionalvna.org

The Lee VNA is an independent nonprofit agency serving patients in 28 communities in Central and South Berkshire and the adjacent hill towns since 1912. More than 1,100 clients have received services from field staff that covers more than 121,000 miles. Staff includes 17 full-time and 32 part-time practitioners, therapists, social workers, aides, and administrative and support staff. The agency has a budget of $2.7 million. Aside from nursing and support systems available for clients at home, the agency provides nurses at some schools; runs a caregiver support group; provides nutrition counseling; screens for diabetes, lead, and tuberculosis; and administers immunizations against childhood diseases, flu, and other communicable diseases. The agency recently undertook a capital campaign with a goal of $1 million to continue to meet the home health care needs of area residents. Funds will help to establish a $700,000 endowment that will be used to pay for care for patients who have no insurance or who are not Medicare/Medicaid eligible; $250,000 for technology and training that allows all field staff to use laptop computers to record and share information about patients; and $50,000 for new programs to provide care for chronically ill patients.

Visiting Nurse Association and Hospice of Northern Berkshire Inc.
535 Curran Memorial Highway (Massachusetts Highway 8), North Adams
(413) 664-4536

In 1911 nurse Mary Bridgman Quinn made home visits on foot. Her service, called the North Adams Community Nursing Service, later became the North Adams Visiting Nurse Association. Williamstown's formal visiting nurse services date from 1918, with the incorporation of the Community Nursing Association. The organization became the Williamstown VNA in 1954. In 1985 the Visiting Nurse Associations of North Adams and Williamstown merged to form the nonprofit VNA of Northern Berkshire, Inc. In 1997 the VNA and Hospice of Northern Berkshire became part of Northern Berkshire Health Systems family of health-care providers. As before, the VNA provides comprehensive home health-care services to help residents recuperate from illness, injury, or childbirth or to manage an acute or serious medical condition while enjoying the comfort and security of their own home. In addition, trained professionals and volunteers offer physical, emotional, spiritual, and bereavement support plus companionship and respite for the terminally ill and their families through the hospice program. The VNA also reaches out to the community through educational programs, free health screenings and fairs, communicable disease immunizations, and follow-up visits.

ALTERNATIVE HEALTH-CARE PROVIDERS AND SUPPORT SYSTEMS

Berkshire Doula Guild
142 Oak Hill Road, Pittsfield
(413) 443-5867

A doula aids women and their partners by providing nonmedical emotional and physical support during pregnancy, birth, and the postpartum period. This network of women also provides breast-feeding support and teaching, newborn/infant care and teaching, and help with household tasks and the care of small siblings.

LaLeche League
The Guthrie Center
Great Barrington
Breast-feeding classes, phone consultations, and informational sessions are offered through this group.

Tapestry Health Systems
211 Main Street, Great Barrington
(413) 528-4238

100 Wendell Avenue, Pittsfield
(413) 443-2844

85 Main Street, North Adams
(413) 663-8846
Reproductive health care, through the auspices of the Family Planning Council of Western Massachusetts, is offered at these three locations. General gynecological services, including birth control, emergency contraceptive, pregnancy testing, and full option counseling are available. Screening for sexually transmitted diseases may be arranged. There is a sliding fee scale.

ACUPUNCTURE AND CHINESE HERBAL MEDICINE

The Massachusetts Board of Medicine licenses acupuncturists just as they do doctors. Applicants must show a special committee that they have graduated from an accredited school. In addition, they must take a clean-needle technique course and pass a national board exam. Foreign acupuncturists must submit transcripts from their schools. Herbalists are not licensed but do have a peer review process through the American Guild of Herbalists, which issues certificates. They may also study at an accredited school and take a national board exam. An acupuncture license also allows the recipient to practice massage and other accessory treatments as deemed appropriate for the client. Massage therapists are not licensed in Massachusetts but are required to get a permit from the town in which they locate. Those who have studied at known schools may apply for a national certification to show they have met the requirements for a license. Generally these services are not covered by insurance. However, some treatments relating to injuries in motor vehicle accidents or at worksites may be covered. A wide range of massage therapists too numerous to list here practice all varieties of techniques, including Reiki, Kryia, and Tsubo. And many of the resorts offer massage therapy to their guests.

South County

The Centre for Acupuncture
105 Main Street, Great Barrington
(413) 528-3514
Linda Jackson holds a master's degree in Oriental medicine from the Oregon College of Oriental Medicine in Portland. She practices acupuncture, herbal medicine, and massage.

Darshan Center for Wellbeing
27 Rossiter Road, Great Barrington
(413) 644-9474
This holistic health center, owned by James and Randy Haskins, offers integrative manual therapy plus the weekly services of an acupuncturist and herbalist. Physical, massage, and craniosacral therapy are performed by a staff of two plus two assistants.

Lonney Jarrett
44 South Main Street, Stockbridge
(413) 298-4221
Lonney Jarrett received his training from the Traditional Acupuncture Institute in Laurel, Maryland, and has been practicing acupuncture and herbal medicine in Stockbridge since 1986. He is a fellow of the National Academy of Acupuncture and Oriental Medicine; is the author of *Nourishing Destiny: The Inner Tradition of*

Chinese Medicine, a standard textbook for teaching acupuncture in English-speaking countries; and teaches Chinese medicine all over the world.

Robert Malik Lawrence
94 West Avenue, Great Barrington
(413) 528-1511
Robert Malik Lawrence is a graduate of Nanjing University, where he studied acupuncture and Oriental medicine. He is also a licensed massage therapist, having graduated from the Florida School of Massage in Gainesville.

Central Berkshire

New England Acupuncture and Herb Clinic
Doctor's Park
197 South Street, Pittsfield
(413) 448-8088
A board-certified acupuncturist and herbalist, Ryan Heath Less received a master's degree in Oriental medicine from the Midwest College of Oriental Medicine in Chicago. He is coauthor of *AIDS and Complementary and Alternative Medicine* and has taught at a number of schools, including the Wisconsin Institute of Massage in Racine. A deep-massage therapist is also located in his office.

Spanda Holistic Center
823 North Street, Pittsfield
(413) 442-0123
Mayer Kirkpatrick holds the equivalent of a master's degree from the New England School of Acupuncture in Watertown and is licensed by the state. He incorporates herbs and energy psychology in his work and has an herbal pharmacy in his office, which is located in a historic home. He has been trained by masters from Japan and offers gentle, sensitive, and effective deep healing for adults and children. He specializes in noninsertion acupuncture methods. Spanda is Sanscrit for "Qi" (pronounced *chee*), the Chinese word for energy.

North County

Sandy Camper
12 Meadow Street, Williamstown
(413) 458-2792
Sandy Camper holds a master's degree from the Traditional Acupuncture Institute in Laurel, Maryland, and completed an additional two-year course on herbal medicine. He has taught clinical Chinese medicine theory.

Northern Berkshire Acupuncture and Chinese Medicine
622 Main Street, Williamstown
(413) 458-3530
Practitioners in this office are Dr. Xingning Zhao and Shaohua Tang. Xingning Zhao holds a doctor of medicine degree from China and is a licensed acupuncturist in Massachusetts and New York. Shaohua Tang is a former professor of acupuncture at Nanjing University. She has a Ph.D. and is a licensed doctor of medicine in both Massachusetts and New York. Both practiced internal medicine combined with Chinese medicine techniques in Nanjing University Hospital of Traditional Chinese Medicine before coming to the United States 12 years ago.

Wellness Center
210 Water Street, Williamstown
(413) 458-0912
Acupuncture, herbal medicine, shiatsu massage, and craniosacral therapy are offered here by Beth Hiam Acheson, who holds a master's degree in Oriental medicine from the Oregon College of Oriental Medicine in Portland.

RETIREMENT

According to the latest census, the number of older people living in the Berkshires is increasing. This may mean that a lot of younger people are leaving the area. But it also could mean that with the recent construction of a number of retirement communities, more retirees are opting to stay here rather than flee permanently to warmer climes or move closer to their children. Additionally, as the cultural attractions in the county expand, there is more to do here year-round than ever before. And there certainly are plenty of support services for seniors of all income levels, enabling many to stay in their homes much longer.

Elder Services of the Berkshires is the main source for information about services for county residents age 55 and older. Every municipality has a Council on Aging, overseen by Elder Services, and many have senior centers where nutritional lunches are served, trips planned, and social activities held. These centers also serve as convenient locations for visiting nurses to check blood pressure, administer flu shots, and provide information about medical issues. Trained representatives from Elder Services also are able to help seniors figure out complex medical bills, income taxes, and other financial quandaries and to advise them of various programs and assistance they might qualify for. In addition to the retirement and assisted-living facilities listed below, several entities and municipalities operate elderly housing complexes. These comfortable and economical apartments, also listed below, are located in a variety of buildings. Each has a community room for socializing, and many run programs and activities for the residents. Some have dining rooms and provide meals on-site. Most senior centers own or share with other communities vehicles that are used to transport the elderly to appointments or shopping. Elders who want to continue learning can choose to take courses offered by area schools and colleges (more about that in the Education chapter).

Who are these retirees? They are from many walks of life. Williamstown's elderly population includes Williams College retirees and alumni returning to the Village Beautiful after leaving their far-flung careers. There also are a number of workers retired—or laid off—from manufacturers like Sprague Electric and Waverly Fabrics. In Central Berkshire, retired GE and Crane & Company workers make up a large part of the aging population. Some members of the Boston Symphony decide to retire here to be near Tanglewood and fellow musicians. Some are from out of the area, having moved into local retirement communities to be near their children. Many second-home owners also retire here. Some eventually sell out and move south permanently, while others head for warmer weather only in winter. But others are opting to stay here year-round. Of course it is debatable whether some retirees do in fact retire. Many professionals serve as consultants in their fields or start a business that has always been in the backs of their minds. Writers, artists, musicians, and other artisans might never really stop producing their work, and many serve as mentors to younger people.

Whoever they may be, retirees are indispensable to the community. They usher at Tanglewood and other cultural venues, are docents at museums, lead tours at historic sites, serve as mentors to businesses and young people, referee at sporting events, serve on boards, support local causes, and volunteer for countless organizations. Some towns allow seniors to volunteer for certain jobs in exchange for a write-off on a portion of their property taxes. They might help out with paperwork in the town hall, volunteer at the school, staff the recycling center, or drive people who have given up their cars to appointments or shopping. Some towns have a corps of volunteers who do small home repairs, bring in firewood, shovel snow, and perform other chores for seniors in their community.

Retirement communities cater to individuals who are capable of getting along on their own but who choose for various reasons to have their basic needs taken care of by someone else. They appeal to people who no longer want to manage property, maintain automobiles, or do their own cooking and housework but who want the companionship of people with like interests. After adding up all the expenses they incur living on their own, they might find a retirement community an affordable and carefree alternative. Assisted-living facilities provide support for those who find it difficult to manage all the routine activities of daily living. Monthly fees for the retirement and assisted-living communities listed below include meals, linens, housekeeping, transportation, and security and emergency medical systems, along with additional services and amenities that vary from place to place. All aim to provide a sense of community, foster independence, and encourage lifelong learning through a variety of activities. Several are owned by the two hospitals in the county, described more fully in the Health Care chapter, and some are run by national chains. Of course the fees listed below are subject to change. Most have waiting lists; all welcome visits. Tours and a sample meal may be arranged by calling ahead.

RETIREMENT COMMUNITIES

Devonshire Estates
329 Pittsfield Road (U.S. Highway 7), Lenox
(413) 637-1700
www.devonshireestates.com

Devonshire Estates opened in 1998 offering several full-service options. Twenty freestanding cottages, some with garages, offer completely independent living but access to all amenities. The cottages, or suites in them, have full kitchens, although residents are entitled to one meal a day in the main dining room. All inclusive monthly rents run from around $2,000 to $2,700 for one, depending on the size. Couples pay an additional $200. There are a total of 108 apartments in the main building in a variety of sizes. All have kitchenettes and may include other features. Apartments run from $1,200 to $1,800 for a studio; $1,800 to $2,100 for one bedroom; and $2,400 to $2,500 for a two-bedroom unit. Add $400 for an additional occupant. There are no buy-in fees or leases. A guest apartment may be rented for $50 a night for friends or relatives visiting from out of the area. A community building includes a library, billiards room, exercise room, and a room for crafts and activities. Meals are served in a large attractively furnished dining room with a restaurant-like atmosphere. Around 90 percent of the residents are from Berkshire County. Operated by Holiday Retirement Corporation, the facility is managed by two couples who live on the premises. Medical care is not offered, but residents may hire outside therapists, visiting nurses, or personal assistants.

Salisbury Estates Retirement Community
165 Tor Court, Pittsfield
(413) 447-9047

Salisbury Estates opened in 1987 with 61 private homes that are leased through a cooperative. To become a tenant, residents purchase shares in the corporation for fees ranging from $150,000 to $155,000. The equity in the stock entitles the tenant to housing in one of the homes and access to all amenities and services, for which a monthly fee of $415 is charged. Security, maintenance, and transportation are included. Each unit has a sunporch, patio, and fully equipped kitchen. Salisbury Estates is managed by

Berkshire Health Systems, but the community is not an assisted-living facility and medical services are not offered.

Sweetwood Continuing Care Retirement Community
1611 Cold Spring Road (US 7), Williamstown
(413) 458-8371
www.nbhealth.org

Founded in 1948 by a local woman, Sweetwood is now owned and managed by Northern Berkshire Health Systems, which also operates the Sweet Brook Nursing Care Center next door and North Adams Regional Hospital. The Sweetwood complex is built on a hill off US 7. Residents on the east side of this imposing structure have magnificent views of Mount Greylock and the valley below. Sweetwood does not bill itself as an assisted-living facility, although healthcare assistance is available if needed. It is more like a gracious hotel geared toward seniors, supplying all their needs. Residents, called guests by the management, are largely independent people who have chosen to live in a safe, carefree, and pleasant environment with stimulating companionship. Among those living at Sweetwood are retired professors, artists, lawyers, and musicians.

One- and two-bedroom suites with varying floor plans have complete kitchens, spacious closets, and private balconies. Additional storage space is available, and there are accommodations for overnight visitors. Above-average meals selected from a diverse menu are served in an elegant dining room, and there is a private dining room for special occasions. There are spacious lounges, a large recreation room with pool and table tennis tables and space for other games, a beauty and barber shop, greenhouse, library, bar, arts and craft center, workshop, computer lab, plus an auditorium for special events and a convenience store. All facilities, including the garage, are connected and enclosed, so residents are always protected from inclement weather. Equipment in the state-of-the-art physical fitness center includes a countercurrent swimming pool similar to the kind used by athletic trainers for injury rehabilitation. A physical therapist will design a personal fitness program to increase strength and flexibility.

With so many cultural resources nearby, residents are never at a loss for things to do in the community. Concerts, art shows, and special events are ongoing, and transportation is provided, if desired. Sweetwood collaborates with Williams College, offering residents the ability to attend classes, lectures, forums, and art programs. Residents pay an entry fee ranging from $198,000 to $371,000, depending on the accommodation chosen. Ninety percent of this fee is returned to either the resident, should he or she decide to leave, or to the resident's estate. The monthly rent varies depending on the kind of residence, ranging from $2,000 for a single unit to $3,000 for the most deluxe. The entry fee for an average two-bedroom apartment with two occupants is around $284,000 and the monthly rent around $2,800.

ASSISTED-LIVING FACILITIES

Cameron House
109 Housatonic Street, Lenox
(413) 637-3100

One of the newest assisted-living facilities, Cameron House was formerly a historic schoolhouse built on property once owned by J. P. Morgan. No longer needed by the town of Lenox, the building was recently restored and renovated by Baran Associates of Wellesley. Benchmark Assisted Living, based in Wellesley Hills, manages this facility as well as 30 other senior living centers in New England. Cameron House is located in a residential area near downtown Lenox. The brick three-story building has been adapted to provide a homelike atmosphere in a state-of-the-art facility. There are 44 studio apartments, which residents may furnish with their own things. Additional spaces include a library, a country kitchen, several lounges, a card and game room, a spacious dining room with table service, and a beauty/barber salon. Computers are provided for residents' use. The landscaped grounds include a gazebo and areas where residents are encouraged to have their own gardens. Round-the-clock staff is on the premises. There are no maintenance or buy-in fees. Month-to-month rents range from $2,500 to $3,100, depending on the size of the unit.

Curtis Manor Retirement Home
83 Curtis Avenue, Dalton
(413) 684-0218
Curtis Manor is located just off Main Street in a tree-shaded residential neighborhood with churches, stores, and the library nearby. The family-owned facility consists of a main house and two cottages. The main house has 23 beds in private or semi-private rooms, some with private baths, and is licensed by the state as a rest home. Assistance with personal care and medications is provided by licensed practitioners on round-the-clock duty. Rooms here are $70 or $75 a day, including meals, housekeeping, and activities. The cottages have kitchens and offer a more independent life style but are connected to the main house by an emergency call system. The rate of $1,000 a month includes the same services offered in the main house. The complex is owned and operated by Joanne and Karen Danforth.

Epoch Assisted Living at Melbourne Place
140 Melbourne Road, Pittsfield
(413) 499-1992, (888) 239-1722
www.epochsl.com
Situated in a rural area on the outskirts of Pittsfield, Melbourne Place offers studio and one- and two-bedroom apartments with a variety of floor plans. There are 125 apartments in all, each with a kitchenette. Owned and operated by Epoch Assisted Living, with corporate headquarters in Waltham, Melbourne Place offers an array of services and activities to provide access to entertainment and new learning experiences. Art exhibits, musical entertainment, afternoon tea and pastries, lecturers, and excursions are scheduled frequently. A wellness clinical director and 24-hour health-care staff attend to medical needs tailored to each resident. In some cases additional fees may apply. A fitness center offers a variety of equipment and therapists to maintain or improve physical abilities.

Meals chosen from a varied menu are served restaurant-style in the spacious dining room. A communal kitchen may be used by residents who miss cooking from scratch. Snacks and beverages are available there at all times. Monthly fees for single occupancy range from $2,600 to $3,000 for a studio apartment and $3,400 to $3,700 for a private one-bedroom apartment. A fee of $750 a month is charged for a second occupant. A two-bedroom apartment occupied by two costs around $2,300 a month. Fully furnished respite apartments may be rented for $150 a day.

Melbourne Place also operates an assisted-living unit for memory-impaired residents based on an enrichment philosophy recently developed for the National Alzheimer's Association. Monthly fees range from $3,900 to $4,500 depending on the type of occupancy and include all personal care.

Rockwell Victorian Assisted Living
219 Church Street, North Adams
(413) 664-8400
www.rockwellvictorian.net
Rockwell Victorian consists of five suites located in a converted carriage house, where homemade meals are prepared by the administrator and chef, Daryl Head. The facility is privately owned and costs $2,500 per month, including all basic services.

Rosewood Homestyle Assisted Living
318-320 Onota Street, Pittsfield
(413) 448-8449
This privately owned home offers a family-like atmosphere to its residents. Located in

a residential neighborhood, Rosewood focuses on maintaining ties to the community. There are 15 private rooms with six shared bathrooms. Monthly rents range from $1,550 to $1,950 depending on the level of assistance needed. A wraparound deck at the rear of the home looks out over a garden with views of the city. Rooms may be rented for short-term stays, providing respite for those who care for their elders at home. There are daily activities and occasional outings to special events.

Side By Side
114 Onota Street, Pittsfield
(413) 443-4274
Side By Side maintains the family feeling that rooming houses used to provide. In fact, it started out as a rooming house that the former owners expanded by purchasing and connecting two adjoining homes more than 20 years ago. Home-cooked meals and snacks are served in an open communal kitchen. Other common areas include spaces for arts and crafts, reading, and hair care. There are 36 rooms, some with private baths, plus a one-bedroom apartment. A long front porch is a popular place for residents to sit in nice weather, watching the comings and goings in this residential neighborhood. At the rear there are three decks. Staff is on hand 24 hours. Rates range from $65 to $100 a day, depending on the accommodations. Side By Side was recently purchased from the founders by Geri and Matt Ravlich and Steven D'Antonio, all of Hancock. A registered nurse, Geri was also employed by Elder Services. Matt is a retired National Hockey League player who played for the Boston Bruins. He and D'Antonio are in the real estate business.

Sugar Hill
45 Main Street, Dalton
(413) 684-0100
www.sugarhillmansion.com
One of the newest senior living communities to open in the Berkshires, Sugar Hill is nevertheless steeped in history. It is located on the 20-acre former estate of Winthrop Murray Crane III, whose 23-room mansion has been restored to its original beauty. Custom wood finishes, marble fireplaces, hand-painted murals, and a grand staircase have been preserved. Suites in the mansion have fireplaces, polished wood floors, and original moldings. Studio apartments are located in a recently completed addition. There are a total 42 units, which may be leased monthly for $3,000 to $4,900. There are no buy-in fees, but residents are asked to pay one month's security and an additional month's rent. Services for both include 45 minutes of personal assistance with bathing, dressing, and medication.

Recreational, educational, spiritual, and social activities and assistance with transportation to shopping and community services are provided. Meals prepared by an executive chef are served in the formal dining room. There are also a library, parlor/lounge, game, and music rooms. A wellness program with regular visits by on-staff nurses is included in the monthly fee. Also available is a secure program for memory-impaired residents. Sugar Hill is owned and operated by Patrick Sheehan, who lives on-site with his wife, Alli LeRoy. Residents who need skilled nursing or rehabilitation services will have preferred status at Craneville Place, also owned and operated by Sheehan.

COMBINED RETIREMENT, ASSISTED-LIVING, AND SKILLED NURSING CENTERS

Berkshire Place
89 South Street, Pittsfield
(413) 445-4056
www.berkshireplace.com
Berkshire Place was established in 1888 by the son of Zenas Crane, founder of Crane & Company. The elder Crane also established the Berkshire Museum, which is right next door to Berkshire Place. The home was incorporated in 1890 as the Berkshire County Home for Aged Women. In 1925

the third floor of the Romanesque-style brick building was expanded and nurses' quarters added. The home was licensed as a rest home by the state in 1950 and renamed Berkshire Place in 1960. Although Berkshire Place is the oldest retirement home in the county, it has kept pace with the latest in assisted living and continues to be locally owned and operated.

There are 20 private bedrooms in the residential-care level. The daily rate depends on whether the room has a half or full bathroom and ranges from $107 to $110. All services, including three daily meals, are included. There are no leases, entry fees, or deposits required. Women living in the residential section have priority admission to the skilled nursing care unit, which costs $147 a day for one of the five semiprivate rooms to $157 for one of the 12 private rooms. A variety of services can be arranged for temporary stays.

Kimball Farms
235 Walker Street, Lenox
(413) 637-7000
www.kimballfarms.org

Kimball Farms is a nonprofit "lifecare" retirement community located on a former estate in Lenox. It is affiliated with Berkshire Health Systems, which owns and operates Berkshire Medical Center in Pittsfield. Situated on the 63-acre campus in New England–style buildings are 150 independent apartments, 48 assisted-living apartments, and a skilled nursing center. The apartments vary in size, floor plan, and location. Some have patios; others have balconies. All are carpeted and have full kitchens and spacious closets. Occupants are free to furnish and decorate as they choose. Kimball Farms requires an entry fee, which ranges from around $13,000 to $230,000 depending on the size and floor plan. Ninety percent of this fee is refunded to the resident, if he or she decides to leave, or to the resident's estate. A monthly service fee is charged, ranging from $665 to $3,700, again depending on the accommodations. Gourmet meals are served in an elegant dining room, and there is a 24-hour professionally staffed health center, and on-site social and recreational opportunities are provided. Walking trails wind through the grounds, and residents are encouraged to maintain gardens for their own pleasure. Residents also may use the pool and other facilities at nearby Cranwell Resort by special arrangement. Communal spaces include a tastefully furnished parlor with a fireplace and numerous private conversation areas, a central auditorium for speakers and cultural events, a library and reading room with a media center, a fitness center, a beauty salon, and a barber shop.

If a resident finds the need for more assistance and moves to PineHill Assisted Living, the monthly fee remains the same. In addition, if the resident needs to move to the skilled nursing center, the fee also remains the same, even if that resident's spouse remains in their apartment. And when medical care enters the picture, a portion of the fee may be tax deductible as a medical expense. PineHill assisted-living apartments and the nursing center also are available to nonresidents. The nursing care center has 74 beds and includes an Alzheimer's unit. Kimball Farm residents are encouraged to contribute to the community, continue their education, and maintain their zest for life while feeling secure that their medical needs will be met as they age.

The Village at Laurel Lake (Hearthstone at Laurel Lake)
600 Laurel Street (U.S. Highway 20), Lee
(413) 243-2727
www.commonwealthcommunity.com

The Village at Laurel Lake consists of 49 assisted-living apartments capable of accommodating 62 residents, a secure Alzheimer's suite for 26 residents, and a rehabilitation and skilled nursing unit with 88 beds. Built in 1999, Laurel Lake is operated by Commonwealth Communities of Needham. The sprawling complex is designed around a central courtyard and is similar to an award-winning facility developed by Commonwealth in Brockton. Assisted living is provided for residents, who rent studio or one-bedroom apartments. Rents range from $2,900 to $4,725. All units have a kitchenette with a cooktop, refrigerator, and microwave and wall-to-wall carpet. Residents furnish and decorate their apartments as they wish. Community areas include a library, an alcove with a fireplace, a cinema, health club, salon, and outdoor porches and patios. Meals, selected from choices offered on a daily menu, are served restaurant-style in the spacious dining room.

In addition to the basics mentioned above, the monthly fee includes 45 minutes of daily personal-care assistance and wellness programs. A short-stay program allows prospective residents to try out assisted living. The adjacent Laurel Lake Center for Health and Rehabilitation provides short- and long-term skilled care. Residents of the assisted-living section have priority access to this unit, which is Medicare and Medicaid certified. The Monarch Special Care Center provides a comprehensive program for seniors with neurological, behavioral, and emotional disorders in a community-like setting that is safe and secure.

NURSING AND REHABILITATION CENTERS

In an effort to eliminate the unpleasant connotations associated with the term "nursing home," facilities that provide such care are now being called nursing centers. Because of the variables affecting costs in these facilities, no pricing is given here. The Massachusetts Department of Public Health inspects Medicare- and Medicaid-certified nursing homes every 9 to 15 months. Thanks to the advent of computer databases and the Internet, the results of these surveys are public and easy to find, although not always easy to decipher. Information includes deficiencies reported and dates corrected, the amount of time staff spends with patients, and a checklist to compare nursing homes. The two main Web sites to check are www.state.ma.us/dph and www.medicare.gov. Elder Services also provides information. (See the Close-up in this chapter.)

BHCS-Affiliated Centers

The following nursing centers are operated by Berkshire Health Care Systems, an affiliate of Berkshire Health Systems, 725 North Street, Pittsfield. For more detailed information visit www.berkshirehealthsystems.org, or call the number listed with each center. See also Kimball Farms above.

i

Most nursing homes and some assisted-living facilities in the county provide short-term care. Unfortunately there is no single clearinghouse to find one to suit specific needs. By calling around, caregivers might find a facility that has a vacancy and can provide appropriate services for when they need respite or must travel.

Fairview Commons
Christian Hill Road, Great Barrington
(413) 528-4560

Fairview Commons offers short- and long-term care, continuing care, and rehabilitation services in a 180-bed facility. Private and semiprivate rooms with private baths are offered. The building has an enclosed courtyard. A homelike atmosphere is provided, and meals are served in the dining room. Visits from pets are permitted. There is a monthly activities newsletter, and staff encourage residents to participate in outings, exercise, and yoga. Services include a secure Alzheimer's and dementia unit and a respite and hospice program for caregivers. Fairview Hospital, also operated by Berkshire Health Systems, is nearby.

Serving the Elderly

Elder Services of Berkshire County Inc. (66 Wendell Avenue, Pittsfield; 413–499–0524; www.esbci.org) began as a private, nonprofit home care corporation and became an Area Agency on Aging in accordance with the Older Americans Act in 1975. In 1997 Elder Services was designated by the state Executive Office of Elder Affairs to be the Aging Services Access Point for all Berkshire County. Its mission is "to provide Berkshire elders the opportunity to live with dignity, independence, and self-determination and to achieve the highest possible quality of life." Services include information and referral, case management, respite care, homemaker and home health assistance, and nursing home prescreening. The agency also operates housing, adult family care, a nursing home ombudsman program, money management, and protective services programs and oversees a senior aide employment program. Depending on income, some services are free or available for modest fees.

Every two years the agency identifies priority needs of Berkshire County's elderly and plans and develops services to address these needs. Each year, more than 1,000 elders receive in-home services, authorized by case managers. Another 1,600 attend one of the 14 congregate meal sites while 1,700 have Meals on Wheels delivered to them. Each day 1,000 to 1,200 meals are prepared in Elder Services' own kitchen. The housing, adult family care, and nursing home ombudsman programs serve an additional 2,161 people. The agency publishes a monthly newspaper, the *Berkshire Senior*, which is circulated to 7,500 individuals throughout the county, and produces a television show.

Elder Services collaborates with local councils on aging, senior centers, certified home health agencies, adult day health and social day care programs, mental health agencies, long-term care facilities, and all area hospitals. As part of its philosophy, the organization recognizes and respects an older person's right to autonomy and is committed to encouraging each elder to control his or her own life and will give the information needed for informed decisions.

Of particular interest to family members who have relatives in nursing homes is the ombudsman program. Massachusetts was among the first six pilot projects for this program when it was established by the federal government in 1973. The goals of the program are to receive, investigate, and attempt to resolve complaints made by or on behalf of residents of nursing and rest homes; to protect residents' rights; to provide information; and to advocate for positive change in the long-term care system. Certified volunteers investigate concerns, work with the home to correct a problem, and report to the Department of Public Health if there are concerns about abuse or neglect.

The volunteer program serves more than 3,600 elders annually with a corps of about 400 folks. Services they may provide include packing or delivering meals to the homebound, grocery shopping, driving elders to appointments or activities, helping with money management, or just providing companionship. Anyone interested in volunteering may call Elder Services for information.

Hillcrest Commons Nursing & Rehabilitation
169 Valentine Road, Pittsfield
(413) 445-2300
Hillcrest Commons is located on Onota Lake on the campus of Hillcrest Hospital, also operated by Berkshire Health Systems. With 265 beds, it is the largest in the county. Residents are encouraged to retain a sense of community and family by bringing in their own belongings. Pets may visit, and there is a resident rabbit. A full range of services is available, including an Alzheimer's unit and long- and short-term care. Rehabilitation services are offered for patients who no longer need hospitalization but who are not ready to return to their homes.

Kimball Farms Nursing Center
40 Sunset Avenue, Lenox
(413) 637-5011
Although this facility is on the grounds of the Kimball Farms Life Care Community, it has a separate address and telephone number. This 74-bed center is open to patients from outside the Kimball Farms community, but those residents have priority should they need nursing care. A secure Alzheimer's care unit also is located here.

Mount Greylock Extended Care Facility
1000 North Street, Pittsfield
(413) 499-7186
Patios, a solarium, and a water fountain add to the pleasant atmosphere at this 100-bed long- and short-term care facility. Rooms are furnished private or semiprivate, and each has its own bathroom. Meals are served in a pleasantly furnished dining room, and there is a lounge and library.

North Adams Commons Nursing and Rehabilitation Center
175 Franklin Street, North Adams
(413) 664-4041
Located in a residential neighborhood near downtown North Adams, this facility provides a homelike atmosphere and offers short-term rehabilitation services with the goal of returning patients to their homes in two to three weeks. Staff assist in arranging home health services and assist in long-term care planning. There are 120 beds.

Williamstown Commons Nursing & Rehabilitation
25 Adams Road, Williamstown
(413) 458-2111
The rehabilitation unit here provides services aimed at returning the patient to the highest level of independence achievable and maintaining that level. The nursing staff is equipped to care for more serious and complicated medical problems that may involve administering intravenous therapy, wound and pain management, peritoneal dialysis, and major orthopedic rehabilitation. The 180-bed facility includes a dedicated dementia care unit.

NBHS-Affiliated Center

Northern Berkshire Health Systems operates the nursing center listed below. NBHS offices are at 71 Hospital Avenue, North Adams. Call (413) 664-5140 or visit www.nbhealth.org for more information.

Sweet Brook Nursing Care Centers
1561 Cold Spring Road (US 7), Williamstown
(413) 458-8127
Affiliated with North Berkshire Health Systems, Sweet Brook is adjacent to Sweetwood retirement community, which NBHS also owns. Residents there have priority for openings in Sweet Brook. There are 184 beds, including an Alzheimer's unit.

Other Centers

The following facilities are not affiliated with BHCS or NBHS.

Craneville Place at Dalton
265 Main Street, Dalton
(413) 684-3212
www.cranevilleplace.com

Craneville Place of Dalton is an 89-bed residential rehabilitation and skilled nursing center providing short-term therapy programs and comprehensive long-term care services, including physical and occupational therapy. The owner, Patrick Sheehan, also owns and manages Sugar Hill assisted living, which is nearby. Residents there have priority at Craneville Place should they need nursing care.

Great Barrington Rehabilitation and Nursing Center
148 Maple Avenue, Great Barrington
(413) 528-3320
This 106-bed facility is owned and managed by Kindred Healthcare Corp., based in Louisville, Kentucky.

Providence Care Center
320 Pittsfield Road, Lenox
(413) 637-2660
www.sphs.com
An affiliate of the Sisters of Providence Health Systems, the center has 69 beds.

Springside of Pittsfield
255 Lebanon Avenue, Pittsfield
(413) 499-2334
There are 112 beds in this privately owned center.

Timberlyn Heights Nursing and Alzheimer's Center
320 Maple Avenue, Great Barrington
(413) 528-2650
Timberlyn Heights is also owned and operated by Kindred Healthcare Corp. There are 78 beds, including 39 dedicated to Alzheimer's care. Arrangements may be made for short stays in the nursing unit.

ELDERLY HOUSING

Subsidized housing for anyone age 62 or older is available throughout the county. Handicapped residents under the age of 62 also are eligible. Potential residents must fill out an application with the authority that operates the complex. Except where noted, individuals whose incomes exceed $29,200 or couples whose joint incomes exceed $33,350 are not eligible. Rent is based on 30 percent of the resident's income. With one exception noted below, there are no limits on assets. Accommodations range from a refurbished grand hotel in Lenox to quite large apartment complexes in Pittsfield and North Adams. More information may be obtained from the agencies listed below.

Adams Housing Authority
4 Columbia Street (Massachusetts Highway 8)
Adams 01220
(413) 743-5924
The Adams Housing Authority office is located in the apartment complex it operates. The facility includes a large common recreation area and other amenities. Residents' assets may not exceed $15,000.

Berkshire County Regional Housing Authority
150 North Street
Pittsfield 01201
(413) 443-7138
Dewey Court in Sheffield is managed by this agency.

Berkshire Housing
74 North Street
Pittsfield 01201
(413) 499-1630
Berkshire Housing manages a total of eight elderly housing complexes in North Adams, Williamstown, Pittsfield, Lee, and Great Barrington.

Berkshiretown Associates
176 Columbus Avenue
Pittsfield 01201
(413) 443-9125

Dalton Housing Authority
293 High Street
Dalton 01226
(413) 684-2493

The authority operates Pomeroy Manor and Pine Grove Manor, both on High Street.

Greylock Apartments
Myrtle Street
Adams 01220
(413) 743-9301

Great Barrington Housing Authority
2 Bernard Gibbons Drive
Great Barrington 01230
(413) 274-1142
The authority is located in Brookside Manor and also operates Flagrock Village in Housatonic.

J. L. Property Management
600 Main Street
Dalton 01226
(413) 684-0043
This company manages River Run Apartments at 600 Main Street. Income levels for residents here cannot exceed $18,250 for individuals or $20,850 for couples.

Lee Housing Authority
Marble Street
Lee 01238
(413) 243-3464
The authority operates Brown Memorial at 155 Marble Street.

Lenox Housing Authority
6 Main Street
Lee 01238
(413) 637-5585
The authority is located in the Curtis Hotel, which it maintains along with Turnure Terrace on Old Stockbridge Road.

Millhouses
73 Commercial Street (MA 8)
Adams 01220
(413) 743-2375
Income limits for this complex are $18,250 for individuals and $20,850 for couples.

North Adams Housing Authority
150 Ashland Street
North Adams 01247
(413) 663-5379
The authority operates four elderly housing complexes in the city: Riverview Apartments, West End Apartments, Ashland Park, and Spring Park.

Pittsfield Housing Authority
65 Columbus Avenue
Pittsfield 01201
(413) 443-5936
The authority manages five apartment complexes in the city, including Columbia Arms, where its offices are located. Others are Francis Plaza, Wahconah Heights, Rose Manor, and Providence Court. Accommodations at Rose Manor and Providence Court include several apartments for congregate living.

Saint Joseph's Court
85 North Eagle Street
North Adams 01247
The income level for residents here is capped at $18,250 for individuals and $20,850 for couples.

Stockbridge Housing Authority
P.O. Box 419
Stockbridge 01262
(413) 298-3222
Heaton Court, at 5 Pine Street, is operated by the authority. Accommodations include one apartment for congregate living.

MEDIA

Rural as the Berkshires are, there are nevertheless many sources for information. Print media includes two daily papers; the countywide *Berkshire Eagle* and the *Transcript,* the latter available only in North County; several weeklies; and a host of monthly publications. Many are free or available by subscription for those who want first crack at the ads or news. Papers from the Springfield area and nearby New York State, along with all the major publications, are available either through subscription or at stores and vending machines throughout the county, but expect to pay a little more for delivery to this fringe area. Some of the smaller stores will reserve copies, which is highly recommended for those who really don't want to miss their Sunday *Times.*

The mountainous terrain often interferes with the transmission of radio and television signals, so reception can vary from place to place. Cable television service is delivered to the more populated areas by three companies. But who sees what is dictated largely by the cable company and the networks, so it's entirely possible for folks in one town to see something that their neighbors down the road never receive. The Berkshires are considered part of the Albany, New York, market by the powers that be in television, so much of what we receive is beamed from that area via antennae on Mount Greylock or satellite. Some residents know more about New York politics than what's going on in Massachusetts.

Until recently, the nine commercial radio stations in Berkshire County were divided among four companies, three of them independent and locally owned. Now Vox Radio Group, based in Claremont, New Hampshire, and Wellesley, owns seven of these AM and FM signals. The change is so new that folks are still wondering what effect it will have. Two public radio stations based in neighboring New York State serve most of the county. The more readily available radio stations are listed below. Folks with children in school will tune to their favorite local station for school lunch menus, bus information, and that all-important winter announcement: SNOW DAY!

Special-interest publications along with some specifically aimed at tourists abound and are found at information centers as well as restaurants and other likely places. And of course the Internet has become a valuable tool in disseminating information.

DAILY NEWSPAPERS

The *Berkshire Eagle*
75 South Church Street, Pittsfield
(413) 447-7311, (800) 245-0254
North Adams bureau: (413) 664-4995
Great Barrington bureau:
(413) 528-9708
www.berkshireeagle.com

The *Berkshire Eagle* has been published daily since 1892. The *Eagle* traces its roots back to the *Western Star,* a paper published in Stockbridge in 1789. By 1891 it had become the *Weekly Eagle* and was published in Pittsfield. That year it was purchased by the Miller family, which began daily production as the *Berkshire Evening Eagle.* In the 1970s publication switched to mornings, and in the 1980s the family added a Sunday edition.

In its heyday the *Eagle* covered every aspect of life in the Berkshires in minute detail. Chairmen for everything from bean suppers to town boards had their own write-ups, often with pictures. Record fish catches, divorces, real estate sales, arrests, and convictions were diligently published. The *Eagle* continued to run detailed wedding write-ups long after other papers had stopped describing the gowns, flowers, and other trappings.

The paper also covered national events and in the 1970s earned a Pulitzer Prize for editorial writing. Through the years the reporting and photography staff won numerous awards for coverage of breaking news or investigative projects. Politicians from the Kennedys on down always managed to stop in to meet with the editorial board—and still do.

The Miller family continued to operate the *Eagle* until 1995 when it was sold to Dean Singleton of Denver, Colorado. He formed Media News Group Inc., which includes other papers he has since purchased in the Northeast. The paper and staff have shrunk, but the *Eagle* continues to be the main source of local news, community events, and reviews.

The *Eagle*'s editorial slant is considered to be liberal, much to the disgust of the conservatives in the area, who vent their frustrations in letters to the editor. The op-ed pages carry pieces by local and national columnists of many viewpoints. The news department is fiercely independent of the editorial and advertising departments.

The paper is available by subscription, at a multitude of shops and single-copy vending machines and online. Circulation of around 30,000 climbs to more than 34,500 on Sunday. *Berkshires Week,* a supplement that carries a calendar of events and features, is published weekly in summer. After Columbus Day the supplement becomes *Berkshires Month* until May, when the season picks up again. The advertising department prints many supplements throughout the year focusing on health, elder care, and such. A large supplement featuring real estate is printed monthly. The *Eagle* also operates Eagle Express, a trucking service, and Eagle Printing, Binding and Mailing.

The *North Adams Transcript*
124 American Legion Drive, North Adams
(413) 663-3741
www.thetranscript.com

The *Transcript* began life in 1843 as the *Adams Transcript,* a weekly started by journeyman printer John R. Briggs. In 1878 North Adams spun off from Adams, and the paper changed its name to the *North Adams Transcript.* Daily publication began in 1895. Several partners and owners operated the paper, often leaving to go to work for the *Eagle*. Stability was not achieved until 1898, when the Hardman family purchased the paper. Four generations of Hardmans were active in the firm, and at its zenith there were 12 reporters covering North Berkshire. The family sold the paper in 1977 to the then-owner of the *Boston Globe.* Two years later it was sold to Ingersoll Publications, which in turn sold it to American Publishing. Singleton purchased the *Transcript* in 1996, the year after he bought the *Eagle*. The *Eagle*'s North Adams office was closed and the reporters were moved into the *Transcript*'s building. Business operations are shared, but the two papers still maintain their own small reporting staff and photographers. The *Transcript* is one of the few papers in the country to continue afternoon publication. It is available by subscription or at newsstands north of Pittsfield. Circulation is 8,000.

WEEKLY NEWSPAPERS

The *Advocate*
106 Main Street, North Adams
(413) 664-7900

The *Advocate* bills itself as a "News and Arts Weekly for the Berkshires and Southern Vermont." The paper began life in 1980, started by a local writer. The paper is now owned by Boxcar Media, a locally owned media company. The *Advocate* prints two editions, which are basically the same except for lead stories, opinion columns, and some features. The North County edition focuses on events in Bennington, Vermont, Williamstown, and North Adams. A desk is maintained in Lenox on Church Street for the *South County Advocate,* which is distributed in Central and South Berkshire. The *Advocate* publishes a summer *Guide to the*

CLOSE-UP

A Helping Voice

Folks who have trouble reading or holding print media needn't be in the dark about what's going on locally or nationally, thanks to the Berkshire Talking Chronicle. Affiliated with the Talking Information Center of Marshfield, the Chronicle is a nonprofit organization staffed by volunteers who read daily papers and other print material to listeners who have special receivers in their homes. The Chronicle broadcasts over a special radio frequency that the receivers, provided at no cost to listeners, pick up. Programming runs nearly 24 hours a day, every day of the year. Clients include the sight-impaired and people with dyslexia, Parkinson's disease, mild retardation, and allergies to newsprint. Many are elderly living at home as well as residents of nursing homes, assisted-living facilities, and listeners in community centers who might otherwise feel isolated from the world around them. Readers, who are all volunteers, take turns reading materials live or for broadcast later. The Berkshire Talking Chronicle is located at 8 Depot Street, Dalton 01226. Call (413) 684-0880 or visit www.talkingchronicle.org for more information.

Berkshires, which is distributed at restaurants and other locations where tourists are apt to stop. The paper publishes a weekly arts and community calendar. News stories and the calendar can be viewed online at www.iberkshires.com, an Internet company also owned and operated by Boxcar Media. The news staff covers community events that the dailies are often unable to cover. Williams College publishes a weekly calendar noting lecturers, arts events, and other activities that are free to the public. The *Advocate* is free, but subscriptions are available. Circulation is 21,000.

The *Berkshire Record*
21 Elm Street, Great Barrington
(413) 528-5380

The *Berkshire Record* was founded in 1989 as a community newspaper for southern Berkshire County. With a paid circulation of 5,000, the *Record* is sold at newsstands from Pittsfield to Canaan, Connecticut, and by subscription to readers in all 50 states. Owned by Limestone Publications, a local company, the paper offers news as well as arts and events information and publishes special supplements, including a monthly *Southern Berkshire Real Estate Guide*.

The *Pittsfield Gazette*
38 West Street, Pittsfield
(413) 443-2010
www.pittsfieldgazette.com

Founded in 1991 by Jonathan Levine, a young local journalist and former *Eagle* reporter, the *Pittsfield Gazette* is David to the *Eagle*'s Goliath. Focusing on government and community events, the *Gazette* has a circulation of around 3,000. In its category, it won a New England Press Association award for outstanding local election coverage in a particularly contentious year as well as an award for its community involvement. The paper is the only local source for the Beacon Hill Roll Call, which reports area legislators' votes in Boston. The editorial pages carry the views of local people, accompanied by cartoons drawn by a local artist. While Pittsfield news is its main focus, the paper also covers arts and entertainment regionally during the summer season.

Unlike other newspapers, the *Gazette* does not put news stories on its fairly bare-bones Web site. Instead it publishes complimentary information that is not included in the print edition, such as agendas for the city council and school committee meetings and results of votes on agenda items that are not otherwise reported. Each year it prints the entire city budget line for line. The paper is sold by subscription or single copies, which are available at around 70 stores in Central Berkshire.

MONTHLY PUBLICATIONS

Animal Life
P.O. Box 1842, Lenox 01240
(877) 264-5433
www.animalife.com

Animal Life is chock-full of information for lovers of all kinds of creatures. Along with features and pictures of animals up for adoption, the paper lists shows and publicizes field trips, workshops, lessons, and special events. *Animal Life* includes a full listing of shelters and rescue leagues in Massachusetts, Connecticut, New York, and elsewhere for dogs, cats, horses, and farm animals; birds, rabbits, reptiles, and wildlife. A directory provides sources for a host of services, including training, grooming, pet sitting and boarding, specialty feed, and veterinarians. There is even a kid's section. Animal Life Publications distributes 11,500 copies free at various businesses in Berkshire County and bordering towns and by subscription.

Berkshire Jewish Voice
235 East Street, Pittsfield
(413) 442-4360, (866) 442-4360

Berkshire Jewish Voice is published by the Jewish Federation of the Berkshires, the coordinating organization for Jewish communal activities in Berkshire County. Published 10 months of the year, the *Voice* is a subscriber of the Jewish Telegraphic Agency wire service and prints international and national news that is usually not found in other local media. The paper also is a member of the New England Press Association. Aside from editorials, local news, and features, the paper prints book and music reviews, a listing of services and activities for seniors offered by the federation in conjunction with Elder Services, and a calendar of events. The paper is mailed to 2,000 families in the Jewish community in Berkshire County and neighboring Connecticut, New York, and Vermont and is distributed free at several business locations. It is supported by advertising and voluntary contributions.

Berkshire Senior
66 Wendell Avenue, Pittsfield
(413) 499-0524, (800) 544-5242
www.esbci.org

Berkshire Senior is published by Elder Services of Berkshire County Inc. and, as its name suggests, it provides information on issues and activities of interest to senior citizens. A column on government keeps elders up to date on legislation affecting their lives. Activities and services sponsored by various Councils on Aging in the county are listed. Articles are published on a wide range of topics, including health, safety, and housing. Circulation is 10,000. Copies are mailed to subscribers and distributed free at all senior centers, libraries, and senior housing complexes and at various businesses.

Berkshire Schedules
150 North Street, Pittsfield
(413) 442-4400

As its name implies, *Berkshire Schedules* publishes listings of events of all kinds, including community meetings, events of interest to children, social gatherings, and arts and entertainment listings along with news and tidbits about Berkshire communities. Published by Rhino Publishing Company, the paper is distributed free throughout Berkshire County, portions of western Columbia and Rensselaer Counties in New York, and northern Litchfield County in Connecticut.

Berkshire Trade & Commerce
137 North Street, Pittsfield
(413) 447-7700
Berkshire Trade & Commerce began life in 1986 as the *Berkshire Business Journal.* It was purchased in 1997 by Brad Johnson, who has carried it on as "the Business Journal for Berkshire County." Around 10,000 copies are printed monthly. Of those, 7,000 are distributed free to businesses in Berkshire County via third-class mail. The remaining 3,000 are left at various drops around the county. Subscriptions for out-of-county delivery are available, and back issues are sold. The paper focuses on business news around the county with timely features and guest columnists. Countywide real estate sales provided by Banker & Tradesman are printed each month.

The *Family Beat*
106 Main Street, North Adams
(413) 664-6900
www.thefamilybeat.com
The *Family Beat* focuses on alternative ways to raise children and other family-oriented issues. Features include such topics as breast feeding, midwifery, when to start babies on solids, and providing toxic-free environments. The paper was started in South County by a group of four parents drawn together by the determination to provide "positive influences to support us from new parenthood to seasoned grandparenting." It is now owned by Boxcar Media. *Family Beat* includes stories and games about nature and other educational topics written for children. A monthly calendar lists support groups and family-centered events such as storytelling, crafts, festivals, and nature walks. Around 9,000 copies are distributed free around the county or by subscription.

The *Paper*
New York Highway 23
Hillsdale, New York
(518) 325-4300
Founded in 1982 by Lael Locke, the *Paper* is now owned and operated by RoeJan Acquisition, a division of the Journal Register Company. It is published monthly from October through April and bimonthly May through September. Issues include feature stories by Berkshire-area writers and columns on hiking, cooking, gardening, and arts and entertainment plus a calendar of events. The *Paper* is distributed for free pickup at more than 350 locations in Berkshire County, Litchfield County, Connecticut, and Columbia and Northern Dutchess Counties in New York or by subscription.

The *Women's Times*
323 Main Street, Great Barrington
(413) 528-5303
With a circulation of 12.000, the *Women's Times* is published monthly and distributed free in Berkshire County; northwest Litchfield County, Connecticut; northeast Dutchess and eastern Columbia Counties in New York; and Bennington, Vermont; or by subscription. Created by editor/publisher Eugenie Sills in 1993, the paper's editorial mission is to tell women's stories and to share resources. Each issue focuses on a particular topic of interest to women. In 1999 Sills added another edition distributed in the Northampton area, which has a circulation of around 20,000. Both editions include arts and community events calendars.

RADIO STATIONS

Public Radio

WAMC/Northeast Public Radio
318 Central Avenue
Albany, New York
(800) 323-WAMC (9262), (518) 465-5233
www.WAMC.org

WAMC/Northeast Public Radio is a regional public radio network serving parts of seven northeastern states with stations and transmitters in 10 locations. The two that most Berkshire residents receive are WAMC, 90.3 FM, based at the main studios in Albany, and WAMQ, 105.1 FM in Great Barrington. WAMC/Northeast Public Radio is a member of National Public Radio and an affiliate of Public Radio International. Financial support comes from annual listener contributions and funds raised in special appeals; grants, business underwriters, and governmental sources, including the Corporation for Public Broadcasting and the New York State Education Department. The station operates 24 hours a day. Programming includes NPR favorites *Car Talk, Prairie Home Companion,* and *All Things Considered.* Local programming includes news and interviews. The station carries the Metropolitan Opera and live broadcasts from Tanglewood in summer.

WMHT
17 Fern Avenue
Schenectady, New York
(518) 357-1700
www.wmht.org
Member-supported WMHT-FM offers classical music round the clock on two stations: WMHT-FM 89.1 and WRHV-FM 88.7, which provides better reception in South County. The station proudly proclaims that it is one of the few in the country that broadcasts classical music only. Funds are raised through several drives a year plus business underwriters. Schedules are available on the stations' Web sites. WMHT-TV is one of two public television stations received by county residents. The other is WGBY, based in Springfield. Both offer all major PBS programming along with locally based shows. Which one you see depends on your cable company's affiliation.

Commercial Radio Stations

WBEC (AM 1420), also based in Pittsfield, is owned by Vox. Syndicated shows include *Imus in the Morning,* Dr. Dean Edell, Rush Limbaugh, and Hannity & Colmes. WBEC also broadcasts syndicated call-in shows at night and covers Red Sox baseball and New England Patriots football games.

WBEC (FM 105.5), also owned by Vox, is known as "Live 105." The station features contemporary hit rock and rock classics with local hosts, including veteran Joann Billow in the morning. The station often sets up a portable studio at fund-raisers and special events.

WBRK (AM 1340) in Pittsfield is owned by J. Willard Hodgkins and other investors. The county's first radio station, it was founded in 1938. Fare includes a morning show hosted by longtime favorite Rick Beltaire, with frequent news and weather updates and a lively one-hour weekday talk show led by local gadfly Dan Valenti. The station also carries live play-by-play broadcasts of regional and local sports, including Yankees baseball and Celtics basketball. Sister station WBRK-FM (101.7) features satellite adult contemporary music.

WNAW (AM 1230) in North Adams is a recent Vox purchase. Fare includes local and national news updates, a daily opinion talk show, community service programming, contemporary hit music, and Red Sox baseball games.

WMNB (FM 100.1), also recently acquired by Vox, features hourly national and local news roundups, plus pop standards and music aimed at the adult market in the North Adams area.

WSBS (AM 860) in Great Barrington, another Vox acquisition, operates from 5:30 A.M. to 7:00 P.M. and broadcasts community service programming, including local and national news; talk shows; and high school sports in the South County area.

WUPE (FM 96) in Pittsfield features light adult contemporary music and a morning wake-up show with frequent news and weather updates. Sister station WUHN (AM 1110) operates from sunrise to sunset only and plays country music by satellite. Vox also owns these stations.

CABLE COMPANIES

Adelphia Cable
225 Hodges Crossroad, North Adams
(413) 664-4011
Adelphia serves five communities in North County: North Adams, Adams, Clarksburg, Cheshire, and Williamstown. Programming on public access channels is provided by Willinet in Williamstown (413-458-0900) and North Berkshire Community Television Corp. in North Adams (413-663-9006). In North Adams Adelphia offers high-speed Internet access.

Century Communications
20 Silver Street, Lee
(413) 243-0676
Also owned by Adelphia, Century Communications serves the towns of Lee, Lenox, Stockbridge, Great Barrington, and Sheffield. A community-based public access studio is operated by Community Television for Southern Berkshire (CTSB) on Massachusetts Highway 102 in Lee (413-243-8211). Combining North and South County, Adelphia has approximately 26,000 subscribers. The company also offers long-distance service and a paging service.

Charter Communications
9 Commerce Road
Newtown, Connecticut
(800) 827-8288
www.chartercom.com
In Berkshire County, Charter provides cable television to about 1,600 residents in the populated areas of Lanesborough, Hinsdale, and West Stockbridge. In neighboring New York State, the company serves the Chatham area and residents in Petersburg and Berlin. Charter also serves a number of towns all over Connecticut.

Time Warner Cable
4 Frederico Drive, Pittsfield
(413) 443-4755
Time Warner serves approximately 19,000 subscribers in Pittsfield, Dalton, and Richmond. Dalton and Pittsfield share a public access channel. Programming includes coverage of town and city meetings, a variety of locally produced shows, and a community bulletin board listing events of interest. Dalton Community Cable Association studios are located at 151 Park Avenue (413-684-4441). Pittsfield Community Television's studio is located in Time Warner's facility in Pittsfield but is a separate entity (413-445-4234).

WEB SITES

www.berkshires.org
The Berkshire Visitors Bureau operates this Web site packed with information on its members. It also publishes a number of special-interest guides. The bureau is based in Adams, with a satellite office in Pittsfield in the lower level of the Pittsfield Common, where the Crowne Plaza Hotel also is located. The telephone number is (800) 237-5747.

www.BerkshireWeb.com
This Web site is operated by a local Internet provider, BerkshireNet, based at 126 Fenn Street, Pittsfield; (413) 442-7805. The site includes information on all aspects of the Berkshires.

www.iBerkshires.com
This Web site is operated by Boxcar Media, a locally owned full-service online and print media company located at 121 Union Street, North Adams. Boxcar's phone number is (413) 663-3384; their Web site is www.Boxcarmedia.com. iBerkshires, in conjunction with the *Advocate* newspaper, provides news, weather, arts and entertainment schedules, plus additional information.

WORSHIP

The ethnic and spiritual diversity of the Berkshires is clearly reflected in the wide variety of houses of worship in the county today. There is hardly a faith not practiced in the area. For many, church or temple is a way to keep in touch in this spread-out area and is often the last hope of preserving cultural traditions that might otherwise be lost. Aside from attending to their spiritual needs, the various congregations provide for the needy, host concerts, bring in speakers, and offer educational alternatives. In many of the smaller towns, the church functions as the community center, regardless of faith. Information about services and special events is published in local papers and other media listed in the Media chapter.

Nearly every town in the Commonwealth has a Congregational church, as this was the "official" religion in the 1700s. Taxes supported the church, which also functioned as the town meeting hall, and no man could vote who was not a member of the church. As more religions came to the area, the system of taxation that supported the Congregational Church and controlled political participation came under increasing attack. The "outsiders" had to fight for their share of the taxes or support themselves some other way. In addition, they were kept from voting on town matters. Roger Williams had taken up this issue in the 1600s—and for his efforts was thrown out of the province. He went on to establish the state of Rhode Island. The First Amendment of the Constitution, adopted in 1791, prohibited Congress from making laws pertaining to religion. But it was not until 1868 that the 14th Amendment was added, clarifying that this law applied to everyone, not just the federal government. Berkshire leaders started seeking religious freedom in the early 1800s, but it was not until 1833 that the state adopted the 11th Amendment separating church and state affairs.

John Sergeant was the first minister to bring the Congregational religion to the Berkshires, arriving in Stockbridge in 1734. A missionary to the Mahican Indians, he preached the doctrine of the United Church of Christ in their native tongue and earned their respect as one who was genuinely interested in their welfare. They spent hours in his home, which is preserved as the Mission House Museum and Gardens, a historical treasure that is visited by thousands each year. The Mahicans, later called the Stockbridge Indians, were given a two-volume Bible written in their language. The Mahicans fought with the colonists in the Revolutionary War, but when they returned to Stockbridge they found that their land had been sold out from under them. They started the trek westward, taking their Bible with them. But as the years passed and the trail became longer, the Bible was lost. In the 1930s it was found and purchased by members of the Choate family, who were involved in establishing the Mission House museum. In the 1970s surviving members of the tribe, now the Stockbridge-Munsee located in Wisconsin, visited the Mission House and saw the Bible on display. They began a 20-year fight to get it back, finally succeeding in 1991. Sergeant was followed by Jonathan Edwards, a fire-and-brimstone sort who is credited with bringing Calvinism to the area. A philosopher and prolific writer, Edwards became a role model for other preachers.

A year after Sergeant settled in Stockbridge, the Reverend Jonathan Hubbard set up shop in Sheffield, where he led a Congregational church for 31 years. By 1761, when Berkshire County was formed, there were seven United Church of Christ Congregational churches. Over the next 20 years, another 17 were established. Today there are 25, including the original Old Parish Church in Sheffield. The Second Congregational Church on Pittsfield's west side was formed by a group of black parishioners in 1846 and is still predominately African American. Other churches serving predominately African-American congregations include AME Zion in Pittsfield and North Adams and Victory Temple in Pittsfield.

Berkshire County is credited with launching two organizations that had a lasting impact on missionary efforts here and abroad. The Berkshire and Columbia Missionary Society was formed in 1797 to work with the Indians and westward migrants. And in 1806 a group of Williams College students formed the American Board of Commissioners of Foreign Missions, keeping a vow they made during a violent thunderstorm. They had sought cover in a haystack and had promised to start a missionary movement if they survived the storm. The Haystack Monument on the college campus commemorates this event.

While the United Church of Christ was undergoing philosophical changes in the Berkshires, other religions were moving in. From the west came Dutch Anglicans from Hudson Valley, who established St. James Episcopal Church in Great Barrington in 1762. St. Stephen's in Pittsfield and St. Luke's in what was to become Lanesborough followed. The 1836 stone church in Lanesborough is still used for services in summer.

The Berkshires also were discovered by rugged and brave Baptists who settled in the wild north, forming communities that later became Cheshire, Florida, and Savoy. By 1800 Baptists had established 15 churches in the area, expanding more rapidly than the Congregational Church. Religious diversity continued with the establishment of a Quaker meetinghouse in Adams that is still there and is opened on special occasions. The Quakers are active today in Great Barrington. Methodist preachers from New York organized a church in Pittsfield in 1789. By then the Shakers, led by Mother Ann Lee, had begun to spread out, with settlements in Tyringham, Mount Washington, and Hancock. Due largely to their belief in celibacy, the Shakers are all but extinct. But the herb gardens that yielded the medicines they sold and the woodworking shops where they crafted their simple yet stunning furniture are alive for all to see at the restored Hancock Shaker Village. (See the Attractions chapter.)

The first Catholic parish was established in Pittsfield in 1835. As immigrants came here to work on the railroads and in the mills, Catholicism grew to eventually become the dominant religion in the area. St. Joseph's in Pittsfield was joined by Notre Dame, Holy Family, and Mount Carmel. Russian and Greek Orthodox churches followed. In Adams, mill workers built three Catholic churches, their spires rising higher than the smokestacks on the mills. The Irish started building St. Thomas Aquinas in 1885. Two years later, just down the street, French-Canadian workers organized Notre Dame. By the 1900s there was a large Polish population, and St. Stanislaus Church was built. The three churches are still serving their various populations, testing the endurance and agility of the thinning ranks of Catholic priests. In North Adams, spires also were rising from various houses of worship, giving that city its nickname of Steeple City.

On the first Sunday after Easter, the population of Stockbridge swells by 20,000 as pilgrims flock to the Marian Helpers Shrine of the Divine Mercy on Eden Hill to celebrate Mercy Sunday. The event commemorates Sister Faustina, a Polish nun who received a visitation from the Lord in 1931. The Marians have had a community in the Berkshires since 1943, when they purchased a former estate with the help of many local parishes and private gifts. The shrine was built in the 1950s and is noted for the craftsmanship shown in the wood carvings, murals, and stained-glass windows that adorn it.

The Jews brought their faith here in the early 1800s, first to a small settlement in Sandisfield. The first temple was built in Pittsfield in 1869. Today there are two synagogues in Pittsfield, one in North Adams, and two in South Great Barrington. The

CLOSE-UP

Historic Organs

Fans of pipe organs will find many interesting instruments in historic churches around the Berkshires, some quite old yet still in service. The black walnut Johnson organ in St. Luke's Old Stone Church in Lanesborough was installed in 1862 and may be the oldest in the county. It is hand-pumped and used in summer, when the unheated church is open for services. The Johnson organ in the Church-on-the-Hill in Lenox dates back to 1868. Johnson organs were built in Westfield using the "tracker" system, the mechanical method used to produce sounds for centuries. Some of these systems were changed to electronically operated valves after the 1900s, but the organs mentioned above, along with others around the county, still have their original innards. Larger organs are located in St. James Episcopal Church in Great Barrington and First Methodist in Pittsfield.

The First Congregational Church in Pittsfield houses a four-keyboard Austin pipe organ, often used for special concerts sponsored by the Berkshire Chapter of the American Guild of Organists. The local chapter has around 80 members, including choir directors and other interested individuals, and recently celebrated its 50th anniversary. The group sponsors educational programs, master classes, and special events, including an annual festival that allows participating church choirs to expand their repertoires. Among organists brought to the area for special concerts are the renowned Frederick Swann. The guild chapter also sponsors an annual "Pedals, Pipes and Pizza" event, where young pianists are encouraged to learn more about this somewhat intimidating instrument by climbing in and around the pipes. It is hoped that some will eventually go on to play the organ, replacing the thinning ranks of organists. Funds raised by the chapter are used to award scholarships for further study to a variety of recipients. More about the American Guild of Organists can be learned by checking out their Web site at www.agohq.org.

Jewish Federation of the Berkshires in Pittsfield is the coordinating organization for Jewish communal activities in the county. The Federation publishes a directory that describes the various programs offered by the synagogues and other organizations.

Many other faiths are represented in the Berkshires. A number of Christian churches are listed in the Yellow Pages under nondenominational, interdenominational, evangelical, Pentecostal, and Advent Christian. Jehovah's Witnesses halls may be found in Dalton, Sheffield, and Lee. First Church of Christ Scientist services are held in Pittsfield and Great Barrington. Seventh Day Adventists meet in Lanesborough, and the Unitarians have churches in Pittsfield and Great Barrington.

As they have for the past 200 years, the Berkshire hills continue to attract religious groups looking for a better place, the latest being a convent from Delaware. Seeking to escape the encroaching world,

16 Sisters of the Visitation purchased land in the peaceful Tyringham Valley, built a convent, and took up residence a few years ago.

In addition to the traditional religions, the Berkshires are home to a number of retreats of different philosophies. All will book rooms for a day, a weekend, or longer visits. The Kripalu Center in Lenox offers relief and restoration for the stressed and weary through yoga and meditation. Situated in a former Jesuit monastery on a beautifully landscaped hill overlooking Stockbridge Bowl, the center provides a peaceful atmosphere for reflection and contemplation. Guests also may take part in special workshops for spiritual and physical healing. Also in Lenox, on the grounds of the former Foxhollow resort, the teachings of spiritual leader and visionary Andrew Cohen are studied at the Moksha Foundation. The Kushi Institute in Becket focuses on macrobiotic diet as a way to a healthier, happier life. It is not tied to any one belief and welcomes all. In neighboring New York State, a group of Sufis continue the practices of a branch of a mystic Muslim sect at the Abode of the Message in New Lebanon. Visitors are welcome to participate in meals and meditation and to study the teachings of the founder, an Indian musician. In Canaan, Connecticut, Buddhists offer respite at the Karuna Tendai Dharma Center. The center is open to the community on certain days for meals, meditation, and talks on Buddhism.

Lest you think all this diversity happened without incident, it is worth noting that in the 1800s a group of Mormons was summarily run out of the county. And in the 1940s a Moorish Science Temple that was established in Becket eventually left town after a dispute over whether they had to pay property taxes. More recently, a fundamentalist organization called the Bible Speaks was exposed as a fraud after bilking a local woman out of millions. The sprawling property they occupied in Lenox is now owned by Shakespeare & Company. (See the Attractions chapter.)

INDEX

A

accommodations
- campgrounds/state camping areas, 69–73
- Central Berkshire, 54–57
- Cheshire, 58
- Dalton, 54–55
- Great Barrington, 33–36
- Hancock, 58–59
- Lanesborough, 55
- Lee, 36–40
- Lenox, 40–48
- New Ashford, 59
- North Adams, 59–61
- North County, 58–65
- Pittsfield, 55–57
- Pittsfield Road, 48–49
- resorts and conference centers, 65–68
- Sheffield, 49–51
- South County, 33–54
- South Egremont, 51
- Stockbridge, 51–54
- time-shares and condos, 68–69
- Washington, 57
- Williamstown, 61–65

Adams, 15
Adams Agricultural Fair, 226
Adams Sno-Drifters, 288
Aegean Breeze, 75
air travel, 25
Albany Berkshire Ballet, 169–70
Alford, 5
alternative health care, 326–28
Americana Artisans Craft Show, 226
American Craftsman, An, 193
Amtrak, 24
annual events, 221–31
antiques stores, 124–26, 133–34
Appalachian Bean Cafe, 99
Appalachian Mountain Club, 279
Appalachian Trail, 278
Appalachian Trail Conference, 279
apparel stores, 126–27, 134–36
Applegate B&B, 36
Apple Squeeze, 228
Apple Tree Inn and Restaurant, 40
Arbor Rose B&B, 51–52
Arcadian Shop, 247, 251–52, 280, 289
ARMI@GreatBarrington, 75, 116
Arrowhead, 152–53, 203
arts and culture
- art centers, 184–87
- child-oriented, 213–15
- dance, 169–70
- film, 182–84
- galleries, 187–96
- historic homes, 203–7
- literary arts, 196–97
- museums, 197–203
- music, 170–77
- theater, 178–82

Arugula, 102
Ashley Falls, 6
Ashuwillticook Rail Trail, 249
Asian Antiques, 125
assisted-living facilities, 331–33
Association of Housatonic Artists, 186
Aston Magna Festival, 170–71
attractions, 152–68
ATV trails, 277, 279
Aunti M's Bed & Breakfast, 36–37

B

B. Mango & Bird, 136–37
Baba Louie's, 75–76
Baker Farm Golf Center, 209, 273–74
ballroom dancing, 122
Bare Furniture, 138
Barnes & Noble, 144
Barrington Brewery Pub and Restaurant, 76
Barrington Court Motel, 33
Barrington Outfitters, 126
Barrington Stage Company, 178, 213–14
Bartholomew's Cobble, 209, 232–33
Bartlett's Orchard, 107–8
Bas Ridge Golf Course, 270–71
B&B at Howden Farm, 49
Beach Party, 225
Beartown State Forest, 72, 235
Beaver Pond Gallery, 195
Becket, 6–7
Becket Arts Center, 184
Becket-Chimney Corners YMCA, 218
bed and breakfasts. *See* accommodations
Ben's, 132
Berkshire Area Farmers' Market, 114
Berkshire Art Gallery, 131
Berkshire Artisans, 185
Berkshire Arts Festival, 224–25, 229
Berkshire Athenaeum, The, 20
Berkshire Athenaeum Book Sale, 223–24
Berkshire Bike & Blade, 247
Berkshire Bike Path Council, The, 31
Berkshire Blues Cafe, 117
Berkshire Botanical Garden, 108–9, 153, 212
Berkshire Botanical Garden Plant Sale, 224
Berkshire Canoe Tours, 251
Berkshire Center for Contemporary Glass, 194–95, 212
Berkshire Chamber of Commerce Expo, 222–23
Berkshire Charity Auto Show, 225
Berkshire Choral Festival, 171
Berkshire Community College Circus Camp, 214

Berkshire Concert Choir, 171
Berkshire Cottages, 158–59
Berkshire County 4-H Fair and Horse Show, 227
Berkshire Crafts Fair, 226–27
Berkshire Cycling Association, 31
Berkshire East, 287–88
Berkshire 1802 House, 49–50
Berkshire Family History Association, The, 21
Berkshire Fishing Club, 258
Berkshire Grown, 108
Berkshire Highlanders, 171
Berkshire Hills Coins & Estate Jewelry, 144
Berkshire Hills Motel, 61–62
Berkshire Historical Society, The, 21
Berkshire Horseback Adventures, 280–81
Berkshire Inn, 55–56
Berkshire Lyric Theatre, 172–73
Berkshire Mall, 143, 182
Berkshire Museum, 153–54, 197–98, 211–12
Berkshire Music School, 173, 214
Berkshire National Fish Hatchery, 261
Berkshire Natural Resources Council, 279
Berkshire Nautilus, 267
Berkshire Opera Company, 172
Berkshire Outfitters, 248, 250, 253, 280, 290
Berkshire Pendleton, 144
Berkshire Quilt Festival, 229
Berkshire Record Outlet, 132
Berkshires
  Berkshire County vital statistics, 6–7
  demographics, 5
  history, 18–22
  overview of towns, 5–17
  physical features, 3–4
  weather, 4–5
Berkshire Scenic Railway, 209
Berkshire Snow Seekers, 288
Berkshire Soaps, 138
Berkshire South Regional Community Center, 217, 264
Berkshire Stonewall Community Coalition, 119
Berkshire Talking Chronicle, 342
Berkshire Theatre Festival, 178–79, 214
Berkshire Visitors Bureau, 31
Berkshire Vista Nudist Resort, 65, 69
Berkshire West, 267–68
Berkshire Wildlife Sanctuaries, 279
Berkshire Writers Room, The, 196
Best Value Inn, 37
Best Western Black Swan, 37
Bidwell House Museum, 154–55, 203–4
biking, 30–31, 246–50
Birchwood Inn B&B, 40–41
Bistro Zinc, 83
Bizen Restaurant and Sushi Bar, 76–77
B. J. Faulkner Gallery, 189
Blantyre, 41, 83–84
BMC Follies, 230
boating, 250–53
Bobbie Lefenfeld Gallery, 188
Bob's Country Kitchen, 91
Body & Soul, 264
Bombay Bar & Grill, 81
Bonnie Brae Cabins & Campsites, 69–70
Bonny Rigg Campground, 70
Bookloft, The, 129, 196
Bookstore, The, 137, 196
Bousquet Ski Area, 209, 274, 286
bowling, 253–54
Boy's and Girl's Club of Pittsfield, The, 218
Bradford Galleries, 139
Brewhaha, 99
Briarcliff Inn, 33
Broken Hill Manor, 50
Bruce A. Sikora, 140
Bucksteep Manor Inn, 57, 286
Buggy Whip Factory, The, 141
Burbank Park at Onota Lake, 238
buses, 25
Buster's Entertainment Center, 209–10
Butternut Ski Area, 284–85

C

cable companies, 346
Cafe Lucia, 84
Cafe Reva, 92–93
campgrounds/state camping areas, 69–73
Candlelight Inn, 42, 84–85
Canoe Meadows Wildlife Sanctuary, 238
Canterbury Farm, 285
Canyon Ranch in the Berkshires, 65–66, 264
car rentals, 27
Carriage House Antiques, 131
Casablanca, 134
Castle Street Cafe, 77, 116–17
Catamount, 285–86
Catherine's Chocolate Shop, 129
Celebrate Pittsfield Street Festival, 224
Chambery Inn, 37–38
Chapin Library of Rare Books & Manuscripts, 198–99
Charles H. Baldwin & Sons, 142–43
Charles L. Flint Antiques, 133
Chef's Hat, 102
Chef's Shop, The, 127–28
Chenail's Produce Market, 109–10
Cheshire, 15
Chesterwood, 156, 204–5
child care, 318–19
children, activities for. *See* kidstuff
Chimney Mirror Motel, 62
Chocolate Springs, 138
Christine's Bed & Breakfast and Tea Room, 33–34
churches, 347–50

Church Street Cafe, 85
Church Street Trading Company, 126
Circus Camp Finale, 227
Clarksburg, 16
Clarksburg State Park, 72, 240
Claymania, 188, 212
Close Encounters with Music, 173
Club Helsinki, 117
Club Next Door, 121
Club Red, 119
Clyde Beatty/Cole Bros. Circus, The, 225
Coffman's Antiques Market, 131
colleges, 315–18
Colonel John Ashley House, 153, 203
Colonial Theatre, 182–83
Comfort Inn, 56
Common Grounds Coffeehouse, 119
Concepts of Art, 189
condos and time-shares, 68–69
conference centers and resorts, 65–68
Conroy's B&B, 53–54
Contemporary Artists Center & Gallery (CAC), 185
contradancing, 122
Cornell Inn, The, 42
Corner House Antiques, 139
Cottage, The, 149–50
Cottage of Lenox, 134
Cottage Store, The, 144
Country Charm, 97–98
Country Curtains, 141
Country Dining Room Antiques, 125
Country Fair and Crafts Festival, 229
Court Square Breakfast & Deli, 93
Cove Lanes, 210, 253
Crane Museum of Papermaking, 199
Cranwell, 85–86
Cranwell Resort, Spa and Golf Club, 66–67, 117, 264–65, 269, 286
Crossing Borders, 138
Crowne Plaza Hotel, 56
Crystal Essence, 129–30
culture. *See* arts and culture
Cupboards and Roses, 139

D

Dalton, 14
Dalton Community House, 218, 268
Dalton Fair, The, 224
Dalton House Bed & Breakfast, The, 54–55
Dalton Town Parks, 237–38
dance (performing art), 169–70
Dark Ride Project, 185–86
Dave's Sporting Goods, 262, 282
David M. Weiss Antiques, 138
day and summer camps, 219–20
day care, 318–19
Days Inn, 34, 48
day trips and weekend getaways, 291–300
Department of Environmental Management, 31
Devonfield, 38
DeVries Fine Art Inc., 189
Dick Moon Sporting Goods, 262–63, 280
Dierdre's, 144–45
Different Drummer's Kitchen, 137
Dora's, 99
Dovetail Antiques, 139
Dreamaway Lodge, 118
driving ranges and miniature golf, 273–74

E

Eagles Band, 173
Eastover Resort & Conference Center, 67
EconoLodge, 59
Eden Hill Recreation Center, 265
Edith Wharton Restoration, 197
education. *See* schools
Egremont, 7–8
Egremont Country Club, 269–70
Egremont Inn, The, 51, 88–89
1896 House Country Inn & Motels, 62
Elder Services of Berkshire County Inc., 336
Eleven, 99–100
Elise Abrams Antiques, 124–25
Elizabeth's, 93–94
Elliott and Grace Snyder Antiques, 140
emergency rooms and walk-in clinics, 321
Emporium Antique Center, The, 125
Empty Set Project Space, 192
Essencials Day Spa, 265
Evviva, 134–35
Expeditions, 247, 252, 280, 289
Eziba, 192

F

Falcon Ridge Folk Festival, 177
Fall Festival, 228
Fall Festival of Shakespeare, 231
Fall Foliage Parade, 229
Fall Motorcycle Run, 228
family history, 20–21
Fantasy Realms, 215
farmers' markets, 114
farms and gardens, 107–15, 215
Farshaw's Bookshop, 130
Fellerman and Raabe Glassworks, 192–93
Ferrin Gallery, The, 189–90
Festival of Trees, 231
festivals, 221–31
Field Farm, 241, 244
film (visual art), 182–84
Firehouse, The, 53
fishing
  boats and supplies, 261–64
  Central Berkshire, 257–59

ice fishing, 260
North County, 259–60
overview of, 254–57
fitness centers and spas, 264–68
Florida, 16
Florida Mountaineers, 288
Flower Show, 226
Fontaine's Auction Gallery, 145
Forest Park Country Club, 272
Founders Weekend, 228
Four Acres Motel, 62–63
Fox-Martin Fine Art Gallery &, 188
Fred Garner River Park, 238–39
Freightyard Restaurant & Pub, 100
Frelinghuysen Morris House & Studio, The, 157–59, 199
From Ketchup to Caviar, 81
Front Street Gallery, 188

G

Gables Inn, The, 42–43
Galadriel's, 148
Garden Gables Inn, 43
gardens and farms, 107–15, 215
Gateways Inn & Restaurant, 43, 86
Gatsby's, 126–27
Gay and Lesbian Berkshire Festival, 223
GEAA (General Electric Athletic Association), 119–20, 271
Geffner/Schatzky Antiques, 140
genealogy, 20–21
Gifted Child, The, 215–16
Girls Incorporated of the Berkshires, 218
Glad Rags, 135
golf
Central Berkshire, 270–72
North County, 272–73
practice ranges and miniature golf, 273–74
South County, 269–70
Good & Hutchinson, 139
Gramercy Bistro, 100
Great Barrington, 8
Great Barrington Antiques Center, 125
Great Barrington Farmers' Market, 114
Great Barrington Pottery, 188–89
Great Finds Antiques & Arts Marketplace, 140
Grecian Festival, 226
Greek Pastry Sale, 223
Greenock Country Club, 270
Green River Farms, 110, 215
Green Valley Motel, 63
Grenadier Pottery, 191–92
Greystone Gardens, 141, 145
Gringo's, 121
Guido's Fresh Marketplace, 130, 145–46
Guthrie Center, The, 174

H

Habatat Galleries, 187
Haddad's, 146
Halloween Parade, 230
Hampton Terrace Bed & Breakfast, 44
Hancock, 12–13
Hancock Inn B&B, 58
Hancock Shaker Village, 110–11, 160, 199–200, 213, 222, 223
Harbour House Inn B&B, 58
Harland B. Foster, 248
Harrison Gallery, The, 196
Harvest Festival, 229
Healing Place, The, 265
health care and wellness
alternative care, 326–28
emergency rooms and walk-in clinics, 321
home care, 325–26
hospitals and medical centers, 321–25
Heirlooms, 141
Helsinki Tea Company, 77–78
Hickory Bill's, 100–101
Hidden Valley Campground, 70
Highland, The, 94
High Lawn Farm, 111
hiking/walking
ATV trails, 277, 279
Central Berkshire, 276–77
information sources, 279
North County, 277
outfitters, 280
South County, 275–76
Hill House Antiques, 140
Hinsdale, 14
Historic Valley Campground, 70–71
history, 18–22
Hoadley Gallery, 190
Hoffman Pottery, 195
Holiday Farm, 111
Holiday Inn Berkshires, 59–60
Holiday Inn Express, 34
Holiday Marketplace, 231
Holsten Galleries, 193–94
home furnishings stores, 127–29
home health care, 325–26
homes, historic, 203–7
Hopkins Memorial Festival, 244
Hopkins Observatory, 122–23
horseback riding, 280–81
hospitals and medical centers
Central Berkshire, 322–24
North County, 324–25
South County, 321–22
hotels. *See* accommodations
Housatonic, 8
Housatonic River Outfitters, 261–62
Housatonic River Walk, 233
House of India, 94–95

Howard Johnson Express Inn, 48
hunting, 281–82

I
ice fishing, 260
Images Cinema, 182–83
Imperial Bowl, 210, 253
Inkberry, 196–97
Inn at Laurel Lake, The, 38
inns. *See* accommodations
Interior Alternative, The, 148
Ioka Valley Farm, 111, 215
IS183, 186, 213

J
Jack's Country Squire Shop, 127
Jacks Grill, 80–81
Jack's Hot Dog Stand, 101
Jacob's Pillow Dance Festival, 160–61, 170
Jae's Inn, 60, 101
JB's Lounge, 120
J&D Marina, 262
Jennifer House Commons, 131
Jericho Valley Inn, 58–59
Jiminy Peak Resort, 67–68, 210–11, 274, 286–87
Joga Cafe, 121
John Andrews, 89
John's Fishing Tackle Service Center, 263–64
Josh Billings RunAground, 228

K
K-B Toy Works, 216
Kemble Inn, 44
Kennedy Park, 234
Ken's Bowl, 211, 254
Kenver Ltd., 289
Key West Lounge, 121
kidstuff
  community programs, 217–19
  day and summer camps, 219–20
  farms, 215
  hands on experiences, 211–13
  out and about, 209–11
  performing arts, 213–15
  shopping, 215–17
  swimming, 220
Kim's Dragon Restaurant, 95
Kneebones Steakhouse, 95
Knox Trail Sno-Riders Club, 289
Kripalu Center for Yoga and Health, 266

L
La Bruschetta Food & Wine To Go, 143
La Choza, 78
La Cocina, 120
Lake Mansfield, 233
Lakeside Restaurant & Catering, 98
Lakeview Orchard, 111–12
Lamppost Motel, 55
Lanesborough, 13
Lanesborough Motel, 55
La Pace, 128
Laurel Hill Motel, 39
Laurel Lake, 234
Laurel Ridge Camping Area, 71
Lee, 8–9
Lee Farmers' Market, 114
Lenox, 9
Lenox Antique Center, 138
Lenox Coffee, 86
Lenox Community Center, 217
Lenoxdale, 9
Lenox Fitness Center and Spa, 266
Lenox Gallery of Fine Art, The, 190
Lenox Inn, 48
Lenox Shops, The, 138
Lenox Sportscards & Games, 138
Le Perigord Antiques, 126
Library Antiques, 150
Lilac Park, 235
limousines and taxis, 25–27
Linda's Cafe, 101–2
Lion's Den, 118–19
literary arts, 196–97
Little Cinema at the Berkshire Museum, 183
Locke, Stock and Barrel, 130
Loring Gallery, The, 193
Love Dog Cafe & Apothecary, 138
Lydia Mongiardo, 191

M
Mac-Haydn Theatre, 181
Mahaiwe Performing Arts Center, 182
Main Street Stage, 179
Mansfield, Lake, 233
Maple Terrace Motel, 63
Margaret Lindley Park, 244
Martin's, 78
Mary Stuart Collections, 135–36
Massachusetts Bicycle Coalition, 31
Massachusetts Department of Environmental Management, 279
Massachusetts Division of Fisheries and Wildlife, 279
MassHighway, 31
MASS MoCA, 161–62, 183–84, 200–201, 213
Matrushka Toys & Gifts, 216
Matt Reilly's Pub & Restaurant, 92
Mayor's Downtown Celebration, 227
Mazzeo's Ristorante, 95–96
McLennan Reservation, 237
McTeigue & McClelland Jewelers, 126
Meadowlark, 53
Mean Wheels Bike Shop, 248
media. *See* news media

medical care. *See* health care and wellness
Memorial Field Park, 233
Mercy Sunday, 223
Metro-North (Metropolitan Transportation Authority), 24
Mezze Bistro & Bar, 102–3
Michael's Restaurant & Pub, 89–90
Michele's Salon & Day Spa, 266–67
Miller Marine, 262
Mill on the Floss, 98–99
miniature golf and practice ranges, 273–74
miniature theatre of Chester, 181
Mission House Museum and Gardens, The, 162–63, 205
Mistral's, 128
Mohawk Theatre, 183
Monterey, 9–10
Monument Mountain Motel, 34–35
Monument Mountain Reservation, 233–34
Moon in the Pond Organic Farm, 112, 220
Morgan House Inn, 39, 81–82
motels. *See* accommodations
Mount, The, 112–13, 163–64, 205–6
Mountain Goat, The, 250, 280, 290
Mountain Meadow Preserve, 245
Mountain View Campground, 71
Mountain View Motel, 35
Mount Greylock Ski Club, 287
Mount Greylock State Reservation, 72–73, 242–43
Mount Washington, 10
Mount Washington State Forest, 235–36
Mt. Greylock Bowl, 211, 254
Mt. View Motel, 55
Mullin-Jones Antiquities, 126
museums, 197–203
Music & More in the Meetinghouse, 174
Music Mountain Summer Music Festival, 177
music (performing art), 170–77
Music Store, 131

N

Naoussa Gallery, 194
Natural Bridge State Park, 241
Naumkeag, 164, 206
Neighborhood Diner, The, 78–79
New Ashford, 13
New Marlborough, 10
news media
    cable companies, 346
    monthly publications, 343–44
    newspapers, 340–43
    radio stations, 344–46
    Web sites, 346
newspapers, 340–43
nightlife
    ballroom dancing, 122
    Central Berkshire, 119–21
    contradancing, 122
    North County, 121–22
    South County, 116–19
    stargazing, 122–23
Nora Martin, 141–42
Norman Rockwell Museum, 165, 201, 213
North Adams, 15–16
North Adams Cinema, 184
North Adams Country Club, 272–73
North Adams Farmers' Market, 114
North Adams Museum of History and Science, 202
Northern Berkshire Food Festival, 224
Northern Berkshire YMCA, 219
Northside Motel, 63
Notchview Reservation, 240
Notchview Ski-Fest, 222
nursing and rehabilitation centers, 335–38

O

Oak 'N' Spruce, 68
O'Brien House, The, 53
October Mountain State Forest, 73, 234
Olde—An Antiques Market, 131
Old Inn on the Green & Gedney Farm, The, 88
Old Mill, The, 89
Onota Boat Livery, 252, 263
Orchards, The, 63–64, 122
Ordinary Cycles, 248
Origins Gallery, 194
Otis, 10
Otis Poultry Farm, 113
Otis Ridge, 286
Out of Hand, 128–29
Ozzie's Steak & Seafood, 120–21

P

paintball, 283
Painted Porch Antiques, 140
Pamela Loring Gifts and Interiors, 132–33
Pappa Charlie's Deli, 103
Papyri Books, 121–22, 149, 197
parks
    Central Berkshire, 237–40
    North County, 240–45
    South County, 232–37
Parsonage on the Green B&B, The, 39
Pasko Frame & Gift Gallery, 192
Past & Future, 133–34
Pat's Gun Shop, 282
Paul and Susan Kleinwald Antiques, 125–26
Paul Rich & Sons, 146
Pearl's, 79
Peru, 14
Pilgrim Inn, 39–40
Pine Cone Hill, 138
Pittsfield, 11–12

Pittsfield Fourth of July Parade, The, 225
Pittsfield Precious Metals, 146
Pittsfield Rotary Club Auction, The, 222
Pittsfield State Forest, 73, 239
Pittsfield Travelodge, 56–57
Pittsfield Winter Carnival, 222
Pittsfield YMCA, 218
Plaine's Bike, Ski and Snowboard, 248, 289–90
Pleasant Valley Wildlife Sanctuary, 235
Plum Gallery, The, 196
Ponds at Foxhollow, The, 69
Pontoosuc Lake, 239
Pontoosuc Lake Country Club, 271
Porches Inn, The, 60–61
Porter's Sporting Goods, 263, 282
practice ranges and miniature golf, 273–74
Prime Outlets at Lee, 133
private schools, 313–15
Prospect Lake Park, 71
public schools, 311–13
Purple Plume, 135
Purple Pub, The, 103–4

Q

Quality Inn, 48
Questing, 236
Quirk's Marine, 252, 263

R

Race Brook Lodge, 50–51
radio stations, 344–46
Railway Cafe, 122
Ramada Inn & Suites, 56
Rawson Brook Farm, 113
real estate
  building a home, 308–9
  overview of, 301–4
  property taxes, 303
  Realtors, 304–10
  See also retirement
recreation
  biking, 30–31, 246–50
  boating, 250–53
  bowling, 253–54
  fishing, 254–64
  fitness centers and spas, 264–68
  golf, 269–74
  hiking/walking, 274–80
  horseback riding, 280–81
  hunting, 281–82
  organized sports, 282–83
  paintball, 283
  running, 283
  swimming, 220
  tennis, 283
  winter activities, 283–90
Red Barn Antiques, 140
Red Carpet, 97
Red Devil Lounge, 121
Red Lion Inn, 52–53, 90
Red Lion Inn Gift Shop, 142
Redwood Motel, 61
rehabilitation and nursing centers, 335–38
resorts and conference centers, 65–68
restaurants
  Adams, 97
  Central Berkshire, 91–97
  Cheshire, 97–98
  Great Barrington, 75–80
  Housatonic, 80–81
  Lanesborough, 91–92
  Lee, 81–83
  Lenox, 83–88
  New Ashford, 98–99
  New Marlborough, 88
  North Adams, 99–102
  North County, 97–106
  Pittsfield, 92–97
  South County, 75–91
  South Egremont, 88–89
  Stockbridge, 89–90
  West Stockbridge, 90–91
  Williamstown, 102–6
retirement
  assisted-living facilities, 331–33
  combined facilities, 333–35
  elderly housing, 338–39
  nursing and rehabilitation centers, 335–38
  retirement communities, 330–31
Richmond, 13
Riverfest & Riverworks, 224
RiverRun, 262
Ronnie's Motorclothes, 146–47
Rookwood Inn, 44–45
Rouge Restaurant & Bistro, 90–91
running, 283
R. W. Wise, Goldsmiths, 138, 191

S

Saddleback Antiques Center, 150
Sandisfield, 10
Sandisfield Arts Center, 186
Sandisfield Snowmobile Club, 289
Sandisfield State Forest, 236–37
Savoy, 16
Savoy Kanary Kats, 289
Savoy Mountain State Forest, 73, 240–41
Sawyer's Antiques, 143
schools
  colleges, 315–18
  private, 313–15
  public, 311–13

Second Life Books, 144
Seekonk Pines Inn, 35
senior services. *See* retirement
Serendipity Sweets, 133
Seven Hills Inn & Restaurant, 45, 118
Seven Stones, The, 68
Shady Pines Campground, 71–72
Shakespeare & Company, 165–66, 179–80, 214–15, 225
Shaun Thornton Memorial Bicycle Race, 224
Sheffield, 10–11
Sheffield Art League, 186–87
Sheffield Farmers' Market, 114
Sheffield Pottery, 193
Shiro, 79
shopping
- Adams, 148
- antiques, 124–26, 133–34
- apparel, 126–27, 134–36
- Central Berkshire, 143–48
- Cheshire, 148
- child-oriented, 215–17
- Great Barrington, 124–32
- home furnishings, 127–29
- Lanesborough, 143–44
- Lee, 132–33
- Lenox, 133–38
- Mill River, 138
- North Adams, 148–49
- North County, 148–51
- Pittsfield, 144–48
- Sheffield, 139–40
- South County, 124–43
- South Egremont, 140–41
- Southfield, 141
- Stockbridge, 141–42
- West Stockbridge, 142–43
- Williamstown, 149–51

Silvio O. Conte National Archives and Records Administration, 20
skating, 288
S. K. H. Gallery, 187–88
Skiddoo, 149
Ski Fanatics, 290
skiing, 284–88
Ski Sale, 230
Sky Dome Golf Center, 274
Skyline Country Club, 271–72
snowmobiling, 288–89
South Egremont, 285–86
Southern Berkshire Family Net Family Center, 217
Southern Berkshire Sno-Dusters, 289
Southern Berkshire YMCA, 218
South Mountain Concerts, 174–75
spas and fitness centers, 264–68
Spice Root, 104
Spigalina, 86–87
Splendid Pheasant, The, 140–41
Spoke, The, 250
sports. *See* recreation
Sports Corner, 250, 290
Springside Park, 239–40
Stafford House, 53
StageWorks, 181
stargazing, 122–23
Sterling and Francine Clark Art Institute, 156–57, 198, 213
Steven Valenti Clothing for Men, 147
Stockbridge, 11
Stockbridge Chamber Concerts, 175
Stockbridge Inn, 54
Stockbridge Summer Arts and Crafts Show, 227
Stone House Properties, 306
Stone's Throw Antiques, 134
Stonover Farm Bed & Breakfast, 45–46
Store at Five Corners, The, 150
Storefront Artist Project, The, 192
Studio 21 Fitness Center, 267
Sullivan Station Restaurant, 82
summer and day camps, 219–20
Summit Hill Campground, 72
Sunny Banks Ranch, 281
Super 8 Motel, 40
Susan B. Anthony Days, 225
Sweet Basil Grille, 82–83
Sweet Peas and Petunias, 79
swimming, 220

T

Taconic Golf Club, 273
Taconic Hiking Club, 279
Taconic Restaurant, 104–5
Taft Farms, 113–15
Tala's Quilt Shop, 149
Talbots, 136
Tanglewood, 166–67, 175–76
Tanglewool, 136
Tannery Pond Concerts, 177
taxis and limousines, 25–27
tennis, 283
Thaddeus Clapp House B&B, 57
Thai Garden, 105
theater (performing art), 178–82
Theatre Barn, The, 181–82
time-shares and condos, 68–69
Tokonoma Gallery & Framing Studio, 189
Tolland State Forest, 73, 236
Tom Fiorini, 190
Tom's Toys, 216–17
Tony's Berkshire Boats, 252, 263
Toonerville Trolley, 150–51
tour companies, 30
Town Players of Pittsfield Inc., 180
T. P. Saddleblanket & Trading Co., 127

Tracy Goodnow Art & Antiques, 139–40
trains, 24
Train Station Gallery, 195
transportation
arriving by bus, 25
arriving by car, 23–24
arriving by plane, 25
arriving by train, 24
bicycling, 30–31
car rentals, 27
getting around, 27–30
limousines and taxis, 25–27
tour companies, 30
Trattoria Rustica, 96
Triplex Cinema Theater, The, 184
Trúc Orient Express, 91
Trustees of Reservations, 155, 279
Tub Parade, 227
Tune Street, 130
2 Maple Street, 53
Tyringham, 11
Tyringham Cobble, 237

U
Undermountain Farm, 281

V
Vacation Village, 69
Valley Park Bowl, 254
Ventfort Hall, 167, 206–7
Verdura, 80
Village Inn, The, 46
Villager Gifts, 137–38
Villager Motel, The, 64
Vlada Boutique, 142

W
Wagon Wheel Motel, 49
Wahconah Country Club, 272
Wahconah Falls State Park, 238
Wainwright Inn, The, 35–36
Walk for the Homeless, 229–30
walk-in clinics and emergency rooms, 321
walking. *See* hiking/walking
Washington, 14–15
Waterside Gallery, 195
Water Street Books, 151
Water Street Grill & Tavern, 105
Waubeeka Golf Links, 273
weather, 4–5
Weathervane, 55
Weaver's Fancy, 136
Web sites, 346
weekend getaways. *See* day trips and weekend getaways
wellness. *See* health care and wellness
Western Gateway Heritage State Park, 167–68
West Stockbridge, 11
Wheatleigh, 46–48, 87–88
Where'd You Get That!?, 217
White Knight Records, 132
Whitney Farms, 215
Wild 'n' Wet Sport Rentals, 252–53
Wild 'n' Wet Tours, 288
William Cullen Bryant Homestead, The, 155–56, 204
Williams College Department of Music, 176–77
Williams College Museum of Art, 168, 202–3
Williams Inn, The, 64–65, 105–6, 122
Williamstown, 16–17
Williamstown Farmers' Market, 114
Williamstown Film Festival, 184, 230
Williamstown Jazz Festival, 223
Williamstown Rural Lands Foundation, 279
Williamstown Theatre Festival, 180–81, 215
Williamstown Youth Center, 219
Willows Motel, The, 65
Windsor, 15
Windsor Lake, 241
Windsor State Forest, 73, 240
Windy Hill Farm, 115
Wingate Limited, 131
Winter Brook Farm Antiques, 148
Winterfest Auction, 222
Winterfest/North Adams, 222
winter recreation
outfitters and equipment rentals, 289–90
skating, 288
skiing, 284–88
snowmobiling, 288–89
Wit Gallery, The, 191
Women's Exchange, The, 151
Wood Brothers, 147–48
Woodworkers Guild Furniture Show & Sale, 226
World's Best Imported Chocolate & Art, 191
World Suppers, 228–29

Y
Yankee Inn, The, 48–49
Yankee Suites Extended Stay, 57
Yasmin's, 106
Ye Olde Forge, 92
Yesteryears, 138
YMCA, 268
YMCA Marina, 253
Yours, Mine & Ours, 148

Z
Zanna, 151
Zinc, 118
Zucchinis, 96–97

EX

UT THE AUTHOR

ny Berkshire-ites, Gae
ke Elfenbein is a transplant.
inally from New Jersey, she
e via New York City, where she
d married—Laurence Elfenbein.
er they ran an antiques shop, which
noved lock, stock, and barrel to
sborough in 1972. Their son Curtis
born shortly after. When a fire
stroyed their shop in 1980, Gae
turned to an earlier career in journalism and started writing for the *Berkshire Eagle* while Larry rebuilt the business. Five years later she became a full-time reporter, covering news and writing features until the paper was sold in 1995. After the death of her husband in 2000, she closed the antiques shop but has continued to feed her addiction to old stuff on a smaller scale. She also ran successfully for public office and has been serving on the town's board of selectmen since 2002. When the opportunity to write the first *Insiders' Guide to the Berkshires* presented itself, Gae happily agreed, seeing it as a chance to utilize all she has learned about the area in the past 30-some years—as a parent, a businessperson, a reporter, and, finally, as an elected official. So even though she will never be considered a native, she certainly is a true "insider."